DICTIONARY OF
CANADIAN
MILITARY
HISTORY

DICTIONARY OF
CANADIAN
MILITARY
HISTORY

David J. Bercuson & J.L. Granatstein

Toronto Oxford New York
OXFORD UNIVERSITY PRESS
1992

Oxford University Press, 70 Wynford Drive, Don Mills, Ontario M3C 1J9

Toronto Oxford New York
Delhi Bombay Calcutta Madras Karachi Kuala Lumpur
Singapore Hong Kong Tokyo Nairobi Dar es Salaam
Cape Town Melbourne Auckland Madrid

and associated companies in
Berlin Ibadan

This book is printed on permanent (acid-free) paper ∞

Canadian Cataloguing in Publication Data

Bercuson, David Jay, 1945–
  Dictionary of Canadian military history

ISBN 0-19-540847-0

1. Canada - History, Military - Dictionaries.
I. Granatstein, J. L., 1939–   . II. Title.

FC226.B47 1992   355'.00971   C92-094676-3
F1028.B47 1992

1 2 3 4 – 95 94 93 92

Printed in Canada by Best-Gagné

PREFACE

The authors will be the first to admit that this book is not complete. We were limited to some 1500 entries and that demanded that much be omitted; moreover, many of the entries are very brief, so much so that only barebones data could be included. Others will seem very long to some readers, but we believed strongly that the utility of this book would be greatly increased if, for example, we had good entries on the two world wars and conscription.

We did, however, try to follow certain principles to guide us in the choice of entries. First and most important, we wanted this to be a military dictionary in the broadest sense. Thus, for example, we include entries on the prime ministers whose policies most directly affected the armed forces and the nation's security; we include defence and veterans' affairs ministers, deputy ministers of National Defence and, of course, Victoria and George Cross winners. Less typically, we also include official war artists, important war novels, and entries on security and intelligence topics.

Secondly, our bias was historical rather than contemporary, and we own up to having favoured the twentieth century rather than the earlier period. We make no apology for this and believe that this selection is what the largest group of users of this book will require. That having been said, there is also a good representation of entries on the French, British, and immediate post-Confederation eras.

Thirdly, as ours was a *Canadian* military dictionary, we were obliged to exclude many British, American, and other figures and events that, had we unlimited space, we would surely have included. That also applied to most explanations of terms that were in common military usage. On the other hand, we have tried to include entries on equipment used by Canadians whether or not it was employed by other armies.

Fourthly, space considerations also forced the exclusion of many senior officers, regiments, ships, and air force entries. We tried to include all those officers who commanded major formations in action but could go no further down the chain of command than division commanders (major-generals) or their equivalent. We have tried to encompass all major ships of war and all that were sunk in action, but in many cases we have only been able to approach this area by way of classes of ship. We had hoped to include all the regiments of the army, but space again prevailed; the result is, with rare exceptions, that only regular force units have entries. Our intention was to cover all the significant aircraft used by Canadians; again, we have been forced to omit many.

These omissions bothered us and they will bother many readers. We regret this sincerely. Still, we know that this book gathers together a vast amount of material that, we realize all too well, was hitherto scattered, if not inaccessible. We hope to publish revised editions of this volume in the future and we invite suggestions for additional entries and corrections of those we included.

Many people assisted us in preparing this book. The Directorate of History, National Defence Headquarters, was most helpful. We received research assistance from Dean Oliver, Eric Johnson, Paul Notley, Paul Doherty, and Julie Green. Our thanks to them all.

N.B.: The first appearance of a cross-reference in an entry is signalled by the use of small capital letters.

A

Abbott, Douglas Charles (1899–1986). Born in Lennoxville, Que., he served overseas from 1916–18 and then practised law in Montreal. Elected to parliament as a Liberal in 1940, Abbott became minister of National Defence (Naval Services) in April 1945 and minister of National Defence in August. He served in that post until December 1946, and was responsible for the armed forces' demobilization.

ABC-1. The ABC — American-British Staff Conference — met from 29 January to 29 March 1941 and produced a staff agreement, ABC-1. This arrangement outlined plans for Anglo-American cooperation if and when the U.S. entered WORLD WAR II and recognized that Germany, the most dangerous of the AXIS POWERS, had to be defeated first. Hitherto an important ally of both Britain and the U.S., Canada's dissatisfaction with its relegation to the far sideline of the war led to pressure for a Canadian military mission to be established in Washington.

ABC-22. The 'Joint Canada-United States Basic Defence Plan No. 2' or ABC-22, was drafted by the PERMANENT JOINT BOARD ON DEFENCE as a by-product of the ABC conversations in early 1941. ABC-22 envisaged U.S. cooperation to defeat the AXIS POWERS, not simply the defence of North America. The U.S. military sought strategic control over Canadian forces, but this was resisted successfully, only 'mutual cooperation' being pledged. The plan was approved by Cabinet on 15 October 1941.

Abercromby, James (1706–1781). A Scot and a career soldier from the age of 11, Abercromby came to North America in 1756 as deputy to the Earl of LOUDOUN, the British commander-in-chief. Promoted to major-general, he replaced Loudon in 1757 and the next July led 15,000 troops in a disastrous campaign against a smaller French force commanded by MONTCALM at FORT CARILLON. Recalled and replaced by Jeffrey AMHERST, he saw no further active service.

ACE Mobile Force. First constituted in 1960, the Allied Command Europe Mobile Force is directed from Heidelberg, Germany. It consists of land and air contributions from eight NATO nations and is of brigade strength. The Mobile Force, to which Canada contributes a battalion, is designed to be sent to any threatened NATO territory at short notice.

Ack-ack. Colloquial term for anti-aircraft gun, anti-aircraft fire.

Acting Sub-Militia Council for Overseas Canadians. An advisory body to the department of MILITIA AND DEFENCE on matters relating to the CANADIAN EXPEDITIONARY FORCE, it was created in England by Sir Sam HUGHES in September 1916. Chaired by John Wallace CARSON, the Council was to report directly to Hughes in Ottawa. Its establishment angered and embarrassed the government of Sir Robert BORDEN, then trying to rationalize its cumbersome overseas command arrangements. Three months later, the Council was superseded by Sir George PERLEY's ministry of OVERSEAS MILITARY FORCES OF CANADA, and Hughes tendered his resignation.

Active Militia. The outbreak of the Crimean War sparked a patriotic outburst in British North America that led Sir Allan MacNab to create a commission to reform the MILITIA of the Canadas. The commission recommended in 1855 that an Active Militia of 5000 men be armed, equipped, and paid for ten days' training a year. This recommendation was embodied in the MILITIA ACT 1855 and recruiting began at once. Within three months 1027 had signed on. But three years later, with the economy in a tailspin, enthusiasm had waned. Many of the 1855 units had collapsed and the 1855 Militia Act was not renewed.

Aerial Experiment Association. Formed at Baddeck, N.S., in October 1907 by Alexander Graham Bell and four associates, the

Association successfully flew four flying machines in the U.S. and Canada before its dissolution in 1909. J.A.D. McCURDY's 23 February 1909 ascent in the SILVER DART was the first successful powered flight in Canada.

Afghanistan, UN peacekeeping in. See UNGOMAP.

Agira. A mountain village in central SICILY, Agira was held by a battalion of the 15th Panzer Grenadier Regiment. After a five-day struggle, the PRINCESS PATRICIA'S CANADIAN LIGHT INFANTRY of the 2nd Brigade of the 1st Canadian Division took the town on 28 July 1943. Gen. Guy SIMONDS' troops had been forced by terrain to deploy as many as two battalions against company strength enemy forces. The biggest battle of the campaign in Sicily, the capture of Agira cost 438 Canadian casualties.

Aid to the Civil Power. The legal process by which municipal or provincial authorities call upon the federal government for troops to preserve or restore order. Before Confederation, British troops stationed in British North America frequently provided aid to colonial governments. The MILITIA ACT of 1868 first authorized the calling out of Canadian MILITIA in aid of the civil power. An amendment to the act in 1904 gave this right to call out troops to municipalities, one exercised most often in labour disputes. The local mayor, invariably on the side of order and ordinarily supporting the city's or town's manufacturing interests, could call on the nearest militia unit for assistance, and as a result workers, angry at the breaking of their strikes, came to destest the militia. In 1919 in Winnipeg, for example, militia units may have played as decisive a role as the North West Mounted Police in ending the general strike that paralysed the city. In 1924, the Mackenzie KING government took the right to call out the militia (and PERMANENT FORCE soldiers) from the local magistrates and handed it instead to provincial attorneys-general. The province paid the costs involved. Though there have been more than 160 instances of aid to the civil power since Confederation, the use of troops as strikebreakers has ceased since the Depression, in part because of changing public attitudes, but also because local police (and

the RCMP and provincial police) are generally better trained than hitherto. The right to call on the armed forces, now incorporated in the NATIONAL DEFENCE ACT, was recently exercised by Quebec when substantial units of the army were mobilized in August 1990 during a land dispute with Mohawk Indians precipitated by the town of OKA.

Air Board. Created in 1919 to deal with civil aviation, the Board soon took over Canada's rudimentary military aviation and established a small non-permanent air force on 23 April 1919. The Liberal government did away with the Air Board when the DEPARTMENT OF NATIONAL DEFENCE was created in 1923.

Air Command. Formed on 2 September 1975, Air Command of the CANADIAN ARMED FORCES consolidated control of military air units under a single commander. The move, seen by many as a return to a single service air force, was aimed at improving flexibility, effectiveness, safety, and economy. With headquarters in Winnipeg, Air Command has as its primary function the provision of operationally ready regular and reserve air units to fulfil Canadian commitments.

Aircraft carriers. The ROYAL CANADIAN NAVY first employed aircraft carriers in WORLD WAR II when HMS *NABOB* and HMS *PUNCHER*, both escort carriers, though remaining Royal Navy vessels, were largely manned by RCN personnel. In early 1945, the RCN decided it had a need for light fleet carriers for use in the Pacific, and the British offered HMS *MAGNIFICENT* and *WARRIOR* on loan. Neither ship was completed before the end of the war, but *Warrior* was commissioned in the RCN in 1946. The next year *Warrior* was returned and exchanged for the slightly larger HMCS *Magnificent*, which was commissioned in 1948 and served on NATO exercises and in 1956 to carry Canadian troops and equipment for the UNITED NATIONS EMERGENCY FORCE to Egypt. The carrier was paid off the next year. Her successor was the HMCS *BONAVENTURE*, equipped with an angled flight deck and steam catapults. The 'Bonnie' came into service in 1957 and had her mid-life

2

refit, an expensive one, in 1966–67. The ship was paid off in 1970 and scrapped.

Air Defence Command. A command within the ROYAL CANADIAN AIR FORCE, Air Defence Command grew out of the need in the late 1940s for fighter squadrons to meet the threat posed by the Soviet Union's long-range bombers. ADC cooperated with the U.S. Air Force in NORAD and after UNIFICATION it was a separate functional division of the forces; in 1975, ADC was reduced to an Air Defence Group within AIR COMMAND.

Air Force Cross. The AFC, created in 1918, is awarded to officers and warrant officers for acts of valour, courage, or devotion to duty while flying, though not in active operations against the enemy.

Air Force Medal. This decoration, equivalent to the AIR FORCE CROSS, is awarded to non-commissioned officers and enlisted ranks.

Air Transport Command. In August 1943, the ROYAL CANADIAN AIR FORCE set up a Directorate of Air Transport which took the name Air Transport Command in 1948. The command continued to exist after UNIFICATION, but in 1975 it was reduced to an Air Transport Group under AIR COMMAND. It provides tactical and strategic airlift to Canadian forces worldwide and commands air search and rescue forces.

Aitken, William Maxwell, 1st Baron Beaverbrook (1879–1964). Born in Maple, Ont., but raised in New Brunswick, Aitken was a millionaire when he moved to Britain in the years before WORLD WAR I. Knighted in 1911, Sir Max was a powerful wartime representative of the Canadian government overseas. His duties included that of eyewitness with the CANADIAN EXPEDITIONARY FORCE, General Representative for Canada at the Front, and officer-in-charge of the CANADIAN WAR RECORDS OFFICE. He wrote two volumes of *Canada in Flanders* (1916–17), before becoming Britain's Minister of Information. In WORLD WAR II, by now raised to the peerage and a newspaper proprietor, Beaverbrook held appointments in Churchill's Cabinet, most notably minister for Aircraft Production in 1940–41.
Reading: A.J.P. Taylor, *Beaverbrook* (1972)

Alabama claims. The Confederate warship *Alabama*, built in Britain during the United States' CIVIL WAR, inflicted heavy losses on the Union's shipping. The United States claimed compensation from Britain and the claim went to arbitration, rather than forming part of the negotiations for the TREATY OF WASHINGTON, 1871. The Americans had suggested that the cession of some Canadian territory might be compensation enough, but they settled for $15.5 million in gold as awarded by the tribunal.

Alaska boundary dispute. The location of the boundary between the Alaska panhandle and Canada had long been in dispute between the United States and the Dominion and, before the Alaska purchase of 1867, between Britain and Russia. The Americans claimed a continuous stretch of coastline; Canada demanded control of certain fjords and especially of the Lynn Canal which provided access to the Yukon and its goldfields, a matter of importance after the Klondike gold rush began in 1897. Direct negotiation in the Joint High Commission of 1898–99 failed, and President Theodore Roosevelt was waving his big stick, talking tough, and sending troops to the region. In 1903 a six-member — three American, two Canadian, and one British — international tribunal decided the issue. Thanks to the British member's decision to support the American position, Canada lost most of what it had claimed, though it received two islands at the mouth of the Portland Canal. The incident went some distance to persuading Canadians that they had to look after their own foreign relations and could not rely on Britain, at least not when larger questions of Anglo-American concern were at stake. See also YUKON FIELD FORCE.
Reading: John Munro, *The Alaska Boundary Dispute* (Toronto, 1970)

Alaska Highway. Built in 1942–43 from Dawson Creek, B.C., to Fairbanks, Alaska, the Alaska (or Alcan) Highway was deemed necessary by the United States because of the Japanese threat to Alaska. The idea of a land route to connect British Columbia and the American territory to its north had been mooted for years, not least by B.C. premier Duff Pattullo, by American generals worried about the defence of Alaska, and by President Franklin Roosevelt. Canada had always been leery, fearful that a land link would increase U.S. influence in B.C. and make impossible Canadian neutrality in the event of war between Japan and the U.S. The attack on Pearl Harbor ended those concerns.

The road was a major construction feat. U.S. Army construction engineers built the highway, stretching 2451 km, in just eight months at a cost of $148 million. The CANADIAN ARMY took over maintenance of the Canadian portion of the road in 1946, and in 1964 this responsibility was assumed by the Department of Public Works.

Reading: Ken Coates, ed., *The Alaska Highway* (Vancouver, 1985)

Aldershot. A sprawling British army training camp in Hampshire, England, Aldershot was a major training facility for Canadian army units in WORLD WAR II. Aldershot, N.S. was also used as an infantry training centre.

Alderson, Sir Edwin Alfred Hervey (1859–1927). Alderson enlisted in the British Army in 1878 and saw service in India, the Nile Campaign, and the Boer War. In 1914, he was appointed to command the Canadian Division, and subsequently took command of the CANADIAN CORPS. A plodding officer, Alderson was replaced by General BYNG in May 1916 after the failure at ST ELOI.

Aldwinckle, Eric (1909–1980). This British-born artist trained in Toronto and worked for a design firm. In WORLD WAR II, he initially worked with the Royal Canadian Air Force's camouflage division. After becoming an official war artist, he served with a number of squadrons. As he wrote, the greatest menace was 'aeroplane motors which have several times threatened to blow me over the English Channel together with my materials if I do not keep an ever watchful eye on mechanics who do not see me behind a tail.' Aldwinckle did a number of superb pieces focusing on the D-DAY invasion of France.

Alexander, Ronald Okedon (1888–1949). Born in Ceylon, Alexander was commissioned in the MILITIA before joining the ROYAL CANADIAN REGIMENT in 1910. During WORLD WAR I he served in France and Flanders, commanded a battalion, and served as staff officer with 2ND CANADIAN DIVISION. After the armistice he held staff posts, being promoted brigadier in 1935 and major-general in 1940. He commanded on the west coast from 1940 to 42, having to deal with the JAPANESE CANADIAN EVACUATION and the threat of attack. He was Inspector-General Central Canada 1942–45 and retired in 1946.

Algie, Wallace Lloyd (1891–1918). Algie was a platoon commander in the 20th Battalion, CANADIAN EXPEDITIONARY FORCE, during an attack north of CAMBRAI on 11 October 1918. German machine-gun fire threatened Algie's battalion and the whole brigade attack, but the officer led a small party that eliminated two guns and then forced the surrender of others. While bringing forward reinforcements to ensure his success Algie was killed. He was posthumously awarded the VICTORIA CROSS.

Allard, Jean-Victor (b. 1913). A native of Ste Monique de Nicolet, Que., he was educated in Montreal and Kitchener, Ont. Allard joined the MILITIA in 1933, served overseas with an armoured regiment and with the ROYAL 22e REGIMENT in Italy, and ended the war as a heavily decorated brigadier in the NORTHWEST EUROPE CAMPAIGN. This outstanding soldier remained in the army, serving as military attaché in Moscow, as a brigade commander during the KOREAN WAR, and as commander of a British division in Germany, a signal honour for a Canadian soldier. He then took charge of MOBILE COMMAND and became CHIEF OF THE DEFENCE STAFF in 1966, responsible for putting the policy of UNIFICATION into effect. Allard also worked diligently and with substantial success to remove barriers to francophones in the armed forces. See also FRENCH-LANGUAGE UNITS.

Reading: *The Reminiscences of General Jean V. Allard* (Vancouver, 1988)

Allies, the. In World War I, the alliance of the U.K., France, Italy, Russia, the U.S. and others against the CENTRAL POWERS; in World War II, the alliance of the U.K., the Dominions, the U.S., Russia, France, and China against the AXIS POWERS.

Allison, John Wesley (1862–1924). An Ontario promoter and financier close to Sam

HUGHES, the Militia minister, Allison was implicated in the 1916 SHELL COMMITTEE scandal and accused of reaping huge profits on munitions contracts. Hughes and the Committee were exonerated by a Royal Commission, but Allison was severely censured for deception in his relations with Hughes and the committee.

Amherst, Jeffrey, 1st Baron Amherst (1717–1797). A British army commander, Amherst made his reputation in the SEVEN YEARS' WAR by capturing LOUISBOURG in 1758 and, after his appointment as commander-in-chief in North America in 1759, capturing Montreal in 1760, the latter victory effectively ending French rule in Canada. He later served twice as commander-in-chief of the army and at his death was a field marshal.

Amiens, Battle of (1918). Described by the German General Ludendorff as the 'black day of the German Army', the CANADIAN CORPS' assault on the German trenches around Amiens that began on 8 August was one of the decisive battles of the last months of WORLD WAR I. The corps of four divisions, led by General Sir Arthur CURRIE, mounted a coordinated and intricate assault that featured tanks, aircraft, cavalry and infantry advances skilfully covered by artillery and machine-gun fire. The four-day battle saw the virtual destruction of 15 enemy divisions and began the corps' 'hundred days' that saw huge territorial gains (13 km on the first day) and some of the heaviest casualty tolls of the war.
Reading: G.W.L. Nicholson, *Canadian Expeditionary Force 1914–1919* (1962)

Anderson, Thomas Victor (1881–1972). Anderson graduated from the ROYAL MILITARY COLLEGE in 1900 and then completed an engineering degree at McGill University. He worked for the Algoma Central Railway, taught engineering at RMC, and in 1906 took a commission in the PERMANENT FORCE with the ROYAL CANADIAN ENGINEERS. He served overseas in WORLD WAR I with distinction and was wounded at VIMY RIDGE, losing an arm. After the war, he went to staff college, served in staff posts, and became CHIEF OF THE GENERAL STAFF as

a major-general in 1938. In 1940 he was made Inspector-General, Central Canada, a post he held until retirement in 1943.

Anderson, William Alexander Beaumont (b. 1915). Born into a distinguished Canadian military family, Anderson attended the ROYAL MILITARY COLLEGE and joined the ROYAL CANADIAN HORSE ARTILLERY in 1936. He served overseas in WORLD WAR II, notably on the staff of FIRST CANADIAN ARMY, and after the war he held various appointments including command of the infantry brigade in NATO, Adjutant-General, and commander of MOBILE COMMAND from 1966–69. He retired as lieutenant-general in 1969.

André, Harvie (b. 1940). Born in Edmonton, this combative Progressive Conservative politician taught chemical engineering at the University of Calgary before winning election to Parliament in 1972. He served as Opposition defence critic and was appointed associate minister of National Defence by Brian Mulroney in 1985. He held the post only until the next year, though continuing to serve in Cabinet.

Anglo-Japanese Alliance. Signed betweeen Britain and Japan in 1902, the Alliance bound each nation to come to the aid of the other in the event of war with a third party. This posed special difficulties for Canada which, as a colony, was bound by Britain's adherence to the Alliance. What would happen if Japan and the United States went to war? Canadians asked. Then Britain was bound to fight the U.S., and Canada, as a result, was certain to be exposed to invasion from the south. The Japanese adhered to the Alliance's terms in WORLD WAR I, their ships operating in the Pacific and the Imperial Navy stationing a liaison officer at ESQUIMALT. But in the immediate postwar years, when renewal of the alliance was at issue in London, Prime Minister Arthur Meighen played a substantial role at the Imperial Conference of 1921 in persuading Whitehall not to go ahead. In effect, American friendship was deemed of more importance by London and Ottawa than potential Japanese hostility. The Australians and New Zealanders, out in the far Pacific and exposed to the Japanese fleet, were not happy with this decision.

Reading: C.P. Stacey, *Canada and the Age of Conflict*, Vol. I (1977).

Angus Shops. A large Canadian Pacific railway repair depot in east end Montreal, the Angus Shops were used to build tanks and armoured vehicles in WORLD WAR II. Employing 14,000 workers, the shops built the Valentine, a light infantry support tank, the Canadian-designed RAM, the SEXTON, and a Canadian variant of the SHERMAN, the Grizzly. After the war, the shops reverted to railway repair work; they were closed in 1992.

Annapolis Royal. Located on the Annapolis River, N.S., this town was first settled by the French in 1606 and initially fortified in 1620. Fort Anne was begun in 1687. The town changed hands several times during the French-English conflicts of the 17th and 18th centuries.

Anse au Foulon. A small cove on the north shore of the St Lawrence just above Quebec, Anse au Foulon in 1759 was the site of General James WOLFE's landing. Under cover of a feint elsewhere, Wolfe's bold but risky venture saw his troops scale the cliffs and arrive at the PLAINS OF ABRAHAM in the early morning of 13 September. See QUEBEC 1759.

Anson aircraft. British-designed, the Avro Anson entered service in 1936 and was not finally retired until 1968 after some 11,000 had been produced, many in Canada. During WORLD WAR II, it was the standard aircraft for twin-engined service flying training in the BRITISH COMMONWEALTH AIR TRAINING PLAN. One variant, the Anson V, featured a moulded plywood fuselage and had a speed of 305 km/h.

Arcadia Conference. After the United States was brought into WORLD WAR II by the attack on Pearl Harbor on 7 December 1941, Prime Minister Churchill and some of his senior officers came to Washington on 22 December to make plans and set up combined war machinery with their U.S. counterparts. Canada was excluded from the discussions and from the Combined Chiefs of Staff and Combined Boards that resulted.

The resentment this fostered led to the development of the FUNCTIONAL PRINCIPLE.

Argentia Conference, 1941. Also known as the Atlantic conference, this meeting of U.S. President F.D. Roosevelt and British Prime Minister Winston Churchill took place aboard warships anchored off Argentia, Nfld from 9 to 12 August 1941. The meeting produced the Atlantic Charter of war aims and speeded the process of coordinating the still-neutral U.S. with the Allies' war effort. Canada was not represented, much to Mackenzie KING's chagrin.

Argus aircraft. Designed as a replacement for the LANCASTER and CANSO in ocean surveillance and anti-submarine roles, the Argus first flew in 1957. Built by CANADAIR, the CL-28 Argus maritime patrol aircraft was the largest NATO aircraft of its kind, and the ROYAL CANADIAN AIR FORCE had 33 in service by 1960. The Argus flew for more than two decades in Canadian service.

Argyll House. Headquarters in London of the ACTING OVERSEAS SUB-MILITIA COUNCIL and then the Ministry of OVERSEAS MILITARY FORCES OF CANADA, the 'Argyll House organization' earned a WORLD WAR I reputation for insensitivity, inefficiency, and confusion.

Armistice, 1918. Coming into effect at the eleventh hour of the eleventh day of the eleventh month, the armistice of 11 November 1918 brought WORLD WAR I to a close after more than four years of bloodletting. Units of the CANADIAN EXPEDITIONARY FORCE had entered MONS, the site of the British retreat four years before, and the CANADIAN CORPS suffered its last casualty at 10:55 a.m. when a German sniper killed a private in the 28th Battalion. The defeat of Germany was celebrated in every Allied capital and at the front, and the armistice was followed by a harsh peace, imposed by the victors, at Versailles the next year. November 11 has been celebrated ever since as Armistice Day, with imitation poppies sold by veterans' groups and a minute's silence at 11 a.m. to mark the occasion.

Armoured regiment organization, World War II. Commanded by a lieutenant-colonel, an armoured regiment was usually organized into a headquarters (four SHERMAN TANKS), three squadrons each of 19 Shermans, and a reconnaissance troop ordinarily of 11 STUART light tanks.

Armstrong-Whitworth Atlas aircraft. A single-seat biplane armed with twin LEWIS GUNS, the Atlas was an army cooperation aircraft. Its top speed was 228 km/h. Sixteen were flown by the ROYAL CANADIAN AIR FORCE from 1927 until early in WORLD WAR II.

Armstrong-Whitworth Siskin aircraft. A single-seat biplane fighter built in Britain, and a first-line fighter in its day. Nine Siskins were flown by the ROYAL CANADIAN AIR FORCE from 1928 to 1939. The much more advanced HURRICANE replaced the now obsolete Siskin just prior to the outbreak of war in 1939.

Army Benevolent Fund. Formed in 1947, the Army Benevolent Fund provides financial and educational assistance to WORLD WAR II veterans and their families when assistance is not otherwise available. It reports to the minister of VETERANS' AFFAIRS.

Army, Navy and Air Force Veterans in Canada. The oldest of Canadian veterans' organizations, its roots date to 1837. An advocate for the welfare of veterans and their dependents, the ANAFV (which added air force to its title in 1946) is also a social club with units throughout the country.

Arnell, John Carstairs (b. 1918). Born in Nova Scotia, Arnell served in the army during WORLD WAR II and then became an official in the DEPARTMENT OF NATIONAL DEFENCE. As assistant deputy minister for Finance, he was influential in the debates over INTEGRATION and UNIFICATION.

Aroostook War, 1839. After several incidents created tension, British and American forces converged on the Aroostook River region of the ill-defined Maine-New Brunswick border region. The main issues involved timber rights and the communication lines between the British provinces. A compromise was reached in March 1839 before serious conflict could erupt, and the border

was finally settled in the Webster-Ashburton Treaty of 1842.

Arras, Battle of. During the first battle of Arras in the spring of 1917, the CANADIAN CORPS under General BYNG took VIMY RIDGE. A year and a half later, the second great battle for this northern French region saw Canadian troops drive the Germans from a series of fortified positions in the DROCOURT-QUÉANT LINE.

Arrow, Avro fighter (CF105). During the KOREAN WAR, the government was concerned with the threat posed by Soviet long-range bombers armed with nuclear weapons. By 1953, the CHIEF OF THE AIR STAFF had proposed the development of a supersonic all-weather interceptor and planned to equip the ROYAL CANADIAN AIR FORCE with up to 600 of the aircraft. The engines, armaments, and electronic systems would be secured elsewhere with only the airframe to be developed in Canada. Cabinet agreed to the development of two prototypes by A.V. ROE CANADA in December 1953. In 1954, the pace increased, Ottawa deciding on 11 prototypes and a pre-production order of 29 aircraft at a cost of $190 million. But no suitable engine was available and, with misgivings, the government agreed to develop the IROQUOIS engine. Costs continued to rise, but discussion of scrapping the project and buying a U.S. aircraft was scuppered when the RCAF argued that no available aircraft could handle the difficulties of flying in the north. Nonetheless, in December 1955, the St Laurent government decided to limit the Arrow's development until the design was tested; only 11 aircraft were to be produced and costs were not to exceed $170 million over three years.

Further blows fell. The U.S. Navy cancelled development of the Sparrow missile, with which the Arrow (or CF105) was to be armed; the question of a substitute was simply deferred. Then the Liberals reduced prototype production from 11 to eight. This was the situation when the DIEFENBAKER government took power in 1957. In October, the CHIEFS OF STAFF COMMITTEE recommended the purchase of 29 additional Arrows and continuation of work on the Sparrow. Cabinet agreed, in effect reviving the project. But by this point the missile age was upon us, notably the BOMARC, intended to knock down bombers relatively cheaply. The twin-engine Arrow first flew on 25 March 1958 but with more than $300 million spent, it was estimated that $874 million more would be necessary to complete the project. One answer to the high unit cost was to increase the production run; unfortunately no country would buy the CF105. Thus by summer 1958, the Arrow was all but dead, the Chiefs of Staff Committee recommending its cancellation. But because up to 25,000 jobs might be lost, Cabinet decided to defer a decision. Finally on 17 February 1959, Cabinet agreed to the Arrow's cancellation and to secure instead two Bomarc missile sites. The announcement three days later provoked a furore; A.V. Roe put 14,000 workers on the street that day. The press and public harshly accused the Conservatives of selling Canada short by scrapping an aircraft of superior quality. The Arrow was a beautiful aircraft with splendid flying characteristics equal to those of top-of-the-line U.S. interceptors; it was, however, too expensive for Canada to produce airframe, engines, and armaments on its own, and cancellation was inevitable if the army or navy was ever to secure any new equipment. Prime Minister Diefenbaker had made the right decision; his only fault was not to have taken it sooner.

Reading: J.L. Granatstein, *Canada 1957–1967* (Toronto, 1986).

Art, war. Canadian war art, though little known to the Canadian public, is extraordinarily powerful and evocative. In both WORLD WAR I and WORLD WAR II, the Canadian government employed official war artists in substantial numbers to record the impact of the struggles; the vast body of art produced remains a stark testimonial to the courage and suffering of war.

During World War I, Max AITKEN, Lord Beaverbrook, received permission from Ottawa to establish the CANADIAN WAR MEMORIALS FUND in late 1916. The Fund was to create a collection of photographs, movies, and paintings to give 'a more vivid, truthful, and lasting impression than can be done ever by the written word' of Canadian efforts in the war. Funds were raised by charging admission to a photographic exhibition in London, and using these proceeds the Fund began to acquire paintings of Canadian war interest which, when exhibited,

quickly raised yet more money. Beaverbrook soon obtained permission from Ottawa to appoint war artists with honorary officers' ranks. The official war artists included British painters such as Augustus John, Wyndham Lewis, and Paul Nash and Canadians A.Y. JACKSON, Arthur LISMER, Lawren HARRIS, and Frederick VARLEY, later to be better known as members of the Group of Seven, and others such as Maurice CULLEN and David MILNE. The Fund purchased the works of British artists too, not all on the present war. Paintings acquired included Benjamin West's 'The Death of Wolfe', and Sir Thomas Lawrence's 'Sir Alexander Mackenzie.' At war's end all the paintings were transferred to the National Gallery of Canada.

In World War II, the memory of Beaverbrook's scheme was very much alive, and in 1940, Col. A.F. DUGUID, the head of the Army's Historical Section, apparently acting on his own, commissioned Pte Edward J. Hughes to paint war art under his direction. Orville FISHER later was added to Duguid's empire. In London, meanwhile, Vincent Massey, the Canadian High Commissioner and a collector of note in his own right, found that Will OGILVIE was serving in an armoured regiment. Ogilvie was already an artist of some reputation, and in October 1941 Massey arranged to have him attached to CANADIAN MILITARY HEADQUARTERS for three months to work as a war artist. Massey also arranged for a British artist, Henry Lamb, to paint Canadian troops. In January 1942, Ottawa agreed to promote Ogilvie, Fisher, and Hughes to officer rank. That did not mean that Ottawa was in favour of a war artists' program, however, and a combined effort by Massey, CMHQ, and Lt-Col C.P. STACEY, the army's historian in Britain, foundered. Early in 1943, Ottawa relented and agreed to the appointment of six army war artists. Naval and air force artists were similarly named. The group was first class. Charles COMFORT arrived in Britain in April 1943; Alex COLVILLE came overseas in May 1944; Bruno BOBAK and Molly Lamb BOBAK worked overseas as well. Army artists served in SICILY (notably Ogilvie), in the ITALIAN CAMPAIGN, and in the NORTHWEST EUROPE CAMPAIGN, recording the death and destruction as well as the awesome technology of the war. Others, such as Jack HUMPHREY, painted eerie paintings of the war in the air.

Stacey, under whose control the army artists came, wrote that 'I considered it my job only to provide opportunities to artists. I had no intention of telling them how to paint, and only to a very small extent did I tell them what to paint.' Stacey added, properly enough, that 'the pictures that were produced impressed Massey as good art and me as good history.'

The vast collection of war art, added to with sketches and paintings from the KOREAN WAR, NATO and PEACEKEEPING operations, and the GULF WAR, is now largely housed in storage at the CANADIAN WAR MUSEUM. A very few drawings and paintings hang at the Museum and at the National Gallery, but most of the collection has never been seen by the Canadian people.

Reading: C.P. Stacey, *A Date With History* (Toronto, 1983); Maria Tippett, *Art at the Service of War* (Toronto, 1984)

Artificial moonlight. By bouncing searchlights off the clouds, enough light could be provided to allow armoured attacks to take place at night. This ingenious device, apparently first used by General Guy SIMONDS in Operation TOTALIZE on 7 August 1944, worked, though (despite other navigational aids) units still got lost.

Artillery regiment organization, World War II. A field artillery regiment consisted of three batteries, each with two troops of four 25-POUNDER GUNS, for a total of 24. Medium regiments had 16 5.5-inch guns organized in two batteries, each with two troops of four guns.

ASDIC. An acronym for the Allied Submarine Detection Investigation Committee of 1917, ASDIC (or Sonar in U.S. parlance) was a British echo-sounding device used in antisubmarine warfare. During WORLD WAR II, ASDIC-equipped ships sank 246 German U-boats. Canada produced some 2600 ASDIC sets for its own and other navies.

Ashton, Ernest Charles (1873–1956). Born in Brantford, Ont., and trained as a physician, Ashton served in the MILITIA before 1914. During WORLD WAR I, he served overseas in Britain and in Ottawa, reaching the rank of major-general. He remained in the PERMANENT FORCE, serving in a variety of staff and command posts, most notably as CHIEF OF THE GENERAL STAFF in 1935–38. He retired in 1941 as a lieutenant-general.

Asselin, Joseph François Olivar (1874–1937). A journalist and *nationaliste*, Asselin was nonetheless one of very few French-Canadian supporters of the military. He served with the U.S. forces in the Spanish-American War and overseas with the CANADIAN EXPEDITIONARY FORCE in WORLD WAR I during which he reached the rank of major. He was then secretary to the Canadian military mission in Paris and was attached to the Canadian delegation at the 1919 peace conference.

***Assiniboine*, HMCS.** The first *Assiniboine*, a RIVER CLASS DESTROYER, was acquired by the ROYAL CANADIAN NAVY in 1939 and served throughout WORLD WAR II. 'Bones' helped capture a German freighter in the West Indies in December 1939, rammed and sank a U-boat in August 1942, and was wrecked off Prince Edward Island in 1945 en route to the U.S. where she was to be broken up. The second ship of this name, a *ST LAURENT*-CLASS destroyer escort, was commissioned in 1956, re-commissioned in 1963 after conversion to a destroyer-helicopter carrier, and extensively modernized in 1979.

Assoro. This Sicilian town was taken on 22 July 1943 by the 1st Brigade of the 1ST CANADIAN DIVISION after a daring assault up a steep mountain face. The surprise ascent by infantry of the Hastings and Prince Edward Regiment was key to the Canadian advance.

***Athabaskan*, HMCS.** The first *Athabaskan*, a TRIBAL CLASS DESTROYER commissioned in 1943, served with the Royal Navy's Home Fleet. After assisting in the destruction of a German torpedo boat, she was sunk by torpedo in the English Channel in April 1944 in an engagement with two enemy destroyers. *Athabaskan*'s captain and 128 crew were lost, and a further 83 taken prisoner. The second *Athabaskan*, another Tribal class ship, was commissioned in 1948 and served tours in the KOREAN WAR. She was broken up in 1970. The current ship of this name is an *IROQUOIS*-CLASS vessel armed with guns and missiles and equipped to carry helicopters. Commissioned in 1972,

Athabaskan served in the GULF WAR of 1990–91.

Reading: L. Burrow and E. Beaudoin, *Unlucky Lady: The Life and Death of HMCS Athabaskan 1940–44* (Stittsville, Ont., 1982)

Atlantic, Operation, 1944. II CANADIAN CORPS, under Gen. Guy SIMONDS, attacked German positions south of CAEN, France on 18–19 July as part of Gen. Bernard Montgomery's Operation GOODWOOD. The attack was a success, though Goodwood was largely checked by the Germans.

Atlantic Conference, 1941. See ARGENTIA CONFERENCE.

Atlantic Convoy Conference, 1943. In March, representatives of the British, American, and Canadian navies met in Washington to discuss command organization, tactics, and equipment in the BATTLE OF THE ATLANTIC. As a result, the ROYAL CANADIAN NAVY took control of convoy protection in the Canadian Northwest Atlantic with Adm. Leonard MURRAY as commander-in-chief.

Atlantic Ferry Organization (ATFERO). Established by Max AITKEN, Lord Beaverbrook in August 1940, ATFERO flew North American-built aircraft across the North Atlantic to Britain. Dorval, Quebec City, and Gander, Nfld were the main starting points. The Royal Air Force, with its newly created Ferry Command, took control of ATFERO in July 1941. Selected graduates of the BRITISH COMMONWEALTH AIR TRAINING PLAN received some practical experience of long-range flying and navigation by ferrying aircraft overseas before their postings to operational units; other RCAF personnel (634 of 1330 aircrew in 1944) and Canadian civilians served in Ferry Command.

Autobiography, military. See BIOGRAPHY, MILITARY.

Aviation, military. Canadian military aviation had some indigenous roots, but it was largely a foreign import. The aircraft industry was almost all foreign-owned and, though some original designs were developed in Canada, with few exceptions none had much world sale.

At the onset of WORLD WAR I, although J.A.D. MCCURDY had flown a Canadian-built aircraft a few years before, there was no Canadian air force. Despite the slow start, a substantial number of Canadians — perhaps as many as 23,000 — flew in the ROYAL FLYING CORPS and the ROYAL NAVAL AIR SERVICE, and some of the war's best known pilots were Canadians. Billy BISHOP, Billy BARKER and others were leading aces. Aircraft production in Canada also began in this period, with CANADIAN AEROPLANES LTD in Toronto building training aircraft for the British and some 30 FELIXSTOWE flying boats for the United States.

After the war, the CANADIAN AIR FORCE began in a small way, flying an assortment of aircraft given Canada by Britain and the U.S. The creation of the ROYAL CANADIAN AIR FORCE in 1924 put military aviation on a marginally firmer footing, though the service remained tiny and ill-equipped, devoting much of its effort to aerial mapping, fishery patrols, and the like. By 1939, the RCAF had only a few modern aircraft, some 19 HURRICANES having been purchased from the U.K. that year.

WORLD WAR II changed all this. The RCAF grew to a force of a quarter-million men and women, and Canadians operated 48 squadrons overseas, more at home, and provided tens of thousands of aircrew for Royal Air Force squadrons. Canadian factories produced over 15,000 aircraft, ranging from huge LANCASTER bombers to trainers. The country also largely paid for and ran the BRITISH COMMONWEALTH AIR TRAINING PLAN, a hugely successful scheme that produced 131,553 aircrew, more than half of whom were Canadians.

The postwar years initially saw the Canadian government determined to maintain a strong aircraft industry. Canadian interceptors such as the CF100 and the ill-fated ARROW and small transport aircraft like the BEAVER and the OTTER were created and made in Canada. The smaller aircraft sold well around the world; the interceptors, as the Arrow soon demonstrated, were simply too expensive to produce on small production runs and too hard to sell in the face of British, American, and European competition; the costs involved forced the DIEFENBAKER government to scrap the Arrow, a blow from which Canadian military aviation never recovered.

The RCAF also took a blow from UNIFI-CATION which ended its existence as a separate service. Operating a substantial range of aircraft, the air force had done very well in increasing its share of the defence budget, but equipment needs of the army and navy as well as the pilots' desire for hot new aircraft largely forced defence minister Paul HELLYER to act. Unification clipped all the services' wings, though the air force did continue to get new aircraft: CF5s, CF18s and new anti-submarine aircraft. Even so, it was largely unequal to the logistical, combat, and training demands placed upon it.

So too was what was left of the Canadian aviation industry. DE HAVILLAND AIRCRAFT, Hawker Siddeley, CANADAIR, AVRO — all were either defunct or in attenuated form by the end of the 1980s. Canada had been priced out of the military aircraft business.

Aviation, naval. Canadian naval aviation began in WORLD WAR I when 635 Canadians served in the ROYAL NAVAL AIR SERVICE, a group that included several notable fliers including Robert LECKIE, Wilfred CURTIS, and L.S. BREADNER. In April 1918, as the U-boat campaign continued to cause heavy losses to shipping in the Atlantic, Canadian, British, and American naval officers met in Washington to coordinate plans to fight the submarines, and one result was the beginnings of a Canadian naval air service, approved in Cabinet on 3 May. A recruitment scheme and plans for the setting up of two East Coast bases were drafted, and the United States Navy in September began to fly patrols out of Dartmouth and North Sydney, N.S. At the same time, the Royal Canadian Naval Air Service came into existence, its first 20 cadets going to Boston for training on 27 September. The expectation was that the RCNAS would be fully operational by the spring of 1919, but the end of the war put paid to that plan, and the straitened circumstances of the ROYAL CANADIAN NAVY between the wars guaranteed that no serious attention was paid in Canada to air/sea warfare.

In WORLD WAR II, Canadians served with the Royal Navy's Fleet Air Arm, some, like Lt Robert Hampton GRAY, V.C., greatly distinguishing themselves. In early 1943, the RCN began to consider seriously branching out into naval aviation once more. This led to the decision in 1944 that the RCN would provide the ship's complement (but not the aircraft or air personnel) for HMS *PUNCHER* and HMS *NABOB*, two escort AIRCRAFT CARRIERS. The experience gained in operating these carriers helped the Navy's arguments that the postwar RCN should have a naval air component. The case was strengthened by the formation in June 1945 of 803 and 825 Squadrons, flying SEAFIRE and Firefly I aircraft and intended for employment on the Canadian-operated carriers and, by early 1946, with a very large percentage of their air crew being Canadians.

In the immediate postwar years, the RCN operated HMCS *WARRIOR*, the first carrier with an entire complement of Canadians, including 803 and 825 Squadrons whose shore station was at Dartmouth, N.S. *Warrior* was replaced by *MAGNIFICENT*, and the Navy's last carrier, *BONAVENTURE*, came into service in 1957. Each had an aviation complement of 34 aircraft. By the time Canada had joined NATO and began to play its critical role in anti-submarine warfare defence in the Atlantic, naval aviation had become very specialized indeed. Grumman Avengers and Trackers, equipped with homing torpedoes and depth bombs, and helicopters worked as hunter-killer teams with surface vessels and ROYAL CANADIAN AIR FORCE ARGUS and NEPTUNE aircraft, tracking Soviet submarines. By the 1960s and the time of the CUBAN MISSILE CRISIS, the small but very able RCN was at the peak of its efficiency.

The life of naval aviation was limited, however. The UNIFICATION of the three services in 1968 saw the RCN swallowed up and its naval aviation absorbed in the air arm; the subsequent scrapping of the *Bonaventure* took Canada out of the carrier business. Naval aviation's brief life in the Canadian Forces was over.
Reading: J.D.F. Kealy and E.C. Russell, *A History of Canadian Naval Aviation* (Ottawa, 1965)

AVRE. The Armoured Vehicle, Royal Engineers was one of the FUNNIES, specialized armoured vehicles developed for the D-DAY invasion. Using a CHURCHILL tank, AVREs had many capabilities, including track- and bridge-laying, ditch-filling with fascines, and bulldozing. Some had a 12-inch spigot mortar or petard.

A.V. Roe Canada Ltd (AVRO). An air-craft manufacturing company established in Toronto in 1945, Avro was a subsidiary of Britain's Hawker Siddeley Aviation. The company used the plant of VICTORY AIR-CRAFT, a wartime Crown corporation, and proved to be an inspired design and engi-neering operation though rather less so in its production skills. Avro built the CF100, the air force's longtime interceptor; the Avro Jetliner, a passenger aircraft; and the ill-fated ARROW. The Arrow's cancellation in 1959, the subsequent layoff of most of the compa-ny's 14,000 workers, and the difficult rela-tionship between Avro and the government, led to its ceasing operations.

Axis Powers, the. The mid-1930s alliance of Germany, Italy, and Japan, later including Hungary, Romania, Bulgaria, Slovakia, and Croatia.

B

Badger vehicle. A WORLD WAR II flame-throwing armoured vehicle based on the RAM/KANGAROO, the Badger was issued to units of FIRST CANADIAN ARMY in early 1945. The Badger used Wasp Mk 2 flame-throwing equipment and was not employed for long in the postwar army.

Bagot, Sir Charles (1781–1843). Bagot ne-gotiated the RUSH-BAGOT CONVENTION (1817), with the United States providing for naval disarmament on the Great Lakes and Lake Champlain. Later, from 1841 to 43, he was Governor-General of British North America.

Bailey bridge. Metal lattice bridge of pre-fabricated standard parts; designed for rapid, if temporary, construction by Allied forces in WORLD WAR II.

Bain wagon. In the scramble to equip the first contingent of the CANADIAN EXPEDI-TIONARY FORCE in 1914, Militia minister Sam HUGHES purchased every vehicle and wagon available. The Bain wagon, purchased by one of Hughes' friends, did not conform to British standards, came without spare parts, and could not be readily repaired. The Bains were scrapped shortly after the contin-gent's arrival in England.

Baker, Edwin Albert (1893–1968). Baker, born at Collins Bay, Ont., was blinded dur-ing his service with the ROYAL CANADIAN ENGINEERS in WORLD WAR I. He then founded the Canadian National Institute for the Blind and played major roles in its de-velopment until 1962.

Ballantyne, Charles Colquhoun (1867–1950). A businessman and politician, Ballan-tyne raised and commanded the 1st Battalion, Canadian Grenadier Guards in 1916. From 1917 to 1921, he served as minister of Marine and Fisheries and minister of Naval Service in the UNION GOVERNMENT.

Bangor-class minesweepers. A British-de-signed ocean-going minesweeper that was simple enough to be built in inexperienced Canadian yards, the *Bangor*-class displaced 660 tonnes, was 55 m long, and had a crew of 83. Of 60 built in Canada, the ROYAL CANADIAN NAVY operated 54 during and after WORLD WAR II, one remaining in serv-ice until 1966. Most ships of this class were employed on port defence on both coasts and, notably, on convoy escort, though six-teen swept mines prior to and after the D-DAY invasion of NORMANDY.

Banting, Sir Frederick Grant (1891–1941). The co-discover of insulin was born at Allis-ton, Ont. and served overseas as a doctor in WORLD WAR I during which he won the MILITARY CROSS and was wounded. His 1921–22 discovery of insulin won him a Nobel Prize. Banting worked for the gov-ernment before and during WORLD WAR II primarily on the physiological effects of flying at high altitudes and on bacteriological warfare. In November 1939 he went to England to study British research in these areas. Banting died when a HUDSON bomber taking him to Britain in February 1941 crashed in Newfoundland.

Barker, William George (1894–1930). Born in Manitoba, he served in the ROYAL FLYING CORPS during WORLD WAR I. Billy Barker was a superb pilot, credited with the destruction of 53 enemy aircraft. He won the VICTORIA CROSS for an epic singlehanded struggle on 27 October 1918 against German aircraft over the Canadian lines near Valenciennes. Though wounded three times, he shot down a two-seater and three Fokker D VII fighters. Major Barker's SOPWITH SNIPE then crash-landed behind the British trench lines. After trying civilian life, he joined the ROYAL CANADIAN AIR FORCE and, as a wing commander, was briefly its director and then liaison officer in Britain. He died in an air accident at Ottawa.

Barometer Rising. Published in 1941, Hugh MacLennan's first novel was set around the HALIFAX EXPLOSION of 6 December 1917 which he had witnessed as a child. The story related the travails of Neil Macrae, a Canadian officer accused of refusing to obey an order overseas.

Barriefield Camp. Established in 1936 near Kingston, Ont., Barriefield was used for training purposes by the ROYAL CANADIAN CORPS OF SIGNALS in WORLD WAR II. After the war Barriefield remained in service as the military's main communications training establishment.

Barron, Colin Fraser (1893–1958). Cpl Barron won the VICTORIA CROSS at PASSCHENDAELE on 6 November 1917 for silencing a machine-gun nest that was holding up the advance of his unit, the 3rd Battalion, CEF.

Bastian, Gordon Love (b. 1902) While serving in the British Merchant Navy in 1943, Bastian rescued two firemen on his torpedoed ship. He was awarded the Albert Medal, later converted to the GEORGE CROSS.

Batoche, Battle of (1885). Battle for the capital of Louis RIEL's provisional government during the NORTHWEST REBELLION. On 9 May, General Frederick MIDDLETON and 800 men of the NORTHWEST FIELD FORCE, equipped with a GATLING GUN (hastily purchased in the U.S. at the outbreak of the rebellion) and artillery, attacked the Métis' elaborately dug riflepits around Batoche, located 44 km southwest of Prince Albert. The Métis, led in the field by Gabriel DUMONT, successfully resisted the militiamen until 12 May, when they were overrun in a headlong charge. The Métis defeat, their only decisive one of the campaign, effectively ended the rebellion; Riel surrendered several days later and Dumont fled to the United States.
Reading: Bob Beal and Rod Macleod, *Prairie Fire: The 1885 North-West Rebellion* (1984)

Battalion organization, World War I. An infantry battalion consisted of four companies, each of four platoons ordinarily comprising four sections. Commanded by a lieutenant-colonel, a battalion numbered some one thousand officers and men.

Battalion organization, World War II. Commanded by a lieutenant-colonel, an infantry battalion of 38 officers and 812 men consisted of one support and four rifle companies. A rifle company had a company headquarters of three officers and twelve men and three platoons (each of one officer and 36 men when at full strength) and company strength was six officers and 120 men. The support company was made up of one platoon each of mortars (six 3-inch mortars), carriers (13 Bren carriers), anti-tank guns (six 6-pounder guns), and assault pioneers. Other weapons besides rifles included 63 BREN GUNS, 23 PIATs, and 26 2-inch mortars.

Battle of the Atlantic. Britain was almost wholly dependent on supplies shipped to her by sea. At the beginning of WORLD WAR II, the British received two-thirds of their foodstuffs, 30 per cent of their iron ore, 90 per cent of copper ore, 90 per cent of bauxite, 95 per cent of petroleum, 100 per cent of rubber, and 80 per cent of their soft timber from abroad. If the supplies could not get through, the British would be unable to fight, and cutting those supply lines was thus a major German goal. The Battle of the Atlantic was to determine the outcome.

In WORLD WAR I, German U-boats had come very close to cutting the links between Britain and North America, and only the institution of the CONVOY system and the development of anti-submarine warfare tactics had saved the day. In 1939, the British defences were bolstered by ASDIC, but there were very few ships available to fight submarines. Fortunately, the Nazis had paid scant attention to their U-boat fleet: in September 1939, there were only 57 U-boats in total of which only an average of 14 were at sea at any one time in the next four months; Nazi difficulties continued well into 1940, their losses to the Royal Navy outpacing new construction. Nonetheless, between July and December 1940, U-boats, beginning to use wolf-pack tactics and with access to French bases, sank 1.5 million tons of shipping. The Battle of the Atlantic was thus a race between the Germans' ability to build U-boats and the Allies' ability to construct merchant ships; and between the development of German undersea tactics and the Allies' ability to build escorts and to learn how to defeat the submarine.

This was a desperate struggle that lasted throughout the entire war but primarily between 1940 and late 1943. The Battle of the Atlantic might be said to have begun when the German *Kriegsmarine* took advantage of the fall of France to move its submarine bases onto the Bay of Biscay. From then until May 1941 when British decrypters first managed to start unravelling the German codes, the advantage lay with the U-boats. Sinkings far outran new construction, and the Royal Navy, hard-pressed to handle German attacks on the home islands, and the ROYAL CANADIAN NAVY, reeling from the effects of rapid expansion and with too few CORVETTES and other escorts to protect convoys, were still virtual amateurs.

Moreover by September 1941, the still neutral United States Navy was participating in the submarine war, and the Canadian and British units operating out of Newfoundland were now fighting under USN command. Even so, the battle was a near-run thing. In the first six months of 1941, the U-boats sank another 1.5 million tons of shipping, but in the last six months of the year under half that. On the other hand, German U-boat construction was picking up and in

January 1942 there were 91 operational boats available (though only 22 were at sea in the Atlantic). Then the Nazis received a boost from the inexplicable American unwillingness to use convoys to escort shipping in American waters. The U.S. east coast became a killing ground for the U-boats: in the first six months of 1942, just over 3 million tons of shipping were sunk, almost 70 per cent off the east coast. Convoys were not organized there until the end of April 1942 and then U-boats moved to the Caribbean and sank an additional 840,000 tons of shipping.

The climax of the battle came at the beginning of 1943. The number of U-boats at sea now averaged over one hundred. The RCN, its ill-equipped escorts strained beyond endurance and its training below standard, was pulled out of the struggle for retraining and re-eqipment. (The RCN, however, soon did well against the U-boats on the U.K.-Gibraltar run and in providing escort for the Allied invasion of North Africa in November 1942.) And there was still an air coverage gap off Greenland, met in part by the heroic efforts of the RCAF's Eastern Air Command operating out of Newfoundland. In February U-boats sank 63 ships; the next month they got 108. At the ATLANTIC CONVOY CONFERENCE in Washington in March 1943, command structures were altered, and the RCN's Adm. Leonard MURRAY took over the CANADIAN NORTH-WEST ATLANTIC COMMAND. The tide had begun to turn. Access to German codes, finally complete in March 1943, was one advantage for the Allies. Others were the development of better detection equipment, including short-wave radar that could pick up the low profile of U-boats on the surface, weapons such as HEDGEHOG, standards of training, and the gradual extension of escort and, eventually, air coverage across the whole North Atlantic. In May 1943, Allied ships sank 41 submarines, and the kill rate remained high despite the Germans' best efforts to revive the wolf-pack attacks. By the beginning of 1944, the RCN and RCAF had almost the entire responsibility for surface escort of convoys, thus allowing the allocation of British and Canadian vessels to support the invasion of France. The RCN continued its anti-submarine role until the end of the war, ensuring that the U-boats could never again regain the initiative.

The Battle of the Atlantic, fought mostly between tiny corvettes and U-boats and between merchant seamen, the elements, and the U-boats, was an Allied victory. Convoys had escorted 25,421 merchantmen across the Atlantic in safety. Still, in return for the 788 U-boats they had lost, the Germans had sunk 11.9 million tons of shipping in the form of 2232 ships. Astonishingly, the Nazis had 463 U-boats in service at the surrender in May 1945, many equipped with the new snorkel underwater breathing device.

The RCN's share in the battle had been significant indeed. Despite all the teething troubles, the navy's escorts had learned their trade. RCN ships accounted for 47 U-boats (see Appendix V) and provided half the escorts in the MID-OCEAN and WESTERN LOCAL ESCORT FORCES. In addition, the ROYAL CANADIAN AIR FORCE provided almost all the air coverage from the Maritimes and Newfoundland.

Reading: Marc Milner, *North Atlantic Run* (1985)

Battle of Britain. After Dunkirk and the Fall of France, Britain and the Commonwealth stood alone against Hitler. Before launching an invasion of Britain, the Nazis had to destroy the Royal Air Force, and from mid-July until October the air battle raged. The Luftwaffe initially targeted the RAF's fighters and control headquarters, but before they had crippled those vital elements, they switched their attack to large population centres, notably London. The Blitz killed thousands of civilians, but it allowed the RAF time to recover its breath. RAF losses were 790 fighters, many of the pilots bailing out and surviving to fight again; the Luftwaffe lost 1389 aircraft and their crews. The ROYAL CANADIAN AIR FORCE was not heavily engaged in this struggle. Only No. 1 (later 401) Squadron, flying HURRICANES, participated directly (claiming 31 kills and 43 probables with a loss of 16 of its own aircraft between late August and October 1940), but there were substantial numbers of Canadians serving in the RAF, not least the almost wholly Canadian 242 Squadron, commanded by RAF officer Douglas Bader.

Battle honours. The practice of awarding battle honours to units participating in campaigns goes back centuries. Canadian units that fought in the RIEL REBELLION 1885 or in the SOUTH AFRICAN WAR emblazoned their victories on their colours, but the practice became widespread and tightly controlled after WORLD WAR I. Then, as after WORLD WAR II, committees in Ottawa had to decide who got what, after consultation with Britain and other allies on battle nomenclature. The British, for example, did not want HITLER LINE on their colours, preferring not to commemorate the Nazi tyrant; the Canadians, convinced that they were the ones who had broken the line, were less squeamish; the result was that the British used the name of an Italian town and the Canadian units involved proudly inscribed Hitler Line. Defeats, such as DIEPPE or HONG KONG, were also declared to be battle honours. The practice continued in the KOREAN WAR—the PRINCESS PATRICIA'S CANADIAN LIGHT INFANTRY, for instance, has KAP'YONG on its colours.

Bazalgette, Ian Willoughby (1918–1944). A pilot in the ROYAL CANADIAN AIR FORCE, Bazalgette, a master-bomber in a Pathfinder squadron, showed great skill and courage in flying his LANCASTER, crippled by anti-aircraft fire in August 1944. Killed when the aircraft exploded after its forced landing in France, he was awarded the VICTORIA CROSS.

Beatty, Henry Perrin (b. 1950). Born in Toronto and educated at the University of Western Ontario, Beatty held several portfolios in the government of Brian Mulroney. As Defence minister (1986–89), he proposed sweeping changes in defence policy in a 1987 WHITE PAPER, calling for a hard-line stance versus Moscow and the acquisition of nuclear submarines. Fiscal restraint and the apparent end of the COLD WAR forced the government to delay or cancel almost everything Beatty had proposed.

Beatty, John William (1869–1941). A Toronto artist, Beatty served as a bugler in the RIEL REBELLION 1885 and overseas in 1918 as a war artist with the CANADIAN WAR MEMORIALS. His war art includes sketches of two VICTORIA CROSS winners and landscape-style battle scenes.

Beaumont Hamel, Battle of, 1916. On the opening day of the Battle of the SOMME, 1 July 1916, the 29th British Division suffered more than 5000 casualties attacking this village northwest of the River Ancre. The [ROYAL] NEWFOUNDLAND REGIMENT, serving in the 29th, was virtually annihilated in the assault, losing 710 men.

Beaver aircraft. The DE HAVILLAND Beaver, designed in the late 1940s, was the first Short Take-Off and Landing (STOL) aircraft built in Canada. It saw—and continues to see—service in Canada and abroad.

Beaverbrook, Lord. See AITKEN, WILLIAM MAXWELL.

Beaver Club. A club in London for non-commissioned members of the three Canadian services, it was established in Spring Gardens by a committee of Canadians resident in London, most notably High Commissioner Vincent Massey and his wife Alice, and opened in February 1940. Supported largely by donations and by an annual grant from the YMCA, it served some one thousand meals a day and in its first year was visited by almost a quarter-million men. The club was eventually largely taken over in its operation by the YMCA. A Canadian Officers' Club nearby provided meals and pleasant surroundings for officers.

Beaver Dams. During the WAR OF 1812, a party of Mohawk and Caughnawaga Indians, led by Capt. Dominique Ducharme and Lt James Fitzgibbons, ambushed an American column at Beaver Dams, near the present site of Thorold, Ont. Fitzgibbons had been warned of the oncoming Americans by Laura SECORD, a settler who, myth has it, led her cow through the U.S. lines. The 462 surviving Americans were induced to surrender on 24 June 1813 with promises of protection from scalping.

Beland, Henri Severin (1869–1935). A doctor, Beland was elected to the House of Commons in 1902 as a Liberal. At the outbreak of war in 1914, he served with the Belgian army's medical staff and in 1921 he became minister of Soldiers' Civil Re-establishment and simultaneously of Health, posts he held until 1926.

Bellew, Edward Donald (1882–1961). Born in India, Lt Bellew won the VICTORIA CROSS during the second battle of YPRES in April 1915. Taken prisoner after almost singlehandedly delaying a German advance that swept away much of his 7th Battalion, CEF, Bellew was not released until 1919 when his award was announced.

Benson, Edgar John (b. 1923). A prominent Liberal M.P. and Cabinet minister in the PEARSON and Trudeau years, Benson represented Kingston, Ont., in Parliament. He held the post of Finance minister from 1968–72 and was briefly Defence minister from January to October 1972.

Bent, Philip Eric (1891–1917). Bent won a VICTORIA CROSS at Polygon Wood, Belgium on 10 October 1917 for organizing and leading a counter-attack under heavy enemy fire. He died in the effort and his award was posthumous.

Bernatchez, J. Paul E. (1911–1983). Born in Montmagny, Que., he graduated from the ROYAL MILITARY COLLEGE and joined the ROYAL 22e REGIMENT. Quiet, almost diffident, he went overseas in 1939, took command of the Van Doos in 1941, and led the regiment successfully and with great personal courage through fierce fighting in SICILY and at ORTONA. He was promoted brigadier in 1944 and commanded the 3rd Brigade of the 1st Canadian Division to the end of the war. He served in a variety of postings in Canada and Japan and with NATO. He ended his career as Vice Chief of the General Staff and died playing tennis in Florida.

Beurling, George Frederick (1921–1948). 'Buzz' Beurling, born at Verdun, Que., was rejected by the ROYAL CANADIAN AIR FORCE but joined the Royal Air Force in 1940 and served as a SPITFIRE pilot in England. With two aircraft shot down to his credit, he was posted to Malta in May 1942 where he began to demonstrate his prowess. He destroyed six enemy aircraft in June 1942 and nine more in September. Before he was himself shot down and wounded in October, he had run his total to 29. He then transferred to the RCAF in Britain and scored three more kills. Beurling was awarded the DISTINGUISHED SERVICE ORDER, the DISTINGUISHED FLYING CROSS, and the DISTINGUISHED FLYING MEDAL and bar. A natural pilot and superb shot, he was undisciplined (some nicknamed him 'Screwball'),

so much so that this greatest Canadian ace of the war was released from the RCAF in August 1944. He died when an aircraft he was flying to the newly created state of Israel crashed near Rome in May 1948.
Reading: Brian Nolan, *Hero: The Buzz Beurling Story* (1981)

Beveland, Battle of. Part of the battle to open the SCHELDT and allow Antwerp to be used as a major supply point, the struggle to isolate Beveland took place in foul conditions in October 1944. The task of cutting off Beveland, which was joined to the mainland by a narrow causeway, fell to Gen. Charles FOULKES' 2ND CANADIAN DIVISION. The attack jumped off on 6 October, instantly running into difficulty from the Germans on the only high ground in the area at Woensdrecht and from the slow going through flooded polders. Three successive attacks by Canadian battalions at the causeway's isthmus failed with heavy losses. Then the BLACK WATCH tried once more on 'Black Friday' (13 October) and were wiped out. Not until 16 October when the Royal Hamilton Light Infantry launched a heavily supported night attack was the causeway even partially cut, though only after counterattacks by German paratroopers had come close to wiping out the battalion. The job was finally completed on 24 October, isolating Beveland. The way to WALCHEREN was now open.

Big Bear (1825?–1888). Plains Cree chief, playing an important role in the NORTHWEST REBELLION of 1885. Though he believed that his people had been treated poorly by Ottawa, he tried to control his hotheaded followers but was unable to prevent some from killing white settlers at Frog Lake on 2 April 1885 and from attacking Fort Pitt. After the failure of Riel's rebellion, Big Bear surrendered on 2 July and was tried for treason and sentenced to three years' imprisonment.

Biggar, Oliver Mowat (1876–1948). A prominent Ottawa lawyer, Colonel Biggar was a member of the Military Service Council established to assist the BORDEN government in operating the MILITARY SERVICE ACT. In 1918 he was Judge Advocate General and an important member of the AIR BOARD where he played a prominent role in creating the CANADIAN AIR FORCE. In WORLD WAR II Mackenzie KING named Biggar to head the Canadian section of the PERMANENT JOINT BOARD ON DEFENCE.

Bill 80 (1942). This amendment to the NATIONAL RESOURCES MOBILIZATION ACT was put through by the Mackenzie KING government after the PLEBISCITE of 1942 on CONSCRIPTION. The strong support for compulsory service in English Canada led several key ministers to demand that the NRMA's prohibition on overseas conscription be eliminated. The Prime Minister had to agree, but to appease the virtually unanimous opposition of French Canadians, he offered his famous dictum, 'not necessarily conscription, but conscription if necessary', making clear that he would not enforce compulsion yet. Bill 80's introduction provoked the resignation of P.J.A. Cardin, the minister of Public Works, and King's temporizing almost led to that of Defence minister J.L. RALSTON as well.
Reading: J.L. Granatstein and J.M. Hitsman, *Broken Promises: A History of Conscription in Canada* (l985)

Billion Dollar Gift (1942). Britain's WORLD WAR II purchases in Canada had far outstripped a financially strapped London's ability to pay in dollars by 1941. It was politically impossible to cut off supplies, and such a measure could only have led to heavy unemployment in Canada. After some difficult Cabinet discussions, therefore, the Canadian government decided to emulate the generosity shown by the United States with its Lend-Lease program by offering Britain a gift and by erasing most of London's debt. Anglo-Canadians cheered, but the reaction in French Canada was markedly unenthusiastic, and subsequent contributions to Britain and the other Allies were presented under the label of MUTUAL AID. See also Mackenzie KING.

Biography, military. The art of military biography in Canada is not highly developed. Very few academics have written about military history; even fewer of those who have tried their hands at biography. And few of our generals, air marshals, or admirals have told their own stories.

With the exception of W.J. Eccles' biography of *Frontenac: The Courtier Governor*, studies of the early figures in Canadian military history are hagiographic and/or sparse. Lt-Col George T. DENISON wrote *Soldiering in Canada* which encompasses history and reminiscences from the WAR OF 1812 to the Diamond Jubilee of 1897, while Joseph Lehmann wrote a study of Field Marshal Lord WOLSELEY, *The Model Major-General*, which treats his service in Canada, notably in the RIEL REBELLION 1870. Sam STEELE wrote a memoir of his life and military experiences, *Forty Years in Canada*, and there is a popular biography of him by Robert Stewart. The first Canadian officer of the pre-World War I period to be properly examined is Gen. W.D. OTTER whose biography, *The Canadian General*, was written by his grandson, the historian Desmond Morton.

Of Great War figures, there are more, including studies of Sir Arthur CURRIE by H.M. Urquhart, Daniel Dancocks and A.M.J. Hyatt. Field Marshal BYNG of Vimy is the subject of Jeffery Williams' biography which won a Governor General's award. There are neither autobiographies or biographies of any other senior Great War figures other than W.A. GRIESBACH, whose *I Remember* deals with his militia and war experiences, and army medical doctor H.A. BRUCE's *Varied Operations*. There are, however, autobiographies and studies of other notable figures. Billy BISHOP, the great air ace, has been well covered, notably in *The Courage of the Early Morning* by his son and in Dan McCaffery's book, *Billy Bishop: Canadian Hero*. There are also many volumes such as Reginald Roy's well-edited book, *The Journal of Private Fraser* 1914–1918 of the 31st Battalion, CEF.

For WORLD WAR II the situation is both worse and better. There are as yet no biographies of Generals H.D.G. CRERAR, Guy SIMONDS, E.L.M. BURNS, or Charles FOULKES who commanded the FIRST CANADIAN ARMY and the I and II CANADIAN CORPS in action. There is, however, a long (3 vols), partisan biography of General A.G.L. MCNAUGHTON, the First Army commander, that covers his Great War and interwar service as well. Reg Roy has also written a well-researched study of General George PEARKES, a Great War VICTORIA CROSS winner, a PERMANENT FORCE officer between the wars, and a division commander in World War II. General Burns has told his own story in a well written fashion in *General Mud*, while General Christopher VOKES committed his reminiscences to paper in a less satisfactory and more bombastic way. George KITCHING, another division commander, told of his military life in a straightforward fashion in *Mud and Green Fields*, while General Maurice POPE, one of Canada's best staff officers, wrote *Soldiers and Politicians*, a very effective recounting of his military life and times. Tony Foster wrote in a most innovative way of his father, General Harry FOSTER, combining his biography with that of SS General Kurt MEYER whose troops fought against Foster's brigade in Normandy and over whose court-martial for murdering Canadian PoWs Foster presided. Larry Worthington's biography of her husband, Gen. F.F. WORTHINGTON, *Worthy*, is a story of derring-do, Robert Speaight's of Gen. Georges VANIER is one of veneration while Brig. J.A. Roberts' *The Canadian Summer* is a starkly told and moving account. Another good memoir by a wartime brigadier who rose to be a peacetime CHIEF OF THE GENERAL STAFF is Howard GRAHAM's *Citizen and Soldier*. Other evocative memoirs by more junior officers and soldiers abound. Worthy of note are R.S. MALONE's *A World in Flames* (2 vols.), Farley MOWAT's *And No Birds Sang*, Strome Galloway's *Bravely Into Battle*, Fred Cederberg's *The Long Road Home*, Ben Dunkelman's *Dual Allegiance*, and C.S. Frost's *Once A Patricia*. Not to be missed is the memoir by Charles STACEY, the army's senior historian. His *A Date With History* gives his own story as well as tart, true assessments of military and political figures.

The other services are less well represented in number. One of the finest World War II memoirs published anywhere, however, is by an RCAF veteran. Murray Peden's *A Thousand Shall Fall* is a superb, if still regrettably little known, deeply moving account of one young man's time in the air force from BRITISH COMMONWEALTH AIR TRAINING PLAN trainee to bomber pilot. Also useful, though more hagiographic, is Brian Nolan's *Hero: The Buzz BEURLING Story*. There are no biographies of senior air officers and only one of a senior sailor, James Cameron's *Murray: The Martyred Admiral* about Leonard MURRAY whose career was destroyed by the HALIFAX RIOT. Jeffry BROCK, who served much of the war with the Royal Navy, wrote a two-volume memoir, *With Many*

Voices, that is most useful for his postwar career, while Hal Lawrence's *A Bloody War* evokes the war for the CONVOYS.

For postwar figures, the accounts are even more sparse. There is a good autobiography by General J.V. ALLARD that covers his career through World War II, the KOREAN WAR, and UNIFICATION. General Leonard Johnson wrote a brief memoir, *A General for Peace*, of his time in the RCAF and the unified force, with his conversion to peace activist being the dominant theme. The volumes by Gen. Graham and Admiral Brock are also useful for the 1950s and 1960s.

Bishop, William Avery (1894–1956). Billy Bishop, born in Owen Sound, Ont., attended the ROYAL MILITARY COLLEGE where he was a troublesome cadet who was on the verge of expulsion when WORLD WAR I began. Bishop joined the Mississauga Horse, went overseas with the cavalry, and transferred to the ROYAL FLYING CORPS in 1915. Trained initially as an observer, he did not get to France as a pilot until 1917, but he quickly made his mark. His superb gunnery gave him a fighting edge and his score began to mount. On 2 June 1917 he made a single-handed early morning attack on a German airfield where his claim to have shot down three aircraft won him the VICTORIA CROSS to go with his DISTINGUISHED SERVICE ORDER and bar, his MILITARY CROSS, and his DISTINGUISHED FLYING CROSS. By June 1918, Bishop had been credited with a total of 72 kills, and two months later he was promoted to lieutenant-colonel and sent to join the staff in England. After the war, Bishop worked in business, and in WORLD WAR II as an honorary air marshal he assisted the ROYAL CANADIAN AIR FORCE in its recruiting efforts.

Bishop's reputation was attacked in a 1982 National Film Board production, *The Kid Who Couldn't Miss*, that claimed he had faked the raid that won him his Victoria Cross. This charge caused a furore and sparked protests from veterans' groups and in Parliament. The matter remains moot, though the weight of evidence three quarters of a century later likely favours Bishop.
Reading: W.A. Bishop, *The Courage of the Early Morning* (1966)

Black Rock. A settlement near the Lake Erie end of the Niagara River, Black Rock

was a fortified American position during the WAR OF 1812. On 11 July 1813, a force of 250 British troops and Canadian militia took the town, destroyed two schooners and a sloop moored there, and burned the fortifications to the ground.

Black Watch of Canada (Royal Highland Regiment). This regiment's roots date back to 1862 and the formation of the 5th Battalion Volunteer Militia Rifles in Montreal. The present name was not formally adopted until 1935, after the unit had raised three battalions for service with the CANADIAN EXPEDITIONARY FORCE. In WORLD WAR II, the Black Watch mobilized for active service in September 1939 and saw service in Newfoundland and Britain and in the NORTH-WEST EUROPE CAMPAIGN as part of the 2nd Canadian Division. It suffered very heavy casualties on the road to FALAISE in August 1944 and at BEVELAND on the SCHELDT. After the war, the regiment provided companies to the forces being sent for NATO service, and in 1953 two battalions of the regular force were designated as the 1st and 2nd Battalions of the Black Watch. The Black Watch was dropped from the regular force in the mid-1970s as part of the army's budget-induced cutbacks.

Blais, Jean-Jacques (b. 1940). Elected to the House of Commons in northern Ontario in 1972, Blais held a number of Cabinet posts. He was Defence minister in the Trudeau government from 1983 to 84.

Board of Pension Commissioners. Created in September 1916 after a special parliamentary committee had considered the question of pensions, the Board was placed under the Finance department and charged with deciding all military pension claims arising out of WORLD WAR I service. Its effective head was Major J.L. TODD and he shaped the Board's procedures. The systems employed were precise and rational but soon created enormous grievance among veterans.

Bobak, Bronislaw Josephus (b. 1923). Canada's youngest war artist, Bruno Bobak was commissioned in 1944 after service in the army engineers. His paintings of combat scenes in Italy and Northwest Europe featured an expressive-realist style.

Bobak, Molly Lamb (b. 1922). Trained at the Vancouver School of Art, Molly Lamb joined the CANADIAN WOMEN'S ARMY CORPS in 1942 and in 1945 became the country's first and only female war artist. She is married to Bruno BOBAK.

Bobcat transport. A Canadian-designed mid-1950s armoured personnel carrier, the Bobcat was abandoned a decade later because of high costs and mechanical troubles.

Boer War. See SOUTH AFRICAN WAR.

Bofors gun. A widely used 40-mm anti-aircraft gun, the Bofors was developed in Sweden and subsequently produced under licence in Britain, the U.S., and Canada. During WORLD WAR II it was the army's standard light anti-aircraft piece. As late as 1990, Bofors were mounted on one of the Canadian ships sent to the Persian Gulf.

Bolingbroke trainer. A pre-war design, the Bolingbroke was a Canadian training aircraft variant of the Bristol Blenheim, a light-medium bomber with a top speed of 362 km/h and a range of 3000 km. The first contracts to build the aircraft in Canada were placed in November 1937. A few ROYAL CANADIAN AIR FORCE squadrons flew fighter versions of the Blenheim overseas.

Bomarc missile. An acronym for the Boeing Michigan Aeronautical Research Center, the Bomarc surface-to-air missile had a range of 400 miles. In 1958, the government of John DIEFENBAKER announced plans to deploy two squadrons of the missiles at North Bay, Ont., and La Macaza, Que. as part of Canada's obligations to NORAD and as a replacement for the troubled ARROW interceptor. The Bomarc was effective only with nuclear warheads, however, though this was not immediately apparent. By 1962, there was intense debate in the country and within the Cabinet over the fitting of the warheads to the missiles, especially between Defence minister Douglas HARKNESS and External Affairs minister Howard Green. Diefenbaker's inability to decide between the positions espoused by two powerful ministers and his subsequent delays in deciding to arm the weapons seriously strained relations with the U.S. and led to the loss of a confidence vote in Parliament and electoral defeat in April 1963. The new Liberal prime minister, Lester PEARSON, accepted the warheads which were deployed in December 1963 and phased out in 1971.

Bomber Command. The Royal Air Force's Bomber Command, established in 1936, was the main air weapon used to strike at Germany in WORLD WAR II. At the beginning of the war, the RAF had only slow, small machines that proved notably ineffective, most early raids failing to get near the target areas or, if they did, to hit it; but the development of HALIFAX and LANCASTER bombers gave the RAF effective weapons able to drop high tonnages at night on German cities, though still largely incapable of accuracy. Bomber Command raids killed over 600,000 Germans, but the cost in aircrews was high — some estimates show the Command's 59,423 dead equalling just under half of the aircrew who flew in bombers.

The ROYAL CANADIAN AIR FORCE formed its first bomber squadron in June 1941 and seven more were created in 1942. These squadrons, most initially flying already obsolescent WELLINGTON bombers, were brought together in NO. 6 BOMBER GROUP on 1 January 1943, and the group at its peak included 14 RCAF squadrons. The group lost 4272 RCAF personnel in flying its 41,000 operations and dropping 126,000 tons of bombs. Many other RCAF officers and men flew with and died in RAF bomber squadrons. Total Canadian casualties in the bomber offensive were 9980, of which 8290 were aircrew lost on operations.

Reading: Spencer Dunmore and William Carter, *Reap the Whirlwind* (Toronto, 1991)

Bonaventure, HMCS. This aircraft carrier, launched in 1945 but with work stopped until Canada purchased her in Britain in 1952, came into ROYAL CANADIAN NAVY service in 1957. The 'Bonnie' had an angled flight deck, a steam catapult, and mirror landing sight, all state-of-the-art devices, and her complement consisted of Banshee fighters and Tracker anti-submarine aircraft. The carrier's mid-life refit in 1966–67 was expensive and stirred criticism, but there was more when the Trudeau government sold her for scrap in 1970.

Bonne Entente. Organized by Toronto lawyer J.M. GODFREY, the Bonne Entente movement was an English Canadian businessmen's attempt to secure Quebec support for national service, i.e., increased voluntary enlistment, in WORLD WAR I. Beginning in the summer of 1916, the movement featured a visit to Montreal in October by 48 Ontarians and a return visit to Toronto by French Canadian businessmen in January 1917.

Bonus campaign. Begun with the Calgary resolution of 1919, the campaign was a noisy populist effort by WORLD WAR I veterans to secure a cash grant of up to $2000 a man over and above existing programs from the government. The GREAT WAR VETERANS' ASSOCIATION split over the issue, and the BORDEN government refused to lay out the billion dollars necessary for the bonus. The successor Meighen and KING governments were no more accommodating.

Books, World War I. Publishing in Canada during the Great War tended to focus on carefully censored accounts of the fighting, designed to inspire recruiting rather than to describe the war's horror. Almost nothing was published then (and for many more years) on the Canadian navy's role in the war. On air fighting, there was only Billy BISHOP's memoir, *Winged Warfare.* For the CANADIAN EXPEDITIONARY FORCE, there was more, as was natural given the high percentage of the country's military manpower enlisted therein. Works ranged from regimental and corps histories such as George Adami's *War Story of the Canadian Army Medical Corps* to Max AITKEN, Lord Beaverbrook's account as CANADIAN EYE-WITNESS, *Canada in Flanders.* There were memoirs such as William Boyd's *With a Field Ambulance at Ypres,* J. Harvey Douglas' *Captured,* and Louis Keene's *'Crumps': The Plain Story of a Canadian Who Went to War,* and accounts of the CEF like Ralph Bell's *Canada in War-Paint* and Corringsby Dawson's *The Glory of the Trenches.* There were many books of expurgated letters such as *A Canadian Subaltern: Billy's Letters to His Mother.* And there were government publications galore on the *European War ... Respecting Work of the Department of Militia and Defence* or the *Returned Soldiers' Handbook* or the *Report of the Director of the Military Service Branch ... on the Operation of the*

Military Service Act, 1917. The *Canadian Annual Review* continued its yearly volumes that still provide the best summaries of events as they seemed to unfold to participants, and there were countless magazine and newspaper special editions dealing with aspects of the war. Readers should bear in mind that censorship in Canada during the war was very tight, and it extended to the daily press, magazines, books, and even to photographs and movies. See also BIOGRAPHY, MILITARY; MILITARY HISTORY; WAR NOVELS.

Books, World War II. The literature published in Canada in World War II was not greatly different in character from that of World War I. Regimental histories abounded (including several published in the Netherlands in 1945), and there were far more government booklets and reports than in the earlier war, notably the extremely useful *Canada at War,* published every few months, which provided a digest of statistics of all phases of the national war effort. There was Harold Clegg's *A Canuck in England: Journal of a Canadian Soldier,* as well as *Drive to the Rhine: the First Canadian Army in Action* by Canadian Press correspondents, CBC correspondent Matthew HALTON's book, *Ten Years to Alamein,* and Wallace REYBURN's *Glorious Chapters: The Canadians at Dieppe.* More annoying to Canadian soldiers was Quentin Reynolds' *Dress Rehearsal: The Story of Dieppe* because of the gushing way it treated Adm. Mountbatten, the head of Combined Operations responsible for the raid, and for the prominence it gave the 50 U.S. Rangers who were with the British commandos.

For the ROYAL CANADIAN NAVY, there was again little. Griffith Coale published his *North Atlantic Patrol: the Log of a Seagoing Artist* and Grant Macdonald published his sketches in *Sailors.* J.M. Hitsman set the war in context with his *Canadian Naval Policy* and W.H. Pugsley chronicled life on the RCN's lower deck with his *Saints, Devils and Ordinary Seamen.* The RCAF was if anything even worse served. There were only some instant squadron histories, D.A. MacMillan's *Only the Stars Know,* and Hermann Hagedorn's *Sunward I've Climbed: the Story of John Magee, Poet and Soldier,* an account of an American who died on active service with the RCAF and who wrote one of the war's greatest poems, 'High Flight'. See also BIOGRAPHY, MILITARY; MILITARY HISTORY; WAR NOVELS.

Borden, Sir Frederick William (1847–1917). Born in Nova Scotia and trained as a doctor, Borden served with the MILITIA from 1869 while simultaneously becoming well off as a merchant. He won election to Parliament as a Liberal in 1874, and in 1896 LAURIER named him minister of Militia and Defence, a post he held until 1911. As minister he had terrific struggles with a number of the British GENERAL OFFICERS COMMANDING the MILITIA, and he had the task of putting together the Canadian contingents for the SOUTH AFRICAN WAR (in which his son was killed in action). In 1904, after the last of his battles with the GOC, he pressed for and won the Canadianization of the militia which now would be under Canadian command and control.

Borden, Sir Robert Laird (1854–1937). Prime minister 1911–20, Borden was born at Grand Pré, N.S. He entered Parliament as a Conservative in 1896, became party leader in 1901, and came to power after the reciprocity election of 1911. Borden led the country through WORLD WAR I, an experience of a magnitude and difficulty simply unprecedented in Canadian experience. His Militia minister, Sam HUGHES, did good work in getting the first army contingent overseas, but thereafter enormous difficulties bedevilled military organization, recruitment, and (by 1917) CONSCRIPTION. Borden demonstrated enormous determination in ramming the MILITARY SERVICE ACT through Parliament, forming a UNION GOVERNMENT, and winning the 1917 election. But his insensitivity to French Canadian resistance to compulsory service did terrible damage to unity. Abroad, Borden used the country's enormous military effort to fight for and win greater autonomy for Canada.
Reading: R.C. Brown, *Robert Laird Borden: A Biography*, 2 vols (1975, 1980).

Boscawen, Edward (1711–1761). He joined the Royal Navy in 1726 and had distinguished himself in the West and East Indies before coming to Canada in 1755 with the task of intercepting French efforts to reinforce North America. He participated in the expulsion of the Acadians and in 1758 commanded the navy at the capture of LOUISBOURG.

Boston bomber. The Douglas DB-7 of United States manufacture was the basis of the Boston, a medium-range three-seat attack bomber powered by two 1600-hp radial engines giving a top speed of 490 km/h. The Boston could carry a bomb load of 907 kg and it was armed with four .303-calibre machine guns. The ROYAL CANADIAN AIR FORCE operated several Boston Mk III squadrons from 1941 to 43.

Bougainville, Louis-Antoine, Comte de (1729–1811). A lawyer and mathematician, Bougainville joined the French army in 1750 and served as an aide to General MONTCALM during the SEVEN YEARS' WAR. He was widely blamed for not coming to his general's aid with timely reinforcements at the battle of QUEBEC in 1759. Bougainville subsequently served in the French navy during the American Revolutionary War.

Bourassa, Joseph Henri Napoleon (1868–1952). The grandson of Louis Joseph PAPINEAU, Bourassa was born in Quebec and first elected to Parliament as a Liberal in 1896. Of independent mind, he clashed in 1899 with Sir Wilfrid LAURIER, whose protégé he had been, over Canadian participation in the SOUTH AFRICAN WAR. Bourassa objected to Canada's sending troops for a wholly British war that posed no threat to Canada, and he ridiculed Laurier's claim that this was not a precedent. He continued his opposition to Laurier, whom he was convinced was a tool of British and Canadian imperialists, by fighting his plans for a Canadian navy and putting a *nationaliste* candidate into the field against the Liberal in the DRUMMOND-ARTHABASKA BY-ELECTION of 1910. In 1911, Bourassa's candidates helped drive Laurier from power. But the two great French Canadians came back together in 1917 to oppose CONSCRIPTION and Sir Robert BORDEN's UNION GOVERNMENT. Bourassa stayed active through World War II, continuing to fight against conscription and to campaign for the 'non' side in the PLEBISCITE of 1942.

Bourke, Rowland Richard Louis (1885–1958). In May 1918 his Royal Navy motor launch was badly damaged by enemy fire off

Ostend. Nonetheless, Bourke rescued three comrades and won the VICTORIA CROSS for his valour.

Bowell, Sir Mackenzie (1823–1917). Bowell came to British North America in 1833. He saw service with the militia against the FENIANS. A Conservative, he held ministerial appointments in the MACDONALD and Abbott governments, including minister of Militia and Defence in 1892. He became prime minister in 1894 and remained in that post until 1896.

Boyle, Douglas Seaman (b. 1923). Boyle graduated from the Royal Naval College and entered the ROYAL CANADIAN NAVY in 1941, serving in both Royal Navy and RCN warships during WORLD WAR II. After staff and command appointments, he commanded NATO's Standing Naval Force Atlantic in 1970 and in 1973 he took over MARITIME COMMAND. He resigned as a vice-admiral in 1977, before his scheduled retirement, after severely criticizing the Trudeau government's military spending cutbacks.

Boys anti-tank rifle. The .55-inch bolt-action Boys was developed as an infantry anti-tank weapon in the 1930s. Though largely ineffective against modern armour, the Boys was standard equipment for Canadian units until early 1943 when it was replaced by the PIAT.

Braddock, Edward (1695–1755). A career soldier, he enlisted in the Coldstream Guards at 15 and by 1754 was commander-in-chief in British North America. He was killed and his army routed after being ambushed by French and Indian forces near Fort Duquesne in 1755.

Bras d'Or, HMCS. The first ship of this name, a trawler, was requisitioned by the ROYAL CANADIAN NAVY in 1939 as an auxiliary minesweeper. She disappeared in the Gulf of St Lawrence in October 1940. Her experimental successor, commissioned in 1968, was an open-ocean fast hydrofoil escort that could make 63 knots. The Bras d'Or was de-commissioned as a government economy measure in 1971.

Breadner, Lloyd Samuel (1894–1952). After service as a fighter pilot in World War

I with the Royal Naval Air Service, Breadner held staff posts with the ROYAL CANADIAN AIR FORCE. Bluff and hearty, he became CHIEF OF THE AIR STAFF in 1940, and played a key role in the wartime expansion of the RCAF. From 1944 to the end of the war, he commanded the RCAF overseas, and on his retirement in 1945 he was promoted air chief marshal.

Bren gun. Based on a Czech design, the Bren was a .303-calibre gas-operated, air-cooled light machine gun. The standard infantry light machine gun of British Commonwealth forces during and after World War II, the accurate, durable Bren was mass-produced in Canada.

Bren gun carrier. A tracked light armoured vehicle, the Bren carrier was used by British and Canadian forces in World War II. Ordinarily carrying a crew of four, the carrier had several variants, including a flame-thrower, and was built in Canada in large numbers.

Bren Gun Scandal (1938). The Canadian and British governments awarded contracts to build BREN GUNS to the John Inglis Co. of Toronto. The contract had not been tendered and Conservative politician George DREW wrote and spoke against the government's policy, forcing the government to establish a royal commission to investigate his charges. The report uncovered no evidence of corruption but did find the DEPARTMENT OF NATIONAL DEFENCE's procedures unworthy. It recommended an advisory group of businessmen to assist, leading to the creation of a DEFENCE PURCHASING BOARD in 1939 and competitive bidding. Inglis eventually produced 200,000 Brens.

Brereton, Alexander Picton (1892–1976). Cpl Brereton, a Manitoba-born member of the 8th Battalion, CANADIAN EXPEDITIONARY FORCE, won the VICTORIA CROSS at AMIENS on 9 August 1918 when he single-handedly destroyed a German machine-gun post, killing two enemy soldiers and forcing the surrender of nine more.

Breskens pocket, 1944. As part of the SCHELDT campaign in October 1944 that aimed to clear the approaches to the port of

23

Antwerp, troops of the 3RD CANADIAN DI-VISION struggled in desperate conditions to subdue a pocket of German troops in the low-lying areas north of the Leopold Canal and around the town of Breskens, Belgium. The battle, involving the first use of BUF-FALO amphibious troop carriers and massed flame-throwers, lasted from 16 October to 3 November and caused heavy casualties.

Brigade group organization, Korean War. The brigade group that fought in Korea was commanded by a brigadier and consisted of three infantry battalions, a squadron of tanks, a field regiment of artil-lery, a field squadron of engineers, a squad-ron of signallers, a transport company, and a field ambulance.

Brigade organization, World War I. Led by a brigadier-general, an infantry bri-gade consisted of four infantry battalions and a trench mortar battery. The Canadian Cav-alry Brigade had four cavalry regiments, a machine-gun squadron, and a field ambu-lance.

Brigade organization, World War II. Commanded by a brigadier, an infantry bri-gade comprised three infantry battalions. An armoured brigade was usually made up of three armoured regiments and a motorized infantry battalion.

Brillant, Jean (1890–1918). A lieutenant in the 22e Battalion, CEF, Brillant won the VICTORIA CROSS during the AMIENS offen-sive of August 1918. Brillant led several as-saults on enemy machine-gun and artillery emplacements; though severely wounded he refused to leave his men until he collapsed. He died the next day, 10 August.

Bristol Beaufighter. A two-seat fighter and attack bomber, the Beaufighter came into British service in 1939 and, during the war, was flown by several ROYAL CANADIAN AIR FORCE squadrons. Powered by two very quiet 1375-hp sleeve-valve engines, the 530-km/h. Beaufighter was initially armed with four 20-mm cannons; later, six machine guns were added, making it the most heavily armed fighter flying. The aircraft also had early versions of airborne radar.

Bristol F2a/F2b fighter. A two-seater fighter-reconnaissance aircraft in WORLD WAR I and one of the best fighter aircraft of the war, the 'Brisfit' flew on combat opera-tions initially in April 1917. Britain gave Canada two of the aircraft as a gift at the end of the war.

British Army Staff College. Located at Camberley, the Staff College trained officers, usually of captain or major rank, for staff duties and, ultimately, for higher command. Twelve Canadians attended prior to WORLD WAR I, and after the war two or more Canadians, selected by competitive examina-tion, were usually to be found in every two-year course. One additional officer attended the staff college at Quetta, India, annually from 1924. The shared experiences with Im-perial and Dominion officers virtually guar-anteed that Canada fought WORLD WAR II as a British military clone.

British Commonwealth Air Training Plan. Arguably the major Canadian contri-bution to the Allied war effort in WORLD WAR II, the British Commonwealth Air Training Plan trained aircrew from Canada, Britain, Australia, New Zealand, and other Commonwealth countries, as well as some from the United States and occupied Europe, at air bases across Canada.

Before the outbreak of war in September 1939, the British government had been try-ing for some time to secure Prime Minister Mackenzie KING's agreement to allow the Royal Air Force to train pilots in Canada. King was reluctant to agree to such ap-proaches, arguing that they would prejudice Canada's ability to decide for itself whether or not to join in any war. But once the war began, and Britain, prompted by the Austra-lian and Canadian high commissioners in London, tried once more, the Canadian mood was more receptive. As a politician fully aware of the impact of CONSCRIPTION in 1917, King wanted to avoid a large army and the casualties sure to result when it went into action. Air combat could not be as costly in lives, King believed, and he agreed to open negotiations with London. These were long and difficult, the British wanting Canada to pay the lion's share of the scheme's costs, the Canadians insisting that London should acknowledge that air training was Canada's most important role in the war. Ultimately a compromise was reached on 17 December 1939, significantly King's birthday, though it fudged the question of the disposition of Canadian graduates of the Plan, thus creating the CANADIANI-ZATION issue down the road. In the original agreement, Britain was to pay $218 million, Canada $313 million, Australia $97 million, and New Zealand $21 million. Later changes raised the proposed Canadian share by $40 million. Each month, the initial agreement said, the BCATP was to graduate 520 pilots with elementary training, 544 with service training, 340 air observers, and 580 wireless operator-air gunners.

The ROYAL CANADIAN AIR FORCE, its prewar strength just 4000, ran and controlled the BCATP and carried out the training, initially with the assistance of private flying clubs. It took some time to get underway and the first aircrew were not graduated until late 1940. Shortages of instructors and training aircraft—the British could supply almost none after the beginning of the BATTLE OF BRITAIN—delayed matters. But by 1942 the Plan was in full flight with 107 schools located all across Canada. It was also vastly bigger than the scheme envisaged in 1939. Almost 11,000 aircraft were used, and the Plan employed 104,000 men and women and made a significant economic contribution to hundreds of communities. The final cost to Canada was $1.6 billion out of a total of $2.2 billion, vastly more than that agreed in December 1939. By the time it was shut down at the end of March 1945, the Plan had produced 131,553 pilots, navigators, bombardiers, wireless operators, air gunners, and flight engineers of which 72,835 were Canadians. The Canadian graduates of the Plan staffed some 85 RCAF squadrons at home and overseas and in addition constituted almost a quarter of the Royal Air Force's total strength.
Reading: F.J. Hatch, *Aerodrome of Democracy* (1983)

British 8th Army. General Bernard L. Montgomery's 8th Army had been victorious in North Africa, and it would, with the U.S. 7th Army, invade SICILY in July 1943. The 1ST CANADIAN DIVISION, assigned to the invasion, thus became part of the Eighth Army, as did the 5TH CANADIAN ARMOU-RED DIVISION and I CANADIAN CORPS in the ITALIAN CAMPAIGN in due course. It was a

matter of great pride for the Canadians to be part of 'Monty's army', the first major British formation in WORLD WAR II to score sustained victories in the field.

British Security Coordination. Headed by Sir William STEPHENSON, British Security Coordination was set up in the neutral United States early in WORLD WAR II to conduct counter-espionage against Britain's enemies. The BSC censored letters, forged documents, guarded against sabotage, and trained Allied agents at CAMP X, near Whitby, Ont. BSC's agents also produced some reports on Canada, including one on Japanese espionage that had some influence.

Brittain, Miller (1912–1968). The Saint John, N.B., artist, trained in New York in the figurative Ashcan School, had begun to establish a reputation for his sympathetic, even radical, Depression drawings when he enlisted in the RCAF. He served on HALI-FAX bombers, flying 37 missions. In 1945, he formally became a war artist. His drawings and oils superbly portray his comrades and convey the air war's terror and eerie beauty.

Brock, Sir Isaac (1769–1812). Born in Guernsey, Brock came to British North America in 1802 and in 1811 was promoted to major-general and made provisional administrator of Upper Canada. He was thus in command at the beginning of the WAR OF 1812, and his forces instantly seized the initiative, taking MICHILIMACKINAC and attacking Detroit. His early victories reversed the feelings of hopelessness in the vastly outnumbered colony and led recent American arrivals to keep their heads down and wait on events. His frontier secured, Brock confidently led his troops, including some INCORPORATED MILITIA, against the American invaders on the NIAGARA FRONTIER. At QUEENSTON HEIGHTS he was killed by an American sniper; an impressive monument to him now dominates the battlefield.

Brock, Jeffry Vanstone (b. 1913). Born in Vancouver, Brock joined the naval reserves before WORLD WAR II. He served on loan with the Royal Navy during the war, establishing an outstanding record in anti-submarine operations, then in 1944–45 he was senior naval officer with the Canadian Escort

Group C.6. After the war, he was executive officer on HMCS ONTARIO when there was a NAVAL MUTINY aboard. Brock commanded the first division of Canadian destroyers to serve in the KOREAN WAR from 1950–51, chaired the influential Ad Hoc Committee on Naval Objectives in 1961, and retired as Flag Officer Atlantic Coast in 1964. He vigorously opposed UNIFICATION and wrote a two-volume memoir, *With Many Voices* (1981, 1983).

Brodeur, Louis Philippe (1862–1924). A barrister and politician, Brodeur was minister of Naval Service in the LAURIER government. As such, he introduced the legislation creating the Canadian navy in 1910.

Brodeur, Victor Gabriel (1892–1977). Brodeur joined the Canadian naval service as a cadet in 1909, one of the rare francophones to do so in that era, and saw extensive action during WORLD WAR I while on loan to the Royal Navy. He had his first independent command (HMCS *Champlain*) in 1930, helped suppress a rebellion in Nicaragua, and was Canada's first naval attaché in Washington, 1940–43. In 1942, a rear-admiral, he represented Canada at the ATLANTIC CONVOY CONFERENCE. After commanding on the Pacific Coast from 1943–46, he retired in 1947.

Brooks, Alfred Johnson (1890–1967). A New Brunswick lawyer and politician, Brooks served with the CANADIAN EXPEDITIONARY FORCE overseas, in the interwar MILITIA, and in the army in WORLD WAR II. First elected to the House of Commons in 1935, he was minister of Veterans' Affairs in the DIEFENBAKER government until 1960 when he was called to the Senate.

Brooks, Frank Leonard (b. 1911). Brooks studied art in Canada, Europe, and Mexico and joined the navy in WORLD WAR II. In 1943, he worked on propaganda and war posters; from 1944 he served as a war artist aboard warships in the English Channel and North Atlantic.

Brown, Arthur Roy (1893–1944). A fighter pilot with the ROYAL FLYING CORPS, Brown was born in Carleton Place, Ont. He scored 11 victories on the Western Front, but his fame comes from the belief that he shot down the 'Red Baron', Manfred Freiherr von Richthofen, in April 1918. The claim is not entirely substantiated, many historians arguing that an Australian machinegunner on the ground did the deed. Brown was severely injured in a flying accident soon after and left the Royal Air Force in 1919.

Brown, Harry (1898–1917). Born in Gananoque, Ont., Pte Brown of the 10th Battalion, CEF, carried critical messages forward under heavy fire during the battle for HILL 70 in August 1917. Mortally wounded, he was awarded the VICTORIA CROSS.

Brown, James Sutherland (1881–1951). Born at Simcoe, Ont., 'Buster' Brown joined the militia in 1896, the regular force a decade later, and served with great distinction in WORLD WAR I as an infantryman. He remained in the army, serving most notably as director of military operations and intelligence at Ottawa in the 1920s. There he drafted the army's plans for various eventualities, including DEFENCE SCHEME NO. 1, a plan to send strong mobile columns to attack the United States in event of an Anglo-American war. Much derided by later generations of historians, Brown's plans were, in fact, intelligent ones, prepared in response to his superiors' instructions. He ended his career in 1933 in command in British Columbia as a brigadier; his efforts to get back into uniform in 1939 were unavailing.
Reading: Charles Taylor, *Six Journeys: A Canadian Pattern* (1977)

Browning .50-calibre machine gun. A modification of the U.S.-designed .30-calibre Browning, this air-cooled heavy machine gun was used in WORLD WAR II and is still in widespread use as an infantry support weapon and on armoured vehicles. The weight of the gun is 37 kg, range is 6600 m, and the rate of fire is 450 rounds per minute.

Bruce, Herbert Alexander (1868–1963). Bruce was born at Blackstock, Ont. A surgeon, he founded Toronto's Wellesley Hospital before becoming a colonel and Inspector-General of the Canadian Army Medical Corps in 1916. In Britain, he charged that patronage ruled and produced poor care of the CANADIAN CORPS' sick and wounded; this led to a substantial reorganization. After the war, Bruce served as Ontario lieutenant-governor and, during WORLD WAR II, as a Conservative M.P. who vigorously advocated CONSCRIPTION.

Reading: H.A. Bruce, *Varied Operations* (1958)

BRUSA. The Britain-United States Agreement on Signals Intelligence was signed in May 1943. It brought the senior partners — and Canada as a de facto member — into a system of operational cooperation on signals intelligence and detailed the security regulations that were to apply. BRUSA was succeeded after the war by the UKUSA agreement.

Brutinel, Raymond (1872–1964). Born in France, Brutinel came to Canada in 1904 and worked as a surveyor and journalist in western Canada. In 1914, at the outbreak of WORLD WAR I, he conceived the idea of and raised a motorized machine-gun unit, the Automobile Machine-Gun Brigade No. 1 with a strength of 123, and led it overseas as part of the CANADIAN EXPEDITIONARY FORCE. His innovative ideas of indirect fire and his stress on mobility were proven in action, and in 1916 three additional privately raised machine-gun batteries were added to Brutinel's, the whole named the 1st Motor Machine-Gun Brigade and designated as corps troops. Brigadier-General Brutinel also served as commander of the CANADIAN MACHINE-GUN CORPS and laid down the CANADIAN CORPS policy on the employment of machine guns. A plaque at the Château Laurier in Ottawa commemorates his efforts.

Buffalo landing vehicle. A tracked landing vehicle developed in WORLD WAR II that could transport personnel or stores. The Buffalo could carry a vehicle or a four-ton load at 6 knots, was armed with a 17-pounder gun and a machine gun, and could negotiate fairly steep grades. The Buffalo was used by Canadians in the SCHELDT campaign and in the Rhine crossing.

Buffalo transport (STOL). The de Havilland Buffalo is a medium-size (24 m long), short takeoff and landing (STOL) tactical transport with a top speed of 365 km/h. It is produced in Canada. The aircraft came

into production early in the 1960s and has been sold widely around the world.

Bull, Gerald (1931–1990). Born at North Bay, Ont., Gerald Bull earned a PhD at the University of Toronto and then worked for the CANADIAN ARMAMENT & RESEARCH DEVELOPMENT ESTABLISHMENT on missile development. He became convinced that artillery could put satellites into orbit and this led to the development of advanced and powerful guns. His work for the Canadian and U.S. governments ended in some acrimony and, after a jail term, he set up his own companies and sold his designs to the highest bidders, a group that included South Africa and Iraq. Bull was murdered in Brussels in March 1990.

Burgoyne, John (1722–1792). 'Gentleman Johnny' Burgoyne purchased a commission in the British army in 1740 and came to Quebec as a major-general in 1776. He served under Guy CARLETON in the campaign against the Americans in 1776, and next year he led 8,000 men south alongside Lake Champlain and the Hudson River in an attempt to cut New England off from the rest of the rebels. Although he captured Fort Ticonderoga in June, he ran out of supplies, fought several costly engagements, and was obliged to capitulate at Saratoga, N.Y., after the two major battles of the campaign, on 17 October 1777. His surrender was a turning point of the revolution.

Burns, Eedson Louis Millard [Tommy] (1897–1985). Burns, born at Westmount, Que., graduated from the ROYAL MILITARY COLLEGE in 1915 and at once proceeded overseas with the Engineers. After serving with the 4TH CANADIAN DIVISION, he ended the war as a captain with a MILITARY CROSS. In the tiny PERMANENT FORCE he developed a reputation as an intelligent young officer in a succession of staff posts. Much of his work was in developing air photo survey techniques that proved of value in mapping Canada and in WORLD WAR II. He graduated from the Staff College, Quetta, and attended the Imperial Defence College. After the outbreak of war in 1939, Burns served at CANADIAN MILITARY HEADQUARTERS, London and in Ottawa. Cold and uncharismatic though he was, Burns' rise was swift. Burns commanded the 2ND CANADIAN DIVISION in

England, took over the 5TH CANADIAN AR-MOURED DIVISION in Italy in January 1944 and then the I CANADIAN CORPS in March. His command lasted until the fall when, despite success in conducting operations in the Liri Valley and capturing Rimini, he was relieved, thanks to a certain lack of confidence in him from his British superiors and Canadian division commanders. The rest of his war was spent on rear area duties.

After the war, Burns moved into the DE-PARTMENT OF VETERANS' AFFAIRS first as an adviser on rehabilitation and then as deputy minister. In 1954, he became head of the UNITED NATIONS TRUCE SUPERVISORY OR-GANIZATION (UNTSO) operating on the troubled borders between Israel and its Arab neighbours. In the fall of 1956, Burns took command of the UNITED NATIONS EMER-GENCY FORCE (UNEF) created after the Suez crisis, and he implemented Lester PEARSON's Nobel Prize-winning scheme on the ground. In 1958, he was promoted lieutenant-general and the next year he stepped down from his UNEF post. Burns then became the government's adviser on disarmament in 1960, a post he held for eight years.

Burns was also a writer. His book *Manpower in the Canadian Army* (1956) was an able analysis of the genesis of the CONSCRIP-TION crises of World War II. This was followed by his account of his UNTSO-UNEF experiences, *Between Arab and Israeli* (1962), a book that was unsparing in its criticism of Israeli policy. His memoir *General Mud* (1970) dealt with his wartime career, including his relief from command, with noticeable lack of bitterness.

Burstall, Sir Henry (1870–1945). A graduate of the ROYAL MILITARY COLLEGE and a PERMANENT FORCE officer born in Quebec, Burstall served in the YUKON FIELD FORCE, fought in the SOUTH AFRICAN WAR, and commanded the artillery in the first contin-gent of the CANADIAN EXPEDITIONARY FORCE and then in the CANADIAN CORPS. He took command of the 2ND CANADIAN DIVISION in December 1916 and led it to the end of the war. Highly regarded, he retired as Inspector-General of the army in 1923.

Butler, Sir William Francis (1838–1910). Commissioned in the British army in 1856, he served in Canada during the FENIAN RAIDS. In 1870, as intelligence officer during the RIEL REBELLION, he preceded the British forces west, interviewed RIEL, and then set off on a long reconnaissance of the Saskatchewan country. He later served in Egypt and Africa and retired as a lieutenant-general.

By, John (1781–1836). A British military engineer, Col By served in Canada from 1802 to 1811, working on the Quebec fortifications. In 1826, he was called out of retirement to construct the Rideau Canal from the Ottawa River to Lake Ontario. Bytown, later Ottawa, grew up around his headquarters.

Byng, Julian Hedworth George, Viscount Byng of Vimy (1862–1935). Born in England, Byng joined the British army in 1883 and, as a cavalry officer, served in the Sudan and in the Boer War. In WORLD WAR I, he took command of the CANADIAN CORPS in 1916 and forged this formation, eventually four divisions strong, into a first-class organization popularly known as 'Byng's Boys'. He directed the attack on VIMY RIDGE in April 1917, a brilliantly planned set-piece assault that produced a major victory. He ended the war as an army commander, was appointed Canadian governor-general in 1921 (where he became involved in the constitutional turmoil of 1926), and then became head of the London Metropolitan Police.
Reading: J. Williams, *Byng of Vimy* (1983)

C

Cabinet Defence Committee. The Mackenzie KING government set up a Canadian Defence Committee in August 1936 that met infrequently. At the outbreak of war in September 1939, King created an Emergency Council, replacing it in December with the

Cabinet War Committee, a grouping of the most powerful ministers. Most important, the Secretary to the Cabinet, Arnold Heeney, kept minutes and followed up on decisions. After the war, the Cabinet Defence Committee was reconstituted as one of several Cabinet committees.

Cabinet War Committee. The key Cabinet committee formed to direct Canada's war effort in WORLD WAR II, the war committee derived from the Emergency Council set up at the outbreak of war and was called by this name from 5 December 1939. Chaired by Prime Minister Mackenzie KING, the committee gathered together the seven or eight key ministers, including the three defence ministers, the finance minister, the minister of munitions and supply, and the senior Quebec ministers. The Cabinet secretary prepared the agenda and kept minutes (the first time this had been done in Canada), and officials and senior officers ordinarily attended when needed. The committee brought unaccustomed efficiency and despatch to the nation's war business.

Cadieux, Leo (b. 1908). A Quebec journalist, Cadieux joined the army's public relations directorate during WORLD WAR II, then served as a war correspondent. He entered Parliament as a Liberal in 1962 and became associate minister of National Defence in 1965. Two years later, he was the minister, charged with implementing UNIFICATION. As defence minister he fought Prime Minister Pierre Trudeau's attempts to cut Canadian commitments to NATO but managed only to ameliorate the reductions.

Caen. The high ground west of this city in NORMANDY was intended to be taken on D-DAY, 6 June 1944, by the 3RD CANADIAN INFANTRY DIVISION while the city itself was the D-Day objective of the British 3rd Division. German resistance made the achievement of both objectives impossible, and Caen would not fall for five weeks. The city was the hub of the Nazi defence, protected by heavy concentrations of armour and some of the Wehrmacht's best troops in Normandy. The 3rd Canadian Division struggled to move towards the city in the days after the invasion, but it suffered bloody repulses at Buron, Putot, Cairon, Le Mesnil-Patry and CARPIQUET. Finally, a massive attack on

the city by the Royal Air Force's BOMBER COMMAND was used to precede an attack by the division on 8 July. The city was liberated the next day, the civilian survivors of the bombing emerging to cheer the troops. The Germans had scarcely suffered in the bomber raid, their men sensibly being pulled back to the outskirts; the raid killed Frenchmen and clogged the streets with rubble, impeding the Allied advance.

Cairns, Hugh (1896–1918). Serving with the 46th Battalion, CEF, Sgt Cairns won a posthumous VICTORIA CROSS in November 1918 for singlehandedly killing several enemy soldiers and silencing three machine guns.

Cambrai, Battle of. In November 1917, the British 3rd Army, commanded by General BYNG, attacked the German front at Cambrai. The attack used massed armour for the first time and the follow-up, intended to exploit the breakthrough, included the CANADIAN CAVALRY BRIGADE, part of the British 5th Cavalry Division. The FORT GARRY HORSE played an important cavalry role at Masnières on 20 November, but the other regiments of the brigade were used as infantry. The next year, the city fell to the CANADIAN CORPS on 8–9 October as part of the CANAL DU NORD battle.

Campbell, Sir Alexander (1822–1902). A father of Confederation, Campbell held a number of ministerial posts in the MACDONALD government. He was minister of Militia and Defence in 1880.

Campbell, Frederick William (1867–1915). At Givenchy, France in June 1915, this Mount Forest, Ont., lieutenant won the VICTORIA CROSS for his role in checking a German counter-attack. Firing a machine gun mounted on the back of the only other unwounded soldier, Campbell held his position. He was mortally wounded in the action and died four days later.

Campbell, Hugh Lester (1908–1987). Commissioned in the ROYAL CANADIAN AIR FORCE in 1931, Campbell became director of training plans during the initial stages of the BRITISH COMMONWEALTH AIR TRAINING PLAN in late 1939. He served in the United Kingdom and was director of air staff at RCAF headquarters in 1942. After the war, he was first commander of the NO. I CANADIAN AIR DIVISION in NATO and then CHIEF OF THE AIR STAFF. He retired in 1962 as an air marshal.

Campbell, W. Bennett (b. 1943). A Liberal politician, Campbell served as premier of Prince Edward Island in 1978–79. He won election to Parliament in 1981 and served as minister of Veterans' Affairs until his defeat in the 1984 election.

Camp Borden. Located some 80 km northwest of Toronto in sandy, scrub-covered soil, Camp Borden was established in 1916 as a training base and named in honour of Sir Frederick BORDEN. The following year the Royal Flying Corps established a pilot training station there, and the RCAF took it over in 1924. In the 1930s, several PERMANENT FORCE schools set up shop there. During WORLD WAR II, some 185,000 men and women, soldiers and airmen, trained there. Now known as Canadian Forces Base Borden, the establishment is the country's largest military trades training station.

Camp Gagetown. Located near Oromocto, N.B., Camp Gagetown is a vast army base, the biggest in Canada. Opened in the 1950s, Gagetown was the home of the IST CANADIAN DIVISION, the army's sole postwar divisional formation, which carried out its training there. Its complement much attenuated after years of defence cuts, CANADIAN FORCES BASE Gagetown in 1991 was home to 3425 servicemen and women.

Campney, Ralph Osborne (1894–1967). Campney saw service overseas in WORLD WAR I. He won election to Parliament as a Liberal in 1949, worked with Brooke CLAXTON, the Defence minister, as parliamentary assistant and associate minister, and in 1954 became minister of National Defence, a post he held until 1957. Under his tenure, Canada's military reached its postwar peak.

Camp X. Located near Whitby, Ont., this camp trained spies and saboteurs in WORLD WAR II. Run by William STEPHENSON's BRITISH SECURITY COORDINATION, with headquarters in New York City, Special Training School No. 103 prepared agents from a variety of nationalities for espionage and resistance work in Nazi-occupied Europe. Camp X was also the location of HYDRA, a super-secret communications network linking Britain, Canada, and the United States, and the secure site was the home of Igor Gouzenko and his family for some time after the cipher operator defected from the Soviet embassy in Ottawa in September 1945.
Reading: D. Stafford, *Camp X* (1986)

Canadair Ltd. Begun during WORLD WAR II as a Crown corporation, Canadair built on the foundation of the Vickers Aircraft Co. of Montreal. The company produced PBY-5 aircraft until 1947 when it was purchased by the Electric Boat Co. to form part of General Dynamics Corporation. In this guise it produced aircraft such as the SABRE jet interceptor and the NORTH STAR transport. The company was acquired by the federal government in 1976 and sold once more to a consortium led by Bombardier Ltd in 1986. It now produces water bombers, unmanned mini-helicopters used in surveillance, small jet liners, and Challenger executive jets.

Canada and alliances. Although Canada's only formal military alliances are with the United States and the nations signatory to the NORTH ATLANTIC TREATY, in fact Canada's history might be characterized in two eras: that of the British alliance and that, much more recent, of the American alliance.

The British alliance for all practical purposes began with the conquest of 1759. Canada was part and parcel of the British Empire, automatically involved in Britain's wars. The British fought to defend Canada against the Americans during the REVOLUTIONARY WAR and the WAR OF 1812 and the Royal Navy kept the seas open during the wars with France. Until 1870–71 Britain maintained troops in Canada, and the naval bases at Halifax and ESQUIMALT were maintained for more than three decades more. Canada's contribution to the alliance was slight, as befitted a new country more concerned with establishing its infrastructure. The Canadian Pacific Railway, for example, was usually cited as a major contribution because of the way it could speed British troops from the Atlantic to the Pacific, thus cutting weeks off the sailing time to India. Nonetheless, Canadians did contribute to

British wars—the NILE VOYAGEURS, for example, and the substantial troop commitment to the SOUTH AFRICAN WAR. The massive Canadian effort in WORLD WAR I and in WORLD WAR II, however, demonstrated that Canadians, or at least those of British origin, took the alliance seriously indeed.

But Britain's increasing economic and military weakness had to concern Canada too. This became very obvious after the fall of France in 1940 when Britain seemed doomed to defeat. Canada, forced to look to its own security for the first time, had no option except to strike a defence relationship with the United States. This was sealed with the OGDENSBURG AGREEMENT which created the significantly named PERMANENT JOINT BOARD ON DEFENCE. It was indeed permanent, and the emergence of the Soviet threat after 1945 guaranteed that it remained so. The two North American nations renewed the PJBD in 1947, and they created the NORTH AMERICAN AIR DEFENCE AGREEMENT in 1957–58. At the same time, both nations joined NATO in 1949, stationing troops in Europe in the first peacetime COLLECTIVE SECURITY arrangement for both. NATO, Canadians hoped, might be a counterweight to the U.S.; it turned out to be yet another web binding Canada to the United States as Washington called the tune to which the other signatories duly danced.

While some in Canada were upset by the links to the U.S. war machine, Canada was also part and parcel of the United Nations. That had led us into the KOREAN WAR in 1950, though in truth Ottawa supplied troops, aircraft and ships only because the United States so urged. Forty years later, after Iraq invaded Kuwait, similar reasons obliged Canada to send ships, a hospital unit, and fighter aircraft to the Persian GULF WAR. Alliances, in other words, entail obligations. In return for the support of the super power, first Britain and then the U.S., Canada and Canadians have to respond to the senior partners' requests for assistance.

Canada-United Kingdom defence relations. Britain was responsible for the defence of Canada from the conquest of 1759; Canadian responsibility in any major sense did not begin until the Union of the Canadas, and then, and for some years, this responsibility was shirked. Canadian governments ordinarily refused to spend much money in the effort to secure Canada's borders, and even after Confederation defence was most often treated as something unnecessary. When British-American relations worsened and hotheads to the south talked of seizing Canada, there would be brief flurries of interest in improving the condition of the MILITIA, but such flurries always blew over when the crises disappeared. Instead, successive GENERAL OFFICERS COMMANDING (British officers in command of the militia) tried in vain to persuade governments, Conservative and Liberal alike, to make improvements, almost never with any success. Nonetheless, Canada was important to Britain as a Dominion, as a potential reservoir of troops, as part of the Empire.

This became evident during the SOUTH AFRICAN WAR when London tried very hard to commit Canada to participation and largely succeeded, though Prime Minister LAURIER attempted to declare that his government's decision to send troops was no precedent. Laurier was no imperialist, though he would be painted as such in Quebec for his Boer War actions and when, a decade later, he created a tiny Canadian navy. His successor, Sir Robert BORDEN, was an imperialist, one who was willing to donate $35 million to Britain to build Dreadnoughts, to fight WORLD WAR I at Britain's side to the last man and the last dollar, and to divide Canada in 1917 with the MILITARY SERVICE ACT, his CONSCRIPTION measure. The Great War was the high point of the Anglo-Canadian relationship, but even Borden, fed up with the lack of information from London, complained bitterly about the short shrift Canada received despite its massive contribution.

The war thus changed the relationship dramatically, fostering Canadian nationalism and leading diplomats, soldiers, and citizens alike to demand greater autonomy. Arthur Meighen, Borden's successor, pressed hard and successfully to get Britain out of the ANGLO-JAPANESE ALLIANCE for fear that it would embroil Canada in war with the United States, but Meighen nonetheless favoured a common Imperial foreign policy. It was, therefore, Mackenzie KING who led the drive for autonomy, refusing to offer troops to Britain during the Chanak crisis of 1922 and pressing for a declaration, subsequently enacted into law as the Statute of Westminster 1931, that the Dominions were independent in foreign policy. King's government repeatedly refused to coordinate plans with London as the world lurched to war after 1935, and his policy of 'no commitments' guaranteed that London continued to be puzzled by Canada's attitudes. Still, King took Canada into war in 1939, Canada's last 'colonial' response to the Mother Country. But the defeats of 1940 drove Canada under the American eagle's wing from which she would not emerge. Though British and Canadian troops used the same equipment and fought together in WORLD WAR II, the military relationship was effectively over after 1945. The two countries still cooperate as allies in NATO; they exchange information, and great regiments still maintain brotherly links, but there is little else left. This was evident as early as the SUEZ CRISIS of 1956 when Canada, acting to rescue Britain from its folly, initiated the idea of the UNITED NATIONS EMERGENCY FORCE (UNEF) and shared Washington's outrage at British policy. A generation earlier, militia unit commanders would have telegraphed London to offer their regiments for service; nothing like that happened in 1956, though there was substantial grumbling from Conservatives and their press at Canada's choosing to desert London. The world had changed, and Britain was now just another NATO ally. Canada's major defence relationship, for better or for worse, was henceforth with the United States.

Reading: J.L. Granatstein, *How Britain's Weakness Forced Canada into the Arms of the United States* (Toronto, 1989)

Canada-United States defence relations. Before 1940, Canada's defence relations with the United States, with the exception of some WORLD WAR I cooperation, were limited to the preparation of defences against U.S. attack and constant worry about being dragged into war because of Anglo-American or American-Japanese difficulties. After Confederation — a political agreement brought about in substantial part because of the FENIAN RAIDS and fear that the U.S. might turn northwards for a quick, victorious war to unite it after its CIVIL WAR—Canada warily contemplated its much larger and wealthier neighbour. The TREATY OF WASHINGTON in 1871 resolved most of the Anglo-American problems resulting from the Civil War (at

Canada's expense, Canadians complained), but there were recurring problems that threatened peace. The dispute over Venezuela's border with British Guiana in the mid-1890s, for instance, brought Britain and the U.S. close to war as Washington stood on its dignity and the Monroe Doctrine; that crisis resulted in a brief flurry of rearmament in Canada. The ALASKA BOUNDARY DISPUTE at the turn of the century saw Canada and the United States send troops into the north —and a British judge side with the Americans, resulting in a settlement highly unfavourable to Canada. But the entry of the U.S. into the Great War brought this era of hostility largely to an end, and Canada and the U.S. cooperated to some extent on anti-submarine measures in the Atlantic, the U.S. Navy even providing some vessels to the tiny, hard-pressed Canadian navy. Thereafter, there was nothing of hostility, though war planners in both countries continued to draw up their plans for war with the other. Canadians, notably the CHIEF OF THE GENERAL STAFF in the early 1930s, Gen. A.G.L. MCNAUGHTON, also feared that a neutral Canada might be dragged into a Japanese-American war if either combatant tried to use Canadian soil, and the general argued that this was a reason to improve West Coast defences. The government paid little attention, though British Columbia's defensive weaknesses were a subject of secret talks, the first of their kind, between the two countries' military chiefs in 1938 and 1939.

WORLD WAR II changed everything. Britain's defeat in Belgium and France forced Canada to look to its own defence and obliged the Mackenzie KING government to seek a defence arrangement with the U.S. This was accomplished with the OGDENSBURG AGREEMENT of August 1940, the first defence arrangement ever between Canada and the U.S. The PERMANENT JOINT BOARD ON DEFENCE created there began immediately to plan for war on the Atlantic and Pacific. As President F.D. Roosevelt manoeuvred to bring the still-neutral U.S. into the war, the next year saw the U.S. Navy take over command of the anti-submarine struggle in the western North Atlantic, much to the chagrin of the ROYAL CANADIAN NAVY. After Pearl Harbor brought the Americans into the war, cooperation increased further still. The U.S. sent troops into Canada to build the ALASKA HIGHWAY, Canadian airmen helped protect Alaska, and a brigade of infantry participated in the U.S. attack on KISKA in the Aleutian Islands. There were also a host of American weather stations, the CANOL PIPELINE, and other installations in Canada, for all of which Canada paid in full at war's end to ensure that no U.S. claim remained.

The emerging threat from the Soviet Union guaranteed the continuance of the relationship. The PJBD was reaffirmed in 1947, vast radar networks (the PINETREE LINE and the DEW LINE) were built in the 1950s (the DEW line was renovated in the late 1980s as the NORTH WARNING SYSTEM), and the NORTH AMERICAN AIR DEFENCE AGREEMENT was signed in 1957–58, effectively combining the air forces of the two countries in the defence of North America. But there were tensions too, as became evident during the CUBAN MISSILE CRISIS of 1962, while the government of John F. Kennedy was believed by many Canadians to have helped to bring down the government of John DIEFENBAKER in 1963 because of the Prime Minister's reluctance to arm weapon systems, secured from the U.S., with the nuclear warheads they needed to be effective. Such disputes, however, were highly unusual in their intensity, and the relationship ordinarily was close. There was, however, a continuing tension within the overall cooperation, sparked by such things as concern about U.S. infringements of Canadian sovereignty in the Arctic by nuclear submarines, oil tankers and Coast Guard ships, and resentment over U.S. pressures on Canada to participate in NATO in ways that Canada sometimes found inappropriate, to permit CRUISE MISSILE TESTING over Canada, and to participate initially in the KOREAN WAR and then forty years later in the GULF WAR. The disparity in power between the two countries guarantees that the Americans will always be the senior partner, but Canada's geography is certain to give the smaller nation a certain leverage with Washington. What the end of the COLD WAR will do to the defence relationship remains uncertain.

Reading: J.L. Granatstein and Norman Hillmer, *For Better or For Worse: Canada and the United States to the 1990s* (Toronto, 1991)

Canada-United States Defence Statement, 1947. Simultaneously announced in Ottawa and Washington on 12 February 1947, this statement was the product of the PERMANENT JOINT BOARD ON DEFENCE and of governmental consideration. The PJBD was to continue and five principles were to govern CANADA-UNITED STATES DEFENCE RELATIONS in the post-war years: the interchange of individuals; cooperation and exchange of observers for exercises and equipment development; encouragement of standardization of arms, equipment, organization and training methods; mutual and reciprocal availability of facilities in each country; cooperation without impairing control by either country of activities in its own territory. This was not a treaty and each country was free to determine the extent of its cooperation.

Canadian Active Service Force. In response to the German invasion of Poland, and in accordance with DEFENCE SCHEME NO. 3, the Canadian government on 1 September 1939 ordered the mobilization of the Canadian Active Service Force. Initially consisting of two infantry divisions and ancillaries, the CASF included NON-PERMANENT ACTIVE MILITIA and PERMANENT FORCE units. Later expanded to five divisions, the CASF's name was changed to 'The Canadian Army' in November 1940, though the original name continued in use.

Canadian Aeroplanes Ltd. Created in December 1916 by the British government purchase of the CURTISS AEROPLANE AND MOTORS LTD facilities in Toronto, Canadian Aeroplanes was controlled by the IMPERIAL MUNITIONS BOARD. It was the first mass-producer of aircraft in Canada, turning out some 2900 training aircraft during WORLD WAR I.

Canadian Air Force. Sir Robert BORDEN's tiny Canadian Air Force, established in the final months of WORLD WAR I, was disbanded in mid-1919. The next year the newly created AIR BOARD authorized a small non-permanent force that ideally would be acceptable financially and effective militarily. The CAF became permanent, thanks to the NATIONAL DEFENCE ACT 1922, and in 1923 it became the ROYAL CANADIAN AIR FORCE.

Canadian Air-Sea Transportable Brigade. The CAST Brigade, based on the 5e

Groupe-brigade du Canada (Valcartier, Que.) and two rapid reinforcement fighter squadrons, was from 1967 to 1987 earmarked for deployment to Norway in the event of war as part of Canada's NATO commitment. Critics expressed doubt about the country's ability to get the force to Norway in a war situation, and some wondered at its chances in action there. The 1987 WHITE PAPER ON DEFENCE cancelled the commitment, instead allocating the CAST brigade to a division-sized wartime concentration in southern Germany.

Canadian Armament Research & Development Establishment. Established in WORLD WAR II at Valcartier, Que., CARDE investigated problems involved with ammunition, ballistics, explosives, and ordnance. In the postwar years it worked on rockets and missiles.

Canadian Armed Forces. The CANADIAN FORCES REORGANIZATION ACT which became law on 1 February 1968 ended the legal life of the ROYAL CANADIAN NAVY, the ROYAL CANADIAN AIR FORCE, and the CANADIAN ARMY. In their stead was a single unified service sporting a common uniform of dark green. The process of UNIFICATION was far from smooth as personnel and roles were shifted about but, though there were resignations, the high professionalism of the military was demonstrated and commitments continued to be met.

The Trudeau government, however, disliked some of those commitments, especially deployment of troops and aircraft with NATO. After a sweeping review, the prime minister announced new roles for the forces with the protection of sovereignty at the top and peacekeeping at the bottom. Soon after, the force in Europe was consolidated at Lahr and Baden-Soellingen, West Germany and reduced by 50 per cent to 5000. Overall military strength was reduced by almost a fifth to 82,000. The next decade was not a happy one for the military. The introduction and enforcement of bilingualism upset anglophones, but far more serious were budgetary restraint and the increasing obsolescence of equipment. Ships, aircraft, and tanks all were well past their prime, and though the government did secure German tanks for the NATO force, begin construction of new frigates, and set out on the process of acquiring

a fighter aircraft, there were sighs of relief when the Progressive Conservatives, who had promised to rejuvenate Canada's military, came to power in 1984.

The Mulroney government restored separate uniforms for the ground, air, and sea components of the forces (at a cost high enough to upset the senior officers who preferred new hardware) and cautiously began to unravel unification, but they provided nothing in the way of new funding; the first budget of the new government in fact cut expenditures. A bellicose WHITE PAPER, issued by defence minister Perrin BEATTY in 1987, promised much, including nuclear attack submarines, but was quickly overtaken by the end of the COLD WAR and the country's budget deficit. Though the country's commitment to NATO and NORAD remained, the former was scheduled to be eliminated by the mid-1990s, and the only genuinely credible role left for the forces by the beginning of the 1990s seemed to be PEACEKEEPING. The government, people, and military all seemed interested in seeing that Canada contributed infantry units or substantial numbers of specialists to virtually every peacekeeping operation — and there were many. There was, however, less support for Canada's small but active military role in the GULF WAR against Iraq in 1990–91 and, domestically, for the army's large part in resolving the conflict between Mohawks and Quebec at OKA in the summer of 1990.

Canadian Army. The land forces of Canada before 1946 were known by a variety of names, but the post-WORLD WAR II reorganization gave the simplest of titles. The Canadian Army's strength was fixed at 25,000 in 1946, a small number, to be sure, but much the largest professional army the country had supported to that time. The Soviet threat, the creation of NATO, and the beginning of the KOREAN WAR combined to increase the military strength and give the army new commitments. By 1952, the army had 52,000 members with a brigade group fighting in Korea and another stationed in Germany with NATO. Additional and substantial commitments soon arose, most notably PEACEKEEPING for the United Nations and other bodies. The major deployments were to UNEF (the United Nations Emergency Force) in Egypt, to the Congo

(UNOC), and to Cyprus (UNFICYP), but there was also a major commitment of officers to the INTERNATIONAL CONTROL COMMISSIONS in Indochina.

Highly professional, well-equipped and well-led, the army by the late 1950s was a crack formation. But increasing budgetary difficulties and the difficulty of keeping equipment up-to-date in a rapidly changing technological environment began to pose difficulties by the beginning of the next decade. The move toward INTEGRATION and UNIFICATION in the mid-1960s seemed, to many senior officers, to threaten military values and the regimental system, and there were resignations and protests before it came into force in 1968, effectively ending the Canadian Army's existence.

Canadian Army Active Force. In 1946–47, the Canadian army was reorganized into a MOBILE STRIKING FORCE, an Active Force, and a Reserve Force. The Active Force, the regular army, included the units of the Mobile Striking Force. Five regional commands were established; they were responsible for supervising Active Force units and training the Reserves. Authorized strength was 25,000 but at the outbreak of the KOREAN WAR, there were fewer than 21,000 in the army. The Active Force expanded rapidly thereafter and in early 1952 numbered more than 52,000. In 1954, its name was changed to the Canadian Army (Regular).

Canadian Army Nursing Service. Although the first Canadian nurse went on active service in the NORTHWEST REBELLION of 1885, the creation of the Canadian Army Nursing Service was first mooted in a general order in June 1899. Shortly thereafter, four nurses accompanied the first contingent to the SOUTH AFRICAN WAR and more followed, all being considered to be of lieutenant's rank. When the sisters returned in 1901, the nursing service was inaugurated, with positions offered to these women and to other qualified nurses with effect from 1 August 1901. When the Army Medical Service was reorganized in 1904, the nursing reserve establishment was raised to 25, and in 1906, the first two nurses joined the PERMANENT FORCE. By the beginning of WORLD WAR I, there were five PF nurses and 57 on the reserve list; the war increased the number dramatically, and in 1917 there

were 2030 on strength with a reserve of 203; peak strength overseas was 1886. Six nurses were killed on service, six were wounded, and 15 died of drowning during enemy action. Another 18 died of disease. Between the wars, the nursing service was controlled by the Director General of Medical Services at Ottawa. In WORLD WAR II and after, the nursing service was an integral part of the ROYAL CANADIAN ARMY MEDICAL CORPS.

Canadian Army Occupation Force. At the end of WORLD WAR II, the FIRST CANADIAN ARMY contributed a division-sized force (designated the 3rd Canadian Infantry Division) under Gen. Christopher VOKES to the Allied occupation of Germany. The force consisted of volunteers and men with low priority for repatriation and was withdrawn in the spring of 1946. A separate deployment saw a composite battalion of infantry serve in Berlin for most of July 1945.

Canadian Army Pacific Force. At the September 1944 QUEBEC CONFERENCE Canada agreed in principle to commit ground forces to the war in the Pacific. Final Cabinet approval came in November. The division-sized force was to be organized, equipped, and trained on American lines and was to be made up of volunteers. Command was given to Gen. Bert HOFFMEISTER, a successful division commander in ITALY and in the NORTHWEST EUROPE CAMPAIGN. There were ample volunteers for the force, but training was not far advanced when Japan sued for peace in August 1945.

Canadian Army Special Force. Its creation announced on 7 August 1950, the Canadian Army Special Force was to be used to fulfil Canada's obligations to the United Nations in Korea and in NATO. Raised as part of the CANADIAN ARMY ACTIVE FORCE, it was composed of 18-month volunteer recruits, with a thin leavening of Active Force personnel. Haste and confusion characterized the recruitment drive, but the 25TH CANADIAN INFANTRY BRIGADE was nonetheless in being by November 1950 under Brig. John ROCKINGHAM; it was despatched to serve in the KOREAN WAR in 1951. The 'Special Force' term was seldom used once the brigade was formed.

Canadian Army Staff College. Opened during WORLD WAR II, and continued after the war in Kingston, Ont., the College provides tactical and staff duties instruction for officers. It is now known as the Canadian Land Forces Command and Staff College.

Canadian Arsenals Ltd. Established in September 1945 to operate Crown-owned munitions factories, Canadian Arsenals remained a Crown corporation until 1986 when it was sold to SNC Group for $92 million.

Canadian Aviation Corps. Formed by Sam HUGHES in September 1914, the Corps consisted of three officers and one aircraft. Its commander, Capt. E.L. Janney, had plans to organize a squadron, but the mercurial Hughes lost interest and the CAC disbanded in early 1915.

Canadian Cavalry Brigade. A component of the CANADIAN EXPEDITIONARY FORCE, the brigade was formed in February 1915 under Colonel J.E.B. SEELEY, a British officer. The brigade saw action throughout the war, though it was, like all cavalry units, often in support or waiting for a breakthrough that never came. The Allied offensive of 1918 provided opportunity for more traditional cavalry roles, and the ROYAL CANADIAN DRAGOONS, the FORT GARRY HORSE, and LORD STRATHCONA'S HORSE fought with great valour in the closing months of the war.

Canadian Coast Guard. The Coast Guard's origins lie in the Marine Branch of the Department of Marine and Fisheries, founded in 1867, and in the Department of Transport's fleet. It acquired its current name in 1962, employs over 6,000 men and women, and operates surface vessels, aircraft, rescue ships, and hovercraft. Its responsibilities include icebreaking, search and rescue, maintenance of navigational aids, and northern resupply.

Canadian Corps. The main formation of the Canadian army in France and Flanders in WORLD WAR I, the Canadian Corps established a formidable reputation for itself.

When the first contingent of the CANADIAN EXPEDITIONARY FORCE left Canada for Britain in the fall of 1914, there was no expectation that the war would be long or that additional large contributions from Canada would be needed. But the development of trench warfare and the terrible losses suffered by the 1ST CANADIAN DIVISION at YPRES soon made clear that more men would be required. The arrival of the 2ND CANADIAN DIVISION in England and its move to France in 1915 led to the creation of the Canadian Corps on 13 September 1915, initially under the British Lt-Gen. E.A.H. ALDERSON. Two more divisions, the 3rd and the 4th, arrived in 1916, bringing the Corps to its full strength. Other Canadian units—the CANADIAN CAVALRY BRIGADE, two MOTOR MACHINE-GUN BRIGADES, and railway and forestry troops — did not always serve with the Corps but were for all practical purposes part it.

The Corps fought in the battle for the ST ELOI craters and MOUNT SORREL in early 1916 and then in the terrible battles along the SOMME later in the year. Its triumph, the climactic battle of the war for the Canadians, came when Gen. Byng led it against VIMY RIDGE at Easter 1917, a superb example of a set-piece attack and startling testimony to the Corps staff's efficiency. Byng soon left to take command of an army and Sir Arthur CURRIE, the Canadian-born MILITIA officer, took over. To him fell the task of leading the Corps against HILL 70 and into the appalling conditions of the PASSCHENDAELE front. Then followed the battle of AMIENS in August 1918, beginning the Corps' greatest stretch of unbroken victories, the Hundred Days that saw the Canadians smash a succession of German opponents and end the war on 11 November 1918 at MONS. With its four battalion brigades and with its powerful artillery, the Corps was a superb fighting machine, creative in its tactics, skilful in its use of weaponry, and in a real sense the embodiment of the nation from which it came. Currie added to the Corps' sense of itself by refusing all pressures to break it up into scattered divisions on different parts of the Western Front.

In all, some 424,589 officers, nursing sisters, and men served overseas with the Corps (a figure that includes those who served in the ROYAL FLYING CORPS and ROYAL NAVAL AIR SERVICE). Fatalities in the Corps from all causes were 59,544 while those wounded in battle numbered 138,001. There were 34,784 injuries in non-battle circumstances.

Reading: G.W.L. Nicholson, *The Canadian Expeditionary Force 1914–1919* (Ottawa, 1962)

Canadian Corps Association. Formed in Ontario in 1934–35, the Association is non-political and non-partisan, though it was an active crusader for CONSCRIPTION in WORLD WAR II. Its name refers to the CANADIAN CORPS of WORLD WAR I fame.

Canadian Daily Record. Published by the CANADIAN WAR RECORDS OFFICE, the *Record* was a newspaper for the CANADIAN EXPEDITIONARY FORCE. Its circulation reached 12,500 by mid-1917.

Canadian Defence Committee. Created by Cabinet in August 1936, the committee was chaired by Prime Minister KING and included the ministers of Finance, Justice, and National Defence. It was intended to deal with questions of peace and security more expeditiously than the full Cabinet, but met only infrequently.

Canadian Defence Force. Organized in March 1917, the Force was intended to consist of 49 battalions or some 60,000 men serving on a voluntary basis for home defence. The CDF would thus release men of the CANADIAN EXPEDITIONARY FORCE, defending Canada against attack from German-Americans or Irish terrorists, for overseas service. Volunteers were almost non-existent, however, fewer than 2000 recruits coming forward by June, and the CDF was dissolved in July. Its failure seemed to demonstrate that CONSCRIPTION was necessary to secure sufficient men for the front.

Canadian Defence League. Founded in 1909 as 'a non-political association to urge the importance to Canada of universal physical and naval or military training', the League was a pressure group that sought to arouse interest in national defence. Its aim was universal military service, in effect CONSCRIPTION, for all youths between 14 and 18 years of age. Concentrated in Toronto, the League fought gamely against public indifference but by 1913 it had all but disappeared.

Canadian Defence Quarterly. Launched by General J.M. MACBRIEN in 1923, the *CDQ* was a forum for professional military debate. Under the notable editorship of Colonel Kenneth STUART, especially, it featured debates on tactics and strategy by, among others, Guy SIMONDS and E.L.M. BURNS. The journal stopped publication with the outbreak of war in 1939; it was revived as a commercial venture by John GELLNER in 1971 and is once more a locus of debate on defence policy.

Canadian Expeditionary Force (CEF). When WORLD WAR I broke out in August 1914, the Canadian government offered Britain an expeditionary force of one infantry division. The 31,000 men of this Canadian Expeditionary Force sailed from Quebec in October and, after training in difficult conditions in England, went to France early in 1915, soon to be joined by a second division. By late 1916, the CANADIAN CORPS of four divisions was at full strength with a hard-earned reputation for ferocious effectiveness. In all, 619,636 served in the CEF, including 142,588 conscripted under the MILITARY SERVICE ACT (of whom only 24,132 reached the front). A total of 424,589 officers, men, and nursing sisters served overseas; 59,544 were killed while 172,785 were wounded or injured. The CEF, though half of all those who enlisted in it were British-born, was nonetheless a Canadian army, in effect the nation in process of creation.

Reading: G.W.L. Nicholson, *The Canadian Expeditionary Force, 1914–1919* (Ottawa, 1962)

Canadian Eye-Witness. Sir Max AITKEN's phrase for his position as Canada's 'General Representative' at the front in the early part of WORLD WAR I. His duties included dealing with the records of the CANADIAN EXPEDITIONARY FORCE, reporting on casualties, and giving Canadians an account of their troops at the front. Aitken relinquished the post in January 1917.

Canadian Field Comforts Commission. A voluntary organization formed by two Toronto women who had accompanied the first contingent overseas in 1914, the Commission distributed to the soldiers of the CANADIAN EXPEDITIONARY FORCE gifts received from Canadian firms and individuals.

Canadian Forces bases. As of the beginning of 1992, there were CFBs at Esquimalt, Comox and Chilliwack, B.C.; at Cold Lake, Edmonton, Calgary, Penhold, and Suffield, Alta; at Moose Jaw, Sask.; at Shilo, Portage, and Winnipeg, Man.; at Petawawa, North Bay, Borden, London, Toronto, Kingston, Trenton, and Ottawa, Ont.; at Montreal, St Jean, Valcartier, and Bagotville, Que.; at Moncton, Gagetown, and Chatham, N.B.; at Greenwood, Shearwater, Cornwallis, and Halifax, N.S.; and at Gander and Goose Bay, Nfld and Labrador. Overseas, there were CFBs at Lahr and Baden-Soellingen, Germany. Some of these bases were scheduled for shut-down; others survive only on sufferance.

Canadian Forces Europe. After the Trudeau government's decision in April 1969 to reduce Canadian forces in NATO substantially, the much attenuated brigade and the Canadian air elements were relocated under one headquarters in late 1970. The Commander, Canadian Forces Europe, was now located at Lahr, Federal German Republic, and his land and air elements were there and at nearby Baden-Soellingen. The initial troop strength after the Trudeau cuts was 5000; this grew slowly until at the peak of the Mulroney government's interest in defence there were some 8000. The end of the COLD WAR reduced this to 6600 in 1991, and in 1992 it was announced that all forces in Europe would be withdrawn to Canada by 1995.

Canadian Forces Headquarters. After the INTEGRATION and UNIFICATION of the Canadian forces, the three service headquarters were combined into Canadian Forces Headquarters. In the CFHQ set-up, some considered, there were parallel structures in the DEPARTMENT OF NATIONAL DEFENCE, notably in the organizations of the deputy minister, the CHIEF OF THE DEFENCE STAFF and the Chair of the DEFENCE RESEARCH BOARD, and no clear lines of authority. The system, the Defence minister told Parliament, also tended 'to produce a layering of responsibility between the military and civilian staffs'. This organization lasted until 2 October 1972 when, after the report of the MANAGEMENT REVIEW GROUP was received and digested, a new NATIONAL DEFENCE HEADQUARTERS came into being.

Canadian Forces Reorganization Act. Introduced in Parliament on 4 November 1966, passed in April 1967, and proclaimed on 1 February 1968, this Act abolished the CANADIAN ARMY, ROYAL CANADIAN NAVY, and the ROYAL CANADIAN AIR FORCE and created a single service, the CANADIAN ARMED FORCES. The UNIFICATION of the forces, the idea of Defence minister Paul HELLYER, had been pushed through in the face of opposition within the forces and from veterans' organizations and elements of the media. Its intention was to eliminate triplication and save money which might then be spent for equipment.
Reading: Paul Hellyer, *Damn the Torpedoes* (1990)

Canadian Information Service. Successor to the WARTIME INFORMATION BOARD, this government propaganda organization was created in September 1945 to provide information and news about Canada outside the country. Because of its international mandate, the Department of External Affairs played a major role in its activities.

Canadian Intelligence Corps. The earliest official intelligence unit in the MILITIA was the Corps of Guides, organized in 1903. The Canadian Intelligence Corps was authorized only in 1942, and the Corps provided intelligence and field security sections to units of the FIRST CANADIAN ARMY. Officers and men of the Corps served in the KOREAN WAR and with CANADIAN FORCES EUROPE. The CIC ceased to exist with UNIFICATION.

Canadian intervention in Russia, 1918–19. The 1917 Russian revolutions that overthrew the Czar and installed the Bolsheviks under Lenin were a danger to the Allies in their war against Germany. If Germany could reach a separate peace with Lenin and move the forces it had deployed against Russia to the Western Front, the war might be lost. This, plus a certain fear of Bolshevism as a doctrine, was behind the decision to send troops to Russia both to safeguard supplies provided the Czarist armies and to encourage 'White' forces opposing the Bolsheviks in the hope that the war with Germany might be resumed. Canada was asked to participate and Sir Robert BORDEN agreed, in part at least because he thought Canada might secure commercial advantages in Siberia. From the spring of 1918 to the spring of 1919, approximately 6000 Canadian troops served mainly in Siberia (as the Canadian Siberian Expeditionary Force) and in northern Russia around Murmansk and Archangel, many of the latter engaging in heavy fighting with Soviet troops though only with 24 casualties. This commitment proved highly unpopular in Canada and with the troops, and the operation was ultimately unsuccessful.

Reading: Roy MacLaren, *Canadians in Russia, 1918–1919* (Toronto, 1976)

Canadianization. When the BRITISH COMMONWEALTH AIR TRAINING PLAN came into existence in December 1939, the question of what was to happen to Canadian graduates of the scheme was left unresolved. Prime Minister Mackenzie KING wanted ROYAL CANADIAN AIR FORCE aircrew to be under Canadian control, just as army and navy personnel were; but King also wanted London to pay the cost of RCAF squadrons overseas in return for Britain's share of the BCATP's costs. Fearing that other dominions might have similar demands, London was reluctant. In January 1941, Canada and Britain agreed that up to 25 additional RCAF squadrons would be formed overseas from BCATP graduates; Canadians serving with the Royal Air Force would wear their country's uniforms. That was some progress but Air minister Chubby POWER soon demanded more. He wanted senior RCAF officers to take command positions overseas, he wanted large Canadian formations and better aircraft, and he wanted, contrary to RAF policy, all suitable Canadian BCATP graduates to get commissions. The tough minister largely got his way and one result was the formation of NO. 6 BOMBER GROUP. Still, RCAF aircrew in RAF squadrons were not remustered into RCAF squadrons. By war's end there were 48 RCAF squadrons overseas. What must be added, however, is that substantial numbers of the Canadians serving with RAF squadrons in mixed British-dominion squadrons were reluctant to be remustered into RCAF squadrons. They were Canadian, yes, but they had formed bonds of friendship and trust with their mates.

Reading: C.G. Power, *A Party Politician* (1966)

Canadian Joint Staff, Washington; Canadian Joint Staff Mission, London. In July 1941, because of concern over the command arrangements envisaged in the ABC-I plans, the Canadian government formally sought Washington's permission to establish a military mission in the U.S. The Army and War departments opposed the request, but Ottawa continued to press its case. In March 1942, General Maurice POPE became the Canadian representative to the Combined Chiefs of Staff, and in July the Americans agreed that the mission, to be called the Canadian Joint Staff, could be established. Pope became its army member, the air force and navy also having officers of similar rank there. The CJS(W) continued after the war; it is now known as the Canadian Defence Liaison Staff-Washington. In 1944, Ottawa established the Canadian Joint Staff Mission, London to secure direct communication with the Supreme Allied Commands and, critics charged, to find billets for three surplus senior officers.

Reading: Maurice Pope, *Soldiers and Politicians* (Toronto, 1962)

Canadian Legion. See ROYAL CANADIAN LEGION.

Canadian Legion War Services. In November 1939, the government decided that 'auxiliary services' for the Canadian forces were to be provided by four voluntary organizations, one of which was the ROYAL CANADIAN LEGION. The Legion's specialties initially were education for service personnel, and concerts and entertainments. They were first supported by donations, but after 1941 the federal government picked up the bills for auxiliary services and after 1942–43 the army assumed increasing responsibility for the education program.

Canadian Machine-Gun Corps. The establishment of this corps with its own doctrine and tactics in April 1918 was the logical outcome of Brig.-Gen. Raymond BRUTINEL's innovative use of indirect machine-gun firepower. The Canadians' use of machine guns had been pace-setting from 1914, and in November 1918 the British established their own Machine-Gun Corps, like the Canadian organization a device largely of administrative intent.

Canadian Military Headquarters. The Canadian army's administrative organization in Britain, Canadian Military Headquarters was authorized on 26 September 1939. Though located close to the offices of the High Commissioner for Canada, CMHQ was a separate organization responsible to the Minister of National Defence through the CHIEF OF THE GENERAL STAFF. Formed on the assumption that the army would be fighting on the continent, CMHQ was to handle all routine communications between NATIONAL DEFENCE HEADQUARTERS and both the British War Office and successively the headquarters of the division, corps, and FIRST CANADIAN ARMY. It also commanded Canadian reinforcement units and other static establishments in Britain. CMHQ was never intended to command the field formations and, in fact, it was under the de facto control of Generals McNAUGHTON and CRERAR, the Army commanders, who came to regard it as part of their lines of communications. As far as the Department in Ottawa was concerned, CMHQ with its peak strength of 4073 was its forward echelon. While there was potential for conflict, good sense ordinarily prevailed.

Reading: C.P. Stacey, *Arms, Men and Governments: The War Policies of Canada 1939–1945* (1970)

Canadian Military Mission, Berlin. Created in September 1945, the mission, headed by General Maurice POPE, represented Canada before the Allied Control Commission governing defeated Germany.

Canadian Military Mission, Far East. Established on 22 August 1950 under Brig. F.J. Fleury, the mission arrived in Tokyo in September in advance of Canada's KOREAN WAR contingent. The mission watched over the build-up of base units in Japan, liaised with U.S. and other United Nations forces, and was not finally disbanded until 1957.

Canadian Mounted Rifles. During the SOUTH AFRICAN WAR, the ROYAL CANADIAN DRAGOONS, the PERMANENT FORCE's cavalry unit, raised the 1st Battalion, Canadian Mounted Rifles, for service against the Boers. That unit used the RCD name in South Africa. The 2nd Battalion, organized around a nucleus of NORTH WEST MOUNTED POLICE, fought under the CMR designation.

In WORLD WAR I, four battalions of Canadian Mounted Rifles fought as infantry, making up the 8th Brigade of the 3RD CANADIAN DIVISION.

Canadian National Service League. Formed in April 1916 from an alliance of local recruiting leagues with John GODFREY as chair, it espoused a national registration and more systematic procedures for raising men. The League also spawned the BONNE ENTENTE movement, but soon became a pro-CONSCRIPTION force.

Canadian Naval Mission Overseas. Established on 15 May 1944 under Vice-Admiral Percy NELLES, the Mission dealt with weapons, equipment, personnel, policy and plans, and public relations. It negotiated with the British for ships, including AIRCRAFT CARRIERS and CRUISERS. The end of the war with Japan saw the Mission's numbers reduced and it subsequently was absorbed into the CANADIAN JOINT STAFF MISSION (London).

Canadian Northwest Atlantic Command. At Canadian request, the ATLANTIC CONVOY CONFERENCE of March 1943 reallocated command responsibilities for the submarine war in the BATTLE OF THE ATLANTIC. As a result, the Canadian Northwest Atlantic Command was created on 30 April 1943 under Adm. Leonard MURRAY, headquartered at St John's, Newfoundland. Murray's forces had responsibility for the protection of convoys on the Atlantic from 47 degrees west and south to 29 degrees north or from north of New York City and west of the 47th meridian. The command, through Eastern Air Command, also was responsible for air operations to the maximum range of aircraft based in Newfoundland and on the East Coast. The command's creation meant that the United States Navy commander at ARGENTIA, in command of the NEWFOUNDLAND ESCORT FORCE since September 1941, was now put, in ROYAL CANADIAN NAVY eyes, in his proper place. In fact, the elevation of Murray was the first sign of the Allied recognition of the RCN's growing competence, size, and stature and of its ability to give a good account of itself against the U-boats. In 1952, when NATO's Supreme Allied Commander Atlantic was formed and the RCN became an integral part of the alliance's naval forces, Canada took command of the Canadian Atlantic (CANLANT) Zone, significantly with the same boundaries as the Canadian Northwest Atlantic Command of a decade earlier.

Canadian Officers' Training Corps (COTC). Organized first in 1912 at McGill University, the COTC spread rapidly to other universities in WORLD WAR I, preparing junior officers for war service. The COTC continued in the interwar years; in WORLD WAR II, COTC training was coordinated with the requirements of the army's Officer Training Centres. After the war, the COTC operated into the 1960s before it was allowed to die, a victim of opposition to the Vietnam War and to increasing Canadian lack of interest in defence. See also REGULAR OFFICER TRAINING PLAN.

Canadian Official Record, The. Published by the DEPARTMENT OF PUBLIC INFORMATION from October 1918, the *Official Record* was distributed to the press, politicians, and opinion leaders in Canada. It aimed at 'uplift' and was, in effect, a government propaganda sheet.

Canadian Patriotic Fund. Patriotic funds had begun in Canada during the WAR OF 1812 as devices to raise money to provide assistance to the families of those serving in the forces, to veterans, and to the wounded. The Fund created in 1900 for the SOUTH AFRICAN WAR raised substantial sums and still had $76,000 on its books in 1914. This money passed to a new Fund, established by Parliament on 22 August 1914. The Fund limited itself to assisting soldiers' families.

Canadian Provost Corps. In WORLD WAR I, a Canadian Military Police Corps provided units to the CANADIAN CORPS and wherever men of the CANADIAN EXPEDITIONARY FORCE served. The title 'Canadian Provost Corps' was adopted in June 1940 and given to companies already organized, including one from the RCMP. Military police served in the KOREAN WAR and on PEACEKEEPING operations. The corps ceased to exist with UNIFICATION.

Canadian Red Cross. The Canadian branch of the International Committee of the Red Cross was founded by George S.

Ryerson. He had used the emblem to protect his horse-drawn ambulance during the NORTHWEST REBELLION 1885, and in 1896 he organized a Toronto chapter of the British Red Cross Society. The society was incorporated in 1909 and in both world wars provided relief services, hospitals, recreational facilities, and money to the armed forces and to orphans and refugees.

Canadian Services Colleges. This is the collective name for Canada's three military colleges, the ROYAL MILITARY COLLEGE, ROYAL NAVAL COLLEGE OF CANADA, and LE COLLÈGE MILITAIRE ROYAL DE ST-JEAN. All are tri-service, degree-granting institutions operated by the DEPARTMENT OF NATIONAL DEFENCE.

Canadian Voltigeurs. As the prospect of hostilities with the United States increased in early 1812, Lt-Gen. Sir George PREVOST took steps to secure the defence of Lower Canada. One measure was the raising of a Provincial Corps of Light Infantry, or Voltigeurs. Soldiers of the corps, almost all French Canadians, played a distinguished role at the battle of CHATEAUGUAY on 26 October 1813.

Canadian War Memorials Fund. Established by Sir Max AITKEN in late 1916 and supported by a number of British newspaper magnates, the Fund sought to provide a lasting visual record of Canada's role in WORLD WAR I through the collection of paintings, photographs, and films. War artists were sent into the field and the collection eventually encompassed work from 108 artists. The holdings were transferred to Ottawa after the ARMISTICE.

Canadian War Mission. Established in Washington on 2 February 1918, the War Mission was created to handle the increasingly complex relations between Canada and the U.S. produced by WORLD WAR I, relations that were thought to be beyond the capacity of the hard-pressed British embassy. The Mission's chair, industrialist Lloyd Harris, was 'empowered to represent the Cabinet and the heads of various Departments . . . in respect of negotiations relating to purely Canadian affairs.' The War Mission was an important step on the road to independent Canadian diplomacy.

Canadian War Museum. Established in 1880 but with its collection in storage from 1897 to 1942, the Museum formally began its existence in Ottawa's War Trophies Building during WORLD WAR II. It became a division of the National Museum of Canada in 1958, is now a division of the Canadian Museum of Civilization, and is housed in the former building of the Public Archives of Canada. The Museum holds Canada's superb collection of war art and other trophies.

Canadian War Records Office. Founded by the government in January 1915 and led by Sir Max AITKEN, initially with a $25,000 budget, the CWRO was charged with documenting Canada's WORLD WAR I effort. By 1916 it had a staff of 60, including reporters, photographers, and cinematographers, and its work helped shape how Canadians viewed the war. Its Historical Section also provided a contemporary record of events through amassing a variety of books and pictorial collections, and publishing a daily newspaper for the troops.

Canadian Wives Bureau. Created at CANADIAN MILITARY HEADQUARTERS in WORLD WAR II, the Bureau dealt with the complex problems involved in sending the WAR BRIDES of Canadian soldiers, sailors, and airmen, and their children, to Canada. Between April 1942 and February 1948, the Bureau saw to the despatch of 43,464 wives and 20,995 children, an enduring testament to the Canadian serviceman's presence in Britain and on the Continent.

Canadian Women's Army Corps. Women demanded the opportunity to serve in WORLD WAR II, and the three services, with varying degrees of enthusiasm, were obliged to comply. The CWACs were established in August 1941 to meet this demand but also to free men for combatant roles. A separate branch of the army until March 1942, the CWAC ultimately enlisted 22,000 women who performed a wide variety of roles as clerks, drivers, and signallers and who served in Canada, Britain, and Northwest Europe. See also WOMEN, WORLD WAR II.

Canal du Nord. Part of the great battles for the HINDENBURG LINE and the DROCOURT-QUÉANT LINE in September-October 1918, the struggle for the Canal du Nord was a major test for the CANADIAN CORPS. An incomplete canal passing through flooded marshland, the Canal du Nord was a major obstacle, the far bank held by strong German forces. Wire was used heavily; there were old excavations, dug-outs, and shelters; and beyond the Canal were heavily fortified defensive works. Three Canadian divisions and one British were in the assault on 26–27 September, moving forward with no preliminary barrage and with the aid of a small number of tanks. Though there was very heavy resistance and high casualties, the attack went well and the Germans were obliged to withdraw on 27–28 September. The way to CAMBRAI was now open.

Canex. Formed in 1968, the Canex system of retail outlets operates on CANADIAN FORCES BASES. The revenues generated help fund recreational and welfare programs for military personnel and their families.

Canloan. In early 1944, Ottawa disbanded two home defence divisions, creating a surplus of junior officers. Of these, 673 were loaned to British units, and many served with great distinction in Italy and Northwest Europe; by 27 July 1944, 465 had become casualties.

Canol pipeline. Constructed between 1942 and 1944, this 1000-km pipeline ran from Norman Wells, NWT, to Whitehorse, Yukon, and was intended as a key element in ensuring oil supplies for the defence of the Alaska frontier against Japanese attack. Plagued by cost overruns and construction bottlenecks, Canol was abandoned in March 1945. To ensure Canadian sovereignty, after the war Canada purchased all U.S.-owned facilities.

Canso aircraft. The Canadian version of the Consolidated PBY Catalina patrol-reconnaissance aircraft which entered U.S. service in 1936, the amphibious Cansos were used by the RCAF between 1941 and the 1960s in a variety of roles, but most especially on anti-submarine warfare in WORLD WAR II. With some 14 hours' endurance and a top speed of 200 km/h, RCAF Cansos scored several U-boat kills.

CANTASS. The Canadian Towed Array Sonar System is a high-tech sonar device that can track submarines as far away as 175 km. It is being fitted on new patrol frigates of the *Halifax* class, the first of which came into navy service in 1991.

Canuck. See CF100 AIRCRAFT.

CANUSA. The Canada-United States Agreement on Signals Intelligence was signed in 1949. It defined the terms for bilateral exchange of signals intelligence and formed a de facto part of the overarching UKUSA pact on signals intelligence.

Carden-Loyd carrier. Designed in Britain in the 1920s, the Carden-Loyd carrier was a precursor of the tracked armoured personnel carriers developed in WORLD WAR II. Carden-Loyds were built in several countries under licence. The PERMANENT FORCE, using imported models, operated them in the interwar period.

Cardin, Louis-Joseph-Lucien (1919–1988). Cardin was born in Rhode Island and came to Canada in 1931. He served in the navy during WORLD WAR II, practised law at Sorel, Que., and won election to parliament as a Liberal in 1952. He served as associate minister of national defence from 1963–65, handling the day-to-day running of the department while Paul HELLYER, the minister, planned UNIFICATION.

Caribou, S.S. A passenger ferry operating between Sydney, N.S. and Port-aux-Basques, Nfld, the *Caribou* was attacked by a U-boat on 13 October 1942. In the sinking, 137 men, women and children died. The event stirred popular outrage in Canada.

Caribou aircraft. First flown in 1958, the de Havilland Caribou was a short takeoff and landing (STOL) utility transport with a top speed of 345 km/h. Widely sold abroad, the Caribou was also used by the RCAF on PEACEKEEPING operations in the Middle East and India-Pakistan.

Carignan-Salières Regiment. The regiment's 1100 men were despatched to New France in June 1665 in response to repeated calls for protection against Iroquois attacks. The troops of the 'good regiment' constructed a line of forts along the Richelieu River to block the main attack route from

the south and launched two expeditions against the Mohawks, one a disastrous midwinter campaign that cost more than a hundred lives. After the Iroquois came to terms in 1667 the regiment was recalled, but some four hundred chose to remain in New France. Settling along the Richelieu for the most part, they greatly strengthened the tiny colony.

Carleton, Sir Guy, 1st Baron Dorchester (1724–1808). Carleton joined the British army in 1742 and served under James WOLFE during the SEVEN YEARS' WAR, suffering wounds on the PLAINS OF ABRAHAM in 1759. As governor of Quebec in 1775, he repulsed an American attack after a lengthy siege of the capital, but his pursuit of the retreating enemy was severely criticized. Learning that Gen. BURGOYNE, his second-in-command, was to lead the subsequent campaign against New England, Carleton tendered his resignation. Four years later, he returned as commander-in-chief in British North America and had to preside over the evacuation of New York. He subsequently served as governor-in-chief of British North America from 1786 to 1795.

Caron, Sir Joseph-Philippe-René-Adolphe (1843–1908). A Quebec Conservative, Caron was minister of Militia and Defence from 1880 to 1892. His MILITIA ACT 1883 established a small PERMANENT FORCE and several new training schools. During the NORTHWEST REBELLION of 1885, he directed the mobilization of the Canadian force that fought RIEL, improvising transportation and logistical arrangements, but always paying close attention to political and patronage considerations. He was knighted for his efforts during the campaign.

Carpiquet. A small village and airfield near CAEN, Carpiquet was the scene of vicious fighting between the reinforced 8th Canadian Infantry Brigade and German SS troops during the NORMANDY campaign of July 1944. After several hundred Canadian casualties on 4 July, the attack was called off, leaving the Germans in position to deny Allied use of the air strip until Caen itself fell.

Carrick, John James (1873–1966). Carrick was born in Indiana and came to Canada as a boy. After education at the University of Toronto, he went into business at Port Arthur, Ont. and represented the area in the Ontario legislature and in the House of Commons. A crony of Sam HUGHES, he was his Special Service Officer and Official Recorder, Canadians Overseas with the rank of lieutenant-colonel. In the summer of 1915 he returned to Ottawa headquarters and sat out the rest of the war there.

Carson, Sir John Wallace (1864–1922). A mining and insurance magnate, Carson joined the MILITIA in 1891. During WORLD WAR I, he was sent overseas by Sam HUGHES as his special representative and was soon promoted major-general. Carson was the key administrative figure overseas until 1916, but his ambiguous mandate and difficult personality caused substantial difficulty in Britain and in Ottawa. His reign ended with Hughes', and Sir George PERLEY became overseas minister of Militia in 1917.

Cartier, Sir George-Etienne (1814–1873). The most powerful Quebec politician of his day, Cartier was born at St Antoine, Lower Canada, and practised law at Montreal. First elected to the legislature as a *bleu* in 1848, he worked with John A. MACDONALD to create Confederation. He was minister of Militia and Defence from 1867–73, and had responsibility for establishing the new dominion's forces.

Casa Berardi. A small collection of buildings astride the Orsogna-Ortona road, Casa Berardi was the scene of heavy fighting in December 1943 between troops of the ROYAL 22E REGIMENT and the Germans' 1st Parachute Division. C Company of the Van Doos, reduced to nine men by the battle's end, took the Casa; the company commander, Paul TRIQUET, won the first VICTORIA CROSS awarded to a Canadian in the ITALIAN CAMPAIGN. The capture of this stronghold turned the German flank and opened the route to ORTONA.

CAT gear. A noisemaking device, the Canadian Anti-Torpedo gear was developed hurriedly in 1943 to counter the Gnat, a German acoustic torpedo that homed on the noise created by ship propellers. Towed by an escort vessel to decoy the torpedo, the CAT was a simple solution and most Canadian warships were equipped with it by 1944.

Cavalry School Corps. Organized on 21 December 1883 in an attempt to secure a permanent instructional cadre for the MILITIA, the Corps operated the Cavalry School of Military Instruction. In the NORTHWEST REBELLION 1885, the Corps patrolled the lines of communication of General Frederick MIDDLETON's column. In 1892 the Corps was named the ROYAL CANADIAN DRAGOONS.

***Cayuga*, HMCS.** A TRIBAL CLASS DESTROYER launched in 1945 and commissioned in 1947, *Cayuga* served with distinction during three operational tours of duty during the KOREAN WAR. She played a notable role in the evacuation of Chinnampo, did blockade and escort duty, and engaged in 'trainbusting'. After service on the West and East coasts, *Cayuga* was paid off in 1964.

CC1, CC2 submarines. These submarines, built for the Chilean government at Seattle, Wash., were purchased by the British Columbia government in the excitement generated by the beginning of WORLD WAR I. The secret transaction was consummated at sea on the night of 4–5 August 1914 and was soon ratified by Ottawa which repaid the province the vessels' $1.15-million cost. The submarines saw no action. In 1917, they were ordered to Halifax for deployment to European waters, but the two craft were deemed unfit to cross the Atlantic and remained in Halifax until scrapped in 1920.

Central Powers. In WORLD WAR I, the alliance of Germany, Austria-Hungary, Bulgaria, and Turkey as opposed to the ALLIED POWERS.

Centurion tank. After an impressive performance during the KOREAN WAR, this 1943-designed British-built main battle tank was purchased by Canada in 1952 to replace the now-obsolete SHERMAN. Originally armed with a 17-pounder gun, the armament was upgraded to 105 mm and the armour increased to 120 mm. Reliable and effective, the 51-tonne Centurion stayed in service for more than a quarter century, despite being badly outclassed by newer Soviet and NATO tanks. In 1978, at last, Canada acquired LEOPARD I tanks from Germany.

Cessna Crane aircraft. An American trainer and utility transport with a speed of 290 km/h, the Crane was purchased in large numbers from 1940 onwards for use in the BRITISH COMMONWEALTH AIR TRAINING PLAN. Hundreds of pilots trained on the 800 aircraft that bore RCAF markings.

CF5 aircraft. In July 1965, Canada purchased single-seater Northrup F5 Freedom fighters as replacements for CF104 and CF101 aircraft then in use. In all, 115 of the tough, easy-to-fly fighters with a top speed of 1600 km/h were built under licence by CANADAIR, the first being activated in 1968. CF5 squadrons performed a variety of roles, including rapid reinforcement of NATO's northern flank. Introduction of the CF18 in the 1980s relegated the CF5 to training service.

CF18 aircraft. Canada's current front-line multi-role fighter aircraft, the Hornet was chosen in 1980 by the Trudeau government. The first of 138 of the fighters arrived in October 1982 and went operational in 1984 to replace CF101, CF104 and CF5 aircraft then in service. The aircraft's 1900 km/h speed and capabilities were first tested in combat during the GULF WAR of 1990–91 when an augmented squadron was deployed to Qatar as part of Canada's commitment to the U.S.-led force.

CF100 aircraft. An all-weather twin-jet interceptor designed and built by A.V. Roe Canada, the Canuck was the first indigenously designed military aircraft produced in Canada. The CF100 first flew in January 1950, and almost seven hundred were built, equipping at one point 13 front line squadrons employed on North American air defence. Fifty-three of the aircraft were later sold to Belgium. A few electronic warfare-equipped CF100s remained in service until 1981.

CF101 aircraft. The U.S.-built Voodoo all-weather interceptor was purchased by Canada in 1961 for its NORAD squadrons as a substitute for the scrapped ARROW. With a top speed of 1960 km/h, the Voodoo continued in service until 1984 when it was replaced by CF18 aircraft.

CF104 aircraft. The multi-role, nuclear-capable Starfighter came into ROYAL CANADIAN AIR FORCE service in 1961 and was Canada's main contribution to NATO for over two decades. Produced by CANADAIR under licence from Lockheed and designed as a high-altitude interceptor though capable of the ground-attack role it was employed in by the RCAF, the aircraft had a top speed of 2333 km/h. Although its frequent crashes led it to be dubbed the Widowmaker, the CF104 was nonetheless a favourite of pilots in l Canadian Air Division.

CH14, CH15 submarines. Constructed in the United States for the Royal Navy, these H class submarines were completed too late for WORLD WAR I service. Handed over to the Canadian navy in 1919, they were scrapped in 1927. Ten additional H class submarines were built for the RN at the Canadian Vickers yard in Montreal.

Chairman, Chiefs of Staff Committee. Created in 1951, this post was designed to provide a single officer who could represent Canada on NATO's new Military Committee. It was also intended to improve training and facilitate tri-service coordination. General Charles FOULKES and Air Marshal Frank MILLER were the only two officers to hold the post before it was abolished in 1964.

Champlain, Samuel de (*c.* 1570–1635). Champlain came to Canada in 1603 and held a series of important posts in the formative stages of New France's history. His explorations and his determination to protect French settlements through a system of alliances with local tribes led inexorably to armed confrontations with the Iroquois. In 1615, he was wounded in an unsuccessful assault on an Iroquois fortress. He was captured by the English in 1629 after a siege of Quebec, but he returned as governor in 1633. His success in establishing a fur trading organization laid the foundation of New France's development.

***Charlottetown*, HMCS.** A Flower class CORVETTE, *Charlottetown* was commissioned in December 1941 and sunk at the mouth of the St Lawrence River on 11 September 1942 with the loss of nine of her crew. The second ship of this name, a RIVER class frigate, was commissioned in April 1944 and served on escort duty. She was paid off and sold in 1947.

Chateauguay, Battle of, 1813. On 26 October 1813, a British force of 460, mostly French Canadians, repulsed a much larger American force moving on Montreal by way of the Chateauguay River. The U.S. troops were the vanguard of a 7000-strong army, and their defeat was a turning point in the campaign. Montreal was not seriously threatened again in the WAR OF 1812.

***Chedabucto,* HMCS.** A *BANGOR* CLASS minesweeper commissioned in September 1941, *Chedabucto* served in the North Atlantic and in the Gulf of St Lawrence. She sank on 21 October 1943 after a night collision with another vessel off Rimouski, Que.

Chemical warfare. The first use of gas in warfare fell upon the Canadian Division at YPRES in February 1915. This new weapon, fearsome and frightening, had an instant impact on the battlefield and in the laboratory, speeding research on other disabling or killing gases and on the ways of countering them. Before the end of WORLD WAR I, gas attacks with MUSTARD GAS or CHLORINE GAS were regularly used as one part of the preparations for assaults. Between the wars, however, although nations prepared for chemical warfare, there was such widespread revulsion against its employment that states were cautious. Although Italy used gas against Ethiopian troops in 1935, none of the combatants in WORLD WAR II employed it. Gas stocks were held close to the front by the Allies, for example, in case the Germans struck first, and research was carried on in Britain, the United States, and Canada, notably at the Chemical Warfare Experimental Station at Suffield, Alta, and at the War Disease Control Station at Grosse Ile, Que. Chemical warfare has not been widely used since 1945, though there were some chemical weapons employed in Vietnam by the Americans and in Afghanistan by the Soviets. In the GULF WAR of 1991, fears that the Iraqis might use chemical weapons led to all combatants in the coalition taking serious precautions.

Chief of the Air Staff. This post was created in 1938 and the incumbent represented the ROYAL CANADIAN AIR FORCE on the CHIEFS OF STAFF COMMITTEE. The CAS was responsible for providing military advice to his minister and the government and for the control and administration of the RCAF. The position was abolished in 1964. See Appendix III.

Chief of the Defence Staff. This appointive office was established in 1964 by Defence minister Paul HELLYER prior to UNIFICATION of the forces. The CDS is responsible to the minister of National Defence for the control and administration of the CANADIAN ARMED FORCES. See Appendix III for list of CDSs.

Chief of the General Staff. The administrative and functional head of the land forces since 1904 when the post of GENERAL OFFICER COMMANDING the MILITIA was abolished, the CGS was responsible for providing military advice to the minister and the government. The CGS was also ordinarily an impromptu chair of the CHIEFS OF STAFF COMMITTEE from 1945 to 1951. The position was abolished in 1964. See Appendix III.

Chief of Naval Staff. The CNS was responsible for the control and administration of the navy and for the provision of naval advice to the Defence minister and the government. The post, created in 1928 by changing the name of the DIRECTOR OF THE NAVAL SERVICE, signified that the army's efforts to secure dominance over the navy had failed. The post of CNS was abolished in 1964. See Appendix III.

Chiefs of Staff Committee. Formed in January 1939 by the CHIEF OF THE GENERAL STAFF, the CHIEF OF THE NAVAL STAFF, and the CHIEF OF THE AIR STAFF, the committee was intended to provide unity in the direction and control of the armed forces. In 1951, a CHAIRMAN, CHIEFS OF STAFF, was added. The unity of direction was always largely illusory as each service chief sought a bigger budget for his force. But, at times, there could be cooperation as, for example, when the committee decided in 1958–59 that the ARROW interceptor should be scrapped for fear that it would devour the entire defence budget. The committee ceased to exist in 1964 when the post of CHIEF OF DEFENCE STAFF was created.

Chippewa, Battle of, 1814. During the WAR OF 1812, a U.S. force under Gen. Jacob Brown repulsed a smaller British army of some two thousand near Chippewa Creek, west of the Niagara River. The British under Gen. Phineas Riall suffered 25 per cent casualties in this engagement on 5 July 1814.

Chlorine gas. First used in combat in 1915, chlorine gas causes constriction of the chest, tightness of the throat, swelling of the lungs, and suffocation. It can be detected by its greenish-yellow appearance and strong odour. On 22 April 1915, Canadian troops at YPRES were among the victims of the first German gas attack.

Churchill, Gordon (1898–1985). Born at Coldwater, Ont., Churchill served as a machine-gunner in WORLD WAR I, a school principal between the wars, and commander of an armoured personnel carrier regiment in WORLD WAR II. He entered the House of Commons as a Conservative in 1951 and became a minister in the DIEFENBAKER government. He served as Veterans' Affairs minister from 1960 and, after the nuclear crisis provoked Douglas HARKNESS' resignation in January 1963, as Defence minister.

Churchill tank. A British infantry (i.e., heavy) tank produced in large numbers during WORLD WAR II, it was standard equipment in Canadian armoured units early in the war and went ashore in the DIEPPE RAID. The 43-tonne heavily armoured tank with a 6-pounder gun was subsequently replaced by the SHERMAN.

Citadel, Halifax. Built on Citadel Hill overlooking Halifax, N.S., this star-shaped British fortification made of stone was begun in 1828 on the site of earlier strongholds. Not completed until 1856, it was then largely obsolete because of advances in artillery and naval technology. Canadian troops took over its garrisoning from the British in 1905.

Citadel, Quebec City. Built on Cape Diamond overlooking the St Lawrence River, some of the Citadel's fortifications and buildings date to the late 17th century; most, however, were built under War Office direction between 1820–31. Garrisoned by the British until 1871, the Citadel subsequently served as headquarters of the artillery school and later for the ROYAL 22E REGIMENT. It has also been the Governor-General's summer residence since 1872.

Reading: André Charbonneau et al., *Quebec the Fortified City* (Ottawa, 1982)

Civil defence. The advent of strategic bombing in WORLD WAR II and the post-war proliferation of nuclear weapons greatly complicated the problem of protecting civilians in wartime. Peacetime civil defence co-ordination, begun by the federal government in 1948, included the designation and construction of air-raid shelters, the collection of emergency supplies, and planning for selective evacuation. Civil emergency planning, not taken very seriously now, is presently run by Emergency Preparedness Canada.

Civil War, United States. The American Civil War had substantial impact on British North America. In the first place, though Britain and official opinion in the colonies largely supported the Confederacy, public opinion seemed more disposed to the Union. Certainly substantial numbers of Canadians joined the Union Army, though surprising numbers also enlisted in the Confederate forces. Secondly, the Confederacy used the Canadas as a base for espionage against the north and in the case of the ST ALBANS RAID as a jumping-off point for a raid on a Vermont town. This worsened relations between Britain and Washington, already troubled by the *ALABAMA* incident. Finally, there was concern in all the British colonies that once the war was over a victorious north might turn on Canada; this fear was one of the major impetuses to Confederation on the principle that a united Canada might just be able to resist attack while separate colonies would have no chance whatsoever. The American experience of states' rights, moreover, led the Fathers of Confederation to opt for a strong central government for the new Dominion.

Clark, Greg (1892–1977). A newspaperman and author of 19 folksy books, Clark won the MILITARY CROSS with the 4TH CANADIAN MOUNTED RIFLES at VIMY RIDGE in WORLD WAR I. During WORLD WAR II, he served as a war correspondent with FIRST CANADIAN ARMY.

Clark, Paraskeva Plistik (1898–1986). Born in Leningrad, Clark left the Soviet Union in 1923 and moved to Toronto with her second husband, Philip Clark. A painter, her canvases revealed leftist influences. Though not an official war artist in World War II, she did commissioned paintings of the RCAF Women's Division, striving to record 'with all possible pictorial drama' the 'very special jobs that girls did.'

Clark, Samuel Findlay (b. 1909). Commissioned in the ROYAL CANADIAN CORPS OF SIGNALS in 1933, Clark served overseas in WORLD WAR II, most notably as Chief Signals Officer of II CANADIAN CORPS. He became deputy chief of the General Staff in 1945, served in NATO, and became Quartermaster-General in 1951. In 1958, he became CHIEF OF THE GENERAL STAFF, a post he held until his 1961 retirement as a lieutenant-general.

Clarke, Leo (1892–1916). A corporal in the 2nd Battalion, CEF, this Waterdown, Ont. resident won the VICTORIA CROSS near Pozières, France on 9 September 1916 during the Battle of the SOMME. When the Germans counterattacked his unit, Clarke, though wounded, fought on, even using a captured German rifle, until the enemy had been forced to retreat. He died of his wounds a month later.

Clark-Kennedy, William Hew (1879–1961). As commanding officer of the 24th Battalion, CEF, Lt-Col Clark-Kennedy won the VICTORIA CROSS for his actions on 27–28 August 1918 near Wancourt, France. Though severely wounded, he continued to direct his battalion's operations, finally consenting to be moved to the rear only after the situation on his front was stable.

Claxton, Brian Brooke (1898–1960). A lawyer and politician, Claxton had served overseas with the artillery during WORLD WAR I. He was then active in nationalist organizations and won election to Parliament as a Liberal in 1940. After service in the National Health and Welfare portfolio, this able man became minister of National Defence in 1946 and presided over the cost-cutting budgets of the immediate postwar years as well as over the enormous expansion heralded by the KOREAN WAR and Canada's

NATO commitments. He retired from the defence portfolio and politics in 1954.

Clayoquot, **HMCS**. A *BANGOR*-CLASS minesweeper commissioned in August 1941, *Clayoquot* served in the Gulf of St Lawrence and in the North Atlantic on convoy escort duties until 24 December 1944 when she was torpedoed and sunk by a U-boat. Eight of her crew perished.

Cloutier, Albert (1902–1965). Born in the United States, this largely self-taught painter lived in Canada from infancy. He worked for the WARTIME INFORMATION BOARD and the DEPARTMENT OF NATIONAL WAR SERVICES from 1940–43, then became a war artist with the RCAF until 1946. His paintings show the influence of impressionism and the Group of Seven.

Cloutier, Sylvain (b. 1929). Born in Quebec, Cloutier joined the public service after completing his education. He became deputy minister of the DEPARTMENT OF NATIONAL DEFENCE in 1971 with the task of shaking up its bureaucracy. He did this, working closely with the CHIEF OF THE DEFENCE STAFF. In 1975, he left DND for the Transport department.

Coastal Command. Created by the Royal Air Force in 1936, this Command was nominally under the Admiralty's operational control after 1941, its main task anti-submarine warfare. The ROYAL CANADIAN AIR FORCE contributed seven squadrons to Coastal Command's efforts.

Coates, Robert Carman (b. 1928). A lawyer, Coates was born at Amherst, N.S., and was elected to Parliament in 1957 as a Conservative. In 1984, he became minister of National Defence in the Mulroney government and began to undo UNIFICATION. He resigned from the Cabinet in February 1985 after a newspaper revealed that he had visited a sleazy bar in Lahr while on an official visit to Canadian NATO troops stationed in Germany.

Cockburn, Hampden Zane Churchill (1867–1913). Born in Toronto, Cockburn enlisted in the ROYAL CANADIAN DRAGOONS during the SOUTH AFRICAN WAR. On 7 November 1900, he won the VICTORIA

CROSS for his courage during an engagement at LELIEFONTEIN on the Komati River. Though he was wounded and all of his rearguard party were either killed or wounded, his resistance allowed the remainder of a British column to escape a Boer trap.

Cold War. The Cold War between the Soviet Union and its satellites and the United States and its allies began at the close of WORLD WAR II. During the war, there had been scant trust between the members of the Grand Alliance, and the coalition was already in disarray by the time the Germans and Japanese had surrendered. To some, the Cold War began in Ottawa on the September 1945 day when a Soviet cipher officer, Igor Gouzenko, left his embassy with documents demonstrating that the USSR had been spying in Canada. Gouzenko also made clear that similar espionage was underway in the U.S. and the U.K. and that atomic secrets were high on the Moscow want list.

The tensions soon grew as Moscow evinced no desire to leave the territories it had liberated during the war. Tame governments were installed throughout Eastern Europe, pressure was exerted on Iran and Norway, and by 1948 the former wartime allies were thoroughly demoralized and frightened. The United States' generous Marshall Plan was one attempt to stiffen spines and economies in Europe. Another was the secret defence discussions between Britain, the United States, and Canada that soon turned into the negotiation of a collective security treaty with the nations of Western Europe: the NORTH ATLANTIC TREATY ORGANIZATION. NATO's establishment in 1949 was followed by the formation of the Warsaw Pact, a parallel organization directed from Moscow, and the beginning of the KOREAN WAR in 1950 sped rearmament throughout the west. A country like Canada, hitherto suspicious of foreign commitments in peacetime, in 1951 sent troops and aircraft to Europe for NATO service as well as a brigade to Korea. An integrated NATO command, slowly in formation from 1949, was put on the ground under American direction, and Europe entered a forty-year period of hostility across the Iron Curtain.

There were recurring thaws and freezes in the Cold War. The SUEZ CRISIS of 1956 came close to splitting the NATO alliance, but threats of missile attack from Moscow soon welded the British, French and Americans back together. The CUBAN MISSILE CRISIS of 1962 saw nuclear war a real possibility, and the Warsaw Pact invasion of Czechoslovakia, struggling toward democracy in 1968, briefly threatened the slow move toward detente. By 1969, however, countries were beginning to look at the frozen posture in Europe as one of futility; in that year Prime Minister Pierre Trudeau unilaterally decided to reduce Canadian forces in Europe by half, a move that won him no credit with his allies and little from the Soviets. Still, nuclear arms reduction talks soon began and except for a period of high tension when the bellicose President Reagan led the U.S. and the Soviets shot down a Korean airliner in 1983, the era of hostility seemed to be waning. This became clear when in 1985 Mikhail Gorbachev came to power in Moscow and set out to dismantle the Cold War, in large part because his society's economy had simply buckled under the strain of financing armaments. A succession of meetings with Presidents Reagan and George Bush essentially brought the Cold War to an end, and agreements to reduce nuclear and conventional weapons in Europe were in train. After the tearing down of the Berlin Wall at the end of 1989, the overthrow of the Communist regimes of Eastern Europe, and the reunification of Germany in 1990, the Warsaw Pact dissolved itself, though NATO remained in existence. In September 1991, as a reflection of the changed situation, the Canadian government announced that it was going to shut down its European bases and bring all but a thousand or so of its troops home; the next year, Ottawa decided to remove all its troops from Europe. Whether American forces would remain in Europe much longer was uncertain.

Collective security. The idea of collective security — that aggressors could be deterred or defeated if all other nations combined against them — first found practical expression in the Covenant of the League of Nations. But the League failed because many states, and not least Canada, refused to accept the obligations and enforcement mechanisms that collective security required. The United Nations, set up after WORLD WAR II, tried to handle collective security better, and PEACEKEEPING and a collective international response during the KOREAN WAR and the Persian GULF WAR suggest some success. But UN collective security for years was paralysed by the COLD WAR, and the western democracies turned to NATO to achieve their mutual security and to avoid the possibility of vetoes by communist nations.

Collège Militaire Royal de Saint-Jean. Opened in 1952 at the historic military installation at Saint-Jean, Que., to add a French-speaking dimension to Canada's military colleges, CMR initially offered a preparatory year and two years of university-level training before sending its graduates to the ROYAL MILITARY COLLEGE, Kingston. The bilingual institution now offers undergraduate and graduate degrees.

Collins, Mary (b. 1940). Born in British Columbia and elected there as a Progressive Conservative in 1984 and 1988, Collins became associate minister for National Defence in January 1989, the first woman to hold the post.

Collishaw, Raymond (1893–1976). A fighter pilot during WORLD WAR I, Collishaw's 60 victories placed him second only to Billy BISHOP among Canadian aces. He served with the Royal Air Force in Russia during the anti-Bolshevik intervention and then in the Middle East in the interwar period. At the outset of WORLD WAR II he commanded RAF forces in Egypt. He retired as an air vice-marshal in 1943.

Colonial Defence Committee. Established as a sub-committee of the British Cabinet's Colonial Committee in 1885, the Colonial Defence Committee was a consultative and advisory body with the whole field of colonial defence in its purview. It was hampered by the baulkiness of the colonies, not least Canada, and it was unable to produce a statement of the principles of Imperial defence until 1895. It became a sub-committee of the COMMITTEE OF IMPERIAL DEFENCE in 1904.

Colours. This term for the flag carried by a military unit was first used in Elizabethan times and symbolizes loyalty both to the monarch and to the unit itself. Colours were carried in battle and served as a rallying point; this practice, of course, has long since lapsed, and regimental colours, emblazoned with battle honours, are now carried only in formal ceremonies such as a trooping of the colours.

Colville, Alexander (b. 1920). One of Canada's best-known artists, he studied at Mount Allison University and enlisted in the army in WORLD WAR II. He was a war artist from 1944 to 1946, and his paintings of infantrymen in the NORTHWEST EUROPE CAMPAIGN are hauntingly powerful.

Combe, Robert Grierson (1880–1917). Lt Combe was awarded a posthumous VICTORIA CROSS for leading an assault against German trenches near Acheville, France on 3 May 1917. Though his company of the 27th Battalion, CEF, was decimated, he reached the trench and captured several dozen of the enemy before being mortally wounded.

Combined Committee on Air Training in North America. Created as a result of the 1942 Ottawa Air Training Conference, the Combined Committee, a Canada-U.S. body, first met in early 1943. The committee agreed to exchange information on training, but its work did not lead to a pooling of air training facilities or to U.S. air training in Canada.

Comfort, Charles Fraser (b. 1900). An art professor at the University of Toronto on the outbreak of WORLD WAR II, Comfort joined the army and served as a weapons instructor before becoming the army's senior war artist in 1943. He served in Britain and during the ITALIAN and NORTHWEST EUROPE CAMPAIGNS, turning out dozens of paintings in a stark, modern style.

Commission on the Defences of British North America, 1825. Appointed by the Duke of Wellington on 11 April 1825, the commission headed by Maj.-Gen. Sir James Carmichael Smyth came to British North America to report on the progress made in implementing the Duke's 1819 recommendations for the defence of the colonies. The commissioners foresaw three routes of possible invasion from the south, and they recommended that major fortifications be built south of Montreal, at Kingston, at Halifax, and on the Niagara frontier as well as a number of lesser ones. They recommended a military road through New Brunswick to link Nova Scotia and Canada, and they proposed a number of British offensive operations against the U.S. to forestall American attack in event of war. Some only of the constructions recommended were built, among them the Rideau Canal system.

Reading: J.M. Hitsman, *Safeguarding Canada 1763–1871* (1968)

Commission on the Defences of Canada, 1862. Established by Governor-General Lord Monck to survey the Canadian border from Lake Superior to New Brunswick and to report on a system of fortifications and defences for the colony, the commission of six officers reported on 2 September 1862. The commissioners envisaged a number of possible threats from the south but saw that the main aim of any American attack would be Montreal. The fortifications at Quebec and Kingston were strong, others in decay, and new strong points had to be built at points between Sarnia and Lévis at a cost of £1.6 million. The key to defending Canada, the commissioners maintained, was the acquisition of supremacy on the Great Lakes and a large Canadian MILITIA and British regular force of some 130,000. The response of the Canadian government was cool in the extreme—no compulsory training for the militia because 'No probable combination of regular troops and militia would preserve our soil from invading armies.'

Reading: J.M. Hitsman, *Safeguarding Canada 1763–1871* (1968)

Committee of Imperial Defence. Created in 1904 by the Balfour government in London, the Committee amalgamated the Cabinet Defence Committee and the Joint Naval and Military Committee and had a permanent secretariat. It was intended to consider all questions of Imperial defence from the point of view of the British services, India, and the colonies. The CID was seen by many Canadians as a device to centralize military control to serve British interests.

Reading: R.A. Preston, *Canada and "Imperial Defense"* (1967)

Commonwealth War Graves Commission. Established in 1917 as the Imperial War Graves Commission to set up and provide perpetual care for the Empire's war dead; the name was changed in 1960. The Commission cares for the graves of 1.75 million men and women in 2500 cemeteries and for some 200 memorials in 140 countries. 110,088 Canadians are interred in or commemorated by the Commission's cemeteries and memorials.

Communications Branch, National Research Council. Created in 1946 as the successor to the wartime EXAMINATION UNIT, the CBNRC handled Canada's signals intelligence work, largely monitoring Soviet and other communications. It cooperated closely with Britain, the U.S., Australia, and New Zealand (through the UKUSA and CANUSA agreements). The existence of the CBNRC was secret until 1974 when it was revealed on a CBC television program. The next year, the CBNRC was succeeded by the Communications Security Establishment, equally secretive in its work of protecting Canadian and NATO signals traffic and listening in on other nations'. Its existence was not publicly acknowledged until 1983.

Company of One Hundred Associates. Also known as the Company of New France, it was founded by Cardinal Richelieu in 1627 to develop France's empire in North America. It had a monopoly on the fur trade, but its military reverses at the hands of the English and other difficulties led it to lease its charter away in 1645. In 1663, its monopoly was ended altogether.

Company organization. See BATTALION ORGANIZATION.

Conference of Defence Associations. A coordinating group founded in 1932 to promote the welfare of Canada's defence forces, the CDA consists of several military service associations. It meets annually and lobbies for strengthened reserve forces and stronger defence efforts generally.

Congo, UN peacekeeping in. See UNOC.

Connor, Ralph. See GORDON, C.W.

Conscientious objector. One who, for reasons of conscience, refuses to do military service or to be placed in any situation in which killing of others might be necessary is known as a conscientious objector. Canada granted this status to individuals with religious, ethnic, or moral objections in both world wars, but in WORLD WAR I the MILITARY VOTERS ACT disfranchised them, and in WORLD WAR II most of the more than twelve thousand conscientious objectors were made to perform Alternative Service Work at camps across the country.

Reading: J.A. Toews, *Alternative Service in Canada During World War II* (n.d.)

Conscription. Compulsory enlistment of citizens (and others) for military service dates back to the French regime. During WORLD WAR I and WORLD WAR II, the governments of Sir Robert BORDEN and Mackenzie KING adopted the measure in the face of heavy casualties overseas and heated political debate at home. Though the policy has been considered occasionally since 1945, Canada remains one of the relatively few NATO nations not to use some form of conscription. See also MILITARY SERVICE ACT; NATIONAL RESOURCES MOBILIZATION ACT.

Conscription crisis, 1917. WORLD WAR I trench fighting proved inordinately costly in human life, and casualties were far greater than any of the belligerents had anticipated. This was certainly true for Canada where initial enthusiasm for the war soon was replaced by near-indifference in some parts of the country, such as French-speaking Quebec, and a grim determination to see the struggle through in others. By late 1916 casualties were beginning to create reinforcement problems as recruiting in Canada, hitherto much disorganized, began to slow. For the Prime Minister Sir Robert BORDEN, the war was a sacred cause and victory had to be won; Canada had to do its full part in this. His visits to the front and to Britain in the spring of 1917 convinced him that compulsory service had to be imposed if the CANADIAN CORPS was to be maintained at full strength, and he returned to Ottawa in May determined to move ahead with conscription to secure at least 100,000 men. Borden realized the difficulties this would cause in Quebec and with farmers and labour, and he tried to avoid them by proposing a coalition with the Liberal party; Sir Wilfrid LAURIER refused, fearing that his hold on Quebec would dissolve if he supported compulsion. Borden then introduced his MILITARY SERVICE ACT, securing its passage in August. He then gerrymandered the electoral rolls with the WARTIME ELECTIONS ACT and the MILITARY VOTERS ACT, created a UNION GOVERNMENT that largely excluded French-speaking Canadians, and proceeded to win a landslide victory in the general election of December 1917. To assist him in his victory he promised that farmers would not be conscripted.

Of those eligible for conscription, almost all sought exemption, their cases being heard in local tribunals. In all, some 401,882 men registered. Call-ups of conscripts began only in January 1918 and by the end of the war 124,588 had been put on strength of the CANADIAN EXPEDITIONARY FORCE. Of that number, however, only 24,132 men had arrived in France by the ARMISTICE, though how many were actually incorporated into units is unclear. As a military measure, therefore, conscription was at best a partial success; as a political measure, it was a long-term unmitigated failure (although it did help Borden win re-election in 1917). It embittered Quebec for a generation and its memory shaped policy on manpower in WORLD WAR II. It infuriated farmers who, despite the promises of December 1917, had their exemptions cancelled in the spring of 1918. And it left English-speaking Canadians convinced that their French compatriots were a cowardly race. The price of conscription was high indeed.

Reading: J.L. Granatstein and J.M. Hitsman, *Broken Promises: A History of Conscription in Canada* (1985)

Conscription crisis, 1942. By late 1941, there were pressures for 'total war' everywhere in Canada. At a meeting in November, the opposition Conservative Party selected former Prime Minister Arthur Meighen, the draftsman of conscription in 1917, to be its leader, and the press began calling for conscription for overseas service. Within KING's Cabinet, his minister of National Defence, J. Layton RALSTON, and several of his colleagues supported conscription. The attack on Pearl Harbor and the entry of the United States into the war increased the pressure. But King felt bound by his pledges against compulsory service made to to Quebec, and his solution was to stage a PLEBISCITE in April 1942 to ask the electorate to release the government from its past commitments restricting methods of raising men for military service. This plebiscite, asking all Canada to release King from promises made to one province, outraged French Canadians. A 'non' campaign was run by LA LIGUE POUR LA DÉFENSE DU CANADA that effectively out-organized the feeble 'oui' campaign in Quebec. The result saw Quebeckers heavily vote 'non' while the 'yes' vote won very large majorities in the rest of Canada. King then introduced BILL 80 in Parliament to delete the clause in the NATIONAL RESOURCES MOBILIZATION ACT restricting the use of conscripts to Canada. But his policy, brilliantly expressed in the phrase 'Not necessarily conscription but conscription if necessary', remained unchanged. Canada still would not send conscripts overseas unless it was necessary; the definition of necessity was nowhere specified. Although Ralston threatened to resign, King got him to stay and pushed Bill 80 through Parliament. The conscription crisis was dormant for two years.

Reading: J.L. Granatstein and J.M. Hitsman, *Broken Promises: A History of Conscription in Canada* (Toronto, 1985)

Conscription crisis, 1944. In the fall of 1944, by which time the army was heavily engaged, the issue of conscription rose to its WORLD WAR II climax. Because of GENERAL STAFF miscalculations of the numbers of infantry reinforcements (Canada was relying on outdated British WASTAGE rates) by October 1944 there was a projected shortage of some 15,000 infantrymen. Expedients had already been tried and failed, and the only source for trained infantry seemed to be the 60,000 NATIONAL RESOURCES MOBILIZATION ACT (NRMA) soldiers or ZOMBIES in Canada. An enormous political crisis erupted in late October and November, one that saw KING sack Defence minister J.L. RALSTON in one of the most dramatic Cabinet confrontations in Canadian history. His replacement was General A.G.L. MCNAUGHTON, until late l943 the commander of the FIRST CANADIAN ARMY. McNaughton tried but failed to find the needed infantry reinforcements, and his army commanders in Canada were increasingly restive. King then used the military's unhappiness as the excuse to reverse course on 22 November: the government now would despatch 16,000 NRMA infantry overseas. The reaction of Quebec M.P.s was bitter, and public opinion in French

Canada was angry at what was seen as a betrayal. But King clearly had delayed the inevitable as long as possible, and the anger died away quickly. The 2463 conscripts who reached the front in NORTHWEST EUROPE before the end of the war by all reports served competently.

Reading: J.L. Granatstein and J.M. Hitsman, *Broken Promises: A History of Conscription in Canada* (Toronto, 1985)

Conspicuous Gallantry Medal. This decoration, created in 1855, is awarded to chief petty officers and naval other ranks for courage in action. A Conspicuous Gallantry Medal (Flying) was created in 1942 to honour army and air force other ranks for gallantry while flying in active operations against the enemy.

Convoys. The basic shipping defence against sea raiders, convoys are groups of merchantmen sailing together under the protection of naval vessels. Although convoys had been employed in the Napoleonic Wars and almost certainly in earlier wars, they had fallen out of use (except for such things as the convoyed troopships that carried the first Canadian contingent overseas in 1914) and were not reinstituted until U-boat attacks in WORLD WAR I inflicted huge losses on North Atlantic shipping. Their use in 1917 and the breaking of German codes almost immediately cut losses significantly, though for the small Canadian navy, the HALIFAX PATROL that covered the merchantmen as they formed up and left port with an array of small vessels was a great trial.

In WORLD WAR II, the convoy system was put in place at once. Halifax became the major forming-up point in North America. Using command and defensive systems that developed during the war (see ATLANTIC CONVOY CONFERENCE), the convoys were handed off from escort group to escort group as they worked their way across the North Atlantic to Britain or from Britain to the Soviet port of Murmansk or to Gibraltar. The U-boats too changed their tactics, moving from single submarine attacks to 'wolfpack' assaults by as many as a dozen U-boats against a single convoy. By early 1943, the Nazis had more than 200 U-boats operational and they were inflicting staggering losses on the Allies: in February 63 ships were sunk; in March 103 were lost. For a time at the peak of the BATTLE OF THE ATLANTIC, Canadian ships were pulled out for retraining and re-equipment.

The convoys ordinarily moved in a giant rectangle at the speed of the slowest ship. Around the merchant ships darted the escorts, usually CORVETTES or DESTROYERS, their ASDIC and radar struggling to detect the U-boats which, when found, were attacked with DEPTH CHARGES and, later in the war, HEDGEHOGS. Often, individual convoys were hit hard by the Germans. CONVOY SC-42 in September 1941, for example, consisted of 64 merchant vessels escorted by a ROYAL CANADIAN NAVY destroyer and three corvettes, none of which had radar. Under almost continuous attack, the slow-moving convoy lost 16 ships; one U-boat was sunk. The Canadians, almost all unskilled in their deadly task, learned their trade, however, and by the end of the war, the RCN was escorting half of all convoys across the Atlantic.

Reading: Marc Milner, *North Atlantic Run* (Toronto, 1985)

Convoy SC-42. Consisting of 64 merchant vessels and escorted by four ROYAL CANADIAN NAVY escorts, this slow convoy was attacked off Greenland on 9 September 1941 by a U-boat wolf pack. Without air cover or radar, the convoy lost 16 ships in the next week; the escorts sank but one U-boat. The disaster highlighted deficiencies in Allied and Canadian convoy efforts, demonstrating the need for better training, air cover, and more escorts.

Coppins, Frederick George (1889–1963). A corporal in the 8th Battalion, CEF, Coppins won a VICTORIA CROSS during the AMIENS offensive of 9 August 1918 by silencing a German machine gun that was holding up his platoon's advance. Five men rushed the gun and Coppins, the sole survivor, knocked out the enemy position despite being wounded.

***Cornwallis*, HMCS/Canadian Forces Base Cornwallis.** Located at Deep Brook, N.S., *Cornwallis* was opened in 1943 as a naval training centre for new entry seamen. The base continued as a naval training station until UNIFICATION when, as Canadian Forces Base Cornwallis, it became the armed forces' main recruit training base.

Corps organization, World War II. A Canadian corps, commanded by a lieutenant-general, consisted of from two to five divisions (not necessarily all Canadian), usually supported by an independent armoured brigade and an Army Group Royal Artillery of four or five regiments of field, medium, and heavy artillery. Corps troops included an armoured car regiment, anti-tank and anti-aircraft regiments, a survey regiment, and engineer and signals units.

Corvettes. The ROYAL CANADIAN NAVY's basic anti-submarine vessel of WORLD WAR II, the corvette was a small ship. Displacing 935 tonnes, about 63 m long, this 'Patrol Vessel, Whaler Type' initially had a range of 6436 km at 12 knots (though later versions had almost double that range). A corvette's maximum speed was only 16 knots, but the little ship was manoeuvrable. Her main armament was the DEPTH CHARGE, dropped from two stern chutes or launched from two throwers on each side; there was also one 4-inch gun, a 2-pounder pom-pom, a few machine guns, and later two or more 20 mm Oerlikon guns. HEDGEHOGs were subsequently fitted in many corvettes. The standard crew for this vessel, its design first proposed in Britain in 1938, was 47 officers and men, and the initial estimated cost of building a corvette was a mere £90,000.

The first Canadian Flower class corvettes were ordered in February 1940 when Ottawa asked Canadian shipyards for 64. Simple as they were, corvettes were a challenge for shipyards without much experience. Each took about 700 tonnes of steel plate, 1500 valves and 39 tonnes of copper wiring; somehow, the task was managed and the first 14 corvettes made their way to Halifax before the end of 1940. Before the end of the war, 122 were built in Canadian yards. Others, somewhat larger Castle class corvettes, were acquired from Britain.

Designed for use in coastal waters, the corvettes had never been intended to operate in mid-ocean. Out of necessity in the desperate days after the fall of France, the corvettes fought the submarines that sought out the fat, slow merchantmen in the critical supply CONVOYS. The ships were unstable in the very rough North Atlantic, they were cramped and crowded (especially as the crews increased, often to almost a hundred, as new equipment and armaments were added to them), and the food provided varied from awful to wretched. Most of their crewmen had never been to sea and the officers, apart from the very few professional RCN officers, were ordinarily yachtsmen or merchant captains. The corvettes had a rough time against the U-boats in the first three or four years of the war, but their crews learned their hard trade and won the BATTLE OF THE ATLANTIC.

Reading: Marc Milner, *North Atlantic Run* (Toronto, 1985)

Cosens, Aubrey (1921–1945). A sergeant in the QUEEN'S OWN RIFLES, Cosens was awarded a VICTORIA CROSS for his critical role in the capture of strongly held farm buildings near Mooshof, Germany on 25–26 February 1945. Cosens directed a tank in crashing through one building's wall, then cleared room after room of the enemy. While on the way to report success, he was killed by a sniper.

COTC. See CANADIAN OFFICERS' TRAINING CORPS.

Coughlin, Wlliam Garnet [Bing] (b. 1912). Born in Ottawa, Bing Coughlin worked in display advertising in the United States and went overseas with the Princess Louise Dragoon Guards. He took part in the invasion of SICILY, and in early 1944 joined the army newspaper, *THE MAPLE LEAF*, in Naples and began to produce his cartoons, 'This Army' and 'HERBIE'. A typical soldier, a scrounger, a grumbler, and a genuine 'poor bloody infantryman', Herbie became extraordinarily popular with the troops. Coughlin then took Herbie to Northwest Europe, was made a Member of the Order of the British Empire, and mentioned in despatches.

Courcelette, Battle of. The battle of Flers-Courcelette, launched by two British armies on 15 September 1916 as part of the battle of THE SOMME, took place on a 16-km front protected by strong German defence works. The attack marked the first use of tanks, seven of which supported the CANADIAN CORPS. The feature of the assault was an attack by the 22e Battalion of the CEF that turned into vicious close-quarter fighting and 14 counter-attacks by the enemy. 'If hell is as bad as what I have seen at Courcelette,' the Van Doos' commander, Lt-Col T.L.

TREMBLAY, said, 'I would not wish my worst enemy to go there.' The battle lasted for most of a week, resulted in small gains, and cost the Corps 7230 casualties.

Crerar, Henry Duncan Graham [Harry] (1888–1965). The commander of the FIRST CANADIAN ARMY from the beginning of 1944 through to the end of WORLD WAR II, Harry Crerar was born in Hamilton, Ont., and educated at the ROYAL MILITARY COLLEGE. He served in the MILITIA artillery before WORLD WAR I, then served overseas in France and Flanders, ending the war as a lieutenant-colonel and counter-battery officer at CANADIAN CORPS headquarters. He joined the PERMANENT FORCE, attended the BRITISH ARMY STAFF COLLEGE and the Imperial Defence College, and developed a reputation for his intelligence and as the best staff officer in the army. When WORLD WAR II broke out he was commandant of RMC, but he soon went overseas as senior combatant officer at CANADIAN MILITARY HEADQUARTERS. In 1940, he returned to Canada as vice-chief and then CHIEF OF THE GENERAL STAFF, a post he held until appointed to command the 2nd Canadian Division in December 1941. He at once became a corps commander in England and did well in Exercise Spartan, then briefly directed I CANADIAN CORPS in Italy, and succeeded Gen. A.G.L. MCNAUGHTON at the head of First Canadian Army in England and in Northwest Europe. No brilliant strategist, Crerar was cautious, capable, and wary of grand schemes. He had the brilliant and mercurial Gen. Guy SIMONDS to keep in harness and the able, irascible, and inconsiderate Field Marshal Bernard Montgomery above him. He managed his military tasks with some skill, simultaneously dealing carefully with his political masters in Canada. Though his health broke down just before the SCHELDT battles, he was in command for the HOCHWALD struggles where he did a very good job commanding a huge army of Canadian, British, American, and other countries' troops.

After the war, Crerar handled a number of minor diplomatic roles for the Canadian government, spoke occasionally, and regrettably wrote nothing beyond a few magazine articles advocating CONSCRIPTION. His reputation, highest during the war, has now been almost entirely superseded by that of

Simonds, and it is significant that Crerar, almost alone of Allied army commanders, has not had a biography.

Croak, John Bernard (1892–1918). A Newfoundlander, Croak served with the 13th Battalion, CEF, during the AMIENS offensive. On 8 August 1918 he silenced one machine-gun nest singlehandedly, then led his platoon in eliminating several others. His wounds were fatal, and he became one of only two Newfoundlanders to win the VICTORIA CROSS in WORLD WAR I.

Croil, George Mitchell (1893–1959). He served in the infantry during the early stages of WORLD WAR I, then transferred to the Royal Flying Corps in 1916 and served in Salonika and the Middle East, including a time as pilot for Lawrence of Arabia. Reserved and retiring, he was a major at the end of the war, served with the AIR BOARD and then rose through the ranks of the ROYAL CANADIAN AIR FORCE. He attended the RAF Staff College and the Imperial Defence College, then served as CHIEF OF THE AIR STAFF from 1938–40. He administered the BRITISH COMMONWEALTH AIR TRAINING PLAN in its initial stages but did not get on with C.G. POWER, his minister, and from 1940–44 was inspector-general of the RCAF. He retired in 1944 as an air marshal.

Cross of Valour. Instituted in 1972 as part of a system of Canadian honours, the Cross of Valour honours those, civil or military, who perform selfless acts of courage in the face of great peril.

Cruise missile testing. The Trudeau government's decision on 15 July 1983 to allow the United States to test air-launched cruise missiles over northwestern Canada provoked a major struggle in Cabinet. The Prime Minister supported the testing, and he was attacked by anti-nuclear and environmental groups as a result. The decision was challenged unsuccessfully in the courts in 1985. Test flights have continued at the rate of several a year, thus far without incident.

Cruisers. Fast warships that are in size, weight, and armour protection between a destroyer and a battleship. The cruiser designation has been in use from the 1860s although the modern cruiser did not emerge until the end of the 19th century. Cruisers ranged in displacement from 4000 to 10,000 tonnes and the main armament was ordinarily of 6-inch or 8-inch guns. Canada's naval forces have operated several cruisers—HMCS *NIOBE*, *RAINBOW*, *Aurora*, *ONTARIO*, and *QUEBEC*—at various times between 1910 and 1958. Armament of the 8000-tonne *Ontario*, e.g., included nine 6-inch guns, eight 4-inch guns, three POM-POMS and six single OERLIKONS, as well as torpedoes.

Crysler's Farm, 1813. Located on the St Lawrence River near present-day Morrisburg, Ont., this farm was the site of a major battle of the WAR OF 1812. A large American invasion force under General James Wilkinson was moving on Montreal when its 1800-strong rearguard turned to drive off a pursuing British column of some 800 men on 11 November. The Americans attacked across ground carefully chosen by the British commander, Lt-Col Joseph Morrison, and suffered heavily, losing 439 men. British casualties were 179. Learning of the action, Wilkinson lost his nerve, abandoned the campaign against Montreal, and went into winter quarters.

Cuban Missile Crisis. The U.S. discovery that the Soviet Union had installed missiles in Cuba resulted in a tense military and diplomatic standoff in October 1962, ended only when the Soviets on 27–28 October agreed to dismantle and remove their weapons. For Canadians, the incident was important because of Prime Minister John DIEFENBAKER's role. Informed by President J.F. Kennedy of the U.S. decision to blockade Cuba just 90 minutes before its public announcement, Diefenbaker at first refused to put the Canadian forces on a state of higher alert. On his own, Defence minister Douglas HARKNESS quietly did just that, but official sanction was not given until 24 October when Soviet vessels were on the verge of confronting the American blockade. Diefenbaker's hesitation was much criticized and relations with the U.S., already difficult because of the question of arming BOMARC missiles with nuclear warheads, were exacerbated. Diefenbaker's reputation never recovered from the impression of indecision left by the crisis, though his concern that Canada's NORAD membership entitled it to more consultation was sound.

Reading: J.L. Granatstein, *Canada 1957–1967* (Toronto, 1986)

Cullen, Maurice Galbraith (1886–1934). Born in Newfoundland, Cullen studied sculpture in Montreal and art in Europe. During WORLD WAR I, he served overseas as an official war artist.

Currie, Sir Arthur William (1875–1933). Currie was the first Canadian-born commander of the CANADIAN CORPS in WORLD WAR I and unquestionably one of the best Allied commanders of the struggle. Born in Strathroy, Ont., Currie moved to British Columbia in 1893, taught school for a time, then ran a successful real estate and property speculation business until it was wiped out in the 1913 crash. If his business career had its ups and downs, his MILITIA rise was steady. He had joined up in 1893, established a reputation for efficiency, and at the outbreak of war in 1914 was a lieutenant-colonel. At Valcartier the minister of Militia, Sam HUGHES, gave Currie command of the 2nd Canadian Infantry Brigade, in part at least because of Currie's friendship with his son GARNET HUGHES, and as a brigadier Currie participated in the IST CANADIAN DIVISION's initial battles at YPRES. By September 1915, he was commanding the division, building a formidable reputation for himself and his men, and on 9 June 1917, now a lieutenant-general, Currie became Corps commander.

As a militiaman, operating in a British Army where the professional soldiers ruled, Currie was something of an anomaly. He was also, as a rather pear-shaped man, unusual in that his appearance did not fit that of the Imperial archetype, typified by Sir Douglas Haig. Currie's concern to minimize casualties, his insistence on reconnaisance and careful preparation, and his determination to learn the lessons of previous battles marked him as one of the British forces' leading thinkers. His high point came, not at PASS-CHENDAELE where he had tried to prevent his Corps from being used, but in the war's last hundred days that began on 8 August 1918. Though the casualties were heavy, the Canadian Corps' attacks made spectacular gains and inflicted heavy losses on the Ger-

mans. Currie entered MONS at the head of his troops as the ARMISTICE came into effect.

Never popular with the troops overseas, in part because he was such a shy man, Currie's postwar reputation was clouded by the attacks an embittered Hughes launched against him, claiming that he had wasted lives. This resulted in a major libel suit in 1928, when Currie was Principal of McGill University, that completely vindicated the General, though awarding him only trifling damages. More seriously, Currie had siphoned off regimental funds before the war for his own use and, though this came to Sir Robert BORDEN's attention, he refused to sack his most successful Canadian general of the war.

Reading: A.M.J. Hyatt, *General Sir Arthur Currie* (Toronto, 1987)

Currie, David Vivian (b. 1912). While commanding a squadron of the South Alberta Regiment in August 1944, Currie took and held the village of St Lambert-sur-Dives in the face of repeated counterattacks by Nazi troops trying to escape the FALAISE GAP. He won the VICTORIA CROSS for his gallantry.

Currie, George S. (1889–1953). A chartered accountant and industrial executive, Currie served in WORLD WAR I and won the MILITARY CROSS and DISTINGUISHED SERVICE ORDER. He was executive assistant to Defence minister Col J. Layton RALSTON during the early stages of WORLD WAR II; in 1942, he became one of two deputy ministers (army), a post he held until September 1944. In April 1952, Currie was asked by Defence minister Brooke CLAXTON to investigate irregularities in the army works service and to recommend ways of avoiding them. A draft of an early version reached Opposition members in early 1953 who made hay with charges that the army had 'horses on the payroll'.

Currie Hall. Located at the ROYAL MILITARY COLLEGE, the Sir Arthur Currie Memorial Hall was named after the first Canadian commander of the CANADIAN CORPS. Opened in 1922 as RMC's main assembly room, the hall commemorates the achievements of the Corps in WORLD WAR I and is decorated with portraits of the Corps' leaders and the badge, battle patch, number, and name of every Canadian unit serving on the Western Front at the armistice.

Curtis, Wilfrid Austin (1893–1977). Curtis served in the infantry during WORLD WAR I, then transferred to the ROYAL NAVAL AIR SERVICE as a fighter pilot. He served in the ROYAL CANADIAN AIR FORCE Auxiliary until being called to active service in 1939 as a wing commander. He was air officer commanding in London from 1941–44, where he was embittered by the inability to make progress on CANADIANIZATION and to secure the aircraft the RCAF needed from the U.S., and was CHIEF OF THE AIR STAFF, 1947–53. He retired as an air marshal, subsequently occupying executive positions in aviation, where his wartime experiences guided his conviction that the RCAF had to be supported by a domestic aircraft industry.

Curtiss Aeroplane and Motors Ltd. This subsidiary of Curtiss Aeroplane Co. of Hammondsport, N.Y., began operating in Toronto on 12 April 1915 after an Admiralty order, in deference to Ottawa's wishes, had specified that 50 aircraft be manufactured in Canada. Only 18 twin-engine, three-seat tractor biplanes were produced in Toronto before Curtiss was bought by the U.K. government and transformed into CANADIAN AEROPLANES LTD.

Curtiss Helldiver bomber. American designed, 1194 Helldiver divebombers were built in Canada in WORLD WAR II by Canadian Car and Foundry Co. and Canadian Fairchild Co. The Helldiver, with a speed of 475 km/h and a range of 1875 km with a 454-kg bomb load, was launched from carriers and shore installations.

Curtiss Jenny trainer. The JN-4 Jenny was a two-seat trainer of which almost 3000 were produced by CANADIAN AEROPLANES LTD during WORLD WAR I. The Jenny was the mainstay of the ROYAL FLYING CORPS and Royal Air Force training establishments in Canada, and 680 were purchased by the U.S. government for pilot training.

Curtiss Kittyhawk fighter. The first mass-produced American single-seat fighter aircraft, the P-40 Tomahawk, one of its early names, was flown by the French before their 1940 defeat. Taken over by the British, the aircraft was upgraded to carry four machine guns and given self-sealing tanks. With a top speed of 560 km/h and a new name, Kittyhawk, the aircraft was used after 1941 by the ROYAL CANADIAN AIR FORCE on home defence tasks and in Alaska where RCAF pilots for the first time engaged Japanese in combat. Kittyhawks also shot down Japanese incendiary paper balloons intended to set the Canadian forests ablaze.

Curtiss School of Aviation. Located at Hanlan's Point on Toronto Island, the school operated in 1915–16 and trained 130 pilots. All but two joined the ROYAL NAVAL AIR SERVICE or the ROYAL FLYING CORPS. Many others received partial training at this school.

Cut Knife Hill, 1885. Located west of Battleford, Sask. on the Poundmaker Reserve, Cut Knife Hill on 2 May 1885 was the scene of a battle during the NORTHWEST REBELLION, 1885. A column of 325 soldiers under Col William OTTER clashed with a roughly equal number of Cree and Assiniboine under Chief POUNDMAKER. Otter's attempted punitive raid against Poundmaker saw his column encircled and pinned down in a poor defensive position. After several hours and 22 casualties, Otter was fortunate to be able to withdraw. His command was saved only because Poundmaker forbade his men to pursue the retreating column.

Reading: Bob Beal and R. Macleod, *Prairie Fire: The 1885 North-West Rebellion* (Edmonton, 1984)

Cypress Hills massacre, 1873. A dispute between a band of Assiniboine and a motley collection of white wolf-hunters over a stolen horse led to an attack in late May on the native camp which produced 36 Assiniboine dead. This lawlessness played a major part in convincing Ottawa to create the NORTH WEST MOUNTED POLICE.

Cyprus, UN peacekeeping in. See UNFICYP.

D

Dakota aircraft. The C47 Dakota, the military version of the Douglas DC3, was used by most allied air forces in WORLD WAR II. Three ROYAL CANADIAN AIR FORCE squadrons flew Dakotas as transport aircraft during the late stages of the war, two on the Burma front, and the 'Dak' stayed in RCAF service for years after the war. The Dakota had a maximum speed of 370 km/h and could carry 28 troops or a 4080-kg payload.

Danson, Barnett Jerome [Barney] (b. 1921). Born in Toronto, Danson served in the QUEEN'S OWN RIFLES during WORLD WAR II as a junior officer. Elected to the House of Commons in 1968, he was minister of National Defence in the Trudeau government from 1976–79.

Dare, Michael R. (b. 1917). Dare joined the MILITIA in 1937, then served overseas in WORLD WAR II as an infantryman and with the 4TH CANADIAN ARMOURED DIVISION. He saw action during the KOREAN WAR, and served on PEACEKEEPING missions and in various staff and command positions. Promoted major-general in 1966, he was deputy chief, Reserves at Canadian Forces Headquarters and, as a lieutenant-general, Vice Chief of the Defence Staff. He then served in the Privy Council Office and as director-general of the RCMP Security Service.

D-Day. The WORLD WAR II term for the day an invasion was to go ashore (with H-Hour being the precise time of landing), D-Day has come to symbolize the invasion of NORMANDY on 6 June 1944. Decided upon at the QUEBEC CONFERENCE in August 1943, the invasion was commanded by General Dwight Eisenhower while General Bernard Montgomery was ground commander. The assault, the largest combined operation in history, was to encompass five infantry divisions, one of which would be the 3RD CANADIAN DIVISION, while three airborne divisions landed on the flanks. The lessons of the DIEPPE RAID were incorporated in the plan—heavy air and naval bombardment by massive bomber, fighter-bomber, and naval vessels; an assault over open beaches and not at a port; and the use of specialized LANDING CRAFT and armoured vehicles (FUNNIES). In command of the German forces was Field Marshal Erwin Rommel, the Desert Fox, who had galvanized the defenders and greatly strengthened the coastal obstacles.

The attack went in successfully, though stout resistance turned one of the American beaches into a charnel house. Generally, however, the Germans were slow to react, Allied air power plastered those units attempting to move toward the beaches, and the Canadians who had come ashore at JUNO BEACH made the day's best gains. By 12 June, despite heavy fighting and strong Nazi counterattacks, the Anglo-American-Canadian allies had united their bridgeheads into one continuous front 97 km long and some 24 km deep.

Reading: J.L. Granatstein and Desmond Morton, *Bloody Victory: Canadians and the D-Day Campaign 1944* (Toronto, 1984)

'D-Day Dodgers'. After the D-DAY invasion of France, Nancy, Lady Astor, a British M.P., referred to the Allied armies fighting in the ITALIAN CAMPAIGN as 'D-Day Dodgers.' This stung, and the forgotten armies, by the time of the NORMANDY assault having been engaged in bitter fighting for 11 months, bitterly resented the slur. A song popular with the troops used the phrase.

De Carteret, Samuel Lawrence [Sydney] (1885–1956). General manager of Canadian International Paper Co., the New Zealand-born de Carteret, a Yale University-trained engineer, was made deputy minister of National Defence for Air in 1941 and held the post until 1944. He supported his minister, Chubby POWER, in pressing for CANADIANIZATION.

De Chastelain, Alfred John Gardyne Drummond (b. 1937). De Chastelain was born in Britain and graduated from the ROYAL MILITARY COLLEGE in 1960. An infantryman, he served in the army in Canada, the Middle East, and with NATO where he commanded the 4th Mechanized Brigade Group from 1980–82. He became vice-chief of the Defence Staff in 1988 and CHIEF OF THE DEFENCE STAFF the next year. He had the task of dealing with the OKA crisis, the GULF WAR, and the Mulroney government's major defence cuts.

Defence of Canada Regulations. Drafted in 1939 by an interdepartmental committee and proclaimed on 3 September 1939 under authority of the WAR MEASURES ACT, the DOCR gave Ottawa wide-ranging powers to control dissent and guard against subversion in WORLD WAR II. INTERNMENT and the JAPANESE CANADIAN EVACUATION, 1942 occurred under DOCR authority.

Defence Construction (1951) Ltd. Created by C.D. HOWE in the rearmament boom sparked by the KOREAN WAR, this Crown corporation is the contracting and supervisory agency for the DEPARTMENT OF NATIONAL DEFENCE's major construction programs. It obtains tenders, makes recommendations on contracts, and administers construction and maintenance projects. It is now informally known as Defence Construction Canada and is under the control and supervision of National Defence.

Defence Council. Established by order-in-council in 1922, the Defence Council was chaired by the minister of National Defence and included the deputy minister of National Defence, the CHIEF OF THE GENERAL STAFF, the DIRECTOR OF THE NAVAL SERVICE and the navy's comptroller. The Council met infrequently until the outbreak of war in 1939 when its composition was changed to include the CHIEFS OF THE NAVAL STAFF and AIR STAFF. The Council had no powers independent of the minister and chiefly concerned itself with personnel and admninistrative matters. After UNIFICATION, the Council was altered to include the deputy minister of National Defence, the CHIEF OF THE DEFENCE STAFF, the chair of the DEFENCE RESEARCH BOARD, and other officers. It provides a channel of communication between the Defence minister and his senior military and civilian officials.

Defence Department. See DEPARTMENT OF NATIONAL DEFENCE.

Defence Production, Department of. See DEPARTMENT OF DEFENCE PRODUCTION.

Defence Production Sharing Agreement. Negotiated by the government of John DIEFENBAKER in 1958, this agreement with the United States looked to the achievement of a long-term balance in defence trade. The DPSA exempted Canada from some clauses of the 'Buy American' legislation by permitting duty-free entry into the U.S. of Canadian defence products.

Defence Purchasing Board. Established by the KING government in 1938 to supervise defence-related purchases and prevent profiteering, the DPB was an attempt to counter criticism resulting from the BREN GUN SCANDAL. The Board initially had a rule limiting profits to 5 per cent but this cap was removed after the outbreak of war. The DPB was superseded by the Department of MUNITIONS AND SUPPLY in 1940.

Defence Research Board. Established in 1947, largely at the insistence of General Charles FOULKES, the CHIEF OF THE GENERAL STAFF, the DRB was responsible for defence research (e.g., missile development, explosives, chemical warfare) and for advising the DEPARTMENT OF NATIONAL DEFENCE on scientific and technical questions. DRB's research, administrative activities, and staff were absorbed by DND in 1974.
Reading: D.J. Goodspeed, *DRB: A History of the Defence Research Board of Canada* (Ottawa, 1958)

Defence Research Telecommunications Establishment. This scientific research body in the DEPARTMENT OF NATIONAL DEFENCE played a key role in the evolution of the Canadian space program in the 1950s and 1960s. The DRTE designed and built the Alouette I and II and ISIS I and II satellites. DRTE's name was changed in 1968 to the Communications Research Centre, and it is now part of the Department of Communications.

Defence Scheme No. 1. Developed by Col J. Sutherland BROWN, the PERMANENT FORCE Director of Military Operations and

Intelligence 1921–27, this plan outlined the steps necessary to defend Canada in the event of hostilities between Britain and the U.S. which would involve Canada. One of its proposals was a limited offensive into the U.S. and a fighting withdrawal pending the arrival of Imperial reinforcements. The plan was not cancelled until 1931.

Defence Scheme No. 2. This plan involved the direct defence of Canada against Japan. Work began immediately after WORLD WAR I but no detailed plans were made until the early 1930s when the focus changed to protection of Canadian neutrality in event of a U.S.-Japan conflict.

Defence Scheme No. 3. This plan, first circulated in 1931, looked to both home defence and the despatch of a large expeditionary force overseas. Approved by the Conservative government in 1931 and by the Liberals in 1937, the plan argued that the needs of national self-defence involved commitments beyond Canada's borders. This was in fact the plan put into effect in September 1939, but the ambiguous phrasing of the scheme caused some governmental conflict.
Reading: Steven Harris, *Canadian Brass* (Toronto, 1988)

Defence Scheme No. 4. In the 1920s, Col J. Sutherland BROWN, the army's Director of Military Operations and Intelligence, began to plan for the despatch of a small expeditionary force for imperial campaigns. Later in the 1930s, the scheme was refined to cover Canadian assistance for small imperial wars. The planning was never completed, the likely necessity for Defence Scheme No. 4 being small and the political support necessary for any action under it unlikely to be secured.

Defence Structure Review. In 1974, the Trudeau government ordered a review of the CANADIAN ARMED FORCES' tasks and the resources necessary to carry them out. Conducted by a committee of senior officials and officers, the DSR put hard operational needs first and committed the government to increasing capital expenditures by 12 per cent a year for five years.

De Havilland Aircraft of Canada Ltd. First incorporated in Canada in 1929 as a branch of the British manufacturer of the same name, de Havilland developed a number of highly successful small and medium-size transport aircraft and pioneered in STOL (short takeoff and landing) technology. The BEAVER, CARIBOU, OTTER, Dash-7, and Dash-8 were all world leaders in their areas and sold widely. In 1974, the federal government purchased the company from its U.K. owners, Hawker Siddeley Aviation, and in 1986, over much protest, Ottawa sold it to Boeing Corp., the giant American aircraft manufacturer. In 1990, Boeing in turn announced that it was in negotiation with Aerospatiale of France and Alenia of Italy for the sale of the Canadian operation. Almost two years later, that sale having fallen through, Bombardier Inc. and the Ontario government bought the company, apparently safeguarding the jobs of its 3760 employees.

Demobilization, World War I. Discussion of the ways and means of demobilizing the CANADIAN EXPEDITIONARY FORCE had begun in 1916 at the Department of MILITIA AND DEFENCE and the OVERSEAS MILITARY FORCES OF CANADA. The decision to demobilize was taken immediately the ARMISTICE was signed, the first to be released being CEF units in Canada. Original estimates had been that it might take 18 months to bring all the boys home, but two-thirds had returned within five months and within a year repatriation was all but complete. Such difficulties as there were came from shipping shortages and the inability of the Canadian railways to move more than 25,000 troops in a month (a figure later raised to 45,000 after government pressure on the railway companies). This pace was not fast enough for the troops, and there were 13 riots at camps in England, most notably at KINMEL PARK in 1919.

In the CANADIAN CORPS units returned as entities; otherwise the principle of first in, first out was in effect (though some breaches in the principle stirred great resentment). Each soldier chose his destination in Canada, received a WAR SERVICE GRATUITY, and was given demobilization leave. A Department of SOLDIERS' CIVIL RE-ESTABLISHMENT, created in February 1918, had also prepared plans. Veterans who wished to take up farming could receive long-term loans, some 30,000

so choosing. There were pensions, medical treatment, and vocational training for the disabled. By the end of 1919, 59,865 pensions had been granted; twenty years later there were 98,000 pensions for Great War service in force — with the most generous benefits in the world, the government said. In 1919, moreover, 8000 veterans were receiving medical treatment and 23,000 had enrolled for vocational training. The burden of pensions would remain until the last World War I veteran passed away. Although governments considered that the CEF had received its due from a grateful Canadian public and a weary taxpayer (in 1919, veterans' benefits amounted to 21.3 per cent of government expenditures and 20 years later they were still absorbing 10.7 per cent), veterans and the organizations they formed to lobby for them were far from convinced.
Reading: D.P. Morton and G. Wright, *Winning the Second Battle: Canadian Veterans and the Return to Civilian Life 1915–1930* (Toronto, 1987)

Demobilization, World War II. As in the earlier war, demobilization after victory in 1945 was much more rapid than expected. The ROYAL CANADIAN NAVY reported at the end of March 1946 that it had discharged 76,905 all ranks, the ROYAL CANADIAN AIR FORCE that it had released 147,263, and the Army 342,361 officers and men. With the largest number of service personnel to be released, the army had devised a point-score system (2 points for each month of service in Canada, 3 points for each month of service overseas, plus 20 points for the married or those with dependent children). While there were complaints, this system worked much more equitably than that used in the Great War.

In Canada, meanwhile, the Department of Pensions and National Health, which had replaced the Department of SOLDIERS' CIVIL RE-ESTABLISHMENT in 1928, had begun planning for demobilization in December 1939, and it had created a General Advisory Committee on Demobilization and Rehabilitation which worked out the government's policies. Benefits came to include rehabilitation grants, a clothing allowance, out of work grants, and thanks to the WAR SERVICE GRANTS ACT 1944, cash payments depending on length of service. The last act was a product of the newly-established Department

of VETERANS' AFFAIRS. Moreover, educational or vocational training was offered, and if a veteran chose not to accept this, he or she could take re-establishment credits instead which could be used, e.g., to buy a home or start a business. There were also pensions for the disabled and for the dependents of those killed, and medical care for the wounded and injured. The official historian of the army noted that 'In point of generosity,' Canadian veterans' benefits 'compared very favourably, on the whole, with those given their counterparts in other Commonwealth countries and the United States.'
Reading: C.P. Stacey, *Arms, Men and Governments: The War Policies of Canada 1939–1945* (1970)

Denison, Frederick Charles (1846–1896). He joined Denison's Horse (later the Governor General's Body Guard) in 1864 and took command of the unit in 1884. Denison served in the FENIAN RAIDS 1866, with WOLSELEY in the RED RIVER EXPEDITION 1870, and commanded the NILE VOYAGEURS in the Sudan in 1884–85. Denison later went into Parliament, sitting as a Conservative from 1887–96.

Denison, George Taylor (1783–1853). Denison came to Canada in 1792, served in the MILITIA during the WAR OF 1812, and commanded a troop of dragoons during the REBELLION OF 1837. This troop developed into Denison's Horse, a volunteer cavalry formation, which he commanded. Denison played a critical role in the organization of the Canadian MILITIA.

Denison, George Taylor II (1816–1873). Denison joined the MILITIA in 1834 and succeeded his father in command of Denison's Horse in 1853. By 1860 he was a colonel commanding the 5th and 10th military districts, and at his death he was senior militia officer in Ontario. Denison served in the REBELLION OF 1837, commanded the Toronto garrison during the FENIAN RAIDS, and worked for the militia in the face of governmental indifference. His son John rose to admiral's rank in the Royal Navy, while his son Septimus Julius Augustus became a major-general in Canada's pre-World War I PERMANENT FORCE.

Denison, George Taylor III (1839–1925). The eldest son of G.T. Denison II, he served in the family cavalry unit and commanded it, as the Governor-General's Body Guard, 1857–68 and 1876–98. He served in the FENIAN RAIDS and the NORTHWEST REBELLION of 1885. Denison wrote military history, including a prize-winning history of cavalry, and was a leading spokesman for the MILITIA and IMPERIAL DEFENCE.

Denonville, Jacques René de Brisay, Marquis de (1642–1710). Denonville came to New France in 1685 as governor after three decades' service in the army. He launched pre-emptive strikes against the English and the Iroquois, capturing English forts on James Bay and destroying Seneca villages. His efforts to improve the colony's defences were hampered by a lack of reinforcements and by the outbreak of KING WILLIAM'S WAR which destroyed chances for an honourable peace and produced, in addition, a surprise Iroquois attack on Lachine in 1689 and the abandonment of FORT FRONTENAC. Denonville was recalled in late 1689.

Department of Defence Production. Created in 1951 to handle the rearmament induced by the KOREAN WAR and the intensifying COLD WAR, the Department was initially the property of Canada's 'Minister of Everything', C.D. HOWE. The Department, working closely with the DEPARTMENT OF NATIONAL DEFENCE, placed contracts for military equipment. The Department was disbanded in 1969, its functions assumed by the Department of Supply and Services.

Department of National Defence. Created on 1 January 1923 by the amalgamation of the DEPARTMENTS of NAVAL SERVICE and MILITIA AND DEFENCE, and the AIR BOARD, the formation of this department brought the three services under a single minister. The department continues to exist with a single minister (though during WORLD WAR II and until 1946 each service had an associate minister of its own) who is responsible, *inter alia*, for certain civil emergency powers. DND has one of the largest operating budgets and, with its civil and military personnel, the largest staff of all departments. Initially, the deputy minister handled the management of the department and the service chiefs ran their own forces; after 1951, a CHAIRMAN, CHIEFS OF STAFF was put atop the military hierarchy, and with INTEGRATION in 1964, his title changed to CHIEF OF THE DEFENCE STAFF. Then in 1972, the department's civil and military branches were merged at NATIONAL DEFENCE HEADQUARTERS with a co-equal deputy minister and Chief of the Defence Staff at its head.

Department of National Defence Act. This act, assented to on 28 June 1922 and effective 1 January 1923, created the DEPARTMENT OF NATIONAL DEFENCE. It arose out of a desire for cost effectiveness and better service coordination in the years after WORLD WAR I. The proposed inclusion of the RCMP under DND was considered but dropped after heated parliamentary debate.

Department of Naval Service. Created on 4 May 1910 to run the new Canadian navy, the department was to be headed by the minister of Marine and Fisheries who was also designated minister of Naval Service. In February 1922, the minister's powers were transferred to the minister of Militia and Defence and both offices were abolished when the DEPARTMENT OF NATIONAL DEFENCE was created on 1 January 1923.

Department of Public Information. Created in November 1917, significantly just a month before a general election, the Department was the federal government's propaganda agency. It supplied the press with information about overseas events and the government's domestic policies. By August 1919 when it shut down, the Department had spent some $150,000 on publicity.

Depth charge. An explosive-filled cylinder designed to explode at a pre-set depth, the depth charge for use against underwater targets was developed in WORLD WAR I. Depth charges were dropped from stern chutes or launched from throwers amidships in patterns of ten or more. Mass-produced in Canada, they were extensively employed against U-boats in the BATTLE OF THE ATLANTIC and, in much modified form, are still standard equipment on Canadian naval vessels.

De Rottenburg, Francis, Baron (1757–1832). Born in Poland, he initially served in the French army. After joining the British army, he saw service around the world before coming to Canada as a major-general in 1810. During the WAR OF 1812, he held important posts, including that of commander in Upper Canada. Cautious but competent, he was recalled in 1815.

De Salaberry, Charles Michel d'Irumberry (1778–1829). Born in Canada, he served in the British army during the Napoleonic wars. He returned to Canada in 1810 as aide-de-camp to General DE ROTTENBURG, raised the CANADIAN VOLTIGEURS in Quebec and led them at CHATEAUGUAY. In that action, he defeated a much larger American force.

Desbarats, Georges J. (1861–1944). Born in Quebec City, Desbarats entered the civil service as director of the Government Shipyards at Sorel, Que., in 1901. Six years later he became deputy minister in the department of Marine and Fisheries, and in 1910 he was named deputy of the new DEPARTMENT OF NAVAL SERVICE. After the creation of the DEPARTMENT OF NATIONAL DEFENCE, he became its deputy minister and held that post until retirement in 1932.

Desert Storm, Operation. See GULF WAR.

Desjardins, Alphonse (1841–1912). Elected as a Conservative in 1874, this lawyer and editor served briefly as minister of Militia and Defence for four months in 1896. He was defeated for re-election later that year.

DesRosiers, Henri (1880–1963). DesRosiers served with distinction in WORLD WAR I and made an important career in business after the war. He was president of Imperial Tobacco when he was appointed associate acting deputy minister (Militia) on 8 September 1939. In 1942, he became deputy minister (Army), in substantial part so a French-speaking Canadian could be seen to be in a key position at Defence, and held the post until war's end.

Destroyer escorts. Similar to but smaller than DESTROYERS, these ships were equipped primarily for escort duty and antisubmarine warfare. There have been several classes in Canadian service since 1945, though most have been converted to destroyer helicopter escorts with the addition of hangars, flight decks, and helicopters. Though the DEs now in service are obsolete, they continue to provide the backbone of Canada's surface fleet. The original DEs of the ST LAURENT CLASS displaced 2227 tonnes, had a 28-knot speed, and carried a crew of 249. They were armed with two twin 3-inch guns, two 40-mm guns, homing torpedoes, and two anti-submarine mortars.

Destroyer Life Extension Project [DELEX]. A Trudeau government program to modernize Canada's aging fleet of 16 anti-submarine DESTROYERS, DELEX began in 1979.

Destroyers. Small, fast, lightly armed and unarmoured, destroyers originated in the late 19th century as ships designed both to destroy torpedo boats and to launch torpedoes of their own. Larger than a FRIGATE and smaller than a CRUISER, destroyers have been a mainstay of the ROYAL CANADIAN NAVY, most notably during WORLD WAR II and the KOREAN WAR. TRIBAL CLASS DESTROYERS (e.g., *HAIDA*) displaced 1900 tonnes, made 36 knots, and had a crew of 259. They carried three twin 4.7-inch guns, two 4-inch guns, six 20-mm OERLIKONS and four 21-inch torpedo tubes, plus anti-submarine weapons.

Destroyers for Bases Deal. In August 1940 the Roosevelt administration and British Prime Minister Winston Churchill agreed to exchange 50 U.S. destroyers for 99-year leases on bases in several British possessions in North America and the Caribbean. Included were sites in Newfoundland where the United States continued to operate military bases after Confederation in 1949. Only the base at ARGENTIA continues as an American base today (1991). The warships, obsolete and ill-equipped, augmented British strength at a critical period; some were commissioned into the ROYAL CANADIAN NAVY.

Detroit, Surrender of (1812). Led by General Isaac BROCK, a small force of British troops, MILITIA, and natives forced the precipitate surrender of Detroit by General William Hull on 16 August 1812. Hull gave up the well-built fort and his 2500 troops virtually without a fight, and the victory greatly heartened Upper Canada at the outset of the WAR OF 1812.

Devil's Brigade. See SPECIAL SERVICE FORCE, CANADIAN-AMERICAN.

Dewar, Daniel Bevis (b. 1932). Born in Ontario and educated at Queen's University, Dewar joined the public service in 1954. After service at the Treasury Board, he first came to the DEPARTMENT OF NATIONAL DEFENCE in 1973 and, after stints elsewhere, became deputy minister in 1982. He held this post until 1990 through years of cutbacks and the end of the COLD WAR.

DEW Line. The Distant Early Warning Line, announced in 1954 and completed in 1957, consists of a series of radar tracking, warning, and control stations stretching across the northern Arctic from Alaska to Baffin Island. Along with the PINETREE LINE and the MID-CANADA LINE, the Canadian and U.S.-built DEW Line was designed to detect incoming Soviet bombers. The rapid evolution of intercontinental missiles, submarine-launched missiles, and cruise missiles greatly lowered its effectiveness. The NORTH WARNING SYSTEM, another joint project designed to improve detection of low-flying aircraft and missiles, is now under construction.

DeWolf, Harry George (b. 1903). A graduate of the ROYAL NAVAL COLLEGE OF CANADA, DeWolf joined the fledgling Canadian navy in 1918. In WORLD WAR II, he commanded destroyers in action, including *HAIDA* during the English Channel operations that made her famous, and also filled senior appointments in Ottawa and Halifax. After the war he captained the RCN's aircraft carriers, *WARRIOR* and *MAGNIFICENT*. A rear-admiral by 1948, he held several senior staff posts, culminating as chief of naval staff from 1956–60. He retired a vice-admiral, widely thought to be Canada's greatest naval officer for his superb leadership in war and peace.

Dextraze, Jacques Alfred (b. 1919). A legendary fighting soldier, 'Jadex' was born in Montreal and enlisted in the Fusiliers Mont-Royal as a private in 1939. He served with distinction (DSO and bar) in NORTH-WEST EUROPE, rising to command his regiment in 1944. He left the army in 1945 but rejoined during the KOREAN WAR where he led the 2nd Battalion, ROYAL 22e REGIMENT. He held staff posts, then served in the UN PEACEKEEPING force in the Congo (UNOC) in 1963 as chief of staff. After further senior positions in Canada, he became CHIEF OF THE DEFENCE STAFF in 1972, a post he held until 1977. Dextraze fought to get his forces the equipment they needed, but his success in the Trudeau era of military unconcern was limited.

DH2 fighter. This WORLD WAR I single-seat fighter, built by de Havilland, was first introduced in large numbers in February 1916. Highly manoeuvrable, the DH2 was outclassed by later German fighters and was phased out a year after its introduction. The DH2 was flown by many Canadian pilots in the ROYAL FLYING CORPS.

DH4 bomber. A two-seat bomber, the de Havilland DH4 was a successful WORLD WAR I aircraft that also saw service as a reconnaissance and anti-submarine aircraft. Canadians flew DH4s extensively, and after the armistice several were given as a gift to Canada.

DH9 bomber. De Havilland's DH9 two-seat bomber was designed to replace the DH4. Although there were problems with its design, more than 4000 were produced, as well as 2500 of the modified DH9As. DH9s equipped one of the two squadrons of the CANADIAN AIR FORCE in England, 1918–20, and Britain gave 12 to Canada at the end of the war. Three of these aircraft participated in the first trans-Canada flight in October 1920.

Dick, Paul Wyatt (b. 1940). A lawyer, Dick was elected to the House of Commons as a Conservative in 1972. He was associate minister of National Defence from 1986–89 in the Mulroney government.

Dickey, Arthur Rupert (1854–1900). This Conservative lawyer was elected to Parliament from Nova Scotia in 1888. He was taken into the Cabinet in 1894, became minister of Militia and Defence from 1895–96, and then Justice minister. He drowned in Nova Scotia in 1900.

Diefenbaker, John George (1895–1979). Prime minister from 1957 to 1963, Diefenbaker was born at Neustadt, Ont., but grew up in Saskatchewan. After Great War service that saw him injured in a training accident, Diefenbaker became a lawyer and a politician, though he failed to win election to Parliament until 1940. In 1956, he was chosen leader of the Progressive Conservative party and the next year, in a stunning upset, he took power.

Diefenbaker's six years in office were bedevilled by defence questions. He took Canada into NORAD in his first days as prime minister, bowing to the urgings of his defence minister and his military advisers. That at once embroiled him in difficulty, for the Opposition was angry that Parliament (and the Department of External Affairs) had not been consulted about an important treaty with the United States. Soon after, his government cancelled the Avro ARROW, the country's supersonic fighter project, after its costs skyrocketed; this correct decision unfortunately was handled ineptly and Diefenbaker was blamed for putting thousands on the dole and destroying the country's aviation industry.

Most important, the Diefenbaker government decided to purchase a number of weapons systems (BOMARCs, CFIO4S, HONEST JOHNS) from the United States and to accept the nuclear warheads that came with them and made them effective. But because of a split in the Cabinet between the External Affairs minister, Howard Green, and the Defence minister, Douglas HARKNESS, over whether Canada should have nuclear weapons, Diefenbaker began to vacillate. By late 1962, after the CUBAN MISSILE CRISIS had revealed the unready state of the armed forces and demonstrated that Ottawa's policy toward defence matters was very different from Washington's, the nuclear controversy burst into the open. Public and private pressures from the Kennedy administration on Ottawa were becoming intense, the issue was stirring great controversy in Parliament and the press, and the government fell apart in February 1963, suffering defeat on a confidence vote and the resignation of several ministers. In April Diefenbaker lost power to Lester PEARSON and the Liberals. The 'Chief' stayed as leader until 1967, and remained a powerful, if divisive, figure in the House of Commons until his death.

Reading: John Diefenbaker, *One Canada*, 3 vols (Toronto, 1975–77)

'Diefenbunker'. Built at the height of the COLD WAR at the beginning of the 1960s, the nuclear bomb shelter intended for the prime minister, Cabinet ministers, and senior officials was located at Carp, 20 km west of Ottawa. Derisively labelled after John DIEFENBAKER, in whose time it was built, the four-storey underground concrete bunker is still maintained.

Dieppe Raid. On 19 August 1942, 4963 Canadians of the 2ND CANADIAN DIVISION, along with British commandos and a few American Rangers, landed at Dieppe, France in a major raid. The result was a disaster with some 70 per cent of the Canadians killed, wounded, or taken prisoner. There has been continuing controversy in Canada in consequence.

There were many reasons for the raid. Planners at Lord Louis Mountbatten's Combined Operations Headquarters wanted to test theories of amphibious warfare and establish whether a fortified port could be taken by storm. The Americans, the hard-pressed Soviet Union, and many ordinary citizens wanted a Second Front in Europe at the earliest possible moment. The Canadian generals and some politicians wanted their troops to see some action after years of training in Britain. The result was that in April 1942 the British suggested that Canadians make up the attacking force and General A.G.L. MCNAUGHTON, commanding FIRST CANADIAN ARMY, and General H.D.G. CRERAR, commanding I CANADIAN CORPS, agreed; their choice fell on the 2nd Division under General J.H. ROBERTS. The assault on Dieppe was originally scheduled for July but poor weather forced cancellation. The plan ought to have been dropped then, but for reasons that remain in debate, Mountbatten revived the scheme, now code-named Jubilee: the assault would go in on 19 August.

The attack plan called for six squadrons of fighter-bombers aloft and eight destroyers and one gunboat in the English Channel to provide support. Infantry from the Essex Scottish and the Royal Hamilton Light Infantry and CHURCHILL tanks of the Calgary Regiment were to land on the beach in front of Dieppe; to the east at Puys, the Royal Regiment of Canada and three platoons from the BLACK WATCH were to touch down; on the west at Pourville were the

South Saskatchewan Regiment and the Queen's Own Cameron Highlanders. The Fusiliers Mont-Royal were the floating reserve, while British commandos were to destroy batteries further to the east and west. The plan went awry at once when the raiders ran into a German coastal convoy. That alerted the German defenders. The landing at Puys at 5:10 a.m. was shattered by concentrated fire from two platoons of Germans on a cliff to the flank of the beach and the survivors surrendered at 8:30 a.m. At Pourville, there was light opposition on the beach but the South Sasks ran into heavy fire at the River Scie. Here Lt-Col C.C.I. MERRITT won his VICTORIA CROSS, urging his men across the bridge. The advance went perhaps 1850 m inland before the withdrawal order came. On the main beach where the infantry landed about 5:40 a.m., all was disaster. Germans atop the cliff to the left of the beach devastated the landing craft and slaughtered those who got ashore. The tanks had trouble in the water and on the pebbled beach though many managed to get across the seawall before being abandoned at water's edge. Roberts received faulty information and sent his reserves ashore at 7 a.m., adding to the casualty toll. Evacuation began at 11 a.m. and survivors were lifted off in the face of heavy fire.

The cost was terrible. Of the 2,211 Canadians who returned to England, almost half had never gone ashore. There were 907 killed and 1946 prisoners of war among the remainder. The lessons learned at Dieppe were said to have been put into effect in SICILY and especially on D-DAY, 6 June 1944. *Reading*: Brian Villa, *Unauthorized Action: Mountbatten and the Dieppe Raid* (Toronto, 1989)

D'Iberville, Le Sieur. See LEMOYNE, PIERRE.

Dieskau, Jean-Armand, Baron de (1701–1767). A Saxon soldier in the French service, he came to Canada as a major-general in command of the regular troops in 1755. In September 1755, he was captured by the British after a stalemated battle at Lake George, and he remained a prisoner until 1763.

Dinesen, Thomas (1892–1979). A private in the 42nd Battalion, CANADIAN EXPEDITIONARY FORCE, the Danish-born Dinesen won the VICTORIA CROSS on 12 August 1918 for repeatedly leading bayonet charges against German machine guns. On five occasions, he singlehandedly destroyed enemy posts, killing 12 of the enemy.

Director of Public Safety. In October 1918, in the closing weeks of WORLD WAR I, the government of Sir Robert BORDEN appointed C.H. Cahan as Director of Public Safety and directed him to watch efforts by 'revolutionaries' to overthrow constituted authority in Canada. Cahan soon secured adoption of an order-in-council (PC 2384) banning 14 revolutionary or ethnic organizations.

Director of Naval Service. The NAVAL SERVICE ACT of 1910 created the DEPARTMENT OF NAVAL SERVICE and provided for a Director to be the professional head of the service. The first was Rear-Admiral Sir Charles KINGSMILL who held the post until 1921. The title was changed to CHIEF OF THE NAVAL STAFF in 1928.

Directorate of Public Information. This predecessor of the WARTIME INFORMATION BOARD was organized in December 1939 as the government's propaganda arm within Canada. Rather unstructured and narrow in its focus, this agency was nonetheless viewed with suspicion, and it disappeared in September 1942.

Distant Early Warning Line. See DEW LINE.

Distinguished Conduct Medal. This decoration was awarded to army enlisted ranks for 'distinguished service and gallant conduct in the field'.

Distinguished Flying Cross. An award given to air force officers 'for an act or acts of valour, courage, or devotion to duty performed whilst flying in active operations against the enemy'.

Distinguished Flying Medal. Similar to the DISTINGUISHED FLYING CROSS; the medal is awarded to non-commissioned officers and men.

Distinguished Service Cross. A naval award for 'meritorious or distinguished services before the enemy' by officers below the rank of lieutenant-commander.

Distinguished Service Order. Awarded to officers of all three services, the DSO was given for 'meritorious or distinguished service in war'. If won by an officer below the rank of lieutenant-colonel, the DSO was considered only slightly less meritorious than the VICTORIA CROSS.

Division organization, World War I. A Canadian infantry division, led by a major-general, comprised three infantry brigades of four battalions each. The division also included two brigades of field artillery (each of three batteries of field artillery and one of howitzers), three trench mortar batteries, a machine-gun battalion, and the requisite arms and services.

Division organization, World War II. A Canadian infantry division, commanded by a major-general, consisted of three infantry brigades of three battalions each. The division also had a armoured reconnaissance regiment, three field artillery regiments, an anti-aircraft and an anti-tank regiment, a machine-gun battalion, and a full array of arms and services. An armoured division ordinarily had one armoured brigade with three armoured regiments and a motorized infantry battalion, one or two infantry brigades of three battalions, an armoured reconnaissance regiment, two field artillery regiments, and the requisite arms and services.

Dollard des Ormeaux, Adam (1635–1660). A soldier and garrison commander of Ville-Marie (Montreal), Dollard was born in France and served in the French armies. Though the evidence of motivation is sparse and conflicting, he led a party of 17 Frenchmen on an ambush against the Iroquois, who were believed to be preparing to attack the settlement. Joined by 44 native allies at the Long Sault rapids, they were discovered and trapped in a derelict palisade by a larger force of 300 Iroquois. After a siege of a week marked by a stout defence of their tiny enclosure, Iroquois reinforcements, a lack of water, and a gunpowder explosion within the fort led to their complete defeat. Nine

survivors were tortured and eaten. The grisly but gallant episode became a staple of *nationaliste* historiography, the sacrifice of a few to save the settlement of New France. The Iroquois were reputed to have said that 'If seventeen Frenchmen dealt with us in that fashion when they were in such a wretched hole, how shall we be treated when we have to attack a strong building? Let us go home.' Myth or reality, the settlement of New France survived.

Dominion Arsenal. Established in 1882 at Quebec City by the federal government, the Arsenal was to provide the MILITIA with ammunition. A second factory was built at Lindsay, Ont. (not coincidentally the home-town of Militia minister Sam HUGHES), in WORLD WAR I, and under the Department of MUNITIONS AND SUPPLY additional facilities came into operation during WORLD WAR II. In 1945, all the arsenals were consolidated into CANADIAN ARSENALS LTD, a Crown corporation.

Dominion Veterans' Alliance. A federation of veterans' organizations formed in 1922 largely through the efforts of Grant MACNEIL, the DVA was intended to press the new and little-trusted Liberal government of Mackenzie KING to improve veterans' benefits. The Alliance, a patched-together association of rival organizations, lasted until it was absorbed by the new ROYAL CANADIAN LEGION in 1925–26.

Douglas, Campbell Mellis (1840–1909). A doctor and soldier, Douglas was born at Grosse Ile, Que., and educated at Laval and Edinburgh Universities. He joined the British army in 1862 and won a VICTORIA CROSS for saving 17 of his comrades under attack by natives in the Little Andaman Islands. Though he retired from the army in 1882, he settled in Ontario and served in the NORTHWEST REBELLION 1885 as a medical officer.

Douglas Digby aircraft. Used by the ROYAL CANADIAN AIR FORCE as maritime patrol aircraft, the American-built Digby entered service in 1940 with Eastern Air Command. The aircraft, flown by 10 Bomber Squadron, had a range of more than 550 km and some 12 hours endurance.

Doyle, Sir Charles Hastings (1804–1883). Born in Britain and educated at Sandhurst, Doyle saw active service in the East and West Indies before his appointment in 1861 to command troops in Nova Scotia, a task of some importance during the tensions that arose between Britain and the U.S. during the Civil War. In 1867 he became lieutenant-governor of Nova Scotia, a post he held until 1873.

Drew, George Alexander (1894–1973). An Ontario and national politician, Drew was born in Guelph, Ont. He served overseas in WORLD WAR I with the artillery and was wounded. After the war he became a lawyer, a municipal politician in his home town, and a prominent member of the MILITIA. By the 1930s, he was well known for his writings on the war and for sparking the inquiry into the BREN GUN SCANDAL. Elected leader of the Ontario Conservatives in 1938, Drew continued to press for stronger defence and CONSCRIPTION and his charges played a major role in forcing Ottawa to set up a ROYAL COMMISSION ON THE CANADIAN EXPEDITIONARY FORCE ... TO HONG KONG. Drew became Ontario premier in 1943 and national Conservative leader in 1948.

Drocourt-Quéant Line. A heavily defended portion of the Germans' HINDENBURG LINE north of St Quentin and west of Douai, the Drocourt-Quéant line was attacked by the 1ST and 4TH DIVISIONS of the CANADIAN CORPS on 2 September 1918, using tanks. Skilfully planned and led by Gen. Sir Arthur CURRIE, the Corps' first efforts broke the line on a 6400-m frontage. The next day the advance continued, the Germans pulling back to the east. This was one of the most stunning accomplishments of the Corps' triumphant Hundred Days, accomplished, however, at a cost of more than 5600 casualties.

Drummond, Sir Gordon (1771–1854). Born in Quebec, the son of a British officer, Drummond himself joined the British army in 1789. He served throughout the Napoleonic Wars until, in 1811, as a lieutenant-general he was made second in command to Sir George PREVOST in Canada. He commanded on the Niagara Frontier in the latter stages of the WAR OF 1812 and was wounded at LUNDY'S LANE. In 1814, he succeeded Prevost in command in Canada, a post he held until 1816.

Drummond-Arthabaska by-election. The issue in this by-election in Quebec (3 November 1910) was Quebec nationalism against Sir Wilfrid LAURIER's policy of pan-Canadianism. Laurier was attacked for creating a Canadian navy, and a vote for the Liberal, J.E. Perrault, was declared to be a vote for war. Henri BOURASSA, campaigning for nationalist candidate Arthur Gilbert, said 'A day will come when draft officers will be scouring the country and compelling young men to enlist' to fight Britain's battles. Gilbert won with a small majority, a major defeat in Quebec for Laurier.

Drury, Charles Mills [Bud] (1912–1990). Born in Montreal and educated at the Royal Military College and McGill University, 'Bud' Drury practised law in Montreal until the outbreak of war in 1939. He served in the artillery and as a staff officer with the 2ND CANADIAN DIVISION and the 4TH CANADIAN ARMOURED DIVISION, reaching the rank of brigadier. From 1948 to 1955, a critical period of rearmament, he was deputy minister of National Defence. In 1962 he won election to Parliament as a Liberal and, among other portfolios, served as minister of Defence Production from 1963–68. He retired from the House in 1978.

Duck Lake. The site of the first battle of the NORTHWEST REBELLION of 1885, Duck Lake is situated some 50 km southwest of Prince Albert, Sask. The Métis, led by Louis RIEL and Gabriel DUMONT, inflicted 23 casualties on the Canadian force of NORTH WEST MOUNTED POLICE and white settlers led by Supt L.N.F. Crozier. Riel's force had only five losses, and the victory guaranteed that the rebellion would intensify.

Duff, Sir Lyman Poore (1865–1955). A justice of the Supreme Court of Canada from 1906, Duff was born at Meaford, Ont. and practised law in Victoria, B.C. Appointed Chief Justice in 1933, Duff was named to head the ROYAL COMMISSION ON THE CANADIAN EXPEDITIONARY FORCE ... TO HONG KONG in 1942. His report largely exonerated the government but found that several senior military officers had not acted with sufficient despatch or efficiency.

Duguid, Archer Fortescue (1887–1962). Born in Scotland and educated at McGill University, Duguid served overseas in WORLD WAR I. In 1921, he took over command of the Directorate of History at Army Headquarters, Ottawa, a post he held until 1947. His task was to write the history of the Great War, but he managed only to get one volume of text (covering August 1914 to September 1915) and one of documents out before the beginning of the new war in 1939. His successor, Col Charles STACEY, would see the job to completion and much more.

DUKW. First used in the invasion of SICILY in 1943, the DUKW was an American-designed and built 2-1/2-tonne amphibious truck, partially constructed from wood, that could operate on water at a speed of 8.7 km/h or on land at 80 km/h. It was ordinarily used to transport supplies from ship to shore.

Dumbells. The 3RD CANADIAN INFANTRY DIVISION'S troupe of entertainers and female impersonators regaled Canadian and British troops in France and Flanders with satirical skits about army life during WORLD WAR I. Formed in 1917, the Dumbells were the creation of Merton Plunkett, a YMCA entertainment director with the division. They became widely known in Canada and the United States after the war when, joined by veterans of other CEF entertainment shows and latterly by female entertainers, they toured the vaudeville circuit from 1919 to 1932.

Dumont, Gabriel (1837–1906). Born at the Red River, buffalo-hunter Dumont was a natural leader. Though he did not participate in the RED RIVER REBELLION, 1870, he became adjutant-general of the 300-man Métis army in the NORTHWEST REBELLION, 1885. He calculated that in order to resist the better armed MILITIA, his men had to be a guerrilla force and, if forced to stand, they had to dig in. This and his tactics of surprise worked well in the victories at DUCK LAKE and FISH CREEK, but at BATOCHE the Métis were simply overwhelmed by weight of numbers and arms. Dumont fled to the U.S. after the surrender and returned to Canada after the amnesty of 1888.

Duncan, James Stuart (1893–1986). Born in Paris, France, Duncan worked for the Massey-Harris Co. and was general manager of its Canadian operations in 1939. He joined the DEPARTMENT OF NATIONAL DEFENCE in spring 1940 as acting deputy minister (Air) and galvanized the BRITISH COMMONWEALTH AIR TRAINING PLAN. Asked to join the Cabinet as Air Minister in June, Duncan declined. Though he returned to the corporate world at the end of January 1941, Duncan continued to serve the government in industrial mobilization capacities.

Dundonald, Cochrane Douglas Mackinnon Baillie Hamilton, 12th Earl of (1852–1935). Dundonald served in the British army from 1870, becoming major-general in 1900. He came to Canada in 1902 as GENERAL OFFICER COMMANDING the Canadian MILITIA, but he quickly fell afoul of the LAURIER government by denouncing the influence of patronage in the militia. He was dismissed in 1904, and the Dominion government acted to put officers under its control in charge of the forces. Dundonald continued his army service in Britain and in the Great War.

Dunlap, Clarence Rupert (b. 1908). Born at Sydney Mines, N.S. and educated as an engineer at Acadia University and Nova Scotia Technical College, Dunlap joined the RCAF in 1928. After working on aerial survey and qualifying as an armaments specialist, he went overseas to Britain in 1942. The next year he commanded an RCAF wing of WELLINGTON bombers in Tunisia and, after his return to the U.K., took over first a medium bomber wing and then RCAF bomber bases. After the war he rose steadily, serving as NATO's Deputy Chief of Staff, as CHIEF OF THE AIR STAFF (1962–64), and as deputy commander of NORAD.

Dunn, Alexander Roberts (1833–1868). Born at York, Upper Canada, Dunn joined the British army. He became the first Canadian recipient of the VICTORIA CROSS when in 1856, as a lieutenant in the 11th (Prince Albert's Own) Regiment of Hussars, he showed great gallantry in the charge of the Light Brigade at Balaklava during the Crimean War. He helped raise the 100th (Prince of Wales' Royal Canadian) Regiment in Canada, served as its commanding officer at

Gibraltar, and died in a hunting accident in Abyssinia.

Duplex Drive (DD) tank. Developed for the D-DAY landings in Normandy in 1944, DD tanks were SHERMANS fitted with a gearing device that let the engine operate tracks on land and two propellers in water. A collapsible canvas wall around the tank's hull displaced enough water to allow flotation; speed was 4.5 knots. The 1st Hussars and the FORT GARRY HORSE, armoured regiments in the assault waves, each had two squadrons of DD tanks.

E

Eastern Air Command. See NO. 1 GROUP.

Eastern Ocean Meeting Point. After the spring of 1941, Royal Navy escorts shepherded CONVOYS to and from this point where they would be handed over or picked up by naval forces based on ICELAND. The Iceland force then repeated the process at the MID-OCEAN MEETING POINT with convoy escorts based at St John's, Newfoundland. This system lasted until altered by the ATLANTIC CONVOY CONFERENCE of March 1943.

Eccles Hill, Battle of. In May 1870, fear of renewed FENIAN RAIDS led to the mobilization of MILITIA in New Brunswick and Quebec. A small party of the Irish fighters invaded Quebec from Vermont on 25 May but most fled at the first shots fired at Eccles Hill by local Missisquoi volunteers and reinforcements from Montreal. Two Fenians were killed and a few more wounded; the defenders suffered no casualties.

Edwards, Harold [Gus] (1892–1952). Born in Britain, 'Gus' Edwards joined the Canadian navy in 1914 and transferred to the ROYAL NAVAL AIR SERVICE in 1915. Shot down, he was made a prisoner of war in 1916. After the war, he joined the [ROYAL] CANADIAN AIR FORCE. By 1941, he was Air Officer Commanding-in-Chief overseas as an air vice marshal and a fierce advocate of CANADIANIZATION, the policy of his government and minister. Paradoxically, at the same time and like many Canadians, Edwards, now an Air Marshal, was also an imperialist who put himself in great difficulty in Canada for remarks made at a press conference

in September 1942. He was replaced by Air Marshal L.S. BREADNER at the end of 1943 and retired from the RCAF in 1945.

8th King's Regiment of Foot. This British Army regiment was garrisoned along the NIAGARA FRONTIER during the WAR OF 1812 with other British regiments and colonial MILITIA. Nearly two-thirds of the regiment became casualties during the battle with the Americans for FORT GEORGE in 1813.

Elkins, William Henry Pferinger [Perf] (1883–1964). Born in Sherbrooke, Que., 'Perf' Elkins graduated from the ROYAL MILITARY COLLEGE in 1905 and joined the PERMANENT FORCE artillery. He served in France from 1915 to 1919, winning the DSO and bar, and he ended the war as a lieutenant-colonel. In the interwar years, he served in Halifax, Ottawa, Toronto, and Kingston, most notably as Master-General of the Ordnance. During WORLD WAR II he was General Officer Commanding-in-Chief, Atlantic Command until 1943. He retired in 1944.

Emergencies Act, 1988. Passed as a replacement for the WAR MEASURES ACT, the Emergencies Act is subject to the Charter of Rights and Freedoms and provides for compensation for those who suffer loss, injury, or damage as a result of its implementation. The Act establishes four classes of emergencies: public welfare (e.g., floods); public order (e.g., threats to national security); international; and war. In the latter emergency, the government can give any order it believes 'necessary or advisable'.

Emergency Measures Organization. The threat of nuclear attack led the DIEFENBAKER government in 1959 to create the Emergency Measures Organization from the very small civil defence organization established in 1948. The army in Canada was assigned to national survival duties in event of attack, and home shelters were urged on the country. EMO was succeeded by Emergency Planning Canada in 1974 and then by Emergency Preparedness Canada in 1986.

Enlistments, Korean War, 1950–1954. The Canadian Army enlisted 21,940 men for Korean service although more served there after the armistice; 10,208 of these were enlisted specifically for Korean service in the CANADIAN ARMY SPECIAL FORCE. The Royal Canadian Navy enlisted 3,621 for Korea. In addition 22 RCAF fighter pilots served on operations with American units.

Enlistments, South African War, 1899–1902. Canadian enlistments totalled 8372, a number that includes a battalion of the ROYAL CANADIAN REGIMENT raised to garrison Halifax, some 1200 men enlisted in the South African Constabulary, and unofficial units such as LORD STRATHCONA'S HORSE. Only 3500 Canadian served in South Africa at Canadian expense, the remainder being paid from time of enlistment by Britain.

Enlistments, World War I, 1914–1918. Naval enlistments were approximately 7000, while the CANADIAN EXPEDITIONARY FORCE enrolled 730,159 men and women. The latter number includes air crew who served with the ROYAL NAVAL AIR SERVICE, the ROYAL FLYING CORPS, and the ROYAL AIR FORCE.

Enlistments, World War II, 1939–1945. The Royal Canadian Navy enrolled 106,522 officers, men and women; the Canadian Army took in 730,159; and the Royal Canadian Air Force enlisted 249,662.

Esquimalt, B.C. Located on the southeast coast of Vancouver Island near Victoria, Esquimalt has been a naval base since the 1850s and the facility was enhanced by the construction of commercial/Royal Navy drydocks there in the 1880s. There was substantial controversy between Canada and the U.K. over responsibility for the defence of Esquimalt from the 1870s, and these were not resolved for twenty years; the base was transferred to Canadian control in 1906. The base had some importance during WORLD WAR I when German raiders sporadically operated in the Pacific and much more in the late 1930s, WORLD WAR II, and after when Esquimalt was the focus of Canadian defences on the West Coast. The large CANADIAN FORCES BASE there is home to Canada's (now much-attenuated) Pacific fleet.

Esquimalt, HMCS. A BANGOR-CLASS MINESWEEPER, this ship was commissioned at Sorel, Que., in October 1942 but did not come into service until May 1943. She served on the East Coast and was on patrol near Halifax on 16 April 1945 when sunk by a U-boat with the loss of 39 crew.

Estevan Point, B.C. On 20 June 1942, the Japanese submarine I-26 shelled the wireless station and lighthouse at Estevan Point on Vancouver Island. This attack, almost completely ineffective militarily, was the only time enemy shells fell on Canadian soil in either world war. The attack, however, helped increase the sense of fear on the West Coast and this led to substantial military, naval, and air reinforcements being sent to the Pacific coast.

Evans, Thomas Dixon Bryan (1860–1908). Evans was born at Hamilton, Upper Canada. As a militiaman, he served in the NORTHWEST REBELLION 1885 and then joined the tiny PERMANENT FORCE in 1888. As a lieutenant-colonel, he commanded the YUKON FIELD FORCE in 1898; in the SOUTH AFRICAN WAR, he skilfully led two battalions of CANADIAN MOUNTED RIFLES. He died while district commander in Winnipeg.

Examination Unit. Established by the Department of External Affairs in 1941 with its costs concealed in the estimates of the National Research Council, the Examination Unit was a secret wireless interception and code-breaking organization. The unit worked on decoding messages intercepted from the Vichy French legation in Ottawa until Canada broke relations in 1942; it intercepted German messages to agents in South America, and, with Britain and the United States, it cooperated in decoding Japanese military traffic. Although plans had been made to shut down the Examination Unit at the end of the war, the Gouzenko case of 1945 and its revelations of Soviet spying led to its continuance as the COMMUNICATIONS BRANCH, NATIONAL RESEARCH COUNCIL and its beginning work on the interception of Soviet diplomatic and military traffic.

Execution. Set in ITALY during WORLD WAR II, *Execution* (1958) is one of the best Canadian novels to emerge from the war. By Colin McDougall, a wartime major in the PPCLI, the novel won the Governor-General's Literary Award in 1959. It is the story of the execution by firing squad of a mentally deficient private soldier. There are shrewd comments on senior officers, the problems of command, and the experience of battle. The book was made into a TV film (1991), though the setting was transformed to northwest Europe and the execution, curiously, was postponed at the final moment.

F

Fairchild Cornell trainer. An elementary flying training aircraft used in Canada to train pilots under the BRITISH COMMONWEALTH AIR TRAINING PLAN, the Cornell came into use in 1943. An underpowered, single-engine two-seater, the Cornell was nonetheless stable and easy to fly.

Falaise, Battle of. After the invasion of Normandy on 6 June 1944, the allies were stalled for almost two months by fierce German resistance. The Canadian and British armies had the bulk of German armour against them, while the Americans were facing somewhat lesser opposition. By 25 July, the U.S. forces were beginning to break out and while good sense would have demanded that the *Wehrmacht* withdraw to the east across the Seine River, good sense was in short supply at Hitler's headquarters. Instead, the Nazis decided to launch Operation Luttich at the Americans before the end of the first week of August. The critical road junction behind the German lines was at Falaise, and this became the target of II CANADIAN CORPS, led by Lieutenant-General Guy SIMONDS. From its base at CAEN, captured after long and hard fighting, the Corps set out on a series of attacks. The first was Operation TOTALIZE, launched 7 August at night. Using improvised armoured personnel carriers and regimental sized columns directed by searchlights and radio beams, the operation was only a qualified success, and there were heavy casualties from SS General Kurt MEYER's 12th SS. But with Luttich already a failure and with German armies in full retreat to the west, Simonds tried again to reach Falaise, this time with Operation TRACTABLE on 14 August. This attack was disrupted when RAF bombers dropped their loads on Canadian and Polish troops, but most objectives were taken. Two days later the gap between the Canadians and the advancing U.S. troops was only 29 km, and if the circle could be closed the Germans would be caught in the bag. The Falaise Gap was eventually sealed on 18 August, but not before tens of thousands of the enemy escaped. Even so, upwards of 50 per cent of German strength in Normandy had been killed or captured.

Reading: R.H. Roy, *1944: The Canadians in Normandy* (Toronto, 1984)

Falls, Robert Hilborn (b. 1924). A professional naval officer, Falls began his career as a pilot in the RCAF during WORLD WAR II. He transferred to the navy after the war and progressed through increasingly responsible posts, including command of an aircraft carrier and of the Canadian Atlantic flotilla. He became the first naval officer to serve as CHIEF OF DEFENCE STAFF in 1977 and at the end of his term in 1980, he headed the NATO military committee. Outspoken on defence issues since his retirement, Falls heads the Canadian Centre for Arms Control and Disarmament.

Fauquier, John Emilius (1909–1981). Born in Ottawa and a commercial pilot before the war, Fauquier joined the RCAF in 1939 and became one of the most distinguished airmen of the war. He led an RCAF Pathfinder squadron and then commanded the famed Dambuster Squadron of the RAF. Fauquier won a DFC for gallantry and three DSOs, the only Canadian airman so recognized.

Felixstowe flying boats. During WORLD WAR I, the British developed flying boats for anti-submarine patrol work. The F series, developed at Felixstowe, could take off and land in rough seas and had up to seven LEWIS guns for defence. The two-engined aircraft, flown by pilots of the ROYAL NAVAL AIR SERVICE, had a ceiling of 2400–2900 m and a top speed of just over 145 km/h.

Fencibles. During the Napoleonic Wars, the British raised fencible (home service) regiments in Newfoundland, Nova Scotia, New Brunswick, and Canada for defence service anywhere in North America. None of these colonial regular regiments recruited to its authorized strength, the Regiment of Canadian Fencible Infantry, for example, managing to enlist only 124 men between 1803 and 1806. All were disbanded by 1816.

Fenian Raids. The Fenian movement began in 1857 when Irish-Americans organized to help Ireland secure its independence from Britain. The object of the organization, which by the end of the U.S. Civil War had some ten thousand adherents, was to attack Britain's North American colonies and thus to force London to send out more troops. That, in theory, would weaken Britain's hold on Ireland. The first Fenian raid fell on New Brunswick in April 1866 and was, like most of those to follow, a comic opera. Its one main consequence was to bring hitherto hesitant New Brunswickers to consider the benefits of joining in Confederation with Canada.

The next attack came across the Niagara frontier on 1 June 1866, and at RIDGEWAY the FENIANS scored their single victory, routing a body of MILITIA, before retreating back to the U.S. An attack on Canada East at Missisquoi on 7 June was ineffective, and that ended the raiding for some years while the Fenians feuded and re-grouped. Two raids were launched over the Quebec border

in 1870 and a final one was planned for Manitoba the next year, though American authorities blocked this attempt to strike sparks with Métis sympathizers of Louis RIEL.

The Fenians, mainly Civil War veterans, ought to have been more effective militarily; the Canadian militia also should have been.
Reading: Hereward Senior, *The Last Invasion of Canada* (Toronto, 1991)

Festubert, Battle of (1915). On 13 May 1915, heavy artillery began to shell German defences at Festubert, Belgium. A British and an Indian division attacked the enemy line on the night of 15–16 May, achieving partial surprise with the first British night attack of the war. On the 17th, units of the 1ST CANADIAN DIVISION joined in the assault, and for the next two weeks mounted costly and unsuccessful operations. The Canadians had staged five separate attacks and, except for one small foothold, had failed to reach the German trenches, although the front was advanced 550 m along a 1.5-km frontage. The Canadian casualties numbered 2468.

5th Canadian Armoured Division (World War II). Formed in March 1941 and disbanded in June 1945, the division took part in the battle for ITALY as part of the 1ST CANADIAN CORPS before transferring to NORTHWEST EUROPE in February 1945.

5th Canadian Division (World War I). This division was authorized in June 1917 to be formed from Canadian units already in England. It was to be commanded by Garnet HUGHES but it never proceeded to Europe; it was broken up and its components used to reinforce the CANADIAN CORPS in the field. Its divisional artillery was especially effective in reinforcing the Corps firepower.

First Canadian Army. The largest ever Canadian field formation, First Canadian Army consisted of corps, divisions and miscellaneous independent brigades and other units in Europe in WORLD WAR II. For most of the war the majority of units (and troops) serving under First Canadian Army were Canadian but units of other nationalities, principally British and Polish, also served. For example, from the time Army HQ was moved to France during the NORMANDY campaign until early 1945, the two corps under its command were II CANADIAN CORPS and I British Corps. At one point in late 1944, during the SCHELDT battle, Canadian troops were in a minority in First Canadian Army. The principal Canadian units under command of First Canadian Army at one point or another were I and II CANADIAN CORPS, 1ST, 2ND and 3RD CANADIAN INFANTRY DIVISIONS, 4TH and 5TH CANADIAN ARMOURED DIVISIONS. Formed in April 1942, First Canadian Army was initially commanded by A.G.L. MCNAUGHTON (1942–43) and later by H.D.G. CRERAR (1944–45). G.G. SIMONDS commanded it for a period in the fall of 1944 while Crerar was ill.

At its peak strength the Army consisted of three infantry and two armoured divisions, plus two independent tank brigades, a formidable force indeed and one comprising 42 infantry battalions, 12 armoured regiments, and 45 batteries of field artillery as well as an array of other specialized units. The difficulty was how and where to employ the troops. McNaughton wanted the Army kept together as a dagger pointed at Berlin, and he hoped to lead the Canadians in the invasion of Europe. But senior commanders and Ottawa believed that action was necessary and with the decision to send the IST CANADIAN DIVISION to SICILY in 1943 (and soon to increase its strength to a corps), McNaughton had lost the struggle. He soon lost his job too, and by the beginning of 1944, General H.D.G. Crerar was in command. Crerar led the Army through the fighting of 1944–45, often having British, American, Belgian, and Dutch units under command. Not until March 1945 did I CANADIAN CORPS rejoin its compatriots. It was disbanded at the end of July, 1945.

I Canadian Corps (World War II). Formed in July 1940 and disbanded in July 1945, the corps was primarily involved in the campaign for ITALY, which it officially entered in October, 1943. The corps consisted of the IST CANADIAN DIVISION and the 5TH CANADIAN ARMOURED DIVISION and was commanded, in turn, by H.D.G. CRERAR, E.L.M. BURNS, and C. FOULKES. In February 1945 it was transferred to Northwest Europe to join the rest of FIRST CANADIAN ARMY.

1st Canadian Division (World War I). Like all four Canadian divisions formed in WORLD WAR I, the 1st Canadian Division comprised three infantry brigades with four battalions to each brigade, two brigades of artillery, an engineer brigade, a machine-gun battalion, field ambulances, and service corps troops. The 1st Division was formed from the first Canadian contingent which sailed from Canada in October 1914. It recorded 6036 casualties during its first major engagement at YPRES. The division was disbanded in May 1919.

1st Canadian Division (1953). Authorized in September 1953, the division was intended to meet Canada's commitment to NATO. One brigade was to be stationed permanently in Germany; the remaining two brigades were to stay in Canada ready for immediate transfer to Europe in the event of war.

1st Canadian Infantry Division (World War II). Formed in October 1939, the division arrived in England in December 1939. In July 1943 it was added to the order of battle for the invasion of SICILY where it was commanded by G.G. SIMONDS. The division then participated in the battle for ITALY before being transferred to NORTHWEST EUROPE in February 1945 to join the rest of IST CANADIAN ARMY.

1st Commonwealth Division. Formed in KOREA in the summer of 1951, the division fought under UN auspices. It consisted of the 25TH CANADIAN INFANTRY BRIGADE, a mixed British-Australian-New Zealand brigade, and a British brigade, as well as a contingent of medical personnel from India.

Fiset, Sir Eugene (1874–1951). Born at Rimouski, Que., and trained as a doctor, Fiset served gallantly with the ROYAL CANADIAN REGIMENT in the SOUTH AFRICAN WAR and was briefly captured. He served as Director-General of Medical Services, Surgeon-General, and deputy minister of the Department of MILITIA AND DEFENCE from 1906–22. He later was a Liberal M.P. and Lieutenant-Governor of Quebec.

Fish Creek, Battle of (1885). During the NORTHWEST REBELLION, 1885, units of

General Frederick MIDDLETON's MILITIA force moving northwards along the South Saskatchewan River towards the rebel capital of BATOCHE came under attack from some 150 Métis and natives on 24 April. Firing from trenches dug along Fish Creek, and using surprise and cover to good effect, Gabriel DUMONT's ambush was successful, though the fighting became stalemated. The militia suffered heavy casualties, about one in six of the 300 men engaged, while the Métis lost only four dead. The Canadians withdrew to the south, thus delaying the advance against Batoche.

Fisher, Fred (1894–1915). An infantryman in the 13th Battalion, CEF, Fisher was moving forward from St Julien, near YPRES, on 23 April 1915 when he saw a battery of Canadian guns threatened by German infantry. Fisher and his section used their machine gun to hold off the enemy, allowing the guns to escape, though most of the infantry were killed or wounded. Returning to St Julien, Fisher found more men and tried to return to the front. All his men were killed or wounded, but Fisher carried on alone until he was killed. He was awarded the VICTORIA CROSS.

Fisher, Orville (b. 1911). Fisher studied art in Vancouver and joined the Army as a sapper in 1939, serving in the ranks and as a service artist. Commissioned in 1942, he became a war artist in 1943 and was soon assigned to the 3RD CANADIAN DIVISION. Fisher trained with the division for the D-DAY landings and served with it through NORMANDY and into the Netherlands. His work varied from the simple and clear in Canada to the near-phantasmagoric when he portrayed the vicious fighting around CAEN in 1944.

Fisheries Protection Service. Beginning in 1870, the Department of Marine and Fisheries had armed six schooners to prevent Americans' poaching in Canadian waters. Manned by merchant seamen, the Service was not of high professional standard, though after 1901 a few seamen took gunnery courses with the MILITIA. In 1903–04, two steel vessels armed with rapid-fire guns were acquired and personnel were given rudimentary training on the Canadian government ship *Canada*. The ships were transferred to the CANADIAN NAVAL SERVICE in 1910.

5.5-inch gun/howitzer: A WORLD WAR II artillery piece which replaced the 6-inch howitzer used in World War I, the 5.5-inch gun was mounted on a two-wheel carriage. It fired a 37-kg shell up to 17 km at two rounds per minute. The gun was operated by ten men and was transported by a heavy tractor. It was designated a gun/howitzer because of its ability to be fired as a flat-trajectory weapon (gun) or as a high-angle, long-range artillery piece (howitzer).

Flak. Anti-aircraft fire; from the German *Fliegerabwehrkanone* (flyer/defence/gun).

Flank companies. Just before the WAR OF 1812, General Sir Isaac BROCK confronted a difficult task in defending Upper Canada. His untrained MILITIA, like much of the population, was unreliable, but he persuaded the colony's assembly to allow him to train 2000 men, either volunteers or chosen by ballot, as flank companies of militia regiments to serve while most of the colony's manpower stayed home.

Flavelle, Sir Joseph Wesley (1858–1939). Born at Peterborough, Canada West, Flavelle made his fortune as president of William Davies Co., a huge pork-packing empire. During WORLD WAR I, he took charge of Canada's scandal-ridden munitions industry, a legacy of Sam HUGHES' cronyism, and converted it into the IMPERIAL MUNITIONS BOARD, a vast and efficient operation that ran factories, virtually conducted a foreign policy of its own, and negotiated labour settlements. Imperious and aggressive, Flavelle was not hailed for his achievement; instead the 'Baron of Bacon' was denounced for war profiteering.
Reading: J.M. Bliss, *A Canadian Millionaire* (Toronto, 1978)

Fleet Finch trainer. A small, slow, training aircraft used for elementary pilot training, the Fleet Finch was employed until 1943. Its top speed was just over 160 km/h. Over 400 were used in the BRITISH COMMONWEALTH AIR TRAINING PLAN until replaced by the FAIRCHILD CORNELL.

Floody, Clarke Wallace (1918–1989). Born in Chatham, Ont., and raised in Toronto, Wally Floody worked in the gold mines of Kirkland Lake, Ont., before joining the RCAF in 1940. Trained as a SPIT-FIRE pilot, he served with 401 Squadron in Britain until he was shot down in 1941. Taken prisoner and assigned to Stalag Luft III, he became a key member of the escape committee and the 'tunnel king' involved in planning the 'Great Escape' of March 1944 when 76 PoWs broke out. Fifty of the escapees were murdered, a number that did not include Floody who had been transferred to another camp a few weeks earlier. After the war Floody was in business in Toronto.

Flowerdew, Gordon Muriel (1885–1918). While serving in LORD STRATHCONA'S HORSE, Lt Flowerdew received orders to seize MOREUIL WOOD in a rearguard engagement during the great German offensive of March 1918. Flowerdew's squadron came across some 120 Germans, and he ordered a troop to dismount while with the remainder he charged the enemy. The cavalrymen rode through two lines of the enemy, turned, and rode through both lines once more. Almost three-quarters of the men were casualties, but the Germans broke and ran. Flowerdew, grievously wounded, died the next day, 31 March 1918. He was awarded the VICTORIA CROSS.

Flying Boxcar transport. The Fairchild C119 transport aircraft was used extensively by the ROYAL CANADIAN AIR FORCE's Air Transport Command for Arctic re-supply and army support. Orders for the rugged aircraft, which could carry a 9-tonne load for 2800 km, were placed in 1952 and 35 were acquired by the RCAF.

FN rifle. The basic infantry weapon of the CANADIAN ARMY into the 1980s, the FN rifle was adopted in the mid-1950s and made in Canada under licence from Fabrique Nationale, a Belgian company. It used the standard NATO 7.62-mm cartridge, was capable of semi-automatic and automatic fire, and slapped the firer's cheek in a most unpleasant manner.

Foote, Rev. John Weir (1904–1988). Padre of the Royal Hamilton Light Infantry, Foote landed with his regiment in the abortive DIEPPE RAID in August 1942. Through eight hours on the beach, he tended the wounded and continually exposed himself to enemy fire. Though he could have been rescued, he left a landing craft and let himself be taken prisoner so he could continue to minister to the men of his regiment. He was awarded the VICTORIA CROSS, the only one given a Canadian chaplain.

Foreign Enlistment Act. Introduced early in 1937 and given royal assent on 10 April, this act prohibited military assistance to the enemies of a friendly state but allowed the government to apply it to any case where there was armed conflict, civil or otherwise. The measure was designed to prevent Canadian volunteers from fighting in the civil war in Spain.

Fort Beauséjour. Located near present-day Sackville, N.B., the fort was built by the French in the early 1750s. Poorly maintained, the fort came under attack by Massachusetts volunteers and British regulars in 1755 and surrendered after a two-week siege. Renamed Fort Cumberland by the British, the fort repelled an American attack in 1776.

Fort Carillon. Constructed by the French in 1755–56, Fort Carillon (or Fort Ticonderoga as it was known to the English) was strategically located near Lakes Champlain and George and guarded the southern approach to Canada. In July 1758, MONTCALM repulsed a superior British force under Gen. James ABERCROMBY here, inflicting almost two thousand casualties. The following year, Jeffrey AMHERST took the fort. Carillon changed hands several times during the Revolutionary War and was ceded to the United States in 1783.

Fort Chambly. Sited on the Richelieu River near Chambly, Que., the fort was constructed initially in 1665 by the CARIGNAN-SALIÈRES regiment. Though strengthened in 1709, the fort was used only as a warehouse and it was easily captured by the British in 1760. In 1775 it was captured by the invading Americans but was retaken the next year.

Fort Erie. Built at the south end of the Niagara River in 1764, the fort occupied a strategic point along the U.S.-Canadian border. The third fort on the site was taken and destroyed in 1814 by the Americans during the WAR OF 1812.

Fort Frontenac. Located at the mouth of the Cataraqui River near the site of Kingston, Ont., this fort was constructed by Governor FRONTENAC in 1673. Abandoned briefly in 1689, Fort Frontenac was soon restored as the manifestation of French power on Lake Ontario. In the SEVEN YEARS' WAR, the fort served as the arsenal for the French navy on the Great Lakes, but it fell to the British in 1758. It was used in the inter-war years of the twentieth century for MILITIA staff courses, and is now the home of the NATIONAL DEFENCE COLLEGE.

Fort Garry. Built in 1822 at the forks of the Assiniboine and Red Rivers in what is now Manitoba, Fort Garry was a Hudson's Bay Company post. Destroyed by floods and re-built in 1836, the fort was seized bloodlessly by Métis during the RED RIVER REBELLION.

Fort Garry Horse. This cavalry regiment began on 15 April 1912 as the 34th Regiment of Cavalry and acquired its present name in WORLD WAR I, when the FGH served with the Canadian Cavalry Brigade from 1916 to the ARMISTICE. The unit was mobilized for WORLD WAR II in September 1939 and, as an armoured regiment, served with the 2nd Armoured Brigade in the NORTHWEST EUROPE Campaign. After the war, the FGH became a regular force armoured regiment.

Fort George. Located on the Canadian side of the Niagara River at Niagara-on-the-Lake, Fort George was built between 1796 and 1799. Compelled to withdraw from FORT NIAGARA across the river by the terms of Jay's treaty, the British built Fort George instead. The post was captured by the Americans after a fierce struggle in May 1813 during the WAR OF 1812 and was not rebuilt —until restoration as a tourist site began in the 1930s.

Fort Henry. Originally built during the WAR OF 1812 to protect the outlet from Lake Ontario to the St Lawrence River, Fort Henry, at Kingston, Ont., was reconstructed in the 1830s to defend the Rideau Canal. A substantial star-shaped structure, Fort Henry was garrisoned by British regulars until their withdrawal from Canada in 1871. Canadian troops used the fort for another two decades and it was then abandoned, though it was used to house prisoners of war in both world wars. It has since been restored as a tourist attraction.

Fort Malden. Located on the Canadian side of the Detroit River at Amherstburg, Ont., the fort was built between 1796 and 1799 by the British as a naval and military centre in western Upper Canada. Though it was the headquarters for British troops in the region during the early stages of the WAR OF 1812, Fort Malden was abandoned in 1813 and was not reoccupied until the end of the war. It remained a garrison centre until 1851.

Fort Niagara. Initially the site of a British fortification, Fort Niagara sat on the U.S. side of the border where the Niagara River enters Lake Ontario, across from FORT GEORGE. During the WAR OF 1812, a British force of 550 surprised its sentries on 18 December 1813, learned the password, and seized the fort. The Americans lost more than 400 men and the British held the fort until the war's end.

Fort Oswego. Built by the British on Lake Ontario at the mouth of the Oswego River in the early 18th century, Fort Oswego was originally intended to offset French posts at Niagara and Kingston. The fort was captured by MONTCALM during the SEVEN YEARS' WAR but returned to the British when France gave up its North American possessions at the end of that war. During the WAR OF 1812, the fort was captured by British forces under James YEO and Gordon DRUMMOND on 6 May 1814 and sacked for its cannons and military supplies. The war ended before American forces could retaliate; the fort was returned to them by the TREATY OF GHENT.

Fort Prince of Wales. Originally built by the Hudson's Bay Company in 1689 at the mouth of the Churchill River on Hudson Bay, in 1717 the fort was destroyed by fire and rebuilt five miles upstream. A new fortification was constructed after 1733 at the river mouth. In 1782 the French forced its surrender and destroyed it.

Fort Rodd Hill. Located at Victoria, B.C., this fort housed three coast defence batteries, put in place at the end of the 19th century.

Fort Ticonderoga. See FORT CARILLON.

Fort Wellington. Located at Prescott, Ont., this stone fortification was intended to guard the upper St Lawrence. It was built by British troops in 1838–39 on the site of an earlier wooden structure dating from the WAR OF 1812.

Fort York. Built in 1793 by Lieutenant-Colonel John Graves Simcoe on the north shore of Lake Ontario at the present site of Toronto, Fort York was twice attacked by the Americans during the WAR OF 1812 and effectively destroyed in 1813, along with much of the town of York. Allegedly in retaliation for the sack of York, British troops burned Washington, D.C.

Foster, Sir George Eulas (1847–1931). Foster, born in New Brunswick, served in Parliament for both N.B. and Ontario constituencies. He held a number of ministerial posts between 1885 and 1896, and 1911 and 1921. He was a prominent member of Sir Robert BORDEN's wartime administrations, and attended the Peace Conference in 1919. Foster's 1909 motion in the House of Commons that Canada should contribute to the Royal Navy led Sir Wilfrid LAURIER to move to create a Canadian navy.

Foster, Harry Wickwire (1902–1964). Born in Halifax into a military family, Foster attended the ROYAL MILITARY COLLEGE from 1922 to 1924 and joined LORD STRATHCONA'S HORSE in the PERMANENT FORCE. After regimental and staff service, he went to the BRITISH ARMY STAFF COLLEGE and then to France with the first contingent in 1940. In NORMANDY Foster commanded a brigade in the 3RD CANADIAN DIVISION and then commanded the 4TH CANADIAN ARMOURED DIVISION. In December 1944, he took command of the 1ST CANADIAN DIVISION in Italy and later in the war led it in the Netherlands. Foster presided over the trial of SS General KURT MEYER in 1945, then served in Canada until his appointment to the COMMONWEALTH [Imperial] WAR GRAVES COMMISSION in 1950.

Reading: Tony Foster, *Meeting of Generals* (Toronto, 1986)

Foster, William Wasbrough (1876–1954). Born in Britain, Foster came to Canada in 1895 to work with the CPR. He served overseas in WORLD WAR I with great distinction, emerging as a brigadier with the DSO and two bars. He continued to serve in the MILITIA between the wars, then returned to active service in 1939. After setting up auxiliary services overseas and commanding military districts in Canada, he was appointed Special Commissioner in northwest Canada as a major-general. This task involved showing the flag to and keeping an eye on U.S. forces in the Canadian north.

Foulkes, Charles (1903–1969). Born in England, Foulkes came to Canada as a youth, briefly attended the University of Western Ontario, and joined the MILITIA in 1922. He transferred to the ROYAL CANADIAN REGIMENT in the PERMANENT FORCE in 1926. After service in various posts in Canada and at the BRITISH ARMY STAFF COLLEGE, he was still a captain on the outbreak of war in 1939. Thereafter, his rise was meteoric — brigade major, battalion commander, brigadier, division commander, and finally corps commander. Foulkes led the 2ND CANADIAN DIVISION in NORMANDY and was briefly acting commander of II CANADIAN CORPS. He then was posted to Italy as a lieutenant-general and took command of I CANADIAN CORPS which he led through its final actions there and to the Netherlands where he received the German surrender. In 1945, he became CHIEF OF THE GENERAL STAFF instead of the more talented Guy SIMONDS, presiding over the DEMOBILIZATION of the army and its strengthening for NATO and KOREAN WAR service. Foulkes established close links with the United States military, ties he reinforced when, six years later, he was appointed CHAIRMAN OF THE CHIEFS OF STAFF COMMITTEE, a post he held until his retirement in 1960. As such, he was the most powerful military bureaucrat in Canadian history, a politically adept and smooth operator in the corridors of power. He persuaded the DIEFENBAKER government to go into NORAD in 1957 and survived the fallout from that hasty decision.

4.2-inch mortar. Adopted in December 1942, the 4.2-inch mortar fired a 9-kg bomb. It was used by battalion mortar teams as was the 3-inch mortar, a smaller version. The 2-inch mortar was an infantry platoon weapon.

4th Canadian Armoured Division (World War II). Formed in June 1941 and disbanded in June 1945, the division was originally to be an infantry division for home defence but was converted to an armoured division in 1942 for service overseas. The division transferred to France prior to the battle of FA- LAISE, and fought in the balance of the NORMANDY campaign and in NORTHWEST EUROPE.

4th Canadian Division (World War I). The division joined the CANADIAN CORPS at the SOMME in October 1916, assisted in the capture of REGINA TRENCH, and served at VIMY RIDGE. It was disbanded in June 1919.

Francotrain. Established in 1968, Francotrain was the CANADIAN FORCES' training program for francophones. Located at St Jean, Que., Francotrain centralized all French-language recruit and trades training.

***Fraser*, HMCS.** Built in 1932 and purchased by the ROYAL CANADIAN NAVY in 1937, this RIVER CLASS DESTROYER was stationed on the west coast until the outbreak of war. Sent to the east coast, *Fraser* escorted convoys out of Halifax. Ordered to U.K. waters in May 1940, the ship was sunk on 25 June in a collision with the cruiser HMS *Calcutta* in the Gironde River estuary, losing 47 of her crew. The second ship of this name, a DESTROYER ESCORT of the *ST LAURENT* CLASS, was commissioned in 1957, converted to a destroyer helicopter carrier in 1963, and completed the DESTROYER LIFE EXTENSION PROJECT in 1979.

French, Sir George Arthur (1841–1921). Born in Ireland, French served in the Royal Irish Constabulary before taking a commission in the Royal Artillery. He served in Canada from 1862–66, then in 1871 set up A Battery of the Garrison Artillery using stores left by the British who were returning home. In 1873, he became first commissioner of the NORTH WEST MOUNTED POLICE, organized it, gave it its character, and com- manded it on its march to the foothills of the Rocky Mountains in 1874. He left the Mounties in 1876 and saw service in India and Australia.

French-Iroquois Wars. An intermittent series of small wars that lasted throughout most of the 17th century, the fighting between the French and the Iroquois Confederacy of the Mohawk, Oneida, Onondaga, Cayuga, and Seneca tribes centred initially around access to fur trapping areas. As the Iroquois spread their influence further afield to the Ottawa valley, they came into conflict with Algonquin and Huron tribes cooperating with the French. To protect their allies, the French built forts and armed their Indian retainers, but the Iroquois were fiercer, and they scattered their enemies, often killing the black-robed missionaries living among them. Between 1642 and 1653 especially, the Iroquois laid waste to Huron, Neutral, Abenaki, and other tribes before signing a peace with the French. That failed to hold, and fighting erupted once more, the French sending the CARIGNAN-SALIÈRES REGIMENT on punitive expeditions against the Mohawks' villages that forced a treaty in 1667. The fighting flared again in 1680 and then was subsumed in the Anglo-French conflict, culminating in a major raid on Lachine in 1689. Not until 1701 did the Iroquois finally agree to stay neutral in the struggle between Britain and France for control of North America.

French-Language Units (FLUs). Begun in 1968 by Defence minister Leo CADIEUX, FLUs were established in an effort to help retain more francophone service personnel in the CANADIAN FORCES. HMCS *OTTAWA* was the first FLU, followed by No. 433 squadron. A third of the Canadian Airborne Regiment was also so designated. The 5e Groupement de Combat, based at Valcartier, Que. after 1969, was the largest French-speaking formation.

Frigates. In late 1940, the Royal Navy called for a ship that could protect convoys in mid-ocean against wolf-pack U-boat attacks, a job for which the CORVETTE was never intended. Originally known as twin-screw corvettes, the frigates were larger, longer-ranged, and more comfortable. In WORLD WAR II, the ROYAL CANADIAN NAVY had ten British-built frigates and 60 RIVER CLASS ships built in Canada. Frigates displaced 1420 tonnes, had a crew of 141, and were armed with twin 4-inch guns, four 20-mm guns and HEDGEHOGS. They entered service in 1943–44 and became the main anti-submarine warship of the RCN with most organized into special U-boat hunting groups largely employed in British waters. The frigates were decommissioned soon after the war, but in the early 1950s 21 were modernized and, except for three given to Norway, remained in service until the 1960s. At the end of the 1970s, the navy placed orders for 12 highly advanced *Halifax*-class frigates at a cost of $10 billion. The first ship, much bigger than World War II destroyers and linked to them only by designation and because *Halifax*-class ships also have an anti-submarine role, was ready for service in 1991.

Front de Libération du Québec (FLQ). The FLQ was was a terrorist organization that had as its goal the separation of Quebec from Canada by fomenting violent revolution. Always small and made up more of malcontents that trained activists, the FLQ began its campaign in March 1963 by planting bombs in mailboxes, armouries, and federal institutions. Police investigations broke up the organization on a few occasions but new recruits kept the FLQ alive. The highlight of its activities was the OCTOBER CRISIS 1970 when the FLQ kidnapped James Cross, the British trade commissioner in Montreal, and then kidnapped and murdered Pierre Laporte, Quebec Labour minister. Public revulsion and a massive federal intervention killed the FLQ.
Reading: Louis Fournier, *F.L.Q.: The Anatomy of an Underground Movement* (Toronto, 1984)

Frontenac, Louis de Buade, Comte de (1622–1698). Well educated and well trained as a soldier, Frontenac obtained appointment as governor of New France in 1672. Very quickly he realized the profits to be made in the western fur trade as well as the possibilities for expansion of the colony's influence, and he established a post on Lake Ontario, FORT FRONTENAC. Moving his activities further west and south and establishing lightly garrisoned trading posts brought Frontenac into conflict with the Iroquois (and with his masters in Paris). Moreover, by blocking the expansion of the British colonies to the west, he laid the seeds of eventual conflict between France and Britain. He was recalled after a decade in the colony and did not return until 1689. This time he came with orders to fight the Iroquois, orders which therefore involved him with the American colonists, culminating in an abortive attack on Quebec by Sir William PHIPS in 1690, an assault that Frontenac faced down with courage and by a skilful concentration of his forces. The war soon turned into a guerrilla conflict, Frontenac's men becoming as adept as the Iroquois in the art of *petit guerre*. Even so, Frontenac hoped to end the war with the Iroquois by diplomacy but failed, and he led an expedition against them that burned their villages. Plagued by charges that he was subsidizing his profitable fur market activities with military funds, Frontenac was likely facing recall to France when he died in 1698.
Reading: William Eccles, *Frontenac: the Courtier Governor* (Toronto, 1959)

Frost, Ernest Ralph Clyde (1917–1969). When two BLENHEIM aircraft collided at West Raynham Royal Air Force Station in England on 12 March 1940, RCAF Leading Aircraftman Frost managed to rescue the unconscious pilot from one of the burning bombers that soon exploded. Though the pilot later died, Frost was awarded the GEORGE CROSS.

Functional principle. The British and Americans excluded Canada from the formulatiuon of Allied strategy, planning, and economic warfare in WORLD WAR II. The resentment this produced led Canadian diplomats to develop the idea of functionalism which insisted that all small powers could not be treated equally (and badly). In some areas, such as food production or raw materials, Canada was a superpower and demanded to be involved in the planning. This case, formally stated by Mackenzie KING in Parliament on 9 July 1943, had substantial effect and Canada alone of the lesser powers secured a place on the Combined Food Board and the Combined Production and Resources Board.

Funnies. The troops' name for the array of specialized tanks developed by the British in

WORLD WAR II. Such tanks, used very effectively in NORMANDY and after, could swim, explode mines, fill in ditches, build bridges, carry flame-throwers, or fire an enormous howitzer. Most were grouped in the 79th Armoured Division, a British formation that included Canadian units. The United States forces, to their cost, failed to use them.

G

Gander. Originally the Newfoundland Airport, Gander was so named in August 1940 during WORLD WAR II. With its local defence provided by Canada, the airport served as a base for the ATLANTIC FERRY ORGANIZATION.

Ganong, Hardy Nelson (1890–1959). Born into the family of candy manufacturers at St Stephen, N.B., Ganong joined the MILITIA in 1909, then served overseas in WORLD WAR I. He was commanding officer of the Carleton and York Regiment on the outbreak of WORLD WAR II, took his battalion overseas, and in 1941 was promoted brigadier. In 1942 he returned to Canada and, as a major-general, took command of two home defence divisions. For the last six months of the war, he was Commander, Newfoundland and Canadian Military Forces, Newfoundland.

Gardiner, James Garfield (1883–1962). Born in Ontario, Jimmy Gardiner moved to Saskatchewan in 1903. Elected to the legislature in 1914, he served as Liberal premier from 1926 to 1929 and from 1934 to 1935. He joined Mackenzie KING's Cabinet in 1935 and became a powerful minister of Agriculture. In 1940, he took control of the DEPARTMENT OF NATIONAL WAR SERVICES, a post he held until 1941. He was a strong opponent of CONSCRIPTION and supported King in his resistance to it.

Garrisons, British. After 1763, troops garrisoned the British North American colonies, first, to keep the recently conquered French Canadians in check, then as a cautionary measure against increasingly restive American colonists and, after the Revolution, an expansionist United States. The major garrisons were stationed at Halifax, Quebec City, Montreal, Kingston, York, London, Amherstberg, and later at ESQUIMALT. Normally some 7000 troops were based here. By 1871, the legions had been recalled except for those at Halifax and Esquimalt; these two were gone by 1905.

Gascoigne, Sir William Julius (1844–1926). Gascoigne enlisted in the British Army in 1863 and saw service in Egypt and the Sudan. He came to Canada in 1895 as GENERAL OFFICER COMMANDING the MILITIA and served without fuss until 1898. His successors would not be so fortunate.

Gatling gun. A heavy machine gun made by Colt, the Gatling was employed in the NORTHWEST REBELLION 1885 at CUT KNIFE HILL and BATOCHE. It fired .45-calibre bullets from its ten barrels and was capable of 800 rounds per minute.

Gault, Andrew Hamilton (1882–1958). Gault served in the SOUTH AFRICAN WAR with the 2ND CANADIAN MOUNTED RIFLES. On the outbreak of WORLD WAR I, he put up $100,000 to raise and organize PRINCESS PATRICIA'S CANADIAN LIGHT INFANTRY, an infantry battalion in which he served as second-in-command. He was seriously wounded, losing his leg. He later lived in England, served as a Member of Parliament at Westminster, and rejoined the Canadian army in 1939, rising to the rank of brigadier.

'Gee.' A target-finding device for allied bombers in WORLD WAR II, Gee enabled the navigator to determine his exact position by calculating the difference in travel time between three radio signals transmitted by stations on the ground.

Gellner, John (b. 1907). Born in Trieste of Czech parents, Gellner was a lawyer in Czechoslovakia until he came to Canada in 1939. He served with the RCAF in WORLD WAR II as a pilot, winning the DFC, and remained in the service until 1958. Retiring as a wing commander, Gellner became the country's most notable commentator and writer on defence policy in *Commentary* and in *CANADIAN DEFENCE QUARTERLY*. He also played a substantial part as an adviser to the Liberals on defence policy in the early 1960s.

General Officer Commanding (GOC). The term used to describe senior army officers, ordinarily of at least major-general rank, holding designated positions. The term was used to describe a division commander, the officer in charge of a post-1945 command in Canada, or (before 1904) the British officer in command of the MILITIA.

Generals Die in Bed. Written by Charles Yale Harrison and published in 1930, this novel was a spare, realistic story of the experiences of Canadian infantry in WORLD WAR I. 'We have learned who our enemies are,' Harrison writes, 'the lice, some of our officers and Death.' Harrison, an American-born journalist, had served in the CEF with the Royal Montreal Regiment.

Generals' revolt. At the height of the CONSCRIPTION CRISIS 1944, General A.G.L. MCNAUGHTON, the Defence minister, telephoned Prime Minister Mackenzie KING on 22 November. 'The Headquarters staff here,' King wrote in his diary recording McNaughton's words, 'had all advised him that the voluntary system would not get the men.' In effect, McNaughton meant that the ZOMBIES or NATIONAL RESOURCES MOBILIZATION ACT home defence conscripts could not be persuaded to volunteer for overseas service to relieve the shortage of infantry recruits in units of FIRST CANADIAN ARMY. King declared McNaughton's 'the most serious advice that could be tendered', persuaded himself that CONSCRIPTION for overseas service now was necessary, and that this had been forced on him by a revolt, 'the surrender of the civil government to the military', a 'palace revolution'. The generals' revolt, in other words, was largely King's justification to himself for reversing a policy that had become untenable.
Reading: J.L. Granatstein and J.M. Hitsman, *Broken Promises: A History of Conscription in Canada* (Toronto, 1985).

General Staff. The planning and directing body of an army, the term General Staff has been used in Canada since before the Great War and the appointment of the first CHIEF OF THE GENERAL STAFF. In fact, it is arguable that Canada has never had a general staff in its true sense. At the onset of WORLD WAR II, for example, there was scarcely any intelligence assessment capacity, something that guaranteed disasters such as HONG KONG. And in both wars and in the COLD WAR, Canada has been so locked into alliances where great powers did the strategic planning that the General Staff's role was little more than the provision and supply of units and equipment.

George Cross. Second only to the VICTORIA CROSS, the George Cross was instituted in 1940 to honour conspicuous acts of bravery not in the presence of the enemy. It was intended primarily for civilians but could also be given to members of the armed forces for actions for which military honours were not ordinarily awarded. Eight Canadians have won the award. See Appendix IV.

George Medal. Awarded for great bravery not in the presence of the enemy, the George Medal was intended, as with the GEORGE CROSS, primarily for civilians but could be awarded to military personnel.

German invasion fears, 1914. At the outbreak of WORLD WAR I, genuine fear existed in Ottawa and generally in Canada that German-Americans might invade Canada or engage in sabotage. Reports from the British ambassador in Washington fuelled this concern, and troops were posted to guard strategic points near the border. By late 1915, the scare was dying out, reports from the Dominion police suggesting that no serious threat existed. The burning of the Parliament buildings in 1916, however, was attributed to German sabotage by some. Ottawa maintained up to 50,000 troops in Canada for home defence, testimony to the nervousness abroad in the land.

Ghent, Treaty of. See TREATY OF GHENT.

Gibson, Colin William George (1891–1974). Gibson attended the ROYAL MILITARY COLLEGE, practised law, and then served in WORLD WAR I with the British army. Elected to Parliament as a Liberal in 1940, he served as minister of National Revenue from July 1940 to March 1945 when he become minister of National Defence (Air), a post he held until December 1946.

Girouard, Sir Edouard Percy (1867–1932). A leading imperial figure, Girouard was born in Montreal and educated at the ROYAL MILITARY COLLEGE. He joined the Royal Engineers in 1888 as a railway expert and saw service in the Sudan, Egypt, and South Africa. In 1907 he became High Commissioner in Northern Nigeria and two years later governor of British East Africa. During WORLD WAR I he was Director General of Munitions Supply in London.

Glassco Commission. The Royal Commission on Government Organization, appointed in 1960 and chaired by John G. Glassco, reported in 1962–63 that the armed forces had never been properly coordinated. The administrative 'tail' was too large in comparison to the fighting 'teeth', and there were too many committees at NATIONAL DEFENCE HEADQUARTERS. Moreover, Glassco argued that the service chiefs had too much control over the work of the CHIEFS OF STAFF COMMITTEE. Glassco proposed a transfer of power to the CHAIRMAN OF THE CHIEFS OF STAFF.

'Go Active'. The slogan of a campaign launched by government—and with substantial unofficial public and media support—to encourage home defence army conscripts or ZOMBIES enrolled under the NATIONAL RESOURCES MOBILIZATION ACT (NRMA) to volunteer for overseas service during WORLD WAR II.

Godfrey, Albert Earl (1890–1982). Godfrey served with the Royal Air Force in France in WORLD WAR I and commanded a training camp at Beamsville, Ont. He served as navigator on the first Montreal-Vancouver flight, set up the ROYAL CANADIAN AIR FORCE's Air Training Command in 1938, and played an important part in establishing the BRITISH COMMONWEALTH AIR TRAINING PLAN. He led WESTERN AIR COMMAND from October 1939 until 1942, when he was posted to Ottawa. Then in 1943 he led Eastern Air Command until his retirement in 1944. In February 1945 he ran unsuccessfully as a CCF candidate against Defence minister Gen. A.G.L. MCNAUGHTON in a by-election in Grey North, Ont. won by the Progressive Conservatives.

Godfrey, John Milton (1871–1938). A lawyer, Godfrey played an important part on the HOME FRONT in WORLD WAR I. He was active in civilian recruiting leagues in Toronto, president of the CANADIAN NATIONAL SERVICE LEAGUE, organizer of the BONNE ENTENTE movement that tried to encourage Quebec enlistments, and Ontario head of the Win-the-War League.

Good, Herman James (1887–1969). A corporal in the 13th Battalion, CEF, Good charged a machine-gun nest on his own at AMIENS on 8 August 1918. He killed or captured the German crew, then discovered a battery of 5.9-inch guns and organized and led an attack on them with but three other soldiers. The battery surrendered. Good was awarded the VICTORIA CROSS.

Goodwood, Operation, 1944. General Bernard Montgomery's Goodwood, launched on 18 July 1944 southward from CAEN toward Bourguebus Ridge, dominating the road south to Falaise, pitched three British armoured divisions against the well-entrenched Germans. The II CANADIAN CORPS' simultaneous Operation ATLANTIC met with somewhat better success.

Goose Bay. Built as an air station by Canada in 1941 on the inhospitable terrain of Labrador, 'Goose' was an important stepping stone for the ferrying of aircraft to Britain via the Great Circle route from North America and an alternate to GANDER. In May 1946, Canada, which had a 99-year lease on Goose, agreed to let the United States use the base and the Americans soon stationed nuclear-armed heavy bombers there. The U.S. pulled out completely in 1991, leaving Goose Bay to be used as a NATO low-level air training base, causing enormous protests among Innu and their supporters.

Goranson, Paul (b. 1911). The first Canadian war artist of WORLD WAR II, Goranson joined the air force in 1941 after training in Vancouver. Until 1943 and his posting overseas, he did sketches and oils at stations in Canada. For the last two years of war, now commissioned, Goranson served with RCAF squadrons in North Africa, Italy, and Northwest Europe, flying on bomber missions. His style was heavily documentary, and he concentrated on the relationship between men and machines. His postwar career was largely spent in New York.

Gordon, Charles William (1860-1937). Under the pen name of Ralph Connor, he wrote enormously successful novels from 1899 through WORLD WAR I, in which he served as a chaplain. His wartime books, *The Sky Pilot in No Man's Land* and *The Major* are crudely drawn and reflect the racism of the time, pointing to the brutality of Germans (and German-Canadians) and the nobility of Anglo-Saxons.

Gordon, James Lindsay (1892-1940). Born in Montreal, Gordon learned to fly in 1915 and served overseas with the ROYAL NAVAL AIR SERVICE (winning the DISTINGUISHED FLYING CROSS) and the ROYAL AIR FORCE. He then served with the AIR BOARD, and was acting director of the CANADIAN AIR FORCE in 1922-23, before joining the ROYAL CANADIAN AIR FORCE. He directed Civil Government Air Operations between 1927 and 1933, attended the RAF Staff College in Britain and the IMPERIAL DEFENCE COLLEGE, and commanded the army's Military Districts in Regina and Winnipeg, the first air force officer to so.

Gothic Line. Extending across the entire width of Italy from north of Pisa on the Ligurian Sea to just south of Rimini on the Adriatic and based on the Apennines, the Gothic Line was the Germans' major defensive barrier in northern Italy. After two months' rest the I CANADIAN CORPS, commanded by Gen. E.L.M. BURNS, went in to the attack against the Adriatic anchor of the line on 25 August 1944. The objective was Rimini but there were six rivers, each well defended, between the start line and the ultimate objective. To reach the outworks of the Gothic Line took four days of heavy fighting. On 30 August, the Corps attack

went directly at the German line. Costly though it was, the assault was largely successful, the Canadians' 1ST and 5TH DIVISIONS gaining a foothold by the 31st and forcing the Germans to pull units from other sectors to slow their advance. Rimini was taken on 21 September and the Gothic barrier was finally breached the next day, and the north Italian plain stretched before the Canadians. The cost to the corps of a month of fighting was 2511 casualties.

Reading: Daniel Dancocks, *The D-Day Dodgers: The Canadians in Italy, 1943-1945* (Toronto, 1991)

Graham, George Perry (1859-1943). A journalist and businessman, Graham served in the Ontario legislature and in the House of Commons. He became minister of Militia and Defence and minister of Naval Service in the Mackenzie KING government in 1921, and he was briefly the first minister of National Defence after the proclamation of the DEPARTMENT OF NATIONAL DEFENCE ACT 1922. He was named to the Senate in 1926.

Graham, Howard Douglas (1898-1986). Born at Buffalo, N.Y., Graham served in the army in WORLD WAR I and then practised law at Trenton, Ont. Active in the MILITIA, in WORLD WAR II he went overseas with the Hastings and Prince Edward Regiment of the IST CANADIAN DIVISION. He led the 1st Brigade in Sicily and Italy, narrowly surviving sharp disputes with his division commander, Gen. Guy SIMONDS; he was relieved when his health broke down, and served in Ottawa. He remained in the postwar army and was Simonds' successor as CHIEF OF THE GENERAL STAFF from 1955-58.

Reading: H.D. Graham, *Citizen and Soldier* (Toronto, 1987)

Grand Army of United Veterans. Formed in 1920 or 1921 from two smaller WORLD WAR I veterans' organizations, the GAUV, like other veterans' groups, sought a bonus and other benefits for its members and tended to gather the disgruntled into its ranks. Some of its members resisted absorption into the ROYAL CANADIAN LEGION in 1925-26.

Grant, Harold T.W. (1899-1965). Educated at the ROYAL NAVAL COLLEGE OF CANADA, Grant served at sea during WORLD

WAR I. He commanded HMCS *SKEENA* just before the outbreak of war in 1939, became staff officer (operations) at Halifax, then chief of personnel at Naval headquarters. In 1944, he commanded the HMS *Enterprise*, an unusual honour for an RCN officer, and then the cruiser HMCS *ONTARIO*, and led the ROYAL CANADIAN NAVY's fleet in the Pacific. From 1947 to 1951, he was CHIEF OF NAVAL STAFF. He retired in 1951 as vice admiral.

Gravell, Karl Mander (1922–1941). Born in Sweden, Gravell was a Leading Aircraftman on flying training in Alberta in November 1941. On a routine flight, the aircraft plunged to the ground in flames. Severely injured, Gravell went back to the burning trainer to attempt to rescue the pilot. Gravell died of his burns, and was awarded the GEORGE CROSS.

Gray, Robert Hampton (1917–1945). From Nelson, B.C., Lt Gray was a Corsair pilot flying from a British aircraft carrier. On 9 August 1945, the day an atomic bomb levelled Nagasaki and just days before Japan sued for peace, Gray participated in an attack against a destroyer at Onagawa Wan, Japan. Despite heavy anti-aircraft fire which hit his airplane, Gray held his course and flew to within fifty feet of the enemy ship before dropping his bombs. The destroyer sank at once, but Gray was killed. He had already been MENTIONED IN DESPATCHES for his role in an attack on the German battleship *Tirpitz*, and he won a DISTINGUISHED SERVICE CROSS for an earlier attack on a Japanese naval vessel. For the attack in which he lost his life, Gray was awarded the VICTORIA CROSS, the only one won by a member of the ROYAL CANADIAN NAVY in WORLD WAR II.

Gray, Roderick Borden (1917–1944). Flying Officer Gray of the RCAF was navigator of a WELLINGTON on anti-submarine patrol in the Atlantic. On 27 August 1944 the bomber attacked a U-boat but was shot down by its gunfire. Despite a broken leg, Gray rescued two of his crewmates from their sinking bomber, then remained in the water to allow his comrades to stay in the tiny, overcrowded dinghy. By dawn he had died of exposure; three survivors were rescued. Gray was awarded the GEORGE CROSS.

Great War Veterans Association. Formed in Winnipeg in 1917, the GWVA became the major spokesman for CANADIAN EXPEDITIONARY FORCE veterans. Its initial leaders were wounded veterans who, naturally enough, put their highest priority on care for the disabled. But by the ARMISTICE 1918, large numbers of able-bodied returned men wanted better benefits from Ottawa, and their radical demands for a $2000 bonus split the GWVA and were inevitably turned down flat by a budget-conscious BORDEN government. By 1925, the still-divided GWVA had been swallowed whole by the ROYAL CANADIAN LEGION controlled by former senior officers.

Greene, Lorne Hyman (1915–1987). From 1939 to 1942, Ottawa-born Greene read the CBC news, his sonorous tones in that dark period giving him the sobriquet of the 'Voice of Doom.' After wartime service, he returned to radio, the theatre, and television, establishing himself as a mainstay of 'Bonanza', one of the most successful TV shows of all time.

Gregg, Milton Fowler (1892–1978). This extraordinary New Brunswicker went overseas as a stretcher-bearer in WORLD WAR I and, after being twice wounded, became an officer with the ROYAL CANADIAN REGIMENT. He was wounded a third time and won the MILITARY CROSS and bar and the VICTORIA CROSS for gallantry. He worked, among other things, for the SOLDIERS SETTLEMENT BOARD between the wars, then served overseas in WORLD WAR II as a battalion commander and in Canada as commandant of officer training units. He retired as a brigadier in 1944, served as president of the University of New Brunswick, and then won election to Parliament as a Liberal in 1947. He was minister of Veterans' Affairs from 1948–50, and after his retirement from politics in 1957, served as a diplomat abroad until 1967.

Griesbach, William Antrobus (1878–1945). Born at Fort Qu'Appelle, Northwest Territories, this son of a Prussian army officer enlisted in the CANADIAN MOUNTED RIFLES for SOUTH AFRICAN WAR service. He then practised as a lawyer in Edmonton and in 1914 went overseas as a major, rising to command the 1st Brigade of the 1ST CANA-DIAN DIVISION. In 1921 he was promoted to major-general. Griesbach was named to the Senate in 1921 by Prime Minister Meighen and was a constant critic of (Liberal) defence policy. Recalled to service as Inspector-General, Western Canada in 1940, Griesbach retired in 1943.

Griffon. The first ship to sail the upper Great Lakes, she was launched in August 1679 on the Niagara River. Armed with seven guns, this tiny barque sailed to Michilimackinac and Green Bay under the command of René-Robert Cavalier de la Salle. The ship was lost on its return voyage.

Gulf War, 1990–91. On 1 August 1990, Iraq invaded Kuwait, its neighbour and the possessor of much of the world's oil supply. This surprising assault produced shock, not least in the United States where President George Bush was quick to react. At the United Nations and in capitals all over the world, the Americans quickly began to put together a diplomatic and military coalition to force Iraq's Saddam Hussein to disgorge his conquest. Canada was soon involved, Prime Minister Brian Mulroney on 10 August offering the destroyers HMCS *Terra Nova* and *ATHABASKAN* and the supply ship *Protecteur* to participate in a blockade of Iraq. The obsolescent ships, with 934 crew — including 27 women, the first Canadian servicewomen to be sent into an area of potential danger—left Canada on 24 August after hurried preparations to bring them close to the standard of armament necessary for combat. The next day, the UN imposed tough economic sanctions on Iraq. But Baghdad made no attempt to accommodate itself to the growing pressure and, as the Americans began to move the first of hundreds of thousands of troops into Saudi Arabia, Canada increased its role on 14 September, this time offering a CF18 squadron with some 450 personnel from Canada's NATO force in Germany. The squadron went operational, flying patrols over the multinational Persian Gulf naval force on 8 October, and its operations were helped by despatch of a Boeing 707 air-to-air refuelling tanker. On 29 November, the UN agreed to use 'all necessary means' to compel Iraq to withdraw if it had not done so by 15 January 1991, and the deadline passed with Saddam hanging tough.

The result on the night of 15 January was the start of devastating air attacks on Iraq's military installations and civilian infrastructure. Canada's CF18s did not initially share in the Allied assault, but on 1 February they were allowed to provide air cover and on 24 February to engage targets on the ground. Meanwhile, Ottawa agreed to despatch a field hospital (with 530 officers and enlisted personnel) on 24 January to handle the heavy casualties expected when the ground assault began. That attack, Operation Desert Storm, began on 24 February, but the Iraqis quickly surrendered in droves and a ceasefire came into effect on the night of 27–28 February. There were few Allied casualties—and none among the Canadians—but the estimates of Iraqi losses were as high as 200,000 dead. The war was over, the Canadians had played a limited but credible role, and all that remained was peacekeeping and peacemaking. Those would prove harder to achieve than the desert victory.

Guthrie, Hugh (1866–1939). Guthrie was born in Guelph, Ont. and represented the area in Parliament from 1900 until 1935. He served as minister of Militia and Defence in Arthur Meighen's governments (1920–21 and 1926) and in a number of other Cabinet posts.

Gwatkin, Sir Willoughby Garnons (1859–1925). Born in England and educated at Cambridge, Gwatkin took a commission in the British army in 1882. Seconded permanently to Canada in 1911 as a colonel, he devised mobilization plans for the raising of a small force for extra-Canadian service; this plan was scrapped by Sam HUGHES at the outbreak of WORLD WAR I in 1914. Gwatkin became CHIEF OF THE GENERAL STAFF in 1913 and had the difficult task of working with Hughes, countering his devotion to the ROSS RIFLE, mobilizing the CANADIAN EXPEDITIONARY FORCE, and handling both volunteers and conscripts. Retiring as Chief of the General Staff in 1919, this quiet, witty officer became an air vice-marshal and the Inspector-General of the newly established CANADIAN AIR FORCE before retiring to England.

Gzowski, Sir Casimir Stanislaus (1813–1898). Born at St Petersburg, Russia,

Gzowski came to Canada in 1841 and worked as an engineer. He became superintendent of public works for the United Canadas, creating canal and railway projects. Gzowski was an advocate of the strengthening of the MILITIA, seeing in this the only way of defending the country. He played a leading part in mobilizing the country against the FENIAN RAIDS and a major role in establishing the Dominion of Canada Rifle Association, and he rose to the rank of colonel.

H

Haida, HMCS. This most famous ROYAL CANADIAN NAVY vessel of WORLD WAR II was commissioned in August 1943, one of a series of TRIBAL CLASS DESTROYERS built in England for the RCN. For a year from January 1944, *Haida* operated off the French coast under command of Commander Harry DEWOLF and provided supporting fire at the D-DAY invasion of NORMANDY. The destroyer also participated in several notable and successful engagements with German naval craft, sinking two destroyers, a minesweeper, a submarine, and fourteen other warships. The ship also took part in the rescue of survivors of her sister-destroyer, *ATHABASKAN*, sunk on 28 April 1944. Refitted, *Haida* served in the KOREAN WAR from 1952 to 1954 and continued in service until 1963. The ship was then purchased by admirers and, taken over by the Ontario government, moored at Toronto as a memorial.

Halifax bomber. Built by Handley-Page in Britain, the Halifax, along with the LANCASTER, was the backbone of the Royal Air Force's BOMBER COMMAND from its introduction in 1941. Equipped with four engines, the bomber had a speed of 365 km/h at 4115 m and was greatly loved by its crews because of its extremely rugged reliability. The Halifax could not carry as heavy a bomb load — just 5900 kg — as the Lancaster, though its defence in the air was similar — nine .303-calibre machine guns. Replacing the WELLINGTON, the Halifax was used from late 1943 by many of the squadrons in the ROYAL CANADIAN AIR FORCE's No. 6 Bomber Group.

Halifax Citadel. See CITADEL, HALIFAX.

Halifax explosion, 1917. The Belgian ship *IMO* and the French munitions vessel *MONT BLANC* collided on 6 December 1917 in Halifax harbour. Twenty-one minutes later, the French ship's cargo of some 2750 tonnes of explosives ignited, producing the greatest man-made explosion in history to that point. The city, a major convoy port and naval base of WORLD WAR I, was devastated. The populous north end of the city was virtually levelled by the blast and the fires that followed as stoves and furnaces set the wreckage alight. Across the harbour, Dartmouth was also hard hit and the noise of the blast was heard in Prince Edward Island. Ships at sea felt the tidal wave it produced.

The misery of survivors was compounded by fierce winter weather. The statistics of the disaster were appalling: of an urban population of some 50,000, almost 1600 died and over 9000 were injured; more than 13,500 buildings were destroyed or severely damaged; and 6000 were left homeless. The estimate of the cost of the damage was $35 million. Early relief had to be improvised, but there was a heartfelt effort from all across Canada and the U.S., amounting in all to some $30 million. The Halifax Relief Commission was incorporated in April 1918 to supervise the city's reconstruction.

Halifax garrison. A British naval and military base from its founding in 1749, Halifax's garrison, centred around the CITADEL, was a factor in imperial and Canadian defence into the 20th century. The garrison was maintained after all other British troops were withdrawn in 1871, but by 1903 the British had decided to withdraw entirely from Halifax. Canada undertook to accept the base in 1905.

Halifax patrol. A tiny fleet of small ships rushed into service as anti-submarine warfare vessels in 1917, the Halifax patrol was commanded by Capt. Walter HOSE (and in fact operated out of Sydney, N.S., for half the year and was called the Gulf of St Lawrence patrol). In May, the Americans provided eight patrol vessels to the Canadian navy, though only six of these submarine chasers were serviceable. Newly built escorts arrived the next month, finally giving Hose a reasonably adequate force to counter the Germans' U-boat cruisers.

Halifax riot, 1945. The city of Halifax had not been a happy posting for service personnel during WORLD WAR II. The population of 65,000 had been almost doubled by an influx of some 60,000 servicemen and women, and housing was short, the liquor laws were primitive, and good entertainment facilities were few. On V-E Day, 8 May 1945, businesses, restaurants, and stores shut down to celebrate the end of the war in Europe. Unfortunately neither civil nor military authorities had thought about planning for the celebrations, and the result was a military riot. Sailors, soldiers, and airmen sacked Keith's Brewery and looted 65,000 bottles of liquor from the government liquor stores. Now roaring drunk, the rioters turned their attention to some five hundred businesses, including taverns and restaurants. There was fighting and rape and three died while two hundred were arrested. The mayor blamed the ROYAL CANADIAN NAVY; the navy scapegoated Adm. L.W. MURRAY, in command in the city, and his career was effectively ruined.

Hall, Frederick William (1885–1915). Born in Ireland, Hall enlisted in the CANADIAN EXPEDITIONARY FORCE and served overseas with the 8th Battalion as a company sergeant major. At the battle of St Julien on 24 April 1915 he went into no man's land in an attempt to rescue a wounded soldier. He was killed by machine-gun fire and was awarded the VICTORIA CROSS.

Hall, William (1827–1904). Hall, a Black, was born in Nova Scotia and served in the Royal Navy. At Lucknow, India, he and one officer worked their gun under heavy fire, sending shot against Shah Najaf, a large fort held by Indian mutineers, until the infantry

secured it. He was awarded the VICTORIA CROSS.

Halton, Matthew Henry (1904–1956). The Alberta-born Halton established a reputation as Canada's pre-eminent foreign correspondent in the 1930s. With the outbreak of WORLD WAR II, he continued to file his despatches to the Toronto *Star* until he joined the CBC as its senior war correspondent. His graphic reports of fighting from SICILY, the ITALIAN CAMPAIGN, and the NORTHWEST EUROPE CAMPAIGN did much to bring the war home to Canadians.

Hampden bomber. The Hampden was designed in the mid-1930s by Handley-Page in Britain to achieve a top speed of 410 km/h. Some 160 Hampdens were built in Canada after 1938 by Canadian Associated Aircraft. About half those constructed here were used for training purposes (though the aircraft lacked dual controls) in Canada; the remainder went overseas and early in the war were employed on bombing raids; later, Hampdens were primarily used on anti-shipping operations.

Hanna, Robert (1887–1967). Born in Ireland, Company Sergeant-Major Hanna served with the 29th Battalion, CEF. On 21 August 1917 at HILL 70, Hanna took command after his company's officers had been killed and led the assault against a German strong point. He killed four defenders, silenced a machine gun, and held a trench against repeated counter-attacks. Hanna was awarded the VICTORIA CROSS.

Harkness, Douglas Scott (b. 1903). Born in Toronto, Harkness farmed and taught school in Alberta until WORLD WAR II when he served overseas with the artillery and won the GEORGE MEDAL. Elected to Parliament as a Progressive Conservative in 1945, he entered the DIEFENBAKER Cabinet in 1957 as Agriculture minister. He became Defence minister three years later, and soon clashed with External Affairs minister Howard Green over the acquisition of nuclear warheads to arm BOMARC antiaircraft missiles, the arming of CF101 aircraft with NORAD and HONEST JOHN surface-to-surface missiles, and the service of CF104 aircraft in Europe under NATO. For more than two years the struggle went on in the secrecy of the Cabinet; the first inkling that something might be wrong came in the CUBAN MISSILE CRISIS of October 1962 when Canada's NORAD defences were slow to go on alert. The Prime Minister, it turned out, had refused Harkness' request to follow the U.S. lead; the Defence minister, however, acted on his own and issued the orders to go on alert. This effectively destroyed relations between the two men, and when Diefenbaker continued to dither on accepting the nuclear warheads, Harkness resigned. His departure helped lead to the government's defeat in the House; other ministers quit, and the government lost the election of April 1963 to the Liberals (who accepted the warheads). Harkness remained in Parliament until 1972.

Harris, Lawren Stewart (1885–1970). A founder and leader of the Group of Seven, Harris was born in Brantford, Ont. He studied art in Berlin and then began to paint the Canadian landscape. During WORLD WAR I, he was a Canadian war artist, and the bleak canvases he produced in France and Flanders captured the misery of war. Harris' career flourished in the postwar years, and he eventually moved from landscapes to more abstract compositions.

Harvard trainer. In August 1939, agreement was reached to build the Harvard aircraft under licence in Canada, and it came into service in 1940, many being built by Noorduyn Aircraft of Montreal or Canadian Car and Foundry at Fort William, Ont. The Harvard had a top speed of 340 km/h. Difficult to fly but rugged, the two-seater Harvard was known wryly and affectionately as the 'Yellow Peril', and was used by the RCAF as an advanced trainer for a quarter-century.

Harvey, Frederick Maurice Watson (1888–1980). Irish born, Harvey was a lieutenant in LORD STRATHCONA'S HORSE in WORLD WAR I. The Canadian Cavalry Brigade of which the LSH was part was supporting the Fourth British Army's advance on the SOMME on 27 March 1917. Near Guyencourt, Harvey dismounted, ran into a wired trench and captured a machine gun, killing its gunner. He was awarded the VICTORIA CROSS.

Hazen, Sir John Douglas (1860–1937). A lawyer, born at Oromocto, N.B., Hazen won election to the House of Commons in 1891. He turned to the provincial field in 1899 and became premier of New Brunswick in 1908. He returned to federal politics in 1911, becoming minister of Marine and Fisheries and minister of Naval Affairs until 1917. He then served as chief justice of New Brunswick.

Heakes, Francis Vernon (1884–1989). Born in Toronto, Heakes served with the CANADIAN EXPEDITIONARY FORCE until transferring to the ROYAL FLYING CORPS. He left the forces at the end of the war but joined the ROYAL CANADIAN AIR FORCE in 1923 and, as a wing commander, helped set up RCAF headquarters in Britain in 1939. After service in Ottawa, he became an air vice marshal and Air Officer Commanding No. 1 Group in Newfoundland in 1942 and then Air Officer Commanding in Western Canada in 1944. He retired in 1946.

Hedgehog mortar. An antisubmarine warfare weapon developed in 1941 by the Royal Navy and belatedly installed on CORVETTES and escort vessels of the ROYAL CANADIAN NAVY in 1943, the Hedgehog was a 'spigot mortar' that threw a circular pattern of 24 30-kg depth charges 210 m ahead of the vessel. The Hedgehog permitted more accurate fire control by ASDIC than did standard depth charges.

Hellyer, Paul Theodore (b. 1923). Born at Waterford, Ont., Hellyer served in the RCAF during WORLD WAR II. Because of a surplus of aircrew, he was released and entered the army, being obliged to undergo basic training yet again. After the war he became a successful property developer, won election to Parliament as a Liberal in 1949, and served briefly as associate minister of National Defence in 1957. In Opposition, he continued his interest in defence and was instrumental in persuading Liberal leader Lester PEARSON to drop his opposition to nuclear warheads, a switch that helped bring down the DIEFENBAKER government in 1963. After Pearson's election victory, Hellyer became Defence minister and soon launched the military on a process of INTEGRATION and UNIFICATION that lasted until 1968 and produced enormous controversy.

Senior officers resigned; old soldiers, sailors, and airmen organized and lobbied, and the House of Commons and its committees debated the issue endlessly. But Hellyer persisted, convinced from his own wartime experience that the forces were rigid and hidebound. The resulting unified force, with a single uniform, was intended to reduce the costs imposed by service triplication and hence to allow more of the defence budget to be spent on equipment than hitherto; there were briefly some gains. Hellyer left Defence in 1967 before the final implementation of unification, failed to win the party leadership in 1968, and resigned from the Trudeau government in 1969. He started a new political party, Action Canada, then launched an unsuccessful bid for the Progressive Conservative party leadership in 1976. *Reading*: Paul Hellyer, *Damn the Torpedoes!* (Toronto, 1990)

Hendry, James (1911–1941). Born in Scotland, Cpl Hendry was serving in No. 1 Tunnelling Company, ROYAL CANADIAN ENGINEERS, employed on construction of a tunnel at Loch Laggan, Scotland on 13 June 1941. Seeing a fire at the powder house, Hendry shouted warnings and, though aware of the danger, proceeded to fight the blaze. The magazine exploded and he was killed, but his warning and actions saved lives. He was awarded the GEORGE CROSS.

Hennessy, Ralph L. (b. 1918). Born in Scotland, Hennessy joined the ROYAL CANADIAN NAVY in 1936 and served at sea in WORLD WAR II, winning the DISTINGUISHED SERVICE CROSS for his role in destroying the Nazi submarine U-210. He held a number of senior appointments in the forces after UNIFICATION, notably comptroller-general and chief of personnel. He retired as a vice-admiral in 1970.

Herbert, Ivor John Caradoc (1851–1917?). Herbert enlisted in the British Army in 1870 and served in Egypt and the Sudan, and in the Boer War. Although only a colonel, he came to Canada in the local rank of major-general to be GENERAL OFFICER COMMANDING the MILITIA in 1890 and held that post until 1895.

'Herbie'. The most popular cartoon character in the FIRST CANADIAN ARMY, Herbie was the creation of Bing COUGHLIN. In training, in action, or on leave, Herbie was always in trouble. Shrewd, brave when necessary, always griping about officers and non-commissioned officers (NCOs), Herbie personified the Canadian soldier. A book of Herbie cartoons was published in 1946 and reprinted in 1959.

Hercules aircraft. The Lockheed C130 Hercules began RCAF service in 1960 and continues to fill a variety of roles for the CANADIAN FORCES. The aircraft serves Canada's troops in NATO, flies scheduled runs in Canada and overseas, serves as a search and rescue aircraft, and is used for training navigators. The four-engine aircraft is able to carry heavy loads, can drop paratroops, and can fly at 618 km/h.

Hertzberg, Halfdan Fenton Harboe (1884–1959). A professional soldier, Hertzberg was born in Toronto of Norwegian descent and educated at the University of Toronto from which he graduated in engineering in 1907. While he worked as an engineer, he served in the MILITIA and on the outbreak of war he joined the 1ST CANADIAN DIVISION. He rose rapidly and by the end of the war was the much decorated chief engineer of the division. Hertzberg stayed in the PERMANENT FORCE, serving in staff posts between the wars until he was promoted to major-general in 1938 and became quartermaster-general. Although he had hopes of being given command of a division, this was not to be; instead from 1940–44, 'Hertz' was a much-loved commandant of the ROYAL MILITARY COLLEGE. He retired in 1945.

High Frequency Direction Finding. HF/DF or 'Huff-Duff' sets were used in WORLD WAR II by the Allied navies to pick up high frequency U-boat radio signals and to pinpoint their locations. The technique had been used in WORLD WAR I and a system of shore radio detection finding stations had been established on Canada's East Coast in the latter part of the war. In the 1939 war, this was used from the outset, Canada playing a substantial part. Ship-borne sets, developed in Britain in 1941 and much improved by 1942, gave CONVOY escorts a much better chance at determining the bearing of U-boats closing in for an attack. The ROYAL

CANADIAN NAVY was slow to fit the equipment to its ships, a tardiness that contributed to its difficulties in 1942–43.

High White Forest, The. Ralph Allen's novel of WORLD WAR II was published in the U.S. in 1964 and contained large portions of an earlier novel, *Homemade Banners*, that found only a Canadian market. The novel is notable for its description of the NATIONAL RESOURCES MOBILIZATION ACT soldiers, or ZOMBIES, and the pressures put upon them in training by General Service volunteers and their officers.

Hill 70. General Sir Arthur CURRIE's CANADIAN CORPS was directed to capture Lens, France on 7 July 1917. The destroyed coal town was dominated from the north by Hill 70, and Currie managed to get his orders changed so that the height would become the major objective. Bad weather delayed the carefully planned assault by two divisions until the pre-dawn darkness of 15 August. The attack was successful, the Canadians reaching their initial objectives (the Blue Line) with relative ease and by 6 a.m. most units had reached the ultimate (Green Line) objective. Casualties numbered some 3500 in the first day's fighting. German counterattacks soon began and lasted until 18 August. Currie called the Hill 70 struggle 'altogether the hardest battle in which the Corps has participated'.

Hindenburg Line. Running from Arras through St Quentin to the River Aisne near Soissons, the Hindenburg Line was built by 65,000 men after September 1916. The defences incorporated two lines, each of two trench lines, and used reverse slopes wherever possible to provide protection against artillery fire. In March 1917, the Germans surprised the Allies by withdrawing more than 32 km into the formidable new position. In September 1918 it fell to the CANADIAN CORPS to attack the Hindenburg Line.

The first attack on the DROCOURT-QUÉANT Line on 2–3 September was successful, the Canadians pressing on toward the high ground overlooking the River Sensée and the incomplete CANAL DU NORD. The canal was a formidable and well-defended obstacle, overlooked from high ground to the east. Gen. Sir Arthur CURRIE's plan was to take Bourlon Wood and the high ground to the north and then to cross the canal. The attack went in on 27 September under a rolling barrage, some of the infantry battalions accompanied by tanks, and was successful, the Canadians pressing on towards CAMBRAI which was taken after heavy fighting on 8–9 October. In all, the Corps suffered almost 31,000 casualties in the six weeks of fighting from 22 August.

Hitler Line. On 23 May 1944, I CANADIAN CORPS, fighting as a corps for the first time in the war, launched a major attack against the Adolf Hitler Line south of Rome. The French Expeditionary Corps had pushed through a lightly fortified part of the line six days earlier, but the defences facing the 1ST CANADIAN DIVISION under Gen. Christopher VOKES and the still-untried 5TH CANADIAN ARMOURED DIVISION under Gen. Bert HOFFMEISTER remained unbreached and strong. Based on earthworks, concrete pillboxes, bunkers, mines, and concertina wire in huge concentrations, the Hitler Line was hit first by the 1st Division. A gap opened, and the tanks of the 5th Armoured, soon to be dubbed 'Hoffy's mighty maroon machine', poured through. The Germans broke, their defences crumbled, and the Canadians followed in pursuit. But the 5th Division and the Corps headquarters, under Gen. E.L.M. BURNS, contributed to a massive traffic jam that greatly slowed the advance. Rome was taken on 4 June by American troops. The attack on the Hitler Line proved unquestionably to have been one of the decisive battles of the ITALIAN CAMPAIGN.
Reading: G.W.L. Nicholson, *The Canadians in Italy* (Ottawa, 1956)

HMCS. Acronym for His (or Her) Majesty's Canadian Ship.

Hobson, Frederick (1875–1917). Serving with the 20th Battalion, CEF, in the struggle for HILL 70 on 18 August 1917, Sgt Hobson resisted a German counter-attack by digging out a Lewis gun and putting it into action. The gun jammed, but Hobson charged the enemy with a bayonet, singlehandedly holding them off until he was finally killed. He had left 15 enemy dead around his position, and he was awarded the VICTORIA CROSS.

Hochwald, Battle of, 1945. Located on a ridge in front of Xanten, Germany, the Hochwald, a densely wooded forest, was the target of Operation Blockbuster on 26 February 1945. FIRST CANADIAN ARMY, its attack spearheaded by the 2ND and 3RD CANADIAN DIVISIONS of Gen. Guy SIMONDS' II CANADIAN CORPS, used tanks or KANGA-ROOs to transport the infantry under ARTIFICIAL MOONLIGHT. The Germans resisted with great skill and ferocity, inflicting heavy casualties on the attackers, especially at Mooshof. After two days, the Canadians were into the Hochwald itself, a rabbit warren of bunkers and mines. After heavy casualties, the forest was cleared by 4 March; Xanten fell on the 8th, and by the 10th all enemy resistance west of the Rhine River had been eliminated.
Reading: C.P. Stacey, *The Victory Campaign* (Ottawa, 1960)

Hoffmeister, Bertram Meryl (b. 1907). Arguably the most successful Canadian division commander of WORLD WAR II, Hoffmeister was born in Vancouver. He worked in the lumber industry before the war and served in the MILITIA with the Seaforth Highlanders, with whom he went overseas in 1939 as a major. By 1942 after a staff course, he was commanding the Seaforths and led the battalion in SICILY. In November 1943 he became a brigade commander, and in March 1944 was a major-general commanding the 5TH CANADIAN ARMOURED DIVISION, 'Hoffy's Mighty Maroon Machine'. A general who led from the front, Hoffmeister won three DSOs and the regard of his troops whom he led through tough fighting in the LIRI VALLEY, the smashing of the GOTHIC LINE, and in the Netherlands. After V-E Day he was named to command the 6th Division destined for service in the Pacific. He returned to the business world after the war.

Holland, Edward James Gibson (1878–1948). While serving with the ROYAL CANADIAN DRAGOONS during the SOUTH AFRICAN WAR, Sgt Holland was involved in a fierce action at LELIEFONTEIN on 7 November 1900. Manning a Colt machine gun, he held off the Boers until his ammunition ran out. Then, to deny the gun to the enemy, he lifted off its very hot barrel and rode away with it under his arm. He was awarded the VICTORIA CROSS.

Holmes, Thomas William (1898–1950). While serving with the 4th CANADIAN MOUNTED RIFLES at PASSCHENDAELE on 26 October 1917, Pte Holmes singlehandedly ran forward and threw hand grenades, killing or wounding the crews of two enemy machine guns holding up a Canadian attack. He then returned to his own men for another grenade, rushed forward once more and attacked a pillbox, compelling its 19 occupants to surrender. He was awarded the VICTORIA CROSS.

Homefront, World War I. The shock of the Great War on the Canadian people was likely much greater than that of WORLD WAR II a quarter century later. No one in 1914 had any inkling of what lay ahead, and the popular expectations were for a short war and a glorious march on Berlin. Few had any doubts about the justice of the cause, and German *kultur* was quickly painted as evil and the Kaiser as a villain beyond compare. The Germans' 'rape' of Belgium, their alleged cutting off the breasts of Belgian nuns and destruction of great university libraries was seen as merely what could be expected of a newly demonized foe. And in such a struggle many, perhaps most, English Canadians thought of themselves as Britain's ally, not its colony. This was not true in Quebec, where French Canadians had only the faintest links to France and felt scarcely any allegiance to Britain, or in Canada's ethnic communities, whose members in many cases were German or from the Austro-Hungarian Empire. The seeds of trouble were there from the onset.

The economy was in recession when the war began and the initial shock of the conflict, with its interruption of trade, made things worse. It was not until late 1915 that the war-induced boom began to pick up, that grain sales began to increase, and that the first products from munitions factories began to be sold. Canada's munitions production, largely consisting of artillery shells and after November 1915 wholly controlled by the IMPERIAL MUNITIONS BOARD, a British agency operating in Canada, amounted to more than $1 billion worth by the armistice. This was widely seen as a miracle, and it may have been; if so, it was largely attributable to Sir Joseph FLAVELLE who whipped industry and labour into line.

The war created labour shortages, drawing young men and women from rural areas into the factories in the cities. That deprived farmers, struggling to bring in large crops for which, for once, good prices could be secured, of their labour force, and greatly increased tension between cityfolk and country-dwellers. The wartime pressure for a 'New National Policy' of lower tariffs and the postwar Progressive party explosion had their roots in this strain. Another factor, of course, was CONSCRIPTION, something much sought after in urban English Canada from 1916 on. To farmers, conscription could only worsen the labour shortage they faced, and their arguments that food was as much a war-winning weapon as a soldier with a rifle, while true, received little credence in the fevered atmosphere of 1917. Victory was everything, and Canada needed every man at the front. To the élites in English Canada, even more than the farmers, that meant French Canadians. Quebec's sons had not volunteered for war in anything like the numbers of their British-born and British-origin compatriots. French Canadians, however, fostered their own grievances, pointing to Ontario's Regulation 17 which limited French-language schooling as evidence that the Prussians were at large in Canada—only in Ontario, they said, was the French language truly threatened. In the circumstances, why should they go overseas to fight in a war that was of no real interest to Canada? This came to its head with the passage of the MILITARY SERVICE ACT 1917, the formation of the UNION GOVERNMENT, and the virulently racist 1917 general election that saw Sir Robert BORDEN returned to power at the head of a wholly English-speaking administration. For good measure, and to ensure their victory, the Bordenites had passed the WARTIME ELECTIONS ACT to disfranchise recent immigrants and to give the vote to women relatives of soldiers. Two weeks before the election, moreover, the Union Government exempted farmers from the conscription call-up. That helped in the election but when, in the spring of 1918, the government withdrew its exemptions just at the time of planting, rural rage was awesome.

The war also saw the emergence of social reform. The federal women's franchise, even if granted in a purely partisan way in 1917, was a step forward. Some provinces had already given the vote to women whose wartime services had tended to wash away male resistance. Similarly, prohibition triumphed everywhere, the people scarcely daring to use grain for alcohol that could be used to win the war. And the first federal-provincial shared-cost program, one to counter venereal disease which was rampant among the troops at home and abroad, was similarly a wartime necessity.

What the war did above all, however, was to create an enormous gap between those who fought and those who didn't. The bitterness with which the troops returned, leaving 60,000 comrades behind, the inchoate rage against slackers, immigrants, and French-Canadians, was to embitter Canadian life for a generation. Conscription in World War II, something that was arguably never necessary, became an issue precisely because of the memories of the Great War. *Reading*: R.C. Brown and Ramsay Cook, *Canada 1896–1921* (Toronto, 1974)

Homefront, World War II. The Canadian attitude at the beginning of World War II was one of resignation. The memory of the heavy casualties in WORLD WAR I naturally weighed heavily on the nation. The Great Depression had devastated the economy for ten years and continued unabated in its severity. And French-speaking Canadians, bitterly resentful of the way in which the English Canadian majority had imposed CONSCRIPTION 1917, had no desire to see Canada enter into another 'British' war in Europe that might lead to heavy casualties and renewed demands for compulsory military service. On the other hand, many, perhaps most, English Canadians still assumed that when Britain was at war, Canada was at war. The Liberal government of Mackenzie KING managed to bring this reluctant, divided country into the war through its prime minister's political skill, a feat that was accomplished by promising that there would be no conscription for overseas service and by pledging a war of 'limited liability'. Those attitudes prevailed for ten months. Not until the fall of France did most Canadians, including their government, take the war seriously as a struggle for survival; not until the summer of 1940 did war orders from Britain or the Canadian government begin to reach the factories in quantity. From that point until the victory over Japan in August 1945, the Canadian war effort increased exponentially.

The economy in 1939 was still in the doldrums. Official estimates had 400,000 workers unemployed and a million Canadians on direct relief. On 1 October 1939, only 3.8 million were gainfully employed, with 2 million men and women in agriculture and the rest in non-agricultural industry or self-employed. The country's Gross National Product was $5.6 billion. The war dramatically altered these numbers. The GNP in 1945 was $11.8 billion, a figure slightly below the 1944 total. Unemployment had disappeared and 5.1 million were gainfully employed, with 3.2 million in non-agricultural industry and 1.9 million working in agriculture. The manufacturing sector of the economy had almost doubled, and war industry at its peak in October 1943 employed 1.2 million men and women or 13.3 per cent of the total population over 14 years of age.

Production increased dramatically in virtually every sector. In agriculture, good weather helped produce bumper crops of grain — 556 million bushels in 1942, for example. The production of pork more than doubled and that of beef increased by more than a third; and agricultural exports rose more than threefold. In the iron and steel sectors, increases were similarly dramatic. Pig iron and steel ingot production more than doubled between 1939 and 1944, and this fuelled astonishing developments in war industry. A country that in 1939 had built no merchant ships by 1944 had produced 345; aircraft production was 14,700 by the end of 1944, while 707,000 military vehicles and 45,710 armoured vehicles were built. Plant expansion was heavily financed by government which established numerous Crown corporations and financed corporate expansion.

The total of war production in Canada was $10.9 billion by 1945, fourth among the Allies. Canada's war production amounted to one-seventh of total British Commonwealth production, but only 30 per cent of this production was used by the Canadian forces. Virtually all the rest was given freely to Canada's allies as gifts or under MUTUAL AID, with the lion's share going to Britain. Mutual Aid was a contribution to the Allied

war effort, but it was also an investment in full employment in Canada.

Extraordinarily, the economic war effort had simultaneously raised living standards to peaks never before attained. It was not that wages rose so much as that there was work for everyone. Full employment and all the overtime anyone wanted meant that families, often with every member over the age of fifteen gainfully employed, had the money to eat better, even with rationing of meat, butter, sugar, tea, and coffee. Moreover, the fact that consumer goods were unavailable meant that savings rose, a cushion for the expected postwar downturn. (On the other hand, the fact that money was on hand in an age of scarcity meant that a black market grew up.) The government's tough economic policies controlled inflation well. From the beginning of the war until October 1941, when wage and price controls were slapped on, the cost of living had risen by 17.8 per cent; but from October 1941 to April 1945, the percentage increase was a mere 2.8 per cent. This was the most successful record of all the belligerents'.

Prime Minister KING shaped domestic politics during the war. He withstood a challenge to the war effort from Quebec when, in September 1939, Premier Maurice Duplessis called a snap election and charged that Ottawa was using the conflict as an excuse to pursue centralist policies. Extraordinarily, the federal ministers from Quebec told the province's voters that they would resign if Duplessis was re-elected. That, they said, would leave Quebec exposed to conscription. The voters listened and elected a Liberal government. In January 1940, by contrast, the Ontario legislature voted to condemn the federal government's lackadaisical war effort. King seized the opportunity to call a snap election of his own for 26 March which he won with a huge majority. As important, King had the election out of the way before the phony war turned into an Allied disaster. The defeats of April and May 1940 put enormous pressure on the government to step up the war effort, and King responded with the NATIONAL RESOURCES MOBILIZATION ACT (NRMA) which authorized conscription for home defence and called for a NATIONAL REGISTRATION. King pledged again that his government would not implement conscription for overseas service. While there was some opposition in French

Canada to the NRMA, the prompt INTERN-MENT of the mayor of Montreal, Camilien Houde, who had urged his compatriots not to register, ended it. The question of conscription, however, did not go away and there were CONSCRIPTION CRISES in 1942 and 1944 that almost wrecked the government and severely damaged national unity.

Still, the question of conscription aside, the Liberal government ran the war superbly. The Liberals in September 1943 had announced their intention to create a social welfare state, largely because the mandarins of the federal bureaucracy had concluded that only through government outlays could a postwar return to depression be averted. Family allowances were introduced, offering mothers a cash payment for each child. Through an order-in-council (PC 1003, 17 February 1944), employees' rights to join and form unions were confirmed and machinery for defining and certifying bargaining units laid out. In effect, Canadian labour had its Magna Carta. At the same time, massive sums were pumped into housing, the re-establishment of veterans, and export promotion. The government even pledged itself to the goal of full employment early in 1945. Thus when the federal election was held on 11 June 1945, fortuitously after the war in Europe had ended and before Canada's promise of a division for the Pacific war had time to be implemented, King's government was re-elected with a bare majority.
Reading: J.L. Granatstein, *Canada's War: The Politics of the Mackenzie King Government 1939–45* (Toronto, 1990)

Home War Establishment. The ROYAL CANADIAN AIR FORCE was responsible for Canada's air defence during WORLD WAR II and took its role seriously. In 1939, of 23 squadrons to be mobilized, 17 were to remain in Canada largely to defend the Atlantic and Pacific coasts. At the end of 1940, there were 12 squadrons in Canada and three overseas. But the Japanese threat to the West Coast after December 1941 forced the government to increase strength there, and in March 1942, Ottawa decided on a Home War Establishment of 49 squadrons, 25 of which would be on the coast. Though this total was not reached, by 1943 there were 39 squadrons in Canada (compared to 38 overseas). The number fell off dramatically thereafter as the threat declined. The Home War Establishment was re-named Western Hemisphere Operations in 1944.
Reading: W.A.B. Douglas, *The Creation of a National Air Force* (Ottawa, 1986)

Honest John. The DIEFENBAKER government decided to equip the Canadian brigade group in NATO with the Honest John surface-to-surface missile. Of American design and manufacture, the missile was designed only to carry a nuclear warhead for use against troop concentrations. The Honest John warheads, required by U.S. law to be kept under American control, thus were part of the nuclear crisis of 1962–63 that brought down the Progressive Conservative government; the Liberals' acceptance of the warheads allowed the Honest John to become operational in 1963.

Honey, Samuel Lewis (1894–1918). While serving in the 78th Battalion, CEF, Lt Honey, as the sole remaining officer, took command of his company and reorganized the men at Bourlon Wood on 27 September 1918. He singlehandedly rushed a machine-gun nest and captured the guns and ten prisoners. Honey then organized the company's defences, repelled four counterattacks, and led a raid on the enemy that resulted in the taking of three machine guns. Finally on 29 September, Honey led his men against another German position; he died of wounds the next day. He was awarded the VICTORIA CROSS.

Hong Kong. When Japan launched itself into WORLD WAR II on 7 December 1941, on the next day its powerful forces attacked the British Crown Colony of Hong Kong, located near Canton. Among the tiny possession's defenders were two battalions of Canadians, the Royal Rifles of Canada and the Winnipeg Grenadiers, and a brigade headquarters commanded by Brig. J.K. LAWSON. The decision to send the troops was taken in haste in the fall, as Ottawa responded to a request from London for a reinforcement of the colony's defences that, it was hoped, might indicate to Tokyo that Britain was serious about defending its position in the Far East. Neither battalion was especially well trained, Gen. H.D.G. CRERAR, the CHIEF OF THE GENERAL STAFF, apparently believing that Hong Kong would not be a theatre of action. If that was a misjudgment, it was an understandable one: London's dark assessments of the indefensibility of the colony were not passed to Ottawa, and Canada had no intelligence assessment capacity of its own.

The Canadians arrived on 16 November, their transport scheduled to follow them a few weeks later. Before they had time to more than sample the fleshpots of the city or to become acclimated to the weather and the steep hills, the Japanese 38th Division's attack fell on them and the 12,000 British, Indian, and local defenders. Without air cover, with few heavy weapons, and no transport (the Canadian vehicles were diverted to the Philippines), the defenders were outclassed, and the Japanese rapidly broke through the still-incomplete Gin Drinkers' Line on the Kowloon or mainland side and forced the British back to Hong Kong island. An amphibious assault put the Japanese ashore on 18 December and the Canadians, split up among their own commanders and the British, found themselves engaged in a hopeless defensive struggle. Short of food, water, and medicine, they took part in a series of gallant but ineffective counter-attacks, all the while being forced back into shrinking perimeters.

There were many examples of great courage. Company Sergeant-Major John OSBORN of the Winnipeg regiment fell on a Japanese hand grenade and absorbed its blast, thus sparing his men. He won a posthumous VICTORIA CROSS. And Brig. Lawson, his headquarters overrun on 19 December, went out, armed only with a pistol, to 'fight it out'. He too was killed. By the time of the British surrender on Christmas Day, the Canadians had lost 23 officers and 267 men killed with with another 483 wounded. That was almost forty per cent of the 1975 Canadians on the island.

The ordeal was just beginning for the survivors. The Japanese army showed dreadful brutality in its treatment of prisoners, bayonetting wounded, raping nurses, and randomly killing many. Those who were spared endured foul conditions in prison camps, trying to survive on rations that were little more than 800 calories a day. Prison guards were as brutal as the infantry and one, KANAO INOUYE, a Canadian-born Japanese known as the 'Kamloops Kid', took special pains to persecute and torture Canadians. Another 287 Canadians died in PoW camps in Hong Kong and Japan; the survivors were in a pathetic and weakened condition on their liberation in September 1945. See also ROYAL COMMISSION ON THE CANADIAN EXPEDITIONARY FORCE ... TO HONG KONG.

Reading: Carl Vincent, *No Reason Why* (Stittsville, Ont., 1981)

Hornell, David Ernest (1910–1944). RCAF Flight Lieutenant Hornell was pilot of a twin-engined amphibious aircraft on anti-submarine patrol off the Shetland Islands on 24 June 1944. He spotted a surfaced U-boat and attacked and sank it with depth charges, although the submarine's gun badly damaged his plane. Hornell managed to bring it down on heavy seas, organized his crew to take turns in the one dinghy, and by the time of rescue the next day was exhausted and blind. He died very soon after being picked up. He was awarded the VICTORIA CROSS.

Hose, Walter (1875–1965). Born at sea, Hose served in the Royal Navy for 21 years before transferring to Canada's fledgling navy in 1912. During WORLD WAR I he was captain of the *RAINBOW* on the west coast; then he commanded defences on the Atlantic. He became DIRECTOR OF THE NAVAL STAFF in 1921 (a title changed to CHIEF OF NAVAL STAFF in 1928), a post he held until his retirement in 1934. As director, he was obliged to resist persistent efforts to starve his tiny fleet or to eliminate it altogether.

Howe, Clarence Decatur (1886–1960). One of the most powerful politicians in Canadian history and the minister responsible for mobilizing Canada's war production in WORLD WAR II, Howe was born in Waltham, Mass. A civil engineer, he came to Canada in 1908 and taught at Dalhousie University, then formed a company to build grain elevators and prospered. Howe ran for the House of Commons in 1935 and became a minister in Mackenzie KING's government. In 1940, King put him in charge of the new Department of Munitions and Supply, and Howe was in his element. With the fall of France, the cap came off Canadian war spending. The direct and brusque Howe negotiated with the business world and, using a cadre of 'dollar-a-year' businessmen and working closely with the WARTIME PRICES

AND TRADE BOARD, created Crown corporations galore to build everything from aircraft to ships to shells. Howe's influence extended to virtually every aspect of Canada's manufacturing industry. Resources were diverted to the places they were needed, the labour force was controlled, and the goods poured forth in an astonishing stream, so much so that Canada delivered one-seventh of all Commonwealth war production. In 1944, Howe took the additional post of minister of Reconstruction which gave him effective control of the conversion of Canadian society from war to peace. This task was similarly well handled and the feared return of the depression of the 1930s did not occur. In 1948, Howe became minister of Trade and Commerce in Louis St Laurent's government and right-hand man to the new prime minister. The outbreak of the KOREAN WAR saw him take on the newly-created DEPARTMENT OF DEFENCE PRODUCTION in 1951, and Howe once again plunged into the task of mobilizing the country for defence. Working closely with the United States in industrial mobilization, he nonetheless encouraged the development of aircraft manufacturing, spurring production of the CF100 and the ARROW. By 1957, the advent of the missile age and the escalation of development costs began to make it clear that concern over the Arrow's cost could not be overcome. Howe was beginning to move toward cancellation of the project, but events—the defeat of the Liberal government —intervened and spared him the decision. His power had been very great, but his methods and his open arrogance in Parliament were perhaps better suited to the urgent necessities of war.
Reading: Robert Bothwell and W. Kilbourn, *C.D. Howe* (Toronto, 1979)

Howitzer. A short-barrelled artillery cannon firing low-velocity shells.

H2S radar. A target-finding device for WORLD WAR II bombers, the H2S's 10-cm radar bounced an echo off the ground, producing a 'map' of the area below on a screen in the bomber. Its maritime operation adaptation was known as ASV III, the initials standing for air-to-surface vessel.

Huff-Duff. See HIGH FREQUENCY DIRECTION FINDING.

Hughes, Garnet Burk (1880–1937). The son of Sam HUGHES, he was educated at the ROYAL MILITARY COLLEGE and worked as an engineer while serving in the MILITIA. At the outbreak of WORLD WAR I he served as a brigade-major in the 1ST CANADIAN DIVISION and rose rapidly until he was commanding the 5TH CANADIAN DIVISION in Britain by 1917. But General Sir Arthur CURRIE, in command of the CANADIAN CORPS, refused to have Hughes, hitherto his good friend, as one of his division commanders, and he remained in England until his division was broken up for reinforcements. This deeply embittered Sam Hughes' relations with Currie.

Hughes, Sir Samuel (1853–1921). One of the most contentious figures in our history, Sam Hughes was born at Darlington, Canada West and educated in Toronto. He made his way in property speculation, purchased a newspaper in Lindsay, Ont., and won election to Parliament as a Conservative in 1892. A stalwart of the MILITIA and a convinced believer that professional officers, British or Canadian, were inherently inferior to commonsensical amateurs, he wormed his way into a staff job during the SOUTH AFRICAN WAR over the opposition of the Department of MILITIA AND DEFENCE. His role in the war was highly creditable, though it probably did not live up to Hughes' claim that he was entitled to one and perhaps two VICTORIA CROSS awards. A firm proponent of the ROSS RIFLE, the strongly nationalist and imperialist Hughes became minister of Militia and Defence in the government of Robert BORDEN in 1911. His energy and drive led to great improvements in the efficiency of the militia, and his role in mobilizing the CANADIAN EXPEDITIONARY FORCE in August 1914 for WORLD WAR I was, while it threw away existing plans, nonetheless an astonishing feat. Where Hughes went truly wrong, however, was in allowing patronage and cronyism to influence officer appointments and the placing of equipment and munitions contracts; the resulting scandals caused great difficulty for the government. By 1916, his behaviour had become increasingly erratic and Borden, driven near to distraction, finally sacked him in November 1916.
Reading: R.G. Haycock, *Sam Hughes* (Waterloo, 1986)

Humphrey, Jack Weldon (1901–1967). Born at Saint John, N.B. Humphrey's grittily realistic paintings had begun to give him a reputation prior to WORLD WAR II. During the war his paintings of air force life—and death—verged on the surrealistic as did his spectral and eerie scenes of night raids against Germany.

Hunters' Lodges. Founded in 1838 to liberate British North America from British rule, the Hunters' Lodges were the creation of Canadian rebels who had fled to the United States after the failure of the REBELLIONS OF 1837. They soon drew American support and in 1838 the Lodges launched a number of raids over the border, all of which were defeated. Efforts to provoke tension between Britain and the U.S. (including the blowing up of BROCK's monument on the Niagara frontier) also failed to succeed, and after a (belatedly) stern presidential warning in 1841, the Lodges went out of business.

***Huron*, HMCS.** A TRIBAL CLASS DESTROYER, *Huron* was commissioned in 1943 and served with the British Home Fleet, escorting convoys to Murmansk. Then *Huron* served in the English Channel and on escort duties. The war with Japan ended before the ship was ready for Pacific duty. Paid off in 1946, *Huron* was recommissioned in 1950 for KOREAN WAR duties and had two tours there. The ship was finally paid off in 1963 and broken up. The second ship of this name, an *Iroquois* class DDH280 helicopter-equipped destroyer escort, was commissioned in 1972.

Hurricane fighter. The RCAF's first monoplane interceptor, the Hawker Hurricane was the main aircraft used during the BATTLE OF BRITAIN. A few were purchased in Britain and brought into service in Canada in 1939; during the war, 1400 of the aircraft were built at Fort William, Ont. The single-seat Hurricane went through various designs; it had a top speed of 530 km/h and carried eight .303-calibre machine guns; later versions were armed with cannons.

Husky, Operation. The codename for the invasion of SICILY, Husky was a British-American-Canadian invasion from the sea that went in on 10 July 1943. The IST CANADIAN DIVISION under General Guy SI-MONDS landed near PACHINO and took its objective, the airfield there, almost at once and with very light casualties.

Hutcheson, Bellenden Seymour (1883–1954). Born in the United States, Capt. Hutcheson, a doctor, served in the Canadian Army Medical Corps on attachment to the 75th Battalion, CEF. On 2 September 1918, his unit participated in the attack on the DROCOURT-QUÉANT LINE. Hutcheson dressed the wounds of an officer under heavy fire and evacuated him to safety. He then rushed forward in full view of the enemy to attend to a wounded sergeant. He was awarded the VICTORIA CROSS.

Hutton, Sir Edward Thomas Henry (1848–1923). Major-General Hutton came to Canada as GENERAL OFFICER COMMANDING the MILITIA in 1898. He complained loudly (and correctly) about the inefficiency of the patronage-wracked militia, and at the outset of the SOUTH AFRICAN WAR he went behind the LAURIER government's back to organize a Canadian contingent. The government was on the verge of demanding his ouster when London offered him a command in South Africa.

Hyde Park Declaration. On a 'grand Sunday' in April 1941, President F.D. Roosevelt and Prime Minister Mackenzie KING met at the president's home in Hyde Park, N.Y. Canada was in serious difficulty because her imports from the still-neutral United States had increased greatly as a result of WORLD WAR II, and the country was short of the U.S. dollars to pay for them. At Hyde Park on 20 April, the two leaders decided that the United States would buy more raw materials in Canada, thus easing the dollar shortage. More important still, Roosevelt agreed that Britain's account would be charged under the Lend-Lease Act for industrial components sent to Canada for incorporation into munitions destined for Britain. This agreement, made without reference to Congress or Parliament, effectively freed Canada of financial worries for the remainder of the war. On the other hand, it undoubtedly linked the two North American economies more closely together, something that carried over into the peace.

Hydra. Located at CAMP X, near Toronto, Hydra was a wireless communications centre used by the British in WORLD WAR II for the transmission of top secret information across the Atlantic. Hydra was linked by land lines to the headquarters of BRITISH SECURITY COORDINATION in New York City.

I

Iceland. The stunning German victories in Denmark, Norway, the Low Countries, and France in April and May 1940 raised concerns in London about the safety of Iceland, critically located in the North Atlantic. In May, Whitehall asked Canada to garrison the island, and the first Canadian troops of 'Z Force' under Brig. L.F. Page arrived on 16 June 1940. One battalion remained over the winter of 1940–41, but the remainder of the brigade committed to Iceland left for England on 31 October. The island was frequently used by ROYAL CANADIAN NAVY vessels, and the ROYAL CANADIAN AIR FORCE's 162 Squadron was based there from 1943–45 for anti-submarine operations.

Ile aux Noix. An island in the Richelieu River, Ile aux Noix was a strategic point on the route northward from Lake Champlain to Montreal. MONTCALM made it one of his major defensive posts in 1759; it was taken by the Americans in 1775, and it was garrisoned during and after the WAR OF 1812 as Fort Lennox. After 1819, the British modernized the fortifications on the island.

Imo. A Belgian relief ship of Norwegian registry, the *Imo* was leaving Halifax for the open sea when she collided with the French freighter *MONT BLANC*, carrying 2300 tonnes of picric acid, 60 tonnes of guncotton and 220 tonnes of TNT. The explosion produced by the collision levelled much of the city of Halifax. See HALIFAX EXPLOSION.

Imperial defence. Britain's world-wide empire was costly to defend and from the mid-19th century onwards London was increasingly interested in passing part of the burden on to its colonies. In Canada, there were advocates of Imperial defence, those who reckoned that by contributing Canada could keep Britain involved in North America and hence a defence against the United States; others supported it in the hope that Canada, huge and potentially rich as it was, might some day inherit the entire empire; still others simply assumed Canada was British and had to do its bit. The impact of WORLD WAR I largely put paid to the concept of Imperial defence, though Canada's military forces continued to be modelled on those of Britain. Mackenzie KING, who opposed the idea of Imperial defence and automatic military commitments, nonetheless was a believer in the British way and wanted his country to go into any major war at Britain's side. Thus it was he who took Canada to war again in 1939, a decision made with the support of English-speaking Canada.

Imperial Munitions Board. A creation of London's Ministry of Munitions, the Board was set up in November 1915 to handle British contracts for munitions and supplies in Canada. Headed by Toronto businessman Sir Joseph FLAVELLE, the IMB placed contracts for shells, ships and aircraft, entered into agreements with U.S. government departments after 1917, and established and operated its own factories when private industry was unable to produce the goods.

Imperial War Cabinet. Convened on 2 March 1917 by British prime minister David Lloyd George, the Imperial War Cabinet discussed matters relating to the conduct of WORLD WAR I. Sir Robert BORDEN attended for Canada, using the trip as an opportunity to visit troops in Britain and at the front. So impressed was he by the gravity of the war situation that he returned to Canada

determined to impose CONSCRIPTION. Borden's later description of the War Cabinet was that it was a 'Cabinet of Governments. Every Prime Minister . . . is responsible to his own Parliament and to his own people.' Borden also looked to this meeting as a harbinger, seeing in it 'the genesis of a development in the constitutional relations of the Empire, which will form the basis of its unity in the years to come.'
Reading: R.C. Brown, Robert Laird Brown: A Biography, Vol. 2 (Toronto, 1980)

Imperial War Conference. Convened in London by British Prime Minister Lloyd George in March 1917, the Imperial War Conference discussed imperial questions unrelated to WORLD WAR I and met concurrently with the IMPERIAL WAR CABINET. At Sir Robert BORDEN's initiation, the conference passed Resolution IX that proclaimed the dominions to be 'autonomous nations' entitled to 'an adequate voice in foreign policy' and 'continuous consultation'.

Income War Tax. Introduced as a temporary measure by the government of Sir Robert BORDEN in 1917 to help pay for WORLD WAR I, this was Canada's first direct tax on personal and business income. The government had suffered much criticism for its willingness to implement CONSCRIPTION of men but not the conscription of wealth; the income tax was the response. The levy initially was very light, but the temporary measure became permanent.

Incorporated militia. Created from FLANK COMPANIES during the WAR OF 1812, the incorporated militia formed several battalions and were as credible a force as the amateur Canadian MILITIA could produce.

India, UN peacekeeping in. See UNIPOM, UNMOGIP.

Industrial Defence Board. Appointed by order-in-council on 20 April 1948, the Board was to advise 'on all matters relating to the industrial war potential of Canada' and worked to coordinate Canadian planning with the National Security Resources Board in Washington. In April 1949 the Joint U.S.-Canada Industrial Mobilization Planning Committee came into being to further the coordination.

Infantry School Corps. After the British government withdrew its troops from Canada in 1871, the country had only its largely untrained and ill-equipped MILITIA for defence. A dozen years later, the government established a permanent instructional unit, the Infantry School Corps, in effect Canada's first professional soldiers. The three companies of the Corps, under Lt-Col W.D. OTTER, were the forerunner of the ROYAL CANADIAN REGIMENT.

'In Flanders Fields'. Composed by Lt-Col John McCRAE of the CANADIAN EXPEDITIONARY FORCE in a few minutes during the battle of YPRES on 5 May 1915, this poem became the best known single piece of poetry of WORLD WAR I and was first printed anonymously in the British weekly Punch.

Influenza epidemic. In 1918–19, just at the end of WORLD WAR I, an epidemic of Spanish influenza spread across the globe. Estimates are that some 20 million people died, of whom 50,000 were Canadians. Governments, municipal and provincial, imposed heavy restrictions on public meetings and cut down public services; the wearing of masks and quarantines were also mandated.

Inouye, Kanao (1916–1947). Born in Kamloops, B.C., Inouye lived in Canada until 1935 when he went to Japan. He served as an 'honorary corporal' at the Shamshuipo prisoner of war camp in HONG KONG and then worked for the secret police. He was notoriously cruel to Canadian PoWs (who called him the 'Kamloops Kid'), and three died as a direct result of his malice. As a Canadian citizen, he was tried for treason in Hong Kong and executed on 25 August 1947.

Integration. Defence minister Paul HELLYER's goal from 1963 on was to eliminate the waste caused by the triplication of services in the armed forces. The concept of integration, introduced in Hellyer's WHITE PAPER 1964, was expected to liberate funds for equipment by creating a more effectively coordinated force. This policy, generally well received, soon was followed by UNIFICATION, which was much more contentious.

International Control Commission. See INTERNATIONAL COMMISSION FOR CONTROL AND SUPERVISION; INTERNATIONAL COMMISSIONS FOR SUPERVISION AND CONTROL.

International Commission for Control and Supervision. On 27 January 1973, the United States, North Vietnam, and South Vietnam signed the Paris agreement that was to bring the Vietnam War to its end. To supervise the truce, the ICCS was established with Canada, Indonesia, Poland, and Hungary as members. Ottawa was reluctant to get involved but, anxious to see the war end, felt it had no alternative. Still, the commitment was for brief, renewable terms, and Ottawa ordered an 'open mouth' policy, one that saw harsh judgments offered publicly whenever breaches of the truce or stonewalling by commission members occurred. The Canadian commitment of some 300, civilian and military, arrived in February 1973 and remained until 31 July. The truce was more honoured in the breach than the observance, and the 'balanced' nature of the commission rendered its work almost impossible; there was, however, substantial success in repatriating prisoners of war, a matter of great urgency to the Americans.

International Commissions for Supervision and Control. The untenable military position of France in Indochina in 1954 troubled the great powers. At a conference in Geneva, three commissions were set up to supervise a truce, the exchange of prisoners, and population movements in the independent successor states of Laos, Cambodia, and Vietnam. To its surprise, Canada was asked to participate along with India and Poland. The commissions in Laos and Cambodia did their tasks with relative ease (though the former did not wind down until 1974 and the latter until 1969), but the Vietnam commission turned into a draining commitment as the north, under communist leadership, fought bitterly with the south, under U.S. influence. The Vietnam War made its role a farce, but the commission continued until 1972 when it collapsed in acrimony. There was substantial embarrassment for Ottawa when the *Pentagon Papers* (1971) confirmed that Canadian commission members had been carrying American threats and blandishments to Hanoi for years.

Reading: D.A. Ross, *In the Interests of Peace: Canada and Vietnam 1954–73* (Toronto, 1984)

Internment. The forcible confinement of persons in time of war, internment was employed by Canada in both world wars. During WORLD WAR I, Germans, Austro-Hungarians, and subjects of the Turkish Empire were deemed subject to internment if there were 'reasonable grounds' to believe they were or might be committing espionage or otherwise acting illegally. In all, some 8579 men were interned in 24 camps across the country, a number that included 2009 Germans, mostly reservists, and 5954 Galicians or Ukrainians, along with 81 women and 156 children who went to the camps voluntarily. The camps were administered initially by General Sir William OTTER for the Department of Militia and Defence; in 1915, the Justice Department took over, though Otter remained in charge.

Many of the internees were Ukrainians, then citizens of the Austro-Hungarian Empire. Very few were loyal to Vienna (though a Ukrainian bishop in Winnipeg in 1914 urged his flock to rally to their emperor), but the government used a broad-brush approach to internment and swept up many unjustly. Many were released when labour shortages emerged by 1916.

In WORLD WAR II, internment was expanded further in its terms, thanks to pre-war planning by committees of civil servants and military officers who prepared the DEFENCE OF CANADA REGULATIONS. Now anyone acting 'in any manner prejudicial to the public safety or the safety of the state' could be interned, a definition covering both enemy aliens and citizens. Lists of Nazis, fascists, communists, and Japanese Canadians suspected of willingness to serve Canada's enemies were in preparation before the outbreak of war. By January 1941, 763 Germans, most members of Nazi front organizations, had been interned and after appeals had been heard by a review committee, 127 were freed; for Italians, suspected of being active supporters of the Mussolini government, the numbers were 586 and 105; for communists, 87 and 5; in addition, 28 domestic fascists were interned, as was the mayor of Montreal, Camilien Houde, who had advised his compatriots not to adhere to the terms of the 1940 NATIONAL REGISTRATION.

Once Japan entered the war on 7 December 1941, the RCMP immediately arrested 38 Canadian Japanese suspected of harbouring subversive intentions. Later an additional 720 Canadian Japanese were interned, most at Angler, Ont., a group that included some members of the Nisei Mass Evacuation Group, who opposed the Canadian government's policy to Japanese Canadians, and active supporters of Japan or *gambariya*. Contrary to widespread public belief, all Japanese Canadians were not interned; JAPANESE CANADIAN EVACUATION from the British Columbia coast was quite different. At war's end, 425 internees remained at Angler.

In all, there were 26 internment camps in World War II, though most held prisoners of war and civilian internees sent to Canada by Britain, a group that included anti-Nazi Germans who were sometimes quartered with active Nazis; most Canadian internees were at Angler or Petawawa, Ont. Responsibility for the camps was shared by the army and the department of the Secretary of State.

The government of Prime Minister Mulroney has apologized to and offered compensation to all Japanese Canadians interned or evacuated, including those internees who supported Japan in the war. An apology has similarly been given Italian Canadians interned in World War II, including those who were fascist supporters. Ukrainian Canadians have also been seeking an apology and compensation for their internment in World War I.

Iran, UN peacekeeping in. See UNIIMOG.

Iraq, UN peacekeeping in. See GULF WAR; UNIIMOG.

Iroquois, **HMCS.** A TRIBAL CLASS DESTROYER, the ship was commissioned in 1942 but was not fully operational until the next year. *Iroquois* carried out escort duties on the Murmansk run, participated in actions against Nazi surface ships, served in the D-DAY fleet, and was being prepared for Pacific service when Japan surrendered. The ship was paid off in 1946, recommissioned in 1949, served two tours during the KOREAN WAR, and was finally paid off in 1962. The second *Iroquois*, a DDH280 helicopter-equipped destroyer, was commissioned in 1972.

Iroquois engine. In 1953, Avro Gas Turbine Division of A.V. ROE CANADA LTD, began development of an aircraft engine designed to give a maximum performance of Mach 1.5 at 15,240 m. Final detailed design was completed on 1 May 1954 and the engine, now called the Iroquois, was first lit-up on 15 December. The engine was tested in a B-47 bomber and was to be installed on the ARROW interceptor; the Arrow project was cancelled before this could be achieved.

Israel, UN peacekeeping in. See UNDOF, UNTSO.

Italian Campaign. After the successful conquest of SICILY in the summer of 1943, the Allies moved into Italy, with the intent of forcing Mussolini's ouster and Italy's capitulation, as well as tying down large numbers of German troops. These limited aims, designed to assist the Russians in their struggle on the Eastern Front and to weaken German resources in NORTHWEST EUROPE prior to an invasion of France, were soon to be partially frustrated. The Italian terrain, much like that of Sicily, favoured defence, and the cumbersome Allied command advanced very slowly and at great cost up the Italian boot.

The invasion of Italy began on 3 September 1943 when General Bernard Montgomery's EIGHTH ARMY, including the 1ST CANADIAN DIVISION under General Guy SIMONDS, came ashore at Reggio di Calabria. Six days later British airborne troops landed at Taranto and British and American forces assaulted Salerno. The initial advances, except at Salerno, were rapid, as the Germans fell back to the north to a defence line south of Rome, dubbed in its various components the Winter Line, the Gustav Line, and the HITLER LINE. The Canadians, originally scheduled to return to Britain after their part in the Sicilian fighting, instead were now to be joined by the 5TH CANADIAN ARMOURED DIVISION and I CANADIAN CORPS headquarters. For the 1st Division, however, now led by General Christopher VOKES (Simonds having taken command of the armoured division), the immediate task in the month of December was to cross the MORO RIVER and take the small port city of ORTONA. This was a major task, for the German defenders were skilled and efficient paratroopers and as usual the terrain favoured the enemy. The infantry bore the brunt of the struggle as they fought from farm house to farm house on the outskirts and then literally from house to house in Ortona. Mouseholing—boring holes between the adjoining walls of row houses — and trapping the other side was the order of the day, and the town was not cleared of the Germans until the night of 27–28 December. The Canadian division had been decimated in the heavy fighting, losing 1372 dead; the German losses were heavier still.

The campaign continued after a winter lull. During the early spring, the Corps, now led by General E.L.M. BURNS, was secretly moved to the LIRI VALLEY, near Cassino, to assault the Hitler Line. The initial Canadian attack went in on 16 May 1944, and the entire corps was committed a week later. Vokes' division cracked the line, and the 5th Armoured, skilfully led by General Bert HOFFMEISTER, poured through. Despite traffic jams, the road to Rome was now open; its capture, almost simultaneous with the D-DAY invasion of NORMANDY, was a sign that the war's outcome was inevitable; unfortunately, for the troops fighting in Italy, the war in France now captured all the attention, and the Italian campaigners were more than a little bitter when they called themselves the 'D-DAY DODGERS in forgotten Italy'.

The next major Canadian actions came well to the north where the GOTHIC LINE now blocked the Allied advance. The Corps was on the Adriatic shore, aiming for Rimini. There were six rivers to cross, each well defended with concrete emplacements. The Canadians now were a superbly trained and equipped force, however, and in heavy fighting that extended from 25 August 1944 for more than a month, they cracked the Apennine barrier. Then the weather deteriorated, turning the landscape into a cold, muddy quagmire, effectively paralysing the advance. The Canadians sat in the mud, their final actions being limited to clearing the line of the Senio River, north of Ravenna, in January 1945 before settling into winter quarters. The next month the corps began to move to northwest Europe to rejoin FIRST CANADIAN ARMY for the final assault on Hitler's Reich. The Italian campaign had been long and costly, and it had likely absorbed more Allied resources than it had tied down German ones. Thanks to skilful generalship, the Nazis had dragged out the struggle and inflicted heavy casualties.

Not least on the Canadians. In all, 92,757 Canadian soldiers served in the Italian campaign, and more than one in four became casualties. There were 5399 killed, 19,486 wounded, and 1004 captured; another 365 died from other causes, mainly disease or road accidents.

Reading: G.W.L. Nicholson, *The Canadians in Italy* (Ottawa, 1957)

J

Jackson, Alexander Young (1882–1974).This member of the Group of Seven was born in Montreal and studied in Paris. He went overseas in 1915, was wounded, and then became a war artist on the western front. His reputation spread after the war and the Group's first exhibition in 1920.

Jamieson, Donald Campbell (1921–1986). Born in Newfoundland, Jamieson was a radio broadcaster and anti-Confederate. He first won election to Parliament in 1966 and entered the Cabinet in 1968 as minister of Defence Production, a post he held for less than a year. He then served in a number of important portfolios in the Trudeau government and as High Commissioner to Britain.

Japanese Canadian Evacuation, 1942. By 1941 there were 23,000 persons of Japanese origin in Canada, almost all living in British Columbia. Slow to integrate, Japanese Canadians had stirred fears of the 'Yellow Peril' which increased exponentially as Japan turned expansionist in the 1930s. A Special Committee on Orientals, appointed in 1940, ordered their registration and barred them from military service. There were, however, no plans for their mass evacuation from the coast or internment in event of war with Japan, though Canadian and American officials discussed the need for coordinated action at the PERMANENT JOINT BOARD ON DEFENCE in autumn 1941. After the Japanese attack on Pearl Harbor and the fall of HONG KONG, fears increased, local political and military leaders called for action, and on 14 January 1942, Ottawa decided to move male Japanese nationals of military age inland. As Allied defeats continued, public pressure mounted; on 24 February the government ordered evacuation of all Japanese Canadians, men, women, and children, British subjects and enemy aliens. Over the next months, their property confiscated, Japanese Canadians were moved to inland British Columbia communities. Men worked on road gangs, though before long labour shortages led Ottawa to encourage a move eastward to Alberta or central Canadian manufacturing plants and farms. Evacuation resisters and Japanese patriots were interned in camps in northern Ontario. On 4 August 1944, the government decided to repatriate 'disloyal' Japanese Canadians to Japan and later to encourage others to return; after protests, 3964 went. The remainder, once the repatriation policy was cancelled, established new lives east of the Rockies.

Reading: Patricia Roy et al., *Mutual Hostages: Canadians and Japanese during the Second World War* (Toronto, 1990).

Jeep. The ubiquitous and widely popular general purpose (and hence GP or jeep) vehicle was produced by Willys Overland in the United States during WORLD WAR II. The four-wheel-drive jeep was used in all Allied armies.

Jefferys, Charles William (1869–1951). This artist, born in England, came as a child to Canada in 1879 and became the leading authority on the pictorial side of Canadian history. While he taught in the architecture school at the University of Toronto, his careful research into military history, especially his detailed sketches of uniforms and equipment, graced many books about Canada's wars and are still reproduced frequently.

'Johnny Canuck'. A comic book character who was popular during WORLD WAR II, Johnny Canuck was a heroic Canadian soldier who fought Nazis and Japanese with great success. Because of government restrictions, this and other comics could not be printed in colour and were known as 'Canadian whites'.

Johnson, Sir John (1742–1830). A notable Loyalist, he was born in New York, the son of Sir William JOHNSON. When the colonies rebelled, Johnson raised the King's Royal Regiment of New York and played a large part in the border raids of the Revolutionary War. In 1782, he became superintendent-general in the British Indian Department and held that post for 46 years. After helping settle Loyalists in Canada, he commanded a MILITIA battalion during the WAR OF 1812.

Johnson, Sir William (1715–74). Born in Ireland, he came to America in 1738 where he inherited vast estates in New York. He was superintendent of Indian Affairs in New York, and he led Six Nations fighters and irregulars in expeditions against the French in 1755, 1759, and 1760.

Johnston, Francis (Franz) Hans (1888–1949). Johnston studied art in Toronto and Philadelphia, and worked in New York. In 1917, the CANADIAN WAR MEMORIALS commissioned him to cover the activities of Canadian airmen training in Canada for overseas action. After the war, he was a founder of the Group of Seven, though he did not long remain a member.

Joint Industrial Mobilization Committee. See INDUSTRIAL DEFENCE BOARD.

Joint War Production Committee. Created in October 1941 as the Joint Defence Production Committee by Canada and the United States, the committee's name was changed on 2 January 1942. The committee coordinated and integrated war production in the two countries and produced sweeping recommendations to speed the flow of goods across the border. Separate committees and sub-committees dealt with specific production programs.

Jones, Alfred Gilpin (1824–1906). A Nova Scotia anti-Confederate, Jones won election to Parliament in the 1867 and 1874 elections. He was minister of Militia and Defence in 1878 in the government of Alexander Mackenzie.

Jones, George Clarence (1895–1946). Jones was born in Halifax, N.S., and graduated from the ROYAL NAVAL COLLEGE OF CANADA in 1913. He served through WORLD WAR I on Royal Navy vessels and with the ROYAL CANADIAN NAVY during the lean postwar years commanding destroyers. At the outbreak of WORLD WAR II he was in command of HMCS *OTTAWA*; he then served as commanding officer Atlantic coast, vice-chief of Naval Staff and, after 1944, CHIEF OF NAVAL STAFF in the rank of vice-admiral.

Juno Beach. The Allies returned to Northwest Europe on 6 June 1944, D-DAY. The NORMANDY invasion employed British, American, and Canadian troops, the latter the 3RD CANADIAN DIVISION commanded by Gen. R.F.L. KELLER and supported by the tanks of the 2nd Canadian Armoured Brigade. The Canadians were assigned to Juno Beach located on the Norman coast between the tiny hamlets of Grave-sur-Mer and St Aubin-sur-Mer; a few miles inland were the historic cities of Bayeux and CAEN.

The plan of attack called for two brigades, the 7th and 8th, to land in the first wave on Mike and Nan sectors; on their right and left would be British divisions. As soon as the beachhead was consolidated, the Canadian infantry and armour were to move inland up to ten miles to seize the high ground to the west of Caen. By this time, the 9th Brigade, in reserve, would be ashore ready to help beat off the anticipated German counter-attacks. The troops were to be supported by massive fire from ships offshore and heavy bombing by allied aircraft.

The Canadian assault on Juno Beach went relatively well. The first landing craft touched down just after 8 a.m. and, though the defenders had not been eliminated, the beachhead was seized. Some units ran into heavy opposition where the bombardment failed to destroy the concrete emplacements built by the Germans for their heavy guns; others did not; but all took their immediate objectives and moved inland. Some Canadian battalions in fact exceeded their intermediate D-Day objectives, the only ones of the invasion force to do so. The next day the counter-attacks began, and Canadians who had come in sight of Caen on 6 June would not again near the city until July.

D-Day casualties were 340 killed, 574 wounded, and 47 captured.

Reading: J.L. Granatstein and Desmond Morton, *Bloody Victory* (Toronto, 1984).

K

Kaeble, Joseph (1893–1918). Cpl Kaeble served with the [ROYAL] 22E REGIMENT at Neuville-Vitasse, France. On 8–9 June 1918 his unit was under heavy artillery fire, and Kaeble and one other were the only men unwounded in his section. He jumped over the parapet with his LEWIS GUN and, though wounded several times, emptied magazine after magazine at some 50 advancing Germans, completely blunting the attack. He was finally mortally wounded while continuing his defence, and he was awarded the VICTORIA CROSS.

Kangaroo carriers. In preparing for Operation TOTALIZE, Gen. Guy SIMONDS, commanding II CANADIAN CORPS in NORMANDY in August 1944, hit on the idea of using armoured personnel carriers to transport infantry through the fireswept battlefields. Simonds took the guns from U.S.-made PRIEST self-propelled artillery pieces—defrocked Priests, they were called—and converted them into 'Kangaroos', a brilliant solution to a hitherto insoluble problem. The Kangaroos, each carrying 11 men, were used in the operation on 7–8 August to transport a battalion of infantry. They were soon formed into a regiment. Later versions were made from RAM tanks.

Kap'yong, Battle of, 1951. The PRINCESS PATRICIA'S CANADIAN LIGHT INFANTRY, serving with Britain's 27th Infantry Brigade during the KOREAN WAR, was assigned to protect the withdrawal of a South Korean division through the Kap'yong valley. On 24 April 1951, the advancing Chinese Communist forces attacked the hilltop defences of the PPCLI and of the Royal Australian Regiment to the east. The Australians were forced to withdraw, but the Princess Pats held their position over the night of 24–25 April in the face of repeated assaults and checked the enemy advance. The battalion suffered 10 dead and 23 wounded, and the PPCLI received a Distinguished Unit Citation from the U.S. government.

Keefler, Ralph Holley (1902–1983). Born at Weston, Ont., Holley Keefler was a MILITIA 'success' in WORLD WAR II. He graduated in engineering from the Universitry of Toronto and while employed with Bell Telephone he served in the militia artillery and went overseas as a captain. Two years later he was a colonel and director of military training in Ottawa. In 1943, he commanded an artillery regiment, became a brigade commander in the Netherlands, and was promoted major-general in command of the 3RD CANADIAN DIVISION in March 1945. After the war he returned to the Bell Telephone Co.

Keller, Rodney Frederick Leopold (1900–1954). Born in England and educated at the ROYAL MILITARY COLLEGE from which he graduated in 1920, Keller served with the PRINCESS PATRICIA'S CANADIAN LIGHT INFANTRY in the PERMANENT FORCE in a variety of regimental and staff posts. A major in 1939, he went overseas with the 1ST CANADIAN DIVISION and progressed rapidly. By 1942 he was a major-general commanding the 3RD CANADIAN DIVISION which landed in NORMANDY on D-DAY. His health breaking down, he was on the verge of being relieved when he was wounded in an errant bombing by U.S. aircraft in August 1944. He died during a pilgrimage to Normandy ten years after the invasion.

Kemp, Sir Albert Edward (1858–1929). Born at Clarenceville, Canada East, Kemp was the owner of a successful sheet-metal manufacturing business in Toronto when he went into politics. Elected as a Conservative in 1900, he was named by Sir Robert BORDEN to succeed Sir Sam HUGHES as minister of Militia and Defence in late 1916. The next year, he went to London as minister of the Overseas Military Forces of Canada, a post he held until 1920. Kemp's task in both his wartime portfolios was to clean up the mess left by Hughes, a task at which he was largely successful.

Kerr, George Fraser (1894–1929). Serving in the 3rd Battalion, CEF, at Bourlon Wood, France on 27 September 1918, Lt Kerr was in command of his company. Far in advance of his men, he rushed a strong point single-handedly and captured four machine guns and 31 prisoners. He was awarded the VICTORIA CROSS.

Kerr, John Chipman (1887–1963). Pte Kerr was in the 49th Battalion, CEF, at COURCELETTE, France on 16 September 1916. Advancing into an enemy position, Kerr found himself in the midst of an exchange of hand grenades and, though wounded, moved along the trench in full view of the Germans, tossing grenades and firing his rifle. He took 62 prisoners. Kerr was awarded the VICTORIA CROSS.

Khaki University. In both world wars this educational institution was established in England to serve the needs of Canadian troops. The WORLD WAR I university was the idea of Henry M. Tory, the president of the University of Alberta, and he headed it from 1917, initially under YMCA auspices. In all, some 50,000 men took courses and in 1918 the army took over its operation. In WORLD WAR II, the Khaki University began operations in 1945 under Brig. G.E. Beament, an Ottawa lawyer who had played a senior staff role at FIRST CANADIAN ARMY. Beament's organization offered first and second year university-level courses both in residence and by extension from a campus at Leavesden, near Watford. The university was a unit of CANADIAN MILITARY HEADQUARTERS OVERSEAS, and its faculty included such academics as Maxwell Cohen and Claude Bissell.

King, William Lyon Mackenzie (1874–1950). Leader of the Liberal party from 1919 to 1948 and prime minister for more than 22 years, Mackenzie King was the country's most extraordinary public figure in the first half of this century. A complex man of deep insecurities, a believer in the crown and the empire and simultaneously a nationalist and a continentalist, King embodied in his person the conflicting attitudes of the whole country.

King was born in Berlin, Ont. to the daughter of William Lyon MACKENZIE and her husband, John King, a lawyer. His education at Toronto, Chicago, and Harvard universities gave him a string of academic degrees, and he had political connections that almost instantly opened doors to him in Ottawa. In 1900, he became deputy minister of Labour; eight years later he won election to the House of Commons, and soon after became minister of Labour. He fought against reciprocity in 1911 and lost his seat as Sir Wilfrid LAURIER went down to defeat. King was working for the Rockefeller Foundation in the United States during the early years of WORLD WAR I (thus fostering rumours that he had gone south to avoid having to enlist), but though he was himself sympathetic to the need for CONSCRIPTION, he returned to Canada to fight the 1917 election at Laurier's side. He again lost his seat, but his reward came in 1919 when he was picked as Liberal leader; two years later he was prime minister.

King's foreign policy slowly became clear. He wanted to cut formal commitments to Britain, an attitude that he made obvious during the Chanak crisis of 1922. Britain sought a commitment from Canada to send troops to resist Turkish expansionism, but King said only that 'Parliament will decide', a brilliant stalling tactic as Parliament was not in session. Moving through formal methods as well, King cut back Britain's residual powers in Canada and though the Statute of Westminster was passed in 1931 when he was not in office, it was his doing. Canada now was formally independent in foreign policy. But King did not want genuine independence — as an imperialist, he *wanted* Canada to go to war when Britain did, and through the late 1930s he manoeuvred brilliantly to create the illusion of choice for Canada. In fact, there was never any doubt that he would take Canada into the war that began in September 1939; the only question was whether he could bring Quebec willingly into the conflict, and King's tactics ensured this was done. There would be no CONSCRIPTION for overseas service in this war, the prime minister made clear. Quebec was gratified and acquiesced in belligerency.

The war effort began slowly. The offer of a division of infantry and the promise of participation in a large and expensive BRITISH COMMONWEALTH AIR TRAINING PLAN, as well as the participation of Canada's tiny navy, were all that Canada could afford—or so said the government in the first months of a 'limited liability' war. But after the fall of France this changed. The stops were pulled, and Canada began to move toward total war. The armed forces ballooned to almost a million men and women organized in a vast air force, the fourth largest navy, and an army of five overseas divisions and two armoured brigades. At the same time, war industry burgeoned, so much so that Canada produced more than it could use and by 1942 was freely giving away the rest to its allies. King, never popular, but widely respected, presided over this extraordinary effort.

What caused the prime minister most trouble, of course, was manpower. Pressures from those who wanted conscription were present from May 1940, and King fought repeated delaying actions. In June 1940, he introduced the NATIONAL RESOURCES MOBILIZATION ACT that put home defence conscription into place. After Japan entered the war in December 1941, pressure increased further, and King called a PLEBISCITE in spring 1942 to remove the clause in the NRMA limiting conscription's use. Quebec, unfortunately for King, voted overwhelmingly 'non' while English Canadians, almost as strongly, said 'yes'. The answer in a brilliant manoeuvre was to eliminate the clause but to say, 'not necessarily conscription, but conscription if necessary', an exact description of his policy that delayed the inevitable for more than two years. Conscription became necessary only in November 1944 after heavy casualties in the NORTHWEST EUROPE and ITALIAN CAMPAIGNS drained the infantry reinforcement pools. King sacked his conscriptionist Defence minister, J.L. RALSTON, and appointed in his place Gen. A.G.L. MCNAUGHTON, the former army commander overseas. But Mc-Naughton could not find the men, and before the month was out King had decided to send 16,000 ZOMBIES overseas. No one was happy, but King and his government survived and even won a narrow re-election in June 1945. In his three postwar years in power, King solidified Canada's defence relationship with the United States, launched the negotiations that created NATO, and brought Canada into the alliance.

His record, dispassionately considered, was extraordinary. He had brought Canada to formal independence, taken her into war, and put together a vast war effort. Few admired his work, however, neither contemporaries nor historians, the peculiarities of his personality seemingly so great as to cloud his accomplishments.

Reading: J.W. Pickersgill, *The Mackenzie King Record*, Vols 1–2 (Toronto 1960, 1968); J.L. Granatstein, *Canada's War: The Politics of the Mackenzie King Government 1939–1945* (Toronto, 1990)

Kingsmill, Sir Charles E. (1855–1935). A Canadian, Kingsmill joined the Royal Navy at age 14 and rose to rear-admiral rank by 1908. In that year he became the head of the FISHERIES PROTECTION SERVICE and in 1910 of the fledgling CANADIAN NAVAL SERVICE. Kingsmill commanded the navy throughout WORLD WAR I, being promoted to admiral in 1917. He retired in 1920.

King William's War. Lasting from 1689 to 1697, this North American offshoot of the WAR OF THE LEAGUE OF AUGSBURG pitted Britain and her colonies against New France. Both sides sought control of Hudson Bay, while the French, initially led by FRONTENAC, raided the English settlements. Sir William PHIPS took PORT ROYAL in 1690, but his assault on Quebec failed. The Treaty of Ryswick (1697) ended the hostilities.

Kinmel Park riots, 1919. Soldiers of the victorious CANADIAN EXPEDITIONARY FORCE were understandably anxious to return to Canada. Shipping was scarce, however, and conditions aboard some of the troop transports appalling. Moreover, Gen. Sir Arthur CURRIE and other senior officers insisted the troops return in battalions so they could receive the cheers of their home towns. The delays in DEMOBILIZATION led

to rising discontent that boiled over in a vicious riot at the Canadian camp at Kinmel Park in northern Wales in March 1919. Five died in the fighting and more were wounded. There were further riots in May and an alarmed British government suddenly found the ships to get the Canadians out of England and home.

Kinross, Cecil John (1896–1957). Pte Kinross of the 49th Battalion, CEF, advanced alone over open ground at PASSCHENDAELE on 30 October 1917, then charged a machine gun and killed its crew of six. His example spurred his company which then advanced a further 300 yards. Kinross was later seriously wounded, but his daring won him the VICTORIA CROSS.

Kirke, Sir David (*c*.1597–1654). Kirke captured Tadoussac from the French in 1628 and sought, but failed to win, CHAMPLAIN's surrender at QUEBEC. Retreating, Kirke took Champlain's supply fleet off the Gaspé coast, and when he returned to Quebec next year, the hungry, weakened French capitulated. In 1632, Kirke was ordered to return Quebec to France, his consolation prize being co-proprietorship of Newfoundland. A pirate as much as a soldier, Kirke died in jail.

Kiska assault. In June 1942, the Japanese occupied Attu and Kiska in the Aleutian Islands, American possessions off Alaska. On 11 May 1943, American forces invaded Attu and, after heavy fighting, completed its recapture on 29 May. For the Kiska assault, Canada provided the 13th Canadian Infantry Brigade based in Pacific Command. Under Brig. Harry FOSTER, the units (which included substantial numbers of home defence conscripts enrolled under the NATIONAL RESOURCES MOBILIZATION ACT) trained for a month, familiarizing themselves with American equipment. D-Day was 15 August 1943, and the attacking force of 34,000 (including the 5,300 Canadians) hit the beaches—only to discover that the Japanese had withdrawn on 28 July.

Kitching, George (b. 1910). Born in Canton, China and educated at the Royal Military College, Sandhurst, Kitching served in the British army before WORLD WAR II. In Canada in 1939, he joined the Canadian army and enjoyed a spectacular rise from lieutenant in 1939 to major-general by February 1944. A protégé of Gen. Guy SI-MONDS, Kitching served with him in SICILY but was ultimately relieved of his command of the 4TH CANADIAN ARMOURED DIVISION by Simonds in the FALAISE fighting of August 1944 in NORMANDY. Kitching worked effectively on staff after this, stayed in the army after the war, and wrote a very good memoir (*Mud and Green Fields*, 1986).

Knight, Arthur George (1886–1918). A sergeant in the 10th Battalion, CEF, Knight won his posthumous VICTORIA CROSS near ARRAS on 2 September 1918. His bombing section held up, Knight dashed forward, bayonetting several German machine-gunners and trench mortar crew. The enemy retreated under fire from a LEWIS GUN Knight brought forward. Seeing 30 Germans enter a tunnel, Knight went forward once more, killed three and captured 20, and then proceeded to rout another enemy party. He died in action the next day.

Knights of Columbus. In WORLD WAR II, the Canadian government asked four national voluntary organizations to provide 'auxiliary services' to the Canadian forces. With the YMCA, the SALVATION ARMY, and the ROYAL CANADIAN LEGION, the Knights of Columbus organized sports, dances, writing rooms, and hostels. The Knights specialized in hospitality and social functions.

Koje-do. An island southwest of Pusan, Korea, Koje-do was the site of a prisoner of war camp for some 160,000 North Koreans and Chinese during the KOREAN WAR. In May 1952, the PoWs seized the U.S. camp commandant and had to be subdued by heavily armed troops. In an effort to spread the burden, the Americans called on Commonwealth units in Korea for assistance, including a company of the ROYAL CANADIAN REGIMENT. The RCRs did their task well for six weeks beginning 25 May, but because Ottawa had not been consulted, and because it was government policy to keep Canadian troops together, a public diplomatic protest was made to Washington.

Konowal, Filip (1887–1959). Born in Russia, Cpl Konowal served in the 47th Battalion, CEF. During the battle for HILL 70,

22–24 August 1917, he led his section in the difficult task of mopping up enemy hidden in cellars and craters. In one struggle, Konowal killed three Germans in a cellar single-handedly; in another, he killed three machine-gunners with his rifle and four with the bayonet. In all, the Corporal despatched 16 Germans and continued fighting until severely wounded. He was awarded the VICTORIA CROSS.

Korean War. On 25 June 1950, North Korean troops crossed the 38th parallel and attacked South Korea. The North had been occupied by the Soviet Union in the aftermath of WORLD WAR II, and the South by the United States. The Korean fighting, therefore, was instantly seen as a major test of the COLD WAR, one involving high principle and grand strategy. The Americans shaped and led the West's response. Because the Soviets were boycotting the United Nations Security Council at the time, the Americans won agreement that the UN would respond to the North Korean aggression in what was described as a 'police action'. Led by U.S. General Douglas MacArthur, the UN put an army into the field, slowly and hesitantly, to be sure. Initially, the war went disastrously. The South Korean army had disintegrated under the first shocks, and the Americans, with only garrison troops from Japan at hand, did little better. By August, the UN forces held only a small perimeter around the port of Pusan. But MacArthur in September launched a surprise sea invasion at Inchon, well to the north, and the hitherto victorious Communists reeled back across the 38th parallel in confusion.

By this time, other UN members were getting troops to the fighting. Canada had initially sent three destroyers and an RCAF transport squadron, but in August, under strong U.S. pressure, the St Laurent government decided to recruit a brigade (the CANADIAN ARMY SPECIAL FORCE) off the street for the war. Commanded by Brig. John ROCKINGHAM, the 5000-strong brigade, many of its members veterans, trained in the United States and, as the war seemed to be all but over in late 1950, its departure was put on hold. Only the PRINCESS PATRICIA'S CANADIAN LIGHT INFANTRY would go to Korea, the battalion arriving there in December 1950 and serving initially with the 27th British Commonwealth Brigade. But by the time the Pats had landed, Chinese Communist armies had intervened massively, and the UN troops were in full retreat, the South Korean capital of Seoul falling to the enemy. The brigade, now called the 25TH CANADIAN INFANTRY BRIGADE, would now go to Korea; it arrived in May 1951.

The fighting against the Chinese was vicious in its intensity, as the PPCLI discovered in April 1951 when it was positioned on the hills overlooking a tiny village called KAP'YONG. A massive assault fell on the Commonwealth brigade's lines, forcing the Royal Australian Regiment to withdraw and exposing the Canadian positions. The Chinese troops poured over the Canadian trenches, forcing commanders to call artillery down on their own lines. That and a stiff, well-organized defence, led to the repulse of the attackers. The PPCLI were awarded a Presidential Unit Citation, the first Canadians to win this high American award.

For two years more, the Canadians and their UN allies fought a long war of attrition. Superior artillery and air support were the UN's advantage; vast numbers, hardiness, and great skill at infiltration were the Chinese trump cards. The battle swayed back and forth without large gains for either side, and the futility of the war was clear to soldiers who watched truce talks, underway at Panmunjon from mid-1951, while they fought and died for two years more. Peace when it came on 27 July 1953 brought the Korean War to its uneasy close. Chinese and North Korean casualties were likely more than a million; UN casualties numbered some 490,000, of which 1588 were Canadian, including 516 dead. In all, 26,791 Canadians served in Korea, the first United Nations war.

Reading: H.F. Wood, *Strange Battleground: Official History of the Canadian Army in Korea* (Ottawa, 1966)

Kuwait. See GULF WAR.

L

LaBrosse, Raymond (1921–1988). Born in Ottawa, LaBrosse joined the army in 1940 and went overseas. In 1942 he was recruited by British military intelligence and trained as a radio operator prior to being dropped in France in February 1943. There he rounded up Allied airmen who had evaded capture and brought 29 aircrew with him to Spain in June 1943. Returned to France, he established an escape route, then fought with resistance units against the Germans. Decorated with the MILITARY CROSS, LaBrosse joned the army again in 1948 and was a lieutenant-colonel when he retired in 1971.

LaFlèche, Léo Richer (1888–1956). Born in Kansas, LaFlèche came to Canada as a youth and joined the ROYAL 22E REGIMENT at its creation. He served overseas, was severely wounded at MOUNT SORREL, and won the DSO. After the war, he was an advocate for veterans, became a highly unpopular deputy minister of National Defence in 1932, and was criticized sharply for his role during the BREN GUN SCANDAL. In 1940 he became military attaché in Paris and in 1942, to the consternation of many in the Cabinet, joined the government as minister of NATIONAL WAR SERVICES. After the war, he served abroad as an ambassador until 1955.

Lahr. The main Canadian NATO base in Germany since 1972, Lahr is located close to the French border in southern Germany. After the Trudeau government's defence review of 1970–71 halved Canada's commitment to NATO, the attenuated ground units were relocated from their north German bases and concentrated here, the air units setting up shop at nearby Baden-Soellingen.

Lake, Sir Percy Henry Noel (1855–1940). He entered the British army in 1873, saw active service in Afghanistan, the Sudan, and Mesopotamia, and became CHIEF OF THE GENERAL STAFF in Canada in 1904 as a major-general. He was then inspector-general of the MILITIA from 1908–10 and, after his return to British service, was a senior commander in the Mesapotamia Field Force's disastrous 1916 campaign.

Lake Champlain, Battle of. An American fleet commanded by Commodore Thomas Macdonough anchored itself at the mouth of Plattsburgh Bay on Lake Champlain on 11 September 1814, facing broadside a British fleet under Captain George Downie. The engagement was fought at close quarters and was bloody, Downie himself being killed. The United States Navy emerged triumphant when Macdonough's ship came about and raked the exhausted British with broadsides.

Lambert, Marcel-Joseph-Aimé (b. 1919). A lawyer and Rhodes Scholar, Lambert served overseas with the Calgary Regiment in WORLD WAR II. Elected to Parliament in 1957 as a Conservative, he was briefly minister of Veterans Affairs in the last three months of the DIEFENBAKER government in 1963.

Lamontagne, J.-Gilles (b. 1919). A RCAF veteran and a municipal politician, Lamontagne was elected to the House of Commons as a Liberal in 1977 and entered the Cabinet the next year. After the Liberals' return to power in 1980, he became Defence minister, 1980–83, and acting Veterans' Affairs minister, 1980–81.

Lancaster bomber. Designed by A.V. Roe Co. and built in Britain and also at Victory Aircraft Ltd at Malton, Ont., the Lancaster originally had four Merlin XX engines, a top speed of 462 km/h at 3505 m, and a bomb load of 6350 kg; later, Hercules radial engines were mounted. In addition, the highly manoeuvrable Lanc's seven-man crew was protected by eight .303-calibre machine-guns in three turrets. Designed for night attacks (and thus lightly armoured and with lower ceiling than comparable U.S. aircraft that were to fly in daylight), the bomber went into service in April 1942, and before war's end had delivered two-thirds of the bombs dropped by British and Canadian squadrons on Germany. Later versions of the aircraft carried increasing bomb loads, up to and including the 10,000-kg 'grand slam' deep penetration bomb. More than 400 Lancs were made in Canada.

Landing craft. Landing craft of many sorts have been used by armies for centuries to convey infantry across water obstacles and land them on beaches or river banks. In WORLD WAR II a number of specialized landing craft were developed. There were Landing Ship Infantry, such as HMCS *Prince David* which carried 550 troops, six Landing Craft Assault, and two Landing Craft Mechanized. The LCAs were wooden vessels designed to put up to 35 troops on a beach; the LCMs were steel-hulled with a ramp bow and carried wheeled and light tracked vehicles. The Landing Craft Infantry had long endurance and could carry 150 troops below decks and put them ashore. The Landing Ship Tank had a ramped bow and could land tanks directly on a beach. All these craft carried Canadian troops at SICILY, in Italy and at JUNO BEACH on D-DAY, and most were operated by the ROYAL CANADIAN NAVY.

Landing Craft Assault (LCA). This vessel was used to bring assault troops from larger ocean-going vessels, usually LANDING SHIPS INFANTRY (LSI), directly to the beach. The lightly armoured, 13-m wooden vessel usually carried 35 men and their personal equipment as well as a crew of five. They had a range of about 140 km.

Landing Craft Infantry (LCI). Also known as the Landing Craft Infantry (Small) or LCI(S), these small boats could carry about 100 soldiers as far as 1000 km at a speed of 12 knots and land them directly on a beach. The vessel was usually armed with three to four 20-mm cannon but was not armoured and was extremely vulnerable to all but small-calibre fire. The ROYAL CANADIAN NAVY manned 24 LCIs in three flotillas. They landed 4600 Canadians at NORMANDY on D-DAY, as well as a number of United States troops, and suffered heavy losses.

Landing Craft Mechanized (LCM). LCMs were steel-hulled with a bow ramp.

They carried wheeled and light tracked vehicles and could land them directly on a beach.

Landing Craft Tank (LCT). These ships were designed to land tanks and other vehicles directly on the assault beaches. Ramped at the front end, LCTs could carry six CHURCHILL or nine SHERMAN tanks. One variant, designed for close support of infantry on the beaches, carried 800 to 1000 5-inch rocket projectors in its cargo hold. This was referred to as the LCT(R). First versions of the LCT were unarmed; later variants carried 20-mm OERLIKON guns.

Landing Ship Infantry (LSI). Canada possessed only two of these vessels during World War II, the *PRINCE DAVID* and *PRINCE HENRY*. Both had once been Canadian National Steamships but were purchased by the government at the outbreak of war for conversion into armed merchant cruisers. Canada's LSIs were well-armed ocean-going ships, capable of conveying up to 550 troops. They also carried six LCAs, used to bring those troops to the beaches, and two LANDING CRAFT MECHANIZED which were somewhat larger than the LCA and which could transport light vehicles ashore.

Landing Ship Tank (LST). First used widely at SICILY and in support of amphibious operations, LSTs were ocean-going vessels of some 3600 tonnes, capable of landing tanks and heavy vehicles directly on beaches. The normal troop-carrying capacity of an LST was 175 at a speed of just under 12 knots. LSTs could also carry LCIs.

Landymore, William Moss (b. 1916). Born at Brantford, Ont., Landymore joined the ROYAL CANADIAN NAVY in 1936 and served through WORLD WAR II and the KOREAN WAR, latterly in command of the destroyer *IROQUOIS*. In 1965, he was commanding on the east coast when he became embroiled in a public dispute with Defence minister Paul HELLYER over UNIFICATION of the forces. He resigned prematurely the next year.

Langemarck, Battle of. A small town near YPRES, Langemarck was the scene of repeated heavy fighting during WORLD WAR I. In late April 1915, the 1ST CANADIAN DIVISION withstood the Germans' first use of gas in the area of the town, and the elements of the division then assisted in an unsuccessful attack east of the Ypres-Langemarck road on 26 April. From 16–18 August 1917 the Battle of Langemarck was a small (but costly) part of the PASSCHENDAELE campaign.

Langevin, Sir Hector Louis (1826–1906). Born at Quebec, Langevin was a lawyer, editor, and political supporter of John A. MACDONALD. In the course of a long, checkered Parliamentary career, he held many Cabinet posts, including Militia and Defence for some five weeks in 1873.

Lapointe, Hugues (1911–82). The son of Ernest Lapointe, a powerful Cabinet minister, he was elected to Parliament in 1940. He served overseas with the infantry in WORLD WAR II, attaining the rank of lieutenant-colonel, then resumed his political career. He held three portfolios in the St Laurent government, notably Veterans' Affairs from 1950–57.

Laurier, Sir Wilfrid (1841–1919). One of Canada's greatest political statesmen, Laurier was leader of the Liberal party from 1887 to 1919 and prime minister from 1896 to 1911. Born at St Lin, Canada East, he was trained in law at McGill University and then, his health poor, he went to Arthabaska to live, practise law, and edit a tiny newspaper. He ran successfully for the Quebec Legislature in 1871 and for Parliament in 1874. Moderate though he was, he was nonetheless so stirred by the NORTHWEST REBELLION of 1885 and the execution of Louis RIEL that he stated that if he had been born on the banks of the Saskatchewan, he too would have shouldered a musket with Riel. That remark did him no good with English-speaking Liberals, but he nonetheless became the first French-speaking Liberal leader in 1887 and nine years later the first Quebecois prime minister.

Laurier had to deal with the realities of Canadian politics as they were: rampant pro-imperialism in English Canada and isolationist nationalism in Quebec. Those two irreconcilable tendencies first came to a head in the SOUTH AFRICAN WAR when the Ontario press and English Canadian ministers demanded full Canadian participation while the Quebecois, convinced that the Boers were a little people beset by the Anglos much as they were, demanded that Canada do nothing. The majority had its way, however, though Laurier weakly argued that no precedent had been set when he committed Canada only to raising men, the great bulk of the costs to be paid by Britain. Laurier had been found wanting in the eyes of many in English Canada, but his charisma and his hold on power were strong enough to last until the free trade election of 1911. That vote reinforced pro-imperial, anti-French, and anti-Catholic sentiments and undercut the base of his support in English Canada. In Quebec, however, the issue was Laurier's NAVAL SERVICE ACT, a modest measure that nonetheless led Conservatives to knock on doors and ask how many men lived there — so they could be registered for CONSCRIPTION for M. Laurier's navy.

Conscription would finally destroy Laurier's career for good. In WORLD WAR I, though he lent his support to the war effort, Laurier was adamantly opposed to compulsory military service. After Sir Robert BORDEN returned from England in May 1917 convinced that only conscription could keep the CANADIAN CORPS reinforced, the drama reached its peak. Offered seats in the Cabinet, Laurier refused, fearful that he might lose his support in Quebec to Henri BOURASSA and his nationalists. After passing the MILITARY SERVICE ACT, Borden rammed through the MILITARY VOTERS ACT and the WARTIME ELECTIONS ACT, thus virtually guaranteeing victory at the polls. Laurier gallantly fought the election of December 1917, though deserted by most of his English-speaking supporters. Borden won, conscription was enforced, and the country was split as it never had been before. Broken in spirit, Laurier hung on as leader through the ARMISTICE 1918 only to die on 17 February 1919. His successor, Mackenzie KING, would continue his work.
Reading: Joseph Schull, *Laurier* (Toronto, 1965)

Law, C. Anthony (b. 1916). An officer with the ROYAL CANADIAN NAVY, Tony Law studied painting in Ottawa. He served as an officer on motor torpedo boats in the English Channel, participating in the D-DAY invasion and follow-up operations. He painted, as he said, 'to keep sane'. For ten weeks in 1943–44, while his boat was being readied for service, he worked as an official war artist, painting in Scapa Flow. He returned to Canada in 1946 and remained in the RCN, retiring as a commander in 1966.

Lawrence, Thomas Albert (b. 189?). Lawrence was born at Creemore, Ont. and enlisted in the CANADIAN EXPEDITIONARY FORCE. He transferred to the ROYAL AIR FORCE and flew fighters. After the war, he joined the AIR BOARD, worked on surveys, and then joined the ROYAL CANADIAN AIR FORCE on its establishment. He did a tour in London as liaison officer to the Air Ministry, and commanded the School of Army Cooperation at Camp Borden and the RCAF station at Trenton, Ont. Promoted to air vice-marshal in 1942, he commanded No. 2 Air Training Command at Winnipeg, a critical post in the BRITISH COMMONWEALTH AIR TRAINING PLAN's operations, and then he was Air Officer Commanding Northwest Air Command in Winnipeg. He retired in 1947.

Lawson, John K. (1890–1941). A WORLD WAR I veteran and a PERMANENT FORCE officer in the ROYAL CANADIAN REGIMENT, Lawson was a colonel and the Director of Military Training in Ottawa when the government decided in the fall of 1941 to send a force of two battalions and a brigade headquarters to reinforce the British garrison at HONG KONG. Promoted to brigadier, Lawson became the force commander, and he was killed when the Japanese overran his headquarters in the fighting that began with Japan's attack on 8 December 1941.

Leach Commission. Led by Major General E.P. Leach, a British army officer with service in Halifax and Montreal, the Leach Commission studied and reported on Canada's defence requirements in 1898. Premised on the need to defend Canada against an American attack, the Leach report saw Canada standing on the defensive, with its forces commanded by British officers and directed by London. The report, immediately shelved, also recommended reorganization of the MILITIA.

Learmonth, Okill Massey (1894–1917). A company commander with the 2nd Battalion, CEF, Major Learmonth led his company in resisting a German counter-attack at HILL

70 on 18 August 1917. Learmonth, though wounded three times, threw bombs and inspired his men to drive off repeated attacks. Finally evacuated, he insisted on being carried to battalion headquarters so he could report though it was apparent he was dying. He was awarded a posthumous VICTORIA CROSS.

Leased Bases Agreement. In September, 1940, the U.S. agreed to transfer 50 World War I-vintage destroyers to Britain in exchange for 99-year leases of military bases in the British West Indies, British Guiana, and Newfoundland. The agreement was signed in March 1941. It gave the U.S. control over six areas in Newfoundland including bases at Argentia, Fort Peperell, and Harmon Field. At the same time a separate but related protocol was signed by Canada, the U.S. and the U.K. recognizing Canada's special interests in, and responsibilities for, the defence of Newfoundland. Also called the destroyers-for-bases agreement. See TOWN CLASS DESTROYERS.

Lebanon, UN peacekeeping in. See UNIFIL, UNOGIL.

Leckie, Robert (1890–1975). Wartime Chief of the Air Staff, Leckie was born in Britain and flew flying boats for the Royal Navy and the RAF in World War I, shooting down a Zeppelin. He came to Canada in 1919 to become Director of Civil Flying Operations but soon went back to the U.K. to continue service with the RAF. In 1940 he returned to Canada to take charge of the BRITISH COMMONWEALTH AIR TRAINING PLAN. He transferred to the RCAF in 1942 and became Chief of the Air Staff in 1944, a position he held until 1947.

Lee-Enfield rifle. The standard infantry weapon of the Canadian soldier in both world wars and even in Korea, though it was obsolete by then. First used by the British Army in the late 1890s, the Lee-Enfield was a bolt-action rifle that fired a .303-calibre bullet. A trained user could fire 10 rounds a minute with an effective range of 831 m. The more common range for the weapon was 550 m.

Leliefontein, Battle of. SOUTH AFRICAN WAR battle which took place 7 November

1900. Ninety officers and men of the ROYAL CANADIAN DRAGOONS and the ROYAL CANADIAN ARTILLERY were assigned to cover the retreat of a British infantry column from Leliefontein farm in the Transvaal. The column was attacked by Boer horsemen and in a short but sharp action three Canadians were killed and 11 wounded. Remarkably, three Canadians were awarded the VICTORIA CROSS for bravery in this battle, a high number for any one action, and especially for one so limited.

Lemieux, Rodolphe (1866–1937). Among the various appointments he held in Sir Wilfrid LAURIER's government, Lemieux was minister of the Naval Service from August to October 1911, a post he held concurrently with that of minister of Marine and Fisheries. He first entered the Cabinet in 1906 and ended his days in the Senate.

LeMoyne, Jacques (1659–1690). Soldier and adventurer, LeMoyne was born in Quebec and spent much of his short life fighting the English alongside his brother PIERRE LEMOYNE. He fought them in Hudson Bay in 1686 and led a bloody raid against Schenectady (now in northern New York State) in 1690. He led the Canadian militia in the defence of Quebec during KING WILLIAM'S WAR and died of wounds inflicted by the retreating British force. See also WAR OF THE LEAGUE OF AUGSBURG, PIERRE LEMOYNE, SIR WILLIAM PHIPS.

LeMoyne, Pierre (1661–1706). Also known as Le Sieur d'Iberville, LeMoyne launched five expeditions against the English on Hudson's Bay to completely disrupt the Hudson Bay Company's trade during the WAR OF THE LEAGUE OF AUGSBURG. He captured YORK FACTORY in 1690 and thereafter lost it and recaptured it twice: in 1694 and in 1697. In a spectacular naval battle in July 1697, LeMoyne, aboard *PELICAN*, sank the English ship *Hampshire* near Hayes River. LeMoyne also tried to oust the English from Newfoundland in 1696 by razing coastal fishing communities and taking residents prisoner. Many of LeMoyne's territorial conquests were returned to England by the Treaty of Ryswick.

Lend-Lease. See HYDE PARK AGREEMENT.

Leonforte, Battle of. During the Allied campaign in SICILY in 1943, Major-General G.G. SIMONDS led the IST CANADIAN DIVISION into bitter fighting to take Leonforte, a strategically located town that was an important road and communications hub near the centre of the island. German forces demolished a bridge over a deep ravine on the approach to the town and, from the hills behind, poured fire down on the approaching 2nd Canadian Infantry Brigade. The first Canadian companies to reach Leonforte engaged in heavy hand-to-hand combat while engineers built a bridge to ferry in reinforcements. The reinforcing units stormed the town 22 July 1943 and eventually succeeded in clearing the town and the heights above it. The Division suffered 275 casualties in the three days of fighting.

Leopard tank. A German-designed main battle tank equipped with a 105 mm cannon. Canada purchased 176 Mk I Leopards in 1976 to replace the aging CENTURION; 128 of the tanks were acquired at a cost of $137 million to re-equip Canada's NATO combat group. By the time the Leopard I was delivered it was considered obsolete, having been replaced by the Leopard II which Canada did not acquire.

Leopold Canal. A waterway south of the Netherlands' West Scheldt estuary. The canal separated German forces in the BRESKENS POCKET, south of the SCHELDT estuary, from the advancing Canadians during the initial stages of the Battle of the Scheldt. On 6 October 1944, the 7th Infantry Brigade of the 3RD CANADIAN INFANTRY DIVISION crossed the canal in assault boats and established two small bridgeheads, about 3 km apart, on the north bank of the canal. Stiff German resistance stopped any further advance for several days. On 9 October the Brigade finally connected the two bridgeheads and resumed its advance north towards the Scheldt Estuary itself. Total casualties for this operation amounted to 533 officers and men.

Letson, H.F.G. (1896–1992). An engineer, Letson joined the MILITIA in 1910 and served in WORLD WAR I. After the war he stayed active in the militia, commanding the British Columbia Regiment and the CANADIAN OFFICERS TRAINING CORPS contingent at the

University of British Columbia while earning a PhD and teaching engineering. During WORLD WAR II he was military attaché to the United States and chairman of the CANADIAN JOINT STAFF MISSION in Washington. General Letson retired from active military service in 1946. In 1954 he headed a committee of former officers studying the organization, training, and role of the reserves in the Canadian armed forces. Their report was referred to as the Letson Review.

Lévis. Located on the south shore of the St Lawrence River, opposite Quebec City, Lévis was used by British forces under WOLFE as a site for artillery batteries during the siege of Quebec in July and August 1759. The French tried unsuccessfuly to retake Lévis 11 July 1759. See also SEVEN YEARS' WAR.

Lévis, François Gaston, Duc de (1719–1787). In the spring of 1760 Lévis led French troops down the St Lawrence from Montreal in an effort to retake Quebec. He defeated a British force at STE FOY and laid siege to Quebec, but was forced to raise his siege when the French fleet, sent to support him and deny the river to the Royal Navy, was destroyed at RESTIGOUCHE.

Lewis machine gun. First used in World War I, the Lewis was still in use by British and Canadian forces in the opening months of World War II. A gas-operated weapon firing a .303-calibre round, the Lewis was fed by a circular, horizontally mounted magazine which held 47 rounds. It was eventually replaced by the BREN in 1940–41. The Lewis was used by the Royal Flying Corps (RAF) on fighters in World War I and by the Navy as an anti-aircraft gun.

Liberator bomber. Four-engine heavy bomber designed and built in the United States. Also known as the B-24. In U.S. service the Liberator was used in great numbers primarily as a strategic bomber. It was armed with .50-calibre machine guns and carried a crew of ten. In RCAF service the Liberator was used as a long-range anti-submarine patrol aircraft in the North Atlantic.

Ligue pour la défense du Canada. Founded by J-E-A. (André) Laurendeau and other Quebec nationalists, the Ligue was an anti-conscription organization formed in Quebec in 1942 to campaign for the 'non' side in the 1942 PLEBESCITE on conscription. The Ligue later became the basis of the Bloc Populaire Canadien, a political party.

Limited Liability War Effort. At the outbreak of WORLD WAR II, Prime Minster William Lyon Mackenzie KING feared the political consequences of placing a large ground army in the field. During World War I that procedure had brought about CONSCRIPTION, which had divided English and French-speaking Canadians with disastrous results for the Liberal Party. It was, therefore, decided that Canada's contribution on the ground would be limited and that Canada's main war effort would be in the training of air crew through the BRITISH COMMONWEALTH AIR TRAINING PLAN and in the provision of raw materials, food stuffs, and munitions to Britain. After the fall of France in May 1940, however, Britain stood alone against Nazi Germany and there was public clamour for a much larger war effort. That, and the German aerial bombardment of Britain in the fall and winter of 1940–41, effectively put an end to any thought of a limited Canadian war effort. See also CONSCRIPTION CRISIS 1942.

Link trainer. A device used to teach flight theory and instrument training in WORLD WAR II. With the trainee pilot seated inside, the machine simulated aircraft motion to test his or her suitability for more advanced pilot training. Recruits disliked the machine because a low Link-trainer score disqualified them without their ever having left the ground. It was used until late 1942.

Lipsett, Louis James (1874–1918). Lipsett joined the British army in 1894, holding a number of staff positions and serving on the northwest frontier of India before coming to Canada in 1911 as General Staff Officer on loan to the Canadian army by the British War Office. On the outbreak of war, Lipsett was given command of the 8th Battalion, CANADIAN EXPEDITIONARY FORCE which he led in battle at 2nd YPRES. He was then promoted to command of 2nd Brigade and eventually, in June 1916, of 3RD CANADIAN DIVISION. He was given this last command over the objections of minister of Militia and

Defence Sam HUGHES who wanted his son Garnet HUGHES to get the post. Lipsett led the division in many key battles such as VIMY RIDGE, PASSCHENDALE, and AMIENS. On 1 October 1918, he took command of the British 4th Division. Two weeks later he was killed in action.

Liri Valley. The site of the opening stages of the battle for Rome; its three rivers, the Liri, Gari, and Rapido, had to be crossed before the formidable defences of the Gustav Line could be assaulted. The Allies were attempting to break a months-long stalemate and help relieve pressure on U.S. forces trapped in the Anzio beachhead perimeter. Units of the the 1ST CANADIAN INFANTRY DIVISION, led by C. VOKES, took part in the battle which opened on 11 May with a massive artillery bombardment of the Gustav Line positions. Initially Canadian armour supported the 8th Indian Infantry Division which crossed the Gari on assault boats and then completed two BAILEY BRIDGES which were crossed by Canadian tanks on 12 and 13 May. During those days and on 14 May the bridgeheads were expanded, while thrusts were mounted deeper into the German positions. On 15 May a particularly vicious battle was fought by the 12th Armoured Regiment (Three Rivers Regiment) near the town of Pignataro. Now in danger of being outflanked, the Germans were forced to withdraw to the HITLER LINE.

Lismer, Arthur (1885–1969). One of the founders of the Group of Seven, Lismer was born in Britain and trained as a painter there and in Belgium before coming to Canada in 1911. As principal of an art school, he taught painting in Halifax from 1916 to 1919 and while there was engaged by the Canadian War Records Office to paint views of Halifax harbour during wartime. Some of his most dramatic scenes were those depicting his city just after the HALIFAX EXPLOSION.

Little Norway. The Royal Norwegian Air Force used Toronto Island airport for a training base from September 1940 until 1943 when it was transferred north to Muskoka. Known as Little Norway, the base was operated independently from the BRITISH COMMONWEALTH AIR TRAINING PLAN by the exiled Norwegian government, and was relocated to Toronto Island in May 1945.

Long range aerial navigation (LORAN). A system for aerial navigation perfected during World War II, it used radio beacons to guide aircraft. The system was particularly useful over water or over large and sparsely inhabited areas such as northern Canada where geographic features are not easily discernible.

Long Sault raid. In April 1660 a mixed French and Indian raiding party led by Adam DOLLARD DES ORMEAUX proceeded up the Ottawa River from Montreal to ambush an Iroquois party and steal their furs. The Iroquois discovered them near Long Sault rapids and attacked them, killing des Ormeaux and taking nine survivors prisoner.

Loomis, Frederick Oscar Warren (1870–1937). Educated at Bishop's College, Loomis joined the MILITIA in 1886 and was commissioned as an officer in 1898. At the outbreak of WORLD WAR I he was given command of the 13th Battalion of the CANADIAN EXPEDITIONARY FORCE which he led during the 2nd battle of YPRES. In 1916 he was promoted to brigadier and in September 1918, he succeeded L.J. LIPSETT as GOC 3RD CANADIAN DIVISION. He retired from the military in 1919.

Lord Strathcona's Horse (Royal Canadians). Canadian cavalry regiment raised by Lord Strathcona (Donald A. SMITH) at the time of the SOUTH AFRICAN WAR. Originally known as Strathcona's Horse, the regiment sent A Squadron of the CANADIAN MOUNTED RIFLES to South Africa. On 1 October 1909, the regiment itself was redesignated Strathcona's Horse (Royal Canadians) and on 1 May 1911, Lord Strathcona's Horse (Royal Canadians). In World War I the regiment contributed infantry to 1ST CANADIAN DIVISION and cavalry to the CANADIAN CAVALRY BRIGADE. The regiment became part of the PERMANENT FORCE between the wars. In World War II it was converted to an armoured regiment and attached to the 5th Canadian Armoured Brigade, part of the 5TH CANADIAN ARMOURED DIVISION. It thus saw service in ITALY and NORTHWEST EUROPE. Units of the regiment also served in the KOREAN WAR.

Loudon, John Campbell, Earl of (1705–1782). Based in Halifax, Lord Loudon commanded British forces in North America in the early period of the SEVEN YEARS' WAR. His failure to capture LOUISBOURG, a powerful French garrison on Cape Breton Island, led to his replacement by General J. ABERCROMBY in 1758.

Lougheed, Sir James Alexander (1854–1925). A Conservative, Lougheed was appointed to the Senate by Prime Minister Robert BORDEN in 1899 and served in a number of minor Cabinet portfolios after the Borden government took office in 1911. Among these was that of SOLDIERS' CIVIL RE-ESTABLISHMENT, 1918–21.

Louisbourg. A French fortification on the southeast coast of Cape Breton Island, Louisbourg was intended to dominate the Gulf of St Lawrence, both to guard the French possessions upriver and to provide a base from which to raid the sea lanes between New England and Britain. Louisbourg, a massive undertaking built primarily of stone and brick, much of which was transported from France, took almost three decades to complete. Located on an isthmus, it included a town, seaport, and military base all protected by massive walls. When finished it was called 'The Dunkirk of North America', after the fortified seaport on the French channel coast, and dominated the French possessions in the region both politically and militarily. To counter it, the British established Halifax as a government centre and naval base.

Despite its massive walls, the fortress was poorly situated and vulnerable to long-range artillery fire from across the harbour and from low hills that lay close by to the west. In 1745, during the WAR OF THE AUSTRIAN SUCCESSION, it was besieged by a mixed force of New England militia and Royal Navy vessels and forced to surrender after six weeks. Louisbourg was returned to France at the end of the war but captured once again in 1758 at the outbreak of the SEVEN YEARS' WAR. This time its downfall was permanent; Cape Breton remained under British rule when the war ended and Louisbourg was razed. It has since been rebuilt as a tourist attraction.

Luard, Richard G.A. (1827–1891). General Officer Commanding the Canadian MILITIA from 1880 to 1884. Luard wanted to expand the tiny PERMANENT FORCE at the expense of the Militia, a politically unwise proposal. His ideas were denounced by the minister of Militia and Defence, Adolphe CARON, as political interference although the government did add to the Permanent Force in 1883. Luard resigned and returned to England shortly after.

Lundy's Lane, Battle of. Site of one of the fiercest battles of the WAR OF 1812. The action began on the night of 25 July 1814, when a mixed force of British regulars and Canadian militia, led by the Canadian-born General Sir Gordon DRUMMOND, met a contingent of American invaders under the command of Major-General Jacob Brown at a location just west of the Niagara River and very close to Niagara Falls. The American force was proceeding north after capturing FORT ERIE. The fight raged for several hours with high casualties on both sides until,

about midnight, Drummond's force compelled the Americans to withdraw to Fort Erie. See also WAR OF 1812.

Lyall, Gordon Thomson (1892–1941). On 27 September 1918, while serving with the 102 Battalion, CEF, Lyall captured 185 prisoners and 26 machine guns in several attacks against German strongpoints in Bourlon Wood. According to his VICTORIA CROSS citation he 'significantly contributed to the capture of Bourlon Wood'. He died while serving with the British Army in Egypt during WORLD WAR II.

Lynch, Charles (b. 1919): After joining Reuters wire service in 1943, Lynch went to London and reported on the D-DAY landings. He later covered the FIRST CANADIAN ARMY and the 2nd British Army in NORTHWEST EUROPE, and the Nuremburg war crimes trials which followed the war.

Lysander. See WESTLAND LYSANDER.

M

MacAdam shield-shovel. Intended as a combination entrenching tool and shield for an infantryman in a prone position, this WORLD WAR I device was modelled on a Swiss invention. It was both heavy and awkward to use and virtually useless as a shield against enemy bullets. The Canadian army ordered approximately 25,000 of these shield-shovels only to sell them for scrap. This was but one example of the poor equipment carried into battle by Canadian soldiers at the start of War War I. See also OLIVER PATTERN WEB EQUIPMENT, ROSS RIFLE.

McBride, Sir Richard (1870–1917). McBride became premier of British Columbia in 1903 and kept that post until 1915. After the outbreak of WORLD WAR I, while Canada and Britain dithered over coastal defence, McBride purchased two submarines from Chile to patrol the west coast. The British

government later reimbursed the province for the $1.15 million spent on the two submersibles, the CC1 and the CC2.

MacBrien, James Howden (1878–1938). Born in Port Perry, Ontario, MacBrien joined the MILITIA in 1901, then saw service with the NORTH WEST MOUNTED POLICE and the South African Constabulary before joining the PERMANENT FORCE as a staff officer, a position he held at the outbreak of World War I. In 1916 he was given command of the 12th Infantry Brigade, one of the very few regular officers to earn a field command during the war. MacBrien became Chief of the General Staff in 1920, a post he held through a period of cut-backs and retrenchment. His clashes with Rear-Admiral HOSE, Chief of the Naval Staff, became legendary. During his tenure the armed forces were reorganized and brought closer together under a new NATIONAL DEFENCE ACT, an initiative MacBrien opposed. He retired in frustration from the military in 1927; four years later, under a new government, he was appointed Commissioner of the Royal Canadian Mounted Police.

McCrae, John (1872–1918). Born in Ontario, McCrae taught medicine at McGill University. At the outbreak of World War I he volunteered his services to the CANADIAN EXPEDITIONARY FORCE as a medical officer. McCrae also wrote poetry, his best known work being 'IN FLANDERS FIELDS', published in 1915. Colonel McCrae died of pneumonia in 1918.

McCurdy, J.A.D. (1886–1961). Pilot of the SILVER DART during the first successful powered flight in Canada, 23 February 1919. In World War II he was assistant director of aircraft production.

Macdonald, Angus Lewis (1890–1954). A veteran of World War I, Macdonald was premier of Nova Scotia from 1933 to 1940 before being invited by Prime Minister William Lyon Mackenzie KING to join the federal government as minister of National Defence for Naval Services, a position he held until 1945. He presided over the rapid build-up of the wartime ROYAL CANADIAN NAVY; the command and equipment difficulties which that expansion precipitated were partly responsible for the poor escort performance of the RCN during the early years of the war.

MacDonald, Daniel J. (1918–1980). Born in Prince Edward Island, MacDonald served in ITALY and NORTHWEST EUROPE in World War II, achieved the rank of sergeant, and was wounded in action. After a brief career in provincial politics, he was elected to the House of Commons in 1972 and appointed minister of Veterans' Affairs from 1972–79, and again for a brief time in 1980.

Macdonald, Donald Stovel (b. 1932). Macdonald entered Pierre Elliott Trudeau's first Cabinet in April, 1968 as minister without portfolio, becoming president of the Privy Council shortly after. In September, 1970, he was appointed minister of National Defence, a post he held for just over a year. Macdonald was chiefly responsible for the

Defence WHITE PAPER of 1971 which, coming shortly after the OCTOBER CRISIS, placed a major emphasis on internal security. He also established the MANAGEMENT REVIEW GROUP.

Macdonald, Edward M. (1865–1940). Macdonald first entered the Cabinet of William Lyon Mackenzie KING in April 1923 and was appointed acting minister of National Defence and minister of National Defence shortly after. He took little interest in the department and his appointment to it was primarily a political gesture to the Maritime Provinces, from whence he came.

McDonald, Hugh (1827–1899). McDonald served four months as minister of Militia and Defence from July to November 1873.

Macdonell, Sir Archibald Cameron (1864–1941). A graduate of ROYAL MILITARY COLLEGE, Macdonell joined the MILITIA in 1886 and then transferred to the ROYAL NORTH WEST MOUNTED POLICE before volunteering for service in the SOUTH AFRICAN WAR. There he was seriously wounded before returning to Canada to resume his position with the RNWMP. Prior to the outbreak of WORLD WAR I, Macdonell joined LORD STRATHCONA'S HORSE which he commanded in 1914. Promoted brigadier in December 1915, he was promoted again to major-general and placed in command of the 1ST CANADIAN DIVISION in June 1917. After the war he served for six years as commandant of RMC before retiring from the service in 1925.

MacDowell, Thain W. (1890–1960). MacDowell served with the 38th Battalion, CEF, during the battle of VIMY RIDGE in April 1917. In that battle he tricked 75 German occupants of a dug-out into surrendering by pretending he had a large force behind him when, in fact, he had only two men. For that he was awarded the VICTORIA CROSS. Earlier, during the Battle of the SOMME, he had won a DISTINGUISHED SERVICE ORDER.

McEwen, Clifford Mackay (1896–1967). Born at Griswold, Manitoba, 'Black Mike' flew fighters with the RAF in Italy in WORLD WAR I, shooting down 27 enemy aircraft. Unlike most wartime pilots, McEwen chose to stay with the military in the interwar years, becoming one of the first pilots to fly with the fledgling Canadian (later ROYAL CANADIAN) AIR FORCE. By 1941 he had reached the rank of Air Commodore with responsibilities for flying operations off Canada's east coast. In early 1944 McEwen was placed in command of NO. 6 BOMBER GROUP (RCAF) which was then suffering from serious morale problems, high loss rates, and a variety of operational difficulties. Within a short time McEwen improved the Group's performance until it was at least on a par with the other bomber groups in Bomber Command. He retired from the service in the spring of 1946.

McGill Fence. See MID-CANADA LINE.

MacGregor, John (1888–1952). MacGregor was awarded the VICTORIA CROSS for subduing a large German machine-gun nest while serving with the 2nd Canadian Mounted Rifles during the battle of CAMBRAI in late September, 1918. The nest had been blocking his company's advance. In the action, Captain MacGregor killed four gunners and took eight prisoner.

McKean, George Burdon (1888–1926). Born in England, Lt McKean was serving with the 14th Battalion, CEF, near Garvelle, France in April 1918, when he destroyed an enemy dug-out, killed eight Germans, and captured two trench blocks during a night raid. For this action he was awarded the VICTORIA CROSS. In yet another escapade in September, he also won a MILITARY CROSS.

Mackenzie, Chalmers Jack (1888–1984). Dr Mackenzie was acting president of the NATIONAL RESEARCH COUNCIL when war broke out in 1939. As such, he presided over a variety of war-related research projects including those designed to develop the Allies' chemical and biological warfare capabilities.

Mackenzie, Sir Colin John (1861–1956). Born in Scotland, Mackenzie was Chief of the General Staff from 1910 to 1913. He resigned after a prolonged period of conflict with the minister of Militia and Defence, Sam HUGHES, who believed strongly in the MILITIA MYTH and wanted to direct resources to the militia rather than to the PERMANENT FORCE. The mobilization plans drawn up under Mackenzie's stewardship were scrapped by Hughes when World War I began.

Mackenzie, Hugh (1885–1917). Serving with the 7th Canadian Machine-Gun Company, Lt Mackenzie was killed in action on 30 October 1917 during the battle of PASSCHENDAELE. Mackenzie drew fire from a German pillbox allowing Sgt G.H. MULLIN, a sniper, to kill the German machine-gunners inside, capture the pillbox, and take the 10-man garrison prisoner. Both he and Mullin (who survived the action) were awarded the VICTORIA CROSS.

Mackenzie, Ian Alistair (1890–1949). A veteran of World War I, Mackenzie served as Defence minister from 1935 until forced to resign in 1939 in the aftermath of the BREN GUN SCANDAL. He became minister of Pensions and National Health and, in 1944, minister of Veterans' Affairs. Mackenzie was one of the key liberal influences in William Lyon Mackenzie KING's wartime Cabinet.

Mackenzie, William Lyon (1795–1861). Born in Scotland, Mackenzie came to Canada after the WAR OF 1812. The publisher of *The Colonial Advocate*, a newspaper espousing governmental reform, he soon became one of Upper Canada's most vigorous advocates of reform but was constantly frustrated by the refusal of British-appointed governors to introduce democratic changes. In 1837 he gathered a small number of reform-minded supporters in an effort to overthrow the government and create an American-style democracy. This was the Upper Canadian version of the REBELLIONS OF 1837. Following defeats at Montgomery's Tavern and Navy Island, Mackenzie fled to the U.S., remaining there until 1849. He then returned to Canada, a spent force in Canadian political life.

Mackenzie-Papineau Battalion. Unit of the Spanish Republican or Loyalist forces battling fascist and conservative forces led by Generalissimo Francisco Franco during the Spanish Civil War (1937–1939). The unit, led by Edward Cecil-Smith and Saul Wellman, arrived in Spain in 1937. It was named for the leaders of the REBELLIONS OF 1837 in Upper and Lower Canada, and consisted of approximately 1300 volunteers. The battalion fought in five battles, suffering heavy casualties before the war ended. The Canadian government disapproved of the battalion and passed the FOREIGN ENLISTMENT ACT to prohibit Canadians from fighting in foreign wars.

McKinnon, Allan B. (1917–1990). While serving in ITALY with the Canadian Army in World War II, McKinnon won a MILITARY CROSS. After the war he stayed in the army, then entered politics. In 1979, following the victory of Joe Clark's Conservatives, McKinnon was appointed minister of National Defence and minister of Veterans' Affairs in the Clark government. He held the posts concurrently. McKinnon's major accomplishment was to establish a task force to review the results of UNIFICATION.

Macklin, Wilfred H.S. (1899–1966). Macklin saw service with the CANADIAN EXPEDITIONARY FORCE in WORLD WAR I. At the start of WORLD WAR II he was posted to National Defence Headquarters. He held a variety of positions there before being sent to British Columbia to command the 13 Canadian infantry battalions, largely composed of NRMA men, there. Later he served at CANADIAN MILITARY HEADQUARTERS in London and in Ottawa. He retired as a major-general.

McKnight, William H. (b. 1940). A wheat and cattle farmer and businessman from Saskatchewan, McKnight was first elected to the House of Commons in 1979 and entered the Cabinet in 1984. In 1989 he was appointed minister of National Defence in the Mulroney government, a position he held until 1991. During McKnight's tenure the plan to purchase up to eleven nuclear submarines which had been suggested in the 1988 WHITE PAPER on defence was scrapped.

MacLaren, Donald Roderick (1893–1988). Born in Ottawa, MacLaren joined the ROYAL FLYING CORPS in World War I and shot down 48 enemy aircraft and six observation balloons in less than eight months. After the war MacLaren served briefly with the CANADIAN AIR FORCE before pursuing a career in civil aviation. He founded Pacific Airways in 1926 and later joined Trans-Canada Airlines.

McLeod, Alan Arnett (1899–1918). A Canadian pilot with the ROYAL FLYING CORPS, Lt McLeod won the VICTORIA CROSS after a hair-raising crash landing when he guided his burning observation plane to the ground in no man's land by climbing on to a wing. The incident took place near the SOMME in March 1918. Although injured, he dragged his badly wounded observer, Lt A.W. Hammond, to safety in the British trenches.

MacLeod, Pegi Nicol (1904–1949). A Canadian artist living in New York, MacLeod returned to Canada to paint scenes of the CANADIAN WOMEN'S ARMY CORPS in the last year of World War II.

McNaughton, Andrew George Latta (1887–1966). Born in Saskatchewan, A.G.L. McNaughton studied engineering at McGill University in Montreal and enrolled in the militia prior to World War I. At the outbreak of war he went overseas with the CEF's 4th Battery, a unit he was soon to command with the rank of major. McNaughton's ability to marry engineering principles to new equipment (such as wireless) for the improvement of his artillery brought success and promotion through the ranks. After commanding a number of batteries, McNaughton was promoted to Counter-Battery Staff Officer in early 1917 and placed in charge of three counter-battery groups. He held this position until the end of the war and must be credited with a share of the success for the effective counter-battery work during the battle of VIMY RIDGE.

Following the war McNaughton joined the PERMANENT FORCE and continued to rise in rank until he assumed the position of CHIEF OF THE GENERAL STAFF in 1929. As such he was in charge of the ill-fated UNEMPLOYMENT RELIEF CAMPS during the early years of the Great Depression. He left the military in 1935 to become president of the NATIONAL RESEARCH COUNCIL. When war broke out in Europe in September, 1939, he returned to the military as GOC 1ST CANADIAN INFANTRY DIVISION.

Certainly innovative in the uses of new technology, especially with respect to artillery, McNaughton was well-liked by the troops. As senior Canadian officer in Britain, it was natural that he would continue to command the Canadian army there as it evolved from one division to a corps and finally to the FIRST CANADIAN ARMY. But as a former militia officer, McNaughton was neither skilled enough, experienced enough, nor a good enough tactician to bear responsibility for an army in the field. He had, for example, approved the plan for the DIEPPE RAID which had been a disaster. In addition, the Canadian Army's first army-sized exercise, Spartan, undertaken in March 1943, was little short of a débâcle. Senior British officers such as Chief of the Imperial General Staff Sir Alan Brooke, Gen. Sir Bernard Paget and Gen. Bernard L. Montgomery began to pressure Ottawa to remove McNaughton from command due to his shortcomings. He was relieved in December 1943.

McNaughton's war service was far from over, however. In early November, 1944, Prime Minister William Lyon Mackenzie KING called on him to replace J.L. RALSTON as minister of National Defence with the express purpose of influencing enough ZOMBIES to GO ACTIVE to allow King to avoid conscription. McNaughton failed at this (as he failed twice to win election to the House of Commons) and CONSCRIPTION was introduced in late November.

After the war McNaughton had a distinguished career as a member of Canada's diplomatic service, serving on the PERMANENT JOINT BOARD ON DEFENCE, as Canada's permanent delegate to the United Nations, and as chairman of the Canadian section of the International Joint Commission, among other posts.

Reading: John Swettenham. *McNaughton*, 3 vols (Toronto, 1968–69).

MacNeil, C. Grant (1892–1976). Born in Ontario, MacNeil served overseas in the CANADIAN EXPEDITIONARY FORCE before being invalided home due to wounds in 1916. He later became active in the GREAT WAR VETERANS ASSOCIATION in Saskatchewan in 1918 and was elected dominion secretary-treasurer of the GWVA in 1919. He served in that post until 1925 when he resigned following charges of financial mismanagement of the organization. In 1935 he was elected to the House of Commons as Cooperative Commonwealth Federation (CCF) member for Vancouver-Burrard.

Macphail, Sir Andrew (1864–1938). A physician, Macphail was born in Prince Edward Island and before World War I taught the history of medicine at McGill University. After the war broke out, Macphail served overseas with the ROYAL CANADIAN ARMY MEDICAL CORPS. He was later commissioned to write the official history of the Corps — *Medical Services, 1914–19*—published in 1925.

MacQueen, John H. (1893–1980). MacQueen served overseas during World War I with the Canadian Ordnance Corps. He remained in the army between the wars and served as Senior Ordnance Officer, Deputy Quartermaster-General and Master General of the Ordnance from 1939 to 1947. After leaving the army, he was appointed president of the government-owned CANADIAN ARSENALS LIMITED.

Magnificent, HMCS. Commissioned in July, 1948 the *Magnificent* was a light fleet carrier designed and built in Britain. She displaced 14,225 tonnes, was armed with 40-mm guns and crewed by 70 officers and 828 men, and had a top speed of 24 knots. For most of her operational life the ship carried a mix of 30 Hawker SEA FURY fighters and Fairey Firefly reconnaisance aircraft. Throughout her service she was Canada's only aircraft carrier, often used to transport aircraft and other military equipment to distant locations, bringing SABRE fighter jets to Britain in 1951 and men and vehicles to Suez for UNEF in 1956. *Magnificent* was used for training cruises before being paid off in June 1957 when she was replaced by BONAVENTURE.

Mahony, John Keefer (1911–1990). Mahony was serving with the Westminster Regiment (Motor) on 24 May 1944 when he took part in the action that won him the VICTORIA CROSS. Despite wounds in the head and leg, Mahony skilfully directed his unit's advance across the Melfa River in Italy and then organized a bridgehead defence.

Mainguy, Daniel N. (b. 1930). Educated at ROYAL ROADS, Mainguy commanded a number of ships and held a variety of senior administrative posts in the ROYAL CANADIAN NAVY and MARITIME COMMAND including vice chief of the defence staff, 1983–85. At one time he commanded the NATO Standing Force, Atlantic. Vice-admiral Mainguy retired from the service in 1986 to become president of Triton Strategies.

Mainguy, Edmund Rollo (1901–1979). Born in British Columbia, Mainguy attended the ROYAL NAVAL COLLEGE OF CANADA. During World War II he commanded the destroyer *ASSINIBOINE* and the cruiser *UGANDA* and was posted as Captain (d) (i.e., destroyers) Newfoundland, in charge of RCN escort duties in the western region of the North Atlantic. In 1949 Mainguy was appointed to chair a commission of inquiry following a number of MUTINIES aboard RCN vessels. The commission's findings were issued in the MAINGUY REPORT, which had a major impact on naval policy in subsequent years. In 1951 Admiral Mainguy was appointed CHIEF OF THE NAVAL STAFF, a post he held until his retirement in 1956.

Mainguy Report. Report of the commission of inquiry headed by Rear-Admiral E.R. Mainguy which studied dissatisfaction within the ROYAL CANADIAN NAVY in 1949 after several MUTINIES had broken out aboard RCN ships. The other two commissioners were civilians—former RCN officer L.C. Audette and former civil servant L.W. Brockington. The Commission recommended greater Canadianization of the navy, improvements in creature comforts for naval ratings, and an end to the strict officer-ratings relationship that had been copied from the Royal Navy.

Malone, Richard S. (1909–1985). Malone founded and edited the Canadian Army newspaper *MAPLE LEAF* during World War II and held command posts with the PRINCESS PATRICIA'S CANADIAN LIGHT INFANTRY. He was also brigade-major with the IST CANADIAN INFANTRY DIVISION, and Director of Public Relations for the Canadian Army during the NORMANDY campaign. Malone wrote a two-volume memoir of his career in the army, *A Portrait of War* (Toronto, 1983) and *A World in Flames* (Toronto, 1984).

Management Review Group. Body established by the minister of National Defence Donald S. MACDONALD in June 1971. The group contained both civilian and military members and was charged with the task of evaluating the internal workings of DND and DND's relationship with other departments of government to ensure effective planning and control within the department.

Manitoba Field Force. See MANITOBA FORCE.

Manitoba Force. The Manitoba Force was formed from the contingent of Canadian militia, about 300 men, left behind when WOLSELEY returned east from Manitoba in the late summer of 1870 after the RED RIVER EXPEDITION had arrived to put an end to the RED RIVER REBELLION. It was the only effective Canadian police or military presence in the area at that time and turned out in October 1871 to defend the colony from a threatened FENIAN attack. To reinforce the garrison, a second militia expedition of some 212 militia and 60 canoemen was sent to Manitoba from Canada in the late fall of 1871. They arrived within four weeks. The Manitoba Force remained responsible for law and order in the province until that duty was undertaken by the NORTH WEST MOUNTED POLICE in 1877.

Mann, C. Churchill (1904–1989). Educated at ROYAL MILITARY COLLEGE, Mann was nominated to Britain's staff college in 1939 and rose rapidly in rank thereafter. He helped plan the DIEPPE RAID and took part in the action as deputy commander. Mann was later appointed Chief of Staff for FIRST CANADIAN ARMY in NORTHWEST EUROPE in 1944–45.

Manning pools. See MERCHANT MARINE.

Manson, Paul D. (b. 1934). Manson joined the RCAF in 1952 and held various senior appointments including Commander of AIR COMMAND 1983–85. He was the Project Manager for the New Fighter Aircraft Program 1977–80, leading to the selection of the CF18 Hornet. From 1985 to 1988 he was CHIEF OF THE DEFENCE STAFF.

Maple Leaf. Founded by Brigadier R.S. MALONE, *Maple Leaf* was published by and for the Canadian Army during World War II. The paper contained news of events at home and the progress of the war in two editions, one for Italy and Northwest Europe (1944–46) and the other for the U.K. (1945–46).

Maple Leaf hostels. Leave hostels in London staffed by the Canadian Red Cross Society during World War II. There were four of them.

MARCOM. See MARITIME COMMAND.

Margaree, HMCS. Originally commissioned as HMS *Diana*, the *Margaree* was a RIVER CLASS DESTROYER acquired by the RCN to replace the FRASER which was sunk in June, 1940. Ironically, some 500 km west of Ireland *Margaree* was sliced in half by a merchant ship she was escorting on her first mission on 22 October 1944; 142 members of the ship's company were lost. The second vessel of that name, a ST LAURENT CLASS DESTROYER, was commissioned in 1957.

Marine Industries Ltd. Ship-building company located at Sorel, Quebec. Marine Industries was awarded a pre-World War II contract from the British government to produce one hundred 25-POUNDER GUN/ HOWITZERS as well as 3.7-inch shells. The contract was intended to foster Canadian war industry, and followed an agreement made at an Imperial conference in 1937. During World War II the company became a major builder of CORVETTES.

Maritime Command (MARCOM). Created in the initial stages of the UNIFICATION program initiated by the minister of National Defence Paul HELLYER in 1964, Maritime Command was instituted in 1966; the ROYAL CANADIAN NAVY disappeared as a separate service in 1968. Usually referred to in DND as MARCOM, Maritime Command assumed responsibility both for the tasks of the pre-unification navy and for the former RCAF's anti-submarine operations. See also MOBILE COMMAND; AIR COMMAND.

Martello towers. Defensive fortifications built by the British between 1796 and 1846 at Kingston, Quebec, Saint John, and Halifax. The towers were round, flat-roofed, and had strong masonry walls at least 2.5 metres —nearly 7 ft—thick. A heavy cannon was mounted on the roof, giving it a clear field of fire. The towers were never attacked. Sixteen of them were built; eleven are still standing.

Masson, Louis F.R. (1833–1903). Masson was first elected to the House of Commons in 1867. In October, 1878, he was appointed minister of Militia and Defence, a position he held until January 1880. In his short term in office Masson unsuccessfully attempted to promote a distinctive style and colour uniform for a proposed French Canadian militia regiment.

Matilda tank. Originally ordered by the British Army in 1937, the Mk I variant had a crew of two, and a top speed of close to 13 km/h. It was armed with a .50- and a .303-calibre machine gun. Later versions were larger, faster, and more heavily armed, and carried a crew of four. At the start of the war, Canadian armoured formations were equipped with Matildas. Although Matildas were last used as gun tanks in North Africa in July 1942, Matilda chassis carried flame-throwers, bulldozer blades, bridging equipment, and other specialized equipment used by all Commonwealth forces for the rest of the war.

Matthews, A. Bruce (1909–1991). Matthews served with the ROYAL CANADIAN ARTILLERY in several capacities in the interwar years. After service in SICILY, from March to November 1944 he was Commander, Corps Royal Artillery in II Canadian Corps. Following that he was promoted to GOC 2ND CANADIAN INFANTRY DIVISION which he commanded until war's end.

Maxim gun. See VICKERS .303.

May, Wilfrid Reid [Wop] (1896–1952). Born in Manitoba, May narrowly missed being shot down by Baron Manfred von Richthofen on the very day that Richthofen was himself killed. After the war he became a well-known bush pilot. In World War II May helped set up the BRITISH COMMONWEALTH AIR TRAINING PLAN.

Medicine, Military. See MILITARY MEDICINE IN CANADA.

'Meet the Navy'. Also known as the Navy show, 'Meet the Navy' was a Canadian stage show put on by members of the ROYAL CANADIAN NAVY during WORLD WAR II. The show was first staged in Canada but went overseas in the final months of the war and opened at the Hippodrome in London on 1 February 1945. It featured dancing, singing, and comedy. The most famous feature of the show was John Pratt singing 'You'll Get Used to It'. After playing in London, 'Meet the Navy' toured England and the continent for a brief time.

Melgund Commission. Also known as the Commission on the Defences of Canada, the Melgund Commission was headed by Lord Melgund (later Lord MINTO), military secretary to Governor-General Lansdowne. It was formed in 1884 by minister of Militia and Defence Adolphe CARON and was supposed to improve communications within Caron's department and between his department and Whitehall, in London. It was largely unsuccessful and met only once.

Melgund, Lord. See MINTO, EARL OF.

Mention in Despatches. A minor honour accorded when a soldier, sailor, or airman was named in official reports as having acted in a meritorious way while engaged in combat.

Mercer, M.S. (1859–1916). A Toronto lawyer and militia officer, Mercer served with the QUEEN'S OWN RIFLES in the NORTH-WEST REBELLION, and was given command of a battalion in 1911. After the outbreak of WORLD WAR I, he rose rapidly through the ranks, especially after distinguishing himself at the 2nd battle of YPRES. Mercer was placed in command of the 3RD CANADIAN DIVISION in December 1915. He was killed on 2 June 1916 during the opening phases of the battle at MOUNT SORREL while he was reconnoitering the front lines. Major-General Mercer was the highest ranking Canadian killed in World War I.

Merchant Marine. Generic term originally used in Allied countries during WORLD WAR II to refer to civilian vessels and sailors who operated directly under the authority of the military; later used to apply to virtually all ships and their crews who carried wartime cargoes to the U.K. and other theatres of war. There was no merchant marine in Canada in World War I despite the initiation of Canada-U.K. convoys in the summer of 1917. In World War II the Canadian merchant marine was created, for all intents and purposes, even before the war began when an order-in-council was issued 26 August 1939 bringing all Canadian-registered ships under the control of the ROYAL CANADIAN NAVY. A wartime system of merchant shipping allocation was devised in cooperation with the British Admiralty while a number of these vessels—the DEMS or Defensively

Equipped Merchant Ships—were armed. In addition to civilian ships, the merchant marine also consisted of government-owned ships as in those vessels operated by PARK STEAMSHIP COMPANY. Just as civilian shipping was mobilized, so too were civilian sailors. Manning pools were created in major ports and training on guns was provided for DEMS crews. Through the manning pools sailors received their pay, were provided with recreation, and were directed to living accommodation. Sailors who ran afoul of regulations could be dismissed by a board of inquiry. The submarine warfare along the NORTH ATLANTIC RUN and elsewhere took a heavy toll of the merchant marine; 1064 Canadian merchantmen were killed in World War II. This was a far lower total than the 31,132 British merchantmen who were lost, but Canada started the war with far fewer merchant vessels.
Reading: Frederick B. Watt: *In All Respects Ready: The Merchant Navy and the Battle of the Atlantic, 1940–1945* (Toronto, 1985)

Merrifield, William (1890–1943). Sgt Merrifield won the VICTORIA CROSS for single-handedly knocking out two German machine-gun nests on 1 October 1918, near Abancourt, France. He was serving with the 4th Battalion, CEF, at the time.

Merritt, Charles Cecil Ingersoll (1908–1979): Commanding officer of the South Saskatchewan Regiment at the time of the DIEPPE RAID on 19 August 1942, Lt-Col Merritt was awarded the VICTORIA CROSS for showing 'reckless bravery'. Despite serious wounds he continued to lead his men in the regiment's crossing of the Scie River. Eighty-one members of the regiment were killed in the battle and Merritt was taken prisoner.

Merritt, William H. (1793–1862). Merritt was a commissioned militia lieutenant who fought at QUEENSTON HEIGHTS and LUNDY'S LANE during the WAR OF 1812. American forces took him prisoner in July 1814 and held him until the end of the war. He later spearheaded the building of the Welland Canal.

Metcalf, William Henry (1885–1968). L.-Cpl Metcalf was serving with the 16th Battalion, CEF, at ARRAS on 2 September 1918, when, according to his VICTORIA CROSS citation, he 'calmly walked across bullet-swept ground guiding a tank and directed its fire against German strongpoints which were holding up the infantry's advance.' His was one of seven Victoria Crosses won that day.

Mewburn, Sydney Chilton (1863–1956). A Hamilton lawyer, Mewburn was a militia officer at the outbreak of World War I. During the war he rose rapidly in rank, although not leaving Canada, until he resigned from the army in 1917 to accept the post of minister of Militia and Defence in the new, pro-CONSCRIPTION, UNION GOVERNMENT. Although a Liberal, he strongly disagreed with the anti-conscription philosophy of Liberal leader Sir Wilfrid LAURIER. He succeeded Sir A.E. KEMP, who had been charged with cleaning up the mess left by Sam HUGHES, when Kemp was posted to London as the new minister of the OVERSEAS MILITARY FORCES. In the December, 1917 federal election he was elected to the House of Commons. He continued to serve in the ministry until January 1920.

Meyer, Kurt (1910–1961). At the time of the early fighting in NORMANDY in June 1944, Meyer was a *Standartenführer* (Colonel) in command of the 25th SS Panzer-Grenadier Regiment (*Hitlerjugend*), which faced the 3RD CANADIAN INFANTRY DIVISION. Later, on 14 June, he was given command of the 12th SS Panzer Division. In fighting on 7 June Meyer's unit took a number of Canadians prisoner; 23 were shot. Later, more Canadian prisoners were executed in the same manner. In December 1945, Canada put Meyer on trial for war crimes before a military court. Meyer claimed he did not know that men of his unit had killed Canadian prisoners of war but he was found guilty on three of five charges. He was given the death sentence but Maj.-Gen. C. VOKES, then commander of the Canadian Occupation Forces in Europe, commuted the death sentence to life imprisonment, arguing that Meyer's responsibility for the deaths was indirect. Meyer was imprisoned in Canada at Dorchester Penitentiary and released in September 1954.
Reading: Tony Foster: *Meeting of Generals* (Toronto, 1986)

Michilimackinac. On the shores of the Mackinac Strait connecting Lake Huron and Lake Michigan, Michilimackinac has been the site of a number of missions, forts, and fur trading posts. The first known European habitation there was Saint Ignace, a French mission established some time in the late 1670s. Since Michilimackinac dominated a strategic waterway, it was constantly fought over, especially during the WAR OF 1812 when the British took control of it. After the war the Americans gained possession, never to lose it.

Mid-Canada Line. Chain of 98 radar stations, most of them unmanned, built along the 55th parallel beginning in 1954. Designed to detect enemy bombers which crossed it, the chain was completed in 1957 at a cost of $250 million. The entire cost of the line was shouldered by Canada. The radar chain utilized the McGill Fence technology, developed at McGill University. It employed an automatic audible alarm system making it unnecessary for all the stations to be manned all the time, thus cutting operational costs. The Mid-Canada Line was closed in 1965.

Middle East, UN peacekeeping in. See GULF WAR, UNDOF, UNEF I, UNEF II, UNIFIL, UNIMOG, UNOGIL, UNTSO, UNYOM.

Middleton, Sir Frederick D. (1825–1898). Born in Ireland, Middleton was posted to Canada in 1868 and became GOC Canadian MILITIA in 1884. Soon after assuming this post, Middleton organized and led the expedition against Louis RIEL's forces during the NORTHWEST REBELLION of 1885. Middleton was both cautious and ponderous. Some of his men thought him too deliberate, even incompetent, in pursuing a vastly outgunned and outnumbered Métis force. However, most of his force were poorly trained and badly led and caution may well have been a wise course.

Middleton divided his force into three columns, the most westerly led by T.B. STRANGE, the central by W. OTTER and his own contingent to the east. His own troops fought an indecisive engagement against the Métis at FISH CREEK before besieging BATOCHE. There, some of his men forced his hand when, after a siege that lasted several days, they broke ranks to rush the Métis positions and bring the battle to a close. In

1890 charges were laid that he had stolen furs confiscated from the Métis during the campaign. He was ruled guilty of 'misjudgement' and forced to return to England. There, he spent his last days as Keeper of the Crown Jewels in the Tower of London, undoubtedly the British government's way of telling Canada that, in its view, Middleton's honesty was unquestioned.

Reading: Desmond Morton, *The Last War Drum: The North West Campaign of 1885* (Toronto, 1972)

Mid-Ocean Escort Force. The designation given in February 1942 to the Anglo-Canadian (with some U.S. warships) escort force responsible for convoying merchant ships across the mid-Atlantic to and from Newfoundland. It replaced the NEWFOUNDLAND ESCORT FORCE. The eastern terminus for the force was Londonderry, Northern Ireland and the western terminus was St John's, Newfoundland. The reorganization had several objectives: shortening convoy routes by shifting them south from the Iceland track; allowing the escort vessels to use the good base facilities at Londonderry rather than at Hvalfjord, Iceland with its bad weather and almost total lack of amenities; and freeing escort vessels from the mid-Atlantic to enable them to be shifted to the coast of North America. The war in the Pacific and U-boat attacks in U.S. coastal waters prompted the United States Navy to withdraw virtually all its escort vessels from the force in 1942. In January 1943 the MOEF consisted of 33 Canadian ships (6 destroyers and 27 CORVETTES), 61 British ships, and only 3 U.S. vessels. See also NEWFOUNDLAND ESCORT FORCE, MID-OCEAN MEETING POINT, WESTERN OCEAN MEETING POINT, EASTERN OCEAN MEETING POINT.

Reading: M. Milner, *North Atlantic Run* (Toronto, 1985)

Mid-Ocean Meeting Point (MOMP). From the spring of 1941 to February 1942, MOMP was the position near Iceland where the NEWFOUNDLAND ESCORT FORCE handed convoys over to escort vessels based in the British Isles. After February 1942, when ships of the MID-OCEAN ESCORT FORCE escorted convoys all the way from St John's, Newfoundland to Londonderry, Northern Ireland, the changeover position was located at the EASTERN OCEAN MEETING POINT, near the U.K.

Mignault, Arthur (1866–1937). An ardent advocate of French-Canadian participation in World War I, Mignault offered $50,000 to raise a battalion for the 2ND CANADIAN DIVISION. The formation—first known as the 22nd (French-Canadian) Battalion—was organized on 7 November 1914. Following the war it became known first as the 22nd Regiment, then as the Royal 22nd Regiment and finally as the ROYAL 22E REGIMENT, or Van Doos.

Military Cooperation Committee, Canada-U.S. A planning committee which functioned in the late 1940s and which was composed of the military members of the PERMANENT JOINT BOARD ON DEFENCE (CANADA-U.S.). In late 1946 the MCC proposed an ambitious air defence plan for North America that was rejected both by Canada and by senior U.S. defence officials.

Military Districts. The 1868 MILITIA ACT divided Canada into nine military districts in the four founding provinces, including two French-language districts in Quebec. Each district was supposed to have its own militia command structure. As other provinces and the population increased, additional districts were created. By the outbreak of World War II, there were 13 districts in all. During the war the eastern and western districts were grouped into the Atlantic and Pacific Commands respectively. See also MILITIA.

Military Cross. Decoration for bravery in action; awarded only to officers.

Military History in Canada. There was no significant Canadian writing on military history until after the WAR OF 1812. That war remained a staple of Canadian military literature until the early twentieth century with works such as William James, *A Full and Correct Account of the Military Occurances of the Late War Between Great Britain and the United States of America* (1818), or John Richardson, *War of 1812, Containing a Full and Detailed Narrative of the Operations of the Right Division of the Canadian Army* (1842). The REBELLIONS OF 1837 also provided material for Canadian military historians, as with Charles Dent, *The Story of the Upper Canada Rebellion* (1885).

Much of the military history of the early and mid-nineteenth century is to be found in general histories of Canada. For example, François-Xavier Garneau's *Histoire du Canada depuis sa découverte jusqu'à nos jours*, 3 vols (1845–1848) contains extensive writing on the various wars fought from the arrival of Champlain to that time. The upsurge of imperialism in the late 19th century, with its attendant strengthening of the MILITIA MYTH, brought a flood of works on Canadian military history, many directed to the War of 1812. This continued following the SOUTH AFRICAN WAR with works such as T.G. Marquis, *Canada's Sons on Kopje and Veldt* (1900), and S.M. Brown, *With the Royal Canadians*. Few of these works were in any way critical histories. They were, almost without exception, written by amateurs, raconteurs, or retired military or militia officers whose chief aim was to glorify and extol, not critically analyse. Even had there been professional historians prepared to produce such works, they would have had little to work with other than militia rolls because the importance of military history was not recognized by the military itself. The war diary was virtually unknown.

Not unexpectedly WORLD WAR I provided substantial grist for the military history mill, much of which was also intended to praise Canada's heroes. This war, however, also gave birth to true institutional history in Canada such as D. Carnegie, *The History of Munitions and Supplies in Canada 1914–1918* (1919). In 1917 the Army Historical Section was created, a reflection of the military's efforts to take its own history far more seriously. War diaries were standard in all field units and an official history was begun after the war. Two volumes eventually appeared; Andrew MACPHAIL, *Official History of the Canadian Forces in the Great War, 1914–1919; The Medical Services* (1925), and A.F. DUGUID, *Official History of the Canadian Forces in the Great War, 1914–1919*, vol. 1 (1938). The latter was intended to span the entire war but the first volume, covering August 1914 to September 1915, was so lengthy and took so long to emerge, that the project was abandoned. It was not until 1962 that a one-volume official history of the CANADIAN EXPEDITIONARY FORCE was produced: G.W.L. NICHOLSON, *The Cana-*

dian Expeditionary Force, 1914–1919 (1962). In addition to these works, however, hundreds of memoirs, regimental histories, and other works also emerged — many privately and commercially printed — which reflected a far more critical attitude toward war in general, and this war in particular, than had hitherto been the case.

WORLD WAR II and the post-war period saw the true birth of critical and professional military history in Canada. The Army Historical Section was headed by C.P. STACEY, a professional historian who had published the only two academic military histories in Canada up to that time. He took care to ensure that diaries and records were faithfully kept by field units, that after-action reports were filed, that interviews were conducted, and that photographs, paintings, and sketches were produced and properly preserved. Stacey oversaw the production of a short introductory history of the Canadian army in World War II — *The Canadian Army: 1939–1945* (1948) — designed to be quickly available after the war, as well as the three-volume official history consisting of Stacey's *Six Years of War* (1955) and *The Victory Campaign* (1960), and Nicholson's *The Canadians in Italy* (1956). Although official histories, those volumes were critically written and not designed to whitewash Canadian errors, downplay Canadian mistakes, or glorify Canadian achievements. Indeed, Stacey's *The Victory Campaign* is regularly cited by British and American historians, reflecting the view that it is one of the best of the official histories to have emerged from World War II in Europe.

Since the war, and with Stacey's work as an example, professional military history began to grow in Canada. It was not until the 1970s, however, that it truly emerged as a sub-field in its own right, practised by a growing number of professional historians and other writers, many of whom have produced solid critical assessments of the performance of the Canadian forces in war and the making of Canadian defence policy in peace.

Reading: O.A. Cooke, *The Canadian Military Experience 1867–1983: A Bibliography* (Ottawa, 1984); Desmond Morton, *A Military History of Canada* (Toronto, 1985)

Military Hospitals Commission. Established in 1915, the commission provided for the demobilization and rehabilitation of veterans in Canada. By 1917 the Commission had 6000 nursing, hospital, and sanitoria beds. The commission's work was taken over by the Department of SOLDIERS' CIVIL RE-ESTABLISHMENT after the war.

Military Intelligence in Canada. Canadian military units in the field collected intelligence in a variety of ways prior to 1901. Most was of an immediate, tactical nature. There was no attempt at coordination until the creation of the intelligence staff in 1901 under a Director of Military Intelligence. Then some work was done in map making, handbook writing, and keeping track of foreign news through reading of newspapers and periodicals. In World War I intelligence consisted mainly of battlefield intelligence, some of which was information gathered by interpreters interviewing prisoners of war. The creation of the CANADIAN CORPS was followed by creation of a corps intelligence staff which disseminated regular reports on enemy dispositions to field units. Some of that information was gained through trench raids. Counter-intelligence in the corps consisted primarily of turning suspected collaborators over to the French. In the inter-war period intelligence ranged from spying on suspected labour agitators to attempting to discern the troop dispositions of the United States, a favourite pursuit of Col J. Sutherland BROWN. For the most part, however, the craft of military intelligence languished.

In World War II an intelligence section was attached to CANADIAN MILITARY HEADQUARTERS in Britain. It was responsible for overall security, censorship, interviewing enemy prisoners, coordinating security liaison with Canada's allies, recruiting and training intelligence officers, and gathering information on British intentions. A CANADIAN INTELLIGENCE CORPS, created in the fall of 1942, was responsible for providing intelligence and field security sections to corps and divisions. Canada also participated with its allies in a number of strategic intelligence-gathering activities such as the interception of enemy wireless communications (see EXAMINATION UNIT; NATIONAL RESEARCH COUNCIL).

Most strategic intelligence information used by Canada in World War II and since has been provided by Canada's allies. Canada has done little in covert intelligence gathering outside its borders and has never had an equivalent organization to the U.S.'s Central Intelligence Agency or Britain's Secret Intelligence Service (MI6).
Reading: S.R. Elliot, *Scarlet to Green: A History of Intelligence in the Canadian Army, 1903–1963* (Toronto, 1981)

Military Medal. Decoration for bravery, awarded to the ranks.

Military Medicine in Canada. A Canadian military medical service took form during the NORTHWEST REBELLION OF 1885 when the minister of Militia and Defence Adolphe CARON appointed Lt-Col Darby Bergin surgeon general. Bergin was a medical doctor who also commanded the Stormont and Glengarry Battalion. Under Frederick BORDEN, a general medical staff was created in 1898, directed by British Col Hubert Neilson who had studied military medicine in Britain and the U.S. Regimental surgeons accompanied the Canadian contingents in the SOUTH AFRICAN WAR and a field hospital company was organized in 1902, the first self-contained Canadian medical unit to serve overseas. In 1904 the Army Medical Corps (later ROYAL CANADIAN ARMY MEDICAL CORPS) was established, and in 1909 the regimental medical system was abolished as the army moved to begin setting up a centralized medical system that would pass wounded men from battalion aid stations up to general military hospitals. The medical services expanded rapidly in World War I and eventually offered wounded Canadian soldiers succour and treatment in an all-Canadian system. By war's end the service contained 1528 officers, 1901 nursing sisters, and 15,624 other ranks. They had treated some 418,052 troops including 144,606 battle casualties. Military medical techniques differed little from those of Canada's allies.

Although the medical services contracted in the inter-war period, they were again called upon to treat large numbers of sick and wounded soldiers overseas in World War II. In that war there was, for the first time, a serious effort to combat the effects of battle exhaustion, or what had previously been known as shell-shock. At the outbreak of war the Department of National Defence created No. 1 Neurological and Neurosurgical Hospital under the direction of Lt-Col

Colin Russel. Russel's hospital went overseas in May 1940. Thereafter there were efforts, sometimes not too vigorous, to assign psychiatrists and psychiatric units to all the Canadian divisions in the field. The treatment of battle exhaustion became a new specialization of military medicine. By the end of the war almost 35,000 personnel served in the medical corps.

In KOREA, the 25th Canadian Field Ambulance accompanied the 25th CANADIAN INFANTRY BRIGADE GROUP across the Pacific. Following unification, the Royal Canadian Army Medical Corps was disbanded.
Reading: Terry Copp and Bill McAndrew, *Battle Exhaustion: Soldiers and Psychiatrists in the Canadian Army, 1939–1945* (Montreal, 1990); G.W.L. Nicholson, *Seventy Years of Service: A History of the Royal Canadian Army Medical Corps* (Ottawa, 1977).

Military Music. The first military music in Canada was probably performed by the fife and drum corps that accompanied the CARIGNAN-SALIÈRES regiment from France in 1665. When the British Army came to Canada in 1760 it was accompanied by a number of regimental bands, many of which made regular public performances. These bands formed the core of what became a number of regimental bands attached to Canadian militia units when, after the withdrawal of British regulars from most of Canada in the 1870s, some British Army bandsmen decided to remain in Canada rather than return to England. There were some 46 such regimental bands in 1869 and bands accompanied the militia during the FENIAN RAIDS, the RED RIVER EXPEDITION, and the NORTHWEST REBELLION. The first regular army band was established by the CANADIAN GARRISON ARTILLERY in 1899. No provisions were originally made for a CANADIAN EXPEDITIONARY FORCE band during World War I, although a merger of the regimental bands of the 10th Battalion and the Winnipeg Light Infantry produced a band in France. This is in contrast to World War II when nine bands were authorized for overseas service with the army, in addition to official bands organized by the navy and air force. Although the number of bands was considerably reduced after the war, bands continue, especially in highland militia regiments. All these bands have traditionally played martial tunes, marches, etc., composed in Britain, the

United States and elsewhere. There is little indigenous military music in Canada.

Military police. See CANADIAN PROVOST CORPS.

Military Service Act, 1917. On 29 August 1917, the Military Service Act was proclaimed into law — introducing conscription to Canada. The legislation decreed that all men 20 to 45 were eligible to be conscripted for overseas service as reinforcements for the Canadian Expeditionary Force. Prime Minister Robert BORDEN introduced the measure in the hope of obtaining 50,000 to 100,000 additional men; instead only 24,000 reinforcements were sent to the CEF in France by the end of the war. See also CONSCRIPTION CRISIS 1917.

Military Voters' Act. Passed in September 1917 to aid Prime Minister Robert BORDEN in the December 1917 federal election, the Act expanded the franchise among military electors. All British subjects in active service regardless of age, sex, or residence were given the right to vote. The Act also allowed the government to allocate the votes of soldiers overseas who declared that they did not know their home constituency to those ridings where the government saw fit. This invariably meant to those ridings where government candidates needed them. See also WARTIME ELECTIONS ACT.

Militia. In Canada as in other countries, the militia has consisted of a part-time, volunteer, armed citizenry which answers the call of government to defend home and hearth and otherwise keep the peace. In Canadian experience the militia has been viewed either as a reserve force to supplement the regular, professional, army (British or Canadian) in times of trouble, or as the backbone of Canada's military, trained by regulars but with the primary mission to defend the country.

The Canadian militia has existed since the days of New France when able-bodied French Canadian males were organized into militia units under a locally elected captain of the militia—one of the few elected positions in the colony. Adopting Indian styles of forest warfare, the militia was used mostly in border raids attacking British frontier settlements, usually in conjunction with Indian allies. Sometimes the militia served together with French regulars but the conflicting styles of fighting could cause severe battlefield difficulties, as on the PLAINS OF ABRAHAM.

Although a Canadian militia continued to exist on paper after the conquest of New France, the militia played little role in defending Canada against invasion from the Thirteen Colonies in the REVOLUTIONARY WAR. Following the arrival of the Loyalists during and after that war, a number of militia units were established in the English-speaking colonies. They, along with a number of French militia units, fought on land and sea alongside British regulars to defend Canada in the WAR OF 1812 although the brunt of the war was borne by British regulars.

Following the War of 1812 the militia languished in the British American colonies. On paper there was a SEDENTARY MILITIA, which was supposed to be composed of all the able-bodied males in the colony capable of being mustered at a moment's notice, and an ACTIVE MILITIA, consisting of those who volunteered, and were paid a small sum, for regular training. The latter was poorly led, badly equipped, and underpaid. After Confederation the first of several MILITIA ACTS was passed in 1868 which established the ACTIVE MILITIA at 40,000 men and provided for a RESERVE MILITIA of almost every other able-bodied male in Canada (i.e., a continuation of the Sedentary Militia). In fact the latter never took any shape at all, while the former's training usually consisted of little more than occasional night and weekend drilling supplemented by a week-long militia camp every summer or so (less often for rural battalions). The country was also divided into a number of MILITARY DISTRICTS for better militia organization.

In 1874 the first General Officer Commanding the Canadian Militia was appointed —Major-General Edward SELBY-SMYTH. The GOC was supposed to combine leadership of the Canadian militia (including training it to operate in conjunction with the British Army) with defence liaison with the U.K., all the while also serving the Canadian minister of militia and defence. Only British officers were appointed in the nineteenth century. Theirs was a most difficult task due to the reluctance of the Canadian government to spend money on defence, and its extreme sensitivity to anything it even remotely considered interference by an Imperial officer in Canadian political affairs. Such interference almost always occurred (at least in Ottawa's eyes) when the GOC tried to get Canada to improve its own defences.

In 1882 the government established permament militia schools, designed to train militia officers. Attendance at those schools was made compulsory the following year but despite this attempt to train militia officers to a respectable standard, appointment of those officers primarily by patronage undermined military efficiency. In fact, attempts by a number of GOCs to eliminate patronage created almost constant friction between them and the government. Although a PERMANENT FORCE began to emerge in the early 1880s, the militia, and not the regulars, was still looked upon as the backbone of Canada's military. This view was reinforced by the MILITIA MYTH to such a degree that for a long time the term 'permanent active militia' was used to designate Canada's professional soldiers, NON-PERMANENT ACTIVE MILITIA being used for the militia itself. As a result, the vast majority of CANADIAN EXPEDITIONARY FORCE and CANADIAN CORPS officers in WORLD WAR I were militia, not permanent force.

Some effort was made between World War I and WORLD WAR II to retain a core of regular soldiers both to train the militia and to provide a nucleus around which the militia could form in time of war. Even so, in World War II militia regiments still formed the backbone of the Canadian army. The militia was retained after World War II but in a much diminished role as reserve troops to back up the regulars. Since 1945 it has been reorganized several times as successive WHITE PAPERS on defence have attempted to re-define its role in Canada's defence. See also Arthur CURRIE, Sam HUGHES, Frederick BORDEN, R.H. O'GRADY-HALEY, Frederick MIDDLETON, E.T.H. HUTTON, W.J. GASCOIGNE, I.J.C. HERBERT, C.D.M.B.H. DUNDONALD, MILITIA COUNCIL.

Reading: Desmond Morton, *Ministers and Generals: Politics and the Canadian Militia, 1868–1904* (Toronto, 1970); Stephen J. Harris, *Canadian Brass: The Making of a Professional Army, 1860–1939* (Toronto, 1988)

Militia Acts. There was little organizational substance to the pre-Confederation militia in the British American colonies because most colonial militia legislation provided only for a *levée en masse*, or call to compulsory service of men ages 16 to 50 when they were required for defence. In 1868 the first of a series of Militia Acts sought to regularize both militia training and the method of calling the militia out. The 1868 Act sought to create an ACTIVE MILITIA of 40,000 volunteers, and a RESERVE MILITIA of every able-bodied male between 18 and 60 years old, unless specially exempted. The 1883 Militia Act provided the basis for the PERMANENT FORCE, i.e., permanent professional soldiers, by establishing training schools with a paid staff for artillery. The 1904 Act, among other things, established a MILITIA COUNCIL to advise the minister of Militia and Defence on military matters, appointed a CHIEF OF THE GENERAL STAFF, and doubled the size of the Permanent Force to 4000. The 1922 NATIONAL DEFENCE ACT brought the three services together and changed the name of the department to DEPARTMENT OF NATIONAL DEFENCE headed by a minister of National Defence.

Militia Council. Modelled on the British Army Council, the Militia Council was established by the MILITIA ACT of 1904. It consisted of both high-level civilian bureaucrats such as the deputy minister of Militia and Defence and military members such as the quartermaster-general and the adjutant-general. It was charged with advising the minister on defence issues and it discussed topics of common interest. The Council effectively halted the public disputes between the minister and senior military officers which had marked previous decades.

Militia and Defence, Department of. Created by the 1868 MILITIA ACT, the department was responsible for all of the country's militia and defence requirements, including personnel and equipment. The often-troubled department was absorbed by the tri-service DEPARTMENT OF NATIONAL DEFENCE which was created by the 1922 NATIONAL DEFENCE ACT.

Militia Lobby. Composed largely of militia officers, many of whom were prominent local leaders, members of provincial legislatures, even members of parliament, the militia lobby pressured Ottawa in the late 19th and early 20th century to spend its meagre defence dollars on the militia, and not on the small PERMANENT FORCE. Since militia officers were largely appointed by patronage, this was completely self-serving, but it was justified by the MILITIA MYTH.

Militia Myth. The myth, developed primarily in the late 19th century, that Loyalist militiamen had saved Canada from the American invasion during the WAR OF 1812. In fact, it had been the well-trained and well-led British regulars who had borne the primary responsibility for successfully defending Canada. The myth produced the further mistaken belief among certain Canadian political leaders, much of the press, and virtually all militia officers that a vigilant, well-armed militia offered Canada's best defence, as opposed to a corps of professional soldiers. The militia myth was self-serving in that it provided a rationale for the government to direct resources towards the maintenance and training of the militia, rather than the small PERMANENT FORCE. Sam HUGHES, minister of Militia and Defence in the BORDEN government believed strongly in the myth. See also MILITIA LOBBY.

Militia Staff Course. One of the reforms of the Canadian defence system introduced by Sir Edward HUTTON during his posting as GOC CANADIAN MILITIA (1898–1900), the four-month course was intended to train staff officers of the NON-PERMANENT ACTIVE MILITIA. The course was not given after 1903 but was begun anew in the interwar years.

Miller, Frank R. (1908–1989). Miller went overseas with the RCAF in 1944 as a station commander, and remained with the air force after the war, becoming vice-chief of the Air Staff in 1951. He left the service for five years to serve as deputy minister of National Defence (1955–60) but returned to become CHAIRMAN, CHIEFS OF STAFF COMMITTEE (1960–64) and CHIEF OF THE DEFENCE STAFF (1964–66). In that post he presided over the beginning of UNIFICATION, a policy he did not agree with and which he did his best to delay.

Milne, David B. (1882–1953). Canadian born, Milne moved to the U.S. to study art and to paint before returning to Canada to join the Canadian Army in 1917. At first he served in the CANADIAN EXPEDITIONARY FORCE as a soldier, not a painter, but after the armistice he did paint war scenes for the army. Upon his return from the war he continued painting in the U.S. until he returned permanently to Canada in 1929.

Milne, William Johnstone (1892–1917). Milne served with the 16th Battalion, CEF. During the Battle of VIMY RIDGE on 9 April 1917, Milne's company was stalled by a German machine gun. Pte Milne crawled toward the gun, disabled its crew, and captured it. Killed in action later the same day, he was awarded the VICTORIA CROSS.

Milroy, W.A. (b. 1920). Milroy served with LORD STRATHCONA'S HORSE as a squadron commander in World War II, attended staff college at Kingston after the war, and in the 1950s and 1960s held a number of important staff positions including Director of Public Relations, Army, Commandant of the Armoured School and Commander, 3rd Infantry Brigade Group. He was appointed Commander of MOBILE COMMAND in 1972 before joining the DEPARTMENT OF NATIONAL DEFENCE as assistant deputy minister, personnel, in 1973. He retired from government service in 1975.

Miner, Harry Garnet Bedford (1891–1918). Serving with the 58th Battalion, CEF, Cpl Miner single-handedly rushed three enemy machine-gun posts at AMIENS on 8 August 1918. He was mortally wounded after his third attack, and was posthumously awarded the VICTORIA CROSS.

Minesweeper. A ship designed primarily to detect and destroy mines, especially contact or magnetic mines which blow up when touched by a passing ship or when a ship's magnetic field is detected. These mines float under the surface, held in place by mooring cables attached to anchors on the ocean floor. They can be laid by ship, submarine, or aircraft. A typical minesweeping operation during WORLD WAR I and WORLD WAR II involved the use of sweeping gear, pulling a steel cable through the water to catch and sever the mine mooring cables. When the mine bobbed to the surface it was destroyed by machine-gun or rifle fire. Initial minesweeping exercises carried out in Canadian waters were conducted by Canadian government steamers as early as 1908.

During World War I minesweeping the approaches to Halifax and Sydney was one of the most important tasks of the fledgling ROYAL CANADIAN NAVY. In 1938 four Canadian-designed and built *Fundy* class minesweepers were commissioned. Sometimes referred to as *Basset* class minesweepers, these vessels displaced 470 tonnes, carried a crew of 38, and were armed with one 4-inch gun. They served until 1945. During World War II the RCN employed *Fundy*, BANGOR, *Algerine*, *Llewellyn*, Lake, and Bay class minesweepers, using them not only for sweeping but also for anti-submarine escort duty. The largest number of wartime minesweepers in RCN service (54) were the *BANGOR*. The *Bangors* were used primarily for anti-submarine warfare, for which they carried 40 depth charges with the appropriate rails and launchers.

Reading: K.R. Macpherson, *Canada's Fighting Ships* (Toronto, 1975)

Minto, Gilbert John Murray Kynynmond Elliot, Earl of (1845–1914). Minto came to Canada as Lord Melgund, serving as military secretary to Governor-General Lansdowne 1883 to 1885. In that role he helped to organize the NILE VOYAGEURS' expedition, served as Sir Frederick MIDDLETON's chief of staff during the NORTHWEST REBELLION of 1885, and initiated the MELGUND COMMISSION. While governor-general (1898–1904), with General E. HUTTON and without consulting the government he drafted a plan to send 1200 men to the SOUTH AFRICAN WAR. He was an outspoken critic of Sir Wilfrid LAURIER's handling of the war; Laurier considered Minto a meddler.

Mitchell, Coulson Norman (1889–1978). Serving with the 4th Battalion, Canadian Engineers at the battle of CAMBRAI in early October 1918, Capt. Mitchell won the VICTORIA CROSS for holding the enemy at bay —killing three men and capturing 12 others —while engineers dismantled explosives on a strategically important bridge.

MOBCOM. See MOBILE COMMAND.

Mobile Command (MOBCOM). Prior to the armed forces' UNIFICATION, Mobile Command assumed control of all army field force units. It was, in effect, the successor to the Canadian Army just as MARITIME COMMAND succeeded the seagoing RCN and AIR COMMAND succeeded the RCAF.

Mobile Striking Force. A response to the challenge of providing for the defence of Canada following deep cuts to the defence budget after 1945, the mobile striking force was to consist of an airborne brigade group, with troops drawn from ACTIVE FORCE units, with the mission of countering a possible enemy lodgement wherever it might take place in Canada. The idea was that reserve and militia units would then be mobilized to reinforce the mobile striking force. Because the ROYAL CANADIAN AIR FORCE's airlift capacity was rather limited throughout the late 1940s and early 1950s, the mobile striking force was a better idea on paper than in reality.

Mobilization, World War I. Although detailed plans for mobilization carried out by the MILITIA DISTRICTS were prepared by PERMANENT FORCE officers prior to the outbreak of World War I, the minister of Militia and Defence, Sam HUGHES, discarded the plans after the outbreak of war and invited the militia regiments to receive volunteers who were then sent to a central location for equipping, training, and formation into operational units. At the same time he decided that regimental contributions would be absorbed into numbered battalions, rather than being sent into the field as distinctive battalions on their own. By September 1914, 25,000 men had been mobilized and sent to a new camp at Valcartier, Quebec. From there the first Canadian contingent of over 37,000 men was sent to England in October 1914. See also NATIONAL REGISTRATION.

Mobilization, World War II. After the German invasion of Poland on 1 September 1939, but before issuing its own declaration of war, Canada mobilized its small professional and part-time military forces. Canada's few destroyers were ordered to patrol the coasts while aircraft went on alert at Halifax. The service chiefs' $500-million mobilization plan, originally based on the idea of dispatching a six-division expeditionary force to war, was slashed in half by the Cabinet; only the RCAF estimates remained untouched. This was in keeping with Prime Minister William Lyon Mackenzie KING's desire to mount a LIMITED LIABILITY WAR EFFORT. Despite this there were initially as many volunteers for the infantry as the army could handle and thus the 1ST CANADIAN INFANTRY DIVISION was sent to Britain in December 1939. By the end of the war the army in Europe had expanded to more than five divisions.

MOMP. See MID-OCEAN MEETING POINT.

Moncel, Robert W. (b. 1917). During WORLD WAR II Moncel served in a variety of command positions with the Royal Canadian Regiment, the 18th Canadian Armoured Car Regiment and the 4th Canadian Armoured Brigade. He became Director of the ROYAL CANADIAN ARMOURED CORPS in 1946 and Director of military training in 1947. By 1966 he had risen to Vice-Chief of the Defence Staff. He retired late that year in opposition to the minister of National Defence Paul HELLYER's UNIFICATION scheme.

Mons, Battle of. The first clash of WORLD WAR I between British and German forces took place in Mons, a city in Belgium, in August 1914; for the CANADIAN CORPS the war also ended there in November 1918 with the Battle of Mons. That battle was part of a larger Allied offensive begun the previous October after the German Army on the western front had started to deteriorate. Spearheaded by the 2ND CANADIAN DIVISION, the Canadian Corps captured the city on 10 November and forced the Germans to retreat toward Antwerp the following day, 11 November which was the day the guns fell silent on the western front. Controversy later developed over whether or not Corps Commander Sir Arthur CURRIE had truly needed to send his forces in for this final assault of the war.

Montague, Percival J. (1882–1966). Trained as a lawyer, Montague saw action with the CEF in World War I and was MENTIONED IN DISPATCHES five times. In the interwar years he commanded the FORT

GARRY HORSE and the 6th Mounted Brigade. During World War II, he served as deputy judge advocate-general and later as judge advocate-general of the Canadian army overseas. He was also chief of staff for CANADIAN MILITARY HEADQUARTERS in London.

Mont Blanc. On 6 December 1917, the French-registered ship *Mont Blanc*, carrying a full load of explosives, collided with the Norwegian freighter *IMO* in Halifax harbour. A cargo of benzol on the *Mont Blanc's* deck caught fire. The ship was rapidly abandoned by its crew and drifted towards the Halifax shipyards. At 9:06 a.m. the ship blew up, causing many deaths and massive devastation. See HALIFAX EXPLOSION.

Montcalm, Louis-Joseph de, Marquis de Montcalm (1712–1759). After a long and distinguished military career which began at an early age, Montcalm was assigned to North America in 1756 to take command of all French troops there at the outbreak of the SEVEN YEARS' WAR. Montcalm was very much a European professional soldier, believing that victory was won by the massed fire power of well-trained infantry, and not by the guerrilla tactics favoured by the French Canadian militia. Outmanned and outgunned by British and British-American forces from the very start, Montcalm took advantage of his shorter internal lines of communication to strike at and subdue British posts along Lake Champlain, thus denying his enemy overland access to the St Lawrence River valley. As good a tactician as he was, however, he could not stop the British under WOLFE from laying siege to Quebec City in the spring of 1759. Despite several inconclusive engagements, the siege dragged on until Wolfe was able to place 4000 men on the PLAINS OF ABRAHAM on the morning of 13 September. Montcalm then committed a major blunder and ordered his men to attack before they were fully prepared. They were repulsed with heavy losses. Both Montcalm and Wolfe were mortally wounded in the battle.

Montmorency Falls, Que. During the siege of Quebec in the summer of 1789, General James WOLFE attempted to overrun French defences at the falls, located east of Quebec City. He intended to seize a redoubt

from which to launch a full-scale attack on the city. Wolfe badly miscalculated French strength at the site and in a clash on 31 July 1759 Wolfe's force suffered over 400 casualties. See SEVEN YEARS' WAR, MONTCALM.

Moose Jaw, HMCS. Corvettes *Moose Jaw* and *Chambly* were part of the escort screen for east-bound CONVOY SC-42 on 10 September 1941, when *Chambly* detected a U-boat. A depth-charge attack was initiated and U-501 surfaced near *Moose Jaw* which rammed it. A party from *Chambly* boarded the stricken sub but could salvage nothing before it sank. Despite this small victory, the convoy lost sixteen ships. During this action *Chambly* was under the command of J.D. 'Chummy' Prentice who was to share in the destruction of three more U-boats before the war's end.

Moraviantown, Battle of. Battle fought during the WAR OF 1812 when disorganized British, Canadian, and Iroquois forces under General Henry PROCTOR retreated from American forces advancing up the River Thames, north of Lake Erie. Under the command of William Henry Harrison, the Americans forced the British to battle on 5 October 1813 and Procter's troops broke. The great Iroquois chief TECUMSEH was killed in the fight. Although the British were routed, the battle was considered inconclusive because Harrison, his supply lines overextended, failed to continue his advance.

Moreuil Wood, Battle of. On 21 March 1918, the German Army mounted a major last-ditch offensive on the western front designed to end the war before the United States could bring its full weight to bear. For the most part the Canadian Corps was by-passed in the fighting, the bulk of which took place to the south of the main Canadian positions. The exception was at Moreuil Wood where all three regiments of the CANADIAN CAVALRY BRIGADE were thrown into action in a desperate bid to stop the German advance towards AMIENS. The advance was slowed but the Canadians suffered heavy casualties in one of the last cavalry charges of the war. See also FLOWERDEW, LT G.M.

Moro River, Battle of. On the east coast of the Italian peninsula, the Moro River flows to the Adriatic and reaches the sea about 3 km southeast of ORTONA. Advancing up the east coast of Italy, the 1ST CANADIAN INFANTRY DIVISION reached the Moro in early December 1943 after fighting its way across the SANGRO RIVER. In order to advance further, the river had to be forded and the town of San Leonardo, about 3 km from the coast, had to be taken. On the evening of 5 December the Division struck. The Hastings and Prince Edward Regiment forced a crossing on the coast, the PRINCESS PATRICIA'S CANADIAN LIGHT INFANTRY crossed some 6.5 km inland and the Seaforth Highlanders assaulted San Leonardo in the centre. Theirs was to be the main attack; the other two were planned as feints to draw off the Germans. The plan failed in the face of stiff resistance and the Seaforths were forced to withdraw although the PPCLI and the 'Hasty Pees' both held small bridgeheads. Two days later, a new attack was launched, this time spearheaded by the 48th Highlanders and the ROYAL CANADIAN REGIMENT. These units, supported by armour, succeeded in expanding the small bridgeheads left after the previous attack and taking San Leonardo on 9 December. The advance on Ortona then resumed.

Mosquito aircraft. World War II twin-engine fighter, night fighter, light bomber, and reconnaisance aircraft designed in Britain by DE HAVILLAND and built there and in Canada, primarily out of plywood. With a bomb load of nearly two tonnes, the plane was a favourite for all types of bombing raids. Its great speed and operational height allowed it to easily evade enemy fighters.

Moth. See TIGER MOTH.

Motor Torpedo Boat. Designed to operate in shallow water, the fast, versatile MTBs carried torpedoes or depth charges and guarded the flanks of invasion forces, blockaded enemy harbours, or raided enemy shipping. Two RCN MTB flotillas were organized in 1944. The 29th Flotilla featured 'G' type MTBs with a top speed of 43 knots, a displacement of 41.6 tonnes, and a crew of 17. The 'G' type was armed with one 2-pounder and two 20-mm guns and two torpedo tubes. The 65th used the larger 'D' type which carried a crew of 32 at a top speed of 30 knots. It displaced 103 tonnes and was armed with two 6-pounders, two 20-mm guns, four .50-calibre machine guns and four torpedo tubes.

Mount Sorrel, Battle of. On 2 June 1916, troops of the 3RD CANADIAN DIVISION, in the line less than two weeks, were occupying positions atop Mount Sorrel when a massive German artillery barrage, combined with the explosion of four mines under the positions, almost wiped the Canadians from the face of the earth. One of those killed was the division commander, Major-General Malcolm S. MERCER. At the same time the Germans launched a flanking attack against Canadian positions in Sanctuary Wood, to the north of Mount Sorrel. The Germans had little trouble taking the high ground and the Canadians suffered very heavy casualties. A Canadian counter-attack the following day was a disaster. The corps commander, Sir Julian BYNG, then gave the task to Arthur CURRIE and his 1ST CANADIAN DIVISION. Currie planned his attack carefully, paying special attention to the use of artillery, and the assault was launched on 8 June. In one hour, and with few casualties, the Canadians regained the position. The Germans counter-attacked two days later but Currie's men held. The fighting for Mount Sorrel cost the CANADIAN CORPS some 8000 casualties.

Mowat, Farley (b. 1921). Born in Ontario, Mowat went overseas as a lieutenant with the Hastings and Prince Edward Regiment in July 1942 and served until the end of the war in the ITALIAN CAMPAIGN and NORTHWEST EUROPE, rising to the rank of captain. After the war Mowat earned fame in Canada and abroad as a writer of non-fiction. His war memoirs, *And No Birds Sang* (1979), and his history of his regiment, *The Regiment* (1955), are among the finest pieces of Canadian writing to emerge from World War II.

Mullin, George Harry (1892–1963). Sgt Mullin served overseas in WORLD WAR I as a sniper with the PRINCESS PATRICIA'S CANADIAN LIGHT INFANTRY. On 30 October 1917, during the battle of PASSCHENDAELE, he and Lt Hugh MACKENZIE of the 7th Canadian Machine-Gun Company both won the VICTORIA CROSS as a result of their attack on a German pillbox. Mackenzie drew the Germans' fire away from Mullin, allowing Mullin to shoot the two German machine-gunners inside, capture the pillbox, and take the ten-man garrison prisoner. Mackenzie was killed in the action.

Mulloy, Lorne (1879?–1932). A teacher from Ontario, Mulloy joined the CANADIAN MOUNTED RIFLES at the start of the SOUTH AFRICAN WAR. He was blinded in action but was able to graduate with a degree from Queen's University in 1907 and later go on to Oxford. He then taught military history at ROYAL MILITARY COLLEGE and helped in WORLD WAR I recruiting drives. After the war he supervised programs for blinded war veterans.

Multinational Force and Observers. The MFO was established as a non-United Nations observation force following the signing of the Israel-Egypt peace treaty in 1980. The force mans electronic listening posts and patrols roads and other strategic locations in the Sinai Peninsula to ensure that the provisions of the treaty respecting the limiting of troops in the Sinai is observed. Canadian personnel have been a part of the MFO since its inception.

Munitions and Supply, Department of. The Department was established on 9 April 1940 and was disbanded on 31 December 1945. C.D. HOWE was its first and only minister. The department coordinated domestic industry during World War II and oversaw the production of munitions and other war supplies for Canadian and Allied forces. The Department created numerous Crown corporations for specific manufacturing and war service tasks and regulated 'essential' supplies. See also VICTORY AIRCRAFT; PARK STEAMSHIPS.

Munro, R. Ross (1913–1990). Munro joined the Canadian Press in 1936 and served as its war correspondent in Europe from 1940 to 1945. In that capacity he followed the Canadian army from SICILY to Spitsbergen and witnessed the DIEPPE debacle. After

the war he published *Gauntlet to Overlord* (1945), a popular history of the Canadian army at war, which won the Governor-General's Award for non-fiction.

Murchie, John C. (1895–1966). A graduate of ROYAL MILITARY COLLEGE, Murchie served in France with the CANADIAN CORPS, was seriously wounded but recovered to return to action. In the inter-war years Murchie held various military appointments in Canada and Britain. In May 1944 he became Chief of the General Staff, a post he held until 20 August 1945. Murchie played a key role in convincing Prime Minister William Lyon Mackenzie KING in November, 1944, that there was no longer any choice but to conscript NRMA men for overseas military service.

Murmansk. See RUSSIAN CIVIL WAR.

Murray, Leonard Warren (1896–1971). Murray joined the navy in 1911 and served in both wars. His operational commands during WORLD WAR II included Commodore Commanding the NEWFOUNDLAND ESCORT FORCE in 1941-42, Commanding Officer, Atlantic Coast in 1942, and Commander in Chief of the Canadian Northwest Atlantic Command in 1943. In this latter post he was the supreme authority over all convoys north of latitude 40 and east of longitude 47 and was thus the only Canadian to command a theatre of war. He was held responsible for the HALIFAX RIOTS on V-E Day and forced into early retirement in 1945.

Murray, James (1721/22–1794). During the SEVEN YEARS' WAR, Murray commanded a battalion at the siege of LOUISBOURG and served as one of WOLFE's brigadiers at the PLAINS OF ABRAHAM. He commanded the British garrison at Quebec City over the winter of 1759–60. In the spring of 1760 he was defeated by the Marquis de LÉVIS at STE FOY but held Quebec because of the timely arrival of British warships. Murray governed Quebec until 1766. He was removed after his failure to implement the Proclamation of 1763, a measure he believed would have alienated the French Canadians because it would have effectively barred them from any participation in public life while handing the task of governing the colony to a handful of English-speaking Protestants.

Mussallem, Helen Kathleen (b. ?). After embarking on a career in nursing education, Mussallem volunteered for the ROYAL CANADIAN ARMY MEDICAL CORPS in WORLD WAR II and served overseas with the rank of lieutenant. After the war she continued her career in Vancouver, receiving the Florence Nightingale Medal in 1981.

Mustang fighter. WORLD WAR II single-engine fighter which originally married a U.S. airframe design to the British-built Merlin engine. The Mustang was not only fast and manoeuvrable, it also had great range, being the first fighter capable of escorting bombers all the way to Berlin and back from bases in the U.K. The fighter saw wide wartime use by the USAAF, both in the escort and air superiority role and to attack German aircraft on the ground. Five RCAF squadrons flew early versions of the Mustang in World War II from June, 1942 to the end of the war. In 1947 the RCAF acquired 130 Mk IV Mustangs as a stopgap until fighter jets could be secured. Some of these aircraft remained in RCAF reserve service until 1961. Equipped with wing-mounted machine guns, the later version of the Mustang could fly at some 700 km/h over a range of 1500 km and had a service ceiling of 12,500 metres.

Mustard gas. The deadliest of the gases employed by both sides during WORLD WAR I, mustard gas was first used in July, 1917. It was made of dichlorethyl sulphide, an oily liquid. It was usually delivered inside artillery shells. The gas caused severe blistering and irritation to skin, eyes, and (if inhaled directly) lungs.

Mutinies, Naval. In late winter of 1949 short-lived mutinies broke out on three Royal Canadian Navy warships. The incidents occurred aboard the destroyer *ATHABASKAN* on 26 February 1949, the destroyer *Crescent* on 15 March 1949, and the light fleet carrier *MAGNIFICENT* on 20 March 1949. The *Athabaskan* incident took place

while the ship was in Manzanillo harbour, Mexico and involved the refusal of 90 of the ship's company of 14 officers and 196 men to perform routine duties for a period of about one hour. The events on the *Crescent* (which involved 83 men out of a complement of 13 officers and 167 men) and the *Magnificent* (32 men out of 70 officers and 828 men) were similar. *Magnificent* was in the Caribbean at the time, *Crescent* at Nanking, China. These mutinies were similar to ones that had taken place during WORLD WAR II on the destroyer *IROQUOIS* and in 1947 on the cruiser *ONTARIO*. As a result, the minister of National Defence Brooke CLAXTON established a commission of investigation under Rear-Admiral E.R. MAINGUY which issued the MAINGUY REPORT in October, 1949. The commission found that the mutinies had occurred as a result of poor shipboard living conditions, unrealistic expectations among the ratings of life in the navy (raised by misleading advertising), the large gap between officers and men, and the Royal Navy-born inclination of RCN officers (many of whom had trained aboard RN ships) to look down on the ratings.

Mutual Aid. The Canadian government provided $2 billion in direct economic assistance to the Allies between 1943 and 1945 in the forms of food, raw materials, and munitions. Most of this went directly to Great Britain. The aid package has been described as an act of enlightened self-interest for a Canadian government concerned with post-war debt in Europe that could inhibit the ability of Europeans, and especially the British, to buy Canadian goods.

Mynarski, Andrew Charles (1916–1944). Born in Winnipeg, Mynarski was a pilot officer aboard a LANCASTER bomber of No. 419 squadron, NO. 6 GROUP, on the night of 12 June 1944 when, on a raid against CAMBRAI, the bomber was attacked by a night fighter and set aflame. Mynarski's clothing and parachute caught fire while he tried to rescue the trapped rear gunner. He was unable to free the man. By the time he jumped he was badly burned. His comrade survived the plane crash but Mynarski died of his burns. He was posthumously awarded the VICTORIA CROSS.

N

Nabob, HMCS. One of two Royal Navy commissioned escort carriers operated by the RCN during World War II, *Nabob* and sister ship *PUNCHER* each carried a mix of twenty torpedo bombers and fighters, as well as a range of defensive armament. *Nabob* was slightly larger than *Puncher*, the former displacing 15,600 tonnes and the later 14,400. Converted merchant ships, these small flattops formed the core of hunter-killer groups that ranged far ahead of North Atlantic convoys to catch U-boats on the surface. On 22 August 1944, *Nabob* was torpedoed near the Norwegian coast where it had sailed on a mine-laying sortie. The crew guided the crippled carrier 1760 km back to its base, but the ship could not be economically repaired and was paid off the following month.

Namibia, UN peacekeeping in. See UNTAG.

National Defence Act. The legislation by which the DEPARTMENT OF NATIONAL DEFENCE is governed. The first National Defence Act was passed in 1922 and united the Department of MILITIA AND DEFENCE, the DEPARTMENT OF NAVAL SERVICE and the AIR BOARD under a minister of National Defence. The act has been modified on a number of occasions when required. Shortly after the outbreak of World War II, for example, ministers of national defence for air and the navy were created to handle the expanded forces.

National Defence College. Established in 1947 at Kingston, the college was founded to offer advanced courses to both civilian and military personnel (usually from the senior bureaucracy and officer corps) in defence and foreign policy and related areas, and in international affairs.

National Defence Headquarters (NDHQ). Following the integration of the three services in 1922, the newly-created DE-

PARTMENT OF NATIONAL DEFENCE established its headquarters in a single structure at Ottawa. When the armed forces expanded and the ministries of national defence for air and the navy were created during World War II, three separate 'temporary' buildings served as NDHQ. Brooke CLAXTON re-integrated NDHQ after taking over as minister of National Defence in late 1946. NDHQ is now housed in the Pearkes building.

National Registration, World War I. Sir Robert BORDEN's government announced voluntary registration, based on a similar British scheme, in late 1916 as a means of establishing a national manpower inventory. Registration began early the following year when cards were distributed to males across Canada; at least 20 per cent of the cards were never returned. Of those that were (1.5 million) only 287,000 came from men eligible for military service.

National Registration, World War II. The NATIONAL RESOURCES MOBILIZATION ACT required all males and females over 16 to register between 19 and 21 August 1940. The information collected provided the government with a basis for compulsory military service. The Department of NATIONAL WAR SERVICES administered the program until 1942 when it was taken over by the Department of Labour.

National Research Council (NRC). Created by the federal government in 1916 to do war-related scientific research, the NRC coordinated and conducted such work until the end of WORLD WAR II. In the inter-war period it was headed for a time by A.G.L. MCNAUGHTON. During World War II, under Dr C.J. MACKENZIE who headed NRC, 1939–1952, it worked on radar, chemical and biological weapons, synthetic fuels, and nuclear fission, among other things. After the war the military function of NRC was assumed by the DEFENCE RESEARCH BOARD.

National Resources Mobilization Act (NRMA). Passed 21 June 1940, the NRMA provided for conscription for home defence and registration of all men and women in Canada over the age of 16. Those conscripts who chose to remain in Canada (i.e., who did not 'GO ACTIVE' or volunteer for overseas service) were known as NRMA men or, more derogatorily, ZOMBIES. The Act was administered by the Department of NATIONAL WAR SERVICES until 1942 when it came under the jurisdiction of the Department of Labour. After the Conscription PLEBISCITE, held 27 April 1942, the government passed BILL 80 to amend the NRMA to authorize it to send NRMA men overseas if need be. Nearly 60,000 NRMA men did volunteer to go active during the war, but a manpower shortage in infantry units which developed after NORMANDY forced the government's hand. Eventually 16,000 NRMA men were ordered sent overseas; 12,908 actually went before the end of hostilities. See also CONSCRIPTION CRISIS 1942, CONSCRIPTION CRISIS 1944.

National Selective Service (NSS). Established in October 1941, the NSS controlled where Canadians worked, when they changed jobs and who was obliged to serve in defence of Canada under the NATIONAL RESOURCES MOBILIZATION ACT. Women 20 to 24 years old came under the NSS's jurisdiction in September 1942. All employees had to give the NSS a week's notice to change jobs, and men age 17 to 45 were barred from 'non-essential' jobs including selling real estate, manufacturing luxury and recreational goods, and driving a taxi.

National Service Board (NSB). The NSB was first established to promote enlistment during the early years of World War I. Later, the NSB helped forecast the effects demobilization would have on the labour market. After the war, demobilization responsibilities were shared among various organizations, but especially the Department of SOLDIERS' CIVIL RE-ESTABLISHMENT.

National War Labour Board. The Board was established in 1941 with national authority to enforce government wage orders and regulate industrial relations in war industries and among civil servants. In 1944, following the recommendations of chairman C.P. McTague, the board was given the authority to increase wages previously held down by the government's wage and price controls. Under order-in-council PC 1003 — the NATIONAL WAR LABOUR ORDER — issued in February 1944, the Board was also given power to certify unions and ensure that employers bargained with them in good faith.

National War Labour Order. An order-in-council (PC 1003) issued in February 1944 which ordered employers to bargain with unions certified by the NATIONAL WAR LABOUR BOARD. The order resulted from recommendations made by NWLB chairman C.P. McTague following mounting unrest in Canadian war industries. It was replaced after the war by the Industrial Relations and Disputes Investigation Act.

National War Memorial. Located in Confederation Square, Ottawa, the cenotaph was dedicated by King George VI on 21 May 1939. Originally designed to honour Canada's war dead from WORLD WAR I, the cenotaph was soon to become the nation's war memorial to the dead of WORLD WAR II and KOREA also. See WAR MEMORIALS.

National War Services, Department of. Department of government established 12 July 1940 under minister J.G. GARDINER to oversee a variety of governmental activities during wartime. At one point the department was responsible for the Canadian Broadcasting Corporation, the National Film Board, and the Canadian Travel Bureau. From the time of the passage of the NATIONAL RESOURCES MOBILIZATION ACT until 1942, National War Services administered that act as well. As the war progressed, many of the most important activities administered by National War Services were placed under the authority of other departments. See also LAFLÈCHE.

National Survival Training. During the late 1950s and early 1960s, when fear of a Soviet atomic attack on North America was at its height, the government launched a program that purported to tell Canadians what to do in case of such an attack. It encouraged Canadians to build fallout shelters (and provided them with plans and lists of provisions to stock in them). The armed forces underwent special training for this possibility.

NATO. See NORTH ATLANTIC TREATY OR-
GANIZATION.

Naval Aid Bill. Sir Robert BORDEN introduced the bill in December 1912 to authorize
a $35 million payment to Britain for con-
struction of three Dreadnought-type battle-
ships for the Royal Navy. This 'emergency
contribution' to the RN was as much for
Britain's defence as Canada's and Borden
hoped it would give Canada a greater say in
imperial defence policy. The Liberals fought
bitterly against the measure since it would
effectively end the LAURIER naval building
program which had been initiated in 1910
with the NAVAL SERVICE ACT. In the House
of Commons they forced Borden to use
closure for the first time in Canadian history.
Since Liberals dominated the Senate, in May
1913 they were able to kill the legislation
altogether.

Naval Boarding Service. Established in
Halifax in 1940 under the authority of the
NAVAL CONTROL SERVICE, the Service's
original task was to examine cargo manifests
of merchant ships in harbour and and keep a
close watch for explosives or saboteurs
aboard ships about to sail. Its name derived
from its mandate to board vessels in pursuit
of its objectives. After a time it also began
to look after the welfare of merchant seamen
in port, using its motor launches to deliver
warm clothing, magazines, and other amenities to ships anchored in harbour.

Naval Control Service (NCS: naval control of shipping). During World War I, the
British Admiralty took control of the movement of British merchant and government
vessels, rerouting them clear of U-boat infested areas and eventually establishing a convoy system. In Canada the ROYAL
CANADIAN NAVY developed its own shipping
control organization to organize convoys in
Canadian ports. At the outbreak of World
War II, a similar method was quickly put
into place for organizing and routing merchant shipping. The Naval Control Service
in Canada began to organize trans-Atlantic
convoys as early as December 1939. The
NCS was also responsible for the operations
of the NAVAL BOARDING SERVICE.

Naval Service Act. At the 1909 Imperial
Conference, British Admiralty officials told

Dominion prime ministers that Britain
needed help in its naval race with Germany.
LAURIER's answer was the Naval Service Act
of 1910. The Act established the DEPART-
MENT OF NAVAL SERVICE and set up a small
Canadian navy which would serve with the
Royal Navy in time of war. The Act was
unpopular with both imperialists, who believed it did not go far enough, and Quebec
nationalists, who decried any military help
for Britain. The Act was one cause of Laurier's 1911 defeat at the hands of Robert
BORDEN. Borden's solution was the NAVAL
AID BILL—a cash contribution to Britain instead of an independent Canadian navy. Before Laurier was defeated, however, the
crusiers *NIOBE* and *RAINBOW* were acquired
from the RN, marking the effective beginning of the ROYAL CANADIAN NAVY.

Naval Service, Department of. See DE-
PARTMENT OF NAVAL SERVICE.

Navy League of Canada. A volunteer organization founded in 1896 and affiliated
with the Navy League of the British Empire
which had been established two years earlier.
The League organized and trained sea cadets,
provided sailors' comforts during wartime,
and generally promoted Canada's naval and
maritime interests.

Navy Show, The. See 'MEET THE NAVY'.

Nazi. A member of the German National
Socialist Party; during World War II a pe-
jorative term for the German forces.

Nelles, Percy W. (1892–1951). After holding a series of operational commands, Nelles
became CHIEF OF THE NAVAL STAFF in 1934
and guided the ROYAL CANADIAN NAVY
through the years of its greatest expansion,
1934–44. Although Nelles cannot be blamed
for many of the RCN's shortcomings in the
early phases of the war, he clearly did not
appreciate the importance of acquiring the
latest in anti-submarine detection and warfare technology for RCN vessels. Following
a disagreement with the minister of National
Defence for Naval Services A.L. MACDON-
ALD about the growth of the navy and its
tardiness in adopting new technological in-
novations such as the latest RADAR, Nelles
resigned his post and was transferred to

London as head of the Canadian Naval mission in the U.K. He retired from the navy in 1945.

Nelson River, 1697. See YORK FACTORY and PIERRE LEMOYNE.

Neptune, Operation. Title given to the actual landing phase of Operation OVERLORD. Neptune saw the movement of approximately 5000 ships of every size into the Bay of the Seine on 6 June 1944. Canada's naval contribution to Neptune included 11 destroyers (nine RIVER CLASS and two TRIBAL CLASS), 11 frigates, 19 CORVETTES, and two LANDING SHIPS INFANTRY.

Neptune aircraft (P2V-7). Twin-engine anti-submarine and coastal patrol aircraft built by Lockheed in the United States. The Neptune was acquired by the ROYAL CANADIAN NAVY beginning in 1958 to replace ageing LANCASTER bombers which had been converted to maritime patrol duty. Neptunes were based at Greenwood, N.S. and Summerside, P.E.I.

Newfoundland Escort Force. Convoy escort force established by the Admiralty with help from the ROYAL CANADIAN NAVY in May 1941. The NEF was set up to counter the growing number of U-boat attacks in the western Atlantic and was organized with its eastern terminus at St John's and its western at Hvalfjord, Iceland. The Force escorted convoys from St. John's to the vicinity of Iceland where it handed them over to escorts from the British Isles, and then headed for harbour in Hvalfjord. In June 1941 the Force was composed of 16 British vessels, mostly CORVETTES, and 23 RCN ships—six destroyers and 17 corvettes. Canada also supplied the shore bases and aircraft to provide air cover for the convoys as far out to sea as the aircraft could manage —about 650 kms at that stage of the war. In early 1942 the escort system was reorganized and the NEF was absorbed into the MID-OCEAN ESCORT FORCE.

Newfoundland Patriotic Association. Organization consisting of Newfoundland Governor W.E. Davidson and fifty prominent citizens invested with the authority to recruit and equip Newfoundland volunteers to serve with the [ROYAL] NEWFOUNDLAND REGIMENT in World War I. The body operated until 1917 when it was dissolved because of its inability to raise enough troops voluntarily. Conscription was then introduced.

Niagara, **HMCS.** TOWN CLASS DESTROYER acquired by the RCN as part of the LEASED BASES AGREEMENT in September 1940. Originally launched in 1918, the ship had been commissioned in the United States Navy as the USS *Thatcher*. Used initially as a convoy escort vessel with the WESTERN LOCAL ESCORT FORCE, it ended the war as a training ship at Halifax and was paid off in September 1945.

Niagara Frontier. The Niagara frontier is that portion of the Niagara Peninsula (bounded on the east by the Niagara River, on the north by Lake Ontario, and on the south by Lake Erie) which is closest to the United States. Strategically located, the frontier was the scene of much fighting during the WAR OF 1812 including the battles of STONEY CREEK, LUNDY'S LANE, FORT ERIE, QUEENSTON HEIGHTS, and CHIPPEWA. Several important military posts were sited on the frontier, including FORT GEORGE, Fort Mississauga, and Butler's Barracks on the British side and Fort Niagara on the American side. The British posts provided an important line of communication between the frontier and Fort York (later Toronto). During the War of 1812 the forts were garrisoned by Canadian militia and British regulars.

Nicaragua, UN peacekeeping in. See ONUCA.

Nichols, Jack (b. 1921). A Canadian painter who trained with F.H. VARLEY, Nichols was commissioned to paint for the MERCHANT MARINE and for the ROYAL CANADIAN NAVY in World War II. He painted the D-DAY landings at NORMANDY and subsequest action in NORTHWEST EUROPE. His preferred subject was the ordinary serviceman at work.

Nicholson, Gerald William Lingen (1902–1980). One of Canada's most prolific and accomplished military historians, Nicholson wrote *The Canadians in Italy* (1956)and *The Canadian Expeditionary Force 1914–19* (1962) while on staff with the Army's historical section. Among his other major works are *The Gunners of Canada*, 2 vols (1967, 1972) and *Canada's Nursing Sisters* (1975).

Nickerson, William Henry Snyder (1875–1954). Born in New Brunswick, Nickerson served with the Royal Army Medical Corps in the SOUTH AFRICAN WAR. On 20 April 1900 he won a VICTORIA CROSS at Wakkerstroom.

Nielsen, Erik Hersholt (b. 1924). Nielsen won a DISTINGUISHED FLYING CROSS as a pilot with the ROYAL CANADIAN AIR FORCE during World War II and was first elected to the House of Commons in 1957. In 1985 he became minister of National Defence. During his tenure the government of Prime Minister Brian Mulroney initiated a reorganization of Canada's NATO units, re-introduced distinctive uniforms for the three commands, and entered into an agreement with the United States to convert the obsolete DEW LINE into the NORTH WARNING SYSTEM, designed to detect low-flying Soviet bombers armed with cruise missiles.

Nile Expedition. In 1884 Britain mounted an expedition up the Nile River from Egypt to Khartoum, in the Sudan, to relieve C.G. 'Chinese' Gordon who was besieged by the forces of the Mahdi who opposed Britain's presence in the region. Garnet WOLSELEY was placed in charge. Wolseley's force would have to overcome the Nile's cataracts as it moved upriver and Wolseley decided that Canadian boatmen, such as those who had helped move his RED RIVER EXPEDITION in 1870, would be immensely helpful. He called them 'voyageurs' but in fact they were not, true voyageurs having disappeared with the end of the Montreal fur trade in the 1820s. The Canadian government gave Britain permission to recruit such a group and 386 men were signed on and brought to Egypt under the command of Colonel F.C. DENISON. Most of these men returned to Canada some six months later without having taken part in Wolseley's expedition because their contract expired and they refused to re-enlist. The remainder — 89 men — did yeoman work in helping the expedition manhandle its heavy boats through the Nile rapids. Wolseley successful took Khartoum,

but not before Gordon had been defeated and beheaded.

Reading: Roy MacLaren, *Canadians on the Nile: 1882–1898* (Vancouver, 1978)

Nile Voyageurs. See NILE EXPEDITION.

Niobe, HMCS. Following the passage of the NAVAL SERVICE ACT, Canada acquired two obsolete cruisers from the Royal Navy, the *Niobe* and the *RAINBOW*, for use as training ships. With LAURIER's defeat in 1911 and the cancellation of his naval program by BORDEN, the two vessels formed the basic strength of the RCN at the outbreak of World War I. Launched in 1897, *Niobe* was the larger of the two ships, displacing some 11,200 tonnes and carrying a crew of about 700. *Niobe* was commissioned into the ROYAL CANADIAN NAVY in September 1910, patrolled the east coast in 1914–15 as a member of the NORTH AMERICA AND WEST INDIES SQUADRON of the Royal Navy, served as a depot ship at Halifax, and was paid off in May 1920.

Nixon, C.R. (b. 1928). An engineer, Nixon joined the Royal Canadian Navy in 1946 and served until 1963, seeing action in Korean waters. Upon his retirement from the military he joined the government, serving in a number of capacities before assuming the position of deputy minister of the Department of National Defence, a post he held from 1975 to 1982.

Non-Permanent Active Militia. See MILITIA.

Nootka, HMCS. A *Fundy* class minesweeper commissioned at ESQUIMALT in 1938, *Nootka* displaced 470 tonnes, carried a crew of 38 and was armed with one 4-inch gun. The vessel patrolled the west coast after the outbreak of World War II and was transferred to the Atlantic coast where she worked with the Halifax Local Defence Force after April 1940. Renamed *Nanoose* in 1943, the minesweeper was paid off in 1945. The second ship of this name, a TRIBAL CLASS destroyer commissioned in August, 1946, served two tours in Korean waters during the KOREAN WAR and ended her days as a training ship. She was paid off in 1964.

Normandy. The battle for Normandy opened with the D-DAY landings of 6 June 1944 and is considered to have ended with the closing of the FALAISE GAP in the third week of August. Elements of the FIRST CANADIAN ARMY played a significant role in the fighting throughout.

Canadian participation in the Battle of Normandy began on the night of 5/6 June as the 1st Canadian Parachute Battalion, part of the 6th British Airborne Division, took part in airborne landings near Bénouville on the Caen canal, about halfway between the Bay of the Seine and CAEN. Their task was to secure the left flank of the invasion and take the bridges across the canal and the Orne River which parallels it a few tens of metres away. These troops secured their immediate objectives but were unable to advance any significant distance eastward from their bridgehead.

The main Canadian effort was launched on the morning of 6 June when the 7th Canadian Infantry Brigade of the 3RD CANADIAN INFANTRY DIVISION, accompanied by the 6th Canadian Armoured Regiment, landed on Mike sector of JUNO BEACH, while the 8th Canadian Infantry Brigade, along with the 10th Canadian Armoured Regiment, landed east of there on Nan sector. The 9th Canadian Infantry Brigade and the 27th Canadian Armoured Regiment constituted the floating reserve. GOC 3rd Division was Maj.-Gen. R.F.L. KELLER. Until Headquarters, FIRST CANADIAN ARMY, under Lieutenant-General H.D.G. CRERAR, was able to assume control of Canadian formations in Normandy on 23 July, the Canadians fought under the command of Second British Army. At all times from 6 June to the end of the war the Canadians were under the overall control of 21st Army Group, commanded by General Bernard Montgomery.

The initial Canadian objective was the stretch of beach from St Aubin-sur-Mer on the east to about half the distance from Courseulles-sur-Mer to La Rivière on the west. This constituted Juno Beach, which was sandwiched between Sword Beach (British) on the left flank and Gold Beach (also British) on the right flank. Farther to the west lay Omaha and Utah beaches, assigned to the United States forces.

Montgomery's original plan called for a deep, rapid thrust by armour early in the invasion, with the capture of the city of Caen and the rolling country beyond as the major objective. Although the Allies enjoyed overwhelming air superiority, the terrain favoured the defence, many of the German troops were either skilled veterans or fanatical SS, and the German tanks—Panthers and Tigers—were better than the SHERMANS and CHURCHILLS used by the Commonwealth troops. The Canadians fought a major battle on D-plus-1 when they ran into 12th SS Panzer Division (Hitlerjugend) troops under Kurt MEYER at Authie, on the way to CARPIQUET airfield east of Caen. They stopped the German advance but suffered heavy losses.

A German victory over the British 7th Armoured Division at Villers-Bocage, to the southwest of the Canadian positions, allowed the Germans to hold Montgomery's troops before Caen. Thus although the Allies were able to get ashore on 6 June and link up shortly after, and the Americans were able to complete their drive across the Cotentin peninsula by 18 June and capture Cherbourg on 26 June, progress southward was slow and costly. German armour could not easily move by day due to Allied control of the skies, but enough units filtered through from southern France and elsewhere to allow them to hold a line across the base of the Normandy peninsula. This created overcrowding in the beachhead and delayed the arrival of additional Allied reinforcements. The other major Canadian units — the 2ND CANADIAN INFANTRY DIVISION and the 4TH CANADIAN ARMOURED DIVISION were not to arrive in Normandy until early July.

Unable to break through at Caen, Montgomery decided to hold, attempt to attract the bulk of the German armour to his forces, and allow the Americans to the west under Omar Bradley to build up their strength for the eventual breakout. Thus 3rd Canadian Infantry Division did little fighting from 11 June until 4 July when Keller's troops moved against Carpiquet once again. Again they faced bitter resistance from the well-dug-in 12th SS Panzer Division, and suffered heavy casualties. The airfield, posing a threat to the German positions in Caen, was taken but Keller and his staff were harshly criticized by the British for what was thought to be a hesitant and uncoordinated effort.

Such criticisms dogged Canadian officers

then and since. The simple truth was that few of the Allied formations equalled the Germans in skill, and that hesitation in attack and failure to follow through was all too characteristic of many U.S. and British officers as well, even Montgomery. This failure of leadership, combined with the sheer ferocity of the fighting, drove casualty figures up. The Canadians lost almost 1200 dead and wounded in the fight for Carpiquet and the capture of Caen that followed shortly after.

Caen taken, Montgomery ordered his formations to increase pressure on the Germans by pushing south towards Falaise, buying more time for the Americans to prepare for their break-out. II CANADIAN CORPS under Guy SIMONDS played a significant role in this effort, known as Operation GOODWOOD, with the Canadian portion known as Operation ATLANTIC. This was an attack southeast of Caen towards Bourguebus Ridge. These thrusts were followed by further attacks farther south at Verrières Ridge (Operation Spring) on 25 July which was a disaster for the BLACK WATCH (ROYAL HIGHLAND REGIMENT OF CANADA). Many of these assaults were preceded by intense bombing of the German defenders by the heavy bombers of the RAF's Bomber Command and the U.S. Army Air Force. The bombings sometimes helped, but they often also produced many friendly casualties.

On 25 July Bradley's forces launched Operation Cobra—the break-out battle. It was tough going at first but within a few days it was clear that the German lines had been cracked. Then the American forces split; the First U.S. Army drove south and west into Brittany while the Third U.S. Army turned eastward in a wide flanking manoeuvre. The Germans attempted a counter-stroke by attacking westward to choke off the American spearheads but, instead, they found their own forces trapped between Patton's army to the south, and the British and Canadian forces to the north, in the Caen sector.

Montgomery moved to take advantage of the German error by ordering Simonds to launch another heavy attack in the direction of Falaise. This Simonds did, first with Operation TOTALIZE, then with TRACTABLE which finally brought troops of the 2nd Canadian Infantry Division into Falaise on 17 August. Following the break-through, the 4th Canadian and 1st Polish Armoured

Divisions drove east and south of Falaise to link up with Patton's spearheads pushing north. As the gap closed, German troops, vehicles, and tanks streamed desperately to the east to escape. Fighter bombers of the 2ND ALLIED TACTICAL AIRFORCE flew constantly to the attack, wreaking havoc on the enemy. Finally, on 21 August, the gap was closed and the Battle of Normandy was, for all intents and purposes, over. From 6 June to the closing of the Falaise Gap, the Canadian formations had suffered 18,444 casualties, of which 5021 were fatal.

Reading: C.P. Stacey, *The Victory Campaign* (Ottawa, 1960); J.A. English, *The Canadian Army and the Normandy Campaign* (New York, 1991); C. D'Este, *Decision in Normandy* (London, 1983)

Norseman aircraft. Single-engine bush plane designed and built by R. Noorduyn of Montreal. The first Norseman flew in 1935. The aircraft could be equipped with floats or skis, and was popular for its load-carrying ability. About 900 of the aircraft were built both during and after World War II. They were used by the RCAF and seven other air forces, and many are still flying today.

North Atlantic Treaty Organization (NATO). Canada was a charter member of the North Atlantic Treaty Organization, signing the pact in Washington, D.C. on 4 April 1949. NATO originally consisted of the United States, Canada, the United Kingdom, France, Iceland, Italy, Denmark, Luxembourg, Belgium, the Netherlands, Portugal, and Norway. France later withdrew, and Turkey, Greece, the Federal Republic of Germany, and Spain later joined.

The discussions which led to the creation of NATO began among the United States, Britain, and Canada in the spring of 1948. The takeover of Czechoslovakia by the Communists was the foremost reason but the deepening of the COLD WAR formed the larger context. Those European countries that had signed the Brussels Treaty were then added to the talks. The prime objective was to create a military alliance to confront the Soviet Union across the Iron Curtain.

Although the NATO treaty came into force on 24 August 1949, NATO had little real substance until after the outbreak of the KOREAN WAR. NATO countries such as the United States and Britain were convinced that the invasion of South Korea was actually a Soviet test of NATO's resolve. On 19 December 1950, Dwight D. Eisenhower was appointed Supreme Allied Commander Europe to oversee a massive buildup of NATO military power aimed at putting an army of 90 or more divisions in place by mid-1954, supported by a massive air force.

Canada agreed to provide up to two divisions to NATO in the event of a European war. The first was to be the 1ST CANADIAN DIVISION (1953) which originally consisted of the 27TH CANADIAN INFANTRY BRIGADE GROUP (CIB), stationed in Germany, with two additional brigades stationed in Canada. The 27th CIB was transferred to Europe in the fall of 1951. It and its successors were first stationed near Hanover, then at SOEST, later at LAHR. Its designation was later changed to 3RD CANADIAN INFANTRY BRIGADE.

In addition to an army contingent, Canada also agreed to provide an air division of 12 squadrons. These originally consisted of SABRE fighters, later augmented by CF100s. They were based first in the United Kingdom, then in France and later in Germany. Canada also provided ships for SACLANT (the Supreme Allied Commander Atlantic), surplus weapons and other equipment for the NATO mutual aid program, and monetary contributions to infrastructure costs.

Canada supported the NATO decision of December 1955 to equip its forces with tactical nuclear weapons because this was seen as one way of reducing costs. The Canadian contribution to NATO remained relatively steady until the early 1970s when the Trudeau government ordered force reductions following the WHITE PAPER of 1971. Thereafter the Canadian role changed a number of times as Canada attempted to fulfil its commitments with a shrinking number of troops. In the fall of 1991 the government of Brian Mulroney announced that Canada's two bases in Germany were to be closed by 1995 and that only a small force of approximately 1500 troops would remain in Europe operating under NATO Command. Then, in the budget speech of February 1992, Finance minister Don Mazankowski revealed that all Canadian troops would be withdrawn from Europe. See also CANADIAN AIR-SEA TRANSPORTABLE BRIGADE GROUP, NORWAY COMMITMENT.

Reading: E. Reid, *Time of Fear and Hope*
(Toronto, 1977); J.B. McLin, *Canada's Changing Defense Policy* (Baltimore, 1967); D.W. Middlemiss and J.J. Sokolsky, *Canadian Defence: Decisions and Determinants* (Toronto, 1989).

North America and West Indies Squadron, Royal Navy. The squadron was the main RN command in the western Atlantic. It was established in 1830 with its main base at Bermuda but with a major base at Halifax for North Atlantic operations in the summer months. In 1904 the last warship in the squadron was withdrawn; the facility in Halifax was turned over to the ROYAL CANADIAN NAVY in 1910. In 1913 the RN's Fourth Cruiser Squadron was returned to Bermuda for possible use against Mexico. It was there at the outbreak of World War I and was used to counter German raiders in the Atlantic. It was briefly joined by HMCS *NIOBE*. In 1927 the Bermuda facility's designation was changed to America and West Indies Station.

NORAD (North American Aerospace Command). Originally known as the North American Air Defence Command, NORAD was established by Canada and the U.S. in 1957 via an exchange of notes, not by treaty, to oversee and coordinate the air defence of the continent. NORAD headquarters are located at Cheyenne Mountain, Wyoming. Its commander is always an American, its deputy commander is always a Canadian. NORAD receives information on aircraft, missile, and satellite movements from a variety of radar sources. It then determines their identity and, in the case of unknown aircraft, determines a course of action. NORAD has at its disposal a number of fighter jet interceptor squadrons based in both Canada and the United States which can be 'scrambled' to visually check the identity of unknown aircraft, and sophisticated computers to determine trajectories of missiles. It is also connected directly to the office of the President of the United States and can warn of impending missile attack so that U.S. missile and bomber forces can be launched in retaliation.

North Atlantic Run. Informal term for the trans-Atlantic convoy escort system instituted by Britain and Canada beginning in 1940. The run was not a single route; several favoured convoy routings were used depending on the speed of the convoy, its port of origin (i.e., Halifax, St John's, etc.), and its destination. For most of the war the escort duties on the North Atlantic Run were divided among ships—primarily British and Canadian — based in St John's, Newfoundland, Hvalfjord, Iceland and Londonderry, Northern Ireland. See also WESTERN LOCAL ESCORT FORCE, WESTERN OCEAN MEETING POINT, NEWFOUNDAND ESCORT FORCE, MID-OCEAN MEETING POINT, MID-OCEAN ESCORT FORCE, EAST OCEAN MEETING POINT.

'North Atlantic Squadron'. A ribald song with an unknown (but apparently endless) number of verses that was born among RCN escort crews in east coast ports during World War II. It is unlikely that any single one of the verses could have passed muster at a church parade.

Northeast Staging Route. Also known as Project Crimson, the Northeast Staging Route was actually designed as a number of different routes across eastern, central, and northern Canada for the ferrying of short-range aircraft, especially medium bombers and fighters, from North America to Great Britain. Canada authorized construction of the Staging Route airfields in June 1942 and the construction was carried out by the U.S. Army Corps of Engineers. The great distances to be flown on these routes militated against the use of most of them; Goose Bay, Labrador and Gander, Newfoundland saw the bulk of the traffic.

North Star transport (Canadair C4). A four-engine transport plane designed and built by CANADAIR LTD in Montreal after World War II, the North Star was the mainstay of the RCAF's air transport command in the late 1940s and 1950s and was also the backbone of the Trans-Canada Airlines fleet until the late 1950s. The basic design was a marriage of the Douglas C54 Skymaster (the military version of the DC4) airframe to Rolls Royce Merlin engines. The early military version, known as the DC-4M, was unpressurized. It could range more than 6200 km at a cruising speed of 465 km/h. See also KOREAN WAR.

North Warning System. In 1985 Canada and the U.S. formally agreed to upgrade and update the DEW LINE to enable its radars to detect low-flying Soviet bombers or cruise missiles. The system comprises both manned and unmanned radar stations.

North West Air Command (NWAC). Formed 1 June 1944 with headquarters at Edmonton, the command was responsible for maintaining the facilities of the NORTHWEST AIR STAGING ROUTE and replaced No. 2 Wing Headquarters. The first commander was Wing Commander T.A. LAWRENCE. On 1 March, 1947, NWAC took over responsibility for WESTERN AIR COMMAND. On 1 August 1951 NWAC was merged with 1 Tactical Air Group (Winnipeg) to form Tactical Air Group.

Northwest Air Staging Route. The western counterpart to the NORTHEAST STAGING ROUTE comprised airstrips, navigational aids, and radio stations built by the U.S. government in northern Alberta, northeastern British Columbia, Yukon, and Alaska. It was used to ferry aircraft from the United States to the Soviet Union. Generally the route paralleled the ALASKA HIGHWAY. Construction on the route actually began in February 1941 but considerable improvements were carried out soon after Japan attacked Pearl Harbor. By 1943 up to 450 aircraft a month were being ferried to Alaska and the USSR.

Northwest Europe Campaign. The campaign of FIRST CANADIAN ARMY from the closing of the pursuit of the German forces across the River Seine (23–30 August 1944) to the end of WORLD WAR II. In that campaign the Canadians were assigned the left flank of Montgomery's 21st Army Group— the capture of the channel ports from Le Havre to Calais, the securing of the SCHELDT Estuary, the liberation of the Netherlands, the penetration of the German frontier fortifications in the Rhineland, and the crossing of the Rhine River. From the opening of the campaign until the late winter and early spring of 1945, First Canadian Army consisted of II CANADIAN CORPS and I British Corps and included the 1st Polish Armoured Division. It was then joined by I CANADIAN CORPS, which had been fighting in ITALY.

In the opening phases of the campaign the Canadians advanced up the Channel coast capturing or occupying Dieppe, Boulogne, and Calais, and cutting off Dunkirk, which the Germans held to the end of the war. These small ports would be important to ensure that adequate supplies reached the Allied armies, now advancing to the German frontier, but they paled beside the huge port facilities at Antwerp and Rotterdam. The former was captured with its port virtually intact by the Second British Army at the beginning of September while the German 15th Army was put into full flight. Montgomery, however, failed to take advantage of German disarray to seize the Scheldt Estuary by which ships passed from the North Sea to the port of Antwerp. This was because his eyes were fixed firmly on the Rhine bridge at Arnhem and his mind was full of the plans for Operation Market Garden, a combined ground/parachute assault to drive a corridor from the British lines to Arnhem, allowing him to seize a Rhine crossing. The Germans took advantage of Montgomery's mistake to occupy and fortify both banks of the estuary including the island of BEVELAND and the virtual islands (they were joined to the mainland by narrow necks of land) of WALCHEREN and South Beveland.

Following the total failure of Market Garden, Eisenhower ordered Montgomery to devote his resources to the clearing of the Scheldt Estuary. The task fell to First Canadian Army which was considerably augmented by the addition of a number of British and American divisions, and the British 30th Corps. General H.D.G. CRERAR fell ill at the opening stages of the campaign and G.G. SIMONDS moved up from II CANADIAN CORPS to temporarily take command. The battle began with the clearing of the BRESKENS POCKET on the southern bank of the estuary and continued with attacks on South Beveland, North Beveland, and finally Walcheren. By 8 November, the estuary had been cleared.

After a period of rest in winter quarters, First Canadian Army went into action once again in the REICHSWALD. This was followed by the cracking of the Siegfried Line, the fighting in the HOCHWALD, and the crossings of the Rhine River which took place in late March and early April. These battles were fought under extremely difficult late-winter conditions, with snow, mud, frozen polder land, and flooded fields and roads delaying advances and causing severe discomfort to the fighting troops.

From the Rhine crossings to the end of the war the Canadians concentrated on occupying parts of northern Germany and liberating the eastern and northern Netherlands. Total Canadian casualties for the Northwest Europe campaign and the NORMANDY fighting which preceded it were 44,339, of whom 11,336 officers and men were killed in action.

Reading: C.P. Stacey, *The Victory Campaign* (Ottawa, 1960); J.L. Moulton, *Battle for Antwerp* (New York, 1978); W.D. Whitaker and S. Whitaker, *Rhineland* (Toronto, 1989)

Northwest Field Force. The force raised by Canada to put down the NORTHWEST REBELLION of 1885. The force was composed primarily of existing MILITIA units, augmented by volunteers and by the small active force. It was under the overall command of Major-General Frederick MIDDLETON and numbered over 7000. For the campaign, it was divided into three columns: the westernmost, commanded by Col T.B. STRANGE, the central under Col W. OTTER, and the easternmost main body commanded by Middleton. The plan was to have the three columns converge on the Métis capital of BATOCHE. There, on 12 May, the Métis were defeated and the rebellion was effectively ended.

North West Mounted Police. Founded in 1873 by the government of Prime Minister John A. MACDONALD, the NWMP was to be a small force of mounted riflemen with both police and magistrate powers to patrol the far reaches of the prairie west. The force of 318 officers and men was sent west in the summer of 1874 and established a number of police posts along the Canada-U.S. boundary. The NWMP played an important role in the NORTH WEST REBELLION of 1885. Many members also volunteered for service in the SOUTH AFRICAN WAR, serving with the CANADIAN MOUNTED RIFLES. As a token of that service, the force became the Royal North West Mounted Police. In 1919 it was joined with the Dominion Police to become the Royal Canadian Mounted Police.

Northwest Highway System. See ALASKA HIGHWAY.

Northwest Rebellion, 1885. After the end of the RED RIVER REBELLION in 1870, many Métis grievances remained unresolved, especially in the Saskatchewan country. At the same time white settlers moving into the area resented such government policies as the monopoly held by the Canadian Pacific Railway and the tariff on manufactured goods. Natives and Métis were unhappy over government failure to live up to provisions of the treaties by which they had given up title to their lands. In June of 1884 they called Louis RIEL back from his exile in Montana to lead them. He designated Gabriel DUMONT as his military leader and in March 1885 proclaimed a provisional government in the west with BATOCHE as its capital. The first fighting in the rebellion broke out at DUCK LAKE when a mixed detachment of NORTH WEST MOUNTED POLICE and Prince Albert militia attempted to re-take supplies and ammunition stored there. The police and militia were defeated and two Native bands soon joined Riel in his uprising.

When news of the fighting reached Ottawa, the government reacted quickly. GENERAL OFFICER COMMANDING Frederick MIDDLETON was sent west while the minister of Militia and Defence Adolphe CARON supervised the raising and dispatch of a military force. Since the CPR was not yet completed, troops and equipment were transferred across gaps in the line by horse-drawn sleigh.

Middleton mounted a three-fold campaign. He led one column of troops north from Qu'appelle towards Batoche; William OTTER led a second column north from Swift Current, and T.B. STRANGE led the third north to Edmonton from Calgary and then east along the North Saskatchewan River. Movement was difficult because of the spring mud, and Middleton attempted to use the stern-wheeler *Northcote* to bring up supplies. Though the Canadians were better equipped and far more numerous — more than 7000 in total—their leadership was unimaginative, even hesitant. On several occasions they escaped heavy losses only because their enemies failed, or refused, to press home. Battles at Frog Lake, FISH CREEK, CUT KNIFE HILL, and Frenchman's Butte were all, in some fashion, defeats for the militia. Nevertheless, Middleton pressed on toward Batoche, besieged it and captured it on 12 May. Riel was taken prisoner and

eventually hanged for treason; Dumont escaped to the United States.
Reading: G.F.G. Stanley, *The Birth of Western Canada* (Toronto, 1960)

Northwest Territories and Yukon Radio System. A radio and telegraph system manned by the Royal Canadian Corps of Signals and built in a line from Dawson, British Columbia to Hudson Bay in 1923. Personnel at the stations directed ships in the Arctic, ordered supplies for outposts, and provided information to northern communities.

Norway Commitment. From 1951 until 1968, as part of its overall NATO role, Canada committed itself to maintain a brigade group in Germany and to reinforce those troops in the event of war. In 1968 it altered that commitment. The troops in Germany were to remain, but instead of Canada's reinforcements being destined for NATO's central front, they would be committed to the defence of Denmark or Norway. The reinforcements were to be in the form of the CANADIAN AIR-SEA TRANSPORTABLE BRIGADE. In 1976 the Denmark part of the commitment was dropped and in 1986 Canada also dropped the Norway commitment.

No. 6 Bomber Group. At the outbreak of World War II the Canadian government believed that the BRITISH COMMONWEALTH AIR TRAINING PLAN would be one of its major contributions to Allied victory. Indeed, that enterprise turned out over a hundred thousand air crew. Under the original terms of the agreement, Canadian graduates were supposed to be earmarked for service with ROYAL CANADIAN AIR FORCE squadrons once overseas, but the Royal Air Force did not take that stipulation especially seriously and sent a large number of Canadians, especially those destined for service with Bomber Command, to serve with RAF squadrons. That was in keeping with the practice followed with other Commonwealth air crew because the RAF wanted to be a British Commonwealth, not a strictly British, fighting force. The Canadian government believed that the integration of Canadians into the RAF did not give the Canadian contribution to the war sufficient exposure. It insisted that the original terms of the agreement be adhered to and that

Canadians be grouped together into Canadian squadrons. This policy was known as CANADIANIZATION. At first Canada refused to pay the operating costs of these squadrons, insisting that it had already paid its share through the BCATP (Canada was footing more than half the total cost). This delayed Canadianization; when Ottawa began to pay, Canadianization moved forward, although not without British resistance. By the start of 1942 the RCAF could count four bomber squadrons — Nos 419, 405, 408, and 420 — flying with Bomber Command. These were known as Article XV squadrons, named for the stipulation in the BCATP agreement that gave Canada the right to use those air crew in that way. Many of the officers and some of the other ranks in these squadrons were RAF or from other Commonwealth air forces, not RCAF, but most of the ground crew were Canadian. These squadrons took part in early operations such as the THOUSAND PLANE RAID.

In 1942 more RCAF squadrons were formed and the decision was made at the OTTAWA AIR TRAINING CONFERENCE, called to decide on whether or not to extend the BCATP (it was extended to 1945), to form an all-Canadian bomber group to operate within Bomber Command. That decision was accepted by the RAF, but only reluctantly. This was officially done 1 January 1943 when No. 6 Group (RCAF) began operating with headquarters at Linton-on-Ouse. It consisted of eight squadrons on seven stations and flew its first operation — mine-laying near the Frisian Islands — the night of 3/4 January. Thereafter additional squadrons were added until at its peak it counted 14 squadrons, No. 405 having been assigned to No. 8 (Pathfinder) group.

No. 6 Group's first year on operations was not a happy one. Several factors—many the by-products of Canadianization — combined to hold down its operational efficiency and keep its casualties high. For example, a group by definition needed to be based together but, by the time No. 6 Group was formed, all base areas in the U.K. nearest to the continent had been allocated to RAF groups or to the United States Army Air Force. No. 6 Group was, therefore, based in Yorkshire, meaning its aircraft flew farther to target and sometimes even had to refuel in southern England before crossing the Eng-

lish Channel. Since it was a new and somewhat inexperienced group, Bomber Command was reluctant to allocate it new LANCASTER bombers and it continued to fly either older twin-engine aircraft such as the WELLINGTON or the four-engine HALIFAX which had serious design flaws. The Group also had a higher concentration of inexperienced crew members.

In February 1944 the first AOC of No. 6 Group, G.E. Brookes, was replaced by World War I ace C.M. MCEWEN. McEwen was a strict disciplinarian and this, combined with the arrival of better aircraft, changes in operational procedures, and greater experience, considerably improved the Group's performance. By war's end it had flown 41,000 sorties and had dropped 126,000 tons of bombs at a cost of 814 aircraft; 3500 air crew had been killed in action.

Reading: W.A.B. Douglas, The Creation of a National Air Force (Toronto, 1986); C.P. Stacey, Arms, Men and Governments (Ottawa, 1970); S. Dunmore and W. Carter, Reap the Whirlwind (Toronto, 1991)

No. 1 Air Division (Europe). The ROYAL CANADIAN AIR FORCE component of the 4th Allied Tactical Air Force formed under the auspices of NATO. No. 1 Air Division was to consist of four wings of SABRE fighters, with each wing consisting of three squadrons. It was eventually based in France (Grostenquin and Marville) and Germany (Baden-Soellingen and Zweibrucken). The formation became operational on 1 October 1952 although it consisted of only three wings; the last wing became operational at Marville in March 1955. In 1956 and 1957 a number of No. 1 Air Division's Sabre squadrons were replaced by CF100 squadrons due to a shortage of all-weather fighters among the NATO air contingent. The CF100s and the Sabres were replaced by CF104 Starfighters beginning in early 1961 and then by CF18s beginning in 1982. The Division declined from its peak strength of 12 squadrons in the late 1950s as a result of defence cuts in the 1960s. On 1 July 1970, No. 1 Air Division was formally transformed into NO. 1 AIR GROUP, with a strength of three squadrons.

No. 1 Air Group. Based at Zweibrucken and Baden-Soellingen, No. 1 Air Group was the successor formation to NO. 1 AIR DIVI-

SION. Part of Canada's NATO contingent, it consisted of three squadrons of fighter jets assigned a ground attack role.

No. 1 Group (Eastern Air Command). No. 1 Group was formed 10 July 1941 with headquarters at St John's, Newfoundland. It was responsible for all ROYAL CANADIAN AIR FORCE units and facilities in Newfoundland and for the operational support of the NEWFOUNDLAND ESCORT FORCE. In October 1942 No. 1 Group and the Flag Officer, Newfoundland formed the Combined Area HQ at St John's. In the spring of 1943 No. 1 Group was equipped with long range LIBERATOR anti-submarine patrol bombers which helped close the gap between the air cover it was previously able to provide to convoys and that provided by the RAF's Coastal Command. No. 1 Group aircraft participated in the destruction of a number of enemy submarines before the end of the war. It was disbanded at the end of June, 1945.

No. 2 (Negro) Construction Battalion. Known as the Black Battalion, the formation (commanded by white officers) was authorized on 5 July 1916. Recruiting was carried out in all Canadian population centres where Blacks lived. The bulk of the volunteers came from Ontario and Nova Scotia. In March 1917 the battalion was sent to Europe. It arrived in France a short time after and was attached to the Canadian Forestry Corps.

NRMA men. See NATIONAL RESOURCES MOBILIZATION ACT.

Nunney, Claude Joseph Patrick (1892–1918). Born in England, Pte Nunney was serving with the 38th Battalion, CEF in France in September 1918 when his unit came under heavy German artillery fire, preparatory to a counter-attack near the DROCOURT-QUÉANT LINE. Despite the shellfire, Nunney worked his way to company outposts to encourage his comrades to hold firm. They did and, the following day, launched a successful attack of their own. Nunney won a VICTORIA CROSS for his cool and consistent fearlessness.

O

Oboe. Electronic aid to night bombing introduced by the Royal Air Force in 1942. Oboe consisted of two radio beacons, one 'cat', the other 'mouse', transmitted from ground stations in Britain in such a way as to cross over the designated target. The bomber flew the 'cat' beacon towards the target and released its bombs when it crossed the 'mouse' beacon. The effectiveness of Oboe was severely limited because it could not bend to follow the curve of the earth. Targets deep inside Germany were too far away for bombers to be able to pick up Oboe signals, even at the upper levels of their effective operational height. See also H2S.

October Crisis. In October 1970, the FRONT DE LIBÉRATION DU QUÉBEC (FLQ) kidnapped British trade commissioner James Cross and Quebec cabinet minister Pierre Laporte. Prime Minister P.E. Trudeau refused to negotiate FLQ ransom demands. After consultation with Quebec premier Robert Bourassa, he invoked the WAR MEASURES ACT 16 October and sent the army to Montreal to aid the police; 400 people were arrested. In response, the FLQ murdered Laporte whose body was found 17 October; Cross was released on 3 December after the hiding place of his captors had been discovered. The kidnappers of Cross were given safe passage to Cuba; the murderers of Laporte were tried for their crimes and sent to prison.

Odlum, Victor W. (1880–1971). Born in Ontario, Odlum served in the SOUTH AFRI-

CAN WAR and commanded the 11th Brigade, CEF, from 1916 to 1919. In World War II he commanded 2ND CANADIAN INFANTRY DIVISION from 1940 to 1941, but he was clearly not suited to command a division in the field and he left the army to join the Department of External Affairs. As Canadian High Commissioner to Australia in 1942, he tried unsuccessfully to convince the Canadian government to send troops and equipment to Australia.

Oerlikon gun. Light anti-aircraft gun, named for the Zurich suburb where it was manufactured.

Official Histories, World War I. The official history of the Canadian army in World War I is outlined by G.W.L. NICHOLSON in *The Canadian Expeditionary Force, 1914–19*, published in 1962. It is a single-volume study that substituted for what was supposed to be a multi-volume account written by A.F. DUGUID. Duguid published the first volume of that study — *Official History of the Canadian Forces in the Great War, 1914–19* — in 1938, but it covered only the first year of the war. There was no Canadian or Royal Canadian Air Force in World War I, but S.F. Wise has told the story of Canadian participation in that war in *Canadian Airmen and the First World War: The Official History of the RCAF, Vol. I* (1980). The navy's account, *The Naval Service of Canada, Vol. I,* was published in 1948 by G.N. Tucker. Sir Andrew MACPHAIL wrote the official history of the ROYAL CANADIAN ARMY MEDICAL CORPS in *Medical Services, 1914–19,* published in 1925. See also MILITARY HISTORY.

Official Histories, World War II. The magnum opus of Second World War histories is the three-volume *Official History of the Canadian Army in the Second World War*. Prepared under the direction of Col. C.P. STACEY, it consists of *Six Years of War: The Army in Canada, Britain and the Pacific* (1955), and *The Victory Campaign: The Operations in North-West Europe 1944–45* (1960), both written by Stacey, and *The Canadians in Italy* (1956), written by G.W.L. NICHOLSON. The series followed a preliminary volume entitled *The Canadian Army: 1939–1945, An Official Historical Summary* (1948) published to enable Canadians to read of the exploits of their forces as soon after the war as possible. That

volume was never intended to be exhaustive. An additional and connected work is Stacey's *Arms, Men and Governments: The War Policies of Canada 1939–45* (1970) which is, nonetheless, not a volume in the series. W.A.B. Douglas has written *The Creation of a National Air Force: The Official History of the Royal Canadian Air Force, Vol. II* (1986), which is the first of two projected volumes to cover the RCAF in World War II. G.N. Tucker's second volume of *The Naval Service of Canada* includes ROYAL CANADIAN NAVY operations in Canada during World War II, but excludes the story of RCN operations in the North Atlantic and elsewhere. *The Far Distant Ships* (1961) by Joseph Schull is a popularly written official account of Canadian naval operations, especially in North Atlantic waters. A new official history of the ROYAL CANADIAN NAVY in World War II is now under preparation by the Directorate of History, Department of National Defence. See also MILITARY HISTORY.

Official Histories, Korean War. There are only two official histories of Canadian operations in the Korean war. Col H.F. Wood wrote the official history of the Canadian Army in Korea, *Strange Battleground* (1964), while Thor Thorgrimmson and E.C. Russell published *Canadian Naval Operations in Korean Waters* (1965). See also MILITARY HISTORY.

Official Languages Act. Act passed by the federal government in 1969 to give official status to the French language in all federal departments and services in Canada, to make the federal civil service officially bilingual, and to guarantee service in both official languages to Canadians wherever warranted by numbers. Prior to the passage of the Act most French-Canadian military personnel worked in English. After the Act, four new FRENCH-LANGUAGE UNITS were created in the three services and French-language training was made available to all new recruits.

Ogdensburg, Battle of. On 22 February 1813, during the WAR OF 1812, the Glengarry Light Infantry Fencibles, led by Lt-Col 'Red George' Macdonell crossed the icy St Lawrence River to capture and sack the town of Ogdensburg, N.Y. The attack was in retaliation for a raid by Americans on Elizabethtown on 7 February. It was mounted despite orders to the contrary and resulted in 6 dead and 54 wounded. Ogdensburg was not reoccupied by American troops until after the war.

Ogdensburg Agreement. On 18 August 1940, United States President Franklin D. Roosevelt and Canadian Prime Minister William Lyon Mackenzie KING entered into the Ogdensburg Agreement at Ogdensburg, New York. The two met at Roosevelt's instigation following the fall of France and amidst the mounting German threat to Great Britain. Roosevelt was eager to nail down a continental defence pact while King and the Canadian government worried about the implications to Canadian security should Britain give way before the Nazi onslaught. The Agreement established the PERMANENT JOINT BOARD ON DEFENCE, CANADA-UNITED STATES, which was charged with coordinating joint defence planning between the two countries while acting as the major communications route on defence matters between the executives of the two governments. The Agreement was a major step in the shift of Canada out of the British orbit and into the American.

Ogilvie, Will A. (1901–1989). Born in South Africa, Ogilvie came to Canada in 1925 and joined the Canadian Army in 1940. In 1943 he was made an official war artist and attached to the 1ST CANADIAN INFANTRY DIVISION. Held in high esteem by fellow war artists, Ogilvie painted and drew in the field, often under fire. His skill and bravery were recognized with the award of a Medal of the Order of the British Empire.

O'Grady-Haly, R.H. (1841–1911). Born in Ireland, O'Grady-Haly attended the Royal Military Academy at Sandhurst. He was appointed GENERAL OFFICER COMMANDING THE CANADIAN MILITIA in 1900, a post he held for two years. He was considered little more than a stopgap between HUTTON and the Earl of DUNDONALD.

O'Hea, Timothy (1846–1874). A member of the British Army, O'Hea won the only VICTORIA CROSS awarded for action in Canada when he extinguished a fire in a railway ammunition car at Danville, Quebec on 9 June 1866.

O'Hurley, Raymond J.M. (1909–1970). O'Hurley was first elected to the House of Commons in 1957 to represent the Quebec riding of Lotbinière. In 1958 he was named minister of Defence Production, a post he held until his (and the government's) defeat in 1963.

Oka, Siege of. A 78-day standoff between members of the Mohawk Warrior Society from the Kanesetake Reserve, near the Quebec town of Oka, and the Sûreté de Québéc in the summer of 1990. The siege was triggered 7 July 1990 when the Sûreté attempted to storm a four-month-old barricade which had been set up by heavily armed Warrior Society members. The Mohawks insisted that the barricade had been built to protect claims to land that was to be turned into a golf course. In the 7 July mêlée one police officer was killed. At the Kahnawake Reserve, on the south shore of the St Lawrence River near the Island of Montreal, another barricade was set up by Warrior Society members to support their comrades at Kanesetake. It stopped traffic from using the Mercier Bridge to reach Montreal from the south shore. When the Sûreté were no longer able to deal with either situation, Quebec Premier Robert Bourassa sought help from the federal government which sent in the army. The army besieged the barricades in both places, then, after careful preparation, moved in at Kanesetake. They succeeded in dismantling the barricades there. Those Warriors and their supporters who chose not to surrender retreated to an isolated treatment centre on the reserve from which they emerged peacefully 24 September 1990. With the siege at Oka over, the barricades at Kahnawake were also dismantled.

O'Kelly, Christopher Patrick John (1895–1922). On 26 October 1917, O'Kelly led his company of the 53nd Battalion, CEF, to capture six German pillboxes and 100 prisoners during the battle of PASSCHENDAELE. Later the same afternoon he took more prisoners when he seized a hostile raiding party. For these acts he was awarded the VICTORIA CROSS.

O'Leary, Michael (1889–1961). Born in Ireland, O'Leary had been living in Canada at the outbreak of World War I when he joined the 1st Battalion of the Irish Guards of the British Army. On 1 February 1915, Sgt O'Leary attacked and put out of action a German machine gun at Cuinchy, France. He was thus credited with saving many comrades' lives and was awarded a VICTORIA CROSS.

Oliver Pattern web equipment. Web equipment is provided soldiers to carry extra ammunition and other battlefield necessities. Prior to leaving Canada for Britain in October 1914, the first Canadian contingent was equipped with Oliver Pattern web equipment. It was obsolete, inadequate, and uncomfortable, and was soon replaced by British equipment. This was another case of Canadian troops being supplied with substandard equipment at the outbreak of World War I. See also ROSS RIFLE, MACADAM SHIELD/SHOVEL.

100th Regiment (Royal Canadians). A MILITIA regiment that served in the WAR OF 1812 and was later disbanded. In 1858 it was reorganized by descendents of the original regiment and other residents of Canada West. The regiment served in India under British command but with Canadian officers, becoming the first Canadian regiment raised for foreign service. It was later based in Ireland and disbanded in 1922.

105-mm howitzer. See PRIEST.

155-mm howitzer (M-109). The Canadian armed forces acquired 50 American-built M-109 155-mm self-propelled HOWITZERS in the summer of 1968. The weapon was capable of firing a variety of shell types over a range of more than 14 km.

155-mm howitzer (M-114). A towed artillery piece, the American designed and built M-114 could fire forty rounds every hour over a range of 14.6 km. It was served by a crew of 11.

Ontario, HMCS. One of two cruisers to serve with the RCN during and after World War II, *Ontario* was first commissioned as the Royal Navy cruiser *Minotaur*, entering ROYAL CANADIAN NAVY service in April, 1945. *Ontario* displaced 8900 tonnes, carried a crew of approximately 730, had a main armament of nine 6-inch guns, and a top speed of 30 knots. *Ontario* served briefly with the 4th Cruiser Squadron of the Royal Navy in the Pacific. After the war the vessel was used primarily as a training ship and visited Hong Kong, Manila, and Japan before being paid off in 1958.

ONUCA. ONUCA is the Spanish acronym for the United Nations Observer Group that served in Central America between December 1989 and February 1990. It was established following a request from Central American nations for a UN peacekeeping force to help end the war in Nicaragua. ONUCA supervised the disarming of the Contras after the 1990 Nicaraguan election. Canada sent 22 personnel to help with logistical and air support.

Order of Military Merit. Roughly comparable to the Order of Canada, the Order of Military Merit has been awarded since 1972 to Canadian Forces personnel in recognition of exceptional service. Annual appointments to the Order cannot exceed one per cent of total Forces staff. Commanders of the Order, the highest rank, can comprise no more than six per cent of the Order membership, Officers thirty per cent, and Members the balance.

Oregon Crisis. Boundary dispute between Britain and the United States arising in 1845. In 1818 the boundary between the United States and British North America from the Lake of the Woods to the Rocky Mountains was set at the 49th parallel. The area to the west of the mountains, known as the Oregon Country, was to be jointly administered. When American settlers began pouring into what are now the states of Oregon and Washington in the early 1840s, the U.S. claimed the area up to 54°40'. The dispute was primarily settled by the Oregon Treaty of 1846 which extended the boundary along the 49th parallel to the Pacific Coast and thence south and west through the middle of the Straits of Georgia and Juan de Fuca to the ocean. That treaty, however, left ownership of a number of small islands in dispute. See SAN JUAN ISLAND DISPUTE.

Orenda engine. The RCAF commissioned A.V. ROE CO. of Toronto to develop and build a turbojet engine to power the CF100 and the Canadair SABRE. The company delivered the first of 3824 Orendas in 1953. The version of the engine used on the Canadair Sabres Mk 5 and Mk 6 gave that aircraft a superior performance to that of any Sabre then in USAF service.

Ortona, Battle of. Town in ITALY along the Adriatic coast and scene of a key battle fought by IST CANADIAN INFANTRY DIVISION in December 1943. After fighting its way across the MORO RIVER the division moved to capture Ortona, a key road junction with a small harbour. The town was perched on a ledge and contained many old stone buildings, high-walled courtyards, and narrow roads offering good defensive positions for the German 1st Parachute Division's tough, élite troops. On 21 December the battle for the town was joined. Basic German strategy was to use the narrow streets as killing zones; basic Canadian strategy was to avoid the streets by fighting house to house through holes blown in the walls, a technique the troops called 'mouseholing'. Tank and artillery fire was used but the battle was fought by infantry. The drive through the town was carried out by the 2nd Canadian Infantry Brigade, led by the Loyal Edmonton Regiment and the Seaforth Highlanders. While that struggle was going on, the 1st Brigade attacked northwest of the town beginning on 23 December with a view to outflanking the German positions in Ortona. They succeeded in seizing the high ground and, although cut off from the rest of the division for a time, sufficiently threatened German supply routes to force the Germans to begin to withdraw. On the night of 27/28 December, the Germans pulled out. *Reading*: W.G. Nicholson, *The Canadians in Italy* (Ottawa, 1957)

O'Rourke, Michael James (1878–1957). Between 15 and 17 August 1917, during the battle of HILL 70 in France, Pte O'Rourke served as a stretcher-bearer with the 7th Battalion, CEF. His heroic and tireless devotion to this duty was credited with the saving of many lives among the 2432 Canadians wounded in action. For this he was awarded the VICTORIA CROSS.

Osborn, John Robert (1889–1941). On 19 December 1941, C.S.M. Osborn was serving with the Winnipeg Grenadiers during the battle of HONG KONG. After leading a bayonet charge to Mount Butler, he threw himself on a Japanese grenade in order to save the lives of seven of his comrades. He was posthumously awarded the VICTORIA CROSS.

***Ottawa*, HMCS.** RIVER CLASS DESTROYER commissioned into the ROYAL CANADIAN NAVY in June, 1938, *Ottawa* was sunk while on convoy escort duty on 14 September 1942. The vessel went down so quickly that there was no time to launch lifeboats. Some crewmen survived on rafts but 114 were lost. The second ship of the name, a RIVER CLASS DESTROYER, was obtained from the Royal Navy and commissioned into the ROYAL CANADIAN NAVY in March, 1943 as a replacement. It served as a mid-ocean escort and with *Kootenay* helped destroy three U-boats in 1944. She was paid off in November, 1945. A third *Ottawa*, a destroyer escort of the *ST LAURENT* CLASS, was commissioned in 1956.

Ottawa Air Training Conference. In May and June 1942, 14 nations met to review and extend the BRITISH COMMONWEALTH AIR TRAINING PLAN with the intent of including the U.S. in it. The conference agreed on coordinated training, aircraft availability, and training systems, and established a COMBINED COMMITTEE ON AIR TRAINING IN NORTH AMERICA. It was at this conference that the decision was taken to proceed with the establishment of what was to become NO. 6 BOMBER GROUP.

***Otter*.** Hudson's Bay Company vessel chartered by the colony of British Columbia to patrol its coastal waters during the Crimean War (1854–1856) which pitted Russia against Britain and France. British Columbia was unaware that Britain and Russia had agreed to keep the Pacific neutral. The British government eventually paid the *Otter's* £400 rental charge.

***Otter*, HMCS.** Armed yacht commissioned into the ROYAL CANADIAN NAVY in October 1940, *Otter* displaced 425 tonnes, carried a crew of 40 and was armed with one 4-inch gun. *Otter* served with the Halifax local defence flotilla until destroyed by an accidental explosion 26 March 1941. The vessel went down with the loss of 19 lives.

Otter aircraft (DCH-3). A single-engine STOL aircraft built by DE HAVILLAND AIR-

CRAFT OF CANADA in the 1950s for both military and civil use, the Otter was an improvement on the smaller BEAVER and proved versatile for search and rescue missions. The Twin Otter, with its two Pratt and Whitney PT6 turbine engines, first flew in 1965 and provided 50 per cent more speed than the original Otter. Both versions use wheels, floats, or skis.

Otter, Sir William Dillon (1843–1929). Otter is often cited as Canada's first true professional soldier. His military career began with the QUEEN'S OWN RIFLES, a MILITIA unit that saw action at the battle of RIDGEWAY during the 1866 FENIAN RAIDS. Otter joined the small PERMANENT FORCE when it was established in 1883, served as commander of the INFANTRY SCHOOL CORPS, and commanded one of three columns in the NORTHWEST REBELLION of 1885. When Canada committed forces to the SOUTH AFRICAN WAR in 1899, Otter led the first contingent and fought at the battle of PAARDEBURG. Following a succession of British appointments, he became the first Canadian CHIEF OF THE GENERAL STAFF from 1908 to 1910. Otter stayed in Canada during WORLD WAR I to direct INTERNMENT operations. He was knighted in 1913 and was promoted to general in 1922.

Otter Committee. In the spring of 1919 the government appointed Sir W.D. OTTER to head a committee to examine Canada's MILITIA requirements in the post-war period. The other members of the committee were Generals A. MACDONELL, A.G.L. MCNAUGHTON, and E.A. Cruikshank. The committee recommended that the militia be organized into 11 infantry and four cavalry divisions, a total of 140,000 men.

Ouimet, Marcel (1915–1978). Ouimet joined the CBC in 1939 and worked in Montreal until sent to Europe as a war correspondent in 1943. He provided vivid coverage from the front as Canadian forces moved through Sicily, Italy, France, Belgium, Holland, and Germany.

Overlord. Code name for the Allied landing on the coast of NORMANDY on D-DAY, 6 June 1944. The 3RD CANADIAN INFANTRY DIVISION, accompanied by the 2nd Canadian Armoured Brigade, was assigned the task of landing on JUNO BEACH. See also NEPTUNE, QUADRANT.

Overseas Military Forces of Canada, Ministry of. In October 1916 Prime Minister Robert L. BORDEN created the ministry of Overseas Military Forces to provide a clear link between the CANADIAN CORPS, the CANADIAN EXPEDITIONARY FORCE, and the government in Ottawa. This had become necessary because of the constant mismanagement of the war effort by the minister of Militia and Defence Sir Sam HUGHES. Borden's intent was to establish a Cabinet post in Britain with direct responsibility for the supply, maintenance, and command structure of both the CEF and the Canadian Corps. All other military matters would remain in the hands of the minister of Militia and Defence and the minister for the Naval Services in Ottawa. The first minister was Sir George PERLEY, who served in the post from 31 October 1916 to 11 October 1917. He was succeeded by Sir Edward KEMP. Outraged by the loss of his control of the forces overseas, Hughes resigned his post just prior to Perley's appointment.

P

Paardeburg, Battle of. On the Modder River in the Orange Free State, Paardeburg was the site of the first significant action of the Canadian contingent in the SOUTH AF-RICAN WAR. The Canadians—the 2nd Battalion of the ROYAL CANADIAN REGIMENT under the command of Col W. OTTER — were part of the 19th Brigade of the British

9th Division commanded by Lt-Gen. Sir Henry Colville. Not long after arriving in South Africa this unit began to advance north towards the Modder River in an effort to cut off Boer General Piet Cronje's troops, then laying siege to Kimberly. In late February, 1900, Cronje made a stand at Paardeburg Drift. He held the British troops at bay for ten days, at one point inflicting heavy casualties on the Canadians who had made a charge on the Boer positions over open country. In the early hours of 27 February, six companies of the RCR led a final assault which brought about Cronje's surrender. The regiment suffered more than 125 casualties including 34 killed.

Pachino. On 10 July 1943, an Allied force which included the 1ST CANADIAN INFANTRY DIVISION, landed at the southern tip of SICILY with both air and naval support. The Canadians' first-day objective was the capture of Pachino airfield, on the Pachino Peninsula. Due to an almost total lack of Italian resistance, they were able to achieve this within hours of the landing.

Pakistan, UN peacekeeping in. See UNGOMAP, UNIPOM, UNMOGIP.

Palestine, UN peacekeeping in. See UNTSO.

Papineau, Louis-Joseph (1786–1871). Papineau was the leader of the REBELLION OF 1837 against British rule in Lower Canada. Leader of the Parti Canadien, later the Parti Patriote, Papineau first tried to force the British to concede more liberal and democratic government by using the French majority in the Lower Canadian assembly. When this failed, he and many of his followers concluded that an American-style revolution was necessary. The rebellion was launched in the fall of 1837 but after a number of defeats, notably at ST DENIS and ST CHARLES, Papineau fled to the United States and the rebellion was crushed. See REBELLIONS OF 1837.

Papineau, Talbot Mercier (1883–1917). A great-grandson of Louis-Joseph PAPINEAU, Papineau joined the CEF in 1914. In an open letter to his cousin Henri BOURASSA, he requested greater French-Canadian support of the war. He worked at CANADIAN CORPS headquarters in France 1916–17 and was killed in action at PASSCHENDAELE in October 1917.

Parkin, J.H. (1891–1981). An engineer, Parkin worked on a variety of weapons research projects during WORLD WAR I and joined the NATIONAL RESEARCH COUNCIL in 1929. During WORLD WAR II he was the head of an aeronautical research team within NRC that worked on jet engine design, among other things. After the war he was instrumental in the establishment of the National Aeronautical Museum.

Park Steamship Company. Crown corporation established by the federal government in April 1942 with a mandate to supervise and control the operation of newly built Canadian cargo ships carrying munitions and other war supplies to the various theatres of war. This was one of the wartime companies operating under C.D. HOWE and the DEPARTMENT OF MUNITIONS AND SUPPLY. The company was so named because merchant vessels built in Canada early in the war bore the names of national parks. At its peak the Park fleet contained 176 vessels.

Passchendaele, Battle of. Passchendaele was the third major battle fought by the entire four divisions of the CANADIAN CORPS and the second under the command of Lt-General Arthur CURRIE. The battle had started in mid-June 1917 with a massive push east by the British 5th Army from positions approximately 3 km west of the Belgian town of YPRES. The immediate objective of the attack was the town of Passchendaele, less than 10 km away, and the ridge beyond. General Douglas Haig, British Commander-in-Chief, had conceived the assault as a way of putting pressure on the Germans at a time when the French Army was in disarray from mutinies in the ranks and Russia was on the verge of collapse. The initial assaults had been carried out by the British, aided by the Australians and New Zealanders, in the face of heavy enemy resistance and at a high cost in casualties. The immense cost in blood had yielded little in the way of results. By mid-September the British lines had been pushed only about half the distance to Passchendaele. By now the town had virtually disappeared from the face of the earth and the battlefield which lay between the British lines and the ridge was a muddy, shell-pocked hell.

In early October Haig called on Currie to bring the Canadian Corps into the fight. Currie agreed, but under a number of conditions: the Corps must fight together; it must not fight under the 5th Army, whose commander Currie thought incompetent, but under the 2nd Army; he and his staff must have sufficient time to prepare the attack. Haig had little choice but to agree since Currie was ultimately responsible to Ottawa and not to him.

Currie's preparations centred on building proper roads to bring up supplies, draining as much of the land as possible prior to the fight, and readying the artillery for massive fire support of the infantry. This last was a typical Currie concern. He believed in expending shells instead of lives; carefully laid out fire support plans and the massive use of artillery marked virtually all his battles. All this was carried out under heavy German bombardment from artillery and from the air. The plan was for the men to advance behind creeping barrages, consolidate their positions, and then advance again after the artillery had been brought forward.

The first attack began on 26 October and lasted two days; 2481 men fell dead or wounded. In the early hours of 30 October, the second assault began. Once again Canadians fell by the hundreds as the Germans put up a furious resistance; once again scant progress was made. This time, 1321 fell dead or wounded. On 6 November, the third attack began; 2238 were killed or wounded this time but the town, or what was left of it, was taken. One last assault was needed to capture the heights of the ridge. This began on the morning of 10 November. The objective was taken by late day and held despite heavy German attacks. The Canadians had accomplished in two weeks what the British had not been able to do in three months but at a total cost of 15,654 dead and wounded.

Reading: D.G. Dancocks, Legacy of Valour (Edmonton, 1986); D. Morton, and J.L. Granatstein, Marching to Armageddon (Toronto, 1989)

Pathfinder Force. An élite unit within BOMBER COMMAND during WORLD WAR II that was responsible for guiding bombers to their targets and marking those targets with a variety of illumination devices. In the latter part of the war all pathfinder crews were grouped together in No. 8 Group. They were always selected from the most experienced Bomber Command crews, equipped with the latest aircraft, and given the most up-to-date navigational and target-finding devices such as H2S. One squadron from NO. 6 GROUP (RCAF)—NO. 405, commanded by J.E. FAUQUIER — was posted to No. 8 Group for much of the latter part of the war.

Patrician, HMCS. Small destroyer which, with the PATRIOT, was loaned to the RCN by the Royal Navy in 1920 to replace the aging NIOBE and RAINBOW. The Patrician displaced 1020 tonnes, carried 80 officers and men, had a top speed of 35 knots and was armed with three 4-inch guns, one 2-pounder gun, and four torpedo tubes. Patrician was stationed at Esquimalt as a training ship from 1922 to 1928, and then paid off. Her strangest assignment was to stop a group of Nanaimo bank robbers fleeing to the U.S. in a motor launch.

Patriot, HMCS. Twin to PATRICIAN, the Patriot was also loaned to the RCN by the Royal Navy in 1920. She served as an east coast training ship until paid off in 1929.

Patterson, James Colebrook (1839–1929). Born and educated in Ireland, Patterson came to Canada in 1857 where he taught school and practised law. A Conservative, he was elected to the House of Commons in 1875 and served there for twenty years. He was appointed minister of Militia and Defence in 1892 and resigned in 1895.

Pattison, John George (1875–1917). Pte Pattison was with the 50th Battalion, CEF, at VIMY. On 10 April 1917 he rushed forward under heavy fire to destroy a German machine-gun position that was holding up the battalion's advance towards Hill 145. His action helped his unit consolidate in a captured German position and he was awarded the VICTORIA CROSS for his bravery. He was killed in action the following June.

Patton, John MacMillan Stevenson (b. 1915). Patton was at Weybridge, England with the ROYAL CANADIAN ENGINEERS when, on 21 September 1940, he removed an unexploded bomb from the Hawker Hurricane factory where it had been dropped by the Luftwaffe after a daylight raid. For this he was awarded the GEORGE CROSS.

PBY. See CANSO.

Peacekeeping. Peacekeeping — the use of armed force either by an international organization or by a group of powers to separate potential combatants—was first conceived by the League of Nations in 1931 with the 'Convention to Improve the Means of Preventing War'. The League was, however, not capable of mounting any peacekeeping operations.

Peacekeeping was clearly envisaged in the United Nations Charter which outlined a mechanism for the mobilization and command, by a UN commander, of forces of member countries when deemed necessary by the Security Council. Although the UN authorized a number of military and armistice observer groups prior to 1956 (e.g. UNMOGIP and UNTSO) the first true UN peacekeeping effort was UNEF, at the time of the Suez Crisis.

Canada has played a continuing role in peacekeeping, both inside the United Nations and outside. Canadians served with UNMOGIP and UNTSO and Canada's Secretary of State for External Affairs, Lester B. PEARSON, proposed UNEF during the SUEZ CRISIS. About 1000 Canadians served with UNEF from its inception to May, 1967 when they were expelled from Egypt by Egyptian President Nasser who accused Canada of siding with Israel in the period leading to the Six-Day War of June, 1967. Canadians have also served in all other UN peacekeeping operations, contributing significant contingents to UNOC (1960), UNFICYP (1964 to present), and UNEF II (1973–1979). Canada also contributed to non-UN peacekeeping efforts on the the the ICSC (1973), ICCS (1954–74), and the MFO (1986-present).

The KOREAN WAR and the GULF WAR were not, strictly speaking, peacekeeping operations but exercises in collective security under the UN banner. Canada sent more than 20,000 armed forces personnel to Korea, with an infantry brigade group, a small naval detachment, and an air transport squadron. A squadron of fighter jets, ground support personnel, and medical personnel were dispatched to the Gulf War.

Since the 1960s, peacekeeping has been considered one of the premier roles of the Canadian armed forces although its importance in defence policy has waxed and waned. The WHITE PAPER 1964 first mentioned peacekeeping as a Canadian defence priority and placed it high on the list. The WHITE PAPER 1971, however, placed it at the bottom. Canadian forces have remained in demand for UN peacekeeping because of special skills in communications and other areas and because of Canada's continuing willingness to use peacekeeping to show the flag and to provide training for its personnel.
Reading: J.L. Granatstein and D.J. Bercuson, *War and Peacekeeping* (Toronto, 1991)

Peace Tower, Ottawa. The original tower in the centre of the Canadian Parliament building (the Centre Block) was destroyed when fire swept through the buildings in 1916. The tower was rebuilt and renamed the Peace Tower in 1933. It contains the Books of Remembrance that record the names of all those killed in action overseas in the service of Canada.

Pearkes, George Randolph (1888–1984). Pearkes joined the NORTH WEST MOUNTED POLICE in 1906, enlisted in the CANADIAN EXPEDITIONARY FORCE in 1915 and ended the war as commander of the 116th Battalion. He received the VICTORIA CROSS for bravery at PASSCHENDAELE in October 1917. After the war he joined the PERMANENT FORCE. He commanded the 1ST CANADIAN INFANTRY DIVISION in Britain from 1940 to 42 and then returned to Canada as general officer commanding Pacific Command. He disagreed with Prime Minister KING about CONSCRIPTION, strongly supporting the measure, and after retiring from the army in 1945 entered federal politics as a Conservative. He was Tory defence critic from 1945 until his appointment as minister of National Defence in the DIEFENBAKER government, a post he held until 1960 when he was appointed Lieutenant-Governor of British Columbia. As minister, he participated in the decision to cancel the Avro ARROW.

Pearson, John (1825–1892). A Canadian, Pearson served with the 8th King's Royal Irish Hussars during the Indian Mutiny and won a VICTORIA CROSS at Gwalior on 17 June 1858.

Pearson, Lester B. (1897–1972). Born in Ontario, Pearson entered the University of Toronto to study history prior to WORLD WAR I but left his studies to enlist in the CANADIAN ARMY MEDICAL CORPS. After service in SALONIKA he joined the ROYAL FLYING CORPS but was invalided home after being hit by a bus in London.

Pearson resumed his studies on return to Canada, won a fellowship to Oxford and then joined the Department of External Affairs in 1928. For the next twenty years he served with great ability and tact, earning an international reputation for his diplomatic skills. In 1945 he was named Canadian ambassador to the United States and in the following year, under-secretary of state for external affairs, the highest ranked bureaucrat in the department.

In 1948 Pearson was appointed secretary of state for External Affairs by Prime Minister Louis St Laurent. In that post he guided Canada into NATO and was one of the strongest exponents in the cabinet of Canadian participation in the KOREAN WAR. In 1956, following the British/French/Israeli invasion of Egypt, Pearson proposed an international PEACEKEEPING force to the United Nations General Assembly and UNEF was born shortly after.

Following the defeat of the St Laurent government by John George DIEFENBAKER in 1957, Pearson was elected leader of the Liberal Party of Canada. He and his party were badly defeated in the 1958 general election but Diefenbaker was unable to sustain his own national popularity; after eking out a narrow victory with a minority government in 1962, Diefenbaker was defeated in 1963 and Pearson became prime minister. One of the prime causes for Diefenbaker's defeat was his dithering on Canadian acquisition of nuclear weapons for three weapons systems that required them—the CF104, the BOMARC, and the HONEST JOHN. In acquiring those systems, Canada had agreed in principle to arm them with nuclear weapons. Although once opposed to nuclear weapons, Pearson reversed position prior to the 1963 election, claiming Canada had no choice but to honour its commitments. For his minister of National Defence, Pearson selected Paul HELLYER who embarked on a major reorganization of the Canadian armed forces which began with the WHITE PAPER of 1964 and ended with UNIFICATION. Following the centennial year of 1967, Pearson resigned in 1968 and was replaced as prime minister by Pierre Elliott Trudeau.

Peck, Cyrus Wesley (1871–1956). Lt-Col Peck served with the 16th Battalion, CEF, during World War I. On 2 September 1918 during an action at Cagnicourt, France, Peck won a VICTORIA CROSS when he made a dangerous reconnaisance to guide British tanks to protect an open flank of his battalion. The tanks in place, he was able to reorganize the battalion and lead them on to their objective, Buissy Switch.

Peden, Murray (b. 1923). Born in Winnipeg, Peden joined the RCAF in 1941 and went overseas as a pilot with BOMBER COMMAND. He was attached to No. 214 Squadron of the Royal Air Force in No. 3 Group. Peden's *A Thousand Shall Fall* is one of the best memoirs of service in Bomber Command to have come out of World War II.

Pelican. Pierre LEMOYNE used this small ship to raid British settlements on the coast of Newfoundland in 1696. The following year he sailed *Pelican* into Hudson Bay. There he engaged a small British flotilla, losing his ship but capturing two larger British vessels and sinking a third.

Pellatt, Sir Henry Mill (1860–1939). A wealthy Toronto entrepreneur, Pellatt joined the QUEEN'S OWN RIFLES in 1880. At his own expense he took the regiment to England in 1910 to take part in annual exercises at ALDERSHOT. Eventually reaching the rank of major-general in 1918, Pellatt later lost his fortune and died virtually penniless.

Pepper, George Douglas (1903–1962). Pepper studied art in Toronto and Europe and taught at the Ontario College of Art before World War II. In 1943 he was appointed Official War Artist and after a term in Canada painting troops in training at Camp Shilo and other places, he was attached to the 2ND CANADIAN INFANTRY DIVISION. In March 1944 he went missing for ten days behind enemy lines before making his way back to British lines. After the war he returned to the Ontario College of Art.

Perley, Sir George Hasley (1857–1938). Perley was educated at Harvard and ran the family lumber business before entering politics. He was first elected in 1904 to represent Argenteuil in Quebec. In 1911 he entered the BORDEN cabinet as minister without portfolio and in 1914 was sent to London as Canadian High Commissioner. In October 1917 Perley was named to head the new Department of OVERSEAS MILITARY FORCES, a post he held until October 1917. Perley acted quickly to clean up many of the difficulties that had been caused in the administration of the CEF by Sir Sam HUGHES and built a good working relationship between himself and the CANADIAN CORPS in France.

Permanent Active Militia. Official name for the PERMANENT FORCE.

Permanent Force. The 1904 MILITIA ACT established a 4000-member permanent force to garrison coastal fortifications and train the MILITIA. This was the professional army which continued the traditions first established in 1883 by the founding of the CAVALRY SCHOOL CORPS and the INFANTRY SCHOOL CORPS. On 1 April 1914, the force comprised 3110 soldiers belonging to various regiments and service and administrative personnel. Some Permanent Force officers saw service with the CANADIAN EXPEDITIONARY FORCE during World War I, but the bulk of the Corps' officers were from the militia. Between the wars the Permanent Force numbered approximately 4000 all ranks; WORLD WAR II senior officers were mainly found from the PF.

Permanent Joint Board on Defence. The PJBD was established as a result of the OGDENSBURG AGREEMENT entered into by U.S. President Franklin D. Roosevelt and Canadian Prime Minister William Lyon Mackenzie KING on 18 August 1940. The Board was intended to provide direct liaison and joint military planning between the two governments, something that was needed more than ever in the wake of the capitulation of France. It has continued to the present as a useful body for intergovernmental consultation on defence matters. In the United States the PJBD reports to the president through the Secretary of State. In Canada the Board formally reports directly to the prime minister. The Board consists of military and civilian members. The Canadian Section almost always contained a high-level

representative from the Department of External Affairs, a permanent chairman (usually a civilian), and a number of military representatives and representatives of the DEPARTMENT OF NATIONAL DEFENCE. For close to a decade after World War II, Gen. A.G.L. MCNAUGHTON chaired the Canadian Section. Decisions of the PJBD were and are issued as joint, unanimous, numbered recommendations to both governments. In the period 1945 to 1950 the Board accomplished a number of difficult tasks, including a redefinition of U.S. rights at the LEASED BASES and the formulation of Recommendation 36, which provided the basis for all post-war joint defence undertakings. The MILITARY COOPERATION COMMITTEE was a sub-committee of the PJBD.
Reading: J.L. Granatstein and N. Hillmer, *For Better or for Worse* (Toronto, 1991)

Persian Gulf Crisis. See GULF WAR.

Peters, Frederick Thornton (1889–1943). A Canadian serving with the Royal Navy, Captain Peters led the *Walney* into the boom defences at Oran harbour during the Allied landings on the North African coast which began Operation Torch on 8 November 1942. Hit by numerous enemy shells, the *Walney* and her sister ship *Hartland* were sunk. Peters was the only man on the bridge to survive. He was subsequently awarded the VICTORIA CROSS.

Phips, Sir William (*c.* 1650–*c.* 1694). Born in the colony of Maine, Phips led an expedition to capture Quebec from the French under FRONTENAC in 1690 after a successful attack on PORT ROYAL. His combined land and sea force numbered over 2000 infantrymen and 32 ships. Frontenac put up a successful resistance and Phips was forced to withdraw. In 1692 he was appointed governor of Massachusetts.

PIAT. See PROJECTOR, INFANTRY ANTI-TANK.

Pig War, 1859. See SAN JUAN ISLAND DISPUTE.

Pimple. A northern extension of VIMY RIDGE, the Pimple contained a maze of trenches and tunnels. Canadian forces attacked the feature in the early hours of 12

April 1917, three days after the main assault on the ridge itself. It took about an hour for the 10th Brigade to capture the Pimple, but the Canadians sustained almost 50 per cent casualties.

Pinetree Line. The Pinetree Line was a chain of radar stations built in southern Canada, primarily along the 49th parallel, which tied in with the U.S.'s continental defence radar system and which was designed to give advance warning of Soviet bombers approaching from the north. The line was agreed to by Canada and the United States in 1951 and completed in 1954 at a cost of $450 million, two-thirds of which was paid for by the United States. When completed it provided coast-to-coast radar coverage.

Plains of Abraham. Located to the south and east of the walled citadel of Quebec, the Plains were named after the farmer who once owned them. They were the site of the battle which took place 13 September 1759 and which was eventually to decide the fate of New France. That battle was the culmination of a siege mounted by the British under the command of General WOLFE and Admiral SAUNDERS which began on 26 June 1759 when a British fleet anchored between the Isle d'Orléans and the south shore of the St Lawrence, just downriver from Quebec. The French, under MONTCALM, planned to defend Quebec by holding the escarpments along the north shore from the Montmorency Falls, below Quebec, at least as far as STE FOY, upriver from the citadel. This gave the British the opportunity to bombard Quebec at will from the south shore. Outnumbered, out gunned, and with no fleet available to help him, Montcalm's task was simple — hold out until the onset of winter when the British would be compelled to withdraw. As summer waned, Wolfe made several failed attempts to gain a decisive victory. Then, on 9 September, he decided to place 4800 men with supporting artillery on the Plains of Abraham, using the small cove at ANSE AU FOULON as a landing spot. Through the incompetence of the local commander the cove was left unguarded by the French and, under cover of darkness on the night of 12/13 September, Wolfe's troops gained the shore, scaled the heights, and arrayed themselves on the plains. Montcalm should have waited for reinforcements but

decided to attack immediately with the troops available — a mixed force of regulars and Canadian militia. He himself led the attack. As the French line neared the British, the Canadian militiamen took cover while those Canadians in the ranks of the regulars lay prone to reload, leaving gaps in the line and weakening the mass of fire that the French were able to bring to bear on their opponents. Under British fire, they broke; Montcalm and Wolfe were both mortally wounded. Governor VAUDREUIL ordered the city surrendered, allowing the British to control the mouth of the St Lawrence. In the spring of 1760 the French almost succeeded in recapturing Quebec but were thwarted by the early arrival of the Royal Navy.

Reading: C.P. Stacey, *Quebec: 1759* (Toronto, 1959)

Platoon organization. The organization of the infantry platoon did not change between WORLD WAR I and WORLD WAR II. A full strength infantry platoon contained 35 men. It was commanded by a lieutenant who was supported by the platoon sergeant. It consisted of three sections of 11 men, each section led by a corporal. Three platoons made up a rifle company which, in the Canadian army, was normally commanded by a major with assistance from a captain.

Plattsburg, Battle of. In September 1814, in the closing stages of the WAR OF 1812, General Sir George PREVOST led a land/water attack against upper New York State from Quebec. At his disposal were some 11,000 troops against about 4000 for the Americans. The land attack was to be preceded by a naval assault on the town of Plattsburg on upper Lake Champlain, but the British naval forces attacked early and were driven off by American vessels. When Prevost heard of the naval failure, he called off the attack and retreated back up the Richelieu River toward Montreal.

Plebiscite, 1942. On 27 April 1942, Prime Minister Mackenzie KING held a plebiscite asking Canadians to release his government from its pledge not to use CONSCRIPTION to raise forces for overseas military service. Pressure to do this had started to mount after the fall of France in May, 1940 and had increased after the Nazi attack on the USSR in June, 1941 and the Japanese attack on

Pearl Harbor in December, 1941. In Quebec the LIGUE POUR LA DÉFENSE DU CANADA campaigned effectively for the 'non' side: 73 per cent of Quebec residents voted 'non'. Elsewhere in Canada, however, 80 per cent of the electorate voted 'yes'. Released from his anti-conscription promises, King introduced BILL 80 which amended the NATIONAL RESOURCES MOBILIZATION ACT to allow the government to send NRMA men overseas if necessary. This was not done until November, 1944. See REINFORCEMENT CRISIS.

Pom pom gun. Two-pounder rapid-fire anti-aircraft gun mounted on Allied naval vessels during WORLD WAR II.

Pontiac (*c.*1720–1769). As chief of the Ottawa Nation, Pontiac led an Indian alliance in a series of successful attacks on British outposts in 1763. When the alliance disintegrated later that year, Pontiac signed a number of treaties with the British. He was later assassinated by those who claimed that his treaties amounted to a betrayal of his people and a surrender of Indian land. See also PONTIAC'S WAR.

Pontiac's War. Disgruntled with unfair treatment at British fur-trading posts, PONTIAC organized discontented Ottawa, Potawatomi, and Ojibwa Indians into an alliance in 1763. They attacked Fort Detroit, killing 46 British soldiers garrisoned there. The alliance then widened and so did the scope of the attacks: eight British garrisons fell in a short period, 2000 settlers were killed and more were taken prisoner. At Bloody Run on 29 July, Pontiac's group overran a 260-man column of reinforcements en route to Detroit. As winter approached, however, and help promised by French traders failed to materialize, the alliance disintegrated. Pontiac then chose to conclude a number of treaties to end the war in the summer of 1765.

Pope, Georgina Fame (1862–1938). Pope volunteered to serve as a nurse with British forces in the SOUTH AFRICAN WAR and sailed from Quebec with four colleagues in 1899. She later joined the CANADIAN ARMY NURSING SERVICE, serving first with the reserve force and later with the PERMANENT FORCE. During World War I Pope worked at hospitals in Britain and France.

Pope, Maurice Arthur (1889–1978). After World War I service with the ROYAL CANADIAN ENGINEERS, Pope stayed with the PERMANENT FORCE in the inter-war years and became vice chief of staff in 1941. He then sat on the PERMANENT JOINT BOARD ON DEFENCE, chaired Canada's JOINT STAFF MISSION in Washington (1942–44), and represented Canada on the Allied Control Council which governed occupied Germany after World War II. Pope later wrote a personal memoir, *Soldiers and Politicians* (1962), and was Canada's ambassador to Belgium and Spain (1950–1956).

Popular Music (Boer War). Popular music in the SOUTH AFRICAN or Boer WAR era tended to be jingoistic, reflecting imperialistic sentiment in Britain and Canada (at least among many English-speaking Canadians). Songs played and sung in Canada were almost completely British due to the strong ties of culture, immigration, etc., that still held most English-speaking Canadians close to their mother country. But one exception was the very popular 'Goodbye Dolly Gray' which had been adapted from an American song sung during the Spanish-American War. Other favourite songs included 'Just as the sun went down', 'Under the same old flag', 'The British bulldogs', and 'John Bull's letter bag'. The anti-Boer racism in many of these ditties was palpable.

Popular Music (World War I). Popular music of the World War I period reflected the changing public mood during the four years of fighting. Early songs were filled with the enthusiastic British-Empire patriotism that marked the first days of the war with titles such as 'Canada fall in', or 'The Canadian forever'. Later, when war weariness set in, the popular music reflected that too; some song titles of 1917 and 1918 were 'I pray that you'll come back', and 'I want to see if my daddy's home'. The vast majority of the more than one hundred World War I songs listed in *Musical Canadiana: A Subject Index*, compiled by the Canadian Music Library Association, have strong, imperial, patriotic themes and touch on duty, sacrifice, and honour. Few deal with personal longing, separation, or loss.

Popular Music (World War II). World War II came in the middle of the Big Band Era and the bands kept on playing throughout the war both in North America and Britain. Unlike the popular music of World War I, that of World War II was rarely militaristic or patriotic; even when it was, its war-time theme was rarely over-stated ('American Patrol', 'When the lights go on again', 'G.I. Jive'). Instead there was a heavy dose of melancholy in much of the music ('I'll never smile again', 'As time goes by', 'I don't want to walk without you'). There were few Canadian homes without a radio and popular music was disseminated on records, not sheet music as it had been in previous wars. Thus most of what Canadians listened to and played was either American or American-style Big Band. Some of the most popular wartime songs included 'A string of pearls', 'Blues in the night', 'White Christmas', and 'Paper doll'.

Port Royal. The earliest settlement in Canada, Port Royal was established by the French in 1605 near the mouth of the Annapolis River in what is now Nova Scotia. Abandoned in 1607 and re-established three years later, the site was occupied by both the French and English at different times through the rest of the seventeenth century. It remained in British hands after 1710 and was renamed ANNAPOLIS ROYAL.

Post-Hostilities Advisory Committee. Established by the Canadian government at the end of 1943 to study a variety of problems that were anticipated to occur after the war, the Committee consisted of the under-secretary of state for External Affairs, the service chiefs, and the secretary of the Cabinet. It was to guide the deliberations of the WORKING COMMITTEE ON POST-HOSTILITIES problems and to report its findings to the CABINET WAR COMMITTEE.

Poundmaker (1842–1886). A Stoney Indian, Poundmaker was the adopted son of Crowfoot, a Blackfoot chief, and nephew of an important Cree chief. Poundmaker cast his lot with the Cree and became a band chief in 1878, the same year he signed Treaty No. 6 after some initial reluctance. During the 1885 NORTHWEST REBELLION, Poundmaker tried to restrain his followers from joining RIEL or committing acts of violence.

He was, however, ignored and members of his band plundered Battleford and besieged the police post there. They then engaged OTTER's column at CUT KNIFE HILL, inflicting 23 casualties and forcing Otter to retreat. Poundmaker surrendered to MIDDLETON at Battleford 23 May. He was charged with felony-treason, but served only one year of his three-year sentence and died shortly after his release.

Power, Charles Gavan [Chubby] (1888–1968). Seriously wounded during service with the CEF (he won a MILITARY CROSS for gallantry) in WORLD WAR I, Power returned to Canada in the fall of 1917 a determined opponent of CONSCRIPTION and ran for the Liberals in the December 1917 federal election. He was elected to represent Quebec South, a seat he held until appointed to the Senate in 1955. Power entered the Cabinet as minister of Pensions and National Health in 1935. In May 1940 he was appointed minister of National Defence for Air, primarily responsible for the BRITISH COMMONWEALTH AIR TRAINING PLAN. He also served as associate minister of National Defence (1940–44), and as acting minister of National Defence for one month in 1940 following the death of Norman ROGERS. He was the driving force behind the government's CANADIANIZATION policy, a policy that eventually resulted in the establishment of NO. 6 BOMBER GROUP. In November, 1944, Power resigned from the Cabinet in protest over the introduction of conscription.

Powley, A.E. (?–?): After fifteen years as a newspaperman in Toronto, Powley joined the CBC in 1940 and three years later was sent overseas to take care of the network's war reporting from Europe and the United Kingdom. He produced 'Eyes Front', a regular report on the war and, in an administrative role, kept track of CBC correspondents and forwarded their reports to Canada. His book *Broadcast from the Front* (Toronto, 1975) details his experiences and those of his colleagues.

PPCLI. See PRINCESS PATRICIA'S CANADIAN LIGHT INFANTRY.

Prevost, Sir George (1767–1816). Prevost became governor of British North America and commander-in-chief of British forces in the Canadas just prior to the WAR OF 1812. In 1814 he led 11,000 experienced British troops in an attack on the American naval base at PLATTSBURG on Lake Champlain. After a minor skirmish, however, he returned to Montreal. He was recalled to England shortly after.

Prideaux, John (1718–1759). A British army officer who took part in the SEVEN YEARS' WAR, Prideaux laid siege to the French in Fort Niagara in 1759 and was killed by a shell burst.

Priest howitzer. A self-propelled 105-mm howitzer used by Canadian artillery regiments during WORLD WAR II. Earning its nickname from the pulpit-like machine-gun mount, it carried a seven-man crew and could travel up to 38 km/h. The gun was capable of firing a 15-kg shell up to 10,615 m. See also KANGAROO.

Prince David, HMCS. A former Canadian National Steamships liner on the Pacific coast, *Prince David* was one of three such vessels commissioned in the ROYAL CANADIAN NAVY as an armed merchant cruiser in 1940. *Prince David* displaced 5800 tonnes and was radically altered before entering RCN service. The top two decks were removed, and the vessel was fitted with a cruiser-style superstructure and bridge, and given a main armament of four 6-inch guns. *Prince David* served in the Atlantic and Caribbean in 1941 but was transferred to the west coast in May 1942 where she patrolled until 1943, seeing service in Aleutian waters after the Japanese occupation of Attu and KISKA. Withdrawn from the Pacific and converted to a LANDING SHIP INFANTRY, mounting two twin 4-inch mounts and a number of anti-aircraft weapons. In 1944 she saw service at NORMANDY and in the Mediterranean. The vessel was damaged by a mine in December 1944, repaired, and then sold in 1945. See PRINCE HENRY, PRINCE ROBERT.

Prince Henry, HMCS. One of three Canadian National Steamships liners commissioned into the ROYAL CANADIAN NAVY as armed merchant cruisers in 1940, *Prince Henry* was the twin of *PRINCE DAVID*. *Prince Henry* patrolled the west coast as far south as Peru where, in April 1941, she intercepted two German merchant vessels

which scuttled themselves to avoid capture. Like her sister ships, *Prince Henry* was deployed to Aleutian waters after the Japanese occupation of Attu and KISKA in 1942. Converted in 1943 into a LANDING SHIP INFANTRY with the same configuration as *Prince David*, she was then sent to Europe in 1944 to take part in the NORMANDY landings. After 1945 the vessel served the Royal Navy as an accommodation and transport ship.

Prince Robert, HMCS. One of three Canadian National Steamships liners commissioned into the ROYAL CANADIAN NAVY in 1940, *Prince Robert* was somewhat smaller than PRINCE HENRY and PRINCE DAVID, displacing 5765 tonnes. While stationed at ESQUIMALT, *Prince Robert* captured the German vessel *Weser* without a struggle 15 September 1940. *Prince Robert* escorted the convoy which took Canadian troops to HONG KONG in late 1941 and served in Aleutian waters in mid-1942 after the Japanese occupation of Attu and KISKA. *Prince Robert* was then converted into an auxiliary anti-aircraft cruiser, mounting five twin 4-inch guns, eight 2-pounder POM POMS and twelve OERLIKONS. In that guise she saw extensive duty on convoy runs from the United Kingdom to the Mediterranean. After the war, *Prince Robert* was one of the ships bringing released Hong Kong prisoners back to Canada.

Princess Patricia's Canadian Light Infantry (PPCLI). Hamilton GAULT of Montreal donated $100,000 to organize the regiment, comprised of British ex-soldiers resident in Canada, in August 1914. The PPCLI fought for a year under British army command before joining the 3RD CANADIAN DIVISION of the CANADIAN CORPS in France in 1915. The regiment served in all the major battles of WORLD WAR I and three of its members earned the VICTORIA CROSS. After the war, the PPCLI became part of the PERMANENT ACTIVE MILITIA. In WORLD WAR II, the regiment fought with the 1ST CANADIAN INFANTRY DIVISION in SICILY, ITALY and NORTHWEST EUROPE. The 2nd Battalion of the PPCLI was earmarked for service in the Pacific in 1945 but the war ended before it could participate. Following World War II the PPCLI was designated as an ACTIVE FORCE unit, converting to airborne in 1949 so as to be part of the MOBILE STRIKING FORCE. It saw action in the KO-

REAN WAR and its 2nd Battalion won a Presidential Unit Citation for its role in the battle of KAP'YONG. The regiment is based in Calgary.

Prince, Thomas George (1915–1977). A descendent of Chief Peguis of the Saulteaux, Sgt Prince was the country's most decorated Native soldier of World War II. He served with the ROYAL CANADIAN ENGINEERS and the 1st Canadian Parachute Battalion 1940–45, and with the PPCLI in Korea. His decorations included the MILITARY MEDAL and the American Silver Star.

Prisoners of War (Canadian). 2818 Canadians are recorded as having been taken prisoner on the western front during WORLD WAR I and approximately 8000 during WORLD WAR II. In most cases these PoWs were treated according to international conventions on prisoners of war concluded at Geneva and the Hague in 1864, 1899, 1907, and 1929, although there was one instance during World War II when, after a mass escape from a German prison camp, approximately fifty escapers, Canadians among them, were executed. There was also a period of several months in the fall of 1942 when Canadian prioners were manacled in retaliation for the shackling of German PoWs. In the KOREAN WAR 32 Canadians were taken prisoner and although subject to constant efforts at political re-education, they were generally treated well when the overall ration levels and living conditions of the Chinese troops themselves is taken into consideration. UN soldiers, like the Canadians, captured in Korea after the spring of 1951 were held by the Chinese; Americans and others who had been held by the North Koreans in the first six to eight months of the war had been harshly treated, many being executed or starved to death.

Prisoners of War in Canada. Far from the fighting front, Canada became a favourite place for PoW camps holding Axis prisoners during WORLD WAR II. Most PoW camps were located in western Canada which was thought far enough away to discourage escape attempts. About 30,000 prisoners in all were held. A number of Axis prisoners were put to work as agricultural labourers on western farms during the war, and a surprising number returned to Canada as immigrants in the late 1940s and early 1950s.

Private War of Jacket Coates, The. Novel, written by Lt-Col H.F. Wood and published in 1966, telling the story of a mythical member of the first contingent of the 25TH CANADIAN INFANTRY BRIGADE GROUP which served in the KOREAN WAR. Wood was the author of *Strange Battleground*, the official history of the Canadian Army in Korea, and it has been surmised that his novel told those parts of the story of the Canadian Army in Korea that he did not wish included in the official history.

Proctor, Henry (?–1822). British Army commander during the WAR OF 1812. Proctor led a force of British regulars, Canadian militia, and Indians that defeated an American army under William Henry Harrison attempting to recapture Detroit in January 1813. Harrison avenged his defeat in October of that year by defeating Proctor at MORAVIANTOWN. Proctor's disappointing performance at Moraviantown resulted in his court martial and a six-month suspension without pay.

Projector, Infantry Anti-Tank (PIAT). A cross between an anti-tank rifle and the U.S.-designed bazooka (an anti-tank rocket fired from a re-usable tube held over the shoulder), the PIAT was issued to all Commonwealth forces during World War II. The PIAT was a shoulder-fired weapon, like the bazooka, but was heavy (15 kg), had a large recoil, and had to be used within 90 m of its target. To be effective, its projectile was best fired directly at a tank's side armour.

Propaganda, World War I. In August 1914 Britain established the War Propaganda Bureau, under the direction of C.F. Masterman, to coordinate its propaganda effort. That effort was aimed at rallying British public support for the war, suppressing the dissemination of potentially damaging war news from the front, and influencing public opinion in the U.S. to support the Allies. Posters and pamphlets, some produced by leading British writers and artists (e.g., Sir Arthur Conan Doyle and Sir Gilbert Parker) stressed alleged German war atrocities in Belgium and elsewhere. Since news from the front was strictly controlled and heavily censored, the public relied on government-generated news for its information. This was equally true in Canada where much of this material was distributed. Canadian writers such as Ralph Connor also contributed to this effort. The Canadian government created a Department of Public Information in 1918, although press censorship had been carried out for some time before that by the Chief Press Censor for Canada. Canadian propaganda efforts were closely coordinated with those of the British government.

Reading: P. Buitenhuis, *The Great War of Words* (Vancouver, 1987)

Propaganda, World War II. In contrast to World War I, Canada entered the propaganda business early in World War II with the creation of the Bureau of Public Information (1939–1942) which was followed by the WARTIME INFORMATION BOARD. The government's main aim was to foster a united, national war effort by creating a shared sense of community. As the war progressed, the entire range of available media was used including radio, newspapers, magazines, pamphlets and broadsheets, and film. The enemy was portrayed as deceitful, aggressive, and violent. After the Soviet Union entered the war, Canadian propaganda stressed the nationalism behind the Soviet war effort, downplaying the brutality of the Communist dictatorship. When Japan attacked Pearl Harbor, anti-Japanese propaganda assumed strongly racist overtones. The National Film Board, under John Grierson, added immensely to these efforts with the series *Canada Marches On* and other productions. Such efforts were also designed to impress Britons and Americans with the extent of Canada's war effort.

Reading: G. Evans, *John Grierson and the National Film Board* (Toronto, 1984)

Provincial Corps. Active MILITIA established in Canada by the British government at the end of the eighteenth century, on the eve of the Napoleonic Wars. The corps worked up to four days a week building roads and forts, and training. It was disbanded in 1802, and revived for the WAR OF 1812. See also ROYAL NOVA SCOTIA REGIMENT and ROYAL CANADIAN VOLUNTEERS.

Provincial Marine (Upper Canada). First established by the British during the SEVEN YEARS' WAR to provide lake transportation for military personnel and supplies, the provincial marine was essentially a lake schooner service. It became moribund after 1775 but was revived as a sort of naval militia at the time of the WAR OF 1812.

Public Information, Department of. See DEPARTMENT OF PUBLIC INFORMATION.

PULHEMS. System used by the Canadian Army in World War II to classify the medical fitness of personnel. 'PULHEMS' is an acronym for physique, upper extremities, lower extremities, hearing, eyesight, mental capacity, and stability. Each recruit was examined and interviewed (sometimes cursorily) and then assigned a score in each category. The standard score for infantry was 1111221.

***Puncher*, HMCS.** Built on the U.S. west coast for the Royal Navy, *Puncher* was an escort carrier commissioned into the ROYAL CANADIAN NAVY in February 1944. The vessel displaced 14,400 tonnes, carried a crew of approximately 1000, and had a top speed of 18 knots. In operational service she was designed to carry 20 aircraft. In the summer of 1944 *Puncher* ferried 40 U.S. Army Air Force fighters from the U.S. east coast to North Africa. In February 1945, the vessel was stationed at Scapa Flow from where she sortied on a number of occasions so that her aircraft could interdict enemy shipping in the North Sea. *Puncher* served as a troop ship after the war in Europe and was returned to the U.S. Navy in 1946. See also *NABOB*.

Q

Quadrant. Code name given to the Anglo-American summit conference held at Quebec City beginning on 15 August 1943 and attended by Churchill and Roosevelt. Canada's Prime Minister William Lyon Mackenzie KING had his photo taken there with the two leaders but did not participate in the meetings. At the conference the decision was made to proceed with the invasion of France in 1944.

***Quebec,* HMCS.** See *UGANDA*, HMCS.

Quebec, 1629. British merchants interested in the trading posibilities of the St Lawrence River funded two expeditions to capture Quebec in the late 1620s. The first, led by Jarvis Kirke, resulted in the capture of 11 French supply ships and 600 prisoners in 1628, although not the taking of Quebec. In the spring of 1629 Jarvis' brother DAVID KIRKE found CHAMPLAIN's settlers at Quebec starving and willing to surrender. A French naval force sent to help Champlain arrived too late and Kirke's force occupied the settlement. Nevertheless, Quebec was returned to the French in 1630.

Quebec, 1759. Since Quebec City dominated the St Lawrence River narrows, it controlled access to virtually all of New France and, therefore, was an obvious objective for British troops in the SEVEN YEARS' WAR. In fact, an attack on Quebec by land and naval forces was part of Britain's threefold strategy for the conquest of New France. The other aspects of the plan were the reduction of the French posts in the west, primarily by the British-American militia, and an assault on Montreal from New York by AMHERST. The British land forces sent to take Quebec were commanded by WOLFE, the naval forces by SAUNDERS. MONTCALM was well aware of the strategic importance of Quebec and ordered batteries set up to guard the approaches to Quebec from the Gulf of St Lawrence, but New France's governor, VAUDREUIL, failed to act on Montcalm's orders, possibly believing

that treacherous currents would prevent the British passage. The few French vessels in the area were upriver from Quebec where they were unable to deny passage to Quebec by the Royal Navy. The British made their way upriver and anchored off the Isle d'Orléans in late June 1759. They then proceeded to lay siege to Quebec until the decisive battle of the PLAINS OF ABRAHAM. Although the French lost Quebec in that battle, they nearly recaptured it in the early spring of 1760 when de LÉVIS moved downriver from Montreal, defeating the British at STE FOY and laying siege to Quebec. After the spring break-up, however, it was Royal Navy vessels, not French ones, that first appeared in the river near Quebec. That rendered de Lévis's position untenable and he was forced to withdraw.
Reading: C.P. Stacey, *Quebec: 1759* (Toronto, 1959)

Quebec, 1775. The American revolutionaries were no less aware of the strategic importance of Quebec City than the British had been before them. After the first shots were fired in the AMERICAN REVOLUTION in April 1775, a scheme was hatched by the Continental Congress to attempt to bring Quebec into the revolution; military action to accomplish this was authorized in June, 1775. Having effectively no navy, or at least none that could match the power of the Royal Navy, the Continental assault on Quebec was to be almost wholly a land affair. At the end of August 1775 an invasion force numbering approximately 2000 men left Crown Point, at the northern tip of Lake Champlain, to move against Montreal. The force was commanded by generals Philip Schuyler and Richard Montgomery. On 4 September they reached and besieged a mixed force of British regulars, Loyalists fighting in British Army uniform, and French Canadian militia at ST JEAN. The siege lasted until 3 November when the British were forced to capitulate. Governor Guy CARLETON then ordered Montreal evacuated and retired to Quebec where a second Continental force,

under General Benedict Arnold, was approaching. Montgomery occupied Montreal and then proceeded to join Arnold at Quebec in early December. Like St Jean, Quebec was defended by British regulars, Loyalists, and French Canadian militia. The Continental forces did not have the men, artillery, or supplies for a long winter siege and attempted to force a capture. They launched their assault early on 31 December 1775 but suffered heavy losses; Montgomery himself was killed. The Continentals were determined to keep the pressure on. George Washington told Schuyler that Quebec had to be taken before the spring break-up and additional troops were sent there. But in early May British ships appeared off the besieged city and the Continental troops were forced to withdraw.
Reading: G.F.G. Stanley, *Canada Invaded: 1775–1776* (Toronto, 1973)

Quebec Conferences. Sir Winston Churchill and Franklin Roosevelt held two wartime conferences at Quebec City to plan Allied strategy. Canada hosted but did not participate in the conferences, held 17–24 August 1943 and 10–15 September 1944. See also QUADRANT.

Queen Anne's War. Also known as the WAR OF THE SPANISH SUCCESSION (1702–13), the conflict, which started and was primarily fought in Europe, spilled over into North America. Most of the action involved border raiding by guerrilla forces acting in concert with Indian allies. Without the resources to conduct an assault on Boston or New York, the French in Canada carried out guerrilla raids against frontier settlements such as Deerfield and Haverhill in Massachusetts. In Newfoundland they destroyed Bonavista in 1704 and captured St John's in 1708. The Acadians and their Indian allies raided Wells and Casco Bay in New England. In counterraids the British took Port Royal and Acadia in 1710. The TREATY OF UTRECHT ended the skirmishing by settling the war in Europe.

Queen's Own Rifles. Organized at Toronto in 1860 from six independent rifle companies, the QOR fought at RIDGEWAY during the 1866 FENIAN RAIDS. The unit served with W.D. OTTER's force during the NORTHWEST REBELLION in 1885 and sent volunteers to the SOUTH AFRICAN WAR together with the 2nd Battalion of the ROYAL CANADIAN REGIMENT. The regiment fought with the 1ST CANADIAN DIVISION in France during WORLD WAR I and raised five battalions of reinforcements for the CEF. In WORLD WAR II the QOR fought with the 3RD CANADIAN INFANTRY DIVISION in the NORTHWEST EUROPE CAMPAIGN. One battalion served with the CANADIAN ARMY OCCUPATION FORCE 1945–46. The QOR were a postwar regular force infantry regiment but are now a militia unit.

Queen's Regulations and Orders (QRs). Body of rules and regulations by which the armed forces of Canada are governed. The Rules and Regulations are established by Parliament and govern the day-to-day administration of the military by the military. They are distinct from the NATIONAL DEFENCE ACT which established the overall structure of the DEPARTMENT OF NATIONAL DEFENCE and set out the place of the military within that structure.

Queenston Heights, Battle of. Battle during the WAR OF 1812 which began 13 October 1812, when American militia crossed the Niagara River intending to capture Queenston Heights preparatory to a general invasion of Canada. British General Sir Isaac BROCK led a combined force of British regulars and colonial militia in a charge aimed at dislodging the Americans from a position they had established at the top of the cliffs. Brock died leading that first charge and his second-in-command died in a second unsuccessful effort. The British eventually prevailed, however, when General R.H. SHEAFFE, with reinforcements from FORT GEORGE, circled the cliff unobserved and attacked the American force from behind, trapping them. The British and Canadian forces sustained 105 casualties and took 1000 Americans prisoner.

R

Radar. Acronym for radio detection and ranging, radar was invented in Britain before the outbreak of WORLD WAR II. Radar works by sending out radio beams which bounce off an object. A radar receiver then picks up some of the return signal or echo, allowing the operator to determine the object's location. Radar in use at the outbreak of the war was primitive, indicating direction but not the height of an aircraft. During the war advances in radar allowed it to be used to detect surfaced U-boats as well as other surface vessels. Radar was the basis of the RAF's H2S blind bombing system.

***Rainbow*, HMCS.** Royal Navy light cruiser acquired by the fledgling ROYAL CANADIAN NAVY, along with the *NIOBE*, in 1910. *Rainbow* displaced 3660 tonnes, had a top speed of 17 knots, and carried approximately 300 officers and men. The main armament consisted of two 6-inch guns, six 4.7-inch guns and two torpedo tubes. *Rainbow* actively patrolled the west coast from San Francisco to Prince Rupert during August, 1914 although she would have been no match for a German cruiser. The vessel continued to guard coastal shipping until 1917. Then used as a depot ship, she was paid off in 1920. The second ship of that name, purchased from the United States Navy in 1968, was a World War II-vintage diesel-powered submarine used for anti-submarine training exercises. She carried 8 officers and 74 men, had a top speed of 10 knots submerged and 20 on the surface, and was armed with ten torpedo tubes. She was paid off in 1974.

Ralston, James Layton (1881–1948). After serving as a battalion commander with the CANADIAN CORPS in WORLD WAR I, Col Ralston was elected to Parliament in 1925. He first entered the cabinet as Prime Minister Mackenzie KING's minister of National Defence in 1926 and kept the post until the Liberal defeat in 1930. Although re-elected in 1930 he retired from politics in 1935 to resume his law practice. He re-entered poli-

tics at the start of the war and was appointed minister of Finance in September 1939. He held that post until his appointment as minister of National Defence in July 1940. Aided by the ministers of National Defence for Naval Services (Angus L. MACDONALD) and of National Defence for Air (C.G. POWER), Ralston presided over the expansion of Canada's armed forces during the war. He was a strong supporter of CONSCRIPTION and threatened to resign from the Cabinet if the measure was not introduced during the CONSCRIPTION CRISIS OF 1942. On a tour of European battle zones in the fall of 1944 he was convinced by the military that conscription could no longer be delayed. That sparked off the REINFORCEMENT CRISIS because when he made his views known to King after his return to Canada, King forced him to resign on 1 November 1944. He was replaced by A.G.L. MCNAUGHTON.

Ram/Kangaroo. Armoured personnel carrier constructed from the chassis of the RAM TANK. The turret of the Ram was removed and hand holds were welded to the inside of the hull. In this configuration, the vehicle carried 11 infantrymen as well as a crew of two.

Ram tank. WORLD WAR II-era tank built in Canada from a Canadian-British design, the Ram was intended to equip Canadian armoured formations. Manned by a crew of five, early models mounted a 2-pounder gun. The Ram II used a 6-pounder as its main armament and had a top cross-country speed of 40 km/h. Because the U.S.-built SHERMAN was considered a superior tank, it, and not the Ram, was used to equip Canadian armoured units. The Ram chassis was used successfully, however, as the basis for a number of important specialty vehicles including the SEXTON self-propelled gun and the RAM/KANGAROO armoured personnel carrier.

Rayfield, Walter Leigh (1881–1949). While serving with the 7th Battalion, CEF at ARRAS, France in early September 1918,

Pte Rayfield overran and occupied two enemy trenches, taking 30 prisoners. He also risked his life to save a wounded comrade. For these acts he was awarded the VICTORIA CROSS.

Rayner, H.S. (1911–1976). Rayner first entered the Royal Canadian Navy as a cadet in 1928. He served in a number of capacities during World War II both in staff positions and at sea commanding the destroyers *ST LAURENT* and *HURON* in action in the North Atlantic, on Arctic convoys to the USSR, and in the English Channel before and during the NORMANDY landings. After the war he commanded the *MAGNIFICENT*. He continued to rise through the ranks becoming CHIEF OF THE NAVAL STAFF in 1960 but he was retired from that position by the minister of National Defence, Paul HELLYER in 1964 because of his strong opposition to Hellyer's UNIFICATION policies.

RCAF. See ROYAL CANADIAN AIR FORCE.

RCAF Staff College. Originally a junior staff college, the institution opened in Toronto in 1943. Now called the Canadian Forces Command and Staff College, it trains officers from all three services for command and staff positions at the lieutenant-colonel level.

RCEME. See ROYAL CANADIAN ELECTRICAL AND MECHANICAL ENGINEERS.

RCMP. See NORTH WEST MOUNTED POLICE.

Reade, Herbert Taylor (1828–1897). Taylor, a Canadian surgeon who served with the British Army's 61st Regiment of Foot, won Canada's second VICTORIA CROSS at Delhi, 4 September 1857, during the Indian Mutiny. Taylor led an attack on mutineers who were firing at his hospital, capturing three cannons and clearing the way for the British re-occupation of Delhi.

Rebellions of 1837. In 1837 armed revolts against British rule took place in both Upper and Lower Canada. In Upper Canada the revolt was led by William Lyon MACKENZIE, a newspaper publisher and political radical who favoured the establishment of an American style of government in the British

American colonies. In Lower Canada the revolt was headed by Louis-Joseph PAPINEAU who also favoured an American-style political system because he believed that under such a system French Canadians would be guaranteed their liberty and survival. In both colonies the revolts followed many years of growing political tension and agitation which pitted reformers against the British governor and his conservative local allies — the Family Compact in Upper Canada, the Château Clique in Lower Canada — who constituted the colonial élites and who most benefited from British rule. And in both colonies these disputes involved a heavy element of rural vs town dwellers with the farmers tending to support the reformers.

The revolt in Lower Canada was the first to break out when in November, 1837 the government moved to arrest leading French-Canadian reformers and their allies (the *Patriotes*). Many fled to the countryside and troops were dispatched to seize them. The first battle was fought at ST DENIS on 23 November; government forces were repelled. The rebels, however, were defeated in battles that followed at ST CHARLES and ST EUSTACHE, and Papineau fled to the U.S.

In Upper Canada on 5 December, a brief battle was fought on Yonge Street north of Toronto when about 800 of Mackenzie's followers ran into a roadblock manned by militia and other loyalist volunteers and were dispersed. A second skirmish followed a few days later in Brantford. The rebels were defeated again and Mackenzie fled to the U.S. In both colonies the rebels made unsuccessful efforts to renew the rebellions in the months that followed the 1837 battles. Both Mackenzie and Papineau eventually returned to Canada but a number of their followers were executed or deported to Australia.
Reading: William Kilbourn, *The Firebrand* (Toronto, 1956); Joseph Schull, *Rebellion: The Rising in French Canada 1837* (Toronto, 1971)

Recruiting leagues. Highly competitive private recruiting leagues arose in Canada after August 1915 to find volunteer reinforcements for the CANADIAN EXPEDITIONARY FORCE. The leagues drew nearly 124,000 men to the CEF but only 40 of the 170 battalions formed by private recuiters actually reached full strength. See also Arthur MIGNAULT and J.M. GODFREY.

Red River Expedition. Expedition commanded by British Col Garnet WOLSELEY, sent from Canada to Red River in the spring of 1870, to put down the RED RIVER REBELLION which had been launched the previous fall by Louis RIEL. At first the British government was reluctant to provide military aid for this purpose. They were in the process of withdrawing troops from Canada and also believed the uprising a Canadian responsibility. They nevertheless agreed to send Wolseley and a contingent of 400 men from the British Army's 60th Rifles in return for Canada's assurances that it would negotiate with Riel. Wolseley's men were augmented by militia from Ontario and Quebec. The expedition could not begin until early May 1870, by which time a political solution to the uprising had been negotiated. The expedition's purpose, therefore, was to take formal control of Red River for Canada, seek out rebels who had not been granted amnesty, and restore law and order. The expedition experienced many difficulties in its journey to Red River. The Americans would not allow it to pass through the canal at Sault Ste Marie, forcing an overland portage there, and once at Thunder Bay it had to negotiate its way to the Prairies via rivers and streams, with many difficult portages. The expedition arrived in Red River in late August, 1870. By then Riel had fled. Wolseley quickly left the Canadian contingent as an occupying force and returned east for eventual departure with his troops for England. The Canadian militia who remained formed the MANITOBA FORCE.

Red River Rebellion. The rebellion of the Métis at Red River against transfer of Rupert's Land to Canada was precipitated in October 1869 by the arrival of a survey party from Canada. It ended in the summer of 1870 when the Manitoba Act was proclaimed and the RED RIVER EXPEDITION, commanded by Garnet WOLSELEY, arrived to impose Canadian law in the area.

The major cause of the rebellion was the conclusion of an agreement between the Hudson's Bay Company, Britain, and the new Dominion of Canada for the transfer to Canada of Rupert's Land on 1 December 1869. The Métis were not consulted and objected that their lives and livelihoods would be directly affected by a process they had had no part of. Under the leadership of Louis RIEL, a Métis who had been educated in Montreal, the English and French-speaking Métis living in the area of the Red River colony united to stop the transfer. Riel's aim was to force Canada to negotiate with his community. Riel and his followers formed the National Committee of the Métis, seized Lower Fort Garry (a Hudson's Bay Company post) and erected barricades to stop the Canadian-designated Lieutenant-Governor from entering the area. They then imprisoned a number of Canadians who had been actively agitating for annexation to Canada and declared a provisional government. One of the prisoners, Thomas Scott of Ontario, escaped capture, joined a small party attempting to reach Portage La Prairie, and was then recaptured and summarily executed as an example to the other colonists. This action enraged Scott's Orange Lodge compatriots in Ontario and elsewhere.

Canadian Prime Minister John A. MACDONALD stopped the transfer of Rupert's Land to Canada as soon as he heard of the uprising and insisted that the British send a military force to put it down. The British agreed, but only on the condition that Canada negotiate with Riel. Thus the RED RIVER EXPEDITION was dispatched in May, 1870. Macdonald negotiated with the Métis through Donald A. SMITH, a Hudson's Bay Company principal who agreed to act as intermediary. The negotiations with the Métis were basically successful in that Riel and his followers gained many of the guarantees they sought and agreed to allow Rupert's Land to become part of Canada. The terms and conditions of the agreement were contained in the Manitoba Act which was proclaimed on 15 July 1870, creating the new, albeit then tiny, Province of Manitoba. See also MANITOBA FORCE.

Reading: G.F.G. Stanley, *The Birth of Western Canada* (Toronto, 1936)

Re-establishment Credit. Veterans of World War II who did not take advantage of the federal government's offer of subsidized vocational retraining or education, or resettlement on the land under the VETERANS' LAND ACT, were entitled to spend an equivalent sum on a home, furniture, or business. The credit was not payable in cash.

Regalbuto, Battle of. Town in SICILY captured by the 1st Canadian Infantry Brigade of the 1ST CANADIAN INFANTRY DIVISION in conjunction with the British 231st Brigade in the final stages of the Sicilian campaign, on 2 August 1943. The Canadians and the British 1st Brigade launched their attack during daylight on 1 August but were caught in the open by heavy tank and mortar fire directed at them by the Hermann Göring Panzer Division. They reached the town the following day and after a pitched battle dislodged the Germans who withdrew to the heights southeast of the town.

Régiment d'Artois. French regiment stationed at LOUISBOURG which defended New France during the SEVEN YEARS' WAR with the assistance of the TROUPES DE LA MARINE. See also TROUPES DE LA TERRE.

Régiment de Bourgogne. Regiment of French regulars which, along with the RÉGIMENT D'ARTOIS, fought to defend New France during the SEVEN YEARS' WAR. See also TROUPES DE LA TERRE.

Regimental histories. Histories of individual Canadian regiments have been a popular form of military writing in Canada for some time and although most such histories have been written and published by amateurs, a number of distinguished Canadian writers and scholars have also contributed their talents. The first recorded Canadian regimental history to be published was *Historical Record of the Governor General's Body Guard* (1876), written by F.C. DENISON which was followed, some twenty years later, by Thomas Champion's *History of the 10th Royals and of the Royal Grenadiers from the formation of the regiment until 1896.* A number of other histories were written prior to World War I, all of militia units. These works were primarily intended as souvenirs for members and former members, and about ten were published before 1914. Not surprisingly World War I produced a large array of regimental histories, as did World War II.

Currently histories are available of all the permanent regiments and most of the militia regiments. The quality of regimental histories is, at best, uneven. Some attempt to devote space to virtually every officer, cover every action engaged in by the unit, and always cast the regiment and its leaders in the best possible light. Others are serious works of historical scholarship based on primary sources and interviews and make critical judgments about commanding officers and other regimental notables. One of the best examples of the genre, one which combines superb writing with historical accuracy, is *The Regiment* (Toronto, 1955) by Farley MOWAT.

Regina Trench. During the battle of the SOMME Canadian soldiers made six attempts between September and November 1916 to capture this German-held trench. Running southwest to northeast roughly 1.5 km north of the French town of COURCELETTE, the trench was thought to be an important site from which further attacks could be launched against German positions. The CANADIAN CORPS made abortive efforts to capture the trench on 26 September, 1 October, and 8 October 1916. In each of these attacks artillery preparation to smash the barbed wire guarding the heavily defended trench proved ineffective, and the wire trapped advancing soldiers, allowing the German machine-gunners to kill them in large numbers. Only a handful of attackers ever reached the trench and they were eventually forced to retreat. Better artillery preparation for an attack on 21 October allowed the CEF's 11th Brigade, under Victor ODLUM, to capture part of the trench 15 minutes after zero hour but the rest of the position remained to be taken. Although the Canadians took 1000 prisoners, the Germans vigorously defended the position when the CEF's 44th battalion attacked again 25 October. That battalion lost 200 killed or wounded. Finally, on 11 November, after two days of remorseless artillery bombardment of the German positions, the 4TH CANADIAN DIVISION captured and held the rest of the trench. The battle cost the Canadian Corps over 3000 casualties.
Reading: Desmond Morton and J.L. Granatstein, *Marching to Armageddon* (Toronto, 1989)

Regular Officer Training Plan (ROTP). Scheme for officer education introduced in 1954 by which young men would be subsidized by the government while attending university in return for three years in the service of their choice after their education was completed. At the end of the three years they could accept permanent commissions or return to civilian life. See also CANADIAN OFFICERS' TRAINING CORPS.

Reid, George Agnew (1860–1947). Reid studied art in Canada, the United States, and France before taking up a teaching post at the Ontario College of Art in 1890. From 1912 to 1918 he was principal of the College. He was designated an official war artist in 1918, painting a number of scenes of Canadian war memorials.

Reid, Howard Emerson (1897–1962). Soon after graduating from the ROYAL NAVAL COLLEGE OF CANADA in Halifax, Reid took command of *RAINBOW*. He was then sent overseas where he served aboard British destroyers in the North Sea and the English Channel until the end of World War I. He stayed with the RCN in the interwar years, rose in rank and was Commanding Officer, Atlantic Coast at the outbreak of World War II. During the war he was vice chief of the Naval Staff, 1941–42, and Flag Officer Newfoundland, 1942–43. In the latter position he was immediately responsible for the ROYAL CANADIAN NAVY groups in the MID-OCEAN ESCORT FORCE. He then served as the naval member of the CANADIAN JOINT STAFF in Washington, 1943–46, and CHIEF OF THE NAVAL STAFF until he retired in 1946–47.

Reinforcement crisis. The shortage of infantry which developed in the ranks of the FIRST CANADIAN ARMY after D-DAY is sometimes referred to as the reinforcement crisis, although it was an integral part of the ongoing struggle over whether or not Canada was to introduce CONSCRIPTION for overseas military service in WORLD WAR II. The reinforcement crisis stemmed from a shortage of trained infantry to replace losses suffered in line rifle companies. The fighting units of First Canadian Army had been organized on the assumption that the rate of infantry casualties (the 'WASTAGE' rate) after the invasion of Europe would be roughly those which had been suffered by the British Eighth Army in the North African desert in 1942–43. Those assumptions were, however, quite wrong. The mobile warfare of the desert produced lower infantry casualties than did the grinding battles in the towns, forests, and flooded polder lands of NORMANDY and NORTHWEST EUROPE. More men were allocated for armour, artillery,

supply, and other duties than were necessary, while fewer were earmarked for reinforcement of the line rifle companies. Thus the CONSCRIPTION CRISIS of 1944 was not produced by a general manpower shortage in the Canadian Army but by a specific shortage of infantry replacements. That shortage began to become acute in the last stages of the Normandy battles and reached crisis proportions during the SCHELDT campaign.

Before conscription was resorted to, the army attempted to 'remuster' men from other duties by retraining them as infantrymen and assigning them to forward units. The process was too slow, however, because retraining took many weeks. Since reinforcements were badly needed, and quickly, the alternatives were either to convince the NRMA men, many of whom were trained infantrymen, to GO ACTIVE or to conscript them. When the first course of action failed, the second was utilized on 23 November 1944 when Ottawa ordered 16,000 NRMA men overseas as reinforcements.

Reading: J.L. Granatstein and J.M. Hitsman, *Broken Promises: A History of Conscription in Canada* (Toronto, 1977)

Remember Me. Edward Meade's novel, published in 1946 in England and in 1965 in Canada, stands as one of the best fictional portrayals of the Canadian army in WORLD WAR II. The hero, Corporal O'Rourke, serves in a ROYAL CANADIAN ARMY SERVICE CORPS transport company. In NORMANDY he is killed in action. The novel is distinguished by Meade's familiarity with the details of army life and the fine rendering of O'Rourke's long-distance relationship with his wife who lives on the prairies. See also WAR NOVELS.

Remembrance Day. Originally designated as the memorial day for soldiers killed in WORLD WAR I, it now also recognizes those killed in WORLD WAR II and the KOREAN WAR. The date and period of the minute of silence — 1100 hours, 11 November — is derived from the hour and date of the signing of the ARMISTICE, which ended the fighting in World War I: 11 November 1918 at 11:00 a.m. In the U.S., war dead are remembered on Memorial Day, the last Monday in May.

Rennie, John (1920–43). During grenade-throwing practice at a Canadian training camp in England on 29 October 1943, Acting Sgt Rennie attempted to throw back a grenade that had failed to clear a protective embankment. Although he prevented serious injuries to others, he died of his wounds and was posthumously awarded the GEORGE CROSS.

Research Enterprises Ltd. A Crown corporation established by the DEPARTMENT OF MUNITIONS AND SUPPLY in World War II to manufacture radar components, optical glass, range finders, and binoculars. Headed by W.E. Phillips, it sold $220 million worth of equipment between 1940 and 1946.

Reserve army. The reserve army was the World War II successor of the NON-PERMANENT ACTIVE MILITIA in that its members had voluntarily enlisted for service in reserve units, i.e., they had not been conscripted for duty under the NATIONAL RESOURCES MOBILIZATION ACT, nor had they specifically volunteered for active overseas service. Many reservists were volunteers too young for active service (they were between 17 and 19 years of age) or too old. The reserves were used for home defence at what were thought of as vulnerable points (bridges, locks, etc.). After Canada declared war on Japan, a reserve brigade was organized in each of the 11 military districts. In December 1940, the reserve army reached a peak of almost 112,000 thousand.

Reserve Militia. The 1868 MILITIA ACT divided Canada into nine military districts and established the reserve MILITIA, a voluntary force whose chief duty was to come to the aid of the British garrison in time of war. The reserve militia was basically a continuation of the pre-Confederation SEDENTARY MILITIA (which effectively existed only on paper). It differed from the ACTIVE MILITIA whose members volunteered to serve with specific militia regiments, to train, and to attend militia camps.

Restigouche, HMCS. Nicknamed 'Rustyguts', this RIVER CLASS DESTROYER was commissioned in the RCN from the Royal Navy in 1938 and served at both ESQUIMALT and Halifax before World War II. In the latter stages of the battle of France in May, 1940, *Restigouche* was sent to British waters to assist the Royal Navy in the evacuation

of Allied troops from the continent. The ship's war service included escort duty with the NEWFOUNDLAND ESCORT FORCE, minesweeping with the British Western Approaches Command, and anti-submarine operations during OVERLORD. The destroyer was used for troop transport after the war and was paid off in October, 1945. The second ship of this name was a destroyer escort commissioned into the ROYAL CANADIAN NAVY in June, 1958. The destroyer was the first of seven *Restigouche* class vessels commissioned between June 1958 and November 1959. Each displaced 2400 tonnes, carried a crew of nine officers and 200 men, and had a top speed of 28 knots. They were armed with two 3-inch guns, two 40-mm guns, and a variety of anti-submarine rockets and homing torpedos. These vessels were near-twins of the *ST LAURENT* CLASS DESTROYER ESCORTS.

***Restigouche* Class Destroyer Escorts.** See *RESTIGOUCHE*.

Restigouche River, Battle of (1760). Following the defeat of the French at the PLAINS OF ABRAHAM in September 1759 the Duc de LÉVIS tried to retake Quebec City in the spring of 1760. He defeated the British at STE FOY and laid siege to Quebec, but the British fleet arrived in early May, 1760, forcing him to withdraw. A small French flotilla carrying reinforcements attempted to move upriver the following July, but was defeated by the British at the mouth of the Restigouche River.

Returned Soldiers, World War I. During and after WORLD WAR I the term most commonly used to describe men returning from duty with the CANADIAN EXPEDITIONARY FORCE was 'returned soldiers' (in WORLD WAR II 'veteran' was used). The first of the eventually 267,813 returned soldiers to arrive back in Canada were invalided home due to illness before Christmas 1914. In 1915 the government established the MILITARY HOSPITALS COMMISSION to rehabilitate and reintegrate returning soldiers, who were arriving back in Canada at the rate of about 100 per week. In February, 1918, the federal government created the Department of SOLDIERS' CIVIL RE-ESTABLISHMENT under Sir J.A. LOUGHEED to oversee pensions and other programs designed to re-integrate the returned men into society. Not a great deal was done for these men, however, and pressures grew for better pensions and other forms of compensation for the men. Much of this was organized and directed by the GREAT WAR VETERANS ASSOCIATION. Bitterness prompted some returned men to participate in riots directed against enemy aliens and union leaders. Returned men were prominent in the wave of strikes which swept across Canada in the spring and summer of 1919. See also SOLDIER SETTLEMENT ACT, SOLDIER SETTLEMENT BOARD.

Reading: Desmond Morton and Glenn Wright, *Winning the Second Battle* (Toronto, 1987)

Returned Soldiers, World War II. See VETERANS.

Revolutionary War, 1775–87. Also known as the American Revolution and the American War of Independence, the Revolutionary War had an important impact on Canada and Canadian military history.

The first fighting in the Revolutionary War took place on 18 April 1775 at Lexington, Mass., but it could not have been a surprise to the British military in Canada which had been preparing for just such an event. For example, the Quebec Act (1774) had been designed, in part, to curry favour with the élites of the former French colony of New France to ensure their support in the event of hostilities between Britain and its British American colonies, while Britain's governor in Quebec, Guy CARLETON had been laying plans for the defence of Quebec and the raising of a colonial militia for some time.

Even before the American Continental Congress issued its Declaration of Independence (4 July 1776), American forces moved to occupy Quebec. Under General Richard Montgomery they first struck north in September 1775 taking the well-known invasion route up the Hudson River and Lake Champlain towards Montreal. Carleton tried to muster the militia to stop them but few Quebeckers rallied to the British flag despite the entreaties of Bishop Briand. The defence of the colony was thus left to a handful of British regulars supported by some militia and volunteers.

Montgomery succeeded in capturing Montreal in mid-November after forcing the sur-

render of Fort ST JEAN, then moved upriver to Quebec City where he joined Benedict Arnold and a force of about 700 riflemen. An assault on the city on 31 December was turned back (Montgomery was killed) ending the threat to Canada for the duration. Thereafter Canada was used mainly as a British base of operations against the American revolutionaries by commanders such as BURGOYNE. In Nova Scotia there was considerable sympathy for the rebels but the powerful British presence at Halifax ensured the colony's loyalty.

The British defeat at Jamestown, Virginia in 1781 brought the end of the war which was confirmed by the TREATY OF PARIS (1783).

Reading: G.F.G. Stanley, *Canada Invaded: 1775–1776* (Toronto, 1973)

Reyburn, Wallace (b. 1913). A British novelist, sportswriter, and newspaper reporter, Reyburn worked as a war correspondent for the *Montreal Standard* from 1941 to 1945.

Rhineland. The Rhineland is that portion of Germany which lies to the west of the Rhine River. By the beginning of February 1945, with the Battle of the Bulge behind them, and the SCHELDT battle having secured access to the port of Antwerp, the Allies began to clear German forces west of the Rhine in preparation for forcing a crossing of that river. FIRST CANADIAN ARMY'S portion of that offensive opened on 8 February.

The Canadian plan was to push southeast along the Rhine River from the Nijmegen Salient which the Allies had captured during the ill-fated Operation Market Garden the previous September. That advance was to form the northern pincer of a combined attack mounted by the Canadians and the 9th U.S. Army which was under the overall command of Field Marshal Bernard Montgomery's 21st Army Group. The American attack was dubbed Operation Grenade. The Canadian assault was mounted in two phases, Veritable (8–21 February) and Blockbuster (22 February–10 March). In both operations First Canadian Army was considerably strengthened by the addition of 30th British Corps. In the first assault the Canadians succeeded in pushing through the Reichswald and reaching the German city of

Goch. In the second, they pushed past Goch through the formidable HOCHWALD and Balbergerwald to a point opposite the city of Wesel.

As the attack progressed, German resistance stiffened. At first they were surprised that the major Allied assault in the northern sector of the Rhineland had come from the Canadian portion of the front and were expecting a more southerly attack. Once alerted, however, they quickly recouped and were aided both by the terrain and by the weather. Late winter thaws, rain, and deliberate flooding of polder land along the river forced the attackers to advance through seas of mud and waterlogged fields, reminiscent of the conditions the Canadians had fought in during the Scheldt battles. The thick forests made movement of armoured vehicles difficult and provided ample ambush and sniper opportunities.

The Canadians eventually succeeded in their objectives. They cracked the Siegfried Line, captured the thickly forested terrain west of the Rhine, and forced the Germans across the river. But they paid a steep price: total Canadian casualties in the Rhineland battle were approximately 5304.

Reading: J. Williams, *The Long Left Flank* (Toronto, 1988); W.D. Whitaker and S. Whitaker, *Rhineland: The Battle to End the War* (Toronto, 1989)

Rice, Ingraham [Gitz] (1891–1947). One of the best known songwriters of WORLD WAR I, Rice was born in New Glasgow, Nova Scotia. After studying at the McGill Conservatory, Rice enlisted in the CANADIAN EXPEDITIONARY FORCE in 1914. He joined the PRINCESS PATRICIA'S CANADIAN LIGHT INFANTRY's entertainment troupe and, after 1917, was put in charge of entertainment for troops in Canada. Among his songs were 'Keep your head down, Fritzie Boy', 'I want to go home' and, purportedly, 'Mademoiselle from Armentières'. The DUMBELLS performed many of his songs. See also POPULAR MUSIC, WORLD WAR I.

Richardson, Arthur Herbert Lindsey (1873–1932). At Wolve Spruit with LORD STRATHCONA'S HORSE during the SOUTH AFRICAN WAR, Sgt Richardson braved enemy fire to rescue a companion who was trapped under his dead horse. For this he was awarded the VICTORIA CROSS.

Richardson, George (1831–1923). A Canadian serving with the British Army's 34th (Cumberland) Regiment of Foot, Richardson won a VICTORIA CROSS 27 April 1859 at Kewarie Trans-Gogra during the Indian Mutiny.

Richardson, James Armstrong, Jr (b. 1922). As a pilot during World War II, Richardson flew LIBERATORS over the North Atlantic for the RCAF. After the war he joined the family grain and investment business where he worked until his election to the House of Commons in 1968. Following his entry into federal politics he served as minister of National Defence 1972–76. During his tenure the government established the DEFENCE STRUCTURE REVIEW to provide DND with broad objectives, establish new equipment priorities, and generally to try to solve the department's funding problems. In 1976 he resigned from the government in a dispute over language policy.

Richardson, James Cleland (1895–1916). On 8 October 1916, during the battle of the SOMME, Piper Richardson stood in the open and played his bagpipes with complete disregard for German bullets, in an effort to rally his comrades of the 16th Battalion, CANADIAN EXPEDITIONARY FORCE, to renew their attack on REGINA TRENCH. He was killed and posthumously awarded the VICTORIA CROSS.

Richelieu River. After establishing a base at Quebec in 1608, CHAMPLAIN joined (or was dragooned into) a war party consisting of some 60 Huron and Algonquin who intended a raid against the Iroquois. He and his two French comrades-in-arms, armed with arquebuses, proved to be the decisive factor in defeating 200 Iroquois at a summer battle near the Richelieu River in 1609.

Ricketts, Thomas (1901–1967). On 14 October 1917, while serving as a machine-gunner with the [ROYAL] NEWFOUNDLAND REGIMENT at Lys, Belgium, Pte Ricketts braved heavy machine-gun fire to bring up ammunition for his LEWIS GUN. At age 17, he was Canada's youngest VICTORIA CROSS winner.

Rideau Canal. After the WAR OF 1812, Col John BY was assigned the construction of the

Rideau Canal, between present-day Ottawa and Kingston, Ontario, as an alternate military route between Kingston and Montreal. The canal was completed in 1832 at nearly five times its budgeted cost and was used almost exclusively for shipping freight rather than military supplies and personnel.

Ridgeway, Battle of. Lt-Col Alfred Booker led 900 Canadian militia into battle against 800 FENIANS at Ridgeway, in the Niagara Peninsula on 2 June 1866. The Fenians, led by 'General' John O'Neil, had crossed the Niagara River near FORT ERIE and were marching west toward Port Colborne when they were intercepted at Ridgeway. Many of the Fenians were veterans of the U.S. Civil War; the Canadian MILITIA were mostly university students. The Canadians fared well at first and were on the verge of victory when Booker, mistaking Fenian scouts for cavalry, ordered his men into a square formation in a defile. The Fenians took advantage of Booker's confusion to mount a bayonet charge that left 10 Canadians dead and 38 wounded. O'Neil thus won the battle but instead of pursuing the Canadians, he retreated to the Niagara River, re-crossed into the U.S., and was interned.

Riel, Louis David (1844–1885). Born in Manitoba and educated in St Boniface and in Montreal, Riel was 1/8 Native. He studied both law and the priesthood before returning to Red River in 1868. Along with many Métis, he objected to the transfer of Rupert's Land to Canada, and as leader of the National Committee of the Métis, initiated the RED RIVER REBELLION of 1869. He proclaimed a provisional government in the fall of that year, seized Fort Garry, imprisoned a number of Canadian settlers, and executed Thomas Scott. Prime Minister John A. MACDONALD was forced by Britain to negotiate with him in return for the dispatch of the RED RIVER EXPEDITION, led by Garnet WOLSELEY. Although the negotiations were a success, Riel fled Canada the following summer to avoid arrest by Wolseley's men. Riel was subsequently elected twice to the House of Commons, but was expelled from Parliament and banished from the country for five years for his role in leading the rebellion. After 1870 Riel spent some time in a Montreal mental institution before settling in Montana in the United States where he taught school in a Métis settlement. He also developed religious delusions, imagining himself a prophet of a new religion that was a cross between Prophetic Judaism and Catholicism. Riel returned to Canada in 1884 on a 'divine mission' to help the Métis of the North Saskatchewan River valley after they, many Indians, and some white settlers invited him to return to help them press their varous claims in Ottawa. In March, 1885, he initiated the NORTHWEST REBELLION by again proclaiming a provisional government, this time at BATOCHE, and challenging the authority of Canada in the region. Macdonald responded by sending the NORTHWEST FIELD FORCE under MIDDLETON. Riel and the Métis were defeated. Riel was captured, found guilty of treason, and hanged at Regina 16 November 1885. See also Gabriel DUMONT, W.D. OTTER, FISH CREEK, BATOCHE, CUT KNIFE HILL.

Reading: G.F.G. Stanley, *Louis Riel* (Toronto, 1963); T. Flanagan, *Louis 'David' Riel: 'Prophet of the New World'* (Toronto, 1979)

Riel Rebellion, 1869. See RED RIVER REBELLION.

Riel Rebellion, 1885. See NORTHWEST REBELLION.

Ring knockers. Term used to describe graduates of the ROYAL MILITARY COLLEGE, allegedly from the practice of knocking their graduation rings on the table. The term refers to the 'old boy' network that is said to characterize RMC classmates in the service.

River Class Destroyer. The River class destroyers commissioned by the RCN between 1931 and World War II were not true 'class' types in that they were not duplicates of one prototype. Rather, they were similar vessels all named after Canadian rivers. The first two were *SAGUENAY* and *SKEENA*, built in Britain specifically for the ROYAL CANADIAN NAVY and commissioned in 1931. Each displaced 1360 tonnes, had a top speed of 31 knots, was crewed by 181 officers and men, and carried four 4.7-inch guns as main armament as well as a number of smaller rapid-fire guns (when acquired). *Skeena* later underwent modification of its main armament, reducing the number of 4.7-inch guns to two but adding more rapid-fire weapons. In 1937 two Royal Navy C-class destroyers, similar to the *Saguenay* and *Skeena*, were acquired by the RCN. These were renamed *FRASER* and *ST LAURENT*. These ships were slightly larger and faster but carried the same main armament. One year later two more C class destroyers were purchased from the RN and were re-named *RESTI-GOUCHE* and *OTTAWA*. In 1939 the larger HMS *Kempenfelt*, designed as a flotilla leader with extra accommodation, was also acquired from Britain. It was renamed *ASSIN-IBOINE*. This completed the pre-war River class acquisition program. During the war the RCN acquired seven additional C class destroyers — *MARGAREE* (sunk in 1940), *Chaudière, Gatineau, Kootenay, Qu'Appelle, Saskatchewan*, and *Ottawa II* to replace *Ottawa* which was sunk in 1942.

The River class destroyers were important vessels in the history of the RCN. They were the first modern destroyers acquired by the navy in the inter-war period and the first built specifically for the RCN. During the war they did yeoman duty supporting the Royal Navy in the evacuation of Allied troops from France at Dunkirk in the last stages of the Battle of France, on escort duty with the NEWFOUNDLAND ESCORT FORCE and the MID-OCEAN ESCORT FORCE, and on anti-submarine patrol in the English Channel during and after OVERLORD. Four River class destroyers were lost during World War II—*Fraser, Skeena, Ottawa*, and *Margaree*.
Reading: K.J.R. Macpherson, *Canada's Fighting Ships* (Toronto, 1975)

River Class Frigate. Built in Canada during World War II, River class frigates were specially designed as anti-submarine vessels, not unlike the U.S. destroyer escorts although slower. These ships mounted two 4-inch guns as their main armament, displaced 1470 tonnes, had a top speed of 19 knots, and carried 140 to 160 men. They were armed with both DEPTH CHARGES and HEDGEHOG anti-submarine mortars. Sixty River class frigates were built in Canada; the first—*Waskesiu*—was commissioned in June, 1943. Seven River-class frigates were acquired from the Royal Navy. These vessels were nothing if not long-lived; the last in service—*Beacon Hill*—served with the RCN for more than 23 years before being paid off in September 1967.

Roberts, J.A. (1907–1990). A businessman, Roberts joined the MILITIA in 1933 and commanded the Manitoba Dragoons and the 8th Canadian Infantry Brigade during WORLD WAR II. After the war he returned to the world of business but entered government service with the Department of Trade and Commerce in 1958. Among the positions he held was Deputy Secretary General of NATO (1964–1968).

Roberts, John Hamilton (1891–1963). Roberts won a MILITARY CROSS for action with the CEF in World War I and served with the PERMANENT FORCE between the wars. He was in command of the 2ND CANADIAN INFANTRY DIVISION on 19 August 1942 when it mounted a raid on DIEPPE that resulted in 907 fatal casualties and 1946 men taken prisoner. Because of poor conception, preparation, and execution of the raid, the Division ran into heavy and effective German resistance and failed to take any of its objectives. Although Roberts was given the DISTINGUISHED SERVICE ORDER for his part in the attack, he was relieved of his post in command of the division in April, 1943 and placed in charge of Canadian reinforcement units in England. The government claimed he was not being used as a scapegoat for the Dieppe disaster even though he never held another operational command.

Robertson, James Peter (1883–1917). Pte Robertson served with the 27th Battalion, CANADIAN EXPEDITIONARY FORCE at the battle of PASSCHENDAELE. On 6 November 1917, he destroyed an enemy post to clear the way for his platoon to advance. He was killed the same day while rescuing a wounded comrade and was posthumously awarded the VICTORIA CROSS.

Robson, Henry Howey (1894–1964). Born in England, Robson was serving with The Royal Scots (British Army), at Mount Kemmel, France on 14 December 1914 when he won his VICTORIA CROSS. He moved to Canada at the end of World War I and died in Toronto.

Rockingham, John Meredith (1911–1988). Born in Australia, Rockingham served in the NON-PERMANENT ACTIVE MILITIA before WORLD WAR II. During the war he was with the Canadian Scottish and the Royal Hamilton Light Infantry before assuming command of the 9th Canadian Infantry Brigade in 1944. He saw extensive action in NORTHWEST EUROPE. He left the army in 1945 to return to civilian life but in August, 1950 agreed to assume command of the 25TH CANADIAN INFANTRY BRIGADE GROUP in the KOREAN WAR. He held command of that unit until completion of its first rotation in 1952. Thereafter he was placed in charge of the 3rd Canadian Infantry Brigade.

Rogers, Norman McLeod (1894–1940). Born in Nova Scotia, Rogers was educated at Acadia University and Oxford. After service in WORLD WAR I he taught history at Acadia, then served a stint as William Lyon Mackenzie KING's private secretary (1927–1929) before moving to Queen's University to teach political science (1929–1935). In 1935 Rogers was elected to the House of Commons. He entered the Cabinet that year as minister of Labour before becoming minister of National Defence in 1939. In 1940 Rogers' career was cut short when he was killed in a plane crash.

Rogers, Robert (1731–1795). Born in Massachusetts, Rogers organized Rogers' Rangers, a guerrilla MILITIA which fought alongside the British in the WAR OF THE AUSTRIAN SUCCESSION and also in the SEVEN YEARS' WAR. During the REVOLUTIONARY WAR, Rogers sided with the British.

Rohmer, Richard (b. 1924). Rohmer flew fighters with the RCAF in World War II and joined the air reserve in Toronto after the war. He also pursued a career as a lawyer and writer, primarily of fiction but producing one work—*Patton's Gap* (1974)—on the history of the NORMANDY campaign. In 1976 he was named commander of the Air Reserve Group, Air Command and was promoted to Chief of Reserves in 1978. He retired in 1981.

Rollo, Andrew (1703–1765). Col Rollo came to Canada with the British Army in 1757 during the SEVEN YEARS' WAR. He participated in raids on French settlements on the New York frontier that year, and in the siege of LOUISBOURG in 1758. After the British conquest of Isle St Jean (Prince Edward Island) he was placed in charge of the

forced evacuation of some 2200 French inhabitants to France. He joined General James MURRAY at Quebec in 1760 and helped in the capture of Montreal.

Ross rifle. A military version of a Canadian-designed and built bolt-action hunting rifle, developed by Sir Charles ROSS, was adopted by the Canadian militia in 1901 although it had been rejected as unsuitable for military service by the British War Office, the U.S. Army, and the NORTH WEST MOUNTED POLICE. Sir Sam HUGHES promoted the use of this .303-calibre rifle on the grounds that it was manufactured in Canada. The Mk I proved problematic and was recalled in 1906. The Mk II was produced in large numbers beginning in 1910 despite continuing British pressure to adopt the LEE-ENFIELD. In action during World War I, the Ross rifle jammed with repeated firing and in less than ideal conditions. The Ross rifle was withdrawn and the CANADIAN CORPS re-equipped with the Lee-Enfield in 1916.

Ross, Arthur Dwight (1907–1981). Ross was awarded a GEORGE CROSS when he led a group of five men to rescue a pilot and gunner from a plane that had crashed into another carrying bombs at an RAF airstrip in Yorkshire England on 28 June 1944. Ross lost his right hand during the rescue; two other men were also injured.

Ross, Sir Charles (1872–1942). Scottish-born aristocrat who developed the ill-fated ROSS RIFLE, an adequate hunting rifle but a failure as a military weapon. After minister of Militia and Defence Sam HUGHES decided to adopt the rifle for the Canadian MILITIA, Ross obtained government contracts to produce over 400,000 of the weapons at his Quebec City plant. When in 1917 the government decided to abandon the Ross, it expropriated Ross's plant and paid him $2 million for it.

Ross, William (1824–1912). A Liberal, Ross served a brief stint as minister of Militia and Defence (November 1873 to September 1874). He was appointed to the Senate in 1905 and served there until his death.

ROTP. See REGULAR OFFICER TRAINING PLAN.

Royal Canadian Air Cadets. The Royal Canadian Air Cadets were established in 1946 as part of the post-war reorganization of the ROYAL CANADIAN AIR FORCE. The organization was the successor to the Air Cadet League of World War II. It is composed of young people aged 12 to 18 who are provided preliminary ground or flight crew instruction. In World War II, the League attracted more than 30,000 young men. It was integrated into the RCAF in 1943.

Royal Canadian Air Force. More than 20,000 Canadians served in the various British air services in WORLD WAR I and several, such as W.A. BISHOP, and Raymond COLLISHAW, earned fame as top Allied aces. In 1918 a short-lived Royal Canadian Naval Air Service was established to patrol Canadian coastal waters, but it was quickly disbanded as was a Canadian Air Force, set up to give air support to the CANADIAN EXPEDITIONARY FORCE.

After the war the government studied the question of the establishment of a separate air service. An AIR BOARD, chaired by A.L. Sifton, recommended that it do so and a CANADIAN AIR FORCE was established once again, this time for good. In 1923 its name was changed to Royal Canadian Air Force.

The RCAF was not much of an air force between the wars. Most of its operations were non-military — flying supplies in the north, for example. Its aircraft were few, were usually civil and not military types, and were generally kept in operation until well past their prime. In 1926, for example, the RCAF received the first of what would eventually be 12 single-engine ARMSTRONG-WHITWORTH SISKIN biplanes and flew them for more than a decade, by which time they were completely obsolete. Not until February 1939 did it begin to receive the modern HURRICANE fighter.

As with Canada's other two services, the RCAF spent the inter-war years preparing both for home defence and, in the event of a major European war, to fight alongside Britain's Royal Air Force. Thus RCAF officers were constantly shuffled back and forth across the Atlantic to receive training and staff education in Britain. There were almost no opportunities to do either in Canada.

Following the Munich Crisis in the fall of 1938 the RCAF began to gear up for a possible conflict. The senior RCAF officer was designated Chief of the Air Staff, reporting directly to the minister of National Defence. Modern aircraft were ordered and regular squadrons were expanded as was the RCAF AUXILIARY. At the outbreak of war there were 8 squadrons in the RCAF, 12 in the Auxiliary.

During WORLD WAR II the RCAF expanded rapidly and became a full service air force. It even had its own minister — the minister of National Defence for Air—from May 1940 on. In North America RCAF aircraft patrolled both coasts, and took part in the KISKA operation. Two RCAF transport squadrons served in Burma while a CANSO squadron flew from Ceylon. At home the RCAF operated the BRITISH COMMONWEALTH AIR TRAINING PLAN which turned out over 131,000 air crew during the war. In Europe RCAF bombers flew with NO. 6 GROUP of BOMBER COMMAND—a result of the government's CANADIANIZATION policy—while RCAF fighters played a major role in the 2ND ALLIED TACTICAL AIR FORCE. In fact, the RCAF was part of the air action almost from the beginning of the war; its No. 1 Squadron, later renamed No. 401, equipped with Hurricanes took part in the BATTLE OF BRITAIN. More than 200,000 men and women served in the RCAF during the war, operating aircraft or supporting flying operations in some 48 separate squadrons overseas and 40 squadrons at home.

The post-war RCAF shrank almost as rapidly as the wartime RCAF had expanded. But following the outbreak of war in KOREA and with the increase of COLD WAR tensions, the RCAF grew once again. A full air division, equipped initially with the SABRE, later augmented by the CF100, was sent to Europe while No. 426 transport squadron played a part in the Korean campaign. In Canada the RCAF worked closely with the USAF to defend the continent, providing approximately 10 squadrons and operational training units to the overall effort. The RCAF role in continental air defence was formalized with the signing of the NORAD agreement in 1958.

From its peak in the early 1960s, the RCAF slowly declined in strength and aircraft as budget cuts took hold. After the government's 1959 decision not buy the CF105, U.S. fighter jets were purchased as were BOMARC air defence missiles.

Like the other services, the RCAF was drastically affected by UNIFICATION. In 1968 the service formally ceased to exist, its functions for the most part assumed by AIRCOM. *Reading*: S.F. Wise, *Canadian Airmen and the First World War* (Toronto, 1980); W.A.B. Douglas, *The Creation of a National Airforce* (Toronto, 1986); S. Dunmore and W. Carter, *Reap the Whirlwind* (Toronto, 1991); C. Shores, *History of the Royal Canadian Air Force* (London, 1984)

Royal Canadian Air Force Auxiliary. Known prior to World War II as the Non-Permanent Active Air Force, the auxiliary in pre-war days was the RCAF's equivalent to the non-permanent active MILITIA. In 1932 three army-cooperation squadrons were formed, the first time that the auxiliary was given a definite organizational shape. After the war the Auxiliary was one of four branches of the RCAF—the Regular Force, the Reserves, the ROYAL CANADIAN AIR CADETS, and the Auxiliary. It was to provide a ready reserve of air personnel and aircraft on a moment's notice if needed. Post-war reorganization provided for 15 Auxiliary squadrons.

Royal Canadian Armoured Corps. The corps was created 13 August 1940 as the Canadian Armoured Corps to train and hold reinforcements for armoured regiments on active service. It had and has no combatant role. In 1945 the designation 'Royal' was added to its title. Its primary role is to train regimental staff and to administer the Canadian Forces' armoured units.

Royal Canadian Army Cadets. In 1908 the department of MILITIA AND DEFENCE provided instructors, arms, books, and exams to school-age males in an effort to standardize the many cadet training programs that already existed in secondary schools in Ontario and Quebec. This was the genesis of the Cadet Corps. By 1913 there were 40,000 cadets in six provinces, including Quebec. From 1909 on the Royal Canadian Army Cadets were administered and trained by the Cadet Services of Canada, originally known as the Corps of School Cadet Instructors (Militia).

Royal Canadian Army Chaplains Corps. A militia unit authorized in 1921, the Chaplains Corps was a continuation of the World War I-era Canadian Chaplain Service. The Service and the Corps provided chaplains to the armed forces in both world wars and the KOREAN WAR, and in various PEACEKEEPING operations. In 1948 a Regular component of the Corps was also established. See also J.W. FOOTE and F.G. SCOTT.

Royal Canadian Army Medical Corps. First established in 1904; the designation 'Canadian Army Medical Corps' was authorized in 1909, the 'Royal' being added in 1919. The RCAMC provided field ambulances and casualty clearing stations for the CANADIAN EXPEDITIONARY FORCE in France during WORLD WAR I. Its members served throughout the world during WORLD WAR II in field surgical teams, hospitals, convalescent homes, and field ambulances. After the war RCAMC personnel were sent to KOREA and served on a variety of PEACEKEEPING operations.

Royal Canadian Army Pay Corps. Organized in January 1907, the corps served as paymasters and cashiers to Canadian forces overseas in World War I. Some members also served in Siberia. During and after World War II, the RCAPC provided personnel and pay services to Canadian forces in various parts of the world.

Royal Canadian Army Service Corps. First organized in 1903 as the Canadian Army Service Corps; the 'Royal' designation was added in 1919. The RCASC provided, and provides, a variety of transport and supply services to Canadian troops.

Royal Canadian Artillery. See ROYAL REGIMENT OF CANADIAN ARTILLERY.

Royal Canadian Corps of Signals. The Corps provides signals communications for the Canadian Army. Although the Corps was not formally established until 1919 (and not given the Royal designation until 1921), the ROYAL CANADIAN ENGINEERS formed a number of signals companies in France during World War I. In World War II, signals companies were attached to the five Canadian divisions, the two Canadian corps, and the 1ST CANADIAN ARMY.

Royal Canadian Dental Corps. In World War I dental services were provided to the personnel of the CANADIAN EXPEDITIONARY FORCE by the Canadian Army Dental Corps, a MILITIA unit. It was briefly disbanded after World War I but re-established in 1921. The 'Royal' designation was added in 1947.

Royal Canadian Dragoons. Incorporating the CAVALRY SCHOOL CORPS, the RCD was organized in 1883. The regiment served with the NORTHWEST FIELD FORCE and the YUKON FIELD FORCE, and in the SOUTH AFRICAN WAR. The RCD fought with the 1ST CANADIAN DIVISION in World War I and with the 5TH CANADIAN ARMOURED DIVISION in World War II. After the war, the RCD served as part of the regular army.

Royal Canadian Electrical and Mechanical Engineers. Founded 1 February 1944, the RCEME provided recovery units, mobile workshops, and other field repair services to detachments overseas and in Canada during and after World War II. Members of the RCEME converted 76 PRIEST self-propelled guns into KANGAROO armoured personnel carriers in only three days in preparation for Operation TOTALIZE in early August, 1944, during the NORMANDY campaign.

Royal Canadian Engineers. The Corps was established in 1903. Its personnel—called 'sappers'—served in both world wars building roads, bridges, railways, and airfields, tunnelling, and planting and removing mines. Peacetime work included land surveys and DEPARTMENT OF NATIONAL DEFENCE construction projects.

Royal Canadian Horse Artillery. Formed in 1905, the RCHA was modelled after the Royal Horse Artillery which had been part of the British Army since 1793. The RCHA was equipped with smaller, more mobile artillery, capable of being drawn quickly to battle by fast horses and of accompanying the cavalry. After the phasing out of both the cavalry and horse-drawn artillery, the RCHA was equipped with smaller field pieces drawn by trucks, such as the 25-POUNDER GUN, and with self-propelled guns such as the SEXTON and the 105-MM GUN.

Royal Canadian Infantry Corps. Formed in 1942, the RCIC held reinforcements for active service battalions. In the modern Canadian Forces it plays a role for infantry similar to that performed by the ROYAL CANADIAN ARMOURED CORPS for armoured units.

Royal Canadian Legion. A disparate group of veterans' organizations, including the GREAT WAR VETERANS' ASSOCIATION, came together to found the Canadian Legion in 1926. In the period immediately after World War II, the Legion concerned itself mainly with the re-establishment of VETERANS.

Royal Canadian Mounted Police. See NORTH WEST MOUNTED POLICE.

Royal Canadian Naval College. See ROYAL NAVAL COLLEGE OF CANADA.

Royal Canadian Naval Reserve. Established in 1923, the reserve was authorized originally to enlist 500 men in nine port divisions, later reduced to five — Charlottetown, Halifax, Montreal, Quebec, and Vancouver—but its actual strength between the wars never amounted to more than half that. The members of the Naval Reserve were to be from maritime occupations and to possess a professional knowledge of ships and the sea. Each year they were given four weeks of naval training aboard RCN vessels.

On the outbreak of war in 1939, a large number of professional seamen volunteered for service with the RCNR and by May, 1941, approximately 3800 members of the service were on active duty.

Royal Canadian Naval Volunteer Reserve. In order to train volunteers for naval service, in 1923 15 reserve companies of the RCNVR were organized across the country, a number subsequently increased to 19. Unlike the members of the ROYAL CANADIAN NAVAL RESERVE these men were amateurs—yachtsmen, etc.—with an interest in the sea and ships but no professional expertise. An RCN instructor provided 30 evenings' training through the winter followed by two weeks at sea in the summer. The service was often called 'the wavy navy' because rank stripes on the cuff of the officer's uniform were wavy, and not straight as in the RCN. Between the wars the RCNVR never numbered more than 1500, all ranks. After the outbreak of war the RCNVR played a key role in the RCN's expansion, providing some 88 per cent of the RCN's total wartime personnel.

Royal Canadian Navy. The RCN was born on 4 May 1910 with the passage of the NAVAL SERVICE ACT. The government of Prime Minister Sir Wilfrid LAURIER planned to build a small navy for coastal waters protection which would also be able to fight alongside the Royal Navy in the event of war. To this end the RCN's first two ships, the RAINBOW and the NIOBE, both built for the Royal Navy in the 1890s, were commissioned into the RCN later that year, primarily as training vessels. The Laurier government lost power in 1911; Sir Robert BORDEN, who succeeded Laurier, decided not to proceed with the construction of ten modern warships, as called for in Laurier's original plan, but to make cash contributions to the Royal Navy instead. Thus the RCN entered WORLD WAR I with virtually no vessels.

During World War I the RCN grew to some 7000 men. Most of its ships were converted civilian vessels such as armed yachts or armed trawlers used as small sub chasers, although it did operate two SUBMARINES, the CC1 and CC2, and the Niobe and Rainbow. Anti-submarine patrols and convoy duty were the RCN's chief preoccupation during the conflict. In 1917 the RCN embarked on an ambitious plan to construct more than 172 small anti-submarine craft for use in Atlantic coastal waters. Most of these vessels were in use by the summer of 1918.

After the war the RCN suffered from the same deprivation that affected the other armed services. It possessed only a handful of ships (six in 1928), but only two — ex-RN destroyers — of any significance, one on each coast. Most of its officers trained with the Royal Navy at one time or another. In 1923 the ROYAL CANADIAN NAVY RESERVE and the ROYAL CANADIAN NAVAL VOLUNTEER RESERVE were both formed.

The inter-war navy was a destroyer navy. Until 1931 the RCN's destroyers had always been cast-off RN vessels but in that year the service received the first ships built expressly for it — the SAGUENAY and SKEENA. Built in British shipyards and following a standard British design, these were the first of Canada's RIVER CLASS DESTROYERS. The RCN

possessed seven of these vessels at the outbreak of war, five having been purchased from the Royal Navy.

At the outbreak of war, the total strength of the RCN, the RCNR and the RCNVR was fewer than 3500 personnel. But the declaration of war was quickly followed by a rapid expansion program as the navy acquired destroyers, minesweepers, frigates, cruisers, and other vessels, even escort and light fleet aircraft carriers. The mainstay of the RCN during the war was the CORVETTE, a small sub-chaser never intended for more than coastal duty. The U-boat onslaught and the demand for Royal Navy escort vessels in other theatres of war placed the RCN's corvettes front and centre on the NORTH ATLANTIC RUN. These vessels were mostly unsuitable for that duty and, in the first three years of the war, their crews were largely untrained and inexperienced. As a result they were not always effective in preventing U-boat attacks. Nevertheless, the RCN was responsible for the bulk of the North Atlantic escort work throughout the war.

RCN destroyers of the TRIBAL CLASS fought alongside RN ships in the Bay of Biscay and took part with other Canadian and Allied vessels in the D-DAY landings — over 100 Canadian ships took part. Other RCN ships, including corvettes, sailed on the Murmansk run to the USSR, the Gibraltar run, and in the Caribbean. One ship, the cruiser UGANDA, saw action in the Pacific. By the end of the war more than 106,000 men and women had served in the RCN. Of its some 900 ships, 375 were combatant vessels and most had been built in Canada, a tremendous feat considering that Canadian shipyards at the outbreak of war were not capable of building anything much more sophisticated than the corvette. The service had lost 24 ships and 2024 men, but had sunk or participated in the sinking of 33 enemy submarines.

The RCN shrank rapidly after the war and at one time had fewer than 15 ships in commission, but it began to rebuild after the outbreak of the war in KOREA. By the mid-1950s modern destroyers had been added to a fleet which still possessed two cruisers — ONTARIO (paid off in 1956) and QUEBEC (paid off in 1958) — and an aircraft carrier — the MAGNIFICENT, replaced in 1957 by the BONAVENTURE. The latter was decommissioned in 1970. At its post-war peak in the early 1960s, the RCN possessed some 45 principal warships and was staffed by some 20,000 officers and ratings. The RCN disappeared as a separate service with UNIFICATION and was replaced by MARCOM.

Reading: G.N. Tucker, *The Naval Service of Canada*, 2 vols (Ottawa, 1952); M.L. Hadley and R. Sarty, *Tin-Pots and Pirate Ships* (Montreal & Kingston, 1991); W.A.B. Douglas (ed.), *RCN in Transition* (Vancouver, 1988)

Royal Canadian Ordnance Corps. Founded in 1903, the corps provided mobile workshops and divisional armourers' shops to the CANADIAN CORPS in France during World War I and services ranging from beach detachments to mobile laundries during World War II and after.

Royal Canadian Regiment. Formed from three companies of the INFANTRY SCHOOL CORPS, the regiment operated under a number of names before receiving its current designation in 1901. The regiment served under the command of W.D. OTTER with the NORTHWEST FIELD FORCE in 1885, while men from the regiment also served with the YUKON FIELD FORCE. Two battalions were formed, again under Otter, and served in the SOUTH AFRICAN WAR, one with particular distinction at PAARDEBURG. The RCR joined the 3RD CANADIAN DIVISION in France in December 1915, taking part in all major divisional battles from then until the end of the war. In World War II the RCR served with the 1ST CANADIAN INFANTRY DIVISION in SICILY, ITALY, and NORTHWEST EUROPE. As a post-World War II ACTIVE FORCE regiment, the RCR also sent three battalions to fight in KOREA.

Royal Canadian Rifles. The British government raised the Royal Canadian Rifles in 1840 from British Army veterans living in Canada with at least seven years of prior army service. The Rifles garrisoned Kingston, Montreal, Quebec and FORT GARRY. The unit was disbanded in 1870 when the British withdrew their forces from Canada.

Royal Canadian Volunteer Regiment. When Britain went to war against France in 1793, the British recruited two battalions of volunteers in Lower Canada to help defend the colony in the event the U.S. decided to take advantage of the situation and invade. The first battalion was staffed and equipped at Quebec while the other was made up of English-speaking troops from Montreal. Never called upon to fight, the battalions disbanded in 1802.

Royal Commission on the Bren Gun Contract. Both the Canadian and British governments signed contracts in 1938 with the John Inglis Co. of Canada to produce 12,000 BREN GUNS. The contract was awarded without having been put up for tender. After complaints from the opposition, the government of William Lyon Mackenzie KING established a Royal Commission to investigate the matter. It recommended that the government establish competitive bidding for defence contracts. See also DEFENCE PURCHASING BOARD; Ian MACKENZIE.

Royal Commission on the Canadian Expeditionary Force to . . . Hong Kong. Known as the Duff Commission after Chairman Sir Lyman P. Duff, Chief Justice of the Supreme Court of Canada, the commission was established by order-in-council in February 1942 to inquire into the disaster that befell the Canadian troops dispatched to HONG KONG. The hearings were held *in camera* and the evidence remained secret until after the war. The Commission reported in June, 1942. Duff judged that, on the whole, the troops had been well trained and equipped but that more vehicles could have been sent. The only person censured in the report was E.J.C. SCHMIDLIN, the Quartermaster-General. Many of the government's detractors claimed the report was a whitewash.

Royal Flying Corps. Perhaps 20,000 Canadians joined the RFC during WORLD WAR I because Canada did not have an air force of its own at the time. Canadian pilots flew the entire range of war missions and many, such as W.A. 'Billy' BISHOP, Billy BARKER, and Mike MCEWEN distinguished themselves in combat.

Royal George. A frigate belonging to the PROVINCIAL MARINE of Upper Canada in the WAR OF 1812, the *Royal George* mounted 22 guns.

Royal Military College. Originally staffed by British army officers, RMC opened at Kingston in 1876 to train Canadian officers, some of whom later joined the PERMANENT FORCE as regulars. The curriculum was designed to reflect military education offered both at Sandhurst, where British officer cadets are educated, and West Point, where the U.S. Army trains its officers. Emphasis at the start was on military engineering but other courses, including an arts stream, are now offered. In the late nineteenth century it was standard practice for a small number of RMC graduates to serve with the British Army where they received operational training. Hundreds of RMC graduates served with the CANADIAN EXPEDITIONARY FORCE in France, many of them with distinction. After 1919, RMC graduates were required either to join the Permanent Force or MILITIA as a condition of their enrolment. RMC closed during World War II because of an inability to provide officers for training. When reopened after the war it did so as a tri-service college. It also provided (and provides) third- and fourth-year education for students who had entered either ROYAL ROADS MILITARY COLLEGE in Victoria, B.C., or COLLÈGE MILITAIRE ROYAL DE ST JEAN in St Jean, Quebec. At one time RRMC and CMR were both two-year institutions; currently students there can complete a four-year program but some choose not to do so. In 1959 RMC acquired degree-granting status. It began training female cadets in 1979.

Royal Naval Air Service. Nearly 1000 Canadians flew with the naval wing of the ROYAL FLYING CORPS, established in June 1914. Among these were the members of the famous Black Flight, headed by Raymond COLLISHAW. At first the RNAS served as a naval auxiliary, playing a major role in the fight against German U-boats; later in the war it was given the task of air defence of Britain and support of land operations, especially in Italy.

Royal Naval College of Canada (Royal Roads). The NAVAL SERVICE ACT of 1910 provided for the college which opened at Halifax in 1911 to train cadets for the ROYAL CANADIAN NAVY. After the Halifax explosion of 1917, the college moved to Esquimalt. Closed from 1922 to 1942, the college reopened as the Royal Canadian Naval College, located at HMCS *Royal Roads*. In 1948 the institution was re-named Canadian Services College, Royal Roads. After unification, the name ROYAL ROADS MILITARY COLLEGE was used. See also ROYAL MILITARY COLLEGE.

Royal Newfoundland Regiment. Formed in Scotland in 1915, the regiment served with British units in the Middle East, where it took part in the Gallipoli campaign, and in France, where it was decimated on the first morning of the Battle of the SOMME, 1 July 1916. The regiment was disbanded after World War I. A volunteer MILITIA force raised for guard duty and artillery training in 1939 was divided in two during the war —the Newfoundland Regiment consisting of the active force and the Newfoundland Militia which was the home guard or reserve. The active force unit was the nucleus from which the re-born RNR was organized in 1949. The RNR is presumed to have inherited the traditions of all those who served with British units raised in Newfoundland prior to Confederation in 1949.

Royal North West Mounted Police. See NORTH WEST MOUNTED POLICE.

Royal Nova Scotia Regiment. Sir John Wentworth, Lieutenant-Governor of Nova Scotia, raised this MILITIA unit in 1793 from Loyalist veterans of the REVOLUTIONARY WAR. The regiment did garrison duty and built various fortifications. The regiment was disbanded in 1802 without ever seeing combat.

Royal Regiment of Canadian Artillery. The overall artillery arm of the Canadian army. The original MILITIA component of the regiment dates back to 1855 and to batteries of garrison artillery formed at Kingston, Quebec, and Victoria. In 1871 the regular component of the regiment came into existence when A and B batteries, located at Quebec City and Kingston, were authorized. These batteries served both training and defence purposes. In the general militia reorganization of 1883 they were designated as the Royal Schools of Artillery, a third battery at Victoria, B.C., was authorized, and the three batteries were formed into the Regiment of Canadian Artillery, sometimes referred to as the Artillery School Corps. In 1893 the designation 'Royal' was added. The regiment has served with Canadian forces in every major engagement since the FENIAN raids, providing field and garrison artillery at home and abroad. See also ROYAL CANADIAN HORSE ARTILLERY.

Royal Roads Military College. See ROYAL NAVAL COLLEGE OF CANADA.

Royal Twenty-Centers. Following an idea of Chief of the General Staff A.G.L. MC-NAUGHTON, the DEPARTMENT OF NATIONAL DEFENCE opened relief camps for single, un-employed men across the country in the early 1930s. The camps provided board and 20 cents a day wages for work on public projects. The camp residents derisively re-ferred to themselves as 'royal twenty-cen-ters'. They were, for the most part, unhappy about living in isolated places, under military discipline, and provided fertile ground for agitators anxious to embarrass the government.

Royal 22e Regiment. Organized in No-vember 1914 as the 22nd (French Canadian) Battalion of the CEF, this French-speaking regiment fought with the 2ND CANADIAN DIVISION in most of the major battles of WORLD WAR I. Colloquially known as the 'Van Doos', from their numeral in French—*vingt-deuxième* — the unit disbanded after the war but was reorganized as the 22nd Regi-ment, part of the PERMANENT ACTIVE MILI-TIA, in 1920. It was given the designation 'Royal' in 1921. During WORLD WAR II the regiment served with the 1ST CANADIAN IN-FANTRY DIVISION in SICILY, ITALY, and NORTHWEST EUROPE. After World War II, the regiment was designated as part of the ACTIVE FORCE. Three battalions of the regi-ment saw service in KOREA (1950–53) while other units have served with Canadian forces in Germany and elsewhere. The Van Doos became a parachute regiment in January 1950.

Royal Winnipeg Rifles. The first compo-nent of this regiment was formed as the 90th Winnipeg Battalion of Rifles in 1883. It served with MIDDLETON's column during the NORTHWEST REBELLION of 1885 and contributed volunteers to the Canadian con-tingents serving in the SOUTH AFRICAN WAR. A second militia regiment, the Win-nipeg Light Infantry, formed in 1912, was also later incorporated into the RWR. Both components of the regiment sent battalions to serve with the 1ST CANADIAN DIVISION in France in WORLD WAR I. In 1935 the Win-nipeg Rifles received the 'Royal' designa-tion. In World War II the Royal Winnipeg Rifles raised a battalion for service with the 3RD CANADIAN INFANTRY DIVISION. The two regiments were merged as the Royal Winnipeg Rifles in 1955.

Rural Battalions. Generic designation for those late-nineteenth century volunteer MILI-TIA units from rural areas who attended the annual militia training camps only every two years or so.

Rush-Bagot Convention. After the WAR OF 1812, the U.S. and Britain agreed to establish strict limits on the number of naval vessels each would station on the Great Lakes and Lake Champlain: two ships each on the upper lakes and one each on Lakes Champlain and Ontario. The agreement was embodied in notes exchanged in 1817 by U.S. Secretary of State Richard Rush and the British minister in Washington, Sir Charles Bagot. Despite limits on naval ves-sels, construction of land fortifications con-tinued on both sides of the border.

Russian Civil War. At the request of Brit-ain, Prime Minister Robert BORDEN agreed to send Canadian troops to Russia to aid British and other anti-Soviet forces at the start of the Russian Civil War in 1918. The Canadian Siberian Expeditionary Force sailed from Vancouver in October 1918. While most of the 5000 Canadians in that force were volunteers, some were drafted under the provisions of the MILITARY SERVICE ACT. At Vladivostok, Canadians cooperated with the Japanese and Americans in attempting to train anti-Bolshevik forces and to guard sup-ply and rail lines in western Siberia. They were almost always hampered by shortages of munitions and supplies. Other Canadians also took part in the Russian Civil War. On the western front at Archangel and Mur-mansk, 4000 Canadian troops participated in an effort to deny these key ports to Bolshe-vik forces. Other Canadians, including pilot Raymond COLLISHAW, fought against the Bolsheviks in the vicinity of the Black Sea.

All Canadians were withdrawn from Russia between April and June 1919.

Rutherford, Charles Smith (1892–1989). During a CANADIAN MOUNTED RIFLES advance on Monchy-le-Preux, France, on 26 August 1918, Rutherford single-handedly silenced enemy machine guns and captured 70 prisoners. Besides the VICTORIA CROSS, won for this feat, Lt Rutherford also earned a MILITARY CROSS and MILITARY MEDAL in the course of the war.

Rutter. Rutter was the initial code name for the DIEPPE RAID which was originally conceived in April, 1942, then cancelled on 7 July 1942 due to inclement weather. When the project was revived later that same month, it was given the code name *Jubilee*.

S

Sabre fighter. U.S.-designed fighter jet originally built in the U.S. by North American Aviation and designated the F86. The swept-wing fighter first entered RCAF service in August, 1950. The original U.S.-built Sabres were capable of a top speed of 1090 km/h with a ceiling of 15.2 km. The RCAF acquired both A and E models from the U.S. prior to the production of Sabres by CANADAIR of Montreal. When engined with the ORENDA turbojet (Mks 5 and 6), the fighter outperformed its U.S.-built cousins. Canadair produced about 1800 Sabres in four series between 1950 and 1958. The Mk 5 entered RCAF service in 1954; the RCAF used Sabres until 1970. The Canadair Sabre also saw service with the air forces of several NATO and Commonwealth countries.

Sackets Harbor. Located at the east end of Lake Ontario, the harbour was the major base for American military operations on the lake during the WAR OF 1812. The British made several attempts to take the harbour, most notably on 28–29 May 1813, but were never successful.

SAGE (Semi-Automatic Ground Environment). SAGE was an early air defence computer designed in the 1950s. It utilized information fed to it from existing RADAR systems to provide a comprehensive visual display of air traffic in a designated area. SAGE was designed to operate in conjunction with the BOMARC anti-aircraft missile which Canada acquired in the late 1950s from the U.S. and which was based at La Macaza, Quebec and North Bay, Ontario. Canada's SAGE was housed at the latter site.

St Albans Raid. In October 1864, 20 Confederate agents based in Canada raided St Albans, Vermont, looted a number of banks, and then returned to Canada. They hoped Union troops would pursue them, arrest them on Canadian soil, and violate British neutrality. The Canadian government ignored this ploy, arrested them itself and held them for trial. Tension between Britain and the U.S. increased, however, when they were released on a technicality. See also *ALABAMA*; TRENT AFFAIR.

St Charles, Battle of. Skirmish between British forces and troops loyal to PAPINEAU during the REBELLIONS OF 1837. The clash took place 25 November 1837 at the town of St Charles, 12 km south of St Denis on the Richelieu River after a column of British regulars, led by Lt-Col F.A. Wetherall, had marched north from Chambly. Wetherall's effort was part of a two-pronged offensive designed to drive the *Patriote* forces out of the Richelieu River valley. The other part of the operation was a southward thrust from Sorel to ST DENIS, led by Col Charles Gore. Gore was defeated at St Denis on 22 November but Wetherall pressed on, defeating the rebels. The British victory gave them control of the Richelieu region.

St Croix, HMCS. TOWN CLASS DE-
STROYER transferred to the Royal Navy and
subsequently to the ROYAL CANADIAN NAVY
in 1940 as part of the DESTROYERS FOR
BASES DEAL. The vessel sank one U-boat and
shared in the destruction of a second before
being herself sunk 20 September 1943. On
that date *St Croix* was helping to escort
convoy ONS 18/ON 202 when she was hit
with an acoustic torpedo. HMS *Itchen* managed to collect 81 survivors from the *St
Croix* but was soon also hit. When *Itchen*
went down, she carried 80 of the *St Croix*'s
81 survivors with her.

St Denis, Battle of. Battle which took
place on 23 November 1837 at the Lower
Canada town of St Denis, on the Richelieu
River, between British regulars under Lt-Col
F. Gore and followers of PAPINEAU during
the REBELLIONS OF 1837. Gore was advancing southward from Sorel as part of a two-
pronged campaign to clear rebels from the
river valley. Another column was advancing
northward to ST CHARLES from Chambly.
The *Patriote* forces in St Denis were led by
Wolfred Nelson. Gore advanced slowly, giving Nelson time to fortify two stout buildings on the route of march. Gore attacked
the rebel barricades for five hours but could
not prevail and was forced to withdraw,
leaving a 12-pound cannon in the town.

St Eloi, Battle of. Sometimes referred to as
the 'St Eloi Craters', the battle was a fight
between 2ND CANADIAN DIVISION troops
commanded by Maj.-Gen. R. TURNER and
the Germans for control of large craters left
after mines had been blown in no man's
land and under German positions in a previous British attack. The craters had been
captured by the British in hard fighting; the
Canadians were brought into the line to
defend them on 4 April 1916. Two days
later, the Germans attacked, capturing all the
craters but one. The Canadians counter-
attacked in turn and heavy fighting continued until 19 April when they were dislodged
from all but one of the craters with losses
totalling 1373 killed, wounded and missing.
The battle engendered controversy since
some of the Canadian troops had defended
the wrong craters, leaving them vulnerable
to German attack, and their mistake had not
been corrected by divisional headquarters.
Although the battle clearly demonstrated

Turner's failures as a field commander, it
was Corps commander A.E. Alderson who
was relieved, not Turner. Turner was not
relieved largely because he was a Canadian
and it was thought that his dismissal might
have caused political difficulties. He was finally removed from command in November
1916 after the SOMME fighting.

St Eustache, Battle of. In the last battle
of the REBELLIONS OF 1837 in Lower Canada, Sir John Colborne's army of 1200 regulars, organized in two brigades, attacked
the *Patriotes* at the town of St Eustache,
northwest of Montreal on 14 December,
1837. The Patriotes were led by Amury
Girod and Dr Jean-Olivier Chenier. Aided
by cannon, the British inflicted heavy losses
on the rebels, killing Chenier and 70 of his
followers and taking 118 prisoner.

Ste Foy, Battle of. After MONTCALM's
defeat at the PLAINS OF ABRAHAM in September, 1759, the Duc de LÉVIS assembled a
5000-man force to retake Quebec in the
spring of 1760. Marching upriver from Montreal, he met and defeated a 3900-man British force led by General MURRAY at Ste Foy
on 28 April 1760. However, the arrival of
British supply ships in early May, ahead of
the French fleet, forced Lévis to retreat to
Montreal.

St Jean, Battle of. At the outbreak of the
REVOLUTIONARY WAR Continental forces
under Montgomery and Schuyler were dispatched up the Richelieu River valley to
launch an assault on Montreal to be followed
by a march upriver to Quebec City. The
British commander, Sir Guy CARLETON, decided to defend Montreal by garrisoning Fort
St Jean, on the Richelieu River south of
Montreal. The garrison of more than 650
regulars, volunteers, and militiamen was
commanded by Major Charles Preston.
When they failed to capture St Jean, the
Continentals besieged it. The siege lasted
from 19 September until 3 November when
Preston was forced to surrender due to supply shortages. Shortly after, Carleton ordered
the evacuation of Montreal and the Continentals occupied the town in preparation for
a march downriver to Quebec.

St John's, 1696. On 30 December 1696,
during the WAR OF THE LEAGUE OF AUGS-

BURG St John's was captured by Pierre LE-MOYNE who then burned the town, killing 200 people and taking 700 prisoners. The French occupation of St John's lasted less than a year, the settlement being returned to Britain at the conclusion of the war.

St Laurent, HMCS. The RIVER CLASS DE-STROYER, purchased from the Royal Navy in 1937, served on the NORTH ATLANTIC RUN for most of World War II. Credited with a share in the destruction of two U-boats, 'Sally' was also instrumental in helping to save some 860 people, mostly German and Italian prisoners of war, who had survided the sinking of the SS *Arandora Star* in July, 1940. The second ship of this name, and the first of the *ST LAURENT* CLASS of DESTROYER ESCORTS, was commissioned into the ROYAL CANADIAN NAVY the end of October, 1955 and paid off in June, 1974.

St Laurent class destroyer escorts. The first of the RCN's post-war generation of escort vessels, and the first substantial warships ever designed and built in Canada, the *St Laurent* was laid down in the shipyards of Canadian Vickers in Montreal in 1950 and commissioned in October 1955. With a displacement of 2300 tonnes and a top speed of 28 knots, *St Laurent* was the first of the class. Six other *St Laurent* class destroyer escorts were eventually commissioned between 1955 and 1957 — *Assiniboine, Fraser, Margaree, Ottawa, Saguenay,* and *Skeena.* Though called 'destroyer escorts' they were much larger and faster than World War II-era destroyer escort vessels and were specifically designed as anti-submarine destroyers able to counter the newest Soviet submarines then extant. In their original configurations, they were armed with four 3-inch guns, two 40-mm guns, and a number of anti-submarine weapons. In the early 1960s all seven ships were extensively refitted with helicopter landing decks aft and each carried a Sea King anti-submarine helicopter. The ships were designed to withstand the shock of an atomic explosion and to keep their crews safe from radio-active fallout. The seven *Restigouche* class destroyer escorts, four *Mackenzie* class, and two *Annapolis* class helicopter destroyers were near-twins of the *St Laurent* class ships although a bit larger. They were commissioned in 1958 and 1959.

St Pierre and Miquelon Affair. The small islands of St Pierre and Miquelon, off the south coast of Newfoundland, passed under the authority of the pro-Nazi Vichy government after the fall of France in the spring of 1940. Free French forces sailing from Canada under the command of Admiral Muselier easily captured the strategically important islands on 24 December 1941. Because of the possibility that German agents could use the islands as a vantage point for reporting on Allied convoys bound for Britain, Canada had also made plans to invade the islands, but had backed off. The U.S., which was still trying to maintain diplomatic relations with the Vichy government, charged that Canada and Muselier were in collusion and demanded the Free French be removed. Canadian Prime Minister William Lyon Mackenzie KING's aides persuaded him not to back down and the crisis soon evaporated.

Saguenay, HMCS. One of the first ships built expressly for the RCN, the destroyer *Saguenay* was a RIVER CLASS DESTROYER commissioned in 1931. On 1 December 1940, while escorting a convoy from Gibraltar, the destroyer was badly damaged and lost 21 crew members when hit by a torpedo fired from an Italian submarine. The vessel was repaired and resumed escort operations until November, 1942 when she was accidentally rammed by a Panamanian freighter and lost her stern when a depth charge exploded. She limped back to port, to be used as a training ship until paid off. A second *Saguenay* was commissioned as a *ST LAURENT* CLASS DESTROYER ESCORT in 1956.

Salaberry, Charles-Michel d'Irumberry de (1778–1829). De Salaberry joined the British army in 1794 and served in a variety of theatres during the Napoleonic Wars. He returned to Canada in 1810 and subsequently raised and commanded a unit of the French-Canadian militia during the WAR OF 1812. At the BATTLE OF CHATEAUGUAY in 1813, his troops held off a numerically superior American force. He retired from the military in 1815 and was appointed to the Legislative Council of Lower Canada.

Salisbury Plain. Located in flat country south of London, Salisbury Plain is the site of the pre-historic Stonehenge monument. It was also the location for a large number of

Canadian army camps during WORLD WAR I. The rain of winter turned the plain into a morass, a situation made worse by the unavailability of permanent shelter; the troops were forced to spend the winter in tents. In the spring of 1915 more than 1000 men from the 1ST CANADIAN DIVISION were forced to return to Canada as invalids as a result of the poor conditions on the plain.

Salmon, H.L.N. (1895–1943). Salmon joined the army in 1914 and served overseas with the CANADIAN CORPS in World War I, winning a MILITARY CROSS and bar. He filled a variety of staff and command positions in the inter-war years. In September 1942 he was promoted to major-general as commander of the 1ST CANADIAN INFANTRY DIVISION. At the end of April, 1943, just before the invasion of SICILY, he died in a plane crash and his place was assumed by Gen. Guy SIMONDS.

Salonika. Although no Canadian combat troops participated in campaigns in the eastern Mediterranean in WORLD WAR I (the [ROYAL] NEWFOUNDLAND REGIMENT did fight at Gallipoli but Newfoundland was not then a part of Canada), some 450 Canadian officers and nursing sisters and a thousand men staffed five Allied hospitals at Salonika, Greece.

Salvation Army. A private religious organization, the Salvation Army maintained canteens for Canadian soldiers in Britain during both World Wars.

San Juan Island Dispute. In 1859 a pig owned by a Hudson's Bay Company official on San Juan Island, in Puget Sound, strayed into a potato patch owned by an American farmer and was killed. The farmer claimed the island was U.S. territory. So did the U.S. government. The 1846 Oregon Treaty, which had settled the OREGON CRISIS, had specified that the boundary between U.S. and British territory ran through the 'middle of the channel' of the Strait of Juan de Fuca, but no one was sure where that was. To strengthen its claim to the island, the U.S. landed troops there; Britain soon followed suit. The status of the island was not officially settled until 1872 when it was awarded to the U.S. in an arbitration. The pig's owner was never compensated.

Sangro River. River in Italy that flows from the Apennine mountains in the centre of the peninsula to the Adriatic Sea south of ORTONA. In the late fall of 1943 the Germans anchored their defensive positions on the Sangro, which became the scene of heavy fighting between them and British units of the British 8th Army. One of those units, the 78th Division, was able to force a crossing of the lower Sangro in mid-November but in the following days lost heavily in the intense fighting aimed at broadening the bridgehead. The 1ST CANADIAN INFANTRY DIVISION was then shifted from the Campobasso area, farther inland, to the coast to take over from the 78th Division. Leading elements of the division crossed the Sangro on 1 December and passed under the command of the 78th Division. In heavy fighting, the Canadians relieved the 78th, brigade by brigade, until they had taken control of the entire bridgehead. By 4 December the relief operation had ended and the Canadians had pushed northwest along the coast to the MORO RIVER.

Sansom, E.W. (1890–1982). Sansom joined the militia in 1906 and served overseas with the CANADIAN CORPS in World War I. He held a number of staff and command positions after the war and went overseas in 1939 as a staff officer with the 1ST CANADIAN INFANTRY DIVISION. He commanded II CANADIAN CORPS but was relieved when he fell ill. In 1945, he was named Inspector-General, and made a three-month tour of Europe to report on the reinforcement needs of the army. He retired from the army shortly after V-E DAY.

Saratoga, Battle of (1745). Following the capture of LOUISBOURG by Massachusetts militia and Royal Navy forces in 1745, the French retaliated by attacking Saratoga, New York with their Abenaki allies. In November 1745 a 600-man raiding party destroyed the town, killed 30 settlers, and took 100 prisoners, but the raid had no lasting effect on the war. See WAR OF THE AUSTRIAN SUCCESSION.

Saratoga, Battles of (1777). In the spring of 1777, during the REVOLUTIONARY WAR, the British general 'Gentleman Johnny' BURGOYNE led an advance south from Canada along the classic Richelieu River-Lake

Champlain-Hudson River invasion route. His force consisted of British regulars (with German mercenaries), Indian allies, and Canadian MILITIA. At Saratoga Burgoyne met a much larger American force and was obliged to halt. After two unsuccessful attempts to force his way through the Americans, and when no help was forthcoming from other British commanders in New York, Burgoyne surrendered on 17 October 1777.

Saunders, Charles (*c.* 1713–1775). Commander of the British fleet at Quebec 1759. Saunders joined the Royal Navy in 1727 and earned considerable experience at sea before being named to command the British fleet bound for QUEBEC in January, 1759 during the SEVEN YEARS' WAR. He was instructed to work closely with General James WOLFE so as to mount an effective amphibious operation. Wolfe joined him aboard his flagship on 13 February 1759, four days before the fleet sailed for Canada. Saunders sailed first to HALIFAX before proceeding to LOUIS-BOURG to make final preparations for sailing upriver. After a difficult upriver passage that took all Saunders' skill, his fleet arrived near Quebec at the end of June. Deciding that the possibility of French naval intervention was slight, he brought his ships as close to the landing areas as possible. After the landings and through the long siege, Saunders cooperated closely with Wolfe and his officers. Following the battle of the PLAINS OF ABRAHAM Saunders did everything he could to strengthen the British positions at Quebec before leaving the river for the winter. He was knighted in 1761 and promoted to admiral before leaving the navy for a career in politics.

SCEAND. See STANDING COMMITTEE ON EXTERNAL AFFAIRS AND NATIONAL DEFENCE.

Schaefer, Carl Fellman (b. 1903). An official war artist with the RCAF during WORLD WAR II. Schaefer studied painting at the Ontario College of Art in the early 1920s and later taught there. His work was influenced by Group of Seven members ARTHUR LISMER and J.E.H. MacDonald.

Scheldt. On 4 September 1944, British troops captured the Belgian city of Antwerp,

one of the two most important ports in NORTHWEST EUROPE (the other was Rotterdam), capable of handling 40,600 tonnes of cargo a day. The Allied armies, having smashed the Germans in NORMANDY, had pursued them almost to the German border. It was difficult enough to supply the Allied pursuit via the small channel ports and from Normandy; it would be impossible to support the next phase of the war — the drive into the heart of Germany — without either Antwerp or Rotterdam.

Having captured Antwerp, however, the Allies could not use it; in his haste to seize a Rhine River Crossing, General Bernard L. Montgomery, who commanded 21st Army Group, delayed a campaign to secure the Scheldt, the estuary which led to the port. He was preoccupied with planning and mounting Operation Market Garden, an airborne assault designed to put him across the Rhine. The Germans took advantage of this blunder to fortify WALCHEREN and South BEVELAND on the north side of the estuary, and the south shore of the estuary, known as the BRESKENS POCKET.

On 12 September 1944, FIRST CANADIAN ARMY was assigned the task of clearing the Scheldt. Without additional Allied help, they were unequal to the task, the Germans having reinforced their positions in the area. It was not until the disastrous collapse of Market Garden, and direct orders from General Dwight D. Eisenhower, that Montgomery began to take seriously the task of clearing the Scheldt and assigned additional British units to fight under the control of 1st Canadian Army. The combined operation actually began 1 October when 2ND CANADIAN INFANTRY DIVISION crossed the Antwerp Canal and the 3RD CANADIAN INFANTRY DIVISION began the assault over the Leopold Canal; the plan was to take the Breskens Pocket first, then secure Walcheren and South Beveland. For most of the battle the Canadians (and the British and other units fighting under their command) were commanded by G.G. SIMONDS, who temporarily took command from H.D.G. CRERAR when a stomach ailment hospitalized the latter.

The Breskens Pocket was well defended by determined German troops. Much of the ground in the area had been flooded, forcing troops and vehicles to push their way forward in thick mud or high water. Tactical air support was invaluable in countering effective German artillery fire and blasting out German defenders. By the third week of October, the pocket had been secured.

Meanwhile, to the east, the Canadians began the campaign to take South Beveland and Walcheren. The former was connected to the mainland by a rather wide isthmus which, though flooded, afforded relatively easy passage for men and vehicles. Again the terrain and effective artillery fire aided the German defenders but by the end of October, South Beveland had been taken.

Next came the most difficult part of the campaign, the capture of Walcheren. Walcheren was actually one large sunken island ringed by a dyke and connected to South Beveland only by a causeway. To deprive the Germans of movement, Simonds urged the bombing of the dyke and the flooding of the island. On 31 October, units of the Fifth Canadian Infantry Brigade attempted the first of several assaults over the causeway. The Calgary Highlanders eventually succeeded in establishing a foothold on Walcheren (the east end of the island remained unflooded) but could not push forward and were soon withdrawn. At the same time, landings were made by British troops at Flushing, on the south shore, and Westkapelle on the western tip of the island. This effectively neutralized German resistance. By 8 November the Scheldt battle was over and the task of sweeping German mines from the estuary began. The first allied vessel reached the port of Antwerp on 28 November.

Reading: C.P. Stacey, *The Victory Campaign* (Ottawa, 1960); J.L. Moulton, *Battle for Antwerp* (New York, 1978)

Schmidlin, E.J.C. (1884–1951). Schmidlin joined the ROYAL CANADIAN ENGINEERS after attending ROYAL MILITARY COLLEGE and serving with the British Army in India. He commanded a battalion of engineers in WORLD WAR I and taught and administered at RMC after the war. He was promoted to Quartermaster-General in 1940, a position he held until the report of the ROYAL COMMISSION ON THE CANADIAN EXPEDITIONARY FORCE ... TO HONG KONG criticized him for failing to ensure that the contingent had sufficient vehicles, and effectively ended Schmidlin's military career.

Scott, Frederick George (1861–1944). Canon Scott, born in Montreal and educated at Bishop's College, was ordained to the Anglican ministry in 1886. During WORLD WAR I, Scott served as senior chaplain in 1ST CANADIAN DIVISION. In 1922 he published his recollections in *The Great War As I Saw It*.

Scrimger, Francis Alexander Caron (1881–1937). A medical officer with the CANADIAN ARMY MEDICAL CORPS, Scrimger tirelessly helped the wounded during the battle of YPRES, particularly after 3rd Battalion, CANADIAN EXPEDITIONARY FORCE headquarters was shelled and set on fire. When his own dug-out was shelled 25 April 1915, he shielded his patients with his body to protect them from SHRAPNEL. For this action, he was awarded the VICTORIA CROSS.

Seafire fighter. British-designed and built single-engine fighter derived from the Supermarine SPITFIRE. Seafires were acquired by the ROYAL CANADIAN NAVY in 1946 and were kept in service until 1954. A squadron of Seafires served aboard HMCS *WARRIOR*. The aircraft had a top speed of 620 km/h, a service ceiling of 10.6 km, and a range of 690 km.

Sea Fury fighter. Single-engine, propeller-driven fighter used by the ROYAL CANADIAN NAVY from 1948 to 1957. These British-designed and-built aircraft, manufactured by Hawker, were considered the ultimate in propeller warplanes with a top speed of 740 km/h, a range of 1120 kms, and a service ceiling of almost 10.8 km. The Sea Fury was primarily flown from the carrier *MAGNIFICENT*.

2nd Allied Tactical Air Force. Formed on 15 November 1943, the 2nd Allied Tactical Air Force was one component of the Allied Expeditionary Air Force (which had been formed two days before). First commander of 2nd ATAF was Air Marshal Arthur Coningham. The specific role of 2nd ATAF was the support of Montgomery's 21st Army Group which included the 2nd British Army and the FIRST CANADIAN ARMY, before, during, and after the D-DAY invasion and the NORMANDY campaign. Most of the striking punch of the 2nd ATAF was provided by No. 83 and No. 84 (Composite) Groups, consisting of day fighter, fighter-bomber, and fighter-reconnaisance squadrons. Of the nineteen ROYAL CANADIAN AIR FORCE squadrons which served with 2nd ATAF, the majority by far were assigned to No. 83 Group. They flew MUSTANG, SPITFIRE, MOSQUITO and TYPHOON aircraft. Ironically No. 83 Group, considered to have the more experienced squadrons, generally flew support missions for 2nd British Army while No. 84 group, with no RCAF squadrons, supported First Canadian Army. Both Groups, as well as the other Groups in 2nd ATAF — No.2 (Bomber) Group with light and medium bombers, No. 85 (Base) Group with day and night fighter squadrons—on occasion also flew missions in support of U.S. troops.

II Canadian Corps (World War II). Formed in January 1943 and disbanded in June 1945, II Canadian Corps took part in the NORMANDY and NORTHWEST EUROPE CAMPAIGNS. It was commanded first by E.W. SANSOM (January, 1943-January, 1944), then by G.G. SIMONDS. At various times different units of different nationalities, particularly British and Polish, were attached to the corps. The Canadian units with the corps at one time or another were 2ND and 3RD CANADIAN INFANTRY DIVISIONS and 4TH CANADIAN ARMOURED DIVISION.

2nd Canadian Division (World War I). Formed in May 1915 and trained in England, the 2nd Division joined the 1ST CANADIAN DIVISION at ST ELOI in April 1916. Together they formed the CANADIAN CORPS. The division was disbanded in 1919.

2nd Canadian Infantry Division (World War II). Formed in May 1940 and disbanded in October 1945, the division saw action in NORMANDY and NORTHWEST EUROPE. Units of the division took part in the disastrous assault on DIEPPE in August, 1942.

Secord, Laura (Ingersoll) (1775–1868). Born in Massachusetts, Secord emigrated to Upper Canada with her father after the REVOLUTIONARY WAR, settling in the area of what is now the town of Ingersoll, Ontario. In the early months of the WAR OF 1812, Secord rescued her husband who had been wounded at the battle of QUEENSTON

HEIGHTS. The following year, in June of 1813, she overheard a number of American officers discussing an impending attack on the nearby British outpost of Beaver Dams and decided to warn the British officer in charge. After a hazardous journey, and aided by Indians, she arrived at the British encampment on 22 June 1813. Two days later an American force was ambushed by Indians while approaching the British position and forced to surrender. Secord's role in the skirmish did not emerge for many years because the British officer in charge failed to mention her in his report of the battle. It was not until 1860, when she was 85, that her deed finally became known.

Sedentary Militia. Authorized by the 1777 Militia Act, the sedentary militia amounted to a loose form of universal military service although its members lacked arms, uniforms, and training. Technically, all able-bodied males in the colony were to be members of the sedentary militia, obliged to attend one muster parade each year. In fact, however, almost no one participated in it. The REBELLIONS OF 1837 revived some interest in the sedentary militia; garrison units numbered 13,000 in 1838. The MILITIA ACT of 1868 left the sedentary militia in place (with a paper membership of over 600,000), but re-named it the RESERVE MILITIA.

Seely, J.E.B. (1868–1947). Born in Britain and educated at Trinity College, Cambridge, Seely served with the British Army in SOUTH AFRICA before entering politics in Britain in 1900. Under the pre-war Liberal government he rose to Cabinet rank, being appointed Secretary of State for War in 1912, a post he held for two years. During WORLD WAR I he commanded the CANADIAN CAVALRY BRIGADE.

SE5A fighter. The CANADIAN AIR FORCE obtained 12 of these single-seat fighters from the Royal Air Force in May, 1919 for use as advanced pilot trainers. Built by the Royal Aircraft Factory in England, the plane flew up to 197 km/h and had an endurance of 2 1/2 hours. It and an earlier version, the SE5, had been flown during the war by a number of Canadian pilots including W.A 'Billy' BISHOP.

Selby-Smyth, Sir Edward (1819–1896). Selby-Smyth served with the British army in India, Africa, and Ireland, before becoming GENERAL OFFICER COMMANDING the Canadian MILITIA in 1875. In that role he was instrumental in the founding at Quebec City of a government-owned cartridge factory later named the DOMINION ARSENAL. He also suggested a naval reserve. He enjoyed good relations with the government but could not accomplish much due to a depressed economy. He stepped down in 1880.

Select Militia. The MILITIA ACT of 1812 provided for the selection by ballot of 2000 bachelors aged 18–25 who would receive 90 days' militia training each summer for two years. Five battalions of the select militia saw service in the war of 1812. See also MILITIA, SEDENTARY MILITIA, RESERVE MILITIA, NON-PERMANENT ACTIVE MILITIA.

17-pounder anti-tank gun. The 17-pounder was designed to meet a request from the British General Staff for a weapon capable of piercing 12 cm of armour plate. The first operational 17-pounder was ready by 1942, but constant improvements were made in the weapon over the course of the war. Approximately the equal of the much vaunted German 88 (depending on the type of ammunition used), the 17-pounder was the only Allied weapon capable of penetrating the armour of the latest German Tiger and Panther tanks. Seventeen-pounders were used on British-modified SHERMAN tanks, known as Fireflys, in place of the Sherman's original 75-mm gun, to give the Sherman enough punch to destroy the best of the German tanks. The 17-pounder entered Canadian service in November, 1942.

75-mm Recoiless Rifle (RCL). Issued to American troops in the last months of WORLD WAR II the 75-mm RCL was later acquired by the Canadian army and used throughout the 1950s. Mounted either on a tripod or a JEEP, the weapon fired a high-explosive shell over a maximum range of 7000 m.

Seven Years' War. The Seven Years' War (1756–1763) pitted Britain and its allies against France and its allies in what amounted to the first conflict fought around the globe. Fighting took place in Europe, North America, India, and elsewhere. In North America the war actually began in 1754, as British colonists led by George Washington endeavoured to push France out of the Ohio River Valley. Washington led a contingent of Virginia militia into the Ohio country in the late spring of 1754 but was defeated and forced back across the Allegheny Mountains. This clash led to the reinforcement of the British army in America and a second attempt, under BRADDOCK, to expel the French from the Ohio country in the summer of 1755. Braddock met the French near Fort Duquesne and was defeated. The French, in the meantime, responded to the British reinforcement with a reinforcement of their own, sending troops to LOUISBOURG. In much of the fighting that year and in 1756 the French prevailed due to shorter lines of supply and communication and a better knowledge of frontier-style warfare. MONTCALM was sent to America in the spring of 1756 and the string of minor French victories continued. In 1757, though the French did inflict one major defeat on the British at FORT CARILLON the tide of battle turned, mainly because of the arrival of more than 20,000 British regulars. In 1758 FORT FRONTENAC and Louisbourg were reduced and France's Indian allies in the Ohio valley decided to make a separate peace with Britain, forcing France to abandon Fort Duquesne. The stage was set for 1759 when one British force captured FORT NIAGARA, another advanced on Montreal along the Lake Champlain-Richelieu River route, and a third, under WOLFE and SAUNDERS, invested Quebec. That siege ended in September, 1759 with the Battle of the PLAINS OF ABRAHAM. Although Montcalm was defeated (and killed) in that fight, the French were almost successful in retaking Quebec in the spring of 1760 when the Duc de LÉVIS advanced upriver from Montreal, defeated the British at STE FOY, and laid siege to the city. The appearance of the Royal Navy sent him back downriver to Montreal where he later surrendered. The war was ended by the TREATY OF PARIS which confirmed Britain's conquest of virtually all of New France.

Reading: G.F.G. Stanley, *New France: The Last Phase* (Toronto, 1968); G. Fregault, *Canada: The War of the Conquest* (Toronto, 1969)

Sevigny, Pierre Albert (b. 1917). Sevigny became a lieutenant-colonel in WORLD WAR II before leaving the army following the loss of a leg. He was elected to the House of Commons in 1958 and joined the DIEFENBAKER Cabinet as associate minister of National Defence in 1959. He resigned the post in February 1963 because he disagreed with the government's failure to acquire nuclear weapons.

Sexton howitzer. Designed and built in Canada, this self-propelled 25-pounder HOWITZER, mounted on a RAM chassis, was a superior variant of the PRIEST. Impressed with its range and design, the British army adopted the weapon in 1943. It was used extensively in NORTHWEST EUROPE.

Shankland, Robert (1887–1968). Serving with the 43rd Battalion, CEF at PASSCHENDAELE, Shankland captured Bellevue Spur 26 October 1917 and managed to keep control of a number of pillboxes and shell holes in the German line until reinforcements arrived the following morning. This action, for which he was awarded the VICTORIA CROSS, proved important in breaking the main German defence line.

Sharp, F.R. (1915–1992). Sharp joined the Royal Canadian Air Force in 1938, eventually going overseas to command 408 Bomber Squadron of NO. 6 GROUP. After the war he remained in the air force, holding a number of staff positions before becoming CHIEF OF THE DEFENCE STAFF in 1969. He held that post until his retirement from the armed forces in 1972.

Sheaffe, Sir Roger Hale (1763–1851). Born in Boston, Sheaffe spent three tours in Canada with the British Army between 1787 and 1813. In the WAR OF 1812, he led both regulars and Canadian MILITIA to victory over American forces at QUEENSTON HEIGHTS after Sir Isaac BROCK's death. However, he unsuccessfully defended YORK from an American raid in April 1813 and the settlement was captured and burned.

***Shearwater*, HMCS.** Launched in Britain in 1899, *Shearwater* was an unarmoured sloop with a displacement of just under 1000 tonnes. Its main armament was two 4-inch guns and it had a top speed of 12 knots. From 1905 to 1910 it was the only Royal Navy ship stationed at Esquimault; in 1910 it was joined by the sloop *Algerine*. When war broke out its two main guns were put ashore for a time to provide some defence for Seymour Narrows. *Shearwater*'s crew went to Halifax to help man NIOBE. *Shearwater* was commissioned into the ROYAL CANADIAN NAVY on 8 September, 1914 as a tender for the submarines CC1 and CC2. Later in the war it was transferred to Halifax where it was paid off in 1919.

Shell Committee. Sam HUGHES, minister of Militia and Defence in the BORDEN government, created the committee in September 1914 to handle British munitions orders placed in Canada, especially for artillery shells. The committee soon secured shell contracts worth $170 million but by the summer of 1915 only a fraction of the total had been delivered. In November 1915, after rumours of corruption and scandal proved all too true, Prime Minister Borden, in consultation with Britain, replaced the committee with the IMPERIAL MUNITIONS BOARD.

Sherman tank. This American-designed medium tank, designated the M4, was the standard Allied tank in WORLD WAR II. Both Canadian armoured divisions used it in ITALY and the NORTHWEST EUROPE CAMPAIGN. The M4A1 version of the Sherman weighed in at 34 tonnes, used a 75-mm gun as its main armament (supplemented by two machine guns), and was manned by a crew of five. It had a top speed of 46 km/h. Many variants of the Sherman were used during the war and, like the CHURCHILL tank, a large number of specialized vehicles were also produced from the basic Sherman chassis. Even though it was the most widely used of the Allied tanks, it was no match for later model German tanks such as the Panther and the Tiger, both of which had better armour and outgunned it. The British found a partial solution by equipping Shermans with the 17-POUNDER anti-tank gun, a version known as the Firefly. The Firefly was in great demand during the NORMANDY campaign and British factories worked hard to produce them for all Allied forces. Nevertheless, during most of 1944, only two Fireflys were available per troop and the British ensured that their own units were equipped with it before sending it off to the Americans.

Short Sunderland aircraft. Four-engined flying boat used during World War II by both the RAF's Coastal Command and the ROYAL CANADIAN AIR FORCE in Britain for long range anti-submarine patrolling. The Sunderland had a patrol range of 880 km and was able to carry 1 tonne of bombs or depth charges.

Shrapnel. Bomb fragments and debris thrown out by an explosion or explosive device.

Siberia. See RUSSIAN CIVIL WAR.

Sicily. On 3 July 1943 the 1ST CANADIAN INFANTRY DIVISION under the command of G.G. SIMONDS, accompanied by the 1st Canadian Army Tank Brigade (later redesignated the 1st Armoured Brigade) participated in the Allied landings on the south coast of Sicily under the overall command of British General Bernard L. MONTGOMERY's 8th Army. That participation came largely as a result of Ottawa's insistence, since the original order of battle for the invasion had not included a Canadian contingent. The government of William Lyon Mackenzie KING was, however, worried that the lack of significant Canadian participation in the war effort on the ground was hurting morale both at home and in the army overseas. Initially A.G.L. MCNAUGHTON objected to the splitting of his forces (the bulk of the Canadian army was then stationed in Great Britain) but he was won over with the promise that his troops would gain battle experience and that the various elements of the Canadian army would be re-united prior to the expected invasion of the continent. The Canadians were assigned a landing beach near PACHINO airfield, to the right of the Americans and the left of the British. They quickly overcame the rather limited resistance in this sector and drove inland, to the centre of the island. After the British drive towards Messina was stalled by heavy German resistance on the east coast of the island, Montgomery gave the Canadians the task of turning the German right flank. As the Canadians penetrated well into the steep mountainous country in the island's centre, the Germans were able to use the terrain to mount an effective defence using few men or fighting vehicles. Major battles were fought at Piazza Armerina, Valguarnera, LEONFORTE, ASSORO,

Nissoria, AGIRA, and REGALBUTO. Most often the Germans forced the Canadians to battle at strategic towns and villages, exacted a toll in killed and wounded, then withdrew. The Canadians were taken out of the line and placed in reserve at the end of the first week in August when Montgomery shortened the Allied line due to the German withdrawal towards Messina. By then they had suffered 2310 casualties including 562 killed in action.

Reading: D. Dancocks, *The D-Day Dodgers* (Toronto, 1991); G.W.L. Nicholson, *The Canadians in Italy* (Ottawa, 1956)

Sifton, Ellis Wellwood (1891–1917). With the 18th Battalion, CEF at VIMY RIDGE on 9 April 1917, Sifton single-handedly attacked a German machine gun that was harassing his battalion. He leapt into the German trench, killed the crew, and held Germans who were trying to recapture the gun at bay with his bayonet. Later that day he was shot dead by a German he had wounded. He was posthumously awarded the VICTORIA CROSS.

Sifton, Victor (1897–1961). Sifton rose to the rank of major with the 4TH CANADIAN MOUNTED RIFLES before retiring from the army in 1919 and pursuing a career in journalism. He continued to serve in the reserves and during World War II became Master-General of the Ordnance for the Canadian Army.

Silver Dart aircraft. Flying machine sponsored by the AERIAL EXPERIMENT ASSOCATION and piloted by J.A.D. MCCURDY.

Simonds, G.G. (1903–1974). Born in Britain, Simonds graduated from ROYAL MILITARY COLLEGE before pursuing a career in the PERMANENT FORCE between the wars. He was one of the few regular officers to think systematically about tactics during this period, publishing articles on armoured tactics in 1938. Simonds went overseas as a staff officer with 1ST CANADIAN INFANTRY DIVISION in 1939, quickly rising through the ranks to become Brigadier, General Staff of 1 CANADIAN CORPS before going to North Africa to observe Montgomery's 8th Army, thus gaining valuable experience and getting to know the methods of the British commander he would later serve. It was there that he first came to Montgomery's attention as a man of imagination and general all-round ability. When Major-General H.L.N SALMON, slated to command Canadian forces in SICILY, was killed in a plane crash in April, 1943, MCNAUGHTON designated Simonds to take over as commander of 1st Canadian Infantry Division. In general, Simonds did a good job in this position, favouring movement over fire power in his constant efforts to outflank the Germans in the battles for towns, hilltops, and defiles that marked the fighting in the rugged terrain of central Sicily. He held this command until the end of October, 1943 when he was transferred to command of 5TH CANADIAN ARMOURED DIVISION, not yet engaged in fighting in ITALY. At the end on January, 1944, he was brought back to England and given command of II CANADIAN CORPS in preparation for the NORMANDY landings. He held that position until the end of the war except when he took temporary command of FIRST CANADIAN ARMY during the SCHELDT battles in the fall of 1944 when H.D.G. CRERAR fell ill.

Considered Canada's best tactician in World War II, Simonds planned Operation TOTALIZE, which opened the way to FALAISE after the fall of CAEN. In that action he devised the KANGAROO, the first dedicated armoured personnel carrier. He was also largely responsible for what was probably Canada's most important victory in World War II, the opening of the SCHELDT Estuary. Following the war Simonds served as chief instructor at the Imperial Defence College in Britain and as commandant of the NATIONAL DEFENCE COLLEGE in Canada before being named CHIEF OF THE GENERAL STAFF in 1951. He held that position until 1955, working for closer army cooperation with Britain and attempting unsuccessfully to win the government over to conscription.

Sioux, HMCS. A former Royal Navy V-class destroyer, *Sioux* was commissioned to the RCN in February 1944, served as convoy escort on the Murmansk run, participated in fleet operations against the Norway coast, and aided in OVERLORD. Like other V class vessels, *Sioux* was armed with four 4.7-inch guns as main armament, four 40-mm and four 20-mm guns, and eight torpedo tubes. She displaced 1740 tonnes, carried a crew of some 200 officers and men, and had a top speed of 21 knots. Taken into reserve after the war, *Sioux* was refitted and did three tours of duty in Korea, 1951–55. The vessel then served as a training ship until paid off in 1963.

6-pounder anti-tank gun. The 6-pounder became the standard infantry anti-tank weapon in the Canadian army as of the summer of 1943, replacing the 2-pounder. In fighting in NORMANDY and elsewhere it was shown to be ineffective against the armour plate of the newest German tanks, the Tiger and Panther, but it could cripple one of these tanks when fired at the treads.

Skeena, HMCS. A RIVER CLASS DESTROYER, built in Britain to British specification but expressly for the RCN, *Skeena* was taken into commission in 1931 (along with its sister ship *SAGUENAY*). *Skeena* was stationed on the west coast prior to World War II. While serving with the NEWFOUNDLAND ESCORT FORCE in September 1941 *Skeena* was involved in the protracted and disastrous battle of CONVOY SC-42. In late July 1942, *Skeena* shared in the destruction of U-588 with the corvette *Wetaskiwin*. In 1944 the destroyer was driven ashore by a storm and wrecked on a reef near Iceland.

Slemon, Charles Roy (1904–1991). Among the first pilot officers trained by the ROYAL CANADIAN AIR FORCE, Slemon joined the RCAF in 1923 and won his pilot's wings the following year. He became commander of WESTERN AIR COMMAND in 1938 and in 1942 was sent overseas as senior staff officer to organize NO.6 BOMBER GROUP of which he eventually became deputy commander. He was promoted to Chief of the Air Staff in 1953, a post he held until 1957 when he became the first deputy commander of NORAD. He retired from active service in 1964.

Smellie, Elizabeth Lawrie (1884–1968). Smellie joined the Canadian Army Nursing Service and served in Britain and France during World War I. She was MENTIONED IN DISPATCHES in 1916 and awarded the Royal Red Cross in 1917. She was matron-in-chief of the ROYAL CANADIAN ARMY MEDICAL CORPS in 1940, helped establish the CANADIAN WOMEN'S ARMY CORPS, and was the first woman promoted to the rank of colonel.

Smith, Donald Alexander, 1st Baron Strathcona and Mount Royal (1820–1914). Known primarily for his connection to the Hudson's Bay Company and the Canadian Pacific Railway, Smith also raised a unit of mounted rifles at his own expense to serve in the SOUTH AFRICAN WAR. A total of 537 men were recruited to form what later became known as LORD STRATHCONA'S HORSE.

Smith, Ernest Alva (b. 1914). A member of the Seaforth Highlanders, 'Smoky' Smith thwarted two German counter-attacks at a bridgehead over the Savio River in ITALY on 21–22 October 1944. In both actions Smith used his PIAT to good effect, destroying at least two German tanks, killing a number of their crew, and dispersing others. For his exploits he was awarded a VICTORIA CROSS.

Snider Rifle. The British government equipped the Canadian militia with 6300 Snider-Enfield breech-loading rifles in 1866, prior to the FENIAN RAIDS. The Snider replaced the Enfield rifles loaned to Canada by Britain during the American Civil War.

Snipe fighter. Built by Sopwith in England, the Snipe was a single-engine fighter used towards the end of World War I. It was flown by Billy BARKER at the time Barker won the VICTORIA CROSS. It was acquired by the RCAF in 1921 for use as an advanced trainer. Three Snipes were in use at CAMP BORDEN until 1924. The Snipe's maximum speed was 194 km/h and it had a three-hour flight endurance.

Snowbirds. The aerobatic team of the Canadian Forces. Formed in 1971 and based at Canadian Forces Base Moosejaw, the Snowbirds fly the CL41 TUTOR. Normally employing a nine-plane team, the Snowbirds have performed at air shows around the world. They are officially designated as No. 431 Air Demonstration Squadron.

Soest base. Located in Westphalia, Germany, Soest was Canada's first post-war army base in Europe. It consisted of four camps and opened in November 1953. The camp was turned over to the British in 1970 when the Canadian army moved to LAHR.

Solandt, Omand McKillop (b. 1909): Solandt studied physiology in Canada before going to Britain to run a blood bank in 1940. After resolving the problem of why British tank crews were fainting (they were breathing in gun exhaust gases) he was appointed to head the British Army's Operational Research Group. When Canada founded the DEFENCE RESEARCH BOARD after WORLD WAR II, he became its first chairman, a post he held until 1956.

Soldier Settlement Act. Passed in 1919, the Act provided World War I RETURNED SOLDIERS with loans to establish themselves as farmers. Over 25,000 took loans for land, stock, and equipment but many later abandoned their farms because of poor farming conditions and heavy debt loads. The act was administered by the SOLDIER SETTLEMENT BOARD.

Soldier Settlement Board. The Board administered the SOLDIER SETTLEMENT ACT on behalf of the Department of SOLDIERS' CIVIL RE-ESTABLISHMENT. Established in 1919, the three-member Board granted up to 320 acres of land and $1500 for stock, equipment, buildings, and improvements, repayable at 5 per cent interest over 20 years. By 1924, at least one quarter of the 'soldier settlers' had abandoned their farms because of poor farming conditions.

Soldiers' Civil Re-establishment, Department of. Department of the federal government founded in 1918 to provide hospital treatment and vocational training for RETURNED SOLDIERS as well as to administer their pensions, and to re-direct munitions workers to other employment after their services were no longer needed. The SOLDIER SETTLEMENT BOARD was one arm of this department. It was absorbed by the Department of Pensions and National Health in 1928. See also Sir J.A. LOUGHEED.

Somme, Battle of the. When the Somme battle began on 1 July 1916, the CANADIAN CORPS was still in Belgium where it had fought since the early months of 1915. That was just as well since faulty planning produced a slaughter of British attackers on the first day—some 21,000 were killed, most by German machine gun fire. The [ROYAL] NEWFOUNDLAND REGIMENT was not so fortunate; it was caught in a German crossfire near the town of Beaumont Hamel and 310 were killed in a few minutes. Almost none of the first day's objectives were achieved; where the British did gain some success, they were soon forced to retreat due to lack of reinforcements and strong German counter-attacks.

Despite the obvious evidence that the battlefield was not well chosen and that the defenders were well entrenched, well armed, and enjoyed high morale, the British commander Haig pressed forward and the attacks continued throughout the summer. What had once been intended as a break-through attack became a battle of attrition with the intention of wearing the Germans down and destroying their will to fight.

The Canadian Corps entered the Somme battle in September under the overall command of General Julian BYNG. The attack opened in the early morning hours of 15 September with an assault by R.E.W. TURNER's 2ND CANADIAN DIVISION towards COURCELETTE from the south, an attack that was quickly successful, followed in the evening by LIPSETT's 3RD CANADIAN DIVISION, attacking through Courcelette from the west. Using newly developed tactics such as the creeping barrage, and utilizing tanks, they succeeded in capturing the objective and then pushing on beyond it in the first two days of heavy fighting, but rain and mud then hindered the assault as did the well-dug in German machine guns in the trenches beyond. By 22 September this phase of the battle ended; the Canadians had suffered 7230 killed, wounded, and taken prisoner.

Following the battle of Courcelette, the Canadian objective became the capture of the main German defensive position known as REGINA TRENCH, less than 2 km to the north of Courcelette. The first assaults on the trench were mounted by the 1st and 2nd Divisions on 26 September. They did not succeed in capturing the position, but they did advance the Canadian front line closer to the ultimate objective. Additional attacks on 1 October by the 2nd and 3rd Divisions and again on 8 October, by the 1st and 3rd Divisions, also failed, with casualties in the latter action amounting to 1364.

The 4TH CANADIAN DIVISION joined the Corps on 10 October and was given the job of attacking the trench once again. The ground over which the attack was to take place had been pulverized by shellfire. The division's first two attacks failed but the third gained its objective and the trench was taken on 11 November. The Somme battle was effectively over. Though entering late, and after the initial set-backs of July and August, the Corps suffered 24,029 killed and wounded.

Reading: Desmond Morton and J.L. Granatstein, *Marching to Armageddon* (Toronto, 1989); J. Swettenham, *To Seize the Victory* (Toronto, 1965).

Sonar. See ASDIC.

South African War. The South African or Boer War began 11 October 1899 and ended 31 May 1902. It was, in almost all respects, a war for the advancement of British imperial interests in southern Africa. The underlying cause of the war was the growth in power and prestige of the two essentially Boer republics in South Africa, the Transvaal and the Orange Free State, in comparison to the two British colonies that lay on the coast, the Cape Colony and Natal. That development was largely due to the discovery and exploitation of large gold deposits in the Transvaal. The ostensible reason for the war was the refusal of the two Boer republics to grant equal status to non-Boer residents — the *uitlanders* — who had mostly migrated to the interior in search of gold and economic opportunity.

When war began Canadian opinion was sharply divided; imperialists pushed to participate, but Quebeckers were strongly opposed. The GOC, Edward HUTTON, had already drawn up a contingency plan for the dispatch of Canadian troops. Much pressure was put on Prime Minister Wilfrid LAURIER by the Colonial Office which was anxious for representation from the self-governing Dominions. Laurier quickly capitulated and authorized the raising of a contingent of 1000 men, all to be volunteers, provided that the British would pay. The formation, commanded by William OTTER, was designated the 2nd (Special Service) Battalion. The men came from a number of regiments, both PERMANENT FORCE and MILITIA. The first contingent was eventually augmented by some 6000 other volunteers. At least one new regiment — LORD STRATHCONA'S HORSE, funded entirely by Donald Smith,

Lord Strathcona—was raised (it was the third contingent to go to South Africa). Eventually Canada was to contribute almost $3 million to the cost of raising, transporting and maintaining the troops.

The Canadians had their first introduction to battle on 31 December, 1899 when one company of the ROYAL CANADIAN REGIMENT took part in an action at Sunnyside Kopje alongside a number of British and Australian troops. The Boer position there was quickly captured with no losses suffered by the Canadians.

The first significant battle in which the Canadians participated was PAARDEBURG, which took place in late February after a good deal of marching through dry and dusty country. The marching, the heat, the filth, and disease took a heavy toll of the Canadians throughout the war. More than 10 per cent of the Canadian contingent had been eliminated even before the advance to Paardeburg.

The RCR played a significant role in the Battle of Paardeburg and took part in the advance to Bloemfontein which followed. Once again the heat, dust, and constant marching took their toll. In three and a half months, about one quarter of the Canadians had been rendered incapable of fighting. Bloemfontein was taken without a fight — the Boers had retired. In fact, Boer tactics now shifted from confronting the British and Imperial troops in set-piece battles, to classic guerrilla warfare using fast-mounted riflemen to raid British positions and then retire. Still, some savage set-piece battles remained to be fought, as at Israel's Poort on 25 April when the RCRs ran into an ambush and sustained heavy casualties. Other engagements followed at Doornkop, Johannesburg, and Pretoria, the Transvaal capital, which was taken on 5 June 1900. Despite these victories, the war dragged on and a second Canadian contingent was dispatched to aid in the fight which had now become a pure guerrilla war. Many further battles were fought, including some notable ones such as at LELIEFONTEIN in November, 1900, before the war ended.

Canada sent 8372 men to the war; 244 were either killed in action or succumbed to disease, 252 were wounded, and four were awarded the VICTORIA CROSS.

Reading: J.L. Granatstein and D. Bercuson, *War and Peacekeeping* (Toronto, 1971)

South Beveland. See BEVELAND.

Spall, Robert (1890–1918). Serving with the PRINCESS PATRICIA'S CANADIAN LIGHT INFANTRY at Parvillers, France on 12–13 August, 1918, Spall used a LEWIS GUN to hold off a German counter-attack and enable his platoon to withdraw from an isolated position. Spall was killed in action during this engagement and was posthumously awarded the VICTORIA CROSS.

Special Service Force, Canadian-American. Popularly known as the Devil's Brigade, the First Special Service Force was a mixed contingent of Canadians and Americans commanded by Col Robert T. Frederick of the U.S. Army. The group was organized in 1942 as an élite commando unit to undertake especially hazardous missions. Between 600 and 800 Canadians served with the force which first saw action during the KISKA landings. It was then shifted to ITALY where it entered the lines in early December, 1943. From then until the liberation of Rome in June, 1944 it saw heavy action, sustaining many casualties, and earning the praise of General Mark W. Clark, commander of the U.S. 5th Army in Italy.

Spitfire fighter. The British-designed and built Supermarine Spitfire was based on a racing plane. It first became widely known during the BATTLE OF BRITAIN even though it was vastly outnumbered by the Hawker HURRICANE in the ranks of the Royal Air Force. In 1941 the Spitfire replaced the Hurricane as the standard fighter of fourteen RCAF squadrons. Various marks of the Spitfire were used during and after World War II, each representing an improvement in speed, manoeuvrability, or armament over its predecessors. The Mk IX—the version most used by the RCAF during World War II— had a top speed of just over 645 km/h, a service ceiling of 13.2 km, and a range of 660 km. The Spitfire was considered one of the best Allied fighters of the war although its utility as a bomber escort was always hampered by its limited range.

Spitzbergen raid. Six hundred Canadian troops conducted a top secret raid on this strategically important group of Norwegian islands from 25 August to 3 September 1941 to evacuate their 2800 inhabitants and raze the settlements. This was done to prevent Germany from using the facilities there. The raiders laid waste to weather stations, transportation and communications facilities, and the islands' coal mines.

Spooner, Kenneth Gerald (1922–1943). On 14 May 1943, Spooner and three other student navigators from the Air Observers School at London, Ontario were on a training flight over Lake Erie in an Avro ANSON when the pilot fainted. Spooner held the aircraft steady while his colleagues bailed out. He had had no pilot training and was killed when he crash-landed into the lake. He was posthumously awarded the GEORGE CROSS.

Spry, Daniel Charles (1913–1989). Spry attended Dalhousie University and joined the PERMANENT FORCE in the early 1930s. During WORLD WAR II Spry served as a battalion commander with the ROYAL CANADIAN REGIMENT and then as GOC 1st and 12th Canadian Infantry Brigades in ITALY. He transferred to NORMANDY in August, 1944 to assume command of the 3RD CANADIAN INFANTRY DIVISION during the NORTHWEST EUROPE campaign. In 1946 he was named vice-chief of the General Staff.

Squid mortar. An anti-submarine mortar not unlike the HEDGEHOG in that it was mounted ahead of the bridge of an escort vessel and threw its projectiles over the bow of the vessel. Whereas Hedgehog consisted of a large number of small mortar bombs which detonated only if they struck the submarine, Squid threw three depth charges in a pattern intended to crush a submarine's hull even if the submersible was not struck. Squid was usually connected to the escort vessel's ASDIC so that it could be automatically fired when the submarine was at a preset depth, bearing, and range.

Stacey, Charles Perry (1906–1989). Educated at Toronto, Oxford, and Princeton universities, at the outbreak of WORLD WAR II Stacey became the army's official historian and director of the Canadian Army Historical Section in 1945. Under his direction, the OFFICIAL HISTORIES of the Canadian Army in World War II were prepared, and he wrote two of the three volumes. Among Stacey's other books are *Canada and the Brit-*

ish Army (1939), *Quebec 1759* (1959), *Arms, Men and Governments* (1970), *A Very Double Life* (1976) and *Canada and the Age of Conflict* in two volumes (1977, 1981).

Staghound armoured car. Built by General Motors in both Canada and the United States, the Staghound was the standard armoured car used by the Canadian army during World War II. Armed with a 37-mm main gun and two machine guns, it was used for raids, reconnaisance, the protection of truck convoys, and patrols. Plated with 3.2-cm thick armour, the car had a crew of five and reached a maximum speed of 88 km/h.

Standardization. After WORLD WAR II, all three Canadian services began a slow process of conversion from British- to American-style equipment. Efforts were then made to establish standardized weaponry and equipment for Canada, the U.S., and Britain so as to ease problems of supply in wartime. Under the minister of National Defence, Brooke CLAXTON, Canada was a leader in this campaign, which actually produced little in the way of tangible results. For example, the three countries could not even agree on a common rifle round, the British continuing to use the .303-calibre until the adoption of the standard NATO 7.62-mm round, while the U.S. used the .300-calibre until it too adopted the 7.62 standard.

Standing Committee on External Affairs and National Defence. Constituted in 1968, this was one of a number of new committees of the House of Commons created under the new Trudeau government to expedite the business of Parliament. It was replaced in 1985 by the External Affairs and International Trade Standing Committee and by the Defence Standing Committee.

Stanraer aircraft. Built under licence by Canadian Vickers, the Supermarine Stanraer was a twin-engine, biplane-type flying boat used on both coasts for general reconnaissance and submarine patrol at the start of WORLD WAR II. The Stanraer could stay in the air for up to 10 hours, and carried three .303-calibre machine guns and up to 630 kg of bombs or depth charges. In all, 40 were built.

Starfighter. See CF104 AIRCRAFT.

Stedman, E.W. (1888–1957). Born and educated in Britain, Stedman served with the Royal Naval Air Service and the Royal Air Force during WORLD WAR I. In 1920 he was named Technical Director of Canada's new Air Board, the federal agency created to oversee all Dominion flying operations. He served in that post until 1924 when he joined the fledgling ROYAL CANADIAN AIR FORCE. He rose through the ranks to become Director-General of Air Research, a post he held from 1941 until he retired from active service in 1946. In his long career he was involved in many areas of aviation research in Canada, from cold-weather testing to the building of jet engines. His memoirs, *From Boxkite to Jet*, were posthumously published in 1963.

Steele, Sir Samuel Benfield (1849–1919). Steele joined the MILITIA in 1866, took part in the RED RIVER EXPEDITION and served with the artillery before joining the NORTH WEST MOUNTED POLICE in 1873. He served with distinction with the force on the prairies and in the Yukon during the Klondike Gold Rush before volunteering for service with LORD STRATHCONA'S HORSE during the SOUTH AFRICAN WAR. In WORLD WAR I he went overseas with the Second Canadian Contingent in 1915 but was considered too old for a field command. He was appointed general officer commanding the Shorncliffe, England, training establishment in 1916, a post he held until his retirement in 1918.

Stein, C.R.S. (1897–1973). Stein succeeded General E.W. SANSOM as commander of the 5TH CANADIAN ARMOURED DIVISION in January 1943, until a medical board found him unfit for further service overseas. He was succeeded in turn by Generals E.L.M. BURNS and Guy SIMONDS.

Sten gun. 9-mm submachine gun in almost universal use with Commonwealth forces during and after World War II. The weapon was adopted as standard issue for Canadian forces in June 1943 although some Canadian troops had already used it at DIEPPE. The 1ST CANADIAN INFANTRY DIVISION, fighting in ITALY, utilized the much superior American-designed THOMPSON .45-calibre submachine gun. The Sten was light, simple, and cheap to manufacture and could fire ammunition captured from the enemy. It was originally intended for use by commandos and guerrillas. It was not suitable as a standard infantry weapon even though it was used as such. It misfired often and was especially prone to going off accidentally. The troops hated it. It was still in use by Canadian soldiers as late as the KOREAN WAR.

Stephenson, Sir William Samuel (1896–1989). The Canadian-born head of British counter-espionage in the United States, based in New York City, was known as 'Intrepid'. He and his team of agents censored letters, forged documents, guarded against sabotage, and trained Allied agents at CAMP X. He has been the subject of several biographies and much controversy is still generated as to the actual extent of his operations during the war—what is fact and what is fiction.

Stevenson, Leigh Forbes (1895–?). In WORLD WAR I Stevenson served with the 8th battalion, CANADIAN EXPEDITONARY FORCE before transferring to the Royal Flying Corps. He stayed in the military after the war, joining the newly founded ROYAL CANADIAN AIR FORCE. In the early 1930s he attended the Royal Naval Staff College in Greenwich. During WORLD WAR II Stevenson served as Air Officer Commandng the RCAF overseas, 1940–41, and WESTERN AIR COMMAND, 1942–44. He retired from active service in 1945.

Stirling, Grote (1875–1953). A civil engineer and B.C. fruit grower, Stirling was first elected to the House of Commons in 1924 and re-elected three times before joining the Cabinet of Prime Minister R.B. Bennett as minister of National Defence in November 1934. He stayed in the post until the resignation of the government in October 1935.

STOL. Acronym for 'short takeoff and landing'; STOL aircraft are specifically designed to land or take off in a very limited space and thus have many military applications. DE HAVILLAND AIRCRAFT OF CANADA has long been a world leader in the development of STOL technology.

Stone Frigate. Built as part of the British dockyard at Kingston, Ontario, the Stone Frigate became a cadet dormitory at the

ROYAL MILITARY COLLEGE when it opened in 1876. It is still in use, not greatly renovated, as such.

Stoney Creek, Battle of. On the night of 4/5 June, 1813, 700 British troops of the 8th and 49th Regiments together with Canadian MILITIA attacked 3500 Americans at Stoney Creek in the Niagara Peninsula. After a confused but pitched battle, the Americans withdrew to the Niagara River. The battle was a key event in frustrating American ambitions to take control of the NIAGARA FRONTIER.

Storm Below. Novel published in 1949 by Hugh Garner. In this book the death of an Ordinary Seaman aboard the corvette *Riverford* six days out from St John's provokes a series of problems for the crew. Based indirectly on Garner's wartime experience, *Storm Below* offers an empathetic view of life aboard an escort ship on the NORTH ATLANTIC RUN.

Strachan, Harcus (1889–1982). At Masnières, France, under his leadership, the FORT GARRY HORSE overran a German battery on 20 November 1917. At dusk, and with his unit reduced to 40 men, Lt Strachan stampeded his horses to divert the Germans' attention, then led his party away from the German lines on foot. For this action he was awarded the VICTORIA CROSS.

Strange, Thomas Bland (1831–1925). Strange served with the artillery with the British Army in India, seeing action in the Indian Mutiny (1857), before returning to Canada and joining the MILITIA. He was given command of one of the two permanent artillery batteries established by the Macdonald government in 1871. He held that command until he retired in 1882. Col Strange emerged from retirement in 1885 to command one of the three columns of the NORTHWEST FIELD FORCE. In that campaign his troops fought an inconclusive engagement against the Cree at Frenchman's Butte.

Strathcona, Lord. See SMITH, DONALD A.

Stuart tank. The American-built M3 was the first U.S. tank to be used by British and Commonwealth forces in World War II, 84 being acquired by the British 8th Army in North Africa in July 1941. Known in British service as the 'General Stuart', the basic M3 carried a crew of four, utilized one 37-mm gun and three .30-calibre Browning machine guns as armament, and had a top speed of approximately 55 km/h. A number of variants were also produced for use as flame throwers, mine-clearing vehicles, etc. Canadian armoured units in the NORTHWEST EUROPE CAMPAIGN used the Stuart as a light tank.

Stuart, Kenneth (1891–1945). A graduate of ROYAL MILITARY COLLEGE, Stuart served overseas with the ROYAL CANADIAN ENGINEERS in World War I. In the inter-war years, he held a variety of staff positions and edited the *CANADIAN DEFENCE QUARTERLY*. Stuart was chief of staff at Canadian military headquarters in London 1943–44 and was instrumental in the removal of A.G.L. MCNAUGHTON from command of FIRST CANADIAN ARMY. His too optimistic wastage-rate forecasts helped bring on the REINFORCEMENT CRISIS and fuelled the CONSCRIPTION CRISIS, 1944.

Stuart, Ronald Neil (1886–1954): A Canadian, Stuart served with the Royal Naval Reserve aboard the HMS *Pargust* and won the VICTORIA CROSS while at sea on 7 June 1917.

Stursberg, Peter (b. 1913). Born in China, Stursberg began working for the Victoria *Daily Times* as a reporter in 1938. He joined the Canadian Broadcasting Corporation as a news editor in 1941 and went overseas as a CBC war correspondent in 1943. He accompanied 1ST CANADIAN INFANTRY DIVISION in the invasion of SICILY, the first Canadian reporter to cover that campaign. After the war he continued his career as a broadcaster, reporter and writer.

Submarines. Canada acquired its first two submarines, CC1 and CC2, in the early days of World War I when British Columbia Premier Sir Richard MCBRIDE purchased two U.S.-built submersibles (originally destined for Chile) for use as offshore patrol vessels. Shortly after they arrived at ESQUIMALT they were transferred to the ROYAL CANADIAN NAVY. In 1917 they were ordered to Halifax where they were used as training craft until scrapped in 1920. Canada's next two submarines were CHI4 and CHI5, acquired in the summer of 1922 from the Royal Navy. H-class submarines, they had been built for the RN in Groton, Connecticut, during the war but became surplus to the RN's needs when the war ended and were offered to Canada. They were taken out of commission in 1922 and sold in 1927. At the end of World War II the RCN briefly acquired and used two ex-German U-boats, U-190 and U-889. In the 1960s Canada acquired five submarines, all for training purposes: *Grilse* in 1961, *Ojibwa* in 1965, *Onondaga* in 1967, and *Okanagan* and *Rainbow* in 1968, although the RCN never operated more than three at a time. *Ojibwa*, *Okanagan*, and *Onondaga* were *Oberon* class vessels, all built in Britain and the only totally new submarines ever acquired by Canada. They are still in operation.

Suez Crisis. Following the Egyptian nationalization of the Suez Canal in 1956, Israel, Britain, and France invaded Egypt in October after diplomatic efforts to resolve the crisis failed. Prime Minister Lester B. PEAR-SON helped to defuse the crisis by persuading the United Nations to create a UN emergency force (UNEF) to separate the Israelis from the Egyptians and to replace the British and French troops which had occupied much of the former Suez Canal Zone. Pearson put his plan forward in the UN General Assembly on 4 November and it was adopted 6 November. Pearson was later awarded a Nobel Peace Prize for the idea. The first elements of UNEF arrived in Egypt on 24 November to supervise the ceasefire. UNEF's first commander was the Canadian general E.L.M. BURNS.

Suffield Experimental Station. Located near Medicine Hat, Alberta, Suffield has been the site of top-secret weapons research since its establishment in June 1941. During the war it was administered by the NA-TIONAL RESEARCH COUNCIL, a responsibility assumed by the DEFENCE RESEARCH BOARD when it was founded after the war. In its first years of operation it was known as the Canadian Chemical Warfare School and was jointly funded by Britain and Canada. The results of the experimental work done there in chemical, biological, and other 'non-conventional' (though not nuclear) weapons were shared between the two countries and also the United States. Suffield is still an active weapons research centre but little is known of the work done there.

Sutherland, Donald Matheson (1879–1970). A physician by training, Sutherland commanded the 52nd Battalion, CANADIAN EXPEDITIONARY FORCE in World War I. He was elected to the House of Commons in 1925 and entered the Cabinet of Prime Minister R.B. Bennett as minister of National Defence in 1930, a post he held until 1934.

T

Tait, James Edward (1886–1918). With the 78th Battalion, CEF, Tait single-handedly knocked out a German machine-gun post near AMIENS 8 August 1918. His men were inspired by this action and went ahead to capture twelve other machine guns and take 20 prisoners that same day. Tait was awarded the VICTORIA CROSS for this action but did not live to collect it: he was killed in action three days later.

Tait, Sir Thomas (1864–1940). A Montrealer, Tait served with the Victoria Rifles dur-ing the NORTHWEST REBELLION. During WORLD WAR I, he was President of the Montreal Citizens' Recruiting Association and was a strong supporter of CONSCRIP-TION. For a brief time in 1916 he filled the position of director-general of National Service for Canada, responsible for operating the government's REGISTRATION scheme.

Talbot, Thomas (1771–1853). Talbot was an Irish aristocrat who commanded a 500-man MILITIA unit at Long Point in Upper Canada during the WAR OF 1812. In July 1812 he attempted to muster his men for an effort to relieve Fort Amherstburg. Upset about leaving wives and families unprotected, angry at Talbot (their landlord) for the way he had treated them, and confused by the entreaties of pro-American agitators, they mutinied.

Tattoo. A military exposition. A tattoo is usually a large public affair involving parades and various forms of drill. In Canada the armed forces mounted a Centennial Tattoo in 1967 which played to large crowds across the country.

Tecumseh (1768?-1813). Tecumseh was a Shawnee war chief who with other Native leaders joined British regulars and Canadian MILITIA during the WAR OF 1812. He took part in several major battles, including the capture of Detroit in 1812, and in May 1813, fighting alongside the forces of General Henry PROCTOR, he helped defeat the Americans at Fort Meigs. In September of that year British naval forces on Lake Erie challenged the Americans under Commodore Perry and were defeated at Put-in-Bay. As a result, Proctor decided to retreat eastward from Detroit and a reluctant Tecumseh accompanied him. With U.S. General Harrison hard on his heels, Proctor was forced to stand and fight at MORAVIANTOWN. The British were soundly defeated; Proctor fled, and Tecumseh was killed.

Teillet, R.J. (b. 1912). Born in Manitoba, Teillet served with the ROYAL CANADIAN AIR FORCE in World War II before being shot down and held as a prisoner of war. Elected to the House of Commons in 1962, Teillet was appointed minister of Veterans' Affairs in April 1963, a position he held until 1968.

Terrace Mutiny. On 23 November 1944, at the climax of the CONSCRIPTION CRISIS of 1944, the federal government announced that 16,000 NRMA men would be dispatched overseas to solve the REINFORCEMENT CRISIS. Almost immediately there was a series of violent reactions in some of the British Columbia army camps where large numbers of these men were based. The most serious incident occurred at Terrace, home of the 15th Infantry Brigade, beginning on 25 November. There, close to two thousand muti-

neers seized weapons and ammunition from the base magazine and trained 6-POUNDER GUNS on Terrace from a spot overlooking the city. At the time of the mutiny most senior officers were attending an inquiry in Vancouver. When they returned the situation was brought under control and peace restored. Several of the movement's ringleaders were court-martialled and imprisoned for their role in the events.

Thacker, Henry Cyril (1870–1953). Commissioned in the ROYAL CANADIAN ARTILLERY in 1891, Thacker fought in the SOUTH AFRICAN WAR and worked as a military attaché with the Japanese during the Russo-Japanese War. He commanded CANADIAN EXPEDITIONARY FORCE divisional artilleries, 1915–19, and served briefly as CHIEF OF THE GENERAL STAFF, 1927–28.

Thames, Battle of the. See MORAVIAN-TOWN, BATTLE OF.

Theriault, Gerard-Charles-Edouard (b. 1932). Theriault joined the ROYAL CANADIAN AIR FORCE in 1951 and occupied several command positions before becoming head of the COLLÈGE MILITAIRE ROYALE DE ST JEAN in 1970. He later commanded the IST CANADIAN AIR GROUP in Germany and served as Deputy Chief of the Defence Staff, Vice-Chief of the Defence Staff and CHIEF OF THE DEFENCE STAFF, 1983–1986.

3rd Canadian Division (World War I). The 3rd Division joined the CANADIAN CORPS at MOUNT SORREL in June 1916 where the Corps suffered 8000 casualties. It was disbanded in April 1919.

3rd Canadian Infantry Division (World War II). Formed in October 1940 and disbanded in November 1945 to be reconstituted as the CANADIAN ARMY OCCUPATION FORCE, the division served in Europe until June 1946. The division took part in the D-DAY landings and fought in NORMANDY and NORTHWEST EUROPE.

Thompson .45-calibre submachine gun. Designed in the United States in the latter stages of WORLD WAR I as a trench assault weapon, the Thompson became notorious in the 1920s as the weapon of choice of American gangsters. Originally utilizing a drum magazine, the 'Tommy' gun was widely featured in the movies. In World War II, a variety of .45-calibre Thompsons were used as the standard submachine gun of the U.S. infantry. The IST CANADIAN INFANTRY DIVISION used the Thompson in common with other Commonwealth forces in SICILY and ITALY. Other Canadian troops in Europe used the much inferior STEN.

Thousand Plane Raid. In early 1942 the new Commander of the Royal Air Force's BOMBER COMMAND, Arthur Harris, decided to mount a series of massive raids against German targets, partly in retaliation for German attacks on British cities, partly as a morale booster for the RAF and for Britain, and partly in an effort to cripple German industrial production. Harris and his planners also believed that sending a large number of aircraft to a single target would overwhelm the German defenders. Thus was born the 'thousand plane raid' — one thousand aircraft (or close to that number) attacking a single target in one night. The first of these targets was Cologne, hit on the night of 30-31 May 1942. Many of the attacking aircraft were twin-engine bombers and some of the crews were actually still with Operational Training Units. At that point in the war, however, the RAF simply did not have enough aircraft, crews, or ground personnel to sustain these large raids and they were soon discontinued.

Thousand Shall Fall, A. Memoir written by Canadian Murray PEDEN of his service with the Royal Air Force in WORLD WAR II. The book begins with Peden's training with the BRITISH COMMONWEALTH AIR TRAINING PLAN and relates the events of his time with the RAF's 214 squadron. It is one of the best memoirs available of a Canadian airman on flying operations.

Three Cheers for Me. In this 1973 book, also known as 'Volume I of the Bartholomew Bandy Papers', Canadian author Donald Jack lightheartedly recounted the education and corruption of a puritanical Canadian youth who became an ace with the ROYAL FLYING CORPS in WORLD WAR I. The novel was followed by three other volumes, *That's Me in the Middle*, *It's Me Again*, and *Me Bandy, You Cissie*. See also WAR NOVELS.

3.7-inch anti-aircraft gun. The standard Commonwealth heavy anti-aircraft weapon of WORLD WAR II. The gun had a height range of 11.3 km. Like other anti-aircraft weapons (the German 88 is a good example) it was also used against tanks. A number of these weapons were deployed around Quebec City during the Roosevelt-Churchill meetings there in 1943 and 1944.

Tiger Moth biplane. Built by DE HAVILLAND starting in 1936, the two-seater Tiger Moth biplane was the chief elementary training plane used by the BRITISH COMMONWEALTH AIR TRAINING PLAN in WORLD WAR II. Approximately 2000 of the aircraft were built in Canada. The aircraft had a maximum speed of 175 km/h.

Tilston, Frederick Albert (1906–1992). On 1 March 1945, during the battle of the HOCHWALD in the RHINELAND campaign, Tilston led the men of C Company, the Essex Scottish, across 460 m of open ground and over a 3-m-high barbed wire fence to put his unit into German trenches at the edge of the Hochwald forest. Although wounded several times, Tilston was the first man into the enemy positions. He silenced one machine-gun nest with a grenade, and continued to press the attack. He then recrossed an open area several times to reorganize and rally his company and to bring his men ammunition and grenades, before losing both legs in the action. He was awarded the VICTORIA CROSS.

Tin Flute, The. Originally written in French by Manitoba-born author Gabrielle Roy and published as *Bonheur d'occasion* in 1945, the novel depicted life among French Canadians in the St Henri district in Montreal during WORLD WAR II. Roy received a Governor-General's Award for the novel.

Tisdale, David (1835–1911). A lawyer, Tisdale was first elected to represent Norfolk South, in Ontario, in 1887. In May, 1896 he was appointed minister of Militia and Defence in the government of Sir Charles Tupper. He held the post until Tupper was succeeded by LAURIER in July, 1896.

Todd, John Lancelot (1876–?). A tropical medicine specialist, Todd discovered a prevention and treatment for 'tick fever', also known as TRENCH FEVER. He served with the CANADIAN ARMY MEDICAL CORPS in 1915 and later with the Board of Pension Commissioners, 1916–17.

Topham, Frederick George (1917–1974). A medical orderly with the 1st Canadian Parachute Battalion during the Rhine crossings, Topham rescued a wounded man and was himself wounded in the process on 24 March 1945. Later that same day he rescued three other men from a burning carrier where all were at risk from exploding ammunition. He was awarded the VICTORIA CROSS for his bravery.

Totalize, Operation. Totalize was conceived by G.G. SIMONDS as a means to break through German positions south and east of CAEN and expedite the Canadian drive towards FALAISE in early August, 1944. The operation was carefully planned. It was to include the use of armoured personnel carriers — the KANGAROO — for the first time in combat, and was to be carried out under cover of darkness. The attackers were to be aided by the use of ARTIFICIAL MOONLIGHT — searchlights played on the clouds — and tracer rounds fired toward the enemy on both sides of the advancing columns. The first phase of the attack opened with a massive bombardment of German positions by heavy bombers of the RAF's Bomber Command on the night of 7 August. Although there was much confusion as the Canadian armoured columns rolled south, most of the objectives of the first phase of the attack were reached. The second phase of the operation, which began 8 August, was much less successful. Confusion, stiffening German resistance, and the mistaken bombing of Canadian positions by American heavy bombers plagued the attack from the start. This phase was called off by Simonds on 11 August. Totalize was followed within a few days by TRACTABLE.
Reading: J. English, *The Canadian Army in Normandy* (New York, 1991)

Town Class Destroyer. As a result of the LEASED BASES AGREEMENT, also known as the destroyers-for-bases deal, the United States transferred fifty World War I-vintage destroyers to the Royal Navy. These ships were transferred to the RN at Halifax and six were immediately turned over to the

ROYAL CANADIAN NAVY. The RCN acquired two additional vessels of this type later in the war. The British named these vessels after towns in Britain and the U.S. that had the same name, hence the designation 'town class', but the Canadian vessels were almost all named after rivers along the Canada-U.S. border. Long, but with a narrow beam, these vessels were fast but rolled violently in the rough North Atlantic seas. To make them more stable and more suitable for the anti-submarine role, a number of modifications were carried out: three outboard torpedo mounts (with three tubes each) were replaced by one centre-line mount, the three rear-most stacks were cut down by 1.5 metres, and one was sealed. Main armament consisted of three 4-inch guns, three torpedo tubes, one 12-pounder anti-aircraft gun, and depth charge racks. Later in the war, a HEDGEHOG mortar was also fitted. With an average displacement of 1120 tonnes, the vessels could make 36 knots. They carried a crew of 14 officers and 245 men. One of these vessels, the ST CROIX, was torpedoed in 1943 with heavy loss of life.

Townshend, George, 1st Marquess (1724–1807). One of General James WOLFE's brigadiers at QUEBEC, Townshend became commander of the British forces there after Wolfe's death at the PLAINS OF ABRAHAM. He accepted the city's surrender from the French, 18 September 1759. A talented cartoonist, he distributed cartoon sketches in England after the battle which ridiculed Wolfe and other officers, an action for which he was strongly criticized.

Tractable, Operation. The failure of the second phase of Operation TOTALIZE, called off by G.G. SIMONDS on 11 August 1944, necessitated a second Canadian thrust towards FALAISE. This was Tractable, launched 14 August 1944 by the 3RD CANADIAN INFANTRY DIVISION and the 4TH CANADIAN ARMOURED DIVISION, reinforced by the 2nd Canadian Armoured Brigade. Aided by heavy bombers, fighter-bombers, and rocket-firing TYPHOONS of the 2ND ALLIED TACTICAL AIR FORCE, and with the infantry again using KANGAROOS, the divisions advanced 8 km toward Falaise and took 1500 prisoners on the first day; Falaise fell 16 August. In the opening heavy-bomber attack, Allied airforces inadvertently inflicted 400 Canadian casualties.

Tracy, Alexandre de Prouville, Marquis de (1596–1670). A professional soldier, he was commissioned lieutenant-governor of New France in 1663. One of his assigned missions was to vigorously prosecute a campaign against the Iroquois, carrying the war into their home territory, even to exterminate them. To carry out this task Tracy was provided with formidable reinforcements by way of the newly arrived CARIGNAN-SALIÈRES Regiment. The campaign began in 1665 and lasted until late 1666. Iroquois country was ravaged and the Iroquois sued for peace. Tracy left the colony in 1667.

Training Command. One of the joint commands established as a result of the WHITE PAPER 1964, Training Command was an early step towards UNIFICATION. It was given the task of supervising the personnel training of all three armed services.

Trans-Atlantic Ferry Service. The brainchild of Sir Max AITKEN, Lord Beaverbrook, the Trans-Atlantic Ferry Service was operated by Canadian Pacific Airlines during WORLD WAR II. It delivered aircraft and crews from Canada to Great Britain.

Treaty of Ghent, 1814. Signed 24 December 1814, the treaty ended the WAR OF 1812. The treaty returned the territories of Upper and Lower Canada and the U.S. to their pre-war status with boundaries unchanged. The issues of neutral rights, impressment, and Indian land claims in the midwest were unresolved. Outstanding questions about western boundaries were later settled by a commission.

Treaty of Paris, 1763. The treaty, signed 10 February, formally ended the SEVEN YEARS' WAR. France retained fishing rights off the coast of North America and the islands of St Pierre and Miquelon but gave up all title to New France and other French posessions in North America.

Treaty of Paris, 1783. Signed by Britain and the United States 20 September 1783, the treaty ended the REVOLUTIONARY WAR. Britain recognized the independence of the thirteen colonies, boundaries were designated

(some of which remained in dispute for years), the U.S. agreed to compensate the Loyalists, and fishing rights in coastal waters were agreed upon. After the treaty was signed the Americans refused to pay compensation to the Loyalists, and Britain retained a military presence in the west until 1794.

Treaty of St Germain-en-Laye, 1632. Concluded 29 March 1632, the treaty returned the settlements at PORT ROYAL and Quebec, as well as the ships and cargo seized from CHAMPLAIN, to France. Quebec had been occupied for three years following its conquest by David KIRKE. See also QUEBEC 1629.

Treaty of Utrecht, 1713. Signed 11 April 1713 by Britain and France, the treaty ended the WAR OF THE SPANISH SUCCESSION. It shrank the French empire in North America with Britain obtaining the Hudson Bay drainage area, Acadia (including Port Royal), and sole claim to Newfoundland. France retained Cape Breton, on which it later constructed LOUISBOURG, as well as parts of New Brunswick, and Isle St Jean (Prince Edward Island).

Treaty of Washington, 1871. Britain and the United States signed the Treaty of Washington 8 May 1871 to resolve issues outstanding between the two countries which had largely arisen from the American Civil War. The U.S. and Canada each received access to specified inland waterways and U.S. fisherman were to be allowed to fish in Canadian inshore waters. Canada failed to win compensation from the U.S. for losses suffered in the FENIAN RAIDS, but compensation was paid to Canada by Britain.

Tremblay, Thomas Louis (1886–1951). Following a career in the militia, Tremblay served with the ROYAL 22E REGIMENT during World War I and became officer commanding the 5th Brigade, CEF, from August 1918 to May 1919. A civil engineer by training, he served as Inspector-General for eastern Canada 1939–46.

Trench fever. Trench fever was carried by fleas that infested virtually every soldier in the trenches of the western front in WORLD WAR I. The CANADIAN EXPEDITIONARY FORCE recorded approximately 17,000 cases of the disease. Canadian John Lancelot TODD discovered a prevention and cure for the affliction.

Trench foot. Akin to frostbite — an affliction which causes limbs to swell — trench foot resulted from cold, wetness, and secondary infection from the soil. Trench foot was prevented by wearing waterproof boots and clean socks, and rubbing the skin with whale oil. If the disease was unchecked and the foot not cared for, the dead tissue could become gangrenous. About 5000 cases were reported in the CANADIAN EXPEDITIONARY FORCE during WORLD WAR I.

Trent affair. The *Trent* was a British packet boat intercepted and boarded by the Union Navy on 8 November 1861. During the boarding two Confederate agents were discovered and taken into custody. This triggered a serious diplomatic incident between the Union and Britain which threatened to erupt into war. The men were returned to British custody without an apology 26 December.

Triangle Run. Informal term used by seamen during WORLD WAR II to describe the main area of operations of the ROYAL CANADIAN NAVY's WESTERN LOCAL ESCORT FORCE up to September, 1942. Navy veteran and newspaperman James B. Lamb popularized the Triangle Run in his book of the same name published in 1986.

Tribal class destroyer. The Royal Navy developed this destroyer type during the 1930s in response to the building of large 'super' destroyers by other naval powers. These ships were much larger than previous British destroyer types and carried twice the armament. Tribals in service with the ROYAL CANADIAN NAVY during WORLD WAR II had an average displacement of 2000 tonnes, carried six 4.7-inch guns in three double turrets as main armament and were also equipped with two 4-inch anti-aircraft guns, four 2-pounder POM POMs, and six 20-mm guns as well as torpedos. They had a top speed of 36 knots and carried 14 officers and 245 men. The RCN obtained its four wartime Tribals —*ATHABASKAN, HAIDA, HURONS*, and *IROQUOIS* — from British shipyards, ordering them in the early years of the war as a prelude to building a big-ship fleet. These

destroyers were not intended for anti-submarine escort service but as fleet-type destroyers to participate in gun and torpedo actions against enemy ships or shore installations. The RCN Tribals saw action in a number of areas but were most noted for service in the English Channel from the spring to the fall of 1944 in support of the NORMANDY invasion. *Athabaskan* was lost in one of these actions.

During World War II, four additional Tribals were laid down at Halifax. When completed after the war they were the largest and most sophisticated warships yet to emerge from Canadian shipyards. The four —*Micmac, Nootka, Cayuga* and *Athabaskan*— entered service between September 1945 and January 1948. They and their surviving wartime sister ships formed the backbone of the RCN in the late 1940s and early 1950s until the arrival of the *ST LAURENT* CLASS DESTROYER ESCORTS. Six Tribals saw service in the KOREAN WAR, used primarily for fleet escort duty, minesweeping, and attacks on coastal targets in North Korea. The last of the Tribals — *Athabaskan* — was paid off in April 1966.

Triquet, Paul (1910–1980). On 14 December 1943, following the loss of half his company of the ROYAL 22E REGIMENT, Triquet reorganized and led his men forward at CASA BERARDI in Italy to destroy German tanks and machine guns and capture the town. With fewer than 15 men, he held the town until reinforcements arrived the following day. His VICTORIA CROSS was the first of three won by Canadians in the Italian campaign.

Troupes de la marine. The *troupes de la marine* were especially established by France in 1690 to protect its colonial possessions. Thirty companies were sent to North America that year. Specialists in bush warfare, the *troupes* generally fought alongside Canadian militia and Indian allies. Many of these soldiers settled in Canada after their military service was done. See also TROUPES DE LA TERRE.

Troupes de la terre. Contingents of the regular French army sent to North America were known as the *troupes de la terre*. Unlike the TROUPES DE LA MARINE, these soldiers drilled and fought in the conventional European manner, thus their officers were often at odds with the Canadian militia. During the SEVEN YEARS' WAR, 4000 of these troops were sent to defend New France; about half remained in Canada after the conquest. See also CARIGNAN-SALIÈRES, RÉGIMENT D'ARTOIS and RÉGIMENT DE BOURGOGNE.

Turner, Sir Richard Ernest William (1871–1961). Born in Quebec, Turner volunteered for service in the SOUTH AFRICAN WAR and won the VICTORIA CROSS for distinguishing himself with the ROYAL CANADIAN DRAGOONS at LELIEFONTEIN. In WORLD WAR I, he commanded the 2ND CANADIAN DIVISION from August 1915 to November 1916. He performed poorly in the disastrous battle of ST ELOI and should have been removed from command. The British were reluctant to do so, however, because of their fear of starting a political row with the Canadian government. Thus Corps Commander Sir Edwin ALDERSON, who was already in Sam HUGHES's bad graces, was sacked instead. By then, however, there was ample evidence that Turner was not a competent field commander and after the SOMME fighting, he was removed from command of the division and placed in charge of Canadian troops in Britain. After the war he played a leading role in the GREAT WAR VETERANS' ASSOCIATION. '

Turvey. Humorous novel by Canadian author Earle Birney about a Canadian soldier in World War II. The book was published in 1949.

Tutor trainer. The Canadian CL41 Tutor is the basic jet trainer in use with the Canadian Forces. Employing a side-by-side design, the small aircraft was built between 1960 and 1968. The Canadian forces acquired 190 of the aircraft. A number of these aircraft are also in service with the Malaysian Air Force. The Tutor has become famous as the aircraft of the Canadian Forces aerobatic team, the SNOWBIRDS.

25th Canadian Infantry Brigade Group. Trained primarily at Fort Lewis, Washington, the bulk of the 25th CIBG (originally referred to as the CANADIAN ARMY SPECIAL FORCE) went into the line in KOREA in May 1951 under the command of Brig. J.M. ROCKINGHAM. The unit consisted of three infantry battalions supplied by the ROYAL CANADIAN REGIMENT, the PRINCESS PATRICIA'S CANADIAN LIGHT INFANTRY and the ROYAL 22E REGIMENT plus support units such as the 25th Canadian Field Ambulance and tanks from the LORD STRATHCONA'S HORSE. The first unit of the brigade to arrive in Korea was the 2nd PPCLI which disembarked in Korea in late 1950 and which saw action at KAP'YONG in April, 1951. The brigade joined the 1ST COMMONWEALTH DIVISION in July 1951.

25-pounder gun/howitzer. Described as the workhorse of Comonwealth field artillery units during and after WORLD WAR II, this artillery piece was operated by a six-man crew which could get the gun ready for action in a minute. Manufactured in Canada starting in July 1941, the weapon had a range of up to 12 km. It could be used either as a flat trajectory gun firing armour-piercing shells, or as a high angle howitzer firing high-explosive shells.

27th Canadian Infantry Brigade Group. Raised in the summer of 1951 for NATO service in Germany, the brigade consisted of composite battalions made up of companies raised from Canadian reserve units. It arrived in Europe in the late fall of 1951 and was first stationed in Hanover, then at SOEST, and was attached to the British Army of the Rhine.

Twin Otter aircraft. This twin-engine version of the OTTER, built by DE HAVILLAND, first flew in 1966. A STOL aircraft powered by Pratt and Whitney PT6 turbine engines, it is used by the Canadian Forces for light transport and search and rescue operations.

Typhoon fighter. This single-seat fighter was rushed into service in WORLD WAR II without its pilots being made aware of its eccentric flying characteristics; 135 of the first 142 delivered were involved in accidents. When switched to the ground attack role as a fighter-bomber, however, it proved its worth as a stable gun and rocket platform capable of carrying heavy weapons loads. The ROYAL CANADIAN AIR FORCE operated four squadrons of 'Tiffies' which could carry more than 900 kg of ordnance and fly up to 660 km/h.

U

U-boat. Submarine or submersible vessel; from German *Unterseeboot* (under-sea boat).

Uffen, R.J. (b. 1923). A professional engineer, Uffen served overseas with the ROYAL CANADIAN ARTILLERY in World War II. Following the war he pursued careers in the academic world, in private industry, and with government. He served on the DEFENCE RESEARCH BOARD from 1964–1969 and was its chairman from 1967–1979.

***Uganda*, HMCS.** A former Royal Navy ship, this 8940-tonne light cruiser was transferred to the ROYAL CANADIAN NAVY in October, 1944. *Uganda* had a top speed of 30 knots, carried approximately 700 officers and men, and was armed with nine 6-inch and eight 4-inch guns, as well as torpedos and numerous 20-mm and 40-mm anti-aircraft guns. In April 1945, she joined a Royal Navy task force in the western Pacific, serving principally as an anti-aircraft screening vessel on carrier strikes against Japanese targets in the Ryukyu Archipelago and the island fortress of Truk. Late in July *Uganda* was withdrawn to Esquimalt in compliance with government policy that Canadian units in the Pacific war be manned only by those who had specifically volunteered to serve there. Used as a training ship after the war, she was renamed *Quebec* in 1952 and paid off in 1956.

UKUSA Agreement. The United Kingdom-United States Security Agreement was signed in 1948, the COLD WAR successor to BRUSA. Despite its name Canada, Australia, and New Zealand also signed the agreement which outlined spheres of signals intelligence and cryptographic influence, divided responsibility among the participants, and laid down security standards. Canada had the task of covering the northern Soviet Union and part of Europe. The rules for the exchange of information with the United States are codified in CANUSA.

UNDOF. The United Nations PEACE-KEEPING contingent separating Israel from Syria, stationed on the Golan Heights, has been in place since the end of the 1973 Arab-Israeli war. UNDOF's strength is generally about 1,330 men of whom approximately 230 are usually Canadian. The Canadians are chiefly responsible for signals and communications.

UNEF. UNEF was the first UN PEACE-KEEPING force. It was created in the wake of the SUEZ CRISIS following a suggestion of Secretary of State for External Affairs Lester B. PEARSON. It was originally intended both to replace Anglo-French forces which had occupied the Suez Canal Zone and to stand between the Israelis and Egyptians. The former task was no longer necessary after the Anglo-French withdrawal was completed. Thereafter, until May 1967, UNEF supervised a ceasefire between Egypt and Israel, patrolling areas of the Gaza Strip, Sinai Peninsula and Sharm El Sheikh. Canada's original contribution amounted to some 1000 troops. In May, 1967, UNEF was withdrawn on orders from Egyptian president Gamal Abdul Nasser as part of the sabre-rattling that preceded the Six-Day War of that year.

UNEF II. This UN PEACEKEEPING force was created following the disengagement agreements entered into by Egypt and Israel after the 1973 Arab-Israeli war. It remained in place until December, 1979 when it was replaced by the MULTINATIONAL FORCE AND OBSERVERS. Canada normally contributed some 1150 men to this 7000-man contingent.

Unemployment relief camps. Sponsored by the DEPARTMENT OF NATIONAL DEFENCE and the Department of Labour, the unemployment relief camps established by the federal government and operated between 1932 and 1936 were the brainchild of A.G.L. MCNAUGHTON. Located across the country, they housed a combined total of 170,248 single, unemployed men. The camps were operated by DND with military-like discipline. The men were paid 20 cents a day for work on a variety of public projects and were provided with accommodation, meals, clothing, and medical care. The camps were a favourite target for Communist agitators who succeeded in organizing the On-to-Ottawa trek in the late spring and early summer of 1935. This consisted of hundreds of camp-dwellers trying to reach Ottawa via freight car. They were stopped by the Royal Canadian Mounted Police during the Regina Riot of 1 July 1935 when one Regina policeman was killed. See also ROYAL TWENTY-CENTERS.

UNFICYP. Created by the UN in 1964 to stand between the Turkish and Greek communities on Cyprus, this is one of the longest-standing UN PEACEKEEPING contingents in current operations. Once as large as 6500, it is now approximately 2400 strong. The initial Canadian contribution amounted to some 1100 officers and men but that has been reduced by about half. Their duties have included the maintenance of a convoy system and patrolling the Greek-Turkish demarcation line at Nicosia. See PEACE-KEEPING.

UNGOMAP. The United Nations Good Offices Mission in Afghanistan and Pakistan was established for a brief time in 1988 to oversee the withdrawal of Soviet troops from Afghanistan. Canada contributed a small contingent. See PEACEKEEPING.

Unification. There had been a number of efforts to rationalize administrative personnel and functions in the Canadian armed forces dating back to the early 1920s but until the advent of minister of National Defence Paul HELLYER in 1963, no one had seriously considered melding Canada's three services into one. That notion was undoubtedly advanced on the government's agenda by the GLASSCO COMMISSION report of 1963. The commission had been charged with examining waste and duplication in the public service. It claimed that the forces cost too much to administer and pointed to a number of duplicated fuctions as evidence.

The Glassco Report was followed by the WHITE PAPER 1964 which largely reflected Hellyer's own views about the desirablity of eliminating waste and duplication in the services. The process began with the integration of defence headquarters under a single

CHIEF OF THE DEFENCE STAFF replacing the three service chiefs. This step was followed in June 1965 by the creation of six commands, including MARITIME COMMAND, and MOBILE COMMAND to replace separate army, navy and air force functional command structures. Eventually the CANADIAN FORCES REORGANIZATION ACT was adopted in 1968 which created one armed force officially known as the Canadian Forces (not the Canadian Armed Forces, as is commonly held). In the process a number of high-ranking officers resigned in protest, ostensibly over the loss of the distinctiveness of their service. Opposition seemed to be most vigorous among senior naval officers. The first Chief of the Defence Staff after full unification was J.-V. ALLARD.
Reading: J.L. Granatstein, *Canada: 1957–1967* (Toronto, 1986)

UNIFIL. The United Nations Interim Force in Lebanon was created in 1978 to patrol those areas of southern Lebanon vacated by Israeli troops which had invaded the area earlier that year. UNIFIL is still in operation although Canadian participation in the force ended after only eight months. At its peak, that participation amounted to some 120 men out of a force of approximately 7000. See PEACEKEEPING.

UNIIMOG. Canada provided 15 observers and a 525-man signals and support unit to the United Nations Iran-Iraq Military Observer Group in August 1988. The Canadians worked with two headquarters, one in Tehran and one in Baghdad, to observe the ceasefire which followed the Iran-Iraq war and to set up a signals network. Most Canadian personnel withdrew in December 1988. See PEACEKEEPING.

Union government. On 12 October 1917 the Union government — the only coalition government since Confederation — was sworn in. It was led by Conservative Robert BORDEN and was formed expressly to fight the 1917 federal election, due 17 December. The Cabinet initially included nine Liberals and 15 Conservatives, with one nominal labour representative added in 1918.

The Union government was formed primarily to bring CONSCRIPTION to Canada. On a visit to Britain the previous March and April, Borden had decided to introduce the measure. He tried to convince Liberal leader Sir Wilfrid LAURIER to support him but Laurier demurred, whereupon Borden opened discussions with a number of leading Liberal politicians in English-speaking Canada. He was able to attract some of these leading lights to his cause because they too supported conscription. For other Liberals, however, it was Borden's promise of progressive reform that was most appealing. Laurier was economically and socially a conservative and many western Canadian Liberals believed he was out of step with the times.

As negotiations between Borden and the Liberals proceeded, the Tories introduced conscription with the MILITARY SERVICE ACT (29 August 1917) and prepared for the forthcoming election by passing the MILITARY VOTERS ACT and the WARTIME ELECTIONS ACT. The first conscripts were called for medicals on 13 October, the day the Union government took office.

On 17 December, the Union government won 153 seats to the Liberals' 82. The Unionists took only three seats in Quebec and the country was badly divided. The coalition introduced many reforms in the coming year such as civil service reform, temperance, and universal suffrage, but the coalition fell apart when the war ended. Borden retired 10 July 1920 and was succeeded by Arthur Meighen who was badly defeated in the federal election of 6 December 1921, taking 50 seats to 66 for the new Progressive Party and 117 for the Liberals.
Reading: J. English, *The Decline of Politics* (Toronto, 1977)

UNIPOM. The United Nations India-Pakistan Observer Mission was established by the UN in the fall of 1965 and, for a short time, Canada contributed just over half of its 200-man contingent. See PEACEKEEPING.

University Naval Training Divisions. Formed in 1940, the UNTD was designed to operate with the ROYAL CANADIAN NAVAL VOLUNTEER RESERVE to provide basic training for university student cadets intending to hold commissions in the ROYAL CANADIAN NAVY. Students were given basic training on land and then advanced training at sea. The program was continued after the war.

UNMOGIP. The United Nations Military Observer Group India-Pakistan was established by the UN following the Indo-Pakistani violence which broke out during the partition of India and the emergence of India and Pakistan to independence in the 1947–1949 period. The force was specifically authorized to report on the activities in Kashmir, an area claimed by both countries. At its peak Canada contributed some 27 members to this force of about 100. See PEACEKEEPING.

UNOC. A total of 19,000 officers and men was sent to the Congo under UN auspices in July 1960 as the Organisation des Nations Unies au Congo. The force's mandate was to ensure an orderly transition of the former Belgian colony to independence and help the Congolese fight secessionists in mineral-rich Katanga province who were sponsored by Belgian mining companies. Canada contributed some 200 signals and communications specialists to UNOC. In 1964 after a number of incidents in which Canadians came close to being killed or wounded due to the chaos in the region, UNOC withdrew its forces. See PEACEKEEPING.

UNOGIL. The United Nations Observer Group in Lebanon was established in June 1958 to check fears of infiltration from neighbouring Arab states. It patrolled border-area roads, staffed observation posts, and maintained a reserve emergency force. A total of 77 Canadians, including 10 officers, worked with the force of close to 600 men between June and December 1958. See PEACEKEEPING.

UNSF(WI). The United Nations Security Forces (West Irian) was sent by the UN to temporarily administer the former Dutch colony of West Irian from October 1962 to May 1963. A total of 13 RCAF officers and ground crew flew and maintained a shuttle service between Biak and Fak Fak using two OTTER aircraft. See PEACEKEEPING.

UNTAG. The United Nations Transition Assistance Group supervised the withdrawal of South African troops from Namibia in 1989–90. The Canadian contribution to the group included 100 Royal Canadian Mounted Police officers, to help train local police, as well as military observers and infantry whose work included guarding polling stations during the Namibian election in November 1989. See PEACEKEEPING.

UNTSO. The United Nations Truce Supervisory Organization in Palestine was established in 1948 to police the UN-sponsored ceasefires that ended the Israeli War of Independence. Canadians joined the force when it was enlarged in 1954 following fighting along the Israel/Jordan border. One Cana-

dian was killed in 1957 while serving with UNTSO. See PEACEKEEPING.

UNYOM. The United Nations Yemen Observer Mission was authorized by the UN in June, 1963 to supervise a ceasefire in Yemen between forces backed by Saudi Arabia and those supported by Egypt. Canada sent military observers, an air patrol unit, aircraft, and five army officers to work with the force from June 1963 to September 1964. See PEACEKEEPING.

V

Vail, William Berrian (1823–1904). Vail was a Nova Scotia shipper who opposed Confederation. He ran in the 1867 federal election and was elected to the House of Commons. He entered the Cabinet as minister of Militia and Defence in September 1874 and served until January 1878. His most notable achievement was his contribution to the establishment of ROYAL MILITARY COLLEGE.

Valcartier Camp. Located near Quebec City, Valcartier was built from scratch in record time at the start of WORLD WAR I. The first group of volunteers for what later became the CANADIAN EXPEDITIONARY FORCE arrived at Valcartier soon after Britain's declaration of war on Germany in August 1914. In less than a month the new recruits had constructed buildings and rifle ranges to accommodate 30,000 trainees. The first Canadian contingent was sent to Britain in October, 1914. Subsequently, Valcartier was used as the final collection point for most other Canadian units sent overseas. The camp was staffed by officers of the PERMANENT FORCE. Valcartier is still a Canadian Forces Base.

Vampire fighter. The DE HAVILLAND Vampire was the RCAF's first operational fighter jet. Designed and built in Britain, the Vampire was acquired in January 1948

and remained in RCAF service for about ten years. Low and slow, the Vampire had a top speed of 855 km/h and a service ceiling of 13 km. It was used in the air defence role until replaced by the CF-100.

Van Doos. See ROYAL 22E REGIMENT.

Vanier, Georges-Phileas (1888–1967). Educated at Université Laval, Vanier joined the ROYAL 22E REGIMENT in 1915. He won both the MILITARY CROSS and DISTINGUISHED SERVICE ORDER while serving in France and also lost his leg. He later joined the Department of External Affairs, serving during World War II as Canadian minister to the exiled French government in London. He was appointed Governor-General of Canada in 1959, a position he held until his death.

Varley, Frederick Horsman (1881–1969). Born in the U.K., Varley studied art before emigrating to Canada in 1912. In 1918 he was commissioned as a war artist. He subsequently painted scenes of Canadian troops in England and made two trips to the front in France. After the war he became a founding member of the Group of Seven.

Vaudreuil, Philippe de Rigaud de, Marquis de (c. 1643–1725). Vaudreuil served with the French Army in Flanders before coming to Canada in 1687 as commander of

French troops. He fought the Iroquois and was appointed governor of New France in 1703. His primary concern as governor was the military security of the approaches to New France from the south and the assertion of French control over the western fur trade.

V-E Day. V-E or Victory in Europe Day was celebrated in Canada, the U.S. and the U.K. on 8 May 1945 following the unconditional surrender on 7 May of the Nazi government of Germany headed by Admiral Doenitz. The day was marked by massive celebration. C.P. STACEY observed that the celebrations were 'inversely proportional to the physical distance of celebrants from the fighting'. See also HALIFAX RIOTS.

V-E Day riots. See HALIFAX RIOTS.

Vedette aircraft. Canadian Vickers designed and built the Vedette, a single-engine flying boat, at Montreal in the 1920s. It was specifically intended for service with the Royal Canadian Air Force and was used extensively for the type of civil operations which the RCAF engaged in extensively in the inter-war period.

Velvet Glove missile. An air-to-air missile developed at the CANADIAN ARMAMENT AND RESEARCH DEVELOPMENT ESTABLISHMENT, Velvet Glove was a solid-fuel weapon with a range of 4500 m. It was originally intended to arm the CF100 interceptor. Some 300 missiles were produced before production was ended in 1954 because the missile was judged incapable of hitting the latest and fastest Soviet bombers.

Verchères, Marie-Madeleine Jarret de (1678–1747). The daughter of an officer, Verchères defended her family's home against an Iroquois attack in 1692. Verchères later exaggerated her exploits in order to seek personal favour from the government of France.

Veteran. The term used during and after WORLD WAR II to designate a person who had completed military service. It replaced RETURNED SOLDIER, which had been in use during and after WORLD WAR I.

Veterans' Affairs, Department of. A separate ministry of the Canadian government, the department was created in 1944 to oversee a number of veterans' benefit programs designed to rehabilitate and re-establish Canadian VETERANS of WORLD WAR II. Ian A. MACKENZIE was the first minister of the department. The department's mandate once included the provision of medical care to veterans but it has since dropped that task. It is now largely concerned with ensuring the smooth operation of Canada's remaining veterans' financial assistance programs.

Veterans' Charter. Drafted in 1944 by Léo LAFLÈCHE, Ian MACKENZIE and others, the Charter advocated a range of 'rights' for Canadian VETERANS including access to paid education and training, grants to start businesses, the right to return to former jobs with full seniority and pension rights, land grants, and rehabilitation credits for the purchase of household items.

Veterans' hospitals. The first veterans' hospitals in Canada were built towards the end of WORLD WAR I by the Military Hospitals Commission, created in 1915. The Commission began construction of veterans' hospitals in 1917 because there were too many RETURNED SOLDIERS to place in civilian homes or hospitals, which had been the practice up to that time. By early 1920 some 44 hospitals had been constructed or renovated for use by veterans by the commission. Naturally enough the number of beds used declined as time passed but the outbreak of WORLD WAR II started the cycle over again. This time the hospitals came under the jurisdiction of the DEPARTMENT OF VETERANS' AFFAIRS. In 1946 more than 12,100 beds were in use in DVA hospitals but that number also started to decline soon after the war. In 1963 the Department began to transfer hospitals under its jurisdiction to civilian administration, a process that took more than a decade and a half to complete.

Veterans' Land Act. A 1942 update of the SOLDIER SETTLEMENT ACT of the post-WORLD WAR I era, the Veterans' Land Act aimed to avoid the pitfalls of its post-World War I predecessor by structuring loans for land, livestock, and equipment for Canadian veterans in such a way as to avoid imposing a heavy debt load on them. About 140,000 servicemen used the program before it was discontinued in 1977.

Veterans' Rehabilitation Act. Passed in 1945, the Act was one of the cornerstones of the government's veterans' benefit program. It provided for training and rehabilitation grants for a period of 18 months after discharge from the service, a deadline later extended. The Act was later amended to provide for grants for veterans and advances to the universities the veterans were attending for both undergraduate and graduate training. Veterans had to apply for such aid by 30 June 1948.

Vickers machine gun. Designed by American Hiram Maxim, the gun was manufactured in England by Vickers and was thus known as the Vickers .303. The infantry version fired 250 rounds per minute of .303-calibre ammunition. It was belt-fed and water-cooled. An aerial version was also produced which was mounted both on fighters and bombers.

Victoria Cross. For over a century the Commonwealth's foremost decoration for exceptional bravery in the enemy's presence; the Victoria Cross—for all ranks and services —was established by Queen Victoria in 1856. A total of 93 Canadians won the award, which was discontinued in Canada in 1972. See Appendix IV.

Victory Aircraft Ltd. A Crown corporation established and administered during WORLD WAR II by the DEPARTMENT OF MUNITIONS AND SUPPLY, Victory Aircraft succeeded the National Steel Car Company and took over the final stages of production of a number of ANSON and WESTLAND LYSANDER aircraft. Its chief activity at its plant at Malton, Ontario was the production of LANCASTER bombers. The corporation also built a civilian version of the Lancaster known as the Lancastrian for use by Trans-Canada Airlines. A.V. ROE bought the Victory Aircraft plant after the war.

Victory Bonds. During WORLD WAR I, the government of Canada was forced to issue savings bonds, which it called Victory Bonds, to finance the war effort. Initially it hoped to raise $150 million from Canadians, but by 1917 it had sold approximately $500 million worth of bonds. Victory Bonds were also sold during WORLD WAR II. After the war Victory Bonds were exchanged for Canada Savings Bonds, a means of financing the national debt. See also VICTORY LOANS.

Victory Loans. The federal government floated victory loans during both world wars. The 1917 Victory Loan raised $400 million from 800,000 subscribers and was followed by another in 1918 that raised $660 million from a million Canadians. Institutional investors and the public took up these loans by purchasing VICTORY BONDS, WAR SAVINGS STAMPS and War Savings Certificates. Using similar techniques and devices, the government raised $6 billion in World War II.

Vietnam War. Although Canada was not directly involved in the Vietnam War, it was connected to that conflict in numerous ways. For example, Canada provided intelligence information to the United States (information gleaned by Canadian representatives on the INTERNATIONAL CONTROL COMMISSION), allowed Canadian companies to supply weapons and conduct weapons research directly used in the war, and, for a time, supported U.S. air attacks on North Vietnam. Canada also contributed $29 million in aid to South Vietnam while Canadian industry sold some $12.5 billion in ammunition, aircraft parts, napalm, and other war materials to South Vietnam and the U.S. It is estimated that up to 10,000 Canadians fought with U.S. forces in Vietnam, although no reliable figures on such participation are available. Approximately 32,000 U.S. draft dodgers and deserters entered Canada during the war. Canada was directly involved in efforts to mediate the Vietnam conflict, first, after the defeat of the French in the Indo-China War as a member of the International Control Commission (1954), and later, following the negotiation of a ceasefire between the U.S. and South Vietnam on one side and North Vietnam and the Viet Cong on the other, as a member of the INTERNATIONAL COMMISSION FOR CONTROL AND SUPERVISION (1975).

Vimy Memorial. Designed by Walter Seymour Allward, the monument stands atop VIMY RIDGE to commemorate the 3598 Canadians who died there and all who fell during WORLD WAR I. The land was donated to Canada by France. More than 10,000 veterans and their families attended the unveiling of the monument by King Edward VIII in 1936. In April 1992 only a handful of Vimy veterans were left to return to the memorial on the occasion of the 75th anniversary of the battle.

Vimy Ridge. Located in northeastern France on the road from Lens to Arras, Vimy Ridge was the site of one of the epic Canadian battles of WORLD WAR I. The ridge had been held by the Germans from the fall of 1914; forming a salient in the Allied lines, it dominated the countryside for miles around, enabling the Germans to keep watch over a large area of countryside. Several times between 1914 and 1917 French colonial troops and British troops had assaulted the ridge; each time they had been turned back with heavy casualties.

In early 1917, after the end of the SOMME battles, the CANADIAN CORPS was sent to the Vimy sector following a period of rest and recuperation. There, under the leadership of Corps Commander Lt-Gen. Julian BYNG, it prepared for an assault on the ridge as part of a general offensive of the British 1st Army. All four Canadian divisions were to be employed in the assault, and a British division was to be held in reserve.

Byng and the Canadians elected to fight a classic set-piece battle, with heavy reliance on the artillery, and extensive preparations were made. German guns were pinpointed using sound locators and by other methods and were targeted for counter-battery fire. Tunnels were dug to enable the troops to be deployed as far forward as possible before the attack without being observed. Rail lines were laid to expedite the shipment forward of thousands of artillery shells and other needed equipment. A model of the ridge was constructed and detailed maps were drawn to ensure that the troops were well schooled as to their objectives.

On 9 April 1917, Easter Monday, the battle opened with a massive creeping barrage. The Canadian counter-battery work was especially effective in silencing German guns. The four divisions then advanced up the hill, and troops in the 1st, 2nd, and 3rd Divisions, arranged from south to north, made good progress. To the north, however, the 4th Division ran into stiff German resistance at Hill 145 and suffered many casualties. Despite the ordeal of the 4th Division, the Canadians succeeded in capturing and holding the greater part of the ridge on the first day of the assault. By the time the entire battle was over and the whole ridge, including a position known as the PIMPLE was secured, the Canadian Corps lost 3598 killed and 7004 wounded. This was considered Canada's greatest military victory of World War I.
Reading: P. Berton, *Vimy* (Toronto, 1986); K. Macksey, *Vimy Ridge 1914–1918* (New York, 1972)

Vincent, John (1764–1848). Vincent came to Canada in 1802 to command the garrisons of British regulars at York and Fort George. He had had rather limited combat experience when the WAR OF 1812 began. When the Americans attacked FORT GEORGE in May 1813, he ordered the garrison evacuated and withdrew to Burlington Heights. He then commanded his troops in the Battle of STONEY CREEK. After the British defeat at MORAVIANTOWN General Vincent was transferred to Kingston.

Visiting Forces (British Commonwealth) Act. This British legislation passed in 1933 gave the Canadian government and its military staff control of discipline, training, and the internal administration of Canadian Forces stationed in England.

V-J Day. Following the second atomic bombing of Japan by the United States on 9 August 1945 the Japanese government announced its acceptance of Allied demands for unconditional surrender. V-J Day was celebrated the following day although the formal surrender documents were not signed until 2 September.

Vokes, Christopher (1904–1985). Born in Ireland, Vokes attended ROYAL MILITARY COLLEGE beginning in 1921 and stayed in the military after graduation. During World War II he rose rapidly through army ranks to command the 2nd Canadian Infantry Brigade in SICILY and the 1ST CANADIAN INFANTRY DIVISION in ITALY from November 1943 to August 1944. He was then transferred to Europe to command the 4TH CANADIAN ARMOURED DIVISION. He stayed in Europe after the war as commander of the short-lived CANADIAN ARMY OCCUPATION FORCE. Vokes was one of the few high-ranking Canadian officers to publish his memoirs: *My Story* (Ottawa, 1985).

Voltigeurs de Quebec. Founded in 1812, the Voltigeurs were recruited in Lower Canada to fight the Americans. They took part in battles at CHATEAUGUAY and CRYSLER'S FARM. In 1862 a MILITIA unit was established in Quebec and took this name, thus perpetuating the earlier unit. It had a variety of designations between 1862 and 1914, and sent men to fight in WORLD WAR I with the 57th battalion of the CANADIAN EXPEDITIONARY FORCE. The Voltigeurs also served with the Canadian Active Service Force during WORLD WAR II.

Voluntary Militia. Recruited in the 1850s to garrison Halifax, Kingston, and Quebec as British regulars withdrew, the force numbered 10,000 men in 1856 and was charged with the main responsibility of guarding Britain's abandoned military posts.

Voodoo. See CF101 AIRCRAFT.

Walcheren. Island in the SCHELDT Estuary which was assaulted by troops of 2ND CANADIAN INFANTRY DIVISION of FIRST CANADIAN ARMY in the last phases of the Scheldt campaign of October and November 1944. Walcheren dominated the north bank of the East Scheldt, the water route to the Port of Antwerp. The island was attached to South BEVELAND by a narrow causeway at its eastern tip. Most of the island lay below sea level and the sea was kept at bay by a dyke encircling the island. On the western tip lay the small port town of Westkapelle; on the southern shore was Flushing.

The task of capturing Walcheren fell to II CANADIAN CORPS commanded by G.G. SIMONDS. Before he mounted his assault he successfully urged his superiors to bomb the dikes of Walcheren so as to bottle the German defenders up in the few locations above sea level and thus deprive them of movement. Then, after the BRESKENS POCKET and South Beveland had been secured, his soldiers turned their attention to the island itself. Beginning on 31 October troops of the 5th Canadian Infantry Brigade, led by the Calgary Highlanders, attempted an assault over the South Beveland-Walcheren causeway. Despite heavy casualties they were able to get over the causeway, but they could not advance in the face of stiff resistance and were withdrawn. On 1 November, however, the British troops of No. 4 Commando assaulted Flushing while their counterparts of the 4th Special Service Brigade attacked Westkapelle. Once ashore it took them seven more days to advance across the flooded polder land and along the dykes to dislodge the German defenders. Walcheren was secured by 8 November.

Reading: J.L. Moulton, *Battle for Antwerp* (New York, 1978)

Walford, A. Ernest (1896–1990). A chartered accountant, Walford served with the ROYAL CANADIAN ARTILLERY during World War I and with the 1ST CANADIAN INFANTRY DIVISION during World War II before being appointed Deputy Adjutant and Quartermaster-General of FIRST CANADIAN ARMY. He became Adjutant General in 1944 and returned to civilian life in 1946.

Walsh, G. (b. 1909). Educated at ROYAL MILITARY COLLEGE, Walsh was commissioned in the ROYAL CANADIAN ENGINEERS in 1930. He proceeded overseas in May 1940 and served with the 1ST CANADIAN INFANTRY DIVISION and 4TH CANADIAN ARMOURED DIVISION as well as II CANADIAN CORPS. He then returned to Canada to organize the Northwest Highway System. Among other tasks given to him in the post-war period was GOC 27TH CANADIAN INFANTRY BRIGADE GROUP. In 1961 he was named CHIEF OF THE GENERAL STAFF, a post he held until UNIFICATION when he was named Deputy Chief of the Defence Staff.

Wapiti bomber. The RCAF acquired six British-built Westland Wapiti aircraft in the mid-1930s and had 22 when World War II began. The Wapiti was a single-engine bomber used by the Eastern Air Command for both training and reconnaissance. Its obsolescence and poor flying characteristics made it unsuitable for operations and it was quickly withdrawn from service.

War Amputees of Canada. Organization formed in 1921 by RETURNED SOLDIERS who had lost limbs as a result of war service. Initially it aimed to lobby government for employment for its members but it later broadened its mandate to produce a variety of products manufactured by amputees and sold to the public to raise money for appropriate causes.

War Book. A war book is a manual of procedure, compiled from the contributions of appropriate federal government departments, intended to guide government operations during wartime. Usually war books are to be resorted to when the international situation indicates that a conflict is looming. Several departments of the Canadian government began to move to a war footing, following procedures laid out in the war book, as early as the end of July 1939.

War Brides. Label applied to foreign women, usually British, who married Canadian servicemen overseas in both world wars and who subsequently came to Canada to join their husbands. By 1946 nearly 48,000 women, most from the U.K., had accepted the Canadian government's offer of free rail and sea passage to come to Canada.

War Correspondents. The first modern war correspondents were sent by British newspapers to cover the Crimean War. The first Canadian war correspondent on record was Kathleen 'Kit' Blake Coleman who covered the Spanish-American War for the Toronto *Mail and Empire*. She was later the President of the Canadian Women's Press Club. The Toronto *Globe* sent a correspondent to the SOUTH AFRICAN WAR who wrote glowing reports of the battles but who privately criticized the waste, inefficiency, and incompetence of the British military there.

In WORLD WAR I information from the front was closely controlled by all the Allies, Canada included. Newspapers were severely restricted in the information they could gather or publish. Sam HUGHES appointed newspaper magnate Max AITKEN (Lord Beaverbrook) Canada's official 'eye-witness', to gather war news and disseminate it. In addition to Aitken, the Canadian Press usually had at least one reporter in the field.

In contrast to World War I, war reporting in WORLD WAR II was both freer and more widespread. Broadcast and print correspondents accompanied the troops virtually everywhere. Most of the censorship was really self-censorship, exercised by the reporters or by their editors as part of the win-the-war effort. They did not see themselves as neutral. The majority of the reporters worked for the print media but a small number pioneered the techniques of making recordings from the front which were later re-broadcast in Canada by the CBC. Some of the more famous of Canada's World War II war correspondents were Gregory CLARK, who had served with the CANADIAN MOUNTED RIFLES in World War I (receiving the MILITARY CROSS), Ralph Allen, who had served with the ROYAL CANADIAN ARTILLERY, and Matthew HALTON, who had reported for the CBC on the Spanish Civil War and the Russo-Finnish War.

An unglamorous war in a faraway place, KOREA never received the coverage in the Canadian media that World War II did. Among those who did cover this war were Bill Boss for the Canadian Press, René Lévesque for the CBC, Pierre Berton for *Maclean's Magazine*, and Peter Inglis for *Saturday Night* magazine. See also Charles LYNCH, Ross MUNRO, Marcel OUIMET, A.E. POWLEY, Wallace REYBURN, and Peter STURSBERG.

War Industry, World War I. Canada's introduction to war industry began shortly after the outbreak of WORLD WAR I with the creation of the SHELL COMMITTEE. An arm of the British Ministry of Munitions, the Committee was responsible for placing contracts for artillery shells with Canadian manufacturers. Few Canadian companies had any experience with this type of production. The only full-time production facilities in Canada in August 1914 were those at the Quebec arsenal (CANADIAN ARSENALS LTD) which could only turn out a handful of shells a day. Hundreds of thousands were needed, however, and the Committee gave contracts to a wide variety of metal-working establishments, machine shops, structural iron companies, and even railway repair shops. In 1915 the Shell Committee was disbanded due to scandal. It was replaced shortly after by the IMPERIAL MUNITIONS BOARD headed by pork packing magnate Sir Joseph FLAVELLE. Under Flavelle's direction, war production grew in volume and scope. National factories — owned by the IMB — were established to produce what private industry would or could not. By war's end Canada was manufacturing everything from aircraft to ships to shells in support of the war effort. This expansion of war production had a decided impact on the workforce. Many women worked temporarily in war plants while trade union membership doubled across the country. Equally important was the boost war manufacturing gave to Canadian managerial and manufacturing techniques and expertise.

Reading: D. Carnegie, *The History of Munition Supply in Canada, 1914–1918* (London, 1925); M. Bliss, *A Canadian Millionaire* (Toronto, 1978)

War Industry, World War II. During WORLD WAR II Canada became deeply involved in the production of munitions and other war-related goods, far more even than in World War I. C.D. HOWE, minister of Munitions and Supply, oversaw the war production effort. Private industry was harnessed to the task and a large number of Crown corporations were also created to do what private industry could or would not. Examples of the latter would include the PARK STEAMSHIP COMPANY, which built merchant ships, and VICTORY AIRCRAFT, which produced the LANCASTER bomber. Canadian munitions production received a major boost from the HYDE PARK DECLARATION, an agreement reached by U.S. President Franklin D. Roosevelt and Prime Minister William Lyon Mackenzie KING in April, 1941 which committed the U.S. to buy Canadian products and raw materials during the war, thus easing a Canadian shortage of U.S. dollars, and allowed Canadian-built war materials to be purchased by Britain under the U.S.-Britain Lend-Lease agreement. At its peak Canadian war industry employed some 1.2 million people and produced approximately $8.7 billion in products from bullets to bombers.

Reading: J. de N. Kennedy, *History of the*

Department of Munitions and Supply (Ottawa, 1950); R. Bothwell and W. Kilbourn, *C.D. Howe* (Toronto, 1979)

War Measures Act. Federal legislation passed in August 1914 which provided the government with sweeping emergency powers including the suspension of *habeas corpus* during war, invasion, or insurrection. The Act also enabled the government, during the period of emergency, to legislate in areas that would normally be considered provincial jurisdiction. It was used during both world wars and during the OCTOBER CRISIS 1970.

War Memorials. Although a few memorials to Canada's war dead were erected after the WAR OF 1812, the NORTHWEST REBELLION of 1885, and the SOUTH AFRICAN WAR, most of Canada's war memorials were built after WORLD WAR I. This was natural given that Canada's 60,000 war dead in 1914–18 dwarfed the casualty lists of earlier conflicts. The best known of Canadian war memorials are the VIMY MEMORIAL, on VIMY RIDGE in France, and the cenotaph, in Ottawa, which is the national war memorial for the Canadian war dead of World Wars I and II, and the KOREAN WAR.

War Novels. Although some fiction was written by and about Canadian soldiers and battles before 1914, WORLD WAR I saw the effective birth of Canadian war fiction. Over 750 novels were written about this war between 1920 and 1940 alone, and books continued to appear years after the event. At first the writing was heroic, presenting stereotyped romanticized pictures of the war in such books as S. Dancey, *The Faith of a Belgian: A Romance of the Great War* (1916), or Bertrand Sinclair's *Burned Bridges* (1919). Even horrifying disaster received this treatment, as in F. McKelvey Bell, *A Romance of the Halifax Disaster* (1918). One novel, *The Magpie* by Douglas Durkin (1923), told of RETURNED SOLDIERS, labour radicals, and others in the period of the Winnipeg General Strike.

Like other national war fiction, Canadian writing was affected by the anti-war themes explored so effectively in Remarque's *All Quiet on the Western Front*. One of the best Canadian novels in this vein was Charles Harrison's *Generals Die in Bed* (1930), followed by Peregrine Ackland's *All Else is Folly* (1933).

World War I continued to be a significant theme in Canadian literature even after the outbreak of WORLD WAR II. Hugh MacLennan's *Barometer Rising* (1941) was set against the backdrop of the HALIFAX EXPLOSION while Timothy Findley's *The Wars* (1977), winner of a Governor-General's Award for fiction, told the graphic story of a Canadian officer in the war and was later made into a film. Donald Jack's novels *THREE CHEERS FOR ME* (1973) and *That's Me in the Middle* were also set in World War I.

Curiously, WORLD WAR II has not received the same attention from Canadian fiction writers. One writer who used the war as a major theme was Ralph Allen who was both war correspondent and gunner with the ROYAL CANADIAN ARTILLERY during World War II. Allen wrote *Homemade Banners* (1946) and *The High White Forest* (1964). Other writers of Canadian World War II literature include Douglas LePan, *The Net and the Sword* (1953) and *The Deserter* (1964); Hugh Garner *Storm Below* (1949); Earle Birney, *TURVEY* (1949); Colin McDougall, *EXECUTION* (1958), and Gabrielle Roy, *Bonheur d'Occasion* [*THE TIN FLUTE*] (1945). *THE PRIVATE WAR OF JACKET COATES* by H.F. Woods (1966) is the only novel about Canadians in KOREA.

War of 1812. The War of 1812 was preceded by growing tension between Britain and the United States arising out of the Napoleonic Wars. In enforcing an embargo on all trade to the Europrean continent, for example, Royal Navy vessels routinely stopped American ships. Sometimes crew members of those U.S. ships were accused of desertion from the Royal Navy and were forcibly carried off. In the U.S. these hostile British acts were deeply resented. Added to this was the demand of 'warhawks' from western and southwestern states of the U.S. who wanted to expand the U.S. by annexing Canada.

Over the bitter opposition of New England representatives who feared the power of the Royal Navy, Congress voted 18 June 1812 to declare war on Britain. The U.S. military prepared to attack Canada; the British admninistrator of Upper Canada, Major-General Isaac BROCK laid plans for defence.

Although badly outnumbered, the British regulars and colonial militia succeeded in their defence of Upper and Lower Canada. This was partly due to (1) their tactic of continual attack at American weak points, keeping the enemy off balance in his own territory; (2) the timidity and hesitancy both of large numbers of U.S. soldiers and of their leaders; (3) the valuable aid rendered Britain by Indian allies such as TECUMSEH. For most of the war the U.S. effort was hindered by deep national divisions. Some New England militiamen, for example, refused to cross the border to fight in British territory. And while some U.S. generals showed both courage and daring, others were hesitant and incompetent as field commanders.

In Canada the war was essentially fought on five fronts: at MICHILIMACKINAC; along the western shores of Lake Erie; on the NIAGARA FRONTIER; along the St Lawrence River between Kingston and Cornwall; and south of Montreal. Michilimackinac, seized by the British in mid-July 1812 to prevent U.S. passage through its strategic straits, was held for the duration of the war. On the western end of Lake Erie, battles were fought at DETROIT, Fort Amherstburg, Put-in-Bay, Fort Meigs, Frenchtown and MORAVIANTOWN for control of Detroit and the water passage from Lake Huron to Lake Erie. Through aggressive action and with the help of Tecumseh, the British had the advantage in 1812, capturing and holding Detroit, but they lost that advantage the following year after a naval battle at Put-in-Bay where U.S. forces under Commodore Perry took effective control of the lake, forcing the British to withdraw from Detroit. It was during that withdrawal that the battle of MORAVIANTOWN was fought, an American victory, but one they could not follow up.

On the Niagara Frontier, the U.S. invaders were first stopped at QUEENSTON HEIGHTS on 13 October 1812 in a battle in which Brock was killed. That held them for the remainder of the year. In 1813, however, they fared somewhat better. First, they captured and burned YORK in May; then they took FORT GEORGE at the mouth of the Niagara River, holding it until December and using it as a base for operations in the region. They were unsuccessful in pinning down and defeating the British, however, and abandoned the fort in December.

The battles along the St Lawrence and

south of Montreal in the fall of 1813 resulted from an American effort to mount a two-pronged operation aimed at capturing Montreal in preparation for an eventual assault on Quebec City from upriver. One of these prongs consisted of a combined land-sea attack down the St Lawrence, mounted from SACKETS HARBOR, which ended with a U.S. defeat at CRYSLER'S FARM. The other was mounted up the traditional invasion route towards Montreal from the south. It was choked off by a British victory at CHATEAU-GUAY.

The war was also fought on other fronts. British forces occupied much of Maine, captured and burned Washington, and attacked, and were defeated at, New Orleans while a number of important naval engagements took place off the Atlantic coast, on the Great Lakes, and on Lake Champlain. When the war ended with the signing of the TREATY OF GHENT on 24 December 1814, no boundaries were altered and the status quo ante bellum was restored.

The status quo was clearly a moral victory for the British. It was their military leadership, their aggressiveness, their professional troops which had denied the U.S. a victory. The Canadian MILITIA had played a part, but a minor one, in most of the fighting. Nevertheless, the experience of having helped the British hold off a numerically superior foe was to become a major part of Upper Canadian mythology in the decades that followed. It contributed, for example, to the creation of the MILITIA MYTH.

Reading: J.M. Hitsman, *The Incredible War of 1812* (Toronto, 1965); G.F.G. Stanley, *The War of 1812: Land Operations* (Toronto, 1983)

War of the Austrian Succession. Britain and France were already at war over trade when a general European war broke out in 1740 over rival claims to the Austrian throne. Britain and France took opposite sides in the dispute and the war soon spread to their North American colonies. French and Indian war parties raided British settlements on the frontier from Massachusetts to New York, destroying the one at Saratoga. In retaliation a force organized by the governor of Massachusetts seized LOUISBOURG in 1745. The TREATY OF AIX-LA-CHAPELLE, signed in 1748, returned Louisbourg to France.

War of the League of Augsburg. In 1689, Britain, France, and other European states began a nearly decade-long battle, the North American portion of which was known as KING WILLIAM'S WAR. Britain fought France to retain control of Hudson's Bay Company posts and the Newfoundland fishery. Pierre LEMOYNE captured Moose Factory and other HBC posts at the southern end of Hudson Bay in 1686 and defended them against various counter-attacks. YORK FACTORY changed hands several times with LeMoyne wintering there in 1694. He raided ST JOHN'S and neighbouring fishing villages in Newfoundland in 1696 but abandoned them within the year. The Treaty of Ryswick, concluded in 1697, returned Hudson Bay to the British while the French retained Acadia. The peace was short-lived, however, and hostilities resumed in 1702 as QUEEN ANNE'S WAR.

War of the Spanish Succession. See QUEEN ANNE'S WAR.

War Savings Stamps. A form of federal fund-raising to offset the cost of war, war savings stamps were sold during both world wars. During World War II each stamp cost 25 cents. See also VICTORY LOANS.

War Service Grants Act. Passed in 1944, this Act provided grants for VETERANS who had seen active service overseas. It paid $7.50 for each 30 days of service, with an extra 25 cents per day for service outside the western hemisphere. For each six months outside the hemisphere, former servicemen were to be paid a supplement equivalent to seven days' pay. See also RE-ESTABLISHMENT CREDIT; VETERANS' CHARTER; VETERANS' LAND ACT; VETERANS' AFFAIRS, DEPARTMENT OF.

War Service Gratuity. In December 1918 the government announced it would pay single RETURNED SOLDIERS with three or more years service overseas $70 per month ($100 per month for those who were married) for six months after discharge. Home-defence servicemen with one year of experience would be given a straight $70 gratuity.

***Warrior*, HMCS.** Loaned to the ROYAL CANADIAN NAVY by the Royal Navy and commissioned in the RCN in January 1946, *Warrior* was a light fleet carrier. It displaced

13,500 tonnes and was crewed by approximately 1000 officers and men. It had a top speed of 24 knots and carried two small squadrons of aircraft, one of SEAFIRES and one of Fireflys. In 1947 *Warrior* was returned to the RN, to be replaced one year later by *MAGNIFICENT*.

Wars, The. Governor-General's Award-winning novel by Timothy Findley. Published in 1977, the novel told the story of one young Ontario man serving with the CANADIAN EXPEDITIONARY FORCE in WORLD WAR I.

Wartime Information Board. The WIB was a WORLD WAR II federal agency responsible for coordinating and disseminating information on the war to Canadians, especially information that would promote pro-Allied and pro-war sentiment. The WIB was created in 1942 to replace the ineffectual Bureau of Public Information. It reported directly to the Prime Minister. For the duration of the war it produced a variety of publications, conducted secret public opinion polling on war issues, and screened information released to the public on the war. For much of the war it worked in close cooperation with the National Film Board.

Wartime Elections Act. Passed in 1917 to help the victory prospects of Prime Minister R.L. BORDEN's government in the forthcoming federal election, the Act disenfranchised voters who were conscientious objectors and those from 'enemy alien' countries who had immigrated to Canada after 31 March 1902 and who did not have immediate family serving with the CANADIAN EXPEDITIONARY FORCE. At the same time the legislation gave the vote to all women who had husbands, brothers, or sons serving in the Canadian army. The effect was to remove a large number of potential anti-CONSCRIPTION voters from the electorate, while adding a substantial number of pro-conscription voters.

Wartime Prices and Trade Board. Federal agency created in 1939 to monitor the war economy and to regulate all normal trade and commerce. The agency's chief mission was to save the country from the high inflation that had wracked the Canadian economy during and after WORLD WAR I.

The Board had wide-ranging powers to regulate the supply and price of both wholesale and retail products and its influence was felt throughout Canada as a result of its rationing and subsidy programs. Through its management of the economy, the Board kept inflation below 3 per cent per annum during the war — far below the price increases of World War I.

War Veterans' Allowance Act. This 1930 legislation granted a pension supplement to impoverished RETURNED SOLDIERS of WORLD WAR I over 60 (regular pension payments began at age 70) and to those who were unemployed for mental or physical reasons. Single men received $240 and married men received $480 per year.

Wastage. Term used by the British and Canadian military before and during WORLD WAR II to refer to losses of men from military units due to all causes, combat and otherwise. In order to determine how many replacements would be necessary for a unit, it was necessary to estimate the wastage rate for that unit. It was expected that wastage rates would differ according to the nature of the fighting the unit was engaged in. A major cause of the REINFORCEMENT CRISIS was failure to forecast infantry wastage rates for the Canadian army following the D-DAY landings. This was because wastage rate estimates were based on British figures compiled during the fighting in North Africa which was very different from, and produced much lower casualties than, the close-in hedgerow fighting in NORMANDY.

Watson, Sir David (1871–1922). Watson held a variety of command appointments during WORLD WAR I including OC 2nd Battalion and GOC 5th Brigade CEF. As commander of the 4TH CANADIAN DIVISION (1916–19) he led his troops in the capture of REGINA TRENCH during the Battle of the SOMME in November 1916.

Wavy Navy. See ROYAL CANADIAN NAVY VOLUNTEER RESERVE.

Wayne and Shuster. John Wayne and Frank Shuster, both from Toronto, enlisted in the Canadian Army as infantrymen when WORLD WAR II began. They won general acclaim through writing and performing comedy, especially on 'The Army Show', for Canada's forces overseas. After the war they enjoyed tremendous success on radio and television in both Canada and the United States.

WDs, RCAF. See WOMEN'S DIVISION, RCAF.

Wellington bomber. British-designed and built, the Vickers Wellington was a twin-engine bomber employing a special lattice-work airframe designed by famed British aircraft designer Barnes Wallis. The Wellington had a top speed of 376 km/h, was armed with six VICKERS .303-calibre machine guns, and carried 2.5 tonnes of bombs. Many Canadian bombing squadrons used the bomber during WORLD WAR II before converting to the heavier HALIFAX or LANCASTER.

Western Air Command. Formed 1 March 1938 as part of the government's new interest in beefing up the defences of the Pacific Coast, Western Air Command was headquartered in Vancouver and was responsible for all ROYAL CANADIAN AIR FORCE operations west of the Ontario/Manitoba border. After the Japanese attack on Pearl Harbor, the Command was greatly expanded and in June 1942, after the Japanese attack on the Aleutians, units under its command were sent to Alaska. At one time about one-quarter of the aircraft in Alaska were WAC. It was charged with helping to defend Anchorage and assisting the Americans in driving the Japanese out. From 1 January 1944 to 1 June 1944 it was given authority over the NORTHWEST AIR STAGING ROUTE, an authority later transferred to the NORTHWEST AIR COMMAND. On 1 March 1947 Western Air Command was dissolved and its responsibilities placed under the NWAC.

Western Escort Force. See WESTERN LOCAL ESCORT FORCE.

Western Local Escort Force (WLEF). WLEF was organized in January 1942 in part to counter the growing threat of U-boats in North American coastal waters. Since the bulk of escort resources were invariably attached to the MID-OCEAN ESCORT FORCE, the WLEF was not usually assigned first-line equipment and was often under-strength. It was responsible for shepherding

convoys between the east coast and the WESTERN OCEAN MEETING POINT. At its peak strength, the force utilized some 45 frigates and CORVETTES. After 1943 it was known as the Western Escort Force. See also TRIANGLE RUN, NORTH ATLANTIC RUN.

Western Ocean Meeting Point (WESTOMP). WESTOMP was the rendezvous point in the western Atlantic at which the WESTERN LOCAL ESCORT FORCE either handed escort duties over to the MID-OCEAN ESCORT FORCE in the case of eastbound convoys, or assumed those duties in the case of westbound ones. It was located to the east of St John's, Newfoundland.

Western Rangers (Caldwell's Rangers). A unit of the Upper Canada militia commanded by William Caldwell who was a veteran of BUTLER'S RANGERS. Caldwell's Rangers were created in early 1813 by Col Henry PROCTOR to harass the American forces on the Detroit frontier. They saw action in several battles including MORAVIANTOWN.

Westland Lysander aircraft. During WORLD WAR II National Steel Car Corp. of Toronto built nearly 700 Lysanders, a British-designed, high-wing, single-engine aircraft. Carrying two, the Lysander was a multi-role aircraft used for training, army cooperation, artillery spotting, and transporting messengers and passengers. With its STOL-like characteristics, the aircraft was frequently used to fly espionage agents into and out of occupied Europe. The Lysander was capable of speeds up to 320 km/h and was armed with a number of small machine guns.

WESTOMP. See WESTERN OCEAN MEETING POINT.

Whitaker, Denis (b. 1915). Whitaker graduated from the ROYAL MILITARY COLLEGE and served with the army in WORLD WAR II, rising to the rank of brigadier of the 3rd Infantry Brigade after the end of hostilities. He was named Honorary Colonel of the Royal Hamilton Light Infantry in 1973. Whitaker has co-authored three histories of the Canadian army in World War II, *Tug of War* (1984), *Rhineland: The Battle to End the War* (1989), and *Dieppe: Tragedy to Triumph* (1992).

White Paper (1964). Following the downfall of the DIEFENBAKER government in 1963, the new Liberal Defence minister, Paul HELLYER, initiated a review of Canadian defence policies. The White Paper of 1964 was the result. It stressed PEACEKEEPING as an appropriate role for Canada's forces while maintaining that Canadian commitments to NATO and NORAD would be met. The White Paper advocated the revolutionary course of total UNIFICATION of the three traditional services into a single force with a reorganized command structure. This initiated the unification process which was completed with the adoption of the Canadian Forces Reorganization Act of 1967.

White Paper (1971). After the accession to power of the Trudeau government in 1968, major reviews of both defence and foreign policy were conducted. New directions in defence policy were indicated in the 1971 White Paper entitled 'Defence in the Seventies'. In it, minister of National Defence DONALD MACDONALD reversed the defence priorities outlined by Paul HELLYER in his WHITE PAPER (1964). Macdonald put protection of Canadian sovereignty and domestic surveillance at the top of the defence list and PEACEKEEPING at the bottom. In part Macdonald was responding to increased concerns about threats to internal security in the wake of both North American and European unrest in the 1960s. The White Paper introduced new forms of civilian control of the military such as the MANAGEMENT REVIEW GROUP, and the functioning of service chiefs as assistant deputy ministers. It heralded a long period of defence cuts considered necessary by Trudeau to help pay for social programs.

White Paper (1987). The White Paper of 1987 was designed to put a Conservative stamp on Canadian defence policies which had been drifting since the early 1970s. It listed the following priorities in order: deterrence of a nuclear attack on North America, non-nuclear defence of western Europe, protection of Canadian sovereignty, peacekeeping and arms control. Its most radical suggestion was for the purchase of 10 to 12 nuclear-powered submarines to operate in the Atlantic, Pacific, and Arctic Oceans. Although the White Paper stressed the failure of previous governments to close the gap

between Canada's commitments and its capabilities, it too was effectively shelved in the face of a mounting economic crisis.

Wilkinson, Thomas Orde Lawder (1894–1916). Born in the U.K., Wilkinson emigrated to Canada in 1912. At the outbreak of WORLD WAR I, he returned to Britain to join the Loyal North Lancashire Regiment (British Army). He was posthumously awarded the VICTORIA CROSS for bravery in action at La Boiselle, France on 5 July 1916.

Williams, Sir William Fenwick (1800–1883). As commander of British troops in Canada from 1859 to 1865, Williams feared that the Union would annex Canada once the Civil War was over. Acting independently of the Canadian government, he ordered an additional 15,000 British troops to garrison Toronto and Kingston.

Windmill, Battle of the. Members of the Hunters' Lodges — Americans who sympathized with the Canadian rebels who had attempted to overthrow British rule in the REBELLIONS OF 1837—raided Prescott, Upper Canada, in November 1838. They established themselves in a nearby windmill in a first step in the capture of Fort Wellington, on the St Lawrence River. British marines and Canadian MILITIA rushed to the scene. After artillery bombarded the windmill a battle ensued. In all, 80 Hunters were killed and 160 others taken prisoner, of whom 11 were later executed.

Window. A device invented by the British, designed to confuse German air defence radar during WORLD WAR II. It consisted of strips of tinfoil cut to correspond to the wavelengths of the German radar. It was dropped from aircraft either in the bomber stream or on diversionary raids. German radar operators found it difficult to tell whether the pips on their radar screens were 'window' or aircraft. Radar-aimed anti-aircraft guns were rendered useless. Window was most effective when first used in the Hamburg raids of 1943.

Winnipeg Rifles. See ROYAL WINNIPEG RIFLES.

Withers, Ramsey Muir (b. 1930). After serving in the KOREAN WAR and at Northern Region Headquarters in Yellowknife, Withers commanded Canadian forces in Europe in the period 1976–77. He then served as vice chief and CHIEF OF THE DEFENCE STAFF from 1977 to 1983 after which he became deputy minister of the Department of Transport.

WLEF. See WESTERN LOCAL ESCORT FORCE.

Wolfe, James (1727/8–1759). Wolfe came to North America with AMHERST in 1758 to take part in the assault against LOUISBOURG after having campaigned with the British Army in Flanders and Scotland. Amherst was impressed with this young officer and recommended his selection to head the expedition to capture QUEBEC in 1759. Wolfe, however, was anything but impressive during the long siege. He was indecisive, and he did not get along well either with his senior officers or with SAUNDERS who commanded the Royal Navy contingent which was laying siege to the city. An assault mounted by him against French positions at MONTMORENCY at the end of July was a total failure. As the siege dragged on, with summer coming to an end and the prospect of a winter campaign looming, Wolfe began to lay plans for an assault upriver of Quebec. If successful, this would cut French communications with Montreal and force a battle. Wolfe himself chose the little cove of L'ANSE AU FOULON as the best place to land British troops who then climbed to the PLAINS OF ABRAHAM early on 13 September 1759. When they drew up in battle formation, French commander MONTCALM rushed to battle — a fatal mistake for him and one which brought victory for Wolfe. Wolfe, however, like Montcalm, was mortally wounded in the fighting.
Reading: C.P. Stacey, *Quebec 1759* (Toronto, 1959)

Wolseley, Garnet Joseph (1833–1913). Wolseley served with the British Army in India, the Crimea, and China before being posted to Canada in 1861. He was called upon to lead the RED RIVER EXPEDITION in 1870 prior to his leaving Canada along with the bulk of the British regulars. His path crossed that of Canada once again, in 1885, when he was chosen to command the British expedition to relieve Gordon at Khartoum.

Having been impressed with the work of Canadian boatmen in 1870, he sought to recruit a contingent to help transport his troops up the Nile: see the NILE EXPEDITION. From 1895 to 1900 he was commander-in-chief of the British army.

Women, World War I. Women played two basic roles in WORLD WAR I, in industry and as nursing sisters overseas. Contrary to popular myth, few women were engaged in war industry in Canada before the fall of 1916. The Canadian economy had been depressed at the outbreak of war and there were far more men to fill jobs than there were jobs available. It was not until mid to late 1916 that this situation turned around, both because of the expansion of war industry and because hundreds of thousands of men had volunteered for military service. By late 1916 there was a shortage of skilled labour and women began to enter war plants to take the place of the absent male workers. By the end of the war some 35,000 women had worked in some branch of the Canadian munitions industry. Few stayed on after the war was over. Most Canadians of the time, men and women, believed that heavy industry was not an appropriate place for women to work and that female munitions labour was a temporary wartime necessity. Nothing was done to encourage women to stay in these jobs.

There were no special branches for women in the Canadian military during World War I but many women volunteered for service as nursing sisters. By 1918 some 1900 nursing sisters were on strength with the various medical services, hospitals, etc. The bulk of these women served overseas. a large number — some 328 — were awarded decorations of various kinds. Six died as a result of wounds, 18 drowned at sea due to submarine attack, and 18 died of diseases while serving.
Reading: G.W.L. Nicholson, *Canada's Nursing Sisters* (Toronto, 1975); A. Prentice *et al.*, *Canadian Women: A History* (Toronto, 1988)

Women, World War II. Women played a far more extensive role in WORLD WAR II than they had in WORLD WAR I, both at home and overseas. Large numbers went to work in war plants while others took over men's jobs on farms. The number of women gainfully employed in Canada virtually doubled from 600,000 in 1939 to 1.2 million in late 1944. Some 10 per cent of all married women were working in 1941; that figure rose to 35 per cent before the war ended. (The latter figure does not include an estimated 800,000 agriculture workers.) In May 1942 the Women's Division of NATIONAL SELECTIVE SERVICE was created to help the placement of women workers in the war economy.

Despite the significant rate of female participation in the labour force, no long-term change in the male-female ratio of work force participation took place. Within a short time after the end of the war, the figures had mostly reverted to 'normal'. Society's attitudes towards women in the work place had not changed much since World War I and women in war plants were considered a temporary necessity. Thus, not much was done to accommodate women in war industry, other than to provide for the necessities. Day care, for example, was virtually unknown.

Just as women played a more significant role in the work force in World War II than they had in World War I, they also served in greater numbers and at more varied jobs in the military. In July 1941 the WOMEN'S DIVISION, RCAF, was established, and 17,018 women served in it before the end of the war. A CANADIAN WOMEN'S ARMY CORPS was set up in August, 1941, and almost 22,000 women served in it. The WOMEN'S ROYAL CANADIAN NAVAL SERVICE eventually attracted approximately 6781 women, while close to 4500 women served as nursing sisters. Women performed duties as varied as flying aircraft on the TRANS-ATLANTIC FERRY SERVICE to driving trucks. Many non-combat jobs in all three services were performed by women, enabling more men to join the fight.

Reading: R.R. Pierson, *Canadian Women and the Second World War* (Ottawa, 1983)

Women's Division, RCAF. The Women's Division was formed in July 1941 to train women for a variety of tasks from clerking to aircraft maintenance in order to release males for combat. A number of WDs served overseas at ROYAL CANADIAN AIR FORCE headquarters in the U.K. and on stations of NO. 6 GROUP. The organization was disbanded after the war but revived again in the early 1950s. Total wartime enlistment was just over 17,000.

Women's Royal Canadian Naval Service (WRCNS). Established in 1942 and patterned after the British Women's Royal Naval Service (WRNS), the WRCNS had a total wartime membership of 6781. Known as Wrens, its members served throughout Canada and at ROYAL CANADIAN NAVY establishments in Newfoundland, the U.S. and the U.K. Wrens participated in a wide variety of support trades including driving vehicles and food preparation but were especially important in clerical and signals work. In this last capacity they staffed shore-based radio intercept stations that were a key means of detecting U-boats.

Working Committee on Post-Hostilities Problems. Small committee of senior civil servants in key government departments which first met in August, 1943. The self-defined mandate of this committee, which was an offshoot of the POST-HOSTILITIES ADVISORY COMMITTEE, was to originate ideas on what the committee believed the objectives of government should be in the post-war period and how to reach them.

World War I. On 4 August 1914 Britain declared war on Germany and the Austro-Hungarian Empire, and Canada, as a colony of Britain and with no control over its own foreign affairs, was automatically at war. At that time Canada was a young nation with a population of a little more than 7.8 million. The economy was mired in recession and the armed forces, such as they were, were almost totally unprepared for any sort of conflict. Canada had no air force, a navy in name only with two obsolete training cruisers, the *NIOBE* and the *RAINBOW*, and a regular army of some 3000 officers and men backed by a MILITIA of approximately 60,000.

Although the government of Robert L. BORDEN was determined to prosecute the war with all vigour, it had no experience in mobilizing a country for anything like a conflict of this magnitude. Thus much of the Canadian war effort for the first three years was based on voluntarism. This meant not only that recruitment for military service would be voluntary, but that efforts to control inflation, to regulate war production, to control the labour force, etc., would also be voluntary. As the war dragged on, however, voluntarism clearly stopped working. The war was too long and too costly to sustain the sort of patriotic enthusiasm necessary for that. By 1917, therefore, voluntarism began to be replaced by compulsion in many areas of the war effort, not the least of which was CONSCRIPTION.

Borden and his government were determined to put as many fighting men in the field as possible. This was because they truly believed in the nobility of the cause, because they did not want to break faith with the men in the trenches by allowing their units to waste away, and because they began to realize that Canada's emergence from colony to nation would depend on the contribution it made to the war. The Canadian Army effectively entered the war with the second battle of YPRES in April 1915; by the end of 1916 it had suffered tens of thousands of casualties in apparently useless offensives such as the SOMME battles. Thus voluntary enlistments dropped off. In early 1917 Borden sailed for England to attend the IMPERIAL WAR CONFERENCE and pledged to redouble Canada's war effort. This and visits to wounded Canadian soldiers convinced him that he could wait no longer. On his return to Canada at the end of April he announced conscription. The measure was passed 29 August 1917 over the bitter opposition of Wilfrid LAURIER and much of Quebec. Borden then formed a coalition UNION GOVERNMENT with pro-conscription Liberals and carried the country in the federal election of 17 December 1917.

Just as voluntarism was abandoned as a means of recruitment, it was also increasingly abandoned as a means of organizing the nation for war. As the months went by the federal government got more actively involved in matters such as coal production, ship building, etc. The SHELL COMMITTEE, formed under the direction of minister of Militia and Defence Sam HUGHES, was disbanded in late 1915 due to corruption and replaced by the IMPERIAL MUNITIONS BOARD under Sir J.W. FLAVELLE. The IMB was soon involved in all manner of war production from shipping to training aircraft. In 1917 the goverment nationalized the first of several bankrupt transcontinental railways and introduced income tax as a way of paying for the war. These too marked the end of voluntarism.

In 1914 a very large part of the English-speaking population of Canada was either British-born or one or two generations removed from Britain. The call to war was, therefore, a call to Empire obligation for many young men. To others in a recession-wracked economy, it was a call to three square meals a day. Even though Hughes shelved the carefully laid mobilization plans of the MILITIA COUNCIL and called instead on the existing militia regiments to muster, thousands of men were soon gathering at the still-building mobilization and training camp at VALCARTIER. In October, the first Canadian contingent sailed for England. After a miserable winter on SALISBURY PLAIN, the IST CANADIAN DIVISION entered the line in France in March and fought its first major battle in April at YPRES.

The effort to mobilize large numbers of troops was probably hurt more than helped by Hughes. His appointments to the officer ranks were often of cronies or political allies. He insisted on submerging the militia regiments in numbered battalions and in raising replacements in Canada in replacement drafts which went to England as complete units. There they were usually broken up and the men placed where needed in the lines. This left large numbers of surplus officers in Britain. Hughes was also responsible for saddling the Canadian troops with faulty equipment such as the ROSS RIFLE. Borden knew Hughes was creating difficulties but Hughes was an old political ally. It was not until October 1916 with the creation of the MINISTRY OF OVERSEAS MILITARY FORCES that Hughes was sacked and his department reorganized.

It is not clear if the government had any particular size in mind for the CANADIAN EXPEDITIONARY FORCE when the war began; it is clear that the authorized force levels were constantly raised during the first years of the war. By the summer of 1915 the target was 150,000; in his new year's message at the end of 1916, Borden aimed at 500,000, an unrealistic target. Nonetheless, the CEF quickly grew from one division to four in the line in Europe (the CANADIAN CORPS) with a fifth division forming in England. This last was never committed to battle but was, instead, broken up for use as reinforcements. These divisions took part in most of the major battles fought in by the British on the western front including MOUNT SORREL, the SOMME, PASSCHENDAELE, VIMY RIDGE, and the battles of the last 100 days. As the war progressed, the Canadian Corps units were increasingly led by Canadian officers who, though mostly amateur militiamen at the start, quickly learned the art of war. By mid-1917 the Corps was commanded by A.W. CURRIE, a Canadian.

Although Canada made a much smaller contribution to the Allied war effort at sea, many Canadian airmen played an important part in the war. Flying with the Royal Flying Corps and the Royal Naval Air Service, Canadians such as W.A. BISHOP, Raymond COLLISHAW, and W. BARKER achieved fame as top war aces.

Canada achieved much of what Borden sought in the war, including the right to sign the peace treaty as a separate nation and the right to a seat at the League of Nations. But the cost was high. The nation was divided over conscription; 60,000 men had been killed in action and 172,000 wounded out of 620,000 who served.

Reading: G.W.L. Nicholson, *Canadian Expeditionary Force* (Ottawa, 1962); S.F. Wise, *Canadian Airmen and the First World War* (Toronto, 1980); M. Hadley, and R. Sarty, *Tin-Pots and Pirate Ships* (Montreal, 1991); J. English, *The Decline of Politics* (Toronto, 1977); D. Morton, *A Peculiar Kind of Politics* (Toronto, 1982); R.C. Brown and R. Cook, *Canada: 1896–1921* (Toronto, 1974)

World War II. Canada entered World War II on 10 September 1939 with a declaration of war against Germany. By the time the declaration was made the war in Europe was already ten days old and preparations for the conflict were already under way in Canada. At that time Canada was a nation of just under 11.5 million people and one large group—French Canadians—had traditionally shown themselves to be wary of foreign wars. Thus it was that the government of William Lyon Mackenzie KING pledged itself to a LIMITED LIABILITY WAR EFFORT and reiterated earlier pledges, pledges also endorsed by the Opposition parties, that there would be no CONSCRIPTION for overseas military service.

Throughout the war the government utilized the legislative provisions of the WAR MEASURES ACT both to enable it to legislate in areas normally denied it (because they were under provincial jurisdiction) and to jail opponents of the war. The War Measures Act had first been passed in August 1914 but was invoked again shortly before the 10 September declaration of war.

The WMA was only one of many special measures enacted by the government during the war. Another was the NATIONAL RESOURCES MOBILIZATION ACT which allowed the government to regulate the use of man- and woman-power and conscript for home defence purposes. Many other acts, regulations, and orders-in-council were issued as the government kept tight control over the war economy and over war finance. Minister of War Production C.D. HOWE was virtual czar over anything related to WAR INDUSTRY. He had two overall aims: to undermine wartime inflation, and to boost war production for Canada and its Allies both to equip men in the field and to earn hard currency where possible. His efforts were aided by a number of agreements with both Britain and the United States including the HYDE PARK DECLARATION. By the end of the war Canada had become an important part of the total Allied war production picture. Everything from bullets to bombers was being produced and a plethora of Crown corporations had been established to manufacture them.

The limited liability war effort had been conceived to forestall the prospect of conscription but pressures for conscription began to mount in English-speaking Canada beginning with the fall of France in May, 1940. These pressures increased significantly with the German attack on the USSR in June, 1941 and the entry of Japan into the war in December, 1941. Thus King called a plebiscite for 27 April 1942 in which the people of Canada were asked whether or not they favoured releasing the government from its pledges not to conscript for overseas military service. English Canada voted 'yes' in overwhelming numbers, Quebec was just as strongly opposed and the government received the permission it sought by a 3:1 ratio. However, it did not immediately introduce conscription but only amended the NRMA to give it the means to do so if required.

There were no significant manpower drains on the Canadian Army until the D-DAY landings. The fierce fighting in NORMANDY and NORTHWEST EUROPE produced WASTAGE figures much higher than anticipated, bringing on the REINFORCEMENT

CRISIS in the fall of 1944. Minister of National Defence J.L. RALSTON pressed King to introduce conscription and was fired for his troubles. He was replaced by A.G.L. MCNAUGHTON who told King that he might be able to increase voluntary enlistments from among the NRMA men (ZOMBIES) who had thus far refused to GO ACTIVE. When he failed, King was forced to introduce conscription as of 23 November 1944.

At the outbreak of war the Canadian military was in poor shape. The ROYAL CANADIAN NAVY had acquired a number of RIVER CLASS DESTROYERS in the previous decades, but it had fewer than 2000 officers and men and was largely untrained for modern war. The Canadian Army's PERMANENT FORCE had a strength of just over 4200 officers and men, no armoured fighting vehicles to speak of, and almost no modern artillery, machine guns, etc. The NON PERMANENT ACTIVE MILITIA numbered some 51,000. The ROYAL CANADIAN AIR FORCE had just over 3000 officers and men. With the exception of recently arrived HURRICANE fighters, most of its 270 aircraft were obsolete.

Although the 1ST CANADIAN INFANTRY DIVISION was quickly mobilized and dispatched to Britain, the government was, at first, reluctant to send additional ground forces due to its fears of high casualties and, inevitably, conscription. By the end of the war, however, three infantry and two armoured divisions had been formed, along with a number of additional independent brigades, supported by all the necessary support units a modern army must have. These were eventually consolidated under FIRST CANADIAN ARMY.

The first two actions engaged in by Canadian ground troops were disasters—HONG KONG in December 1941 and DIEPPE in August 1942. In May 1943 the 1st Canadian Infantry Division took part in the SICILY campaign over the objections of A.G.L. MCNAUGHTON, GOC FIRST CANADIAN ARMY, who did not want Canadian forces split up. But the prime minister was convinced that Canadians needed to show the flag and McNaughton was overruled. The division was kept in the theatre and was joined by the 5TH CANADIAN ARMOURED DIVISION for the ITALY campaign, again over McNaughton's objections, due to King's belief that the fighting in that theatre would produce fewer casualties than the expected invasion of France. Thus Canadian forces were divided for most of the war. The two divisions in Italy were joined in I CANADIAN CORPS and stayed in the theatre until February 1945, when they were sent to northwest Europe to join the rest of the Canadian forces.

The bulk of the Canadian army fought in France, Belgium, Holland, and north Germany in the NORMANDY and NORTHWEST EUROPE CAMPAIGNS. It was assigned one of the five Allied beachheads on D-DAY, fought in the battles for CAEN, helped close the FALAISE Gap, and then was assigned the task of clearing the English Channel and North Sea ports on the left flank of the 21st Army Group. It cleared the SCHELDT and then fought in the RHINELAND battles before crossing the Rhine, helping to secure the remainder of Holland and occupying parts of the North German plain by the end of the war.

Canada also made a major contribution to the Allied effort in the air. It operated and largely paid for the BRITISH COMMONWEALTH AIR TRAINING PLAN (which turned out over 131,000 air crew), provided crews and later aircraft for NO. 6 GROUP (RCAF) Bomber Command and contributed 19 squadrons to the 2ND ALLIED TACTICAL AIR FORCE. Canadian fighter pilots were part of the war effort as early as the BATTLE OF BRITAIN and fought in most European theatres. Canadian pilots and crews participated in all aspects of the bomber war, flying missions in the Aleutians, anti-submarine patrols over the North Atlantic, and with the RAF's Coastal Command. They could be found as far afield as Ceylon and Burma. At least two-thirds of the Canadian pilots and air crew served out the war in the Royal Air Force and not the RCAF.

The ROYAL CANADIAN NAVY also played a significant role in the Allied war effort. Its destroyers fought the German navy off the coast of Europe and in the English Channel and its escort vessels did convoy duty from the freezing Arctic waters of the Murmansk run to the tropical waters of the Caribbean. But the most important RCN contribution to the war was on the NORTH ATLANTIC RUN where, for most of the war, a large part of convoy escort duty was carried out by RCN CORVETTES and other escort vessels such as destroyers, minesweepers, frigates, etc. By the end of the war RCN escort vessels and anti-submarine aircraft of the RCAF, alone or in conjunction with other Allied units, had accounted for 52 enemy submarines.

The cost of the war was heavy: 42,042 dead and 54,414 wounded out of the 1.1 million who served. Although deaths in battle were fewer than in WORLD WAR I, they came in a much shorter time span. Canadian divisions fighting in Normandy, for example, consistently suffered casualty rates at least as high as those sustained by Canadian units on the Western Front in World War I. Canada also spent almost $22 billion either to purchase war materials itself or in contributions to the Allied war effort. By any measure it was a remarkable performance for a nation so unprepared for war in 1939, guided throughout the war by a prime minister more concerned with high casualties and conscription than he was with an effort aimed at total victory.

Reading: C.P. Stacey, *Six Years of War* (Ottawa, 1955), *The Victory Campaign* (Ottawa, 1960), *Arms, Men and Governments* (Ottawa,

1970); G.W.L. Nicholson, *The Canadians in Italy* (Ottawa, 1956); M. Milner, *North Atlantic Run* (Toronto, 1985); W.A.B. Douglas, *The Creation of a National Air Force* (Toronto, 1986); W.A.B. Douglas and B. Greenhous, *Out of the Shadows* (Toronto, 1977); J.L. Granatstein, *Canada's War* (Toronto, 1975)

Worthington, Frederic Franklin (1890–1967). Born in Scotland, Worthington served with the Canadian Motor Machine-Gun Brigade during WORLD WAR I, and joined the PERMANENT FORCE after the war. Worthington was particularly interested in the use of armoured vehicles in combat and was a pioneer of the CANADIAN ARMOURED CORPS. He commanded the Army Fighting Vehicles Training Centre at the outbreak of war and was later the first commander of the 4TH CANADIAN ARMOURED DIVISION, a post he held until February 1944. He served in the army until 1947 when he resigned his commission to become Canada's first civil defence coordinator.

Y

Yardley, Herbert (1889–1958). Born in the United States, Yardley was an important figure in American cryptology during WORLD WAR I. In 1919 he succeeded in breaking the Japanese diplomatic codes, enabling the U.S. to read radio traffic between Tokyo and the Japanese negotiators at the Washington Naval Conference. Yardley was left unemployed after the U.S. government closed the Cipher Bureau in 1929. He wrote a book, *The American Black Chamber* — the story of the Cipher Bureau—to support himself. This revealed a number of secrets and caused great embarrassment to the U.S. government. After working as a cryptanalyst for China, he was employed by the Canadian government to establish the EXAMINATION UNIT. He was fired in 1941 because the U.S.

would not cooperate with Canada in intelligence efforts as long as he was employed there.

Yemen, UN peacekeeping in. See UNYOM.

Yeo, Sir James Lucas (1782–1818). Yeo commanded the PROVINCIAL MARINE in Upper Canada during the WAR OF 1812. Although he had little war experience, he held control of Lake Ontario until the summer of 1813 when a superior American force blockaded him at Kingston. After a winter of improving his fleet, in the spring of 1814 he recorded naval successes at OSWEGO and SACKETS HARBOR, thus regaining control of the lakes.

YMCA. In WORLD WAR I the Young Men's Christian Association provided reading material and non-alcoholic refreshment to Canadian soldiers from SALISBURY PLAIN to SIBERIA. The YMCA also sponsored the KHAKI UNIVERSITY which offered courses to off-duty soldiers in England. During WORLD WAR II the YMCA provided sports and recreation services to soldiers.

Young, Hugh Andrew (1898–1987). After serving with the CANADIAN EXPEDITIONARY FORCE in WORLD WAR I, Young was commissioned to the ROYAL CANADIAN CORPS OF SIGNALS in 1924. He then embarked on a study of cold weather radio operations, touring both Arctic and Antarctic radio stations run by a number of countries. During WORLD WAR II he commanded the 6th Infantry Brigade in the NORMANDY fighting and then served as Quartermaster-General in Canada.

Young, James Vernon (1891–1961). A graduate of ROYAL MILITARY COLLEGE, Young served with the 3rd Artillery Brigade of the CANADIAN EXPEDITIONARY FORCE during WORLD WAR I. From 1942 to 1945 he was Master-General of Ordnance at NATIONAL DEFENCE HEADQUARTERS.

Young, John Francis (1893–1929). A medical orderly with the 87th Battalion, CANADIAN EXPEDITIONARY FORCE during the battle of ARRAS in early September, 1918, Young worked diligently under fire to dress the wounds of his company. He later organized and led stretcher-bearing parties. For these acts of bravery he was awarded the VICTORIA CROSS.

York, 1813. In the spring of 1813 American forces under Commodore Isaac Chauncey and General Zebulon Pike set out from SACKETS HARBOR with 14 vessels and 1700 men, landing near the Upper Canada capital of York (later renamed Toronto). They quickly overwhelmed the outnumbered defending force of British regulars and colonial MILITIA but an exploding powder magazine killed Pike and a number of his men. The angry Americans then sacked much of the town and burned important public buildings such as the provincial Parliament. They then abandoned the town to campaign westward on the NIAGARA FRONTIER. The British later burned Washington in retaliation.

York Factory. Throughout the WAR OF THE LEAGUE OF AUGSBURG, the British and French contested the ownership of this Hudson's Bay Company fur trade post on the southwestern shore of Hudson Bay. The fort changed hands several times before the French finally took control of it following a naval battle at Hayes River in 1697 during which Pierre LEMOYNE aboard *PELICAN* sank the British ship *Hampshire*. However, York Factory was returned to the English with the peace settlement later that year.

Yukon aircraft (CL44). Built by Canadair in the 1960s, the Yukon was a four-engine turboprop transport the design of which was derived from the British-designed Bristol Britannia. The Yukon featured a swing tail for easy loading of cargo. The Yukon replaced the older NORTH STAR, and a total of 12 were taken on strength by the RCAF up to 1968.

Yukon Field Force. The federal government sent a 203-man contingent from the PERMANENT FORCE to assert Canada's sovereignty in the Yukon in 1898 during the height of the Klondike Gold Rush. The force set out from Vancouver in May, 1898 and proceeded by water and overland trail to Fort Selkirk and Dawson. Half the force was withdrawn in 1899 when the SOUTH AFRICAN WAR broke out. The remainder pulled out in 1900.

Ypres. The second battle of Ypres was the first major battle fought by the 1ST CANADIAN DIVISION in WORLD WAR I. When the battle began on 22 April 1915, the Canadians were in the front lines with a French colonial division on the left and a British division on the right, and the town of Ypres was to the rear. The sector had been quiet for many months and the Canadians had little to do other than to improve their trenches and dig deeper dugouts.

The German attack began in the late afternoon. It was the first gas attack of the war. The Germans lugged thousands of chlorine gas cylinders to the front, waited until the wind was right, then released the gas. Their troops followed behind wearing cloth face masks. Since chlorine is heavier than air, the gas cloud drifted toward the Allied lines, hugging the ground and filling trenches, dug-outs, and gun positions.

The French colonials and the British gunners situated in Kitcheners Wood felt the full impact of the gas and broke and ran, the latter abandoning their field pieces. Some of the gas drifted into the Canadian positions but the Canadians stayed in the line and fought off the German attack. Nevertheless, the left flank of the Canadians was exposed and quick action was necessary to close the gap in the lines. The night of 22 April, R.E.W. TURNER of 3rd Brigade ordered his troops into St Julien, a village on the Canadian left flank. Then General E. ALDERSON, the divisional commander, ordered an attack to re-take Kitcheners Wood. The attack failed with heavy Canadian losses.

The fighting continued all the next day as British units were rushed forward to plug the line while German artillery reduced Ypres to a heap of ruins and killed many of the reinforcements. On 24 April, the Germans used gas again, this time directly against the two Canadian brigades still in the line—Turner's 3rd and A.W. CURRIE's 2nd.

As the Germans advanced the Canadians at first held to their positions despite the thick, choking gas and the constant jamming of their ROSS RIFLES. But confusion reigned among the ranks of the largely untried Canadians. Turner and his brigade-major, Garnet HUGHES, were found wanting in leadership and initiative that day. Currie's role is more controversial because in the midst of battle he went to the rear at his own initiative, ostensibly to bring up reinforcements. This was a highly unusual thing for a brigadier to do and remains unexplained to this day.

By 4 May when the Canadians were pulled out of the Ypres fighting, their casualties numbered more than 6000 out of an effective strength of only 10,000 and the Canadian line had been pushed back two miles. But four Canadians won the VICTORIA CROSS and, more importantly, the Germans had failed to break completely through the Canadian lines.

Reading: D.G. Dancocks, *Welcome to Flanders Fields* (Toronto, 1988)

Z

Zengel, Raphael Louis (1894–1977). At the battle of AMIENS in August 1918, Zengel attacked a German machine-gun position, dispersing its crew and killing an officer. His bravery saved his unit — the 5th Battalion, CANADIAN EXPEDITIONARY FORCE — from heavy casualties. Zengel was awarded a VICTORIA CROSS for this action as were two men who fought with him, A.P. BRERETON and F.G. COPPINS.

Zimmerman, Adam Hartley (b. 1902). An engineer trained in part at ROYAL MILITARY COLLEGE, Zimmerman was director of small arms production and director-general of signals production for the Department of Munitions and Supply, 1941–44. He then headed up the the DND electronics division (1951). Appointed to the DEFENCE RESEARCH BOARD in 1952, he later became its chairman.

Zombies. Derogatory term in popular use during WORLD WAR II to describe men conscripted under the NATIONAL RESOURCES MOBILIZATION ACT (NRMA) who refused to GO ACTIVE.

Zoot suit riots. In 1943 and 1944 riots broke out in Toronto and Hamilton pitting members of the military against 'hepcats' who wore long baggy trousers belted high on the chest, and long jackets that draped to the knees. These outfits were called 'zoot suits' in both Canada and the United States. In the U.S., violence between members of the military and zoot suiters was more frequent.

Zouaves. A 390-man force, raised by the Catholic Church in Quebec for the Papal army that fought from 1868 to 1870 against Italian forces trying to seize the Papal states during the campaign to unify Italy.

APPENDIX I
MINISTERS AND MINISTRIES

Prime Ministers of Canada

Sir John A. Macdonald	Conservative	1 July 1867–5 Nov. 1873
Alexander Mackenzie	Liberal	7 Nov. 1873–8 Oct. 1878
Sir John A. Macdonald	Conservative	17 Oct. 1878–6 June 1891
Sir John Abbott	Conservative	16 June 1891–24 Nov. 1892
Sir John Thompson	Conservative	5 Dec. 1892–12 Dec. 1894
Sir Mackenzie Bowell	Conservative	21 Dec. 1894–27 Apr. 1896
Sir Charles Tupper	Conservative	1 May 1896–8 July 1896
Sir Wilfrid Laurier	Liberal	11 July 1896–6 Oct. 1911
Sir Robert Borden	Conservative	10 Oct. 1911–12 Oct. 1917
Sir Robert Borden	Unionist	12 Oct. 1917–10 July 1920
Arthur Meighen	Unionist-National Liberal and Conservative	10 July 1920–29 Dec. 1921
William Lyon Mackenzie King	Liberal	29 Dec. 1921–28 June 1926
Arthur Meighen	Conservative	29 June 1926–25 Sept. 1926
William Lyon Mackenzie King	Liberal	25 Sept. 1926–7 Aug. 1930
Richard Bennett	Conservative	7 Aug. 1930–23 Oct. 1935
William Lyon Mackenzie King	Liberal	23 Oct. 1935–15 Nov. 1948
Louis St Laurent	Liberal	15 Nov. 1948–21 June 1957
John Diefenbaker	Progressive Conservative	21 June 1957–22 Apr. 1963
Lester Bowles Pearson	Liberal	22 Apr. 1973–20 Apr. 1968
Pierre Elliott Trudeau	Liberal	20 Apr. 1968–3 June 1979
Joe Clark	Progressive Conservative	4 June 1979–2 March 1980
Pierre Elliott Trudeau	Liberal	3 March 1980–30 June 1984
John Turner	Liberal	30 June 1984–17 Sept. 1984
Brian Mulroney	Progressive Conservative	17 Sept. 1984–

Ministers of Militia and National Defence

MINISTER OF MILITIA AND DEFENCE

Sir George Étienne Cartier	1 July 1867–20 May 1873
Hector Louis Langevin, *Acting Minister*	21 May 1873–30 June 1873
Hugh McDonald	1 July 1873–4 Nov. 1873
William Ross	7 Nov. 1873–29 Sept. 1874
William Berrian Vail	30 Sept. 1874–20 Jan. 1878
Alfred Gilpin Jones	21 Jan. 1878–8 Oct. 1878
Louis François Rodrigue Masson	19 Oct. 1878–15 Jan. 1880
Sir Alexander Campbell, *Senator*	16 Jan. 1880–7 Nov. 1880
Sir Joseph Philippe René Adolphe Caron	8 Nov. 1880–24 Jan. 1892
Mackenzie Bowell	25 Jan. 1892–24 Nov. 1892
James Colebrooke Patterson	5 Dec. 1892–25 Mar. 1895
Arthur Rupert Dickey	26 Mar. 1895–5 Jan. 1896
Sir Mackenzie Bowell, *Senator-Acting Minister*	6 Jan. 1896–14 Jan. 1896
Alphonse Desjardins, *Senator*	15 Jan. 1896–27 Apr. 1896
David Tisdale	1 May 1896–8 July 1896
Sir Frederick William Borden	13 July 1896–6 Oct. 1911

Appendix I

Sir Samuel Hughes	10 Oct. 1911–12 Oct. 1916
Sir Albert Edward Kemp	23 Nov. 1916–12 Oct. 1917
Sydney Chilton Mewburn	12 Oct. 1917–15 Jan. 1920
James Alexander Calder, *Acting Minister*	16 Jan. 1920–23 Jan. 1920
Hugh Guthrie	24 Jan. 1920–29 Dec. 1921
George Perry Graham	29 Dec. 1921–31 Dec. 1922

MINISTER OF NATIONAL DEFENCE

George Perry Graham	1 Jan. 1923–27 Apr. 1923
Edward Mortimer Macdonald, *Acting Minister*	28 Apr. 1923–16 Aug. 1923
Edward Mortimer Macdonald	17 Aug. 1923–28 June 1926
Hugh Guthrie, *Acting Minister*	29 June 1926–12 July 1926
Hugh Guthrie	13 July 1926–25 Sept. 1926
James Alexander Robb, *Acting Minister*	1 Oct. 1926–7 Oct. 1926
James Layton Ralston	8 Oct. 1926–7 Aug. 1930
Donald Matheson Sutherland	7 Aug. 1930–16 Nov. 1934
Grote Stirling	17 Nov. 1934–23 Oct. 1935
Ian Alistair Mackenzie	23 Oct. 1935–18 Sept. 1939
Norman McLeod Rogers	19 Sept. 1939–10 June 1940
Charles Gavan Power, *Acting Minister*	11 June 1940–4 July 1940
James Layton Ralston	5 July 1940–1 Nov. 1944
Andrew George Latta McNaughton	2 Nov. 1944–20 Aug. 1945
Douglas Charles Abbott	21 Aug. 1945–11 Dec. 1946
Brooke Claxton	12 Dec. 1946–30 June 1954
Ralph Osborne Campney	1 July 1954–21 June 1957
George Randolph Pearkes	21 June 1957–10 Oct. 1960
Douglas Scott Harkness	11 Oct. 1960–3 Feb. 1963
Gordon Churchill	12 Feb. 1963–22 Apr. 1963
Paul Theodore Hellyer	22 Apr. 1963–18 Sept. 1967
Léo Alphonse Joseph Cadieux	19 Sept. 1967–16 Sept. 1970
Charles Mills Drury, *Acting Minister*	17 Sept. 1970–23 Sept. 1970
Donald Stovel Macdonald	24 Sept. 1970–27 Jan. 1972
Edgar John Benson	28 Jan. 1972–31 Aug. 1972
Jean-Eudes Dubé, *Acting Minister*	1 Sept. 1972–6 Sept. 1972
Charles Mills Drury, *Acting Minister*	7 Sept. 1972–26 Nov. 1972
James Armstrong Richardson	27 Nov. 1972–12 Oct. 1976
Barnett Jerome Danson, *Acting Minister*	13 Oct. 1976–2 Nov. 1976
Barnett Jerome Danson	3 Nov. 1976–3 June 1979
Allan Bruce McKinnon	4 June 1979–2 Mar. 1980
Gilles Lamontagne	3 Mar. 1980–12 Aug. 1983
Jean-Jacques Blais	12 Aug. 1983–16 Sept. 1984
Robert C. Coates	17 Sept. 1984–12 Feb. 1985
Erik Nielsen	17 Feb. 1985–30 June 1986
Perrin Beatty	30 June 1986–8 Dec. 1988
William McKnight	30 Jan. 1989–21 Apr. 1991
Marcel Masse	22 Apr. 1991–

Ministers of Soldiers' Civil Re-establishment and Veterans' Affairs

MINISTER OF SOLDIERS' CIVIL RE-ESTABLISHMENT

Sir James Alexander Lougheed, *Senator*	21 Feb. 1918–10 July 1920
Sir James Alexander Lougheed, *Senator-Acting Minister*	19 July 1920–21 Sept. 1921
Robert James Manion	22 Sept. 1921–29 Dec. 1921
Henri Sévérin Béland, *Senator*	29 Dec. 1921–14 Apr. 1926

John Campbell Elliott	15 Apr. 1926–28 June 1926
Robert James Manion, *Acting Minister*	29 June 1926–12 July 1926
Raymond Ducharme Morand, *Acting Minister*	13 July 1926–22 Aug. 1926
Eugène Paquet	23 Aug. 1926–25 Sept. 1926
James Horace King	25 Sept. 1926–10 June 1928

MINISTER OF VETERANS' AFFAIRS

Ian Alistair Mackenzie	18 Oct. 1944–18 Jan. 1948
Milton Fowler Gregg	19 Jan. 1948–6 Aug. 1950
Hugues Lapointe	7 Aug. 1950–21 June 1957
Alfred Johnson Brooks	21 June 1957–10 Oct. 1960
Gordon Churchill	11 Oct. 1960–11 Feb. 1963
Marcel Joseph Aimé Lambert	12 Feb. 1963–22 Apr. 1963
Roger Joseph Teillet	22 Apr. 1963–5 July 1968
Jean-Eudes Dubé	6 July 1968–27 Jan. 1972
Arthur Laing	28 Jan. 1972–26 Nov. 1972
Daniel Joseph MacDonald	27 Nov. 1972–3 June 1979
Allan Bruce McKinnon	4 June 1979–2 Mar. 1980
Daniel Joseph McDonald	3 Mar. 1980–30 Sept. 1980
Gilles Lamontagne, *Acting Minister*	1 Oct. 1980–21 Sept. 1981
W. Bennett Campbell	22 Sept. 1981–9 July 1984
George Hees	17 Sept. 1984–14 Sept. 1988
George Merrithew	15 Sept. 1988–

Associate Ministers of National Defence

Charles Gavan Power	12 July 1940–26 Nov. 1944
Ralph Osborne Campney	12 Feb. 1953–30 June 1954
Paul Theodore Hellyer	26 Apr. 1957–21 June 1957
Joseph Pierre Albert Sévigny	20 Aug. 1959–8 Feb. 1963
Louis Joseph Lucien Cardin	22 Apr. 1963–14 Feb. 1965
Léo Alphonse Joseph Cadieux	15 Feb. 1965–18 Sept. 1967
Harvie André	20 Aug. 1985–29 June 1986
Paul Dick	30 June 1986–30 Jan. 1989
Mary Collins	31 Jan. 1989–

Other Related Ministries

MINISTER OF THE NAVAL SERVICE

John Douglas Hazen	10 Oct. 1911–12 Oct. 1917
Charles Colquhoun Ballantyne	13 Oct. 1917–29 Dec. 1921
George Perry Graham	29 Dec. 1921–31 Dec. 1922

MINISTER OF THE OVERSEAS MILITARY FORCES

Sir George Halsey Perley	31 Oct. 1916–12 Oct. 1917
Sir Albert Edward Kemp	12 Oct. 1917–1 July 1920

MINISTER OF NATIONAL DEFENCE FOR AIR

Charles Gavan Power	23 May 1940–26 Nov. 1944
Angus Lewis Macdonald, *Acting Minister*	30 Nov. 1944–10 Jan. 1945
Colin William George Gibson, *Acting Minister*	11 Jan. 1945–7 Mar. 1945
Colin William George Gibson	8 Mar. 1945–11 Dec. 1946

Appendix I

APPENDIX II
COMPARATIVE RANKS

RCN	CA	RCAF
Admiral	General	Air Chief Marshal
Vice Admiral	Lieutenant General	Air Marshal
Rear Admiral	Major General	Air Vice Marshal
Commodore	Brigadier	Air Commodore
Captain	Colonel	Group Captain
Commander	Lieutenant Colonel	Wing Commander
Lieutenant Commander	Major	Squadron Leader
Lieutenant	Captain	Flight Lieutenant
Sub Lieutenant	Lieutenant	Flying Officer
Midshipman	2nd Lieutenant	Pilot Officer
	Warrant Officer I	Warrant Officer I
Chief Petty Officer	Warrant Officer II	Warrant Officer II
Petty Officer	Staff Sergeant	Flight Sergeant
Leading Seaman	Sergeant	Sergeant
Able Seaman	Corporal	Corporal
Ordinary Seaman	Lance Corporal	Leading Aircraftman
	Private	Aircraftman First Class
		Aircraftman Second Class

APPENDIX III
CHIEFS OF THE MILITARY FORCES

General Officers Commanding the Canadian Militia

LGen. Sir Edward Selby-Smyth	1875–1880
MGen. R.G.A. Luard	1880–1884
MGen. Sir Frederick Middleton	1884–1890
MGen. I.J.C. Herbert	1890–1895
MGen. W.J. Gascoigne	1895–1898
MGen. E.T.H. Hutton	1898–1900
MGen. R.H. O'Grady-Haly	1900–1902
MGen. the Rt. Hon. the Earl of Dundonald	1902–1904
BGen. the Rt. Hon. Matthew Lord Aylmer (Acting)	1904

Chairmen, Chiefs of Staff

Gen. Charles Foulkes	1951–1960
Air Chief Marshal F.R. Miller	1960–1964

Chiefs of Defence Staff

Air Chief Marshal F.R. Miller	1964–1966
Gen. J.V. Allard	1966–1969
Gen. F.R. Sharp	1969–1972
Gen. J.A. Dextraze	1972–1977
Adm. R.H. Falls	1977–1980
Gen. R.M. Withers	1980–1983
Gen. J.C.E. Theriault	1983–1985
Gen. P.D. Manson	1985–1988
Gen. A.J.G.D. de Chastelain	1988-

Chiefs of the General Staff

MGen. Percy Lake	1904–1908
MGen. W.D. Otter	1908–1910
MGen. C.J. MacKenzie	1910–1913
MGen. W.G. Gwatkin	1913–1919
Gen. Sir Arthur Currie	1919–1920
MGen. J.H. MacBrien	1920–1927
MGen. H.C. Thacker	1927–1928
MGen. A.G.L. McNaughton	1929–1935
MGen. E.C. Ashton	1935–1938
MGen. T.V. Anderson	1938–1940
LGen. H.D.G. Crerar	1940–1941
LGen. K. Stuart	1941–1943
LGen. J.C. Murchie	1944–1945
LGen. C. Foulkes	1945–1951

LGen. G.G. Simonds	1951–1955
LGen. H.D. Graham	1955–1958
LGen. S.F. Clark	1958–1961
LGen. G. Walsh	1961–1964

Directors of the Naval Service

| Adm. Sir Charles Kingsmill | 1910–1920 |
| Commodore Walter Hose | 1920–1928 |

Chiefs of Naval Staff

RAdm. Walter Hose	1928–1934
VAdm. Percy Nelles	1934–1944
VAdm. G.C. Jones	1944–1946
VAdm. H.E. Reid	1946–1947
VAdm. H.T.W. Grant	1947–1951
VAdm. E.R. Mainguy	1951–1956
VAdm. H.G. DeWolf	1956–1960
VAdm. H.S. Rayner	1960–1964
RAdm. K.L. Dyer (Acting)	1964

Air Officer Commanding, Canadian Air Force

| Air Commodore A.K. Tylee | 1920–1921 |

Officers Commanding, Canadian Air Force

| WC R.F. Redpath | 1921 |
| WC J.S. Scott | 1921–1922 |

Directors, Royal Canadian Air Force

WC J.L. Gordon	1922–1924
WC W.G. Barker	1924
GC J.S. Scott	1924–1928
WC L.S. Breadner	1928–1932
SL A.A.L. Cuffe	1932

Senior Air Officers

GC J.L. Gordon	1932–1933
WC G.O. Johnson	1933
AVM G.M. Croil	1933–1938

Chiefs of Air Staff

AVM G.M. Croil	1938–40
AM L.S. Breadner	1940–43
AM R. Leckie	1944–47
AM W.A. Curtis	1947–53
AM C.R. Slemon	1953–57
AM H.L. Campbell	1957–62
AM C.R. Dunlap	1962–64

(Ranks are those held at the time the post was vacated.)

APPENDIX IV
VICTORIA CROSS AND
GEORGE CROSS WINNERS

(*associated with Canada)

Victoria Cross

CRIMEAN WAR

Dunn, Alexander Robert (1833–1868)

INDIAN MUTINY

Hall, William (1827–1904)
Pearson, John (1825–1892)*
Reade, Herbert Taylor (1828–1897)
Richardson, George (1831–1923)*

O'Hea, Timothy (1846–1874) only VC won in Canada

BURMA CAMPAIGN

Douglas, Campbell Mellis (1867–1909)

SOUTH AFRICAN WAR

Beet, Barry Churchill (1873–1946)*
Cockburn, Hampden Zane Churchill (1867–1913)
Holland, Edward James Gibson (1878–1948)
Nickerson, William Henry Snyder (1875–1954)*
Richardson, Arthur Herbert Lindsay (1873–1932)
Turner, Richard Ernest William (1871–1961)

WORLD WAR I

Algie, Wallace Lloyd (1891–1918)
Barker, William George (1894–1930)
Barron, Colin Fraser (1893–1958)
Bellew, Edward Donald (1882–1961)
Bent, Philip Eric (1891–1917)
Bishop, William Avery (1894–1956)
Bourke, Rowland Richard Louis (1885–1958)
Brereton, Alexander Picton (1892–1976)
Brillant, Jean (1890–1918)
Brown, Harry (1898–1917)
Cairns, Hugh (1896–1918)
Campbell, Frederick William (1867–1915)
Clarke, Leo (1892–1916)
Clark-Kennedy, William Hew (1880–1961)

Combe, Robert Grierson (1880–1917)
Coppins, Frederick George (1889–1963)
Croak, John Bernard (1892–1918)
Cruickshank, Robert Edward (1888–1961)*
De Wind, Edmund (1883–1918)
Dinesen, Thomas (1892–1979)
Fisher, Fred (1894–1915)
Flowerdew, Gordon Muriel (1885–1918)
Geary, Benjamin Handley (1891–1976)*
Good, Herman James (1887–1969)
Gregg, Milton Fowler (1892–1978)
Hall, Frederick William (1885–1915)
Hanna, Robert (1887–1967)
Harvey, Frederick Maurice Watson (1888–1980)
Hobson, Frederick (1875–1917)
Holmes, Thomas William (1898–1950)
Honey, Samuel Lewis (1894–1918)
Hutcheson, Bellenden Seymour (1883–1954)
Kaeble, Joseph (1893–1918)
Kerr, George Fraser (1894–1929)
Kerr, John Chipman (1887–1963)
Kinross, Cecil John (1896–1957)
Knight, Arthur George (1886–1918)
Konowal, Filip (1887–1959)
Learmonth, Okill Massey (1894–1917)
Lyall, Graham Thomson (1892–1941)
MacDowell, Thain Wendell (1890–1960)
MacGregor, John (1888–1952)
McKean, George Burdon (1888–1926)
MacKenzie, Hugh (1885–1917)
McLeod, Alan Arnett (1899–1918)
Merrifield, William (1890–1943)
Metcalf, William Henry (1885–1968)
Milne, William Johnstone (1892–1917)
Miner, Harry Garnet Bedford (1891–1918)
Mitchell, Coulson Norman (1889–1978)
Mullin, George Harry (1892–1963)
Nunney, Claude Joseph Patrick (1892–1918)
O'Kelly, Christopher Patrick John (1895–1922)
O'Leary, Michael (1889–1961)
O'Rourke, Michael James (1878–1957)
Pattison, John George (1875–1917)
Pearkes, George Randolph (1888–1984)
Peck, Cyrus Wesley (1871–1956)

Rayfield, Walter Leigh (1881–1949)
Richardson, James Cleland (1895–1916)
Ricketts, Thomas (1901–1967)
Robertson, James Peter (1883–1917)
Robson, Henry Howey (1894–1964)*
Rutherford, Charles Smith (1892–1989)
Ryder, Robert*
Scrimger, Francis Alexander Caron (1881–1937)
Shankland, Robert (1887–1968)
Sifton, Ellis Wellwood (1891–1917)
Spall, Robert (1890–1918)
Strachan, Harcus (1889–1982)
Stuart, Ronald Neil (1886–1954)*
Tait, James Edward (1886–1918)
Tombs, Joseph (1887–1966)*
Train, Charles William (1890–1965)
Wilkinson, Thomas Orde Lawder (1894–1916)*
Zengel, Raphael Louis (1894–1977)

WORLD WAR II

Bazalgette, Ian Willoughby (1918–1944)
Cosens, Aubrey (1921–1945)
Currie, David Vivian (1912–1986)
Foote, John Weir (1904–1988)
Gray, Robert Hampton (1917–1945)
Hoey, Charles Ferguson (1914–1944)
Hornell, David Ernest (1910–1944)
Mahony, John Keefer (1911–1990)
Merritt, Charles Cecil Ingersoll (1908–1979)
Mynarski, Andrew Charles (1916–1944)
Osborn, John Robert (1899–1943)
Peters, Frederick Thornton (1889–1943)
Smith, Ernest Alva (b. 1914)
Tilston, Frederick Albert (1906–1992)
Topham, Frederick George (1917–1974)
Triquet, Paul (1910–1980)

George Cross

Ashburnham-Ruffner, Doreen (1905–1991)*
[Albert Medal]
Bastian, Gordon Love (b. 1902)
Butson, Arthur Richard Cecil (b. 1922)* [Albert Medal]
Davies, Robert (b. 1900)*
Frost, Ernest Ralph Clyde (1917–1969)
Gravell, Karl Mander (1922–1941)
Gray, Roderick Borden (1917–1944)

Hendry, James (1911–1941)
McClymont, John McIntosh (b. 1903)
Patton, John MacMillan Stevenson (b. 1915)
Rennie, John (1920–1943)
Ross, Arthur Dwight (1907–1981)
Spooner, Kenneth Gerald (1922–1943)

APPENDIX V
AXIS SUBMARINE LOSSES TO CANADIAN FORCES

Compiled by Robert Fisher, Directorate of History, Department of National Defence with revised assessment by R.M. Coppock, British Ministry of Defence

DATE	U-BOAT	KILLER	TASK	AREA
1940				
6 Nov.	Faa Di Bruno	HMCS Ottawa, HMS Harvester	Patrol	North Atlantic
1941				
10 Sept.	U-501	HMCS Chambly, Moose Jaw	Escort	North Atlantic
1942				
24 July	U-90	HMCS St. Croix	Escort	North Atlantic
31 July	U-588	HMCS Skeena, Wetaskiwin	Escort	North Atlantic
31 July	U-754	RCAF Squadron 113	Air patrol	Off Nova Scotia
6 Aug.	U-210	HMCS Assiniboine	Escort	North Atlantic
28 Aug.	U-94	HMCS Oakville US Squad. 92	Sea/Air Escort	Caribbean Sea
1 Sept.	U-756	HMCS Morden	Escort	North Atlantic
30 Oct.	U-520	RCAF Squadron 10	Air Escort	North Atlantic
30 Oct.	U-658	RCAF Squadron 145	Air Patrol	Newfoundland
27 Dec.	U-356	HMCS St Laurent, Chilliwack, Battleford, Napanee	Escort	North Atlantic
1943				
13 Jan.	U-224	HMCS Ville de Quebec	Escort	Mediterranean Sea (C. Teneriffe)
19 Jan.	Tritone	HMCS Port Arthur	Escort	Mediterranean Sea (Bougie)
8 Feb.	Avorio	HMCS Regina	Escort	Mediterranean Sea
4 Mar.	U-87	HMCS Shediac, St Croix	Escort	North Atlantic
13 Mar.	U-163	HMCS Prescott	Escort	North Atlantic
4 May	U-630	RCAF Squadron 5	Air Escort	North Atlantic
13 May	U-753	RCAF Squadron 423, HMCS Drumheller, and HMS Lagan	Escort	North Atlantic
4 Aug.	U-489	RCAF Squadron 423	Air Patrol	West of Faroes
19 Sept.	U-341	RCAF Squadron 10	Air Support	North Atlantic
8 Oct.	U-610	RCAF Squadron 423	Air Escort	North Atlantic
26 Oct.	U-420	RCAF Squadron 10	Air Escort	North Atlantic
20 Nov.	U-536	HMCS Calgary, Snowberry, and HMS Nene	Escort	North Atlantic

246

1944

Date	U-boat	Units	Type	Location
8 Jan.	U-757	HMCS *Camrose*, HMS *Bayntun*	Escort	North Atlantic
11 Feb.	U-283	RCAF Squadron 407	Air Escort	North Atlantic
24 Feb.	U-257	HMCS *Waskesiu*	Escort	North Atlantic
6 Mar.	U-744	HMCS *Gatineau*, *St Catharines*, *Chaudière*, *Fennel*, *Chilliwack*, HMS *Kenilworth Castle*, *Icarus*	Escort	North Atlantic
10 Mar.	U-625	RCAF Squadron 422	Air Support	West of Ireland
10 Mar.	U-845	HMCS *Swansea*, *St Laurent*, *Owen Sound*, HMS *Forester*	Escort	North Atlantic
13 Mar.	U-575	HMCS *Prince Rupert*, Aircraft from USS *Bogue*, USS *Haverfield*, *Hobson*, British Squadron 172 and 206	Carrier Sea/ Air Escort	North Atlantic
14 Apr.	U-448	HMCS *Swansea*, HMCS *Pelican*	Escort	North Atlantic
17 Apr.	U-342	RCAF Squadron 162	Air Support	Southwest of Iceland
22 Apr.	U-311	HMCS *Swansea, Matane*	Escort	North Atlantic
4 May	U-846	RCAF Squadron 407	Bay Air Patrol	Bay of Biscay
3 June	U-477	RCAF Squadron 162	Air Patrol	Off South Norway
11 June	U-980	RCAF Squadron 162	Air Patrol	Southwest of Norway
13 June	U-715	RCAF Squadron 162	Air Patrol	East of Faroes
24 June	U-971	HMCS *Haida*, HMS *Eskimo*, Czechoslovakia Squadron 311	Sea/Air Escort	West Channel
24 June	U-1225	RCAF Squadron 162	Air Patrol	North of Shetland
30 June	U-478	RCAF Squadron 162, British Squadron 86	Air Patrol	South of Shetland
6 June	U-678	HMCS *Ottawa*, *Kootenay*, HMS *Statice*	Escort	English Channel
18 Aug.	U-621	HMCS *Ottawa*, *Kootenay*, *Chaudière*	Patrol	Bay of Biscay
20 Aug.	U-984	HMCS *Ottawa*, *Kootenay*	Patrol	English Channel
31 Aug.	U-247	HMCS *Swansea*, *Saint John*	Patrol	Off Land's End
11 Sept.	U-484	HMCS *Dunver*, *Hespeler*	Escort	Hebrides
16 Oct.	U-1006	HMCS *Annan*	Patrol	Faroes
27 Dec.	U-877	HMCS *St Thomas*	Escort	North Atlantic
30 Dec.	U-772	RCAF Squadron 407	Air Escort	English Channel

1945

Date	U-boat	Units	Type	Location
16 Feb.	U-309	HMCS *Saint John*	Escort	Northeast of Scotland

7 Mar.	U-1302	HMCS *Thetford Mines*, *La Hulloise*, and *Strathadam*	Escort	St George's Channel
20 Mar.	U-1003	HMCS *New Glasgow*	Collision	North of Ireland
2 May	U-2359	RCAF Squadron 404, British Squadrons 143, 235, 248 and Norwegian Squadron 333	Air Strike	Kattegat